BERGLUND CENTER FOR INTERNET STUDIES

INTERFACE

THE JOURNAL OF EDUCATION, COMMUNITY, AND VALUES

Volume 10

AF882677

Published by
Berglund Center for Internet Studies
bcis.pacificu.edu

Acknowledgements

Published by Staff of Pacific University Oregon's
Berglund Center for Internet Studies,
Forest Grove, Oregon, USA

Jeffrey G. Barlow, Ph.D., Editor
Theresa A. Floyd, Managing Editor
Jenn Hernandez, Design Editor
Sierra Brummett and Lilly Huynh, Copy Editors
Sebastian Schlumpf and Jeffrey Luong, Publishing Assistants
Ben Griffin, Cover Design

The on-line version of *Interface* was produced by:
Jamaica King, HTML Editor
Meghan Schulz, Assisting HTML Editor
Jeffrey Mazar and Ken Hyland, Systems Operations

http://bcis.pacificu.edu/journal/

Copyright © 2011 by Berglund Center for Internet Studies
Printed in the United States of America
Volume 10
ISBN 978-0-983-43537-2 (paperback)
Interface (Forest Grove, Oregon)
ISSN 1940-915X

All rights reserved. No part of this book may be reproduced in any form or by any electronic or mechanical means including information storage and retrieval systems without permission in writing from the publisher, except by a reviewer who may quote brief passages in a review.

Berglund Center for Internet Studies
Pacific University
2043 College Way, Forest Grove, OR 97116
http://bcis.pacificu.edu

Acknowledgments

As these articles were published on-line in *Interface* we marked our tenth year as an e-journal. That it was ever published at all was due entirely to the generosity of James and Mary Berglund, the far-sighted sponsors of the Berglund Center. Julie Berglund Baker, joined in their support and now serves on the advisory board for the Center. She also serves on the Board of Trustees for Pacific University. It is to Julie that we dedicate this tenth issue. We are also grateful to our founding Director, Joe Howell, and to his successor, Steven Boone, each of whom set us on the proper and highly timely path of studying the Internet. Joe Howell continues to support in his role as our Board Chair.

In addition, we are grateful to the efforts of our present Program Coordinator, Theresa Floyd, who brought this volume from virtual to physical reality. We'd like to thank Jenn Hernandez, the design editor for the *Interface* hard copy, and we are also particularly grateful to Jerry Greenfield, also a member of our advisory board, for his very expert proofreading of this volume.

And of course, we are grateful not only to this year's Berglund Center student staff, but to all the staff members who preceded them for the past decade, many of whom are now employed in the industry or running their own highly successful businesses.

And above all, we are grateful to our writers and editors, who have made the content enclosed here so useful, informative, and entertaining, as it is.

Jeffrey Barlow
Director, Berglund Center for Internet Studies
Pacific University Oregon
March, 2011

Introduction

Interface, the electronic journal of the Berglund Center for Internet Studies, Pacific University Oregon, is written and produced for the broad audience of those interested in the impact of the Internet in all its manifold forms. These include not only such obvious ones as the rapid shift into electronic banking and commerce, but also even very subtle ones as the impact of the Internet on popular film and fiction, social relationships and communications, and even on poetry, and upon the English language itself.

At *Interface*, we study all of these phenomena, and the flexibility of an electronic journal, which can be useful to all audiences, unlike the rigidly determined form of traditional journals, has let us range widely. At the Berglund Center we not only publish the results of our authors' research and thought, but also have the great pleasure of encouraging such productivity through grants and scholarships as well as our payments for articles.

This volume represents the content of our electronic journal, *Interface*, 2010. This publication includes original work from international scholars, as well as members of the Pacific University faculty. For more information on this project, please see our web pages. (http://bcis.pacificu.edu)

This is our third volume of a fully bound hard-copy publication done under a print-on-demand process. This is our fourth such work, the first, Yang Desheng's *Jigsaw III* is now available at Amazon*, as is *Interface*, Volume 9, 2009. We have found this approach useful and practicable, especially for limited edition publications such as this one. This work, too, will soon be available at Amazon. While our work emphasizes the impact of the Internet, we are also aware of the importance of hard copy publications for such purposes as archival durability, assessment and tenure processes, and simply because as much as we love the Internet, most of us still love a good book. We hope that you will find this such a book.

Jeffrey Barlow
Director, Berglund Center for Internet Studies
Pacific University Oregon

**Reference to Amazon throughout this publication implies the on-line retail distributing company. Due to Copyright restrictions we were not allowed to use the correct reference.*

Table of Contents

January – February 2010 – Volume 10, Issue 1

About This Issue

The February 2010 issue of *Interface* is live and on the WWW...

We begin out tenth year of posting *Interface* with this February Issue. It is also, we believe, our 65th posting. Despite these daunting facts, we think this issue is an especially strong one...

Our feature is the first of two parts of Ashley A. Kjos' Master's thesis in the School of Professional Psychology at Pacific University, "*Adults Who Play Violent Video Games and Their Normative Beliefs About Aggression.*" The question of video games and violence is continually a troubling one. We think that Ashley's two part series adds substantially to the scholarship of the field.

Education Editor Steve Rhine of Willamette University offers us "*The Timely Demise of the Paper Textbook*" Steve, who has written more than one book himself, makes a strong argument for e-book readers in education. See also his recent Berglund Roundtable presentation under Announcements...

Chris Macfarlane, Professor of Education at Pacific University, whose field is Special Education and Technology, presents her maiden piece for us, "*Sixty, Female, and Tech-Savvy: One Educator's Journey.*" Chris will be joining us our editorial board and we look forward to additional work from her.

Berglund Student Fellow Nicole Nowlin also offers her first piece for *Interface*, discussing amateur comic publishing, with some implications for copyright violations in "*Scanlations: Copyright Infringement for Literature and Art Fans Brought to You by the Internet.*"

Director Jeffrey Barlow, recently returned from six weeks in China, not surprisingly reviews two works on China. The first review is Marina Yue Zhang's *China 2.0. The transformation of an Emerging Superpower...And the Opportunities.* Zhang argues that the Internet is moving China toward a more open and democratic society and suggests that businesses hoping to succeed in China need to begin relying on Web 2.0 sales operations.

The second review is of Martin Jacques' *When China Rules the World. The End of the Western World and the Birth of a New Global Order.* Jacques' title, while deliberately intended to be provocative, pretty much describes his central arguments and, according to Jeffrey, is a very important book for those who wish to understand the rapidly changing global order.

The editorial is "*Google and China: Minor Incident or Cyberwar?*" As Jeffrey was in China during the beginning of what is rapidly becoming a major issue in Sino-American relations, he was able to discuss the problem with many groups of Chinese Netizens.

See also a series of Announcements related to recent Berglund activities including the showing of our first film...

As always, we hope you find this issue of *Interface* educational and interesting. Look for us again in March...

The Berglund Center for Internet Studies
Pacific University, Oregon

The Timely Demise of the Paper Textbook

Steve Rhine, Ed. D.

Willamette University

As Apple Computers unleashes its version of an e-book reader onto the public, the dawn of interactive screen reading is upon us and the tactile feel of paper is fading away. The field is crowded with options such as Barnes and Noble's "Nook", the Sony e-Reader, the Hearst/Sprint Skiff Reader, and Amazon's Kindle. Sales of the devices are skyrocketing, with $1 billion worth of Kindles expected to be sold in 2010.[1] Jeffrey Barlow has both lamented the loss of the paper book and welcomed the new technology in prior INTERFACE articles, calling the Kindle a "disruptive technology".[2] While schools struggle to survive in a time of recession and to maintain relevance in a digital age, what are the implications of these reading technologies for students? In this article I explore the growing phenomenon of e-textbooks for these reading technologies and how they may disrupt schools as we have known them.

Textbook costs in schools, from Kindergarten to the University, have increased dramatically over the past two decades. Textbooks nearly tripled in price between 1986-2004.[3] College students are forced to spend up to $1,000 a year, further adding to the burden of paying for a higher education. For school districts, the rising cost of textbooks means pushing other school funding priorities to the side, keeping outdated materials for longer, or simply doing without. For instance, even though California spends $400 million per year on textbooks,[4] 500,000 students did not have textbooks to use in class and 2 million could not take their textbook home last year.[5] In response, 34 states have introduced laws that attempt to scale back prices but only six were successful, possibly due to heavy lobbying by the industry.[6]

Schools' efforts to release themselves from the bonds and constraints of textbook publishers are not new. However, with e-books, a number of new developments make purchasing a reading device for students rather than paper textbooks more attractive, particularly as device competition pushes prices downwards. First, the

---

[1] Kindle sales pegged at $1 billion by 2010. http://news.cnet.com/8301-1023_3-10014387-93.html

[2] *To George Orwell: It's the Kindle Baby, it's the Kindle!* (http://bcis.pacificu.edu/journal/2009/04/article.php?id=68).

[3] "*Break on Cost Of Textbooks Unlikely Before Last Bell, 2010.*" http://www.washingtonpost.com/wp-dyn/content/article/2008/08/19/AR2008081903230.html

[4] http://www.opensourcetext.org/

[5] "*ETV14: Decrease the Cost of K-12 Textbooks.*" http://cpr.ca.gov/CPR_Report/Issues_and_Recommendations/Chapter_3_Education_Training_and_Volunteerism/ETV14.html

[6] "*Break on Cost Of Textbooks Unlikely Before Last Bell, 2010.*" http://www.washingtonpost.com/wp-dyn/content/article/2008/08/19/AR2008081903230.html

cost issue drives the market. E-textbooks can be up to 50% less, although the cost difference for many books is currently not significant. As more textbooks hit the e-market, school districts and college students will likely see cost benefits.

Second, and perhaps more importantly for K-12 schools, it makes individualization possible. Three states, California, Florida, and Texas make up 25% of the textbook market. Matt Federoff, the Vail, Arizona School District's Chief Information Officer notes "Textbooks are basically produced by half a dozen manufacturers to be sold as widely as possible to as many districts as possible".[7] If the big three don't like something, it doesn't go in the book. Other states have had to get along with whatever those three states want to put in a textbook. However, with e-textbooks, publishers can cost effectively produce textbooks that align with each state's standards. Books can be customized to state's desires and updated without having to reprint. McGraw-Hill, one of the largest textbook publishers in the United States, already publishes nearly 95% of its books electronically.[8] More than 6,000 colleges and universities now subscribe to CourseSmart's (http://www.coursesmart.com) accumulation of 8,500 e-textbooks. Yet, the market for e-textbooks has been slow to emerge. One of many hurdles to overcome, is that you can't sell back an used e-textbook, so the end cost is not worth it for students yet. However, the growing presence of Kindle-like devices and low cost "subscriptions" at sites like CourseSmart are likely to set the tipping point in motion.

To push the future for K-12 schools a bit more, California has initiated the Open Source Textbook Project (COSTP: http://www.opensourcetext.org/). COSTP's mission is to completely eliminate the $400 million line item for K-12 textbooks, increase the range of content, and end textbook shortages. COSTP plans to access free, already-existing, and widely available K-12 educational content in the public domain, use California's best K-12 teachers to create resources, and use dormant K-12 textbook content. Last year, COSTP released the first group of free, online books to schools that meet state education standards.

Also impacting the growing content side of the equation, Project Guttenberg (http://www.gutenberg.org) was the first site to make ebooks available for free and now boasts 30,000 titles. Any work of Shakespeare, Dickens, or Twain is just a few clicks away. Google is working with such institutions as the University of California at Berkley and the University of Michigan to scan 10 million books.[9] While most of these books will incur some costs, a significant percent will be freely downloadable to schools.[10]

Bottom line, so far, is that e-textbooks readers are becoming more accessible, costs for e-textbooks are coming down, and the content available for these

---

[7] "*Arizona High School Dumps Textbooks for Laptops.*" http://blackchristiannews.com/news/2009/08/arizona-high-school-dumps-textbooks-for-laptops.html

[8] http://www.insidehighered.com/news/2008/01/03/ebooks

[9] http://www.cic.net/home/Projects/Library/BookSearch/Introduction.aspx

[10] Bonk, C. The World is Open. (2009). San Francisco, CA: Jossey Bass.

readers is increasing dramatically. But, does it make educational sense for schools to move towards e-textbooks and how might e-textbooks disrupt schooling? From my perspective, there are three driving forces educationally for e-textbooks to find their place in classrooms: currency, interactivity, and individualization.

First, the easy examples addressing the currency issue are history and science books. Yesterday is today's history. If the textbooks are online instead of in students' hands, discoveries, new perspectives, and influential events can be updated continually without reprinting. Some students are reading ten year old science books. Consider what we have learned about the brain, genes, technology, and global warming in the past decade. It is likely that very few textbooks in the United States are up to date on these critical topics for the next generation. For better or worse, current history is the domain of Wikipedia. Not to knock Wikipedia, but what if thoughtful historians and scientists became resources for schools' textbooks on an ongoing basis? When e-textbooks make state-of-the-art knowledge available to students, school becomes more relevant.

Second, e-textbooks provide interactivity that paper books can't. Don't know that word? "Look it up!" says your teacher. How many students bother to walk over and pick up the dictionary to look up those words and learn their meaning and how they function in the context of the current paragraph? If all a student has to do is click on the word to discover its meaning, learning is at their fingertips. Further, if a student wants to learn more about a topic they are reading about, a linked word can lead them to a reviewed source rather than spending wasted minutes searching on Google to find a questionable site. Also, highlighting and note taking on the reader can lead to increased interaction with the text because it is easy, accessible, and immediately storable. Interactivity ultimately puts increased depth and breadth of learning in students' hands.

Finally, e-textbooks can be individualized. In education, we know that the more you meet a student's individual needs, the more he or she can find success. For example, I visited Howard Elementary School in Eugene, Oregon recently where every student has their own laptop. One of the tasks for the day in a fourth grade classroom was for the students to all read an article about dolphins and then answer some questions. From his laptop, the teacher set the reading level of the article and questions for each individual student on their laptop. Based on their comprehension scores, he can set the next article to a different reading level. The class was able to have a large group discussion about dolphins and work together in small groups on projects. This was possible because they had all read the same content, but tailored to each student's reading skills. Needless to say, their reading scores on the state test have increased.

Whether it is creating appropriately challenging math problem sets, end of chapter questions, or individual readability, e-textbooks have the potential to take students where they are and move them forward. One of the biggest problems in schools is that teachers typically don't have time to individualize teaching, particularly regarding the resources they use, so they necessarily teach to the middle. The result is that lower students struggle and the higher students are not challenged. Teachers care and want to do the best for their students. E-textbooks could facilitate that effort by helping teachers customize learning.

In the end, e-readers make it an interesting and potentially exciting time for schools from Kindergarten to college. My generation generally enjoys the feel of paper when it comes to reading. My fifteen year old son is not so emotionally attached. When I think about the benefits to students that e-textbooks can provide, I'm willing to make the sacrifice, let the demise of paper play out its course, and the Kindle generation begin.

Sixty, Female, and Tech-Savvy: One Educator's Journey

Chris Macfarlane, Ph.D.

Pacific University

It was a serendipitous moment – one I would have never predicted; yet it created a tidal wave of reflection about my career as an educator and corollary expertise in technology. Breakfast, coffee, and the chance to work away from my office for a few uninterrupted hours sounded perfect. I settled into a small table by the window, opened my laptop, laid my smart phone where I could see/reach it (my wireless earpiece in place), and began to tackle email.

The café crowd dwindled. I was concentrating – so much so, I was a little unnerved when a voice beside me said, "You look very nice today." I turned to see a woman about my age kneeling beside me camera in hand. Not quite sure, I responded, "Thank you." She asked if she could take my picture. I must have given her a quizzical look because she quickly followed, actually stammered, to say women of our age weren't usually thought of as being so comfortable with technology. I somehow defied this view.

She was a feminist. She liked to take pictures and was especially motivated to take pictures that could serve as role models for young women. We decided on a non-posed picture. After realizing I was also a professor, she snapped my picture and was gone. In less than 5 minutes I'd been reminded of several perceived stereotypes encountered in my lifetime: female, educated, mature, and technology skilled.

First, am I, in fact, a role model for young women? And, if they need role models, in what areas or ways should we provide role models? Are women considerably less visible in STEM (Science, Technology, Engineering, Math) fields? While more than half of undergraduates are women, we still lag in geosciences, mathematics, and physical science, although degrees in social sciences and life sciences have increased significantly (Rosser, 2009). Unfortunately, the number of women earning degrees in computer science, computer engineering, and engineering has plateaued or dropped since 1984 [Olson, 2000]. The effect is compounded by our increased need for a workforce in a technology-oriented society. Further, women who enter STEM fields, leave sooner than their male counterparts resulting in a significant lack of women in higher-level positions (Vosser, 2009). I would also posit, we need educators who can teach in a technology-oriented society and prepare a future workforce.

The truth is I am a role model; however, I am not in a hard-core scientific field. I am a special educator who prepares teachers. Throughout the course of my career, though, I've developed, utilized, and taught others about technology. The question I've been asking myself is whether this is enough or not?

During 1983-1984, we began to experiment with the use of computer technology with one of my students, a 12 year old with severe cerebral palsy. He used his eyes to communicate yes/no, but we all knew he had more to say. One of the classroom consultants gained access to a TI-99 home computer with a speech synthesizer (Texas Instruments). Using a cassette tape recorder as a linear drive (32K), he developed a communication program for Doug. Doug pushed any key and the computer talked. The first time he pressed a key and told one of his peers to "bug off," he laughed hard; I had goose bumps. Several weeks later at the Christmas program, his mom cried when he pressed the keyboard and sang, "Tomorrow, tomorrow, I love you tomorrow." I knew tomorrow had arrived for students with disabilities and technology would become the great equalizer.

I left the classroom at the end of that year and began my doctoral studies in the Department of Special Education at Utah State University (USU), intent on learning as much about assistive technology as I could. Dr. Alan Hofmeister had received a leadership grant from the US Department of Education to train doctoral students in the use of microcomputers in education. Computer scientists were not knowledgeable about education and educators were not knowledgeable about computers. The idea was to create a cadre of special education leaders who understood computers and how to use them in education.

In addition to working on technology-related research projects, we were required to take courses and participate in a weekly seminar. The first and primary lesson we learned was that the promise of computers in education was not to replicate current paper and pencil tasks. Instead, we were to think of technology as a tool that could improve instruction and create more powerful learning opportunities for students.

My second lesson came in an undergraduate computer science course. Learning program languages did not come easy and I failed the first test, a definite first for me. The 18-year-old males in my class got it. I did not. When I met with the professor, the only empathy he offered was having failed his first test in an undergraduate computer class while a doctoral student – the move from electrical engineering to computer science had been hard for him as well. What he said next, though, was golden. He explained computer scientists really did not know how to teach computer programming. Besides, computer languages were evolving and having learned one, you would probably need to learn more. Thus, learning to program was more about the ability to learn on your own. The most successful programmers were students who could teach themselves or problem-solve. I've never forgotten that insight and I did pass the course. In doing so, I learned to read documentation, poorly written or not, ask others, watch others, and experiment with assurance that I should always save, create a back-up, and keep notes and I really couldn't blow up the computer. The worst thing that would happen, at least in my world, was unplugging the computer in order to start all over. That was my fail-safe reset button.

Opportunities presented themselves during my doctoral studies and eventually led to research positions at USU. I co-authored three expert systems, two funded by federal grants. I was the knowledge engineer on those two expert systems and developed and validated a methodology for determining the content validity of a knowledge base as my dissertation. I provided pre-service and in-service training, wrote manuals, and conducted research on these expert systems. I also wrote a computer-assisted testing system for one of the department's courses. Eventually, I moved into a faculty position and taught the assistive technology course. In addition, I published and presented on technology topics.

One other facet of my USU experience was teaching at the extension campuses. The experience of flying in a small airplane with 3 to 6 other instructors over the Uintah Mountains with all the nuances of the jet stream and changing seasons was unforgettable. I once experienced what felt like 3 seconds of weightlessness as we encountered severe turbulence. During the winter, I needed matches to warm my key enough to unlock my truck when we returned sometime after midnight, if the fog didn't force us to land a canyon's drive away. Thus, when the opportunity presented itself to teach via the early electronic distance learning system (two-way audio; slow-scan, 15-second delay video), I immediately said, yes. Despite a less than optimal learning environment, I reached students throughout the state, saved time, and saved nerves. I was hooked.

In 1991 I arrived at the University of Northern Iowa (UNI) to coordinate the Mental Disabilities Program and begin a tenure-track career. Interestingly, I was back in a small airplane within a year flying to western Iowa.

Consequently, when I learned the state of Iowa was building a statewide fiber-optics network with two-way audio, two-way, real time, full motion video, I immediately met with administrators. I began teaching on the Iowa Communications Network (ICN) fall 1993. When I left in 2000, I had logged more hours on the ICN than any other faculty member. I also developed strategies for supervising at a distance.

The ICN classroom became my research lab. The television monitors resembled computer monitors and I realized I could put the tenets of well-designed computer instruction to work in the delivery of distance learning. US congressman, foreign scholars, fellow faculty, and university administrators observed me teach and demonstrate the capabilities of the system.

My students vicariously learned about technology in their special education courses. I worked diligently to utilize technology in all my class and encouraged/required my students to utilize technology when teaching students with disabilities. I continued to write and present on technology.

In 2000 I came to Pacific University to develop and implement a special education program. I continue to approach technology in education from a problem-solving perspective and as a means to improve learning. In addition to teaching pre-service teachers about assistive technology, I also teach a technology class. I have learned to podcast and use other forms of distance learning. Recently, I observed one of my students teach using SKYPE as the video interface. It was awesome.

Having come to a reflective point in my career and prodded by a stranger in a coffee shop, I realize I've never stopped learning about technology and thinking about how I might use it to promote/foster learning and provide equity for students with disabilities. Each and every time I teach, I am a role model.

I sincerely hope Dr. Hofmeister's vision of computer-savvy special education leaders created the far-reaching sphere of influence he sought. While not a STEM field, I am inclined to think the applied use of technology within education serves the greater good. And, somewhere, out there is a picture of a white-haired lady, comfortable with technology, defying stereotypes and, hopefully, encouraging someone to think.

Scanlations: Copyright Infringement for Literature and Art Fans Brought to You by the Internet

Nicole Nowlin

Student Fellow, Berglund Center for Internet Studies

We've all heard the cries of pain from artists and record labels as dollars are bled from the music industry via illegal downloading and file sharing. We've seen the lawsuits[1] and the evolution of Napster[2] and iTunes. We've more recently seen the news about the multi-million dollar lawsuit against the four biggest members of the Canadian Recording Industry Association for not paying for the rights to music they used – and from which they profited – on compilation CDs.[3]

But do you hear writers and publishers bemoaning their loss of revenue? No. Why writers, you ask? Aside from the plagiarism that is severely punished in our educational system, written works don't have the appearance of dealing with the same pressures of illegal sharing and reduced royalties. Stephanie Meyer's *Midnight Sun* (*Twilight* Series)[4] was illegally distributed while unfinished and she shut down the project – that may be the only thing that comes to mind when people think of books and file sharing, and that is over a year old. It doesn't get much attention, because really... how much work is it to remove the pages from a book and scan them into a PDF or image file? How much work is it to retype a novel? Too much work!

However, it's not too much work for everyone, especially when there are shorter books that are mostly images to be scanned, not manuscripts to be retyped. This is where scanlations come into play. According to Wikipedia,

> **Scanlation** (also **scanslation**) is the unauthorized scanning, translation, editing and distribution of comics from a foreign language into the language of the distributors. The term is most often used for Japanese (manga), and rarely for Korean (manhwa) and Chinese (manhua) comics. Scanlations are generally distributed for free via the Internet, either by direct download, BitTorrent or IRC. The word scanlation is a portmanteau of scan and translation.[5]

---

[1] Straziuso, Jason. "Download lawsuits scare some, but song trading still popular." USA Today. 20 Feb. 2004. Web. 10 Jan. 2010.
[2] Gil, Paul. "Understanding Music Downloading: P2P File Sharing." About.com. Web. 14 Jan. 2010. <http://netforbeginners.about.com/cs/peersharing/a/aap2p.htm>.
[3] Geist, Michael. "Record industry faces liability over 'infringement.'" Toronto Star. 7 Jan. 2010. Web. 7 Jan. 2010. <http://www.thestar.com/business/article/735096--geist-record-industry-faces-liability-over-infringement>.
[4] Meyer, Stephenie. "Midnight Sun: Edward's Version of Twilight." StephenieMeyer.com. 28 Aug. 2008. Web. 15 Jan. 2010. <http://www.stepheniemeyer.com/midnightsun.html>.
[5] "Scanlation." Wikipedia. Web. 11 Jan. 2010. <http://en.wikipedia.org/wiki/Scanlation>.

For an example of scanlations before and after, check out Dan in Japan's blog post.[6] Is this needed?

If it weren't for the Internet, we wouldn't have a lot of things – including so much piracy! The Internet has created a forum through which the world shares everything, legally and illegally. It is a place where one can find anything, and that commonly touted phrase is becoming truer every day. As a Generation-Y 'net fanatic, I can safely say I rarely can't find something for which I am looking... and that includes music downloads, manga scanlations, or artwork. It's very easy, found in archives and repositories growing in volume every day.

The scanlators (those actually doing the scanning and translating) are aware they walk a fine line. In their Frequently Asked Questions section, Mangascreener writes, "Technically it's illegal, but if the series is not licensed, it is normally overlooked. In some ways, scanslations are beneficial: many series get popular through scanslations".[7]Anime News Network includes the illegality and reality of the copyright infringement in their definition, stating "...scanlations are technically illegal copyright infringement, but are a tolerated fan practice so long as distribution of the scanlation ceases when the manga is licensed or the original copyright holder requests it."[8]

From a purely legal standpoint, illegal is the right description. Just as music is illegally downloaded, printed materials like manga – turned into scanlations – that are scanned, copied, or downloaded, are subject to copyright infringement. Online repository MangaFox places a disclaimer at the bottom of their site stating, "Copyrights and trademarks for the manga, and other promotional materials are held by their respective owners and their use is allowed under the fair use clause of the Copyright Law." At first blush, this looks kosher – they're aware of copyright and apparently are able to use the materials posted on their site under the aforementioned fair use clause.

Frankly, it's not that simple. Mark Hubert, a copyright lawyer in Portland, OR, explained, "Scanlations, assuming they are unauthorized, would not qualify as 'Fair Use' according to the Copyright Act of 1976, the reproduction of authored works for the purpose of 'criticism, comment, news reporting, teaching, scholarship, or research'." Hubert went on to quote the tests used to determine if the fair use clause is applicable, according to the code: "(1) the purpose and character of the use, including whether such use is of a commercial nature or is for nonprofit educational purposes; (2) the nature of the copyrighted work; (3) the amount and substantiality of the portion used in relation to the copyrighted work as a whole; and (4) the effect of the use upon the potential market for, or value of, the copyrighted work".[9] [10] From this, two things are clear – the materials

---

[6] Johnston, Dan. "Scanlation attempt." Web log post. Dan in Japan. 12 Oct. 2009. Web. 21 Jan. 2010. <http://dan.hellosensei.org/2009/10/scanlation-attempt.html>.

[7] "FAQ (Frequently Asked Questions)." Mangascreener.Com. Web. 15 Jan. 2010. <http://www.mangascreener.com/faq.php>.

[8] "Scanlation." Lexicon. Anime News Network. Web. 15 Jan. 2010. <http://www.animenewsnetwork.com/encyclopedia/lexicon.php?id=71>.

[9] Hubert, Mark. E-mail interview. 14 Jan. 2010.

posted, while generally without profit are not for educational purposes, and most works are posted in their entirety.

The definition of the fair use clause and infringement is further expanded under the Digital Millennium Copyright Act of 1998 to adapt to the increasing use of the Internet.[11] Hubert described it as defending "copyright owners from infringement or infringement through the transfer of digital copies of their protected works." With it came some protections for Internet Service Providers and websites from lawsuits based on user-generated content. It is most likely under the addition of the DMCA that scanlation sharing sites are absolved of wrongdoing, as their content is provided by users, like YouTube videos. In the Terms of Service, these sites claim no responsibility for liability or damages due to user content, explicitly stating:

> You shall be solely responsible for your own User Submissions and the consequences of posting or publishing them. In connection with User Submissions, you affirm, represent, and/or warrant that: (i) you own or have the necessary licenses, rights, consents, and permissions to use and authorize <insert website here> to use all patent, trademark, trade secret, copyright or other proprietary rights in and to any and all User Submissions to enable inclusion and use of the User Submissions in the manner contemplated by the Website and these Terms of Use; and (ii) you have the written consent, release, and/or permission of each and every identifiable individual person in the User Submission to use the name or likeness of each and every such identifiable individual person to enable inclusion and use of the User Submissions in the manner contemplated by the Website and these Terms of Use. **For clarity, you retain all of your ownership rights in your User Submissions.**[12]

When considering that the materials are not posted by the authors, publishers, or anyone else licensed to own the materials, it puts into perspective the fact that the entirety of the manga content on these websites is both illegal and completely accessible. "A lot of the file sharing websites seem to maintain servers in random countries that don't enforce intellectual property rights, but whenever someone in the ol' USA downloads the music, manga, whatever to his/her computer you run the risk that the copyright holder might come looking for you," wrote Hubert via email. "This has just become a huge issue for artists. Due to technology the ability to swap data has completely altered artists' ability to enforce their copyrights."

In an article in The Comic Journal, Dirk Deppey interviewed several amateur scanlators. "Scanlation isn't simple piracy -- not always, anyway," he wrote. One of his interviewees gave an excellent comment to lighten the dark view on the legality of this issue, a suitable closing to this examination of the copyright infringement on the manga industry. Jill Schlicher, former scanlator, explained to

---

[10] 17 USC 107. 1976.
[11] H.R. 2281, 105th Cong. (1998) (enacted). Print.
[12] MangaFox. "Terms of Service." Web. 12 Jan. 2010. <http://www.mangafox.com/terms.php>.

Deppey the positive side of scanlations – essentially, what the scanlators and fans are attempting to do. "There are many great series that are not commercially available in the States, but if somewhere some small group of fans really love it, it can become accessible to others who may not be able to read Japanese and may not even have ready access to Japanese bookstores where the raw comics could be bought. It may be illegal and offensive to some companies, but I do think it's actually more likely to be beneficial to them in the end by promoting an interest in comics and related merchandise. And for big companies and small fans alike, that really is a lovely thing for everyone."[13]

Glossary of Terms

- Manga – Japanese comics or graphic novels
- Manhwa – Korean comics or graphic novels
- Manhua – Chinese comics or graphic novels
- Scanlation (scanslation) – a scanned translation of a work originally published in another language
- Scanlator – the person(s) who scan and translate the works
- IRC, BitTorrent – downloading and file sharing services

---

[13] Deppey, Dirk. "Scanlation Nation: Amateur Manga Translators Tell Their Stories." The Comics Journal #269 (2005). Web. 14 Jan. 2010. <http://archives.tcj.com/index.php?option=com_content&task=view&id=343&Itemid=48>.

Adults Who Play Violent Video Games and Their Normative Beliefs About Aggression, Part I

Ashley A. Kjos

Introduction

On December 6th 2007, 16-year-old Heather Trujillo and 17 year old Lamar Roberts were babysitting Trujillo's 7 year old sister Zoe Garcia when they hit, kicked and body-slammed the child in an attempt to re-enact various scenes from the video game Mortal Kombat. Garcia received a broken wrist, more than 20 bruises, swelling of the brain, bleeding of her neck muscles and spine, and ultimately died from her injuries. The teens faced a possible sentence of 48 years in prison if convicted of murder (Lubich, 2007).

On April 20th, 1999, Eric Harris and Dylan Klebold entered Columbine High School in Littleton, Colorado to embark on a shooting rampage that killed 13 and left 23 others wounded before turning the guns on themselves. Although it is impossible to know what exactly caused these teens to attack others, it is possible that one contributing factor was exposure to violent video games. Both Harris and Klebold spent a great deal of time playing violent video games such as Doom and Wolfenstein 3D. Harris actually created his own video game that contained characters, weapons, and situations that were eerily similar to the events that occurred during the actual shootings at Columbine (Pooley, 1999).

Are violent video games to blame for the senseless and aggressive actions taken by Trujillo and Roberts against a 7 year old or for the actions of Harris and Klebold at Columbine High School? Although many factors may have contributed to these teens acting in aggressive and violent ways, numerous researchers have suggested that violent video games are in fact related to increases in aggressive behavior and affect (Anderson & Bushman, 2001; Anderson & Dill, 2000; Anderson & Murphy, 2003; Bartholow & Anderson, 2002; Bartholow, Sestir, & Davis, 2005; Colwell & Payne, 2000; Gentile, Lynch, Linder, & Walsh, 2004; Persky & Blaskovich, 2007; Sherry, 2001). This does not mean that playing violent video games was the only possible explanation for these teens acting aggressively but that the violent games these teens played may have been a contributing factor. These tragedies and others like them have definitely brought the spotlight to the problem of video game violence and researchers have begun to look at what effects this form of media may have on children's and adult's behaviors and feelings.

The research regarding aggression and violent video games is sparse but there are a growing number of researchers adding to the field of knowledge. As previously noted, there are numerous studies showing a positive relationship between aggression and violent video game play (Anderson & Bushman, 2001; Anderson & Dill, 2000; Anderson & Murphy, 2003). Sherry (2001) found an overall effect size ($d = .30$) suggesting there is a relationship between video game play and aggression. Although many researchers have studied actual aggressive behaviors exhibited by children and adults who play violent video games, researchers are also determining if there is a relationship between violent media and peoples' beliefs about the acceptability of aggressive behaviors.

Huesmann and Guerra (1997) created a measure to determine children's and adult's normative beliefs about aggression. These researchers found that children's normative beliefs about aggression were positively related to the actual aggressive behaviors they exhibited. Krahe and Moller (2004) studied normative beliefs about aggression and video games and found that the normative acceptance of physical aggression increased with an increase in exposure to violent video games. More research is needed to determine exactly what relationship exists between video games and beliefs about the acceptance of violence. There is also evidence that there are gender differences in the types of aggression displayed (Anderson & Huesmann, 2003), the types and length of video games played (Colwell & Payne, 2000), and beliefs about acceptance of aggression (Krahe & Moller, 2004).

Aggression

Aggression is an attribute commonly found in animals and humans and has been present since the beginning of existence. Aggression can be defined as "behavior intended to harm another individual who is motivated to avoid that harm" (Anderson & Bushman, 2001, p. 356). This definition excludes accidental acts that lead to harm but includes intentional acts to harm even if the attempt fails. For example, it is considered an aggressive action if a person attempts to fire a gun at another person but the gun jams. Violence is defined as aggression that has extreme consequences as its goal, such as death or murder. This means that all violence is aggression but not all types of aggression are violent. Aggression can take many forms and is often used in diverse ways to achieve different outcomes. Physical aggression is the actual use of physical force upon another person to cause intentional harm, such as punching or kicking another person. Verbal aggression is the use of words to cause intentional harm, such as spreading rumors or lies about another person. Past studies have found that females are more likely to resort to verbal aggression to harm another individual while males are more likely to resort to physical aggression to harm another individual (Anderson & Huesmann, 2003). Although the definition and types of aggression can be easily understood, the mechanisms underlying aggression are still a cause of debate among psychologists and sociologists.

Theories of Aggression

There are numerous models and theories to explain how aggression develops within children and adults. Although an exhaustive discussion of all these theories is beyond the scope of this paper (see Anderson & Huesmann, 2003 and Anderson & Bushman, 2002a for more detailed information regarding theories of aggression), three theories that have been well documented in the study of aggression will be examined specifically social learning theory, script theory, and the general aggression model (GAM).

Social Learning Theory

Bandura's (1973) social learning theory suggests that people learn from one another through observational learning, imitation, and modeling. This means that people learn through observing others' behaviors and outcomes of behaviors. For example, if a child observes a parent being physically aggressive with another individual and that parent is reinforced for this action, the child may deem this behavior as acceptable and may later be aggressive due to observing aggressive models. Bandura's infamous bobo doll experiment (1961) demonstrated that if children witnessed an aggressive display by an adult model, they imitated the aggressive behavior when given the opportunity. In this experiment, 36 boys and 36 girls witnessed an adult act either aggressively or non-aggressively towards a bobo doll and were then observed playing with numerous toys including a bobo doll to determine what behaviors the children would imitate. The results suggested that children who viewed an aggressive model made more aggressive responses toward the bobo doll than children who viewed a non-aggressive model. Also, boys made more aggressive responses than girls overall. These results support Bandura's social learning theory by showing that children can learn aggression through the process of observational learning which is watching the behavior of another person.

Although most studies of the social learning theory involve determining how children develop and learn, some studies have determined how the theory applies to adult behaviors. Anderson et al. (2004) suggest that observational learning remains a powerful mechanism for acquisition of new social behaviors throughout maturity and into old age. Phillips (1974) found that the national level of suicides increased for brief periods following suicide stories being publicized in the newspaper. He concluded that suicide rates increased following publicized suicide stories because people are imitating the publicized suicide story. Phillips (1979) also showed that daily California motor vehicle fatalities increased significantly following front-page suicide stories and these results were replicated by Bollen and Phillips (1981) in Detroit. Another study by Phillips (1982) found that suicides, motor vehicle deaths, and nonfatal motor vehicle accidents all show significant increases just after a character on a soap opera commits suicide. All of the results from the previous studies cited suggest that adults may use the social learning theory to imitate aggressive acts and suicidal behaviors publicized in the media. Other theories also include observation as means of learning aggressive behaviors and thoughts.

Script Theory

Script theory suggests that aggressive scripts are learned through observing violent acts (Huesmann, 1986). The violent acts that lead to the formation of scripts can be executed by various people in various situations such as parents at home, strangers in public, or all forms of mass media. A script can be defined as a sequence of expected behaviors for a certain situation (Abelson, 1981). Behavioral scripts are subroutines the brain executes in a way that enables it to accomplish predictable tasks without thinking too much about them. By rehearsing and practicing a script, the brain begins to form stronger links between situations and behaviors which enables a person to generalize this behavior to various conditions and circumstances. In other words, aggressive scripts can be learned through the observation and replication of a behavior which then becomes a well practiced routine. Aggression then becomes the reaction behavior to many types of situations and circumstances. For example, violent video games are a type of stimulus that can teach aggressive scripts which in turn develop into aggressive and reactive behavior in everyday circumstances. Laboratory evidence suggests that scripts for social behaviors are often encoded from patterns of behaviors that are observed. Just as individuals may encode a motor program for throwing a football from observing others, individuals may encode a script for hitting or kicking those who victimize them from observing video games that depict this type of aggression (Huesmann, 1988).

The General Aggression Model

The general aggression model (GAM) appears to be the most unifying theory, acquiring applications from previous ideas and putting them together in a concise model. The model has four main advantages over past theories of aggression: it is more parsimonious, it is a better explanation of multiple causes for aggressive actions, it aids in the creation of interventions for aggression, and it adds insight into child development and child rearing practices (Anderson & Bushman, 2002a). GAM focuses on the person in the situation, meaning GAM explains how situational and personal variables interact to affect a person's internal state. The internal state includes thoughts, feelings, and physical arousal. All of these influence each other and each will have an effect on an individual's interpretation of an aggressive or violent act (Anderson et al., 2004).

GAM research has focused on what biological, environmental, psychological, and social factors influence aggression and cause aggressive behavior (Anderson & Bushman, 2002a). Researchers have found that various personal and situational factors play a role in aggressive behavior. Person factors include all characteristics a person brings to the situation such as beliefs, values, long-term goals, attitudes, personality traits, and certain genetic predispositions which can all play a role in the aggressive preparedness of an individual (Anderson & Huesmann, 2003). Situational factors include important features of the situation such as presence of provocation or an aggressive cue (Anderson & Bushman, 2001). Aggressive cues are objects that prime aggressive related concepts in memory, making aggressive actions more likely. Provocation, frustration, pain, discomfort, drugs, and incentives are all situational factors that have been shown to play a role in aggressive actions of individuals (Carnagey & Anderson, 2005). These two variables, person factors and situation factors, influence the final outcome of behavior by effecting a person's cognitions, affect, and arousal. Although there are many situational and personal factors that can influence a person's behavior, Huesmann, Lagerspetz, and Eron (1984) have suggested the most aggressive children will have certain characteristics. According to these researchers, aggressive children will have parents with lower education and social status, have a more aggressive mother, perform poorly in school, and will be unpopular with peers. These aggressive children will also watch more violent television programs, believe these programs portray real life, and strongly identify with the aggressive characters in the shows. The previous cited research points to numerous situational and personal factors that can influence children's and adult's amount of aggressive behavior.

Social learning theory, script theory, and the general aggression model all describe various ways in which aggressive behaviors may be learned and acted upon by an individual. These theories however do not necessarily take into account what an individual believes is acceptable behavior towards another individual. In order to determine what people believe are acceptable behaviors and what behaviors are intolerable and overly aggressive, researchers need to assess normative beliefs about aggression.

Normative Beliefs About Aggression

Although aggression itself can be a physical or verbal behavior that can be easily observed and assessed, peoples' normative beliefs about the acceptability of aggression may not be as explicit. A normative belief can be defined as an individual's cognition about the acceptability or unacceptability of a behavior (Huesmann & Guerra, 1997). Normative beliefs serve as guides for action, meaning they provide shortcuts in deciding how to behave in given situations. Although a person's normative beliefs may differ from what others believe is an acceptable behavior, there is usually considerable overlap between an individual's normative beliefs and the normative beliefs of relevant peers, family members, social groups, and societal institutions (Huesmann, Guerra, Zelli, & Miller, 1992; Souweidane & Huesmann, 1999). Therefore, normative beliefs about aggression are beliefs about the acceptability or unacceptability of aggression in situations, and these beliefs are influenced by a person's family, peers, and culture.

Although normative beliefs about aggression are usually stable and consistent once developed, these beliefs are in a great state of flux when we are children. Huesmann and Guerra (1997) found that there appears to be no stability in children's normative beliefs between the first and second grade and found moderate stability in the fourth grade. However, these researchers did find that even in the first grade, children's normative beliefs about aggression and their actual aggressive behavior were highly correlated. Even though children's beliefs may change rapidly, their behaviors reflect what beliefs they are endorsing at the time. So if a child accepts that aggression is a normal response, he or she will act more aggressively, but if later that same child believes that aggression is not an acceptable response, his or her aggressive behavior will decrease. There is also evidence that in elementary classrooms where peers and teachers discourage aggression, children behave less aggressively which is possibly because they have learned that aggression is an unacceptable response (Henry et al., 2000). Although normative beliefs about aggression are unstable and in flux in children, by the time adolescence is reached these beliefs are more firm and stable but still adjustable. Werner and Nixon (2005) found that adolescents who endorsed aggression as an appropriate response reported more aggressive behavior in comparison to those who believed aggression was not an acceptable behavior. It has also been shown that high levels of anger and strong beliefs supporting aggression significantly contribute to the frequency of physical aggression as well as lower endorsement of the belief that aggressive behaviors and antisocial acts are wrong (Sukhodolsky & Ruchkin, 2004). Little research has been conducted regarding adult normative beliefs about aggression but one study has found a positive correlation between adults' aggressive behaviors and their endorsement of aggression as an appropriate response (Sigurdsson, Gudjonsson, Bragason, Kristjansdottir, & Sigfusdottir, 2006). Due the instability of the normative beliefs in children and the insufficient number of studies conducted with adults, more research needs to be conducted in order to determine what the relationship is between adults' aggressive behaviors and their normative beliefs about aggression.

Just as normative beliefs about aggression can vary depending on the age of the individual, these beliefs can also vary depending on gender of the individual. Boys and girls appear to hold differing standards when it comes to what they believe is appropriate in aggressiveness of behavior. It has been shown that the correlation between normative beliefs supporting aggression and the use of aggressive behavior is significantly higher in boys than in girls (Huesmann & Guerra, 1997; Huesmann et al., 1992). Some researchers have suggested that the gender differences seen in the attitudes related to aggression are associated with the type of aggression exhibited. Females tend to view relational and verbal aggression as a normative aggressive response while males tend to view physical aggression as a normative aggressive response (Crick, Bigbee, & Howes, 1996; Krahe & Moller, 2004). This provides additional support to the differences between males and females in not only beliefs about aggression but also in aggressive behaviors.

So far what has been discussed has been primarily concerned with what aggression is, some theories about how aggression is produced, and some of the beliefs about aggression. There are many aspects of daily existence that can perpetuate aggressive behaviors and beliefs, some of which include the various types of media which display aggressive language, actions, affects, and behaviors and the ability to access these forms of media.

Violent Media

Media can be viewed in many forms including newspapers, magazines, music, art, the Internet, television, movies, and video games, all of which have genres that are aggressive and violent. Exposure to violent media can increase the likelihood of aggressive behavior occurring and can influence the development of aggression related knowledge structures and aggressive personalities (Anderson & Bushman, 2001; Bartholow et al., 2005; Eron, Huesmann, Lefkowitz, & Walder, 1972; Huesmann, Moise-Titus, Podolski, & Eron, 2003). Each time a violent movie or television show is watched or a violent video game is played, aggressive scripts are rehearsed that teach and reinforce vigilance for enemies, aggressive actions against others, expectations that others will behave aggressively, positive attitudes towards the use of violence, and beliefs that violent solutions are effective and appropriate (Bushman, 1998). It has also been shown that repeated exposure to violent video games can increase players' aggressive outlook, perceptual biases, attitudes, beliefs, and behavior (Anderson & Dill, 2000). The effects of violent media on aggressive behavior and affect have been studied for many years beginning with the popularity and accessibility of television people's daily lives.

Television

The television was first introduced to Americans in 1928 and since that time almost every American home has at least one television. Just as the popularity of the television has grown over time, the programming being broadcast on the networks has become increasing violent and aggressive since the introduction of television. Researchers began to notice an increase in the aggressive behaviors of children and launched research to determine whether viewing media violence had any effect on these behaviors. Television was not introduced to all communities at the same time so researchers took advantage of this to determine what differences existed between aggression in communities with or without television. Hennigan et al. (1982) compared crime rates in numerous American cities in which television was introduced and in cities where television was not yet available. He found that the presence or absence of television did not significantly affect violent crime rates. Centerwall (1989a, 1989b, 1992) examined the relationship between homicide rates and the introduction of television in South Africa, Canada, and the United States. The results suggested that 15 years after the introduction of television, homicide rates for Caucasians increased dramatically in the United States and Canada. It was concluded from these various studies that the introduction of television, combined with frequent portrayals of violence, increased interpersonal violence in the United States and Canada. Although these studies attempted to determine if the introduction of television created any differences in crime rates, various researchers have also attempted to determine what relationship television viewing has on aggressive behaviors and thoughts.

Eron, Huesmann, Lefkowitz, and Walder (1972) wanted to determine if children's preferences for violent television at age eight would be positively related to adulthood aggressiveness. The researchers found that the more violent television programming preferred and viewed by males at age eight, the more aggressive their behavior was at that time and ten years later. These same effects were not found for females. These results suggest that the influence of watching violent television is not confined to only short-term effects but can influence a person's behavior for a life-time. Another study by Huesmann, Lagerspetz, and Eron (1984) found a positive relationship between viewing violent television and aggressive behavior among boys in both Finland and the United States and among girls in the United States only. They also found that a boy's violence viewing and identification with a character is a good predictor of later aggression, while a boy's initial level of aggression is not a good predictor of viewing violent television and identification with characters. These results suggest that children's viewing of violent television programs is related to aggressive behavior but aggressive children do not necessarily watch more violent television. Since the beginning of violent television research, investigators have repeatedly found that viewing violent television is positively related to increased aggressive behavior and affect among children and adults (Anderson, 1997; Bushman & Green, 1990; Bushman & Huesmann, 2001; Comstock, 1980; Huesmann et al., 2003; Josephson, 1987).

There have also been longitudinal studies conducted to determine what the long-term effects of violent television viewing are. Huesmann and Eron (1986) studied the effects of television violence in five countries: Austria, Poland, Finland, Israel, and the United States. They examined children at three times as they grew from ages 6 to 8 or from 8 to 11 years of age. The results suggested that there was a small to moderate relationship between aggression and overall exposure to television violence in all five nations. The extent to which earlier viewing of television violence predicted later aggression varied substantially between genders and among countries. A 15 year follow-up of 300 American participants suggested a delayed effect of media violence on serious physical aggression (Huesmann et al., 2003). The researchers found a significant relationship between television violence viewing during childhood and aggressive behaviors as adults in both men and women. Another longitudinal study by Johnson, Cohen, Smailes, Kasen, and Brook (2002) assessed the total amount of time people spent watching television and amount of physical aggression displayed from age 14 to age 22. The results suggested that television viewing at age 14 significantly predicted assault and fighting behavior at age 16 and age 22. The researchers concluded that television watching may have long-term aversive effects lasting into adulthood. In fact in a meta-analysis conducted across 42 tests involving almost 5,000 participants, Anderson and Bushman (2002b) suggested that high levels of violent television viewing in childhood could promote aggression in later childhood, adolescence, and adulthood.

Although there are scores of studies suggesting that viewing violent television is related to increases in aggressive affect and behavior, other forms of media have not been as extensively researched. Additional categories of media such as music, video games, magazines, and the Internet have been implicated as media that increase the aggressive behavior and affect of those who consume them. Besides television, video games have received the most attention from researchers among all forms of violent media.

Video games

The video game industry has grown significantly since the introduction of Pong, a nonviolent game of table tennis, in 1972. Although the first video game was not violent, it did not take the industry long to determine that violent games led to increased sales. The first violent video game was Death Race and was released in 1976 (Gentile & Anderson, 2006). The goal of the game was to run over stick-figured pedestrians who would then scream and turn into gravestones. The public was outraged by the violent content of this game and some communities even banned its use, but the controversy surrounding this game actually increased sales tenfold (Kent, 2001). This was the first indication to game developers that violence sells and this began the creation of numerous violent games. With technological advancements during the 1980s and early 1990s, video games became increasingly violent and realistic. First-person shooter games were developed at this time which enabled the player to "see" the video game through the eyes of the character being controlled making the games more realistic and making the player feel more involved in the game (Kent, 2001). Video games also began to depict more violent images when characters were injured or killed in the game with splatters or pools of blood and extremities being removed.

Not only has the amount of violence increased in the gaming industry, the overall value of the industry has increased significantly. In less than 30 years the video game industry has grown into a multi-billion dollar industry with annual sales totaling $20 billion worldwide and almost half of these sales ($9.4 billion per year) are in the United States (Carnagey & Anderson, 2004). In a recent survey of over 600 8th and 9th grade students, children averaged nine hours of video game play per week, with boys averaging thirteen hours per week and girls averaging five hours per week (Gentile et al., 2004). Due to the amount of money spent annually and the amount of time per week people spend playing video games, this form of media requires much more research in order to determine what effects these games may be having on behavior and affect. One way to determine these effects maybe to look at the differences and similarities between viewing television and playing video games.

Although television and video games have some similarities in terms of content and graphics, the differences between these forms of media are extensive and they may explain how aggressive behavior may result from certain types of media. One main difference between television and video games is that television is viewed in the third person, meaning that the viewer does not have a viewpoint from a character within the show and does not actively participate in the events taking place in the show. Most video games on the other hand can be viewed in the first person, meaning the player actually sees the activities of the game through the eyes of a character. This first person point of view that video games utilize creates many differences between television and video games. Players of video games are active in the game having control over the actions of the characters whereas viewers of television are passive and have no control over what happens to the characters in the shows being viewed. This also means that players can control the amount of violence they see and the amount of violent actions the characters exhibit in the games; in television the viewers have no control over the amount of violence involved. Television can present real people who are acting out scenes and behaviors while video games only portray animated characters whose behaviors are controlled by the player. Despite these characters being animated, the graphics on video games are becoming much more realistic every year which may increase a player's involvement with the characters. Players can even create their own characters that can look identical to themselves so that players truly feel like they are in the game.

Another difference between television and video games is that viewers of television are passive spectators of the events being portrayed and are not rewarded when characters act more aggressively, but players of video games are rewarded for the violent actions of characters. For example, most shooter and first-person games score how many hits or kills a player has and in most games players cannot advance until they conquer a certain character or group of characters which requires using aggressive behaviors. These rewards combined with the realism of the graphics and characters in the games could help to explain how aggression may develop and how beliefs about the acceptability of aggressive behaviors increase in video game players.

The previously discussed theories of aggression show how playing violent video games could potentially lead to aggressive behaviors of individuals. Social learning theory would suggest that while playing violent video games, players are learning aggressive behaviors through observing in the first person how the characters behave and how the characters are rewarded for violent actions. Players are more likely to repeat these behaviors because the characters in the game were not punished for the actions but were actually rewarded and the player felt rewarded by being able to continue to another level of the game therefore reinforcing the belief that aggressive behaviors are acceptable. After playing many violent games, players may begin to form scripts around what types of behaviors are appropriate for certain situations and because most video games are played in the first person these scripts have been well rehearsed while playing the game so script theory would suggest that players are more likely to react aggressively in various situations in their lives. Although theories of aggression appear to explain what effects playing video games could have on behavior, researchers are still trying to determine exactly what effects playing violent video games have on aggressive behavior and affect.

The final part of this analysis will be posted in March 2010 in Interface.

Editor's Note: This reference list includes sources related to the forthcoming Part II of this article.

References

Abelson, R. P. (1981). Psychological status of the script concept. *American Psychology*, 36, 715-729.

Anderson, C. A. (1997). Effects of violent movies and trait hostility on hostile feelings and aggressive thoughts. *Aggressive Behavior*, 23, 161-178.

Anderson, C. A., & Bushman, B. J. (2001). Effects of violent video games on aggressive behavior, aggressive cognition, aggressive affect, physiological arousal, and prosocial behavior: A meta-analytic review of the scientific literature. *Psychological Science*, 12, 353-359.

Anderson, C. A., & Bushman, B. J. (2002a). Human aggression. *Annual Review of Psychology*, 53, 27-51.

Anderson, C.A., & Bushman, B.J. (2002b). Media violence and the American public revisited. *American Psychologist*, 57, 448-450.

Anderson, C. A., Carnagey, N. L., Flanagan, M., Benjamin, A. J., Eubanks, J., & Valentine, J. C. (2004). Violent video games: Specific effects on violent content on aggressive thoughts and behavior. *Advances in Experimental Social Psychology*, 36, 199-248.

Anderson, C. A., & Dill, K. E. (2000). Video games and aggressive thoughts, feelings, and behavior in the laboratory and in life. *Journal of Personality and Social Psychology*, 78, 772-790.

Anderson, C. A., & Huesman, L. R. (2003). Human aggression: A social-cognitive view. In Hogg, M. A. & Cooper, J. (Eds.), *The Sage Handbook of Social Psychology* (pp. 296-323). Thousand Oaks, CA: Sage Publications, Inc.

Anderson, C. A., & Murphy, C. R. (2003). Violent video games and aggressive behavior in young women. *Aggressive Behavior*, 29, 423-429.

Archer, J., & Latham, M. (2004). Variation in beliefs about aggression as a function of relationship to the opponent. *Personality and Individual Differences*, 37, 33-41.

Arriaga, P., Esteves, F., Carneiro, P., & Monteiro, B. (2006). Violent computer games and their effects on state hostility and physiological arousal. *Aggressive Behavior*, 32, 358-371.

Bandura, A. (1973). *Aggression: A social learning theory analysis.* Englewood Cliffs, NJ: Prentice-Hall.

Bandura, A., Ross, D., & Ross, S. A. (1961). Transmission of aggression through imitation of aggressive models. *Journal of Abnormal and Social Psychology*, 63, 575-582.

Bartholow, B. D., & Anderson, C. A. (2002). Effects of violent video games on aggressive behavior: Potential sex differences. Journal of Experimental Social Psychology, 38, 283-290.

Bartholow, B. D., Sestir, M. A., & Davis, E. B. (2005). Correlates and consequences of exposure to video game violence: Hostile personality, empathy, and aggressive behavior. *Personality and Social Psychology Bulletin*, 31, 1573-1586.

Bollen, K. A., & Phillips, D. P. (1981). Suicide motor vehicle fatalities in Detroit: A replication. *American Journal of Sociology*, 87, 404-412.

Bushman, B. J. (1998). Priming effects of violent media on the accessibility of aggressive constructs in memory. *Personal and Social Psychology Bulletin*, 24, 537-545.

Bushman, B. J., & Green, R. G. (1990). Role of cognitive-emotional mediators and individual differences in the effects of media violence on aggression. *Journal of Personality and Social Psychology*, 58, 156-163.

Bushman, B.J., & Huesmann, L.R. (2001). Effects of televised violence on aggression. In D. Singer & J. Singer (Eds.), *Handbook of children and the media* (pp. 223-254). Thousand Oaks, CA: Sage Publications.

Buss, A. H., & Perry, M. (1992). The aggression questionnaire. *Journal of Personality and Social Psychology*, 63, 452-459.

Carnagey, N. L., & Anderson, C. A. (2004). Violent video game exposure and aggression: A literature review. *Minerva Psichiatrica*, 45, 1-18.

Carnagey, N. L., & Anderson, C. A. (2005). The effects of reward and punishment in violent video games on aggressive affect, cognition, and behavior. *Psychological Science*, 16, 882-889.

Centerwall, B.S. (1989a). Exposure to television as a cause of violence. In G. Comstock (Ed.), *Public communication and behavior* (Vol. 2, pp. 1-58). New York: Academic Press.

Centerwall, B.S. (1989b). Exposure to television as a risk factor for violence. *American Journal of Epidemiology*, 129, 643-652.

Centerwall, B.S. (1992). Television and violence: The scale of the problem and where to go from here. *Journal of the American Medical Association*, 267, 3059-3063.

Colwell, J., & Kato, M. (2005). Video game play in British and Japanese adolescents. *Simulation and Gaming*, 36, 518-530.

Colwell, J., & Payne, J. (2000). Negative correlates of computer game play in adolescents. *British Journal of Psychology*, 91, 295-310.

Comstock, G. (1980). New emphases in research on the effects of television and film violence. In E.L. Palmer & A. Dorr (Eds.), *Children and the faces of television: Teaching, violence, selling* (pp. 129-148). New York: Academic Press.

Crick, N. R., Bigbee, M. A., & Howes, C. (1996). Gender differences in children's normative beliefs about aggression: How do I hurt thee? Let me count the ways. *Child Development*, 67, 1003-1014.

Deselms, J. L., & Altman, J. D. (2003). Immediate and prolonged effects of videogame violence. *Journal of Applied Social Psychology*, 33, 1553-1563.

Entertainment Software Association (2006). Entertainment Software Rating Board (ESRB). Retrieved January 26th, 2008 from http://www.esrb.org

Eron, L. D., Huesmann, L. R., Lefkowitz, M. M., & Walder, L. O. (1972). Does television violence cause aggression? *American Psychologist*, 27, 253-263.

Farrar, K. M., Krcmar, M. & Nowak, K. L. (2006). Contextual features of violent video games, mental models, and aggression. *Journal of Communication*, 56, 387-405.

Ferguson, C. J. (2007). Evidence for publication bias in video game violence effects literature: A meta-analytic review. *Aggression and Violent Behavior*, 12, 470-482.

Fleming, M. J., & Rickwood, D. J. (2001). Effects of violent versus nonviolent video games on children's arousal, aggressive mood, and positive mood. *Journal of Applied Social Psychology*, 31, 2047-2071.

Funk, J. B., Flores, G., Buchman, D. D., & Germann, J. N. (1999). Rating electronic games: Violence is in the eye of the beholder. *Youth and Society*, 30, 283-312.

Funk, J. B., Hagan, J., Schimming, J., Bullock, W. A., Buchman, D. D., & Myers, M. (2002). Aggression and psychopathology in adolescents with a preference for violent electronic games. *Aggressive Behavior*, 28, 134-144.

Gentile, D. A., & Anderson, C. A. (2006). Violent video games: The effects on youth and public policy implications. In Dowd, N., Singer, D. G., & Wilson, R. F.

(Eds.), *Handbook of Children, Culture, and Violence* (pp. 225-246). Thousand Oaks, CA: Sage Publications, Inc.

Gentile, D. A., Lynch, P. J., Linder, J. R., & Walsh, D. A. (2004). The effects of violent video game habits on adolescent hostility, aggressive behaviors, and school performance. *Journal of Adolescence*, 27, 5-22.

Haninger, K. & Thompson, K. M. (2004). Content and ratings of teen-rated video games. *Journal of the American Medical Association*, 291, 856-865.

Hartmann, T., & Klimmt, C. (2006). Gender and computer games: Exploring females' dislikes. *Journal of Computer-Mediated Communication*, 11, 910-931.

Hennigan, K.M., Del Rosario, M.L., Heath, L., Cook, T.D., Wharton, J.D., & Calder, B.J. (1982). Impact of the introduction of television on crime in the United States: Empirical findings and theoretical implications. *Journal of Personality and Social Psychology*, 42, 461-477.

Henry, D., Guerra, N., Huesmann, R., Tolan, P., VanAcker, R., & Eron, L. (2000). Normative influences on aggression in urban elementary school classrooms. *American Journal of Community Psychology*, 28, 59-81.

Huesman, L. R. (1986). Psychological processes promoting the relation between exposure to media violence and aggressive behavior by the viewer. *Journal of Social Issues*, 42, 125-140.

Huesmann, L. R. (1988). An informational processing model for the development of aggression. *Aggressive Behavior*, 14, 13-24.

Huesmann, L. R., & Eron, L. D. (1986). *Television and the aggressive child: A cross-national comparison*. Hillsdale, NJ: Erlbaum.

Huesmann, L. R., & Guerra, N. G. (1997). Children's normative beliefs about aggression and aggressive behavior. *Journal of Personality and Social Psychology*, 72, 408-419.

Huesmann, L. R., Guerra, N. G., Zelli, A., & Miller, L. (1992). Differing normative beliefs about aggression for boys and girls. In Bjorkqvist, K. & Niemela, P. (Eds.). Of Mice and Women: Aspects of Female Aggression (pp. 77-87). San Diego, CA: Academic Press, Inc.

Huesmann, L. R., Lagerspetz, K., & Eron, L. D. (1984). Intervening variables in the TV violence-aggression relation: Evidence from two countries. *Developmental Psychology*, 20, 746-775.

Huesmann, L. R., Moise-Titus, J., Podolski, C. L., & Eron, L. D. (2003). Longitudinal relations between children's exposure to TV violence and their aggressive and violent behavior in young adulthood: 1977-1992. *Developmental Psychology*, 39, 201-221.

Johnson, J.G., Cohen, P., Smailes, E.M., Kasen, S., & Brook, J.S. (2002). Television viewing and aggressive behavior during adolescence and adulthood. *Science*, 295, 2468-2471.

Josephson, W. L. (1987). Television violence and children's aggression: Testing the priming, social script, and disinhibition predictions. *Journal of Personality and Social Psychology*, 53, 882-890.

Kent, S. (2001). *The ultimate history of video games*. Roseville, CA: Prima.

Krahe, B., & Moller, I. (2004). Playing violent electronic games, hostile attributional style, and aggression-related norms in German adolescents, *Journal of Adolescence*, 27, 53-69.

Lubich, M. (2007, December 26). Vigil finds 'little girl lost' amid chaos of death. The Johnstown Breeze. Retrieved from www.johnstownbreeze.com/modules/php?name=news&file=article&sid=2499

Olson, C. K., Kutner, L. A., Warner, D. E., Almerigi, J. B., Baer, L., Nicholi, A. M., & Beresin, E. V. (2007). Factors correlated with violent video game use by adolescent boys and girls. *Journal of Adolescent Health*, 41, 77-83.

Oser, K. (2004). Moms are unsung players in gaming world. *Advertising Age*, 75, 56-57.

Persky, S., & Blascovich, J. (2007). Immersive virtual environments versus traditional platforms: Effects of violent and nonviolent video game play, *Media Psychology*, 10, 135-156.

Phillips, D. P. (1974). The influence of suggestion on suicide: Substantive and theoretical implications of the Werther Effect. *American Sociological Review*, 39, 340-354.

Phillips, D. P. (1979). Suicide, motor vehicle fatalities, and the mass media: Evidence toward a theory of suggestion. *American Journal of Sociology*, 84, 1150-1174.

Phillips, D. P. (1982). The impact of fictional television stories on the U.S. adult fatalities: New evidence on the effect of the mass media on violence, *American Journal of Sociology*, 87, 1340-1359.

Pooley, E. (1999). Portrait of a deadly bond. *Time*, May, 26-32.

Sherry, J. L. (2001). The effects of violent video games on aggression: A meta-analysis. *Human Communication Association*, 27, 409-431.

Sigurdsson, J. F., Gudjonsson, G. H., Bragason, A. V., Kristjansdottir, E., & Sigfusdottir, I. D. (2006). The role of violent cognition in the relationship between personality and the involvement in violent films and computer games. *Personality and Individual Differences*, 41, 381-392.

Souweidane, V., & Huesmann, L. R. (1999). The influence of American urban culture on the development of normative beliefs about aggression in Middle-Eastern immigrants. *American Journal of Community Psychology*, 27, 239-253.

Sukhodolsky, D. G., & Ruchkin, V. V. (2004). Association of normative beliefs and anger with aggression and antisocial behavior in Russian male juvenile offenders and high school students. *Journal of Abnormal Child Psychology*, 32, 225-236.

Thompson, K. M., & Haninger (2001). Violence in E-rated video games, *Journal of the American Medical Association*, 286, 591-598.

Werner, N. E., & Nixon, C. L. (2005). Normative beliefs and relational aggression: An investigation of the cognitive bases of adolescent aggressive behavior. *Journal of Youth and Adolescence*, 34, 229-243.

Marina Yue Zhang and Bruce W. Stening's *China 2.0. The Transformation of an Emerging Superpower...And the Opportunities.*

Review by Jeffrey Barlow

Berglund Center for Internet Studies, Pacific University

One of the pleasures of working out of Hong Kong for even a few days, as I have recently done, is being able to browse shelves of books in English dealing with contemporary Asia. Online ordering is useful, but usually I wait for a book to be noticed by others before I invest. At my favorite Swindon's outlet in Kowloon, I recently discovered Marina Yue Zhang's *China 2.0*, published in Singapore.

Briefly put, the work is a valuable one, which offers the insights of a very well trained and highly experienced expert in management who has impeccable cultural credentials as well. Maria Zhang is a native speaker of Chinese who attended college in Beijing (B.A. Biological Sciences, Beijing University), then went on to get her MBA and a Ph.D. in Management at Australian National University. The author's special area of interest is high-tech, and she has lectured widely in Asia, and now lives once again in Beijing.

Zhang approaches her subject sympathetically in that she feels, as do I, that Western perspectives on China are all too often warped by centuries of accumulated preconceptions, making it difficult to understand China during periods of rapid change like the present. At the same time, sympathetic or not, she has an excellent grasp of the subject and views it both broadly and objectively. For example, Zhang was directly and personally involved in the Beijing spring protests of 1989, but has decided that China's recent economic and political success has benefitted more from a stable regime than it would have benefitted from idealistic attempts to somehow graft Western democratic institutions onto such an ancient and highly developed culture.[1]

This position, which will seem paradoxical to many American readers, stems from Zhang's belief that China is, because of its stability, achieving staggering economic progress, which is the only way that the hugely overcrowded and formerly poverty-stricken country could possibly have come to the point where substantive political reform could ever be considered a realistic project. China 2.0 does an excellent job of describing recent progress, not only in the data-driven language of economists, but also with numerous insights and anecdotes made possible by the author's residence in China and her ability to follow Chinese blogs and other popular cultural materials.

One of Zhang's many strong points is that she is able to decipher the language of Chinese political slogans such as calls to achieve "a Harmonious Society" and

[1] Zhang xix-xx.

therefore understand the underlying models for reform which they represent.[2] She also understands the issues that vex foreign corporations and political leaders in trying to come to terms with China's sudden economic clout both at home and abroad. She discusses in some detail all the usual aspects of such stresses, from intellectual property rights to currency manipulations, and in doing so greatly illuminates their meaning for China, and for the rest of the world.

The book is ambitiously organized. It's part chronicle of China's rise and part a how-to manual for Western businesses hoping to take advantage of this booming economy. The end result may be that it will appeal primarily to very serious scholars or businesspeople seeking detailed explanations of various elements of the Chinese economy in the context of the global economy.

The overarching metaphor of the book, "China 2.0," is an apt one in that the work focuses on the impact of interactive social media on all aspects of Chinese life, with an emphasis upon the changing Chinese customer and his or her orientation toward life and politics, as well as upon changing consumption patterns. The author's many public appearances and consulting jobs have also given her a great deal of insight into not only Western firms in China, but also into Chinese ones, and into the minds of those who direct both. Her close analysis of many such firms, such as those involved in the milk scandal in China, also give her a micro- as well as a macro-perspective. Her analysis gives the reader a very good sense of who operates the Chinese economy now, and how they have changed substantially from the grey Maoists of the past.

Zhang shows that Chinese society is making a transition from the sort of broadcast version of Chinese society emanating from the top (the Communist Party) to an interactive one which is empowering common Chinese people, using the tools of the World Wide Web, to begin to impact the Chinese political system in a manner which amounts to forcing serious and substantive reforms. Ordinary people are now routinely challenging corruption and authority, and the state is hurrying to catch up with them rather than be left in their wake.

In the West in general, and in the United States in particular, these events are invariably reported as though they are mere cracks in the totalitarian façade of one party-rule, remarkable precisely because they are exceptional. By reporting them in this fashion, we emphasize not change, but continuity: China is still totalitarian. Zhang rather argues that such events are becoming, not exceptions, but part of the daily fabric of Chinese life. This is not to say, as the author cautions us, that the results will bear much resemblance to Western ideas of democracy.

The metaphor of 2.0 is also important, the author argues, for businesses trying to succeed in China. The old ways of doing business—spray advertising and pray—will not work much longer. The more successful businesses are those which take advantage of interactive processes, such as facilitating customer responses to

---

[2] Zhang 31-37.

sales campaigns, utilizing every possible social media, and those which will see Chinese production facilities, not as an entrée to the Chinese market, but as part of an international production chain which will inevitably shape the corporation globally.

One very serious shortcoming of the book is that it was edited much too hurriedly. This might be thought by some readers to be a minor issue but in this case it sometimes becomes an exercise in the surreal as a reader begins to feel that he or she has already read a given sentence or paragraph. It is as though two different versions of the manuscripts were hurriedly pasted together in an attempt to make a publishing deadline.

I read much of the work in the economy class dungeon of an aged jetliner on an extended transpacific flight. Repeatedly experiencing the reader's equivalent of déjà vu, I initially feared that I was losing my mind from bad air, bad lighting, dangerous noise levels, inadequate nutrition, and overcrowding and might soon begin to gnaw off body parts in an effort to escape. I was relieved to encounter a paragraph of some six or eight sentences ending with the two identical sentences with which it had begun, proving definitively that it was the editor who had lost his or her mind, not me.[3] One expects more from a John Wiley publication, particularly from a relatively expensive one (36 USD). One can imagine that the author is very tired of jokes about the quality of outsourced work in Singapore, where the book was edited.

But despite the cavalier treatment the press gave it, *China 2.0* is a remarkable book, which should be read by all those trying to understand the effects of the rapid economic, political, and social changes which China is undergoing, and their effects upon the world.

[3] Zhang, top of page 264

Martin Jacques' *When China Rules the World. The End of the Western World and the Birth of a New Global Order.*

Review by Jeffrey Barlow

Berglund Center for Internet Studies, Pacific University

Martin Jacques' work, *When China Rules the World*, is an important one. It argues that the global order is in the process of rapid and fundamental changes. China, as a new economic giant, will begin to be much more influential, particularly in East and Southeast Asia, but also globally. This will necessarily result in major changes in the international economic and political order.[1]

From the above summary, *When China Rules the World* might be thought to be one of a series of such cautionary analyses of the "rise of China." However, this work is very different. Jacques argues not that China is on the rise, but that it is re-attaining the dominant position it has usually enjoyed in the world economy. In making this argument, Jacques redefines many critical issues. For example, most Western analysis prefers to see the brief period of Western world domination as a natural result of cultural superiority. That is, the Judeo-Christian tradition produced a culture uniquely capable of rapid advances in science, exploration, and business, whereas non-Western countries like China were doomed to backwardness, unless, of course, they adopted Western institutions.

Jacques believes, correctly, in my opinion, that Western dominance was largely a result of European colonialism. The 19th and 20th centuries saw the West at its strongest, and Asia at its weakest; this was particularly the case for China. China remained politically divided and backward until the mid-twentieth century. From that point forward, it has grown steadily, despite the slowdowns caused by Maoist extremism from 1958-68.

The banking crises of 2009 created an environment where it suddenly has become obvious, in Jacques' perspective, that there is in fact more than one path and, perhaps, infinitely many paths, to development. This may seem a simple truism. But Jacques argues that along with China's return to prominence the world order is itself being changed by the mere presence of the successful Chinese model. In addition, as China is not a new player at the top of the global order, it will come to the table with a great deal of previous experience, even with institutions which served it well in the past. These are quite alien to the Western models to which it temporarily was forced to conform by the violence of colonialism.

---

[1] For a good review of the book, see "Waking Dragon," by Joseph Kahn (A former U.S. ambassador to Beijing), The NYT, December 31, 2009, at: http://www.nytimes.com/2010/01/03/books/review/Kahn-t.html?ref=review

These arguments are staggering in their implications, and suggest that a very conflict-ridden period may lie ahead of us as China pushes its way into the world order on significantly different terms than other recent arrivals. It may be a harbinger of similar stresses accompanying the imminent arrival of the other "BRICS"---Brazil, Russia, India, and China herself.

Jacques' credentials are impeccable. He has the familiarity with Asia necessary to understand China, and the scholarship to build on much previous work. He has been awarded major visiting positions at a number of first-rate Asian and Western universities and is currently a Visiting Fellow at the London School of Economics.[2] He also writes regularly for a number of periodicals and has established, over the years, a circle of contacts whose information and perspectives enrich this work. He is clearly left-leaning and has been associated with a number of moderate Marxist journals. This orientation enables him also to analyze Chinese Communism, which, in sum, he finds largely irrelevant to an understanding of contemporary China.

Jacques is, however, much more than a scholar and a journalist. He has learned a lot from personal circumstances. For example, his wife is an overseas Indian from Malaysia. This causes him to reflect upon Chinese attitudes toward other ethnicities, particularly those with darker skins.

The work, of course, deals with Internet-enabled communications as an important factor in the current international political and economic structure. While Jacques uses an astonishing number of classical and new scholarly resources, he also draws on Chinese blogs and Web pages to sample Chinese opinion on a variety of issues. His personal contacts in Beijing and Hong Kong also prove to be very worthwhile additions to the research base of the work.

Jacques' title is deliberately inflammatory and intended to shock and/or to sell books. But his arguments are very cogent ones. Not all of them are by any means new, but he has assembled them into a highly organized and unified perspective. His key point is simply that China, if it will not actually rule what is, after all, a multi-polar world, will be the first Western equal in Asia, dominant in Southeast Asia, and among the world's ranking powers at a global level. This situation will be unprecedented. Japan, for example, broke into the international political order largely as a Pacific ally of the British. Once Japan truly went its own way, violence began to mount. Adapting to China will also severely stress the international order.

One of Jacques' several key perspectives is that, in understanding China, we should not look at its recent Communist past, but at its ancient Confucian imperial culture. In his opinion, we would do better to understand Confucius than Marx or Mao.

Jacques argues, for example, that China will employ a sort of variant on the old Confucian Tribute System for its relations with other states, and particularly with East and Southeast Asian ones. This system is quite different than the Western

---

[2] See Jacques' Wikipedia biography at http://en.wikipedia.org/wiki/Martin_Jacques

Westphalian order, in which all states are presumed to be equal; China was forced into that order in the mid-nineteenth century as a result of the Opium Wars.

In the Tribute System, other states revolved around China in informal recognition that China was the center of the regional order. China expected these states to play by Chinese rules, such as recognizing Chinese influence as dominant. At the same time, in recompense, China owed subordinate states a stable order and a generous Chinese hand with political and economic support.

This position might seem, to many, to be ludicrous. But in China, ancient symbols have great staying power. I am reminded, for example, of some television footage I saw of a major world conference being held in Beijing, perhaps three years ago. (I was in China at the time, so I have no way of knowing if the footage to which I refer here was seen internationally.) It was customary at these meetings for the guests to wear the costumes of the host. In this case, the guests rode up in their limos, stepped onto a red carpet and walked toward their host, bowing before him—Hu Jintao as I recall, but it may also have been Jiang Zemin, both state and Party leaders at the time.

All the guests wore brightly colored Chinese silk gown—every color but red. Red is reserved for the Emperor, in this case, worn only by Hu Jintao, who laughed with great pleasure as the President of the United States, George W. Bush, bowed before him in a blue robe. To anyone familiar with Chinese culture, the entire ceremony was an obvious 21st-century kotow; the symbolic bow with which foreign emissaries presenting tribute acknowledged the superior power of the Chinese emperor and the moral authority of the Confucian world order.[3] Jacques may indeed have a point here.

The return of China to world prominence will have its costs, both for China, and for the rest of the world. The Chinese, Jacques believes, do not understand that, following the impact of the Internet, there are no longer any issues which can be regarded as purely internal. The Han (the dominant Chinese ethnic group) Jacques argues, are in fact a fictive group and the Chinese insistence on rigid ethnic divisions is merely a political cover for internal control purposes. But for us outside the Chinese system, the Han treatment of minorities is a sort of foreshadowing of how Chinese might well choose to treat us if they had external influence equivalent to their internal influence over other ethnicities.

The author feels, correctly, I think, on the basis of my own experience, that the Chinese are deeply and unthinkingly racist...so much so that a rational debate of prejudice in Chinese policy and attitudes is not even possible. As I was teaching in China while reading Jacques, I tried this idea out on my sophomore students, using some of his examples. What, I asked my class, are we to make of the fact that, as Jacques shows, Chinese newspapers located in diaspora communities all over the world universally refer to the majorities around them as "waiguo ren," foreigners? (That is, to Chinese living in Italy, Italians are "foreigners".) My students found the question puzzling. After all, aren't they, in fact, foreigners?

---

[3] See Wikipedia, http://en.wikipedia.org/wiki/Kowtow

Jacques also argues that there are going to be many changes when Chinese influence begins to increase in the West, as it is already so obviously doing. Many of these will amount merely to a diversification of the previously dominant influences. Chinese language will be used more broadly on the Internet; more people will choose to study it; it will become a major influence on world culture. In addition, Chinese films will begin to compete with Hollywood, extending Chinese cultural influence through a channel hitherto dominated by the United States. We will learn more about important Chinese historical events and famous personages. But some of the changes will be less comfortable ones.

Jacque believes, for example, that the days of the domination of the dollars as a reserve currency are numbered. China clearly intends to make its national currency, the Ren Min Bi, an international one, and to replace the dollar in at least East and Southeast Asia as a reserve currency. This will take some time, of course, as the value of the RMB is now carefully controlled, both to isolate the Chinese economy from harmful surges of "hot" investments which can do great damage to an economy, and to decrease the price of Chinese goods abroad, stimulating the great export machine which the Chinese economy has long been.

But the Chinese now must reorient their economy, given the collapse of effective demand in Western markets. As part of employing their huge dollar surpluses, Chinese will be buying more and more businesses abroad. They will also, one presumes, buy more and more political influence in at least the United States as well.

We once had a Senator from California, William F. Knowland, who was so responsive to Chinese Nationalist interests—represented by Chiang Kai-shek and Madame Chiang---that he was known as "The Senator from Formosa".[4] It is possible that we will also have "Representatives from Beijing" in some Congressional districts when Chinese firms become large employers.

Europe too has some painful adjustment to make as China increases its influence in world political and economic systems. The big problems, however, according to Jacques, will be for Americans. The return of China requires that the United States make room in what has happily been a U.S. dominated world order.

Within the current decade the triumphalist Neo-Cons sincerely believed that the entire international order could and should be redesigned to reflect the undeniable fact of American supremacy. What will it mean, for example, when China becomes the largest aide donor to some countries in the Western hemisphere? It has long been the major donor for many African countries, which has enabled it not only to construct their transportation and port facilities but also to ship out key natural resources to China under favorable contracts. China just became the largest aide donor for the Philippines, which hitherto might safely be regarded as an American colony.

[4] See Wikipedia, http://en.wikipedia.org/wiki/William_F._Knowland

There are, of course, some shortcomings in *When China Rules the World*. Some reviewers have argued that Jacques pays inadequate attention to the many obstacles which China potentially faces as it tries to adjust its economy from a tightly controlled one to a necessarily more open one. It may be that Jacques also overlooks, in his enthusiasm, the restraints China will face in a multi-polar world.

In the imperial era, China never really faced equals so much as inferiors. Vietnam and Korea were the primary tribute states, both sharing land borders with China. Others like Japan were at a sort of secondary remove. The Westphalian order, while ostensibly open and democratic, in fact was carefully stacked to the advantage of a few great Western powers, notably Great Britain and the United States.

China thus went from a superior status to an inferior one in a few decades. It has never really faced a world in which it must conform to international usages while wielding great power and influence. As the current conflict over Google and the censoring of the World Wide Web in China shows, this will not be an easy transition for anybody.

Jacques also posits, in my opinion, too much continuity in Chinese culture. Confucianism is, I agree, a powerful model for explaining even contemporary China, but it will be much changed in the era of the one-child family.[5] Just as Confucianism must adapt, so will many other elements of Chinese culture. The other work reviewed in this issue (pg. 30), Marina Yue Zhang's *China Web 2.0* makes a very powerful argument for the strong democratizing effects of the interactive Web upon China, for example.

The book, to me, was not only highly instructive but also enjoyable. The author has a journalist's ability to explain abstruse elements of history and economics, while leavening them with human-interest stories drawn from his personal experience. *When China Rules the World* should be read by anyone with a serious interest not only in China, but in the future global order. His arguments, if occasionally strained, introduce new and very important issues into the discussions of the "Rise of China."

[5] I have written from China upon this point. See: entry of January 3, 2010" Yea for Confucianism…but what about the Bad Emperor?" at: http://chinatripper.wordpress.com/2010/01/

Google and China: Minor Incident or Cyberwar?

Editorial by Jeffery Barlow

Berglund Center for Internet Studies, Pacific University

I was in China from December 17, 2009 to January 22, 2010, teaching and lecturing at three Chinese universities. In addition, I spent five days in Hong Kong, much of it with very knowledgeable members of the international business community. This was the period when the recent Google incident began-by which I mean Google's charges that attempts had been made to hack the accounts of Chinese dissidents in Gmail, causing Google to state that it would no longer censor its Chinese search results, and would, if necessary, leave China.

I had ample opportunity following these events to discuss the issues with Chinese people. The audiences at my presentations collectively numbered several hundreds, and we had a total of well over three hours of discussions together following my presentations, not counting numerous smaller lunches and dinners. My interlocutors included Chinese undergraduates at a medical school in Wenzhou, a seminar of Chinese graduate students of law in Nanjing, and a graduate and undergraduate group including ethnic minorities, such as Zhuang, Yao, Dong, and Miao in Nanning.[1]

I have also, of course, been writing on issues relating to China and the Internet for several years now, as well as on cyberwar.[2] Given this recent experience in China, and my continued interest in related topics, it may seem probable, then, that I have something profound to say upon the subject of Google and Cyberwarfare. However, perhaps the most profound thing I can say is that in this matter I consider very little is proven, nothing is certain, and not even a deliberately paced move to judgment is warranted.

This uncertainty is inherent to most cyberwarfare incidents. We often will not even be certain that such incidents have occurred; we will rarely know who is responsible, or what their motives were. Part of the cost of the Internet is relative anonymity for the perpetrators of such incidents.

This inherent uncertainty creates a very volatile, even potentially dangerous, situation when such incidents involve the interests of nation states, particularly ones as powerful, and as necessary to a peaceful international order, as are the United States and the People's Republic.

---

[1] For my blog maintained through this entire period, see: http://chinatripper.wordpress.com/. These entries were largely spontaneous and emphatically do not represent the perspectives of the Berglund Center for Internet Studies, nor of Pacific University. I have also rethought some of my positions on the basis of additional evidence.

[2] I more often used the term netwar. See: http://bcis.pacificu.edu/journal/results.php?cx=006538533868481694997%3Am_lmeb1yh-g&cof=FORID%3A9&ie=UTF-8&q=netwar+Barlow&sa=Search&siteurl=bcis.pacificu.edu%252Fjournal%252F#1269

What is Certain?

A brief answer here: almost nothing is certain. There was an incident, or a series of incidents, and these became linked in the media to many other similar but unrelated incidents in an attempt to establish meaning, and to draw audiences. From there everything gets rather murky.

Even Google's motives in raising the issue now are disputed. Particularly in China, Netizens seem mostly to believe that the issue is simply about Google's frustration at its local market share. It is prepared to leave because it was not a winner; it has only about one third of the market for search engines as its closest Chinese competitor, Baidu. This is a very interesting shift in attitudes between Chinese and American people.

After many decades of doing outrageous things for the flimsiest of idealistic or ideological reasons, Chinese now see economic explanations as dominant ones. Americans, after decades of criticizing this Chinese behavior, now believe that Google acted not out of self-interest but out of altruism. And after the event, Google's statement that it was prepared to withdraw from China caused its stock prices to increase markedly, demonstrating, if nothing else, that Americans are prepared to support enthusiastically acts in opposition to Chinese policies.

So, accepting Google's explanations, what do we know about the possible perpetrators? Again, nothing is certain. This, of course, does not prevent the media from not only speculating, but of presenting speculations as certainties.

Media criticisms of China often show some common characteristics which Chinese people, including very thoughtful and learned ones, interpret as due to prejudice. One of these is that while early reports are often carefully nuanced, subsequent pieces accept the earlier tentative ones as rock-hard evidence and a cascade toward certainty ensues. It is also common now that headlines or article headers seem to proclaim certainties while the content is often considerably more tentative.

An important piece by John Markoff in *The New York Times* is almost a classroom example for this sort of process. The article title fairly screams: "Evidence Found for Chinese Attack on Google".[3] Most readers would, like myself I think, immediately assume a smoking gun. This is the only part of the piece that everybody will read; most readers are not going to go much further. Thus we have it, case solved, the Chinese government did it!

This article deserves some close analysis, if only because the stakes are proving to be very high. Secretary of State Hillary Clinton quickly became involved, the Chinese government took a very obdurate position, and soon we have had a major international incident, followed by Chinese anger over U.S. intentions to soon sell major weapons systems to Taiwan, and the Dali Lama

---

[3] Evidence Found for Chinese Attack on Google By JOHN MARKOFF, January 19, 2010 http://www.nytimes.com/2010/01/20/technology/20cyber.html?hp

waits in the wings should Sino-American relations somehow survive the first two disruptions. Those relations have gone in less than a month from quite warm, to very distant, with various important meetings and reciprocal visits being cancelled.

The argument that the Chinese government was responsible is, as best I can tell, based largely upon the evidence cited in Markoff's article.[4] However, the article itself tells us only that the perpetrators are likely Chinese speakers because the malicious code was in the Chinese language and copied from a source that appeared, it is said, only in a Chinese technical journal. Does this in fact prove that the Chinese government did it?

The expert interviewed by Markoff used numerous qualifiers and finally concluded: "Occam's Razor suggests that the simplest explanation is probably the best one." I will suggest below that there are several even simpler explanations, and that, in any event, the simplest explanation may not be the best one. The instant appeal of Occam's Razor here is probably that, as one analyst has said, it is a "mirror of prejudice".[5] That is, to us, the simplest explanation is that the Chinese government did it, because in our opinion, that is the sort of thing they would do. In China there are more than a few who believe, on pretty much the same grounds, that the C.I.A. is responsible.

Who was Responsible?

If not the Chinese government, then who? Markoff's expert wound up appealing to a medieval argument for good reason; that is about the best that we can do. There are so many ways to loop Internet attacks through the web itself that certainty is finally impossible without something other than electronic evidence. There are also many ways to "spoof" identities.

This attack began, it seems, most directly from a computer based in Taiwan, and then it has been followed back to mainland computers. This is an awfully simple route. Hackers and spammers in the private black-hat sector routinely use many more hops than that. Given purported Chinese control of some critical American sites, it would not have been impossible to pass the attack through Pentagon computers, for example. For most analysts, a loop ending at a Chinese Internet Protocol address was as far as it was necessary to go; beyond that, lacking an ability to open up those machines, it was probably as far as they could go.

One argument for it not being the Chinese government is simply that the attacks could have been much more sophisticated and eminently deniable. As Google stated, the attacks were unsuccessful, and all the evidence suggests that the authors simply exploited known weaknesses in a number of computing programs.

---

[4] Google has not, insofar as I am aware, ever stated that in fact the Chinese government was responsible, though that too has entered the discourse as a certainty.
[5] Dieter Gernert, Ockham's Razor and Its Improper Use, Journal of Scientific Exploration, Vol. 21, No. 1, pp. 135-140, (2007). Cited in Wikipedia at: http://en.wikipedia.org/wiki/Occam%27s_razor#cite_note-fn_.28111.29-7

If solid evidence that it was the Chinese government is lacking, for many, such evidence is not necessary. Who else had motive and ability? But this argument fails; there are many possible perpetrators with both motive and ability.

One possible perpetrator is any one of a number of young Chinese nationalists popularly known as "Angry Youth," or, if referring specifically to hacker nationalists, as Hong Ke (Red Guests).[6] These folks think that the government is just not doing enough to stand up to the bad guys, in this case, the former Western imperialists. These people see themselves as a sort of vigilante volunteer force ever ready to respond to slights against China by hacking web pages or computers. I return to them in my conclusion below.

Do any of the Angry Youth have the ability for hacks of the sorts which occurred? Unquestionably. Among their numbers are distributed groups of well-trained and well-equipped I.T. specialists. They can write code and read even highly technical articles, like the one discussed above with the smoking code in it. And, as suggested, these attempts do not in any event seem to have been particularly sophisticated.

Are there other possible suspects? What if we ask the question qui bono---who benefits? Then the list quickly lengthens. Many of the firms targeted in these events, in addition to Google, were large Western corporations. What, then, about commercial rivals? And while we are speculating about commercial rivals, let us remember that the United States itself allegedly once turned electronic espionage techniques upon European corporate rivals, using the National Security Agency's Echelon operation.[7]

All corporations, of course, have strong motives for cracking into their competitors' internal documents. What of Google's competitor in China, Baidu? True it has 60% of the search engine market already, but perhaps it aspires to total monopoly?

If we posit the actions as deliberately misleading and intended to stir up trouble between the Chinese government and Google, or even between the Chinese and American governments, many other possible suspects enter the list: The anti-governmental hacker mirror image of Angry Youth, Chinese dissident youth; or Fa Lun Gong, the Buddhist sect which once took over Chinese Central Television for most of a day, operating, apparently, from a former American air base and listening post in Taiwan. Even Taiwan itself, which will benefit greatly from these events as the U.S. Congress discusses arms sales to it.

---

[6] See Melanie Lee and Lucy Hornby, "Google attack puts spotlight on China's "red" hackers" Reuters, Wed Jan 20, 2010 6:11pm at: http://www.reuters.com/article/idUSTRE60J20820100120

[7] See Richard Barry, "Echelon: The French fight back" ZDNet.co.uk Published: 29 Jun 2000 at: http://news.zdnet.co.uk/itmanagement/0,1000000308,2079852,00.htm See also Wikipedia, "Echelon" at: http://en.wikipedia.org/wiki/Echelon_%28signals_intelligence%29

These latter potential suspects must strike any reasonable person as distant possibilities indeed, but again, nothing is certain in these events. This leads, I think, to the necessary conclusion that great caution is required here.

The need for caution in a period of rising tension

What began as an incident between a single corporation and unknown hackers, who, after all, failed in their goals to open up Gmail accounts, has escalated to the point where the events are often now described as cyberwar.[8] China has responded in turn, by accusing the U.S. of online warfare in the case of the Iranian election, and attacking U.S. motives in opposing censorship as ultimately political ones.[9]

This is a very dangerous time in Sino-American relations and for the Internet as well. Tensions between the U.S. and China are, in my opinion, higher than they have been since 2001 when China forced down an American plane, which supposedly intruded into their air space around Hainan Island in the South China Sea.

One important question is, given that such incidents as these have happened regularly for some time, and that the Chinese have often been accused of committing them, why has the issue rather suddenly become so salient? Many of us think that most nations as well as many non-state groups have engaged in such activities on a regular basis for a very long time. There are millions of hacking attempts every year.

There are no easy explanations, of course, for sudden changes in either media coverage or public opinion. But I think that the international context has changed dramatically since the onset of the recent banking crises about this time last year. As a result of the crises, the Chinese are much less prepared to defer to Western, and particularly, American models, whether they are economic or political ones. Consequently they are, as Martin Jacques has argued in his recent work, When China Rules the World (See the review in this volume, p. 33) prepared to be much more active in redressing what they feel to be long-standing injustices in the global political and economic order.

I found this to be true among the Chinese audiences to which I spoke. There is a very strong feeling of triumphalism among what I would estimate to be about ten percent of Chinese youth, based on my personal experience. These feel that China has long been oppressed, and now has the power to resist additional wrongs, and even to redress outstanding grievances.

---

[8] See reports at: Gerald Posner "China's Secret Cyberterrorism" The Dailybeast, Jan 13, 2010 at: http://www.thedailybeast.com/blogs-and-stories/2010-01-13/chinas-secret-cyber-terrorism/

[9] Tania Branigan "China accuses US of online warfare in Iran" The Guardian, Sunday 24 January 2010 at: http://www.guardian.co.uk/world/2010/jan/24/china-us-iran-online-warfare

The U.S., for its part, has not made any adjustments in either policy or attitudes to the "rise of China." Many Americans think of China's progress as a trick or due to cheating, possibly illusory, or simply a result of the Chinese adopting our system. Included in this mélange of attitudes is a great deal of negativity toward China, and as the Google incident shows, an uncritical readiness to accept the worst possible interpretation of every event. A recent comment I saw in an on-line copy of Business Week rather sums it up for many Americans: "China can kiss my @zz !!!!!!!!".[10]

China is correct that for many Americans the Internet is a tool, which it is hoped, will bring about regime change there. The U.S., in turn, discusses being even more aggressive in utilizing electronic means to influence Chinese internal affairs. Some have suggested funding servers in the U.S. configured to facilitate Chinese Netizens' evasions of their country's firewalls.[11]

To do so amounts to a formal policy commitment to regime change and formal encouragement to Chinese secessionists or revolutionaries. How then, would we respond if China were to create equivalent servers for use by Pakistani supporters of Al Qaeda, which include, apparently the Pakistani military intelligence? Pakistan is, after, all, an ally of China in some important regards.

In addition, Americans are locked in a seemingly insoluble internal political conflict, unable to agree on fundamental issues at a national level, despite the crisis which we all agree is upon us. Teabags and pitchforks have been substituted for coherent national discussions. This is an unfortunate time to have rational debate over cyberwarfare, China policy, or anything else substantive. For Clinton or Obama to raise doubts or cautions at this time would be taken as a lack of resolve, of toughness, even of patriotism.

This conflict is unfortunate in a number of ways, but especially for Chinese democracy. Many Chinese think that the Internet is in fact already steadily encouraging democracy in China (See review of Marina Yue Zhang's work, *China 2.0* in this issue.) This encouragement, however, is done in a manner which permits China both stability and political reform, even if not at the dramatic pace which might satisfy many Americans.[12]

The hardening of both American and Chinese positions and the policy brawls in the U.S. make compromise in this incident unlikely. Google has told China it will not censor search data; China believes that the U.S. spreads disinformation in an attempt to force "regime change" abroad.

---

[10] Jan 19, 2010 8:50 PM GMT (http://www.businessweek.com/globalbiz/content/jan2010/gb20100119_789082.htm)

[11] Nicholas D. Kristof "See Google Takes a Stand" The NYT, 1.14.2010 at: http://www.nytimes.com/2010/01/14/opinion/14kristof.html?pagewanted=all I might well add here that I believe that this is already being done.

[12] See the review of Marina Yue Zhang, China 2.0 at p. 30 for examples of just this argument.

The implications for the worldwide Internet are not good. It may shortly be broken---de facto, if not formally---into national segments and many users will be unable to search outside those national boundaries.

Cyberwar and democracy

The implication of this recent event, and one possible outcome of current developments, is that cyberwarfare will become more or less a constant factor, not so much a specific event as an ongoing reality. It may indeed have been the case that in fact this happened sometime ago---many point to 2005 as the time at which attacks seemingly emanating from China increased markedly. But we are, at present, on the verge of making such mutual electronic warfare part of our national policy.

To do so will raise some serious issues for governance. Civilian control of the military has been a critical issue in American democracy. Douglas McArthur, when commander of U.N. forces in Korea, tried to put the U.S. and China in a position where an American invasion of China was a likelihood, and nuclear war a possibility. President Truman, at considerable political risk, yanked McArthur from command. If cyberwar with China becomes a national policy, given that it is necessarily covert, how are we to assure civilian control of such activities?

And how to be sure that it remains a state function, and not a rapidly accelerating chaotic series of events involving non-state groups such as Angry Youth in China and American cyber-vigilantes hacking away at each other and at the Internet? That genie will be very hard to get back into the bottle.

March 2010 - Volume 10, Issue 2

About This Issue
http://bcis.pacificu.edu/journal/article.php?id=650

Articles
Feature: Chris Pruett - *My Automated Player Feedback Quagmire*
http://bcis.pacificu.edu/journal/article.php?id=643

Social Networking: Jenn Hernandez - *Is THIS the Internet?!: The Technological Generation Shift Separating Siblings*
http://bcis.pacificu.edu/journal/article.php?id=644

Health: Jeff Cain - *Health 2.0: The next big 2.0?*
http://bcis.pacificu.edu/journal/article.php?id=646

Gaming: Ashley A. Kjos - *Adults Who Play Violent Video Games and Their Normative Beliefs About Aggression (Part 2): Video Games and Aggression*
http://bcis.pacificu.edu/journal/article.php?id=649

Book and Site Reviews
Mark Pegrum's *From Blogs to Bombs. The Future of Digital Technologies in Education.*
http://bcis.pacificu.edu/journal/article.php?id=647

Joseph Menn's *Fatal System Error. The Hunt for the New Crime Lords Who Are Bringing Down the Internet.*
http://bcis.pacificu.edu/journal/article.php?id=648

Editorial
Google and China Eight Weeks Later: Where Are We Now?
http://bcis.pacificu.edu/journal/article.php?id=645

About This Issue

The March 2010 issue of *Interface* is live and on the WWW...

Our current issue focuses largely on social impacts of the web, particularly upon game playing.

Our feature is by our Pacific University and Berglund Center alumnus, Chris Pruett, now working as a Google engineer in Japan. Chris has been working on Google's first Android OS-based game. He reports on the process of getting player feedback and the surprisingly complex social and technological issues this raises in "*My Automated Player Feedback Quagmire.*"

Another gaming feature is the second of the two parts of Ashley A. Kjos' Master's thesis in the School of Professional Psychology at Pacific University, "*Adults Who Play Violent Video Games and Their Normative Beliefs About Aggression (Part 2): Video Games and Aggression.*" Ashley's two pieces are an excellent quick review of the current state of research in this highly controversial area.

Berglund Student Fellow Jenn Hernandez gives us insight into the difficulties even a young adult fan of computers faces in keeping up with technology in "Is THIS the Internet?!: The Technological Generation Shift Separating Siblings."

Health Editor Jeff Cain of the University of Kentucky analyzes some of the issues presented by the interactive Web and health information in: "*Health 2.0: The next big 2.0?*" While Jeff protests that he usually refrains from predicting the future, we are confident that some of these issues will indeed be around for some time.

We offer two very different book reviews. The first is Mark Pegrum's *From Blogs to Bombs. The Future of Digital Technologies in Education*. Our reviewer felt that this could be the one book best suited to introduce new teachers to the opportunities and dangers presented by technology in their classrooms.

The second book reviewed perhaps emphasizes the dangers of the Web more than the opportunities: Joseph Menn's *Fatal System Error. The Hunt for the New Crime Lords Who Are Bringing Down the Internet*, is a very well researched history of international cyber-criminal gangs. Our reviewer found this the most comprehensive of the several books we have reviewed on hacking at the Berglund Center.

Our editorial is "Google and China Eight Weeks Later: Where Are We Now?" by Jeffrey Barlow, who summarizes current knowledge on the Google case and the lessons which are to be learned about cyber war from it.

See also Announcements related to recent Berglund activities including the departure of three graduates to teach in China and a notice from the Duboff law firm concerning on-line endorsements.

As always, we hope you find this issue of *Interface* educational and interesting. Look for us again in April...

The Berglund Center for Internet Studies
Pacific University Oregon

My Automated Player Feedback Quagmire

By Chris Pruett

One of the best ways to develop an idea for a game is to build a prototype and have people play it. Being able to watch somebody play a game, even in a prototype form, is extremely valuable. Almost immediately rough spots in the design become apparent; there will be details that players miss, or controls that players have trouble with, or they will discover a method of playing that isn't what the creator had in mind. The very best games are often those that incorporate user testing from a very early stage of development, and use that feedback to tune and modify the design of the game throughout development.

When I worked at a game company, we would often bring children (our target audience was usually 8 to 12 year olds) from the local community in to test our games. Kids are great testers because they don't get frustrated easily and have a higher tolerance for flawed games than adults. We would bring the kids in, hook the game machine up to a VCR, and record the whole play session. Usually the designer would sit in with the kids and talk to them about their play experiences; hearing what they have to say as they play can often be as valuable as the video of the play session itself. After the kid testers have left, the designer would pore over the video recordings, trying to identify areas that were problematic.

The basic goal of these tests is usually to identify frustration points. Frustration is the enemy of fun, and it is very hard to know what players will find frustrating without doing real world tests. Frustration can be the result of the game giving the player unclear goals, or being too difficult, or otherwise arresting the players' progress. Often, frustration happens because some message that the designer intended to communicate to the player does not make it through. A good game is one that is easy to understand yet challenging; a bad game is one that is challenging because it is hard to understand. By watching kids play, a designer can quickly identify these kinds of problems and take steps to resolve them.

For the last year I have been developing a small game in my free time called *Replica Island*.[1] The game is a side-scrolling action game, part of the platformer genre. My day job involves working with Google's Android mobile operating system, and Replica Island is my first Android-based game. Though the game started out as a technical exercise, over the last six months I have been almost totally focused on the design of the game itself; though the basic technology has been in a completed state for a long time, developing the content of the game has proof to be a significant challenge.

Part of the challenge is that I have no way to test my designs on other people. I do not have a local community of kids who are willing to volunteer their time (nor are kids my target audience for this title). I do not have a way to connect my game to a VCR and record a play session; most Android devices are cell phones without any sort of video connectors. And finally, even if I do get somebody to

1 For more information, see http://www.replicaisland.net

play the game, it is hard to see what sort of mistakes they are making without hovering right over their shoulder. So while I know from experience that user testing is really the only way to verify the quality of any given game design, the logistics of testing on my chosen platform are problematic.

After some deliberation, I decided to try a different approach. Rather than record live play sessions, my game now reports statistics about players back to a server, which I can then use to determine which areas are particularly problematic. I released a beta version of my game internally to other Google employees, and several hundred were nice enough to give it a spin. The data I collected from those users has proven extremely useful in tuning the design of the game and identifying frustration spots, and I'm very pleased with the results.[2]

The problem with this approach is that it requires walking a fine line between privacy concerns and test integrity. In order for the data to be reliable, the player should ideally not know that he is being watched. Even though I only send back a very small amount of information (notifications are sent when a player "dies" or completes a stage), being observed causes some players to change their behavior. I've experienced this myself; I find myself playing very differently in games that I know are keeping an internal score card of my achievements compared to those that do not. So in the interests of data integrity, I would rather that my players not be aware of my data recording system.

But on the other hand, any time I send data about a specific person back to a server, I am increasing the potential for somebody to complain about privacy. The average user cannot tell what data I am sending, or how I am sending it, or whether that data could be used to build some sort of personal profile about them. In reality, I have been careful not to include any personal details in the data I send. Each player is assigned a random number and I have no way to tie that number to any sort of personal information. I have been pretty careful to ensure that this data is really just game-related, and even if some nefarious third party got their hands on it, it would not be possible to identify users with it. But the user cannot know that I have taken such precautions—it is natural for an internet-savvy player to wonder a bit about why my game needs an internet connection and what kind of data it is transmitting.

Of course, for the purposes of my test I have only released the game to fellow employees, so there is no real trust problem. But as Replica Island nears completion, I am very strongly inclined to include the data collection system in the final version that goes out to Average Joe users. With this system operating in the wild, I would be able to collect huge amounts of play data and make adjustments to the game even after it is released. That's a really attractive idea; I would love to be able to continue to improve the play experience as my understanding of my players grows.

---

[2] More information about the system I built for Replica Island is detailed on my development blog: http://replicaisland.blogspot.com/2010/01/tuning-with-metrics-redux.html

But, then again, maybe it is not worth the confusion and suspicion that comes with transmitting user data back home. Android lets users know which apps use the Internet, and there is no other Internet-related functionality in my game. It would be a shame if the very system I included to improve the game caused some players to refuse to install it.

I will probably choose a safe middle ground by letting players opt-out of the data collection system via a setting screen. This is not an ideal solution because it lets everybody know that there is a data collection system in the first place, and some players' data will subsequently be influenced by that knowledge. But it is probably a better alternative than trying to be sneaky about it or cutting the system out altogether. Letting the user make an informed decision is probably the best way to go.

At any rate, I plan to release the source code for Replica Island along with the game, so anybody who is interested can pick it apart and see how it works. If I do ship the game with the data collection system enabled, my next challenge will be actually interpreting all of the automated feedback that I receive (and, if the title is popular, keeping my server from crashing). So far, my tests have been limited to a few hundred users; I do not know what will happen when that is expanded to 1000 or 10,000 or 50,000 users. Still, that is a nice problem to have. If 50,000 people decide to play my game, I must be doing something right.

Is THIS the Internet?!: The Technological Generation Shift Separating Siblings Or Sibling Schism: Technology Shifts and Rethinks the Traditional Generation Gap

Jenn Hernandez
Pacific University, Berglund Student Fellow 2006-2011

Isn't it funny how quickly words and phrases fall out of use almost as quickly as the need for them in society does? It's either that, or the hardier of the phrases evolve as circumstances change. "Language, like culture, is a dynamic thing. It was an oral thing once, then became a printed thing and it becoming a digital thing":[1] writing letters gave way to electronic mail, creating the term for the former: snail-mail. Soon even e-mail became obsolete in the wake of the instant message. A block of text can now be condensed to a few lines of sometimes-indecipherable abbreviations and acronyms through text messaging. The key word now is *instantaneous.*

As it is a normal cycle of life for all things, generations are separated from those that came before them, and those that come after. Perhaps the generation gap, technologically speaking, should now be called the, "generational shift," says Ning[2] (a social networking site) co-founder and Web browser pioneer Marc Andreessen.[3] "A whole new generation grows up used to new technologies, and they're just different."[4] As for generation gaps usually separating literal generations like parents and children, the new generation shifts only span a few years.

We all have different needs for technology, but they are often influenced by what we grew up with. I, for instance, having grown up reading any book I could find once or twice, found reading from a Kindle to be not as satisfying as reading printed material (though it is definitely more compact). I find the "*electronic paper*"[5] technology, or whatever it is, to be fascinating. In a New York Times article, the author gives a similarly resonant example of the generation shift:

> My 2-year-old daughter surprised me recently with two words: "Daddy's book." She was holding my Kindle electronic reader. Here is a child only beginning to talk, revealing that the seeds of the next generation gap have already been planted. She has identified the Kindle as a substitute for words printed on physical pages. I own the device and am still not

---

1 _http://www.nytimes.com/2010/01/16/world/americas/16iht-currents.html
2 http://www.ning.com/
3 http://www.ibiblio.org/pioneers/andreesen.html
4 http://www.businessweek.com/magazine/content/07_27/b4041401.htm
5 http://www.amazon. com/Kindle-Amazons-Original-Wireless-generation/dp/B000FI73MA

completely sold on the idea.[6]

The article is titled "The Children of Cyberspace: Old Fogies by Their 20s." Hey...I'm in my 20s. Does that mean I'm old? Technologically speaking, I suppose that would be the case.

Kids are growing up fast nowadays. My 8-year-old cousin has a Facebook[7] which she updates literally with what she is doing at the moment, for instance: "Brooklyn is having a conversation with Doug". Someone should get this kid a Twitter.[8] The truth is probably that this little girl is just as savvy (and will probably become even more so than I or her older sisters are) on the Internet. Don't get me wrong—I started out a savvy little 5-year-old "gamer" (my specialties were Rodent's Revenge,[9] Reader Rabbit,[10] and Minesweeper[11]) and an intrigued encyclopedia CD-ROM user. I was on my way.

I still remember my first encounters with the Internet when I was in the second grade. The page I wanted to look at was going to take at least half an hour to load, even without images, on our poorly equipped connection. I decided that it wasn't really worth it and wondered what the use of the Internet was if it was so slow. Once we actually had a decent connection, I was disappointed to find out that typing a keyword into the AOL[12] keyword search bar didn't automatically direct me to the page I was hoping to read. (I didn't even have an idea of what a web page looked like yet. I also thought that AOL was the Internet at the time.) But, instead it returned white pages after pages with line after line of black and blue text: the search results my keyword turned up. I was surprised. *This is the Internet*?

A child of around the same age today might laugh, feel a little bit embarrassed for my naïveté, and respond through the time-space continuum (because that's how everyone communicates in the future), "*Of course this is the Internet.*" Is it just me, or are my 8-year-old ears burning?

So how are internet companies and search engines catering to the knowledge that more and more young people are beginning to use the Internet? This brings into light an article I recently found about how Google[13] is trying to make searches more understandable, given the way a child's mind works. The article discusses some problems with existing search engines: it can be difficult for users to formulate the right keywords to call up their desired results...that task can be even more challenging for children, given that they do not always have the right context for thinking about a new subject. One 12-year-old boy searching

---

[6]http://www.nytimes.com/2010/01/10/weekinreview/10stone.html?scp=7&sq=january%2010%202010&st=cse
[7] http://www.facebook.com
[8] http://www.twitter.com
[9] http://en.wikipedia.org/wiki/Rodent%27s_Revenge
[10] http://www.reader-rabbit.com/
[11] http://www.mine-sweeper.com/
[12] http://www.aol.com/
[13] http://www.google.com/

for information about Costa Rica used the search term 'sweaty clothes' because that was what he associated with the jungle.[14]

Google and many other search engines are incorporating more visuals, which would've no doubt benefitted the visual learner I was and still am. (Find out what your learning style is, if you haven't already figured it out![15]).

Here is a search I conducted as an example using the keyword "cats".[16] To try it out for yourself, go to Google.com and start a search. Once you get your results, click on "See Options". Under "Standard View" you'll find "Wonder Wheel". It's kind of reminiscent of the brainstorming word webs we used to use in language arts class in elementary school. Remember those?

In an interview with John Carlin,[17] he discusses the generation gap, explaining that, unlike with the minority counterculture of the 60s defining the generation gap, there is no underground anymore. Everything is on the surface—America survives by absorbing rather than rejecting. This is also why the new generation is so hard to see and also why it is so profound. It takes place in a new social arena that only certain people, notably those who grew up with computers, are aware of. ... The gap is more about what an older generation can't see or value than in what a younger generation creates."[18]

It's no secret that the Internet is becoming a big part of most of our lives, whether we are the blossoming social network butterfly, or (on perhaps the opposite end of the technology savviness continuum) the grandparent firing up the old dinosaur-of-a-computer to check that darned e-mail for pictures of the grandkids (please excuse my overt use of stereotyping, or ageism, if you prefer). Point illustrated, is it possible to keep up? Of course it is! It takes practice and patience, just like anything does. However, it's not so wrong to be dumbfounded or even a little bit intimidated by technology, or even to employ it for uses "unimagined by marketing departments".[19] In helping a man at a retirement home use his tape player, and striking up a friendship, Genevieve Zook[20] took, "a lesson from [him], because this may well be how the generations will bridge technology issues. Some will use the technology at hand, ...while yet others will take comfort in the habits of older technologies, unmoved by the latest gadget. Finally, a few... will use any gizmo as a bridge to a human connection. I guess you could say that those folks prefer to socially network in person, which is so 20th century, don't you think?".[21]

---

[14] http://www.nytimes.com/2009/12/26/technology/internet/26kidsearch.html?fta=y
[15] http://www.learning-styles-online.com/inventory/
[16] http://www.google.com/search?hl=en&client=firefox-a&rls=org.mozilla:en-US:official&hs=PDQ&tbo=1&output=search&q=cats&tbs=ww:1&ei=-Id5S4fIF4SAswP0gNHKCA&sa=X&oi=tool&resnum=2&ct=tlink&ved=0CCQQpwU
[17] John Carlin, of Funny Garbage (http://www.funnygarbage.com/about)
[18] http://www.aiga.org/content.cfm/the-new-generation-gap
[19] http://www.llrx.com/features/generationgap.htm
[20] http://www.llrx.com/authors/1119
[21] http://www.llrx.com/features/generationgap.htm

Health 2.0: The next big 2.0?

Jeff Cain

Web 2.0's underlying philosophy of openness, user-driven choices, and connections has been extended to almost every domain that is seeking a new identity. Over the past several years, the 2.0 suffix has been attached to just about every topic imaginable. We now have education 2.0, shopping 2.0, business 2.0, library 2.0, government 2.0 and the list goes on and on and on. The 2.0 placed at the end of a term usually signifies more than just a second generation/version of something; it represents the aforementioned characteristics of Web 2.0.

We should not be surprised that this philosophy has spread to the different areas of our lives. I agree with the statement that most of us are now "e-people". A myriad of everyday tasks such as banking, social conversations among friends, and job searchers can now easily be completed in a digital environment. One of the lesser-known domains, which has not received a lot of attention, is health care.

Health 2.0 is an emerging, broad, and sometimes controversial topic that could be discussed ad nauseam at different levels. With potential changes on the horizon due to stimulus funding and health care reform, Health 2.0 may eventually come to full fruition. The focus of this article will be to briefly explain Health 2.0 and provide a few examples that illuminate the concepts.

What does Health 2.0 look like? What are the distinguishing characteristics? As with most other things labeled 2.0, there is not a definitive answer. Experts in the field still debate over what Health 2.0 actually is. Some focus on the online social connections between health care providers and patients. Others stake the importance on electronic personal health records. A third contingent concentrates on patient/consumer empowerment.

Finding a commonly accepted definition is difficult, but one of the best definitions incorporates numerous aspects of the Web 2.0 philosophy. Health 2.0 (or the broader term, Medicine 2.0) is the compilation of "...Web-based services for health care consumers, caregivers, patients, health professionals, and biomedical researchers that use Web 2.0 technologies and/or semantic web and virtual-reality tools, to enable and facilitate specifically social networking, participation, apomediation, collaboration, and openness within and between these user groups."[1]

The breadth of that definition alone indicates just how massive an undertaking it is to revolutionize the philosophy of the health care industry. Health 2.0 involves all participants in the health care environment, but possibly the most important thing to understand about Health 2.0 is that it is primarily bottom-up and

---

[1] Eysenbach G. Medicine 2.0: Social networking, collaboration, participation, apomediation, and openness. J Med Internet Res. 2008; 10(3):e22.

consumer driven. Unlike other areas of health informatics such as computerized physician order entry (CPOE) that are system driven, the patients are the ones who are pushing for changes in the health care environment.

Examples of Health 2.0 applications

Because we are quickly becoming an e-society, we are beginning to expect the convenience and efficiencies of new media to encompass all aspects of our lives. Who among us has not completed forms at the doctor's office and answered the same set of questions again for the umpteenth time? We also probably know someone who could benefit from peer support of others afflicted with the same medical condition. These are exactly the types of needs/desires that are driving the development of some exciting Health 2.0 applications. Many companies, including Google, are developing applications for patients to retrieve, enter, maintain, store in one online location, and selectively share their own health records and information. Rather than rely on communication among physicians and other medical staff, individual patients can house all of their medical records on their Google Health[2] site and *maintain control* of that information.

PatientsLikeMe[3] is one example of a thriving application developed from one family's desire to provide the best quality of life possible for a young man diagnosed with ALS. This site provides a social community for patients with various disease states to connect with others, describe in detail their afflictions, and discuss treatments and strategies to cope with their disease. Both of these examples highlight the trend toward a patient participatory[4] model of healthcare. The Health 2.0 consumer has more information, more resources, and more control over how s/he seeks, researches, and receives health care. Many of us spend hours online reading reviews of items such as television sets so that we can get the best one at the best price. Why shouldn't we do the same when choosing physicians, hospitals, and forms of medical treatment?

Obstacles to Health 2.0

The road to Health 2.0 is neither clear nor well marked and for even a moderate transformation of the current system to occur, there are numerous obstacles, issues, and barriers to overcome.

First and maybe foremost, is the huge task of breaking down the barriers within and among the health care institutions and firms. While Web 2.0 and Health 2.0 are about openness, sharing, and user-driven choices, health care has traditionally been an inward-focused and closed society. Web 2.0 is about risk-taking. Health care institutions are about risk-aversion. Hospitals, physicians, and drug manufacturing companies do everything within their power to control information in order to avoid harm to the patients, bad publicity, and lawsuits.

---

[2] http://www.google.com/health/

[3] http://www.patientslikeme.com/

[4] medicine. Available at: http://en.wikipedia.org/wiki/Participatory_medicine. Accessed February 25, 2010.

Even the most willing physicians and drug manufacturers are constrained by government regulations that were established to prevent harm and protect patient privacy.[5]

The development of business and financial models for Health 2.0 services is another major hurdle. Developing Health 2.0 applications is one thing, but attracting a critical mass of users and finding funding sources to maintain those systems over time is another. Web servers and programmers cost money and the businesses must find a way to recoup those expenses. In many cases selling advertising space on the site is not enough, and fee-based subscriptions can hinder adoption by users. We are accustomed to not paying for social media services like Facebook, YouTube, and Twitter. Convincing the users of the value gained from fee-based applications is not an easy task.

Similarly, the mechanisms are not there yet for physicians and other health care providers to receive compensation from insurance companies for online and social media involved interventions. Rightfully so, many are reluctant to participate in these types of transactions without receiving just compensation. There is also the ever-present issue of blending personal and professional lives. While some physicians have opted to use popular social media applications like Facebook to interact with patients, there are many who do not want to cloud the physician/patient relationship with online social connections and communications.[6]

Future of Health 2.0

I usually refrain from predicting the future until after it has occurred, but I do have some thoughts on future developments in Health 2.0. First and foremost I believe that the principles behind Health 2.0 will remain. Openness, user control, and connections are highly valued attributes and those will continue to be demanded as younger generations mature and begin to utilize the health care environment more frequently. Younger generations are heavier users of social media than older generations, so one can reasonably expect them to want to continue using them (or their future iterations) as they age. Health 2.0 applications will evolve over time as the technology advances and other user needs are identified.

As mentioned previously, financial sustainability is an issue with many start-ups. Even with a good technical product, an adequate business model is necessary for long-term success. Just like other Web 2.0 applications, there will be more failures than successes. However, some companies will find a niche area to target and develop a method of receiving income for their service. PatientsLikeMe, for example, attracted a critical mass of users who desired the

---

5 Colaizzi, M. Despite regulation, cool things are brewing in healthcare and finance. Available at: http://smartblogs.com/socialmedia/2010/02/08/despite-regulation-cool-things-are-brewing-in-healthcare-and-finance/. Accessed February 24, 2010.

6 Cohen, E. Should you 'friend' your doctor on Facebook? Available at: http://www.cnn.com/2009/HEALTH/09/03/friending.your.doctor/index.html. Accessed February 24, 2010.

peer support and community that the company offered. Secondly, the company understood that there was a market for the information they collected and developed a means to obtain revenue from it.

Finally, there will be lots of angst, consternation, and pessimism by many who cannot envision a healthcare environment in which patients have control of their records, can use online resources to critically evaluate physicians, and can find sources of medical information from other patients. For some, the reasons are based upon the disbelief that companies can successfully implement and maintain these applications. Others may fear negative consequences of transparency across all health care environments. They immediately foresee lawsuits. Still, a third concern stems from a fear that patients will suffer when medical professionals are removed as the gateway to health information.

These are all valid concerns and only some of the issues that must be worked through. However, if you listen closely to the conversations occurring in the social media world, you will realize that there are strong advocates for changes. Many of these advocates utilize social media to continue the conversation and drive change. Within Twitter, you can search for the hashtag #hcsm to receive a rich feed of conversations regarding health care and social media. You can also use Twitter to follow @SusannahFox, @drwalker_rph, and @ePatientDave who are leaders in this field to find out more about the imminent changes upon us.

Adults Who Play Violent Video Games and Their Normative Beliefs About Aggression (Part 2): Video Games and Aggression

Ashley A. Kjos

The first part of this analysis was published in February 2010 in Interface *(this volume, p. 16).*

Video Games and Aggression

Many studies have been conducted in order to help explain the relationship between aggression and video games. However, researchers cannot seem to agree if violent-content video games have an effect on aggression. Through numerous correlational studies, various researchers have found results suggesting that violent video game play is positively related to increases in aggressive behavior and affect (Anderson & Bushman, 2001; Anderson & Dill, 2000; Anderson & Murphy, 2003; Bartholow & Anderson, 2002; Bartholow, Sestir, & Davis, 2005; Colwell & Payne, 2000; Gentile et al., 2004; Persky & Blaskovich, 2007; Sherry, 2001). Sherry (2001) conducted a meta-analysis of studies from 1975 to 2000 to determine the correlation between playing violent video games and aggression. He found that the overall correlation between video game play and aggression was relatively small (r =.15). He also found that the overall effect size of that correlation was small (d =.30), suggesting there is a relationship between video game play and aggression, but that this relationship is smaller than the relationship found between television and aggression (d =.65). This implies that, although there is a relationship between the aggression and video games, the relationship may be small and not as strong as other media devices.

Not every study, however, has found that playing violent video games increases aggressive thoughts and affect. For example, Fleming and Rickwood (2001) found that arousal and mood were negatively correlated with violent video game play, suggesting that playing may rather lead to decreases in aggressive behavior and affect. Ferguson (2007) conducted a meta-analysis of studies completed from 1995 to 2005 to calculate an overall effect size for the relationship between violent video games and aggression and to examine whether there has been any publication bias in the research. He found that there was a positive correlation between violent video game play and aggressive behavior (r =.29) and aggressive thoughts (r =.25). However, the results of the meta-analysis also suggest that there is significant publication bias issues for both experimental and nonexperimental studies of aggression so that the effects found in many past studies many not be completely accurate. For example, many studies implemented measures that may not be reliable or valid for assessing aggression. Ferguson (2007) concludes that researchers have "not provided compelling support to indicate either a correlational or causal relationship between violent game play and actual aggressive behavior" (p. 480). Obviously, this is an area that requires more research that utilizes reliable and valid measures to determine what effect, if any, playing video games has on aggressive affect and behavior.

One related area of video game research that has been the focus of attention is the relationship between the amounts of time people spend playing video games and the amount of aggressive behavior and affect exhibited. As the amount of violent graphics and the popularity of video games has increased, so has the amount of time people are spending playing video games. In the mid 1980s children were spending approximately four hours a week playing video games (Carnagey & Anderson, 2004). Recent estimates of video game usage has increased significantly with eighth and ninth grade students reporting an average of nine hours a week and male college students reporting an average of twenty hours per week (Carnagey & Anderson, 2004).

With the astounding quantity of time people are spending engaging in games, it is important to understand what effects the amount of time spent playing video games has on aggressive behavior. Although many people are playing video games for extended periods of time, researchers have suggested that even short term exposure to violent video games causes temporary increases in aggression (Anderson & Bushman, 2001; Anderson & Murphy, 2003; Bartholow et al., 2005; Colwell & Kato, 2005). Bartholow, Sestir, and Davis (2005) found that participants who had more exposure to violent video games behaved more aggressively than participants who had lower levels of exposure to violent video games suggesting that the amount of time spent playing games with violent content is related to aggressive behaviors.

Researchers have also found that various traits are related to increased amount of time spent playing video games such as lower grades (Anderson & Dill, 2000), lower self-esteem and lower number of friends (Colwell & Payne, 2000), and increased hostility (Gentile et al., 2004). In fact, it has been shown that parental limits on children's use of video games are related to decreases in fights and arguments and increases in school performance (Gentile et al., 2004).

Although most research has suggested that playing violent video games for even short lengths of time can cause increases in aggressive behavior and affect, Sherry (2001) suggests that playing even the most violent video games for extended periods of time may not increase aggression. He proposes that children who play games for long periods of time may transfer less aggression from the game to the external world than those who play for brief periods of time due to arousal levels decreasing over time. Evidently, the relationship between the amounts of time that people spend playing violent video games and aggression is debatable and requires further evaluation.

As stated previously, a video game can have a component that is much different than other forms of media in that it may rewards violent actions performed by the player. Unlike television, video games enable the player to control the movements of a character in a virtual world. Most video games reward players for exhibiting violent behaviors in the characters they are controlling by receiving points, achievements and/or higher status, completing levels, and winning the game. Some video games punish violent behaviors such as when innocent bystanders or "friendlies" are shot instead of the enemy which can result in the player losing points or status or having to begin the level over. Researchers have examined what effects reward and punishment of violent actions in video games can have on later aggressive cognition, affect, and behavior. In a series of three experiments, Carnagey and Anderson (2005) found that rewarding violence in video games can increase aggressive affect, cognition, and behavior. They found that participants who were rewarded for violent actions exhibited more aggressive behaviors than participants who played the same game where violence was punished or did not occur. This suggests that the reward component that is exclusive to video game media may increase aggressive behaviors, affect, and cognitions.

Although researchers have focused primarily on whether playing violent video games that have components of control and reward leads to aggressive behaviors and affects, there is also interest in whether people who play more violent games deem aggression as an acceptable behavior.

Video Games and Normative Beliefs About Aggression

As stated above, normative beliefs about aggression are beliefs about the acceptability or unacceptability of aggression in particular situations. These beliefs are influenced by a person's family, peers, and culture which includes the media within that culture. Eron et al. (1972) found that people who watch many hours of violent television and prefer to watch violent programs do not consider the aggressive behaviors viewed on the shows as deviant. In fact, many of the participants suggested that these behaviors were appropriate ways to solve real-life problems, therefore endorsing aggression as a normal response to everyday problems.

Other researchers have found that the ways in which a person thinks and feels are important in influencing their interest and exposure to violent games, films, and television (Sigurdsson et al., 2006). These researchers also found that people who are accepting of violence as a normal behavioral response are more likely to expose themselves to violent forms of media. These findings suggest that peoples' beliefs and feelings about aggression can cause them to have more or less exposure to violent forms of media (Anderson & Bushman, 2001). Krahe and Moller (2004) found that the normative acceptance of physical aggression increased with an increase in exposure to violent video games. These researchers also found that for both males and females the frequency with which violent video games were played and the amount these types of games were liked were related to the acceptance of aggression as normative. This suggests that there is a positive relationship between normative beliefs about aggression and exposure to violent video games with more exposure related to increased beliefs that aggression is a normal response.

Not only are there differences in beliefs about the normality of aggression among video game players, there are also differences in video game use and aggression between males and females and differences in how games are rated.

Video Games and Aggression: Gender Differences

When people think of typical video game players, males are most likely to come to mind. but females are becoming more involved in the gaming world with an estimated 40% of the gaming market being female (Oser, 2004). Researchers have found that females reported being less experienced with video games than males (Fleming & Rickwood, 2001) and in fact, males reported playing more violent video games for longer amounts of time than females (Colwell & Payne, 2000; Funk et al., 2002; Krahe & Moller, 2004). Even while playing the games, males appear to be more involved overall, but females become more focused and involved when playing a third person rather then a first person game (Farrar, Krcmar, & Nowak, 2006). In a first person game, the player is represented by a given avatar; in a third person game, the player is not represented by any particular avatar but may manipulate groups of avatars or other digital representations. While males tend to prefer video games that contain violent and aggressive content such as *Call of Duty* and *Mortal Kombat* (Funk et al., 2002), females tend to prefer games that have opportunities for social interaction, contain non-sexualized role for the female characters, and have non-aggressive content such as *The Sims* (Hartmann & Klimmt, 2006). Evidently there are differences between males and females who play video games and two areas where there are marked differences is in the amount of aggression contained in the games males and females prefer, and the amount of aggression males and females display.

Males and females may respond differently to exposure to violence and aggression in video games. Arriaga, Esteves, Carneiro, and Monteiro (2006) found that playing violent video games increased the arousal levels of female participants more than male participants, but Fleming and Rickwood (2001) found that both males and females showed increased arousal levels after playing violent video games. Numerous researchers have found that males appear to be more affected by violent video games than females, suggesting that males may become or be more aggressive in general and are more sensitive to aggression. (Anderson, 1997; Archer & Latham, 2004; Bartholow & Anderson, 2002; Buss & Perry, 1992). Deselms and Altman (2003) found that exposure to violence in video games decreased male participants sensitivity to violence while women participants become more sensitive to violent content after playing violent video games. Although both males and females responded to the violence they viewed in the games, this research supports the idea that male sensitivity to violence and aggression may cause them to be more affected by video games by being more aggressive in their actions. In fact, Huesmann et al. (1992) found that boys are more physically aggressive than females and are more likely to believe that aggression is an acceptable behavior across a range of circumstances and targets.

Research has provided evidence that males may be more sensitive to aggression and more likely to behave aggressively than females. It has also been shown that males tend to prefer games with more violent content and aggression than females but one issue that has not been addressed so far is how do consumers of video games know what games are more violent then others? One way to determine what type of content and how much violence a game contains is to look at for which age level the game is appropriate and what rating the game is given.

Video Game Ratings

Rating systems have been put in place for most major forms of media beginning with films in the 1960s, music in the 1980s, video games in 1994, and finally, television in 1996 (Funk, Flores, Buchman, & Germann, 1999). The ultimate goal of ratings is to limit the amount of access vulnerable individuals have to forms of media that contain explicit content such as sex, crude language, and violence. When video games first appeared in the United States in the 1970s, the content and graphics were not a large concern. As technology and the graphics of games have become more violent and realistic, parents and legislators have begun to express concern about the content within these games and pushed for access restrictions for children (Funk et al., 1999).

In 1994, the Entertainment Software Rating Board (ESRB) was established in order to assign video game content ratings which were designed to provide consumers with concise impartial guidance about their age-appropriateness and content (Entertainment Software Association, 2006). ESRB ratings have two equal parts: rating symbols which suggest age appropriateness for the game and content descriptors which indicate elements in a game that may have triggered a particular rating and may be of concern. Upon reviewing and before releasing games, game publishers submit responses to a detailed written ESRB questionnaire regarding the pertinent content in the video game, then raters recommend an appropriate rating category and content descriptors (Entertainment Software Association, 2006).

The ESRB has six different ratings that it assigns to video games which are: early childhood (EC) which is suitable for ages three and older; everyone (E) which is suitable for ages six and older; everyone ages ten and older (E10+); Teen (T) which is suitable for ages thirteen and older; mature (M) which is suitable for ages seventeen and older; and finally, adults only (AO) which is suitable for ages eighteen and older (Entertainment Software Association, 2006).

There are many content descriptors that the ESRB uses when describing video games including alcohol and drugs, blood, gore, violence, language, sex, and nudity and each rating is associated with different types of content descriptors. This means that video games with higher ratings contain more violent content and therefore more content descriptors warning about what will be witnessed while playing the game.

Since the establishment of video game ratings there has been little research conducted to determine how efficient and accurate these ratings actually are but some researchers are looking into these questions. Thompson and Haninger

(2001) wanted to quantify and categorize the depiction of violence, drugs and alcohol, and sex in E rated video games. As stated previously, E rated video games according to the ESRB are suitable for ages six and older. The researchers discovered that 35 of 55 (63%) games involved intentional acts of violence for an average of 30.7% of the game time. In 33 of the games injuring characters was rewarded or required for advancement in the game. Additionally, 14 of 32 (44%) games did not receive a content descriptor of violence from ESRB when they in fact contained numerous acts of violence. The results suggest that even though E rated games have been deemed appropriate for children ages six, there is a significant amount of violence in these video games.

Following the findings of their previous research, Haninger and Thompson (2004) conducted another study in order to quantify and characterize the content in video games that are rated T (for teen). These researchers also wanted to determine if there was agreement between the ESRB content descriptors and the actual content observed in the games. The results suggested that in a random sample of 81 games that were studied, 79 involved intentional violence for an average of 36% of game play, 73 rewarded the player for injuring other characters or required the player to do so, 56 rewarded the player to or required the player to kill, 34 depicted blood, 22 depicted sexual themes, 22 contained profanity, 12 depicted substances, and 1 involved gambling. The researchers' observations identified 51 instances of content in 39 games that warranted a descriptor by the ESRB where none was actually given. This suggests that although the ESRB content descriptors provide a good indication about what types of content one may observe while playing a video game, the absence of a descriptor does not mean the absence of that type of content. Similar to the results found in their study with E rated games, Haninger and Thompsons' (2004) results suggest that there is a significant amount of violence in T rated games and that not all information about the content of the game is always depicted by the content descriptors given by the ESRB.

Obviously there are some differences between the ESRB's and researchers' beliefs about what content descriptors should be included and what the ratings of certain video games should be. Funk, Flores, Buchman, and Germann (1999) wanted to determine if there were similarities between consumer's perceptions of what content descriptors and ratings of video games are and ESRB's actual content descriptors and ratings. The results suggested that when violent content was not a central theme of game or when it was prominent in the game there was strong agreement between consumers and the ESRB on ratings and content descriptors. One area where there was considerable variance between the two groups was in regards to cartoon-type violence depicted in games. Depending on the respondent's age, gender and status as parent or nonparent, consumers rated the games containing cartoon-type violence more or less violent than the ESRB.

The results of these studies together suggests that although the rating and content descriptor system used by the ESRB is helpful in determining what games may be appropriate for certain individuals, many of the games that are rated E for everyone or T for teen depict many violent acts that may not be appropriate for the age level suggested. It is also interesting to note that many players are not necessarily playing games that are appropriate for their age level, either by choice or because they are unaware of what the game is rated or the content depicted. It has been shown that playing M rated video games is very common among children ages 12-14 (Olson et al., 2007). M rated video games are for mature audiences only, meaning ages 17 and older, due to the prevalence of intense violence, blood and gore, sexual content, and strong language. Due to the increasing numbers of people who are playing violent video games, more research needs to be conducted to determine how accurate this rating system is and how accurate players perceptions are regarding the ratings of games being played.

Editor's Note: This is a cumulative References List; some of the works listed below will have been referenced in Part I of this piece, but not in Part II.

References

Abelson, R. P. (1981). Psychological status of the script concept. *American Psychology, 36*, 715-729.

Anderson, C. A. (1997). Effects of violent movies and trait hostility on hostile feelings and aggressive thoughts. *Aggressive Behavior, 23*, 161-178.

Anderson, C. A., & Bushman, B. J. (2001). Effects of violent video games on aggressive behavior, aggressive cognition, aggressive affect, physiological arousal, and prosocial behavior: A meta-analytic review of the scientific literature. *Psychological Science, 12*, 353-359.

Anderson, C. A., & Bushman, B. J. (2002a). Human aggression. *Annual Review of Psychology, 53*, 27-51.

Anderson, C.A., & Bushman, B.J. (2002b). Media violence and the American public revisited. *American Psychologist, 57*, 448-450.

Anderson, C. A., Carnagey, N. L., Flanagan, M., Benjamin, A. J., Eubanks, J., & Valentine, J. C. (2004). Violent video games: Specific effects on violent content on aggressive thoughts and behavior. *Advances in Experimental Social Psychology, 36*, 199-248.

Anderson, C. A., & Dill, K. E. (2000). Video games and aggressive thoughts, feelings, and behavior in the laboratory and in life. *Journal of Personality and Social Psychology, 78*, 772-790.

Anderson, C. A., & Huesman, L. R. (2003). Human aggression: A social-cognitive view. In Hogg, M. A. & Cooper, J. (Eds.), *The Sage Handbook of Social Psychology* (pp. 296-323). Thousand Oaks, CA: Sage Publications, Inc.

Anderson, C. A., & Murphy, C. R. (2003). Violent video games and aggressive behavior in young women. *Aggressive Behavior, 29*, 423-429.

Archer, J., & Latham, M. (2004). Variation in beliefs about aggression as a function of relationship to the opponent. *Personality and Individual Differences, 37*, 33-41.

Arriaga, P., Esteves, F., Carneiro, P., & Monteiro, B. (2006). Violent computer games and their effects on state hostility and physiological arousal. *Aggressive Behavior, 32*, 358-371.

Bandura, A. (1973). *Aggression: A social learning theory analysis.* Englewood Cliffs, NJ: Prentice-Hall.

Bandura, A., Ross, D., & Ross, S. A. (1961). Transmission of aggression through imitation of aggressive models. *Journal of Abnormal and Social Psychology, 63,* 575-582.

Bartholow, B. D., & Anderson, C. A. (2002). Effects of violent video games on aggressive behavior: Potential sex differences. *Journal of Experimental Social Psychology, 38,* 283-290.

Bartholow, B. D., Sestir, M. A., & Davis, E. B. (2005). Correlates and consequences of exposure to video game violence: Hostile personality, empathy, and aggressive behavior. *Personality and Social Psychology Bulletin, 31,* 1573-1586.

Bollen, K. A., & Phillips, D. P. (1981). Suicide motor vehicle fatalities in Detroit: A replication. *American Journal of Sociology, 87,* 404-412.

Bushman, B. J. (1998). Priming effects of violent media on the accessibility of aggressive constructs in memory. *Personal and Social Psychology Bulletin, 24,* 537-545.

Bushman, B. J., & Green, R. G. (1990). Role of cognitive-emotional mediators and individual differences in the effects of media violence on aggression. *Journal of Personality and Social Psychology, 58,* 156-163.

Bushman, B.J., & Huesmann, L.R. (2001). Effects of televised violence on aggression. In D. Singer & J. Singer (Eds.), *Handbook of children and the media* (pp. 223-254). Thousand Oaks, CA: Sage Publications.

Buss, A. H., & Perry, M. (1992). The aggression questionnaire. *Journal of Personality and Social Psychology, 63,* 452-459.

Carnagey, N. L., & Anderson, C. A. (2004). Violent video game exposure and aggression: A literature review. *Minerva Psichiatrica, 45,* 1-18.

Carnagey, N. L., & Anderson, C. A. (2005). The effects of reward and punishment in violent video games on aggressive affect, cognition, and behavior. *Psychological Science, 16,* 882-889.

Centerwall, B.S. (1989a). Exposure to television as a cause of violence. In G. Comstock (Ed.), *Public communication and behavior* (Vol. 2, pp. 1-58). New York: Academic Press.

Centerwall, B.S. (1989b). Exposure to television as a risk factor for violence. *American Journal of Epidemiology, 129,* 643-652.

Centerwall, B.S. (1992). Television and violence: The scale of the problem and where to go from here. *Journal of the American Medical Association, 267,* 3059-3063.

Colwell, J., & Kato, M. (2005). Video game play in British and Japanese adolescents. *Simulation and Gaming, 36,* 518-530.

Colwell, J., & Payne, J. (2000). Negative correlates of computer game play in adolescents. *British Journal of Psychology, 91,* 295-310.

Comstock, G. (1980). New emphases in research on the effects of television and film violence. In E.L. Palmer & A. Dorr (Eds.), *Children and the faces of television: Teaching, violence, selling* (pp. 129-148). New York: Academic Press.

Crick, N. R., Bigbee, M. A., & Howes, C. (1996). Gender differences in children's normative beliefs about aggression: How do I hurt thee? Let me count the ways. *Child Development, 67*, 1003-1014.

Deselms, J. L., & Altman, J. D. (2003). Immediate and prolonged effects of videogame violence. *Journal of Applied Social Psychology, 33*, 1553-1563.

Entertainment Software Association (2006). Entertainment Software Rating Board (ESRB). Retrieved January 26th, 2008 from http://www.esrb.org

Eron, L. D., Huesmann, L. R., Lefkowitz, M. M., & Walder, L. O. (1972). Does television violence cause aggression? *American Psychologist, 27*, 253-263.

Farrar, K. M., Krcmar, M. & Nowak, K. L. (2006). Contextual features of violent video games, mental models, and aggression. *Journal of Communication, 56*, 387-405.

Ferguson, C. J. (2007). Evidence for publication bias in video game violence effects literature: A meta-analytic review. *Aggression and Violent Behavior, 12*, 470-482.

Fleming, M. J., & Rickwood, D. J. (2001). Effects of violent versus nonviolent video games on children's arousal, aggressive mood, and positive mood. *Journal of Applied Social Psychology, 31*, 2047-2071.

Funk, J. B., Flores, G., Buchman, D. D., & Germann, J. N. (1999). Rating electronic games: Violence is in the eye of the beholder. *Youth and Society, 30*, 283-312.

Funk, J. B., Hagan, J., Schimming, J., Bullock, W. A., Buchman, D. D., & Myers, M. (2002). Aggression and psychopathology in adolescents with a preference for violent electronic games. *Aggressive Behavior, 28*, 134-144.

Gentile, D. A., & Anderson, C. A. (2006). Violent video games: The effects on youth and public policy implications. In Dowd, N., Singer, D. G., & Wilson, R. F. (Eds.), *Handbook of Children, Culture, and Violence* (pp. 225-246). Thousand Oaks, CA: Sage Publications, Inc.

Gentile, D. A., Lynch, P. J., Linder, J. R., & Walsh, D. A. (2004). The effects of violent video game habits on adolescent hostility, aggressive behaviors, and school performance. *Journal of Adolescence, 27*, 5-22.

Haninger, K. & Thompson, K. M. (2004). Content and ratings of teen-rated video games. *Journal of the American Medical Association, 291*, 856-865.

Hartmann, T., & Klimmt, C. (2006). Gender and computer games: Exploring females' dislikes. *Journal of Computer-Mediated Communication, 11*, 910-931.

Hennigan, K.M., Del Rosario, M.L., Heath, L., Cook, T.D., Wharton, J.D., & Calder, B.J. (1982). Impact of the introduction of television on crime in the United States: Empirical findings and theoretical implications. *Journal of Personality and Social Psychology, 42*, 461-477.

Henry, D., Guerra, N., Huesmann, R., Tolan, P., VanAcker, R., & Eron, L. (2000). Normative influences on aggression in urban elementary school classrooms. *American Journal of Community Psychology, 28*, 59-81.

Huesman, L. R. (1986). Psychological processes promoting the relation between exposure to media violence and aggressive behavior by the viewer. *Journal of Social Issues, 42*, 125-140.

Huesmann, L. R. (1988). An informational processing model for the development of aggression. *Aggressive Behavior, 14*, 13-24.

Huesmann, L. R., & Eron, L. D. (1986). *Television and the aggressive child: A cross-national comparison*. Hillsdale, NJ: Erlbaum.

Huesmann, L. R., & Guerra, N. G. (1997). Children's normative beliefs about aggression and aggressive behavior. *Journal of Personality and Social Psychology, 72*, 408-419.

Huesmann, L. R., Guerra, N. G., Zelli, A., & Miller, L. (1992). Differing normative beliefs about aggression for boys and girls. In Bjorkqvist, K. & Niemela, P. (Eds.). *Of Mice and Women: Aspects of Female Aggression* (pp. 77-87). San Diego, CA: Academic Press, Inc.

Huesmann, L. R., Lagerspetz, K., & Eron, L. D. (1984). Intervening variables in the TV violence-aggression relation: Evidence from two countries. *Developmental Psychology, 20*, 746-775.

Huesmann, L. R., Moise-Titus, J., Podolski, C. L., & Eron, L. D. (2003). Longitudinal relations between children's exposure to TV violence and their aggressive and violent behavior in young adulthood: 1977-1992. *Developmental Psychology, 39*, 201-221.

Johnson, J.G., Cohen, P., Smailes, E.M., Kasen, S., & Brook, J.S. (2002). Television viewing and aggressive behavior during adolescence and adulthood. *Science, 295*, 2468-2471.

Josephson, W. L. (1987). Television violence and children's aggression: Testing the priming, social script, and disinhibition predictions. *Journal of Personality and Social Psychology*, 53, 882-890

Kent, S. (2001). *The ultimate history of video games*. Roseville, CA: Prima.

Krahe, B., & Moller, I. (2004). Playing violent electronic games, hostile attributional style, and aggression-related norms in German adolescents. *Journal of Adolescence*, 27, 53-69.

Lubich, M. (2007, December 26). Vigil finds 'little girl lost' amid chaos of death. The Johnstown Breeze. Retrieved from www.johnstownbreeze.com/modules/php?name=news&file=article&sid=2499

Olson, C. K., Kutner, L. A., Warner, D. E., Almerigi, J. B., Baer, L., Nicholi, A. M., & Beresin, E. V. (2007). Factors correlated with violent video game use by adolescent boys and girls. *Journal of Adolescent Health*, 41, 77-83.

Oser, K. (2004). Moms are unsung players in gaming world. *Advertising Age*, 75, 56-57.

Persky, S., & Blascovich, J. (2007). Immersive virtual environments versus traditional platforms: Effects of violent and nonviolent video game play. *Media Psychology*, 10, 135-156.

Phillips, D. P. (1974). The influence of suggestion on suicide: Substantive and theoretical implications of the Werther Effect. *American Sociological Review*, 39, 340-354.

Phillips, D. P. (1979). Suicide, motor vehicle fatalities, and the mass media: Evidence toward a theory of suggestion. *American Journal of Sociology*, 84, 1150-1174.

Phillips, D. P. (1982). The impact of fictional television stories on the U.S. adult fatalities: New evidence on the effect of the mass media on violence. *American Journal of Sociology*, 87, 1340-1359.

Pooley, E. (1999). Portrait of a deadly bond. *Time*, May, 26-32.

Sherry, J. L. (2001). The effects of violent video games on aggression: A meta-analysis. *Human Communication Association*, 27, 409-431.

Sigurdsson, J. F., Gudjonsson, G. H., Bragason, A. V., Kristjansdottir, E., & Sigfusdottir, I. D. (2006). The role of violent cognition in the relationship between personality and the involvement in violent films and computer games. *Personality and Individual Differences*, 41, 381-392.

Souweidane, V., & Huesmann, L. R. (1999). The influence of American urban culture on the development of normative beliefs about aggression in Middle-Eastern immigrants. *American Journal of Community Psychology*, 27, 239-253.

Sukhodolsky, D. G., & Ruchkin, V. V. (2004). Association of normative beliefs and anger with aggression and antisocial behavior in Russian male juvenile offenders and high school students. *Journal of Abnormal Child Psychology*, 32, 225-236.

Thompson, K. M., & Haninger (2001). Violence in E-rated video games. *Journal of the American Medical Association*, 286, 591-598.

Werner, N. E., & Nixon, C. L. (2005). Normative beliefs and relational aggression: An investigation of the cognitive bases of adolescent aggressive behavior. *Journal of Youth and Adolescence*, 34, 229-24

Mark Pegrum's *From Blogs to Bombs. The Future of Digital Technologies in Education*

Review by Jeffrey Barlow

Mark Pegrum's short book (146 pages) may be just right for teachers who feel overwhelmed by the knowledge gap between themselves and their students with regard to digital matters. The students, invariably "digital natives"—those who have grown up with computers omnipresent their entire lives—not only know how to do things the teachers have usually only read about, but the students discuss them in a highly specialized language that usually renders those outside the culture mystified.

The main point of the book, however, is to persuade the reader that educators simply must pay more attention to technology in their curricula. The author accomplishes this through a sort of alternative carrot-and-stick approach: do so, and much high-level learning will occur; do not do so and a high social price may be paid. At a higher level, the point of the book is also to produce good policy by making sure the stakeholders in important educational decisions have a very broad view of the issues, and of the possible consequences of their decisions.

From Blogs to Bombs is, however, a great deal more than simply an introduction to the advantages and disadvantages of mainstream digital technologies. Pegrum focuses on the advantages to even a novice teacher of working with digital materials.
As most teachers might expect, the author is a whole-hearted constructivist in his pedagogy, seeing the Web as itself the best possible tool for constructing and sharing meaning between learners. He does, however, see many uses for other pedagogies, such as behaviorism and even perhaps for stimulus-response learning at times. To him, however, knowledge is "...a property of the network." (28)

The work uses the metaphor of "lens" as in "technological lens," "pedagogical lens," "social lens" to make the point that digital subjects usually cross intellectual boundaries rather freely. Pegrum himself then uses these lenses (each organized into a chapter) to unpack the broad impacts of digital technology in schools. For example, one of the lenses is "Many Literacies" which include print literacy, search literacy, information literacy, participatory literacy, visual literacy, audio literacy, media literacy, virtual world literacy, gaming literacy, remix literacy, personal literacy (how to present yourself on the World Wide Web), intercultural literacy, technological literacy and texting literacy. Each of his other lens is equally nuanced and multi-focused.

While short, the work is by no means simple. Pegrum is very familiar with a broad range of research on each of the many issues he raises, and occasionally introduces voices to the discussions which may not be familiar to American readers. He has a strong interest in policy as well as theory and while he cannot dedicate many pages to any given issues, each of them seems to have been very thoroughly dealt with at the last. He is rather critical of conservative positions on issues such as literacy, seeing them as essentially political efforts to maintain the status quo in the interest of maintaining control.

The author is an Australian scholar and, as of the time of writing, an Assistant Professor in the Graduate School of Education at the University of Western Australia. Australia has had considerable controversy over the place of the Web in public life, with a strong governmental impetus toward increasing censorship in the name of first, national security then of the protection of the young.[1] The author's bruises from this conflict are in evidence throughout the work, and the last chapter, "Many baaas & ^^^^" (See the sheep?) is a rather fervent appeal for teacher-directed education on digital issues as a counter-balance for the attempts of governments and corporations to control and exploit the Web, sometimes at the expense of freedom of access. Pegrum's answer to all these issues is simple: "Education". And From Blogs to Bombs might well be the place for many teachers, especially novices, to begin.

---

[1] For a work dealing specifically with those issues, see our review of Beattie, Scott. *Community, Space and Online Censorship. Regulating Pornotopia*, Franham, Surrey, England: Ashgate Publishing, 2009, found at: http://bcis.pacificu.edu/journal/2009/08/article.php?id=109

Joseph Menn's *Fatal System Error. The Hunt for the New Crime Lords Who Are Bringing Down the Internet*

Review by Jeffrey Barlow

Joseph Menn's work, *Fatal System Error*, is an extremely detailed and very well researched investigation into organized cyber crime, with a focus on the years from about 2004-2008. Mr. Menn is well qualified to write this book. A former technology reporter for *The Los Angeles Times*, he has written several other significant works related to the Internet, notably, *All The Rave, The Rise and Fall* of Shawn Fanning's Napster. He was twice nominated for the Pulitzer prize.

The topic is an inherently exciting one. The author focuses upon the protagonists in organized cybercrime, both the "white hats" and the "black hats." The first of the former is an American hacker, Barrett Lyon, who turned from initially protecting gambling sites from Denial of Service Attacks to broader work assisting law enforcement internationally in uncovering criminal cartels. The second white hat is Andy Crocker, an English police officer who came up in the British forces during a period when the Blair government intended to make Britain a model for the protection of on-line commercial activity. The author worked closely with them in researching and writing *Fatal System Error*.

Through Lyon and Crocker's work, often done cooperatively, the reader also meets numerous criminals, some in their real-world identities, others as shadowy pseudonyms on the net. These operate most frequently out of Russian and other former Soviet republics, may of which have effectively become an alliance between organized crime and corrupt local, and apparently, national governments.

Menn[1] worked closely with dozens if not hundreds of actors on both sides of the legal divide and has been able to discuss highly technical details of the endless fight between offense and defense in cybercrime, while simultaneously bringing the individuals alive. The author manages to walk some very tight lines in doing so. It is clear that Lyon has a very mixed past and at some points came very close to himself being a criminal, an issue which Menn skirts while pointing out how very frequently other individuals have worked both sides of the street, now an FBI informant, now a master criminal.

Some might idealize the criminals discussed here. After all, part of the charm of computer crime is that it is white-collar work and intellectually challenging. There is also a sort of pleasure, I am sure, in the power that breaking and entering other's computer systems, not to mention their lives, brings. But these criminals are not Robin Hoods.

---

[1] See Menn's home page at: http://www.josephmenn.com/index.php

The gangs rob the poor as well as the rich; in fact, as the book points out, the poor, or at least the middle class, are much easier to rob than the rich, who have a tendency to spend money to protect their money, sometimes vengefully so. The gangs also murder...daughters of complainants are kidnapped, never to be seen again; those who turn on the gangsters die accidently in the custody of corrupt police forces, and if angered the gangs may destroy your business simply to make an example of you. Even those who write about them may find their lives and those of their family members threatened. The difficulties (and dangers) of the author's research should not be underestimated.

We assume that at least the readers of *Interface* are aware how very serious a problem cybercrime has become. As bad as you might think it is, Menn is able to point out how very much worse the reality has become. The agencies which should be protecting consumers, particularly the banking industry, have managed to make accommodations—such as passing losses onto merchants who in good faith accept bad credit cards—to the point where they now often oppose stricter legislation intended to prevent such crimes in the first place.

Governments, for their part, have found the struggle much too difficult (fewer than one percent of cybercriminals are ever convicted) and have in effect given up. It is telling that both Lyon and Crocker, although young in at least Lyon's case, and both at the top of their game, have essentially retired from the struggle and gone into private industry where they see some hope of making headway. They, like the author, have very low expectations of governmental agencies.

In his last chapter, "Fixing What's Fixable," Menn discusses possible solutions, but like many of the experts whom he interviews, he believes that the current Internet is broken and may have to be supplanted with a new two-track system in which participants either accept restrictions on their privacy or risk being robbed or otherwise exploited.

Of the positive actions which Menn suggests, one is the education of consumers. At *Interface*, we have long argued that such education must be undertaken at the public level as soon as computers begin to appear in the curriculum at any given school. This will mean, as Menn's work suggests, educating future "black hats" as well as future "white hats," but the problem can hardly be worse. At present, the "black hats" are clearly winning and the "white hats," are, as one of Menn's experts puts it, "losing faster."

In addition to those simply interested in cybercrime, the work is worth reading by those who work in the industry. Menn does an excellent job of outlining the rapid evolution of the use of technology by the gangs—among his villains are all the familiar big name companies which refuse to take responsibility for bad software which is distributed with known weaknesses.

These firms, like the banks, have supported laws which relieve them of responsibility. As the consumer does not "buy" the product but in effect "rents" or licenses it, the legal exposure to the producer is far less. The consumer pays at every point. Finally, as the author points out, both the recovery of lost funds and the prosecution of perpetrators is extremely difficult, despite the assurances we are constantly given from the business dependent upon digital transfers of funds:

A Gartner survey found that 30 percent of Americans had been victimized by identity fraud by 2009. They got back an average of 86 percent of the money drained from credit cards and 77 percent of the money stolen from ATM and debit cards. Victims of bogus account transfers, though, recovered only 54 percent of their losses. Small businesses were increasingly targeted in account transfers, and the banks often refused to make up the losses. As for the banking industry's red ink, that was anyone's guess. Convictions remained an extreme rarity, striking far less than half of 1 percent of the perpetrators.[2]

Many of Menn's solutions are perhaps counter-intuitive, another value of the book. The issues are so complex that most of us may choose to oppose legislative proposals which initially might seem ineffective or perhaps even likely to worsen the situation. For example, Menn supports the legalization of on-line gambling on the grounds that on-line gamblers are such fools that they are going to gamble anyway, and that it would be better to license and tax it than simply turn so many sheep over to the wolves annually.

His arguments are compelling. For many years individuals have chosen to gamble on-line with firms that have shown, statistically at least, to simply ignore the players' odds of winning by manipulating the hands dealt. The player turns up three aces; the software is programmed to finally, after betting is closed, deal itself four of a kind, however long the odds against that occurring in fact are. The player whispers “almost!” and plays again.

Fatal System Error shows us a terrible truth about the Internet. It truly is in an important sense, broken. Or perhaps more importantly, it has broken many of our laws and institutions, particularly when viewed internationally. Nation states are simply not sufficiently cooperative to deal with cross-border gangs.

Menn fears that the result may one day be that it will be necessary for given states to isolate themselves from other states where criminals—or politically oriented nationalist hacker groups—flourish.[3] But even this is only a partial solution. Ironically, most gangs choose to operate in the U.S. or Europe where the bandwidth is better and the pickings richer.

The book is not without its flaws. While the author has done tremendous research and made much of it available on the Internet, to see his sources as one reads requires, at least in my Kindle edition, the reader to prowl through the chapter notes at the back, not knowing if the source is, in fact, cited—there are no notes to indicate such. There is a key word index, but not searchable in the

---

[2] Loc. 2889-93 (Kindle edition)

[3] China comes in for much criticism by the author. While it is clear that Chinese nationalist hackers have been very active, I myself think that the tolerance of the PRC for truly organized crime is very low. Such groups have too often been rivals for power and authority in China to be tolerated at more than a local level.

Kindle edition[4] and there are no page numbers added to the key word—the reader knows the topic is covered, but not where nor to what extent.

Some readers are going to find the author's prose a bit breathless...lest the reader miss the significance of the topic or the scale of the research, Menn reminds us frequently in words such as these:

Their (Barrett and Crocker) combined stories shine by far the brightest light yet into a shadow economy that is worth several times more than the illegal drug trade, that has already disrupted national governments, and that has the potential to undermine Western affluence and security. This book is about the triumph of two men who went where none like them had gone before.[5]

Also, the work is not truly up to date. Although the publication date is 2010, the coverage pretty much ends before 2009, though there are a few references to events in 2009. While this early history is necessary to understand the present, we can only hope for periodic updates. This is, of course, a great deal to ask from any author. We all get bored with any one topic, and as exciting as investigating cyber crime must be—the author did on site research in the former Soviet Union, for example—the prospect of a career spent on one topic is a daunting one at best.

At *Interface* we have reviewed several previous works on hackers, and while each has its value, this is by far the most comprehensive of them. See Nuwere, Ejovi and David Chanoff. *Hacker Cracker*. At: http://bcis.pacificu.edu/journal/2004/02/nuwere.php. See also Mitnick, Kevin D. and William L. Simon. The Art of Intrusion. at: http://bcis.pacificu.edu/journal/2005/07/mitnick.php.

---

[4] While, as I have often made clear, I find our Berglund Kindle a great aide in reading and writing, the increasing tendency of Amazon to release Kindle editions without searchable indexes negates one of the great advantages of the format.

[5] Loc. 58-60 (Kindle edition)

Google and China Eight Weeks Later: Where Are We Now?

Editorial by Jeffrey Barlow

In the February issue of Interface, my editorial was on "Google and China: Minor Incident or Cyberwar?"[1] One month after that piece and two months after the incident was announced, I want to revisit the issues here, because it gives us some insight into the notion of "cyber war," if it clarifies little else.
While it is not my intent here to defend my earlier judgments, arrived at during six weeks of working in China, I think it easy enough to do so. My first judgment was simply that nothing is certain.

We now know a bit more, but given the amount of time which has passed, surprisingly little. We do not know, for example, how serious an impact the event will in fact have, either on Google's relationship with China, or China's relationship with the U. S. Google now says that it will be meeting with the Chinese government after the New Year's holidays end there.[2]

Interestingly, Google's focus has apparently become less the incidents themselves than its desire to provide unfiltered searches in China—this is the issue being negotiated. While it is true that Google frequently conflated these issues in the initial responses to the incident, it is somewhat surprising to see the issue boiled down to this. If the incidents are to be used as a bargaining chip with China, it makes sense to make the issue network filtering. I do, however, have a fair amount of experience bargaining with Chinese institutions and officials, and I am very glad that I am not on that Google bargaining team—it will be very hard to get fruitfully from the one issue—"you hacked our servers!" to "And...uh....so we want an end to filtering!"

One reason this bargaining process is surprising is that the change in emphasis amounts in part to an affirmation of the position taken by many Chinese sources who felt that the issue was more a commercial one than a defense of privacy on Google's part. Unfiltered searching, for example, will not provide any additional protection to the Chinese dissidents who were supposedly hacked in the incidents.

But an end to filtering would be very good for Google's share of the search market in China because it would then be the only completely open search engine for Chinese users. Other engines, notably Baidu, which has about two-thirds of the Chinese market to Google's less than one-third, will, as Chinese corporations, be obliged to follow Chinese laws.

---

[1] See "Google and China: Minor Incident or Cyber war?" January-February 2010 – Volume 10, Issue 1. <http://bcis.pacificu.edu/journal/article.php?id=634>
[2] Market watch, The Wall Street Journal, February 23, 2010. <http://www.marketwatch.com/story/google-talks-with-china-officials-to-resume-wsj-2010-02-23?reflink=MW_news_stmp>

We also know a bit more about the origins of the attacks. Google invited the National Security Agency into the investigation in early February.[3] Whether the additional information comes from NSA or not, it is now held that the direct source of the attack was two Chinese educational institutions. However, because of the inherent uncertainties involved in trying to trace artful cyber attacks, our understanding has not in fact been decisively furthered. To quote *The New York Times* statement at the discovery:

"Within the computer security industry and the Obama administration, analysts differ over how to interpret the finding that the intrusions appear to come from schools instead of Chinese military installations or government agencies. Some analysts have privately circulated a document asserting that the vocational school is being used as camouflage for government operations. But other computer industry executives and former government officials said it was possible that the schools were cover for a "false flag" intelligence operation being run by a third country. Some have also speculated that the hacking could be a giant example of criminal industrial espionage, aimed at stealing intellectual property from American technology firms".[4]

These are pretty much some of the possibilities I discussed in February, though the mention of two specific Chinese schools is certainly an important new wrinkle.

I remain suspicious of anybody's ability to identify the source of an attack without being able to access the machine that was directly involved, or, at a minimum, generous assistance from the Internet Providers involved. It is my understanding that to trace the activities taking place on a "captured" computer, that is, one to which a hacker has gained control, it is not enough to merely trace the attacker back to a network. To do so is to leave open the possibility that the attack went to that network, to a specific machine, but from that machine (another captured one) hopped to yet another network and another captured machine, and perhaps another and another. As *The New York Times* put it in part of an article which otherwise tries to build the case against the two Chinese universities:

"Beijing has not announced an investigation, but Web security experts emphasize that the Chinese government would need to be involved to find the ultimate perpetrators of the attacks.

"The U.S. would not be able to trace this" back to the source, said O. Sami Saydjari, the founder of the Cyber Defense Agency, a private Web security firm

---

[3] Ellen Nakashima, "Google to enlist NSA to help it ward off cyberattacks." *The Washington Post*, Thursday, February 4, 2010. <http://www.washingtonpost.com/wp-dyn/content/article/2010/02/03/AR2010020304057.html?wpisrc=nl_politics>

[4] See: John Markoff and David Barboza, "2 China Schools Said to Be Tied to Online Attacks." *The New York Times*, February 18, 2010. <http://www.nytimes.com/2010/02/19/technology/19china.html>

based in Wisconsin. "We cannot trace it beyond borders. We'd need the cooperation of the Chinese".[5]

In China, Internet Providers are both few in number and tightly controlled. If the Chinese government is in any way involved in the attacks—and if it is not, it is difficult to see the point of the issue, it just becomes another of hundreds of thousands of daily hacking events, possibly devoid of political or international significance at all—then it is difficult to imagine the Chinese government pitching in to, in effect, investigate itself.

We have now traced the series of attacks being generally described as the Google attack to two networks in China, but until we are able to actually access the machines directly involved we have stopped short of certainty—that is the hackers may have utilized that machine as a route into yet another undiscovered source. This is why the experts quoted above left open the three possibilities that they mentioned, each of which recognizes the possibility of yet another undetected hop out of the network.

There are also some real shortcomings in the research of the American authorities concerned, which quickly announced that one of the two schools, the Lanxian Vocational School in Shandong, was closely linked to the Chinese military. There is a great deal of controversy over this particular designation[6]—many feel it rather to be a down-at-the-heels junior college equivalent incapable of producing true elite hackers and we must again wait for additional information to accumulate.[7]

The other university, Shanghai Jiaotong, is indeed an elite school, comparable to America's M.I.T. in China. Evidence, however, is largely circumstantial beyond the bare fact that apparently the attack was related to its network at some point.[8] The uncertainties inherent in this incident have provided a feast for news organizations. China is so high on the American media radar at present that the

---

[5] See David Barboza, "Hacking Inquiry Puts China's Elite in New Light" *The New York Times*, February 21, 2010. < https://myaccount.nytimes.com/auth/login?URI=http://www.nytimes.com/2010/02/22/technology/22cyber.html&OQ=_rQ3D1>

[6] Chinese bloggers and students at Lanxiang have been having a great deal of fun with the NYT story; for English translations go

[7] For a supportive view, see Nick Farrell, "Google was brought down by Chinese hairdressers" Curl up and dye westerners, *The Inquirer*, Mon Feb 22 2010. < http://www.theinquirer.net/inquirer/news/1592914/google-bought-chinese-hairdressers>

[8] For the sort of evidence being brought forward against Jiaotong (Entirely circumstantial in my opinion, with the possible exception of the reports initially quoted in the NYT articles quoted here, which have yet to reveal the nature of their evidence.) See Jaikumar Vijayan, "Chinese school linked to Google attacks also linked to '01 attacks on White House site" A former U.S. Army officer linked '01 hacker to Shanghai Jiaotong University. February 19, 2010 07:06 AM ET Computer world.com at: http://www.computerworld.com/s/article/9159258/Chinese_school_linked_to_Google_attacks_also_linked_to_01_attacks_on_White_House_site

story has been repeated endlessly. One recent exhaustive analysis of the news gathering process on this one story by Jonathan Stray of the Neiman Media Labs,[9] made this point:

"We often talk about the new news ecosystem — the network of traditional outlets, new startups, nonprofits, and individuals who are creating and filtering the news. But how is the work of reporting divvied up among the members of that ecosystem?

To try to build a datapoint on that question, I chose a single big story[10] and read every single version listed on Google News to see who was doing the work. Out of the 121 distinct versions of last week's story about tracing Google's recent attackers to two schools in China, 13 (11 percent) included at least some original reporting. And just seven organizations (six percent) really got the full story independently."

That is, of the welter of commentary and reporting on the issue, only a few sources possess real authority.[11] The others are not only repeating secondary reports, but often adding additional commentary and opinion to those original stories. This has been particularly true for the cyber war boffins, both individuals and institutions, including American defense groups, which stand to gain by increased anxieties and the resultant hope of enhancing their budgets.

Shay has a very useful table of the 121 unique stories which he examined from which a number of conclusions can be drawn: *The New York Times* was at least the partial source for the great majority of the stories. A number did access Chinese English-language sources, notably Xinhua, but only 18 of the 121 accessed any Chinese sources at all.

---

[9] Jonathan Stray, "The Google/China hacking case: How many news outlets do the original reporting on a big story?" Neiman Journalism Lab, February 24, 2010. < http://www.niemanlab.org/2010/02/the-googlechina-hacking-case-how-many-news-outlets-do-the-original-reporting-on-a-big-story/>

[10] http://www.nytimes.com/2010/02/19/technology/19china.html

[11]According to Stray: — "Only seven stories (six percent) were primarily based on original reporting. These were produced by *The New York Times* (https://myaccount.nytimes.com/auth/login?URI=http://www.nytimes.com/2010/02/19/technology/19china.html&OQ= rQ3D1), *The Washington Post* (http://www.washingtonpost.com/wp-dyn/content/article/2010/02/19/AR2010021902643.html?hpid=moreheadlines), *The Wall Street Journal* (http://online.wsj.com/article/SB10001424052748703787304575074703728470246.html), *The Guardian* (http://www.guardian.co.uk/technology/2010/feb/19/google-attacks-chinese-schools), *Tech News World* (http://www.technewsworld.com/story/Look-Whos-Not-Talking-About-Chinese-Schools-and-Google-Hack-69382.html?wlc=1299868039), Bloomberg (http://www.financialexpress.com/news/-Fortune-100-cos-were-on-hackers-target-list--too-/581995/), *Xinhua* (China) (http://news.xinhuanet.com/english2010/china/2010-02/21/c_13181326.htm), and the *Global Times* (China) (http://www.globaltimes.cn/www/english/sci-edu/world/2010-02/506319.html)."

What then, at the last, do we learn about cyber war? The lessons to me seem to boil down once again to a very few:

- There is always going to be an element of uncertainty involved where cyber attacks are concerned.
- This uncertainty magnifies the risk of bad judgments.
- Where Sino-American relations are involved, there are major commercial and political interests internal to the U.S. involved, which further complicates the issues.

We are certain that there will be additional issues over the Google events, and we look forward to following them here at *Interface*.

April 2010 – Volume 10 – Issue 3

About This Issue

Our April issue of *Interface* is live and on the WWW.

Since holidays come and go, but *Interface* is forever, we have rigorously avoided all April First humor...at great cost...

This issue is, we think, an outstanding one. This is the time of the year when many long-term projects come to fruition, giving us very well thought-out pieces. Our Feature for this issue is by Anthony Cantu, Chair, Department of Teacher Education at Bradley University. Tony's piece, "Emerging Classroom Technologies: Application of the 2010 Horizon Report to K-12 Education" is a marvelous survey of "...emerging technologies that will be commonplace in American K-12 classrooms by the end of this decade." It is also a very useful introduction to The Horizon Report, a well-considered analysis of emerging technology of particular importance to teachers.

Berglund Research Fellow Professor Lorely French presents here her stunning project, *LIVE—DANCE—PAINT—WRITE: A Multi-Media Project on Romani ("Gypsy") Artist, Writer, Singer, and Educator Ceija Stojka*. This multi-media project is the study of the life and art of a Romani artist. As Lorely began research, she saw that there are not that many authoritative sites on Romani language and culture on the web, and as a very serious and highly-published linguist, undertook to create one. The Berglund Center is proud to have had the opportunity to support this research.

Professor Shawn Davis of Pacific University's School of Professional Psychology, offers us "When our Tools Become our Master: Psychological and Sociological Implications of Rapid Technological Development." Here Shawn fearlessly takes on a number of critical questions in the development of technology, such as how are we to understand the many impacts of technology on the human organism and our social structures?

Media Editor and Electronic/Information Services Coordinator at the Pacific University Library, Lynda Irons, surveys the on-line film viewing scene and its impact on conventional rental businesses in "Netflix: Streaming Ahead." Read Lynda's piece and understand why so many video rental stores are now closing.

Jeffrey Barlow's Editorial, "Cyber War or Cyber Vigilantism" discusses a recent on-line clash he viewed in real time between several highly committed partisan groups. He uses the conflict to try to better understand the limitations of the concept of "Cyber war." He also offers us insights into what Cyber Vigilantism means in the Chinese context.

Our two book reviews are of quite different works appealing to widely varying audiences. The first is Nitesh Dhanjani, et. al.'s, *Hacking: The Next Generation*. Dhanjani's work should be of interest to anyone concerned about the current state-of-the-art in computer intrusions. It is well written and can be read by those with little or no technical skill but would also be of benefit to those with considerable skill and experience.

The second review is a novel by Daniel Suarez, *The Daemon*. The work is the first of two "Techno Thrillers" by Suarez; the second, *Freedom TM*, has just been released. Although fiction, the work is a useful indication of the impact of the Internet because of Suarez' high level of professional skills and experience in the I.T. industry. This is a work for a very geeky audience and has received strong reviews in those quarters.

See also our series of recent announcements, ranging from warnings about a very sophisticated new phishing scam to recent events at the Berglund Center.
As always, we hope you find this issue of Interface both interesting and useful.

The Berglund Center for Internet Studies,
Pacific University

Emerging Classroom Technologies: Application of the *2010 Horizon Report* to K-12 Education

By D. Antonio Cantú
Bradley University

> "The illiterate of the 21st century will not be those who cannot read and write, but those who cannot learn, unlearn, and relearn."
> -Alvin Toffler

American author and futurist Alvin Toffler's sage advice is perhaps even more relevant today, at the dawn of this digital and technological century to which Toffler refers, than it was when he first dispensed it at the close of the twentieth century. This is particularly true when considering the emerging technologies that will be commonplace in American K-12 classrooms by the end of this decade. Teachers who are unwilling to learn, unlearn, and relearn new classroom technologies will soon find themselves to be pedagogically illiterate in the classroom of the twenty-first century where such technologies and online tools are ubiquitous.

While some sources, such as the popular online list of the "Top 100 Tools for Learning," compiled by the Centre for Learning & Performance Technologies, attempt to keep educators abreast of the latest in online tools or technologies, they are snapshots of "what is," i.e., popular technologies already being utilized today.[1] These sources may be of assistance to classroom teachers in identifying online technologies that could potentially serve to enhance the teaching and learning process in their respective classrooms. They are not, however, a predictor or barometer for "what will be," i.e., technologies that are on the horizon. Indeed, classroom teachers should continue to learn more about the technologies and online tools that are currently available to them, however they should also keep one eye on where technology is going, in order to stay one step ahead of the technology curve.

This approach is the same one advocated by former professional hockey player Wayne Gretzky, "The Great One," who when asked how he was able to sustain such an incredibly high level of performance over his twenty-one year NHL career, replied simply, "I skate to where the puck is going to be, not to where it has been." To assist in keeping one eye on where the digital puck is going, each year the New Media Consortium and the EDUCAUSE Learning Initiative publish the Horizon Report, which provides colleges and universities with a summary of technologies that are likely to impact post-secondary teaching and learning over

---

[1] Centre for Learning & Performance Technologies, "Top 100 Tools for Learning 2009," Learning Tools Compendium (November 15, 2009). Available at http://www.c4lpt.co.uk/recommended/.

the next one to five years.[2] This year's *Horizon Report* identifies six emerging technologies that are expected to "enter mainstream use on campuses within three adoption horizons," as follows:

> The **near-term horizon** assumes the likelihood of entry into the mainstream for institutions within the next twelve months; the **mid-term horizon**, within two to three years; and the **far-term**, within four to five years.[3]

While the *2010 Horizon Report* provides academic faculty and IT staff with critical information on the technologies and practices that will be impacting the teaching, learning, and creative processes at their respective colleges and universities in the near future, i.e., where the puck is going, it does not address K-12 education. The purpose of this article is to apply the findings of the *Horizon Report* to the K-12 classroom, providing classroom teachers with the same critical information on where the digital puck is going over the next five years as it relates to their classroom and pedagogical practices. The same three-tier adoption schedule and six categories of emerging technologies found in the *Horizon Report* will be adopted; however, the focus will be on K-12 education.

Near-Term K-12 Horizon (School Year 2010-2011)

The *Horizon Report* identifies two technologies which are likely to enter into "mainstream use for teaching, learning, or creative inquiry" within the next year.[4] The two technologies and practices on the near-term horizon are mobile computing and open content.

Mobile Computing

The *Horizon Report* defines mobile computing as "network-capable devices students are already carrying" (e.g., smart phones, iPod Touch, netbooks).[5] The portability of these devices and easy wireless access to the Internet makes mobile computing devices ideal pedagogical conduits for a variety of teaching and learning activities in K-12 education. The challenge is for K-12 teachers to seize opportunities to integrate mobile computing in the teaching and learning process. Five such opportunities to use mobile computing and learning are outlined in Carly Shuler's book *Pockets of Potential: Using Mobile Technologies to Promote Children's Learning*, as follows:

1. **Encourage "anywhere, anytime" learning**
   Mobile devices allow students to gather, access, and process information outside the classroom. They can encourage learning in a

---

[2] Larry Johnson, Alan Levine, Rachel Smith, and Sonja Stone, The 2010 Horizon Report (Austin, TX: The New Media Consortium, 2010). Available at http://www.nmc.org/pdf/2010-Horizon-Report.pdf.
[3] Ibid, 3.
[4] Ibid, 5.
[5] Ibid, 9.

real-world context, and help bridge school, afterschool, and home environments.

2. **Reach underserved children**
Because of their relatively low cost and accessibility in low-income communities, handheld devices can help advance digital equity, reaching and inspiring populations "at the edges" -- children from economically disadvantaged communities and those from developing countries.

3. **Improve 21st-century social interactions**
Mobile technologies have the power to promote and foster collaboration and communication, which are deemed essential for 21st-century success.

4. **Fit with learning environments.**
Mobile devices can help overcome many of the challenges associated with larger technologies, as they fit more naturally within various learning environments.

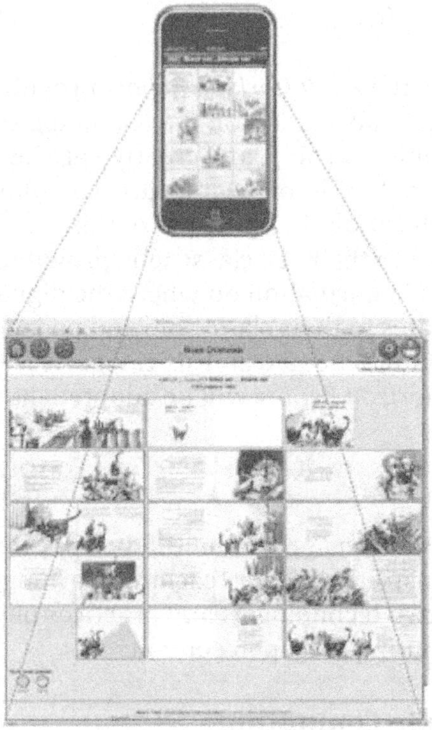

Figure 1 - International Children's Digital Library, iPhone Edition

Source: Carly Shuler, *Pockets of Potential: Using Mobile Technologies to Promote Children's Learning* (New York: The Joan Ganz Cooney Center at Sesame Workshop, 2009), 27.

5. **Enable a personalized learning experience**
Not all children are alike; instruction should be adaptable to individual and diverse learners. There are significant opportunities for genuinely supporting differentiated, autonomous, and individualized learning through mobile devices.[6]

One of the best examples of mobile computing and learning is the International Children's Digital Library ICDL iPhone App, which makes available to users one

[6] Carly Shuler, Pockets of Potential: Using Mobile Technologies to Promote Children's Learning (New York: The Joan Ganz Cooney Center at Sesame Workshop, 2009), 5.

of the largest collections of digitized children's books currently available (see Figure 1).

Another example of mobile computing and learning is the Center for Children and Technology and Center for Science Education's research project "Super Sleuths," which is designed to integrate mobile computing (i.e., Nintendo DSi) in science and literacy education. At the 2009 Institute of Education Sciences Research Conference, researchers distributed the following schematic illustrating the manner in which researchers are using Nintendo DSi as a pocket-sized laboratory in order to develop middle school students' scientific reasoning skills (see Figure 2).

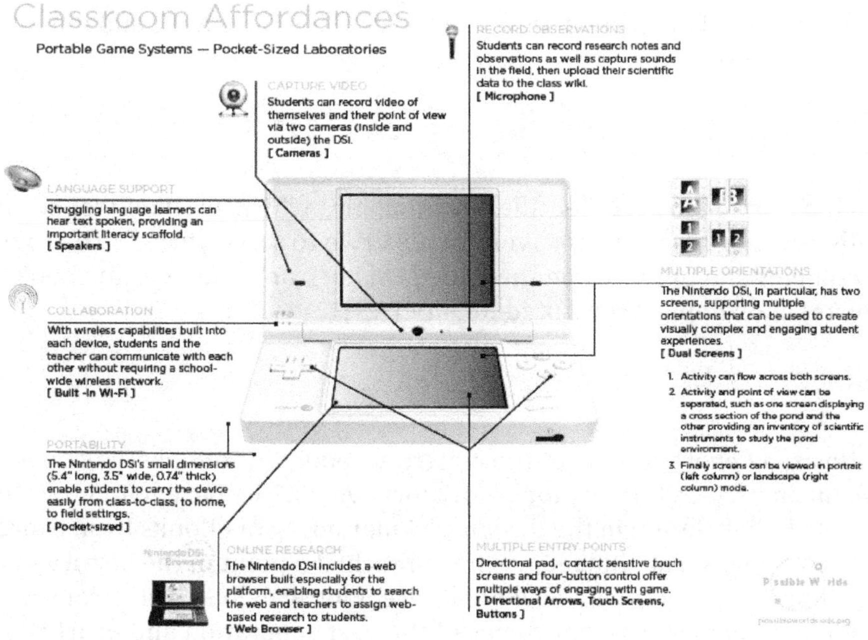

Figure 1 Possible Worlds: Portable Game Systems as Pocket-Sized Laboratories

Source: Center for Children and Technology and Center for Science Education, *Possible Worlds: Research and Overview* (Washington, D.C.: National Research and Development Center for Instructional Technology, 2009), 2

Open Content

The *Horizon Report* defines open content as "customizable educational content" that is made "available for free over the Internet."[7] The pedagogical nature of the open content design allows for K-12 students to not only gain knowledge of the content of the material under examination but also to refine their research and evaluation skills as they analyze the online open content resources. Although most of the Open Educational Resources (OER) is designed for college and university faculty and students, a growing number of sites are beginning to

[7] The 2010 Horizon Report, 13.

integrate K-12 education OER materials and resources. Some of the most popular OER sites for K-12 teachers are as follows:

> Connexions (cnx.org) includes a large collection of Open Educational Resources for K-12 and university educators, arranged in easily accessible clusters or modules.
>
> Teachers Without Borders (www.teacherswithoutborders.org) provides P-12 teachers with a myriad of international OER materials and resources, including early childhood education content and tools.
>
> Open Educational Resources Grapevine (oergrapevine.org/OER_projects) is a wiki designed as a portal to a variety of open educational resources (OER) for K-12 and university educators.

Mid-Term K-12 Horizon (School Year 2011-12 to 2012-13)

Next, the *Horizon Report* identifies technologies which are likely to "see much broader use across academia over the next two to three years."[8] The two technologies and practices on the mid-term horizon are electronic books (eBooks) and Simple Augmented Reality (AR).

eBooks

The *Horizon Report* points out the electronic books, or eBooks, have been available in various formats for nearly forty years. The past year, however, has witnessed a revolution in the design and marketing of eBooks from Amazon's Kindle to Apple's iPad. Indeed, we have reached a point in the history of book publishing where nearly all new books are now available in electronic format.[9] In addition, the most popular tomes of the past generation and nearly all of the classics are available to eBook readers. The multi-billion dollar textbook industry, however, has not been aggressive in pursuing the K-12 eBook market. Therefore, K-12 teachers who want to adopt electronic textbooks in their respective classrooms often find themselves in uncharted territory. To this end, *Education Week*'s Rhea Borja has developed a list of suggestions or tips to assist K-12 educators in the eTextbook adoption process, as follows:

1. Get the administrative green light. Does the administrative leadership in your district or school understand the positive impact virtual textbooks can have on learning?
2. Identify an on-site advocate and expert. You need a teacher, librarian, or other non-administrative staff member at each school to keep classroom teachers focused and to train and support them in e-textbook integration.

---

[8] Ibid, 6.
[9] Ibid, 9.

3. Build a technical-support team. Teachers need classroom hardware and software support so they can focus primarily on creating and teaching academic content, rather than troubleshooting technical problems.
4. Showcase the results of using e-textbooks. Teachers need to see how digital books can help improve instruction at a faster rate than traditional texts.
5. Share ideas and lessons learned. Are other schools or districts using virtual textbooks? What have they learned?
6. Solicit feedback from district curriculum experts. They can look beyond the bells and whistles and measure the usefulness of the e-textbooks' interactive features.[10]

Augmented Reality (AR)

The *Horizon Report* defines simple augmented reality as "blending (augmenting) virtual data--information, rich media, and even live action--with what we see in the real world, for the purpose of enhancing the information we can perceive with our senses."[11] While AR has had its greatest impact in fields of entertainment and marketing, it is beginning to make inroads in education, thanks in large part to the application of augmented reality gaming to K-12 subject or content areas such as history, geography, and anthropology.[12] A couple of the most popular AR apps for K-12 teachers are as follows:

1. Google Sky Map (www.google.com/sky/skymap.html) uses an Android phone's orientation sensors to provide students with a map of the stars and constellations. Sky Map even uses the phone's compass, GPS, and accelerometer to move the map as the student moves his/her hand across the night sky.
2. Wikitude World Browser (www.wikitude.org/world_browser) provides students with information about landmarks and other points of interest in an area through data overlays that appear on a smart phone as the student moves his/her camera view over the surroundings.

Far-Term K-12 Horizon (School Year 2013-14 to 2014-15)

Finally, the *Horizon Report* identifies technologies which are "[not] yet commonly found in campus settings, but the high level of interest and the tremendous amounts of research in both areas indicates that they are worth following closely."[13] The two technologies and practices on the far-term horizon are gesture-based computing and visual data analysis.

---

[10] Rhea R. Borja, "Reviewing E-Books: The Benefits and Drawbacks of Virtual Textbooks," *Education Week*, June 13, 2008. Available at http://www.edweek.org/dd/articles/2008/06/09/01ebooks.h02.html.
[11] The 2010 Horizon Report, 21.
[12] Ibid, 22.
[13] Ibid, 6.

Gesture-Based Computing

Gesture-based interaction with technology has been commonplace for decades, however for most of that period it has been largely restricted to a keyboard, controller, and mouse. In the past few years, however—with the introduction of the Nintendo Wii, in 2006, and Apple iPhone, in 2007—we have witnessed a revolution in gesture-based computing, where now gesture-based interfaces does not even require handheld devices, using instead cameras and motion sensors to track our body movements.[14] While today the most popular forms of gesture-based computing are designed for gaming and simulation/training purposes, there is a growing interest in applying these technologies to K-12 education. Perhaps one of the best examples of such application is the collaboration between Nintendo and the National Association for Music Education to integrate Wii consoles and music software into secondary school music classes.[15] Another example of application of gesture-based technology in the K-12 classroom can be found in Bayside Middle School (Virginia Beach, Virginia) integration of Nintendo Wii consoles and Wii Fit software in physical education classes for special education students.[16] These are but two examples of gesture-based technology integration in the K-12 curriculum; however they have yielded extremely encouraging results. In the coming years, the integration of other gesture-based technologies, such as the Microsoft Natal system, in K-12 education should serve to provide classroom teachers in other subject areas with even more possibilities for incorporating such technologies into their pedagogical repertoire.

Visual Data Analysis

The *Horizon Report* defines visual data analysis as "a way of discovering and understanding patterns in large data sets via visual interpretation."[17] An emerging field for K-12 education, visual data analysis traces its genesis to college and university researchers and scientists who developed such technologies to analyze voluminous amounts of data generated from their investigations and studies.[18] Examples of visual data analysis technologies and sites that have application to K-12 education include the following:

1. Visual Complexity (www.visualcomplexity.com/vc/) is a site for educators who are interested in visualizations of complex concepts and networks to use as heuristics in the classroom to facilitate understanding and enhance the learning process.

---

[14] Ibid, 25.

[15] "Nintendo's Wii Music Strikes a Chord with Music Educators," Business Wire (January 13, 2009). Available at http://www.allbusiness.com/education-training/teaching-teachers-primary/ 11748231-1.html.

[16] John Streit, "Special Physical Education Class Gets Wii Fit," *The Virginian Pilot* (February 24, 2009). Available at http://hamptonroads.com/2009/02/special-physcial-education-class-gets- wii-fit.

[17] The 2010 Horizon Report, 7.

[18] Ibid, 29.

2. Worldmapper (worldmapper.org) is a geographic visualization site K-12 social studies teachers will find of great utility, in particular for the animated maps that combine geographic and demographic data, in some cases along chronological timelines.

Conclusion

While these emerging technologies hold tremendous promise for the classroom, we should also exercise caution when attempting to predict the potential impact of the "latest technology" on K-12 education. Even one of the greatest minds of the twentieth century, Thomas Edison, was unable to avoid the trap of exaggerating the impact technology would have on education when he proclaimed, in 1922, "I believe that the motion picture is destined to revolutionize our educational system and that in a few years it will supplant largely, if not entirely, the use of textbooks."[19]

Consistent with Wayne Gretzky's advice, however, to skate to where the puck is going, K-12 educators will still benefit from examining further these six technologies—many of which are already widely used in American society in different forms and for different purposes—to see which hold the greatest promise for their classroom. To be sure, the technology a high school chemistry teacher may find to be of pedagogical value in his/her classroom may be quite different from the technology a middle school language arts teacher needs to facilitate student learning in his/her classroom. The question in not whether technology will continue to play a role in K-12 education but, rather, what types of technologies will serve to chart the course K-12 teaching and learning takes over the next decade.

---

[19] Larry Cuban, *Teachers and Machines: The Classroom Use of Technology Since 1920* (New York: Teachers College Press, 1986), 9.

Live Dance Write: A Multi-Media Project on Romani ("Gypsy") Artist, Writer, Singer, and Educator Ceija Stojka

Lorely E. French
Pacific University, Berglund Fellow 2009-2010

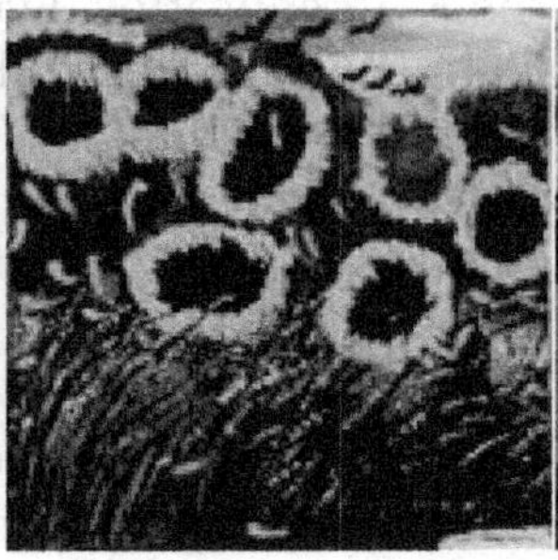

Introduction

The Roma, with their origins in India and populations residing in Europe, the Americas, and the Middle East, are one of the most global ethnic groups in the world and the largest minority group in Europe. Estimates of their entire population range from eight to twelve million people and include numerous diverse groups. Amongst those groups there are at least sixty dialects divided among four major language groups.[1] With the expansion of the European Union into Eastern Europe, where large populations of Roma reside, many governments have seen the need to improve socio-economic situations for Roma. News reports in the past year, however, have made clear that violence and discrimination against the Roma continue[2] Initiatives such as the Decade of Roma Inclusion 2005-2015 show a heightened need for the recognition of the importance of the Roma for future European success.[3]

The Austrian Romani writer, artist, educator, and activist Ceija Stojka was born in 1933 in Kraubath in Austria to a traveling Lovara family. The Lovara are one of six major Romani and traveling groups in Austria[4] She was one of the first Roma to publish her life story in the German-speaking countries. Her paintings, graphic art, and writings depict her life as a traveling Roma before and after World War

---

[1] For information on the history of the Roma see Fraser, Hancock, and the "Patrin" Web site. For information on the language Romany, see the "Romani Linguistics Site" of the Romani Project at the University of
Manchester. http://romani.humanities.manchester.ac.uk/index.html. Accessed 15 March 2010.

[2] Westervelt, 2009.

[3] "Decade of Roma Inclusion 2005-2015." www.romadecade.org. Accessed on 13 March 2010.

[4] Halwachs, 1999.

II, the trauma she and other Roma experienced in Nazi concentration camps (she was interned in Auschwitz, Ravensbrück, and Bergen-Belsen), and the hope she has for future generations to overcome the oppression that plagued her life and that of the Roma.

Project Description

The multi-media project that I undertook as a Berglund Center for Internet Studies 2009/10 Research Fellow built upon the success of the exhibit *LIVE—DANCE—PAINT: Works by Romani Artist Ceija Stojka*, which I and Michaela Grobbel, Associate Professor at Sonoma State University, organized in 2009. The exhibit traveled to three sites in the United States during the year: the Cawein Gallery at Pacific University; the Sonoma State University Library Art Gallery in Rohnert Park, California; and the West Branch Gallery in Stowe, Vermont.

Also included in the exhibit were transcriptions from conversations with Ceija Stojka about each art piece, which I and three students from Pacific University had taped in her apartment in Vienna in January 2009, thanks to the support of the Elise Elliott Trust at Pacific University. At all three sites, the exhibit was accompanied by a program that included interpretive lectures on Romani music, art, history, and culture. The program at Pacific University also included a live flamenco concert and demonstration by professional guitarist Mark Ferguson and Singer Stephanie Sanchez, films, and a final music performance by the Sinti/"Gypsy Jazz" group Hot Club Sandwich.

At Sonoma State University the program included films, live Romani music, and a Romani dance workshop with Sani Rifati from Voice of Roma. The artwork and artist's commentary, as well as information from films, musical performances, literary texts, historical accounts, and linguistic studies, supplied necessary background for developing a sophisticated PowerPoint presentation, a Web site, and a blog.

Before even beginning these projects, however, the entire exhibit needed to be photographed professionally. The Berglund Center helped enlist the time, expertise and skills of Bill Carrigan, faculty member in the art department at Pacific University, and Jennifer Hernandez, Student Intern in the Berglund Center. Bill Carrigan then generously spent countless hours photographing the works and then selecting, cropping, and organizing the photographs so that they were readily accessible for use. He also offered advice on the design and layout of the PowerPoint presentation and the Web site. He recommended Nancy Duarte's insightful book *Slide:Ology* as a guide for design and layout.[5] Photos by Bill Carrigan and John Sappington (SSU) were used for the images on the Web site and in the catalogue that the West Branch Gallery published from the exhibition, the first catalogue in English of Ceija Stojka's artworks.[6]

---

5 See Maria Walters review of slide:ology in Interface, volume 9, Issue 6 (July-August 2009).

6 Ceija Stojka: Live—Dance—Paint, 2009. Two catalogues in German (Ceija Stojka, 1995, Ceija Stojka: Bilder & Texte 1989-1995; and Ceija Stojka, 2009, Auschwitz ist mein

The next step was building the Web site with the help of student interns in the Berglund Center. Maria Walters made the basic template through Word Press, and Jennifer Hernandez built the Flash slide show with Ceija Stojka's artwork and commentary on each piece of art. Jamaica King assisted in the final step of setting the blog up on the site so as to maintain current commentary and updates. My main focus has been writing content for each web page as well as working on visual design as I learn to build on the Web site and blog myself.

In the rest of this article, I will explain the content of the PowerPoint presentation, the Web site, and the blog. I will then reflect on the importance of technology and the Internet for making Romani arts more visible.

PowerPoint Presentation on Ethical Remembrance through Artistic Biographies: The Example of Romani Artist Ceija Stojka

The Berglund Fellowship provided support for me to develop a sophisticated PowerPoint presentation to showcase and analyze Ceija Stojka's artwork in a variety of venues. The first main occasion on which I used the presentation was on October 10, 2009, when Michaela Grobbel and I co-presented our paper "Ethical Remembrance through Artistic Biographies: The Example of Romani Artist Ceija Stojka" at the international conference of the German Studies Association in Washington, D.C. The photographs of the artwork that Bill Carrigan and Jennifer Hernandez had taken were combined with other photographs taken by John Sappington at Sonoma State University through a grant from Interdisciplinary Partnerships for Investigations that Connect the University (IPICU) . These photos, coupled with the technical assistance of the student interns in the Berglund Center made it possible to enhance the presentation with visually powerful imagery as well as with music, links to Web sites, and a short film slideshow of her artwork.

After a theoretical analysis of the notion of ethical remembrance in Ceija Stojka's artwork, we examined eight pieces from the exhibit in detail to demonstrate how

---

Mantel: Bilder und Texte; and), and one in Czech (Ceija Stojka, 2008, Zijeme ve Skrytu: Vyprávení rakouské Romky) have appeared of her artwork.

her artwork is a form of visual memory space. For purposes here, I will concentrate on the self-portrait that Ceija Stojka painted entitled "Ceija nach dem Krieg/Ceija after the War," with which we also ended our presentation. Here Ceija stands in the foreground with depictions of her family with the wagons in the background. This is a scene after the war when the remaining Stojka family resumed traveling.

While those in the background are wearing what Ceija identifies as traditional Romani dress—the women in long, colorful skirts; the men in dark suits and hats—the artist has dressed herself in the traditional Austrian Dirndl. In addition, her hair is colored blond, which she only began doing later in life to be more successful in business. The painting thus amalgamates three different periods in one picture—the past, present, and future—and alludes to the challenges that Roma face as they attempt to maintain their culture but also integrate into today's united Europe and a globalized world.

"Romani Arts" Web site

As the home page of my Web site, entitled "Romani Arts: Artists, Literary Figures, Filmmakers, and Musicians," states, the site is "dedicated to making the visual and literary arts by Roma more visible. That visibility will lead to a better understanding of Romani culture and history as diverse and vibrant. The tight interconnection between the visual and literary arts and language also spurred the idea to include information on Romany, the language of the Roma people."[7] The first highlighted artist is Ceija Stojka because of the relevancy of the recent exhibit and because there are no Web sites on her works.

Most of the existing Web sites on the Roma focus on the minority group's status in individual countries and concentrate on political, social, and economic issues. Moreover, while there are several Web sites promoting various individual Romani artists, musicians, and filmmakers, I have found none that attempt to bring the Romani arts together in one central location. The more I have researched for my own site, the more I have become amazed at the wealth of Romani artists, writers, filmmakers, and musicians, which is both inspiring and

[7] http://bcis.pacificu.edu/roma/

daunting. Such a central site, although very ambitious in nature, seems particularly important as the Roma try both to assert their own identity and integrate into an expanding European Union.

Two Web sites have been particularly helpful in building my own site. The first is that of the First Roma Pavilion at the 52nd Venice Biennale, a prestigious biennial art extravaganza, which marked the importance of Romani art for asserting that identity. This beautiful Web site contains biographies and images of visual arts.[8] There are now plans for a Second Roma Pavilion at the 54th Venice Biennale in 2011. A second Web site was that of the organization Roma e.V. in Cologne, Germany, where a major art exhibit entitled "The Forgotten Europeans: Art of the Romanies. Romanies in Art" occurred from December 5, 2008 until March 1, 2009. The Web site[9] and catalogue of that exhibit[10] provide a wealth of information on Romani artists and their artworks as well as historical background and perspectives on the importance of art in the formation of Romani identity.

As the above quotation from the home page emphasizes, Romani arts cannot be divorced from history, politics, social-economic conditions, and language. Thus, the site attempts to address each of these areas on separate pages and links. Because of the dynamic nature of Romani culture as analyzed in the presentation

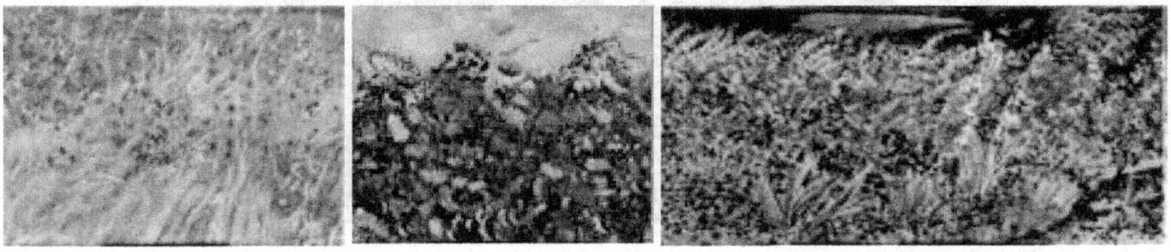

on ethical memory in Ceija Stojka's artwork, the site also needed to have a blog for updates and running commentary.

Reflections on the value of the Internet and technology for Romani arts and Future Projects

There is no denying that the Internet and technology have opened up entirely new spheres of information, networking, and transmission of visual imagery for Romani arts. Multi-media projects disseminated through the Internet and other technological means offer Roma, who have traditionally been an oral, diasporic culture with very little documentation of their works in written format, an important venue to inform others about their rich culture and artistic works. As Michaela Grobbel and I discussed in our presentation on the relationship between memory and visual imagery in Ceija Stojka's works, art contributes to the establishment of a new cultural and political space in which both individual

---

[8] http://www.romapavilion.org/
[9] http://www.romev.de/
[10] Die vergessenen Europaeer: Kunst der Roma. Roma in der Kunst, 2009.

and community memory create and propagate the history of the Roma. The Internet can thus act as a metaphorical and physical territory in which the diasporic (not a word) Roma can build a home.

For my own future projects, there is still information that I must gather to make the Web site more complete, although I now realize that such information will never be exhaustive, nor should it be. If, indeed, we look at Romani arts as a continually evolving, vibrant field, then the methods to convey the value and beauty of those arts must also be continually evolving and vibrant. This has given me as an academic, who is used to publishing books and articles that reach a final stage upon publication, a totally new perspective on the process of information dissemination. This does not mean that we dedicated scholars should be less than thorough and meticulous in the research we post on the Internet. On the contrary, the vastness of the audiences that the information will reach should force us to be even more vigilant and careful in what we present. The blog, I am finding, can be an incredibly useful tool not only for keeping the Web site up-to-date, but also for commenting on the process whereby we find the information and select what to disseminate. As I am seeing from Romani blogs, the blogging process can also be a powerful means to allow others to interact on significant issues. I have just begun to post my own entries on the blog. I would like to enlist commentary from other experts so as to keep the blog fresh, vibrant, and up-to-date. In this way, the project will continue to thrive in the hopeful manner that Ceija Stojka advocates the Roma do as well, that is "say Yes to life."[11]

I wish to thank the Berglund Center for Internet Studies; Maria Walters, Jennifer Hernandez, and Jamaica King, student interns in the Berglund Center; and Bill Carrigan, Instructor of Art at Pacific University; Ceija Stojka; Michaela Grobbel, Associate Professor of German at Sonoma State University; and the Elise Elliott Fund at Pacific University for support and assistance in this project.

References

[11]The quote comes from a poem by Ceija Stojka that was included in the exhibit. The concluding lines are:

Look at the bees buzzing
at the little ants
gathering for their lives
You too should take a deep breath
and say Yes to life
Schau wie die Bienen summen
wie sich die kleinen Ameisen
das taegliche Leben holen
Auch du sollst tief Luft holen
zum Leben Ja sagen

Ceija Stojka. 2003. Meine Wahl zu schreiben -ich kann es nicht/o fallo de isgiri - me tschischanaf les. Translated by Lorely French and Michaela Grobbel, 38.

Ceija Stojka: *Live—Dance—Paint. 2009.* With an essay by Lorely French. Stowe, VT: West Branch Gallery.

Decade of Roma Inclusion 2005-2015. www.romadecade.org. Accessed on 13 March 2010.

Die vergessenen Europäer: Kunst der Rom, Roma in der Kunst. 2009. Ed. Kurt Holl. Cologne: Verlag Rom e.V.

Duarte, Nancy. 2008. *Slide:ology: The Art and Science of Creating Great Presentations.* Sebastapol, CA: O'Reilly Media.

Fraser, Angus. 1992. *The Gypsies.* Oxford UK, Cambridge USA: Blackwell Publishing.

Halwachs, Dieter W. 1999. Romani in Österreich. In *Die Sprache der Roma: Perspektiven der Romani-Forschung in Österreich im interdisziplinaeren und internationalen Kontext.* Edited by Dieter W. Halwachs and Florian Menz. Klagenfurt: Drava Verlag. 112-46.

Hancock, Ian. 2002. *We are the Romani people/Ame same Rromanedzene.* Hertfordshire: University of Hertfordshire Press.

Kenrick, Donald. 2004. *Gypsies: from the Ganges to the Thames.* Hertfordshire: University of Hertfordshire Press.

Patrin: The Patrin Web Journal: Romani Culture and History. http://reocities.com/Paris/5121/. Accessed 14 March 2010.

Rom e.V. http://www.romev.de/. Accessed 15 March 2010.

Romani Arts. http://bcis.pacificu.edu/roma/. Accessed 15 March 2010.

Romani Linguistics Site of the Romani Project at the University of Manchester. http://romani.humanities.manchester.ac.uk/index.html. Accessed 15 March 2010.

Stojka, Ceija. 2009. *Auschwitz ist mein Mantel: Bilder und Texte.* Edited by Christa Stippinger. Vienna: edition exil.
—. 1995. *Ceija Stojka: Bilder & Texte 1989-1995.* Ed. by Patricia Meier-Rogan. Vienna: Graphische Kunstanstalt Otto Sares.
—. 2005. *Träume ich, dass ich lebe?: Befreit aus Bergen-Belsen.* Vienna: Picus.
—. 2003. *Meine Wahl zu schreiben--Ich kann es nicht: Gedichte und Bilder.* Landeck: Emirgan Yayinlari Editions.
—. 2000. *Me Dikhlem Suno.* Vienna: non food factory [CD].
—. 1992. *Reisende auf dieser Welt: Aus dem Leben einer Rom-Zigeunerin.* Vienna: Picus.
—. 1988. *Wir leben im Verborgenen: Erinnerungen einer Rom-Zigeunerin.* 1st ed. Vienna: Picus.
—. 2008. *Zijeme ve Skrytu: Vyprávení rakouské Romky.* Horomerice: Argo.

Westervelt, Eric. (2009). Wave Of Violence Strikes Eastern Europe's Gypsies. National Public Radio, 2 September 2009, http://www.npr.org/templates/story/story.php?storyId=112460670. Accessed 13 March 2010.

Netflix: Streaming Ahead

Lynda Irons
Pacific University

I have not been to a video store in years. There are several reasons for this. First, I am trying to be more energy conscious, relying on public transportation. As a result, it is not very convenient to travel by bus to my nearest video store. Second, the video stores don't often carry what I want to see. Some of the latest releases are those classified as "straight to video," bypassing the theaters. These definitely are not high on my must-see list. Third, I really like having my movie mailed to me. It's fun anticipating that red envelope in my mail box. And now even that is becoming passé as I am rapidly becoming a fan of something else entirely.

I am not the only one who is shunning video stores. The Wilsonville Oregon-based Hollywood Video is going the way of the dodo bird, having filed for Chapter 11 bankruptcy (its second bankruptcy filing in recent years) and closing stores nation-wide. Blockbuster has re-instated their strict late fee policy and shortened their rental period from 7 to 5 days in an effort to raise revenues so as to compete with Red Box. While Blockbuster does offer mail rental services, I fear this may not be an economically feasible business model as even they are closing nearly 1,000 stores.[1]

What is happening to the video market? In two words: video streaming. According to NewTeevee.com, video streaming was "11.2 billion streams while video watchers dropped to 138.6 million unique viewers in October 2009, from 139.3 in September 2009."[2]

Though Netflix is not immune to market forces, they have an edge and are sufficiently flexible to respond accordingly, and they are good at what they do.[3] They reported that "48 percent of its subscribers watched streamed content in the fourth quarter of 2009, up from 41 percent in the third quarter."[4]

Netflix subtly changed their tab order on their customers' login page. The first tab is not the "Browse DVD" tab but rather the "Watch Instantly" tab. This modification illustrates the changing philosophies at Netflix. According to

---

[1] http://www.walletpop.com/blog/2010/03/03/late-fees-are-back-at-blockbuster-good-luck-with-that/

[2] http://newteevee.com/?s=facebook+now+the+no.+3

[3] A friend works for a printing and direct mail company. He said that Netflix has an arrangement with the Post Office. The barcodes are scanned at the Post Office and the information is sent to Netflix. This triggers the mailing the next film in the queue. I haven't confirmed this with Netflix though, but it sounds logical.

[4] Bulik, Beth Snyder. "How Netflix Stays Ahead of Shifting Consumer Behavior: DVD-rental company Expands Streaming Beyond Just PCs as Customer Base Explodes." Advertising Age, 22. February, 2010, 28. LexisNexis(R) Academic. Web. March 14,

the Wall Street Journal, Netflix "fourth-quarter profit in 2009 climbed 36 percent as the DVD streaming and rental company added more than a million subscribers while reducing the costs to keep them."[5]

Right now, we have 22 Watch Instantly movies in our queue. And what's amazing is Netflix' business model: it does not cost any extra beyond our subscription package to watch them. We can watch as many as we want when we want. While I do have a nice Toshiba Satellite laptop, it is not my favorite location to watch a movie. Rather, we have a Roku player. In 3 easy steps, we can watch videos on our 52-inch, HD TV set.[6] Now I have choices and convenience.

However, convenience is a relative term. According to a recent Advertising Age article, Netflix in a "recently renegotiated deal with Warner Brothers gets access to more Warner content to stream; in return, the studio gets a 28-day blackout period on rentals of new DVD releases."[7] I may have to wait a bit for a newly released film, but I am willing to have a time delay for the convenience of not waiting for the mail. According to NewTeevee.com, Netflix spends approximately $600 million a year on postage but with video streaming, they will only spend only a nickel a gig for bandwidth.[8]

And I'm not limited to only a Roku. As Shwiff reported, "The company has begun streaming movies through a wider array of electronic devices as a way to combat increased competition from stand-alone DVD-rental kiosks and online video services.[9] Netflix is expanding their devices to include not only their own Roku player but also Wii, PlayStation 3, Xbox 360, and Blu-Ray players, though it may be some time before you will see anything on your Apple devices.[10]

Netflix is becoming ubiquitous through their nimble responsiveness to meet the ever-changing technological environments.

---

[5] Kathy Shwiff. (2010, January 28). Corporate News: Netflix Profit Surges on Member Jump. Wall Street Journal (Eastern Edition), p. B.3. Retrieved March 15, 2010, from Wall Street Journal.

[6] According to the Roku website, you will "need a high-speed Internet connection with a speed of at least 1.2 Mbps (such as mid-level DSL). You may also need a wired or wireless router if you are unable to connect the player directly to your cable or DSL modem." We have a LinkSys wireless setup in our home. http://www.roku.com/roku-products (Editor's note: Our VuNow box works much the same way and also interfaces with Netflix. See: http://bcis.pacificu.edu/journal/2009/09/article.php?id=127)

[7] Bulik, 28.

[8] http://newteevee.com/?s=forget+tv+everywhere

[9] Shwiff, B.3.

[10] Ibid, 28.

When our Tools Become our Master: Psychological and Sociological Implications of Rapid Technological Development

Shawn Davis, Ph.D.
Pacific University - School of Professional Psychology

Introduction

One of my favorite professors in graduate school often warned me of the danger inherent in relying too heavily on existing theory when interpreting research data that I collect. His concern was with the all-too-common tendency for researchers to only view findings within an existing theoretical framework, thus letting the theory dictate conclusions drawn from the data rather than serve as a guide for interpretation. He would say, "Shawn, theory is like whiskey. It's a wonderful servant, but a horrible master."

While my professor was speaking of the potential misuse of theory, the underlying warning that our tools can easily become our master is one that I carry with me to this day. This concern is ever-present as I spend the majority of my day sitting in front of the computer, often watching the number of e-mails that I receive skyrocket like the national debt. Over the years, I've developed a love-hate relationship with my computer. Granted, my productivity as a researcher and educator has increased exponentially along with advancements in computer technology. The growth of the Internet, in particular, has opened to me a world of possibility that previous generations of academicians couldn't imagine. On the other hand, rather than making my life easier, I often feel that it is because of these advancements that I'm working harder than ever before. I'm learning that there may be a price to pay for advancement and I'm left wondering if my tools have indeed become my master.

The Stage is Set: Tool Development and Adaptation

Thinking and behaviors change with the use of more advanced tools. This idea is central to the social-historical framework for development put forth by Marx and expanded by Lev Vygotsky.[1] Basically, we create tools to better master our environment. Our cognitions, in turn, become more advanced along with these tools.[2] We are free to improve our thinking to match higher levels of environmental mastery, thus the creation of even more advanced tools. For example, in my research I utilize statistical methods (tools in their own right) that are built on the shoulders of their mathematical predecessors. The mean score begat the correlation, the correlation begat the regression, and so on. With

---

[1] Crain, W. (2000). Theories of development: Concepts and applications. 4th Ed. New Jersey: Prentice Hall.
[2] Vygotsky, L. S. (1986). Thought and language. MIT Press.

each generation of statistical advancement, researchers are free to ask increasingly complex questions and think about their data in ways that were not possible with previous methods. The tool precedes thought and is the impetus for future behavior.

Inherent in such development is the propulsive nature of change. That is, there is progression (this does not necessarily imply a positive outcome) and not a return to an earlier way of thinking, in essence a regression. This idea is central to most theories of cognitive growth and development. For example, Piaget wrote often of how an individual cannot return to earlier modes of thought once they achieve a different form of thinking.[3]

This natural tendency is balanced with an integrative phase wherein the individual (or society for that matter) incorporates new ideas into their thinking. New information is associated with existing knowledge and the individual achieves cognitive growth. But the increasingly rapid rate of development that we see in our technologies is problematic for two reasons. First, we are afforded less and less time to achieve this integration and we are, in effect, reacting to this exponential change without successful incorporation of this new mode of thought. Second, changes that we see occurring are not merely quantitative in nature (e.g., increases in processing speed for computers, increases in computer storage capacity, etc.), they are qualitative shifts in the way that we develop, process, and transmit information. We are forced to very rapidly learn new ways to interact with knowledge itself. The nature of our tool use is changing in a way that we cannot easily apply previous learning to current situations, a foundational aspect of adaptation to one's environment. Many individuals are, therefore, placed in a position wherein they are reacting to the tool itself rather than use it to better master and adapt to their changing environment.

Sociological Impact

The full impact of the role of technology and the Internet on our society is well beyond the scope of this article. I will, however, detail two examples that highlight how increasingly rapid development impacts our thoughts and behavior.

First, while we might not like to admit it, television viewing has become a routine part of most individual's daily lives. In fact, it is estimated that the average individual spends roughly 4 hours per day watching television (that's 9 years of a 65-year life!).[4] Contrast that with the finding that, on average, a parent spends as little as 3.5 minutes in meaningful conversation with their children per week.[5] This change has been within the lifetime of many individuals.

Now, consider the move of broadcast media to the Internet. Television broadcasts were a focus of conversation for many individuals as they went about their daily lives. The power of the Internet to deliver broadcast media in the

---

[3] http://viking.coe.uh.edu/~ichen/ebook/et-it/cognitiv.htm
[4] http://www.csun.edu/science/health/docs/tv&health.html
[5] Ibid.

absence of an imposed time structure has changed the nature of this conversational structure. Broadcast viewing has become more under the dictate of an individual's schedule and, as a result, the socially cohesive nature of shared broadcast experience is quickly becoming a thing of the past. We can clearly see how the introduction of new tools by which broadcast media is delivered has brought about changes in our thinking and our behavior, both our individual behavior and the way that we interact with others.

Second, the way we experience musical entertainment has gone through a number of significant developmental changes within a very short time period as well. During my life, I've gone from having my music collection consist of a stack of LP records to a digitally-based format. What once filled a significant corner of my bedroom can now travel with me anywhere I have an Internet connection. Along the way, of course, I've seen the rise and fall of the 8-track tape, the audio cassette, and the CD. Changes in media format are not surprising, but the change in the nature of music ownership is a significant shift, both physically and, as a result, psychologically. I no longer own a physical item that is my music. I purchase the rights to listen to the music rather than possess the music itself. This shift, along with the technological advancements that have allowed such a change, has altered the way that we talk about and think about the concepts of music and music ownership. Our tools have indeed changed our thoughts and behavior.

These two examples of how our technological developments influence both our thinking and our behavior do represent a liberation of sorts; first, from time constraint (as in the case of broadcast media) and second, from physical restriction (as for musical entertainment). As I will now detail, however, the increasingly rapid change in thinking that is the natural outcome of such tool development may have profound and possibly quite negative psychological effects as well.

Psychological Impact

From the dawn of time (one imagines), older generations felt out of touch with their offspring (and even more so for following generations). This perceived generation gap, however, has quickly widened as fewer and fewer individuals "speak" the same language. A fundamental aspect of successful communication is achieving common ground, a shared understanding between both parties in a conversation. As our thought and language change with rapid technological advancement, we see a reduction in common ground between those immersed in new technologies and those who are not. In that our developing technologies are becoming more and more a part of our daily existence, it is not surprising that we see increasing generational distinctions and a reduction in the "passing on" of knowledge from one generation to the next. Not only is this problematic sociologically, this is likely to bring about increased marginalization for those individuals who fail to keep up with the rapid development.

In addition to the very real concern of technology-driven marginalization, there has been reported an increase in negative individual reaction to changes in technology as well.[6] Technophobia is the term coined to represent a fear or dislike of technology in general, or of specific technological devices such as computers or the Internet.[7] The rise in such reactions is not surprising given the ever-increasing dependence on our technologies (both individual and societal) and the qualitatively changing nature of our technological use. Again, we are in danger of marginalizing individuals who are resistant to technological change either intentionally or as a defensive and possibly an individually-protective reaction.

Future Shock?

This situation is not so different from that presented in the book Future Shock, first published by sociologist and futurist Alvin Toffler in 1970.[8] In Toffler's work, future shock is defined as an individual's reaction to the demands of too much change occurring in too short a period of time. According to Toffler, the rapid nature of our technological changes (and resulting social adaptation) will leave many individuals feeling disconnected from their society (and from other individuals). Toffler goes on to detail how a great many of our social problems may very well be symptoms of information overload and a resulting future shock. While Toffler's ideas have been subject to various criticisms—generally the same arguments leveled against many who extrapolate current development to future events—the societal changes and individual reactions to such change previously mentioned give one reason to pause.

Conclusion

The purpose of this article was not meant to be a call to return to snail mail and covered wagons. I'll not be using an abacus to analyze my research data any time soon. This article, however, is a reflection on the often-overlooked impact that our technological advancements have on individuals and society at large. I'm not advocating for development to stop; that is frankly not possible and likely not completely advantageous. The advancements that we've experienced do indeed provide us with opportunities never before imagined.

It is wise, however, for us to take a moment to consider the unexpected ways that the increasingly rapid pace of our advancement might actually be pulling us from an evolutionarily adaptive developmental path that has, to this point, served us well as a species. Tool development and use has opened worlds of possibility that have allowed our species to survive and thrive. If we are not careful, we might find that our natural abilities are stretched beyond their evolutionary limitations and that we are no longer successfully adapting to a rapidly changing environment. We might find that our tools have indeed become our masters.

---

[6] http://www.articlesbase.com/e-learning-articles/dealing-with-technophobia-among-learners-107071.html
[7] http://en.wikipedia.org/wiki/Technophobia
[8] http://en.wikipedia.org/wiki/Future_Shock

Nitesh Dhanjani, et al.'s *Hacking: The Next Generation*

Review by Jeffrey Barlow
Pacific University, Berglund Center for Internet Studies

Recently, after suddenly needing to know much more about hacking,[1] I looked for a book from which I thought I might learn something. At the outset of this review, I should say that Hacking: The Next Generation is way over my head...but my purpose was to learn much more than I knew, and there are very few people out there for whom this book would not serve that same purpose. The principle author, Nitesh Dhanjani, is one of the most highly regarded and successful writers and consultants in the industry.[2]

Using one of the most useful of the functions on my Kindle, I downloaded the first chapter of several highly-regarded works on Hacking, and determined that this was the one I wanted, both in terms of how well it is written and reviews found on the Web. It has not disappointed me. Scared the wits out of me, yes, but disappointed me, no.

The core audience for the book is probably best defined as I.T. professionals in charge of protecting large systems, corporations or institutions. As Dhanjani's closing remarks say:

"For any given corporation, the quest toward risk reduction and information security may seem chaotic to even the most seasoned professionals. The security team must reduce risk without getting in the way of revenue-generating business units, in addition to complying with the plethora of never-ending regulations. To bring some order to this chaos, corporations and individuals need to understand the capabilities of their adversaries. The authors sincerely hope that this book has provided you with a head start in your quest to comprehend the skill set and the mindset of attackers who are out there today."

But the nature of the book also makes it valuable for simply those wishing to be better informed on the threats of hacking. The reference to "...The Next

---

[1] I had been criticized in some foreign language sources on the Web for some of my critical attitudes as expressed in my blog, which made me a bit anxious about my computer security. Once something like that happens every slowdown or weird cycle on your computer is like hearing—maybe—a floorboard creak in your house under that window you think you might have left open.

[2] Dhanjani is the author of "Network Security Tools: Writing, Hacking, and Modifying Security Tools" (O'Reilly) and "HackNotes: Linux and Unix Security" (Osborne McGraw-Hill). He is also a contributing author to "Hacking Exposed 4" (Osborne McGraw-Hill) and "HackNotes: Network Security". Dhanjani has been invited to talk at various information security events such as the Black Hat Briefings, RSA, Hack in the Box, Microsoft Blue Hat, and OSCON. The description is taken from his WWW site at: http://www.dhanjani.com/

Generation" in the title is to hackers who primarily use Web 2.0 functions to accomplish their intrusions. One of Dhanjani's primary arguments is that the "perimeter defense," that is, trying to block all possibly malicious intruders at the firewall, while obviously still necessary, has basically been superseded by new applications and new platforms. This is particularly true within the "cloud," virtual servers created in other people's digital space, such as Google or Amazon's vast server aggregations.

If you intend to move operations to a cloud, as we all eventually surely will, then the authors' discussion of the distinctions between Google's approach and Amazon's—the two principle providers at this time—is probably a must read for your I.T. department.

Web browsers themselves are particularly vulnerable as they need to be able to do so much for the user. Most of us have probably wondered why our particular browser is continually requesting that we download patches and updates. The answer is that intruders are discovering holes at that pace, or better, at an even faster pace as the browser builders have to become painfully aware of a vulnerability before they can fix it.

The much greater importance of social networking in Web 2.0 has also created many new opportunities and greatly leveraged the ability of hackers to "social engineer" intrusions. The authors have many creative examples of such approaches that would probably work on just about anybody. Social networking applications such as Facebook and MySpace now give diligent intruders an opportunity to stealthily enter your "Circle of Trust."

If you already have a healthy fear of hackers and malware and have regarded the Web as the wild frontier, reading this book will take you back several eons in time, making you want to climb a convenient tree to escape the carnivores snuffling around in the dark. This is partly because the hackers themselves have, uh, evolved, to continue belaboring my Darwinian metaphor.

If previous generations were recreational hackers, or merely trying to impress teen-aged peers, today's are hard-eyed businesswomen. (In this choice of gender I am following the authors' sometimes jarring habit of reminding us that girls like to have fun, and make vast amounts of money, too.)

These frequent abrupt switches in voice are part of what makes the book so readable; the authors are continually aware of multiple audiences and segue smoothly from chatty narratives of complex intrusions to introducing the reader to the wide varieties of simple tools available on the market, or worse, for free.

For one example among dozens, want to spoof a caller ID number to prank your brother-in-law? Or perhaps to harass a former boyfriend, or to fool an executive at a major corporation into sending you the fourth quarter balance sheet on the supposition that you are one of his sales men in the field? Start at:

spoofcard.com.[3] This will help you spoof your caller ID, disguise your voice, and record your call in case you want to play back some technical information or strings of numbers later. You can now do it internationally, too!

One of the most interesting elements of the book is that it shows just how easy intrusion can be. The amount of information that can be gleaned simply by using publically accessible materials is remarkable. Google caches things you would not believe, and even a simple search will often turn up reams of financial data from major corporations, lists of credit card numbers, etc.

Want to get into somebody else's Google docs site? Go to "Stealing Documents from Online Document Stores" at Loc. 1151-1210 Kindle edition.

Do you always patch your important applications promptly? Me too! Do you always patch the old ones that you no longer use? Me either! But now I know that a hacker can use minor weaknesses in two different applications to craft one intrusion, a "blended attack." A hole in an application you don't ever use can let the intruder get into one you do use and the next thing you know, he is your daddy! Or at least you are his victim.

I suppose it is a compliment to say that the primary author thinks like a hacker, save for the fact that he is hopefully much more experienced and thoughtful than most of them. Many of the stories he tells are of exploits that he himself created as part of his work as a security consultant. Thankfully, he carefully only reveals weaknesses which have already been corrected in major software or hardware, but the sheer number of them certainly implies that there are abundant additional options out there for the criminally ambitious.

I am aware that this review must seem idiotically simple to the truly knowledgeable in this field. Fear not, the authors will challenge even you. Here is an example of one of their chapter summaries:

> *In this chapter, we examined the crafty and emerging attack techniques that today's new age of sophisticated attackers are employing. Whether they're conducting complex XSS attacks, turning the perimeter inside out by way of CSRF, abusing domain-based content ownership issues, or exploiting the browser software itself, attackers are evolving and learning how to poke holes into the corporate perimeter, turning it into a porous castle. As we demonstrated in this chapter, these exploits are less focused on compromising or infecting entire systems and more focused on stealing corporate secrets and data. This shift in focus allows attackers to bypass all the typical security strategies and protection mechanisms that modern software and information systems employ. Typical protection measures, such as SSL, VPNs, strong password policies, expensive firewalls, and even fully patched systems, will not stop many of these attacks. These exploits will not trigger antivirus alerts, nor will they leave an easy forensic trail for investigators to follow. In most*

[3] I am not going to follow my usual reader-friendly practice of giving formatted links in this review; I would like a running start in the event that readers want to put such information into immediate practice.

cases, once the attacker has successfully carried out the exploit, the victim experiences no noticeable change, as the system has no persistent change to detect[4]*].*

For the novice, the authors have previously painstakingly explained each of the above abbreviations and acronyms, or led you to an online site where even I could understand the issues. If you can't understand the above selection but would like too, the authors make that possible.

If you found the above childishly transparent, play with this one, particularly you Mac users who, like me, probably have felt perfectly safe in our teeny market niche:

> "Finding Protocol Handlers on Mac OS X: Protocol handlers on the Mac are similar to those on Windows-based machines. Various applications, including browsers, can invoke protocol handlers on the Mac. Once a protocol handler is invoked, the operating system provides a mapping between the protocol handler and the application registered with it. Any application can register a protocol handler on Mac OS X by using a program such as RCDefaultApp, or by utilizing the appropriate OS X CoreFoundation APIs. Users wishing to view all of the registered protocol handlers on their Mac OS X machine can use the following program: /* * Compile on Tiger: cc LogURLHandlers.c -o logurls -framework CoreFoundation -framework ApplicationServices or on Leopard: cc LogURLHandlers.c -o logurls -framework CoreFoundation -framework CoreServices */ #include <stdio.h> #include <AvailabilityMacros.h> #include <CoreFoundation/CoreFoundation.h> #if !defined(MAC_OS_X_VERSION_10_5) || MAC_OS_X_VERSION_MAX_ALLOWED < MAC_OS_X_VERSION_10_5 #include <ApplicationServices/ApplicationServices.h> #else #include <CoreServices/CoreServices.h> #endif /* Private Apple API... helpful for enumerating. */ extern OSStatus _LSCopySchemesAndHandlerURLs (CFArrayRef *outSchemes, CFArrayRef *outApps); static void GetBuf(CFStringRef string, char *buffer, int bufsize) { if (string == NULL) buffer[0] = '\0'; else CFStringGetCString(string, buffer, bufsize, kCFStringEncodingUTF8); } int main() { CFMutableArrayRef apps; CFMutableArrayRef schemes; int i; printf("URL Name App (Current Path)\n"); _LSCopySchemesAndHandlerURLs(&schemes, &apps); CFArraySortValues(schemes, CFArrayGetCount(schemes), *CFStringCompare, null); for (i=0; i< CFArrayGetCount(schemes); i++) { CFStringRef scheme = (CFStringRef) CFArrayGetValueAtIndex(schemes, i); CFURLRef appURL = (CFURLRef) CFArrayGetValueAtIndex(apps, i); CFStringRef appName; CFStringRef appURLString = CFURLCopyFileSystemPath(appURL, kCFURLPOSIXPathStyle); char schemeBuf[100]; char nameBuf[300]; char urlBuf[2048]; LSCopyDisplayNameForURL(appURL, &appName); GetBuf(scheme, schemeBuf, sizeof(schemeBuf)); GetBuf(appURLString, urlBuf, sizeof(urlBuf)); GetBuf(appName, nameBuf, sizeof(nameBuf)); printf("%-25s %s (%s)\n", schemeBuf, nameBuf, urlBuf); if (appURLString != NULL)

[4] Highlight Loc. 1385-93

CFRelease(appURLString); if (appName != NULL) CFRelease(appName); } CFRelease(apps); CFRelease(schemes); exit(0); return 0; } When the provided application is compiled and executed, it will offer output similar to that shown in Figure 4-8. Figure 4-8."[5]

I could get really cruel, and for most readers, really boring, by reproducing some of the pages and pages of code in the book or the appendices; but I will forebear. The author takes every reader, whatever their level of ability, through every step of the exploits that he examines. If you think you are too smart to learn from this text, seek counseling, you have a problem.

One of the delights of the work, as suggest above, is that the authors are splendid teachers. Some works of this genre present the material choppily broken down into segments: horror stories, fixes, sites you should visit, annotated list of tools which are probably already outdated, etc. This text is fully integrated, you get the information you need to know in plenty of time to take your level of understanding up a notch, and if you decide to bail off the learning curve as it rockets skyward, you still feel that you accomplished something.

The careful integration and layering of the text means that the book is highly useful for those who despair of ever walking the I.T. walk but desperately need to occasionally decipher the talk, if not actually talk it. If you should worry about the security at your operation, then you probably should read the book just to be sure that those upon whom you depend are aware of the new generations of threats.

In addition to the technical expositions, the work is also a major contribution to a fuller understanding of hacking. Dhanjani gleefully hacks hackers to show the reader how that sphere actually works. He has fascinating information on real-world examples, and again, a great deal of frightening data.

The denizens of that shadowy world are, above all, quite successful. The chances of being caught and prosecuted are miniscule. The most that we can usually hope for is to protect ourselves from becoming victims. For that reason, if you are even mildly curious, let alone if you are justifiably concerned—and we all should be—then consider reading this book.

---

[5] Highlight Loc. 1385-93

Daniel Suarez' *The Daemon*

Review by Jeffrey Barlow
Pacific University, Berglund Center for Internet Studies

The Daemon is a fiction book written by Daniel Suarez, an author with considerable experience in the technology field, particularly as a systems developer.[1] The work is both speculative and highly demanding in that it requires the reader to have a relatively strong grasp of technological issues in order to appreciate the plot.

Nonetheless, *The Daemon* has been quite successful as a mass-market work and inspired the immediate publication of a second book in the series, *Freedom TM*, just released. The books are generally described as "Techno Thrillers," and the appearance and success of *The Daemon* is perhaps one measure of the impact of the Internet.

The plot device is a familiar one which has been with us for quite some time, well before the development of the Internet itself: Machines, in this case an Internet-enabled artificial intelligence capable of not only replicating itself across platforms but also learning very rapidly, threatens the protagonist, if not the world.

The author defines a daemon as "A computer program that runs continuously in the background and performs specified operations at predefined times or in response to certain events." (facing title page) Conventionally a daemon is a background program which responds to network requests, hardware activity or calls from other programs.[2] This particular daemon, however, takes over the entire show, creating additional programming rather than responding to it. This is rather an extensive reach from the current capabilities of such operations.

But what Suarez brings to the genre is sufficient expertise with technology to take this plot device well beyond the usual bounds of belief. A wide range of technological mavens, including Stuart Brand, Billy Brand (The former Director of Cybersecurity and Communications Policy for the White House) and Robin Cook have reviewed it positively, all affirming it as presenting a possible future, given the direction of current technology.[3]

While it is certainly true that the book is solidly based on current technology, I find the extrapolation successful in the limited sense that from where we are now, just about anything might, indeed, happen. But the central plot device, without giving too much away, depends ultimately on one man writing unprecedented amounts of code with thousands if not millions of branches so

---

[1] See book page at: http://thedaemon.com/aboutauthor.html
[2] See description at: http://en.wikipedia.org/wiki/Daemon_%28computer_software%29
[3] To access these reviews, start at: http://thedaemon.com/

that whatever situation develops, his Artificial Intelligence (A.I.) engine can continue to respond successfully.

One scenario, for example, has several hyped-up and weaponized automobiles performing flawlessly without direction. Presumably none of these were Toyotas, and none encountered unexpected circumstances, even at very high speeds. The machines defy not only logic, but the laws of physics as well. While A. I. may indeed improve in geometric progressions, it is unlikely that the laws of physics will change that much.

Nonetheless, the work is worth reading as light fiction, if only to show us how far a plot can now be carried on the basis of a deep understanding of current technology. Obviously there is an audience which is much more prepared for such demanding plot devices than could have possibly been the case a few short years ago.

Part of the appeal is that as the protagonist, Detective Peter Sebeck, tries to solve a series of mysterious crimes, he is taught enough technology by others to begin to appreciate the threat presented by a daemon seemingly programmed by a man believed to be dead. As his understanding grows, it is based on current technology, and the reader finds himself nodding along, affirming the possibilities.

The writing is straightforward and usually unobtrusive, though not by any means particularly evocative. It is technology that carries the work, not character development nor language. The protagonist and secondary characters are at the last eminently forgettable.

Fans of this genre probably owe it to themselves to read the work, if only to see where the field might possibly be going insofar as dependent upon readers' ability to follow complicated technological problems and their solutions within a thriller-fiction context. It will be interesting to see whether the second volume carries the series farther, or provides us more of the same, which could easily become rather mechanical in short order.

Cyber War or Cyber Vigilantism?

Editorial by Jeffery Barlow

Pacific University, Berglund Center for Internet Studies

On the evening of March 15 I saw what many call "Cyber War" might unfold in real time. I was aware of the complexity of the phenomenon loosely labeled as "Cyber War" before the event. But the event persuaded me that much of what we describe with that term should be broken down into at least several other categories.

The "battle space" was a mixed-media event, entitled "*Digital China and Social Media*," a live stream of a New York panel from The Paley Center for Media (http://www.paleycenter.org/special-event-ai-weiwei-jack-dorsey-richard-macmanus) , which we viewed locally in Portland, Oregon. A local panel, including myself, then led local audience discussion. To see the program and its participants described go to the Website of the Northwest China Council, of which I am a member, but for whom I do not speak here.[1]

The topic of the event as announced was:

> "The central question of the event is: What is the relevance of new social networking technologies in our culture and society; and how can we use these tools for digital activism in order to foster positive social change, particularly in China?"

The actual event was quite different than I had expected from the above description. It featured Ai Weiwei, a noted Chinese artist and dissident.[2] He is a remarkable man who has done some wonderful work in Human Rights, at great personal cost, including being attacked by Chinese police in Siquan, an event which required hospitalization in Germany where he now lives.

The panel was late in beginning. In the meantime the Asia Foundation ran—actually began to run a second time as well—an appreciative—if not celebratory—video which featured both Mr. Ai's human rights work and his art.

I had some concerns about the program from the beginning, because of the description offered by the Asia Society: "...and how can we use these tools for digital activism in order to foster positive social change, particularly in China?" This seemed to me to very likely be an example of what I have described elsewhere as "Regime Change Lite," an effort to further peaceful change in China by what are in my mind, heavy-handed and obtrusive means often amounting to

---

[1] http://www.nwchina.org/programs/100315caps.htm

[2] As Mr. Ai is expert in the use of digital media, it is not surprising that there are thousands of references to him on the web. I found the site at http://www.artinfo.com/news/story/32223/who-is-ai-weiwei/ to represent the man I watched for more than 90 minutes in the program under discussion here.

the external encouragement of dissidence in China.[3] I think these efforts ill advised, culturally centric, and ultimately, fruitless.

But, as it is my opinion that the Internet is in and of itself moving China towards a sort of democracy,[4] I agreed to participate on the local panel. I was also interested in seeing such a mixed-media event, which could make experts in specialized topics more widely available to small local audiences around the world. This would be a welcome alternative to noted speakers appearing locally with all the associated costs.

It was clearly the hope of the moderators that this event would be of great interest in China. But fewer than 300 people watched the event worldwide, which put about 10% of the total audience in the room with us in Portland. There we had a good audience of quite sophisticated people. While it is possible that a few of them had not been to China, many were regular business travelers, China-born, or simply very interested in China.

Part of the problem with the audience was surely that at the time the event began it was barely 7 a.m. in China. None were watching from China at the outset, according to the moderators. However, there were soon overseas Chinese involved; they quickly registered for the accompanying Twitter feed and were able to participate in the program. The Twitter feed was shown on both a side bar to the streamed video, and projected on a screen in the Paley Center behind the panel for their local audience.[5]

But we do not know if the Twitter participants were Chinese mainlanders, Taiwanese, from Hong Kong, or foreign-born. Many of them were watching from overseas locations such as Australia and Europe where they were in school. Several were also from the Unites States. These viewers can be fairly described as opposed to the Chinese government; we will use the term "dissident" to describe them here, though this does not imply that they are in any way activists or any more deeply involved than to participate by Twitter in the course of the event.

We were also joined by a number of pro-Tibetan Independence participants. Both pro-Tibetans and dissidents took the opportunity to communicate via the Twitter feed in what was certainly social networking. Their exchanges sometimes had as much to do with flirting as with politics. This produced such odd conversations as apparent offers for blind dates, accompanied by continual

---

[3] See: "Peaceful Evolution in China and the World Wide Web: Part I, Two Democracies?" At http://bcis.pacificu.edu/journal/2009/07/article.php?id=98

[4] See "Peaceful Evolution in China and the World Wide Web: Part II, Factionalism and Democracy" at http://bcis.pacificu.edu/journal/2009/08/article.php?id=108

[5] It was my hope that the entire event would be captured at the Asia Society, and placed on the web so that I could reference it here for the reader. However, more than two weeks later, not only do all references to the event seem to have disappeared from the Asia Society site, but no such video is available. I hope that this is just a matter of delay in processing, though it would surely have been very easy to capture the event in real time for rebroadcast on their site.

celebration of Tibetan independence and the evils of the Chinese government, particularly vis-à-vis Tibet. This was truly mixed media, which sometimes caused laughter in both the New York and local audiences.

The Twitter discussion was dominated throughout by a group of perhaps 15 individuals; the other Twitter members, if any, were silent. The frequent contributors to the Twitter feed had, in common, not surprisingly, a real interest in Twitter, and uniformly saw its blockage by the Chinese government as a major Human Rights issue.

The panel was not, in my perhaps jaded opinion, completely successful as an exploration of the stated topic, but was truly focused on that tag line "...and how can we use these tools for digital activism in order to foster positive social change, particularly in China?" This was unfortunate, because the other members of the panel in addition to Mr. Ai, were quite expert in the topic promised to us.

These included, Jack Dorsey, the co-founder of Twitter and Richard McManus, the founder of ReadWriteWeb, said to be one of the top 20 blogs worldwide, which focuses on web technology. Orville Schell, a Sinologist-journalist of considerable reputation and the Director of the Asia Society Center on U.S.-China Relations who was billed as the moderator, did not appear, without any explanation so far as I am aware. Emily Parker, an Asia Society staff member, also highly qualified by both experience and education, filled in for him.

Despite the presence of McManus and Dorsey, however, the show was almost entirely focused on Mr. Ai, and quickly confirmed my own suspicions of a "Regime Change Lite" performance. The presence of the pro-Tibetan independence group certainly pushed the event even farther in that direction than perhaps even Mr. Ai and the other participants wished. There were occasional discussions of Twitter and the Chinese digital scene, but as the dissident group drove the questioning, it invariably returned to a highly critical stance.[6]

Since the Twitter feed was wide open, it was an irresistible target for spammers. We were soon treated to an attempt to steer traffic to what may have been a pornographic site on the Kama Sutra. Then about 45 minutes in, the feed was disrupted, apparently for political purposes. Cyber War, in short, was flaring up.

A participant subscribed to the Twitter feed, apparently from China, and began spamming nonsense characters. The dissident group excitedly described this disruptive presence as "50 Centers", a play on the Chinese term Wu Mao, which means a netizen paid—at the piece rate of 50 Chinese cents[7]—by the government to either report anti-government content or to post positive pro-

---

[6] See an article on this issue which refers to the events I am discussing here at: http://mashable.com/2010/03/16/Twitter-china/

[7] Wu mao 五毛 or five cents of Chinese RMB, at current rates, about .007 cents U.S)

government comments.[8] A play upon the terms in Chinese, however, also suggests "Five Mao Zedongs," meaning very leftist.

It is important to note that we do not know how many such individuals there were, or their motives. All we saw was repetitive nonsense messages which made no sense in either English or Chinese Romanization so far as I could see. Having been kicked out once, the spammer quickly returned.

The Asia Society had surprising difficulty in dealing with these intrusions, but finally managed to block the IP address from which they were coming.[9]

It seems probable that the spammer was politically motivated, but working alone. A group would surely have used cell phones to coordinate IP hopping and would have effectively shut down the Twitter feed. But whether an individual or a group, whether Wu Mao or not, this incident shows the weaknesses of mixed media-based Regime Change Lite, and says something about Cyber conflict as well. One, or at the most, several poorly organized individuals effectively disrupted a well-planned attempt to stage an interactive discussion worldwide.

However, lest we be over-confident in the rectitude of the dissident group of tweeters, they soon exhibited their own ability to use—if not abuse—the net. Toward the end of the scheduled events questions and comments were invited from the New York audience at the Paley Center. Most of these were intended to elicit more information from the panel, but one well-spoken Chinese-American businesswoman took Mr. Ai to task.

The woman, a native speaker of Chinese who now makes frequent business trips to China in financial services, asked, in the most polite terms possible, how he explained the great gap between his perceptions of a down-trodden fearful Chinese populace, and her own experience. In China she interacted with Chinese friends, colleagues, and relatives who seemed to her to be happy, optimistic, and increasingly well off.[10]

I thought her question of Mr. Ai was a very sensible one.[11] He essentially replied that the Chinese people are so oppressed by their government as to be afraid to speak truthfully and asked—some might say demanded—to know who she was.

---

[8] See the Wikipedia article at: http://en.wikipedia.org/wiki/50_Cent_Party#cite_note-radioau-5 which is, while loosely documented, informative.

[9] I have to observe here, that I think that what this individual shows that it is impossible for anyone to use this particular technology to present many sorts of materials to China, another weakness of Regime Change Lite. If it truly was a Wu Mao group of Chinese netizens, they were remarkably ill organized. Using cell phones and multiple IP addresses, they could have effectively blocked the tweet site indefinitely, and doubtless will do so in the future if another event such as this were planned.

[10] I had hoped to be able to quote her directly here, but as we assumed that the Asian Society was capturing the events and would post them, we did not do so at our end, and the event has not yet been posted.

[11] I note here that her description confirms quite closely to my own experiences in China, and to all those in our local audience who later voiced opinions on the matter. I thought her question of Mr. Ai was a very sensible one.

She gave her name, and in response to another question from him, the name of her firm. He responded, again rather brusquely, that now she was on record.

Mr. Ai's response was less interesting to me than the response of the Twitter audience of dissidents. They immediately began to discuss her name and her firm, attempting to fully identify her as an individual. One of them asked, "Can't we Ren Rou her?" Ren Rou , literally "human meat" with a suggestion of hunting or cannibalism,[12] involves using the World Wide Web to expose Chinese citizens to public anger, in some cases resulting in violence. There is a search engine or engines dedicated to that purpose in China, usually used to punish outstanding examples of violations of widely agreed upon social values[13].

Another dissident stated, "Ha, she underestimates our ability to use Ren Rou." Other statements denounced her for taking a government line and for being a "Wu Mao"—clearly a term which is being used far beyond its original meaning of a paid pro-government flack.

Within several moments a dissident flashed the address of her Chinese offices upon the Twitter feed screen. The event ended soon after this exchange, but it seems possible that the lady may come to regret her inquiry, and her openness. But even if the dissidents do not follow up, the mere fact of having been publically threatened with Ren Rou is certainly a violation of democratic principles which illustrates the almost random nature of some flash conflicts now facilitated by interactive social media and the World Wide Web.

Altogether the presentation was a wonderful real-live example of social networking technologies. But it also very clearly demonstrates the difficulty of typifying Cyber conflicts. Any of the participants on either side, dissident or pro-Chinese government, could well engage in retributive or revenge-driven hacking or harassment, and if successful cause an international incident.

If, for example, someone from China attacks some of Mr. Ai's sites, or those of the Asia Society or the Paley Media Center, will some see such an attack as committed, organized or encouraged by the Chinese government, when it may merely be a Chinese teen-ager inflamed with patriotism?

On the other hand, if the Chinese businesswoman is attacked online, will this suggest an attack from Mr. Ai himself, from the Tibetan independence movement or from overseas Chinese dissidents? Or will it merely be a Chinese dissident youth desiring to court one of the other dissidents whom he met via the Twitter feed at the event by establishing his heroic bone fides and demonstrating his hacker skills?

---

[12]See an explanation at: http://www.hplusmagazine.com/articles/politics/search-and-destroy-engines

[13] See http://caution.wordpress.com/2009/11/30/ren-rou-sou-suo/ for examples, including the notorious killing of a kitten.

This confusion is an inevitable problem with the Web and with social networking. Such conflicts as these are unprecedented and to try to force them into conventional analysis involving state conflict and the metaphor of war is usually senseless and misleading. Cyber War is a term which should be restricted to clearly established state-to-state digital attacks. As these are so difficult to attribute, the term is effectively meaningless.

Cyber Vigilantism seems a more appropriate term, with its overtones of righteous individuals taking the law into their own hands. But, as this event shows, Cyber Vigilantism knows no ethical boundaries. Most of us are probably drawn more to the youthful dissidents than to the Chinese government's side, but either side is capable of behaving in a pronouncedly undemocratic fashion, even in a retributive one.

The Web has taken actions which earlier could be safely described as bullying or slander, behavior usually restricted by law if not by editors in a print environment, into an international, open and largely anonymous environment. It is very important that we are very cautious not to read too much into such incidents, as they will happen increasingly.

Moreover, we need a descriptive typology of digital conflicts which helps us distinguish between the important and the jejune. Suggestions and definitions from the reader are welcome at comments below.

May 2010 – Volume 10, Issue 4

About This Issue

The May Issue of Interface is now posted on the Web.

This is a very busy time for us. Seniors are preparing for graduation with all that implies in a very weak economy. All the other students are preparing for final exams and dreaming of warmer, drier climes. Despite these distractions, however, we have produced what we think is an outstanding issue.

The Feature for this issue is our last Berglund Fellowship Report for the year, Isaac Gilman and Daniel Munoz' *Initial Development of an Online Repository to Facilitate Data Sharing and Collaborative Research: A Berglund Fellowship Report.* They report on a project that has the capacity to entirely change the way research projects involving large datasets are conducted here.

One of our several highly talented Berglund Student Fellows, Valerie Horres, reports again on women and the Internet in *Online and Enabled: Ways the Internet Benefits and Empowers Women.* This is the second article in a series.

Our only self-confessed non-human contributor, IProfess, an avatar from the online game World of Warcraft, discusses in-game hacking and identity theft and how to prevent it in *Naked in the World of Warcraft.*

We have assembled a group of reports from our Legal Editors, Leonard Duboff and Christy King in *Copyright and Trademarks.* They discuss a number of issues of potential importance to those who work with digital materials.

Our book reviews complement each other nicely in that both touch on the impact of Web 2.0. The first is David Shields's *Reality Hunger: A Manifesto.* Reviewer Jeffrey Barlow found it not for everybody but also that reading it was a worthwhile project and months after doing so, some of its epigrams continue to inform his thinking.

The second review, Andrew Lih's *The Wikipedia Revolution*, is an excellent study of the development of *Wikipedia*, which discusses not only the technology and the personalities behind it, but also its very complex and interesting social context. In addition, Jeffrey offers a *Wikipedia* like "stub", a start at a longer piece on how to effectively use *Wikipedia* in academic contexts.

The editorial for this issue, *After Internet Time: A Decade of the Berglund Center/A Call for Proposals*, both discusses the context in which the Berglund Center developed in a particular stage of the Internet, and calls for papers for a series of articles to analyze that context, intended to culminate in a peer-reviewed on-demand book. See the *Call for Papers* at: http://bcis.pacificu.edu/journal/article.php?id=677, as well.

Our announcements cover a number of recent events at the Center.
As always, we welcome comments on the above pieces, and hope that you find this issue of *Interface* useful and entertaining.

The Berglund Center for Internet Studies
Pacific University, Oregon

Initial Development of an Online Repository to Facilitate Data Sharing and Collaborative Research: A Berglund Fellowship Report

Isaac Gilman, MLIS
Pacific University Libraries

Daniel Munoz, Ph.D.
Pacific University School of Professional Psychology

Summary: At Pacific University (Oregon), a project funded by the Berglund Center for Internet Studies was developed to introduce the idea (and benefits) of data sharing to university faculty engaged in research. Pacific is a small, private doctoral/research university (Carnegie Basic Classification) with four campuses in western Oregon and four colleges: College of Arts & Sciences, College of Education, College of Health Professions and College of Optometry. This project systematically evaluated several different approaches to encourage use of data sharing.

Introduction

Research, as defined by the United States Code of Federal Regulations, is "a systematic investigation, including research development, testing and evaluation, designed to develop or contribute to generalizable knowledge."[1] This contribution to knowledge has always been a primary purpose of scientific research and implies the need to communicate the results of research so that others may learn from, and build upon, that work. The traditional model for communicating research has been to analyze collected data and then summarize key points of that analysis for publication in scholarly journals.[2] [3] In an era of paper journals, the necessity of distilling results and only sharing data that was necessary to illustrate or support conclusions was clear - there was a finite amount of space to share each study. However, in today's digital world, where online journals have rendered page fees meaningless and there is seemingly no

---

[1] United States Department of Health and Human Services, Code of Federal Regulations, Title 45: Public Welfare, Part 46: Protection of Human Subjects, Revised January 15, 2009: http://www.hhs.gov/ohrp/humansubjects/guidance/45cfr46.htm (accessed April 13, 2010).

[2] Jim Gray, "Jim Gray on eScience: A Transformed Scientific Method," edited by Tony Hey, Steward Tansley and Kristin Tolle. In *The Fourth Paradigm: Data-Intensive Scientific Discovery*, edited by Tony Hey, Stewart Tansley and Kristin Tolle (Redmond, Washington: Microsoft Research, 2009), xix-xxxiii.

[3] Toronto International Data Release Workshop Authors, "Prepublication Data Sharing," Nature 461, no. 10 (2009): 168-170.

limit to the available space for sharing information, the possibilities for sharing the full extent of research results (and data) are virtually limitless.[4]

Data sharing is not a new practice. For example, professional associations, like the American Psychological Association, encourage their members to make their data sets available to other professionals for re-analysis and in fact codify that aspiration in their code of ethics.[5] Some journals, such as the *American Economic Review*, have explicit policies about requiring published authors to make their data available to other researchers.[6] In the last decade, however, there has been an increased call for research data sets to be made openly available online without the mediating step of requesting access from the data owner(s). Researchers from both the biomedical and social sciences have communicated the necessity of open access to data sets for reasons including "accelerated scientific progress"[7] and the need to ensure the "transparency of analytic work"[8] by providing an additional level of peer review.[9] Recent professional meetings in Toronto and Rome addressed the importance of both prepublication and post-publication data sharing and the need for standards that would make it easy to identify and access available data sets.[10] [11] The benefits to researchers from sharing their data, including potential increased citation rates for associated articles, have also been examined.[12]

Many disciplines have made efforts to provide the necessary infrastructure to encourage data sharing. This infrastructure usually takes the form of a data repository where researchers can deposit their data sets, code books and other materials necessary for others to replicate their original analyses. Examples of disciplinary repositories include arXiv.org, the ICPSR data archive, PsychData, Protein Data Bank, GenBank, PANGAEA and the World Data System.[13] The availability of data sets from researchers around the world in these repositories

---

[4] Jeremy Freese, "Replication Standards for Quantitative Social Science: Why Not Sociology?" Sociological Methods & Research 36, no. 2 (2007): 153-172.
[5] American Psychological Association, "Ethical principles of psychologists and code of conduct," American Psychologist, 57, no. 12 (2002): 1060-1073.
[6] Freese, 2007.
[7] Heather A. Piwowar, Michael J. Becich, Howard Bilofsy and Rebecca S. Crowley, "Towards a Data Sharing Culture: Recommendations for Leadership from Academic Health Centers," PLOS Medicine 5, no. 9 (2008):http://dx.doi.org/10.1371/journal.pmed.0050183 (accessed September 28, 2009), 1315.
[8] Freese, 2007, 154.
[9] Glenn Firebaugh, "Replication Data Sets and Favored-Hypothesis Bias,"Sociological Methods & Research 36, no. 2 (2007): 200-209.
[10] Toronto, 2009.
[11] Paul N. Schofiled, Tania Bubela, Thomas Weaver, Lili Portilla, Stephen D. Brown, John M. Hancock, David Einhorn, Glauco Tocchini-Valentini, Martin Hrabe de Angelis and Nadia Rosenthal, "Post-Publication Sharing of Data and Tools," Nature 461, no. 7261 (2009): 171-173.
[12] Heather A. Piwowar, Roger S. Day and Douglas B. Fridsma, "Sharing Detailed Research Data is Associated with Increased Citation Rate," PLOS ONE 2, no.3 (2007): http://dx.doi.org/10.1371/journal.pone.0000308(accessed September 28, 2009).
[13] Bryn Nelson, "Empty Archives," Nature 461, no. 7261 (2009): 160-163.

encourages collaborative work across institutional and national boundaries and is fundamental to researchers' abilities to solve data-intensive problems that exceed the capabilities of individual scientists, labs or research groups.[14]

For some researchers, contributing data to large disciplinary repositories with global users may initially seem daunting. The benefits of possible collaborations or initiating new projects from existing data can be overshadowed by fears of others' capitalizing on their results for publication glory or of re-analysis revealing mistakes in their methodology or initial analysis. Additionally the need to completely de-identify data that may contain sensitive human subjects or proprietary information (and possibly receive permission from institutional review boards or other oversight bodies to release the data) can present an ethical dilemma for researchers.[15] [16] Of these potential impediments to sharing, the last is certainly valid—but even that may be ameliorated (in most cases) through careful coding and removal of unique identifiers. Education and support is vital to help researchers navigate these concerns about data sharing and encourage them to take the first steps to contributing their information to an openly available collection of research data.

Data Sharing in a Local Context: Motivating Factors

At Pacific University (Oregon), a project funded by the Berglund Center for Internet Studies was developed to introduce the idea (and benefits) of data sharing to university faculty engaged in research. Pacific is a small, private doctoral/research university (Carnegie Basic Classification) with four campuses in western Oregon and four colleges: College of Arts & Sciences, College of Education, College of Health Professions and College of Optometry.

As an institution, Pacific is committed to interdisciplinary and collaborative teaching, service and research. Though the 380 faculty across the four colleges represent a diversity of research interests, experiences and sources of data, there are faculty in different schools and departments who share research interests and who represent potential collaborations. However, there is no central location within the University that faculty (or students seeking advisors/mentors) can access to identify potential collaborators. To meet that need, this project focused on the creation and initial promotion of a searchable database that would house metadata and data sets resulting from faculty research. Such a database will allow faculty and students to identify not only colleagues on campus with similar research interests, but even more micro-level items such as specific protocols or survey questions that may be of interest. By sharing descriptive information about faculty data sets, the database goes beyond simply identifying research interests to identifying aspects of faculty research that would not be captured in a simple "research interest(s)" label on a departmental website. For example, if faculty members identify themselves as having a research interest in "eating disorders", it is likely that others outside of psychology might not envision

[14] Tony Hey, Stewart Tansley and Kristin Tolle, eds., The Fourth Paradigm: Data-Intensive Scientific Discovery (Redmond, Washington: Microsoft Research, 2009).
[15] Piwowar et al., 2007.
[16] Freese, 2007.

potential collaborative opportunities with that faculty member. However, if the faculty member has datasets that, in addition to eating disorder data, includes measures of depression, health behaviors (e.g. smoking, drinking, exercise) and medical history that are searchable through the database's metadata, then the relevance of that faculty member's work expands to a greater proportion of faculty and students. That faculty member and their available research data would be of interest not only to colleagues interested in eating disorders, but also to those with interests in depression, health and medical behaviors—which could attract interdisciplinary collaboration (e.g. with pharmacy, physical therapy, physician assistants, public health, etc.).

A secondary motivator in creating a centralized database for faculty research data is the cost of initiating research. Research at the university level, particularly in the social and health sciences, is dependent on a myriad of funding sources such as institutional, corporate or government grants. In institutional terms, Pacific currently only provides a competitive $3,500 faculty development grant where basic research must compete with applications for travel or materials unrelated to basic research. Corporate foundation and governmental grants (e.g. National Institutes of Health grants) often require a level of infrastructure (i.e. course release time, start-up funding) that is not easily available at Pacific University. Furthermore, to be competitive for foundation or government grants, researchers typically need to demonstrate a consistent and productive output of published research, which, again, may be hampered by the aforementioned limitations. Finally, grant providers are increasingly requiring a multidisciplinary component as part of a fundable proposal. At Pacific University, the time and work demands of each individual discipline often make it difficult for faculty to have the opportunity to initiate conversations that may lead to collaborative research ideas. The database initiated through this project will facilitate access to existing datasets for faculty and students from different disciplines. Analyzing and re-purposing existing data both saves on the costs of initiating new research and also increases the publication productivity that makes researchers more viable prospects for external funding.

It is anticipated that faculty at Pacific will, on the whole, share similar concerns to other researchers related to providing widespread access to their research data. By focusing primarily on these local motivating factors and not pushing prematurely for faculty to deposit full data sets in disciplinary repositories and other widely used venues, the initial objectives of this project have been to introduce faculty to the benefits of openly sharing this type of information and to create a venue that makes it easy to share that information.

Materials & Methods

As technology options, knowledge and opportunities have shifted since the project's conception, the data sharing venue has evolved accordingly and will continue to evolve as participation—and the nature of participation—increases/changes in coming years. This report focuses on the two initial phases of the project—exploration and development—and will provide guidance for further growth/use of the database at Pacific moving forward.

Initial Database Platform

As noted in the introduction, online repositories for sharing datasets and related information are fairly common across multiple disciplines and it would make little sense to reinvent the repository when there are existing platforms available for use. One of the best examples of an existing platform that was created for this purpose is the Dataverse Network software developed at Harvard University (http://thedata.org/). Dataverse Network software is open source, and available for local installation.[17] However, the free, hosted version of the software was utilized for this project. The hosted service is currently used by researchers at large universities, as well as by government agencies, and provides excellent support and services without the commitment of time and resources required by a local installation. Hosted "Dataverses" provide nearly all of the benefits of a local installation, and hosted data is backed up on a daily basis, with the last 6 months of data available on Harvard servers.

The Dataverse Network software is best explained by its creators from the Institute for Quantitative Social Science at Harvard University:

> "Individual Dataverses are self-contained virtual data archives [...] The extensive digital library services of each Dataverse include data archiving, preservation formatting, cataloging, data citation, searching, conversion, subsetting, online statistical analysis, and dissemination. Each Dataverse presents a hierarchical organization of data sets, which might include only studies produced by the Dataverse creator (such as for an author or research project), those associated with published work (such as replication data sets for journal articles), or data sets collected for a particular community (such as for a journal's replication archive, or a college class or subfield)."[18]

The first step in this project was configuring a hosted Dataverse for Pacific University (http://dvn.iq.harvard.edu/dvn/dv/pacificu/). Configuration of the Dataverse included branding with Pacific University colors and logo, the creation of hierarchical collections for all colleges and schools within the University, and the creation of indexing templates to guide the input of data set metadata. Currently, the Dataverse is not openly accessible and requires an account/password.[19] Once a Dataverse is "released" (made openly accessible), all Dataverse Network users are able to see search results from that Dataverse (though restrictions may be placed on the ability to download materials).

---

[17] Gary King, "An Introduction to the Dataverse Network as an Infrastructure for Data Sharing," Sociological Methods & Research 36, no. 2 (2007): 173-199.

[18] The Dataverse Network Project, http://thedata.org/#section-3 (accessed April 15, 2010).

[19] The Dataverse Network will not allow a Dataverse to be "released" (made public) if there are no data files attached to metadata records in the account. This ensures that Dataverse Network users are only searching through records that contain openly available data sets. There are currently no data sets associated with records in the Pacific University Dataverse.

Exploration: School of Professional Psychology Pilot

After configuring the Dataverse, a pilot study to gauge faculty/student interest and response was conducted within the School of Professional Psychology (SPP). SPP was considered an ideal site for the pilot due to the relatively high output of data by its students and faculty. Students in SPP are expected, as part of their thesis and dissertation requirements, to seek out and initiate research projects, at least one of which typically generates quantitative data. Faculty within SPP represents a wide variety of research interests and many diverse research programs are available for student participation. However, there are barriers to connecting interested students with appropriate faculty researchers. There is no centralized list of specific faculty projects, only broad topic areas, and students typically need to initiate contact with each faculty to discover a) whether the faculty member has an active research program and b) if, so, what projects are currently ongoing. In addition, students within SPP may have research interests that do not coincide with active faculty, and thus need to look outside the department; unfortunately, there is no easily accessible database of University-wide research interests and projects. For SPP faculty who may wish to broaden their own research programs (and create opportunities for students) by seeking collaborators from across the College of Health Professions or the University at large, there is no centralized repository of cross-discipline research information.

The first step in the SPP pilot was collection of available data set information from faculty volunteers within SPP. Several emails were sent to the SPP faculty describing the project and interested respondents were directed to a secure online spreadsheet where they entered descriptive information about their respective datasets (i.e. subject population, assessment protocols, summary of findings, etc.). To mitigate possible concerns about sharing actual data, only descriptive metadata about existing data sets was collected for ingest into the Dataverse. The Dataverse records about the data sets provided descriptions of sample size, population and assessment instruments used in the studies. All fields in the database records were searchable, allowing users to look for information about data sets relevant to their interests (and search terms). In total, information about 6 studies from 7 participants was initially available in the Dataverse (as the project has progressed, information about additional data sets has been added).

Concurrent with the collection of data set information, an anonymous survey was sent via SurveyMonkey to all SPP faculty and doctoral students. The purpose of the survey was to determine a) interest in intra- and interdisciplinary collaboration within SPP and b) the current level of research activity within SPP. Two weeks following the initial survey, a second survey was sent to request feedback on the usability of the interface and to determine whether or not any collaborative ideas had been generated through use of the Dataverse. Prior to sending the second survey, Dataverse accounts were created for all SPP faculty and doctoral students to enable them to access the database and potentially upload information. Survey responses are discussed in the Results section of this report.

Development: Usability Testing

Following the SPP pilot, the investigators originally intended to implement a similar study across the College of Health Professions to see if the results from the SPP pilot were confirmed or challenged by faculty and students in different disciplines. However, developments in the available technological resources at the University necessitated a change in the planned methodology.

In June 2009, shortly after this project began, the Pacific University Library purchased a digital repository platform. This platform, Digital Commons®, from Berkeley Electronic Press (bepress), provides a means of preserving and disseminating online Pacific University faculty and student work. *CommonKnowledge* (the chosen name for Pacific's Digital Commons® site) is envisioned as the central portal for users both within and outside the University who would like to access scholarly and creative works created faculty, staff and students. *CommonKnowledge* collections (http://commons.pacificu.edu) are primarily open access, which means anyone with an Internet connection can discover and download materials that have been uploaded to the site. Bepress hosts *CommonKnowledge*(though it is configured to meet local needs), ensures that materials are indexed in online search engines (e.g. Google™), and provides comprehensive usage statistics for items posted on the site.

With the availability of *CommonKnowledge* and its shared objectives with the project (open sharing of information), it became logical to consider *CommonKnowledge* as a possible alternative venue for hosting data set information. Several immediate benefits to using *CommonKnowledge* were readily apparent: as a hosted product for which the University Library pays (as opposed to a free hosted Dataverse site), there is greater flexibility in configuration and available dedicated technical support; faculty across the University were already being exposed to *CommonKnowledge* and receiving education about how to contribute their work to the site; *CommonKnowledge* would not require users to create accounts/log in to view descriptive information about others' data sets (as with the Dataverse Network, which does not allow sites to be public unless they host actual data files); and, finally, *CommonKnowledge* provided a simpler user interface for both searching and uploading information about data sets. Though the first three benefits are fairly clear, the latter required testing of the hypothesized improvement in user experience.

Website usability testing can vary in complexity but, at its core, is usually concerned with the user's ability to comprehend, navigate and utilize functionality on a given site. The usability testing conducted for this project was comparative in nature, asking participants to complete the same tasks on both the Dataverse and *CommonKnowledge* sites, provide feedback as to the usability of each site through an assessment measure and interviews, and finally decide on a preferred site.

A convenience sample of five College of Health Professions faculty members and five College of Health Professions students was selected to participate in the usability testing. SPP students or faculty who had previously participated in the evaluation of the Dataverse site were excluded from participation. The order of use of both sites within each testing session was alternated (first participant used the Dataverse first; second participant used *CommonKnowledge* first, etc.) in an attempt to control for any possible carryover effect/bias that could occur by examining one site first (or last).

After providing basic demographic information to potentially aid in analysis, each participant was taken through a series of four tasks on each website. During the tasks, a think-aloud protocol was used (participants were asked to verbalize their thought processes and reasons for their actions/movements on the site). Immediately after completing the tasks on each site, participants were asked to completed an adapted version of the 10-item System Usability Scale© (SUS), an instrument developed for the purposes of evaluation industrial systems.[20] Though not originally designed for use with websites, it provides a standardized assessment of usability factors that are relevant to website use and design. At the end of the session, each participant was asked to comment on likes/dislikes of each site before providing a final conclusion as to the preferred site (Dataverse or *CommonKnowledge*).

Results

SPP Survey Results

Seventy-one faculty members and students (13 & 58 respectively) responded to the initial survey. Table 1 summarizes findings of interest. In summary, while many respondents report interest in conducting research and engaging in interdisciplinary collaboration, actual engagement was less.

---

[20] John Brooke, "SUS - A Quick and Dirty Usability Scale," UsabilityNet, www.usabilitynet.org/trump/documents/Suschapt.doc.

Survey Item	% Respondents
Average number of papers published/presentations made (2008-2009 academic year)	1.36 (responses from 0-7)
% "somewhat" or "very" interested in conducting research	70.4%
% "somewhat" or "very" interested in interdisciplinary collaboration	56.3%
% engaged in research collaboration with colleagues in other disciplines (2008-2009 academic year)	23.9%
% discusses research with colleagues in discipline ("sometimes" or more)	80.3%
% discusses research with colleagues in other disciplines ("sometimes" or more)	35.2%

Table 1. Findings of Interest

For both faculty and students, time was a significant barrier in conducting research. Students also reported difficulties in finding faculty with similar research interests; difficulties in securing populations of research interest and problems with developing a topic. Figures 1 and 2 summarize faculty and student reported barriers to developing research.

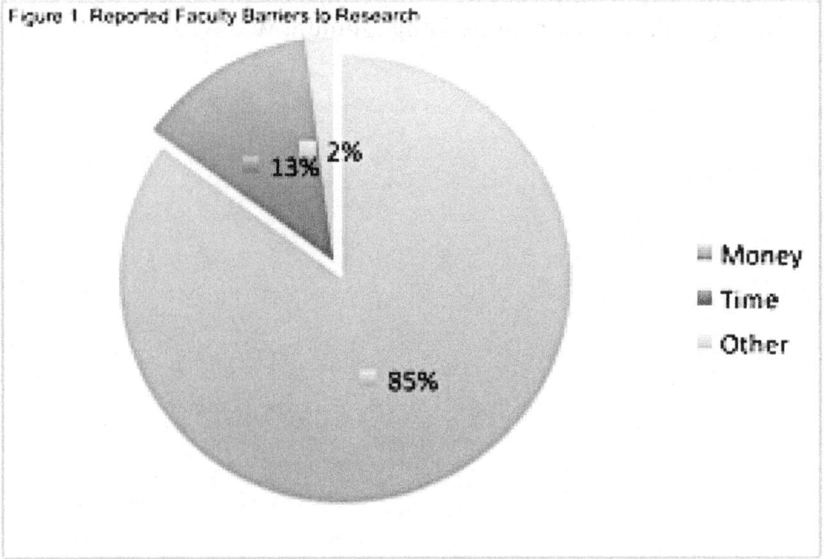

Figure 1 Reported Faculty Barriers to Research

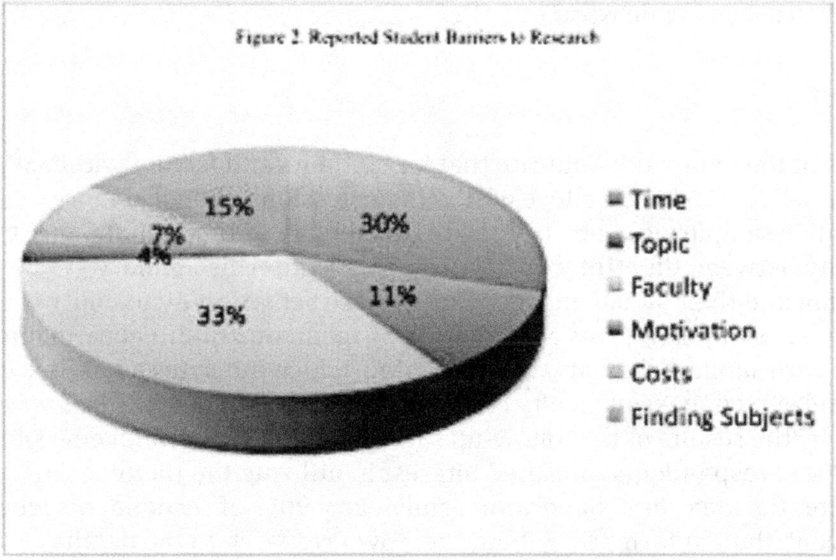

Figure 2 Reported Student Barriers to Research

Four faculty members and 19 students responded to the follow-up survey assessing use of the Dataverse site. Table 2 summarizes their responses.

Usability Testing Results

Participants in the usability testing were predominantly female (the College of Health Professions student body is more than 60% female; faculty gender ratios within the University are closer to even), and ages ranges were between the twenties to fifties (ranges, not exact ages, were reported). All participants indicated using computers on a regular basis for both personal and professional purposes.

Participants showed slightly more difficulty completing tasks using the Dataverse site, but there were specific points of confusion indicated with using both sites, so the error rate is not a significant comparative factor when looking at the two sites. Participants *did*, however, express greater frustration with difficulties experienced on the Dataverse site, which included not being able to determine how to submit information to the database, and difficulty using the search/advanced search functions to locate information about data sets in the database.

The most significant results were found in the SUS scores and the post-test interviews. SUS scores are based on 10 Likert items, with a total (best) possible score of 100. The mean SUS score for the Dataverse site was 51.75, while the mean SUS score for *CommonKnowledge* was 86 (a statistically significant difference: $t(9) = 6.13$, $p < .001$). In addition to this discrepancy in scores, 100% of participants indicated that they preferred the *CommonKnowledge* interface, finding it more "intuitive", navigable and generally easier to use when attempting to search for information or add information to the database. Importantly, most participants also encountered a similar point of confusion on the *CommonKnowledge* site, which is easily rectified and which will make the site even easier to use going forward.

Discussion

The results of the pilot study indicate that for students and faculty within SPP (and, potentially within the College of Health Professions, though a more representative sample would be needed to extrapolate to that population), there is a disparity between their interest in research and interdisciplinary collaboration and their actual engagement in these activities. Availability of resources (especially time) was a barrier to engagement, but difficulty in finding colleagues with similar interests was also noted, which indicates a possible use for a centralized database of faculty research data and information. This was confirmed by the results of the follow-up survey assessing the Dataverse site, in which 100% of respondents indicated interest in utilizing the Dataverse to identify potential ideas or collaborators, and nearly 90% of respondents were willing to contribute information about their own research to the database. These results suggest that a centralized database of research data sets/information may help attenuate barriers (such as time, cost, and knowledge of existing research) and assist in the development of new research collaborations.

While the results of the SPP surveys indicate the conceptual use/viability of a local repository for data sets/research information, the usability testing results suggest that *CommonKnowledge* may be the most appropriate platform for this repository. Though the *CommonKnowledge* platform is not as robust as the Dataverse site in terms of data-related functionality (Dataverse includes built-in analytical functions, more advanced search options and significantly more detailed/complex metadata options), selecting a platform that faculty and students find simple to use is an incredibly important factor in soliciting/sustaining participation in data sharing activities across the University. Using *CommonKnowledge* as the portal for research data information also means that such information will be collocated with faculty publications, presentations and other work - creating a more complete picture of faculty interests and activities that can be searched/accessed by students and colleagues through a single interface.

It is important to note, however, that *CommonKnowledge* does not immediately address some of the key issues identified by data sharing advocates. Altman & King[21] identified six elements that should comprise a basic citation to a data set available online:

1. Author(s)
2. Date of publication/date data was publicly released

---

[21] Micah Altman and Gary King, "A Proposed Standard for the Scholarly Citation of Quantitative Data," D-Lib Magazine 13, no. 3/4 (2007):http://www.dlib.org/dlib/march07/altman/04altman.html_(accessed March 29, 2010).

3. Title
4. Unique global identifier
5. Universal Numeric Fingerprint
6. Bridge service

The first three elements are easily included in a *CommonKnowledge* metadata record; the last three are not (at present). A unique global identifier (e.g. a Digital Object Identifier (DOI®)) provides a persistent identifier/access point for a digital object, irrespective of whether the URL of the object's hosting website changes or the location of the object changes. Altman & King[22] recommend the Handle (HDL) System®, upon which DOI® is based, for assigning unique identifiers. HDL identifiers must be assigned by an organization that has registered as a Resolution Services Provider (RSP);[23] currently, neither Berkeley Electronic Press nor Pacific University is a RSP.

While a unique global identifier provides a persistent means of accessing a digital object, a Universal Numeric Fingerprint (UNF) addresses the issue of changes in/multiple versions of a data set. A UNF is "is an algorithmic tool used to verify that a data matrix or related digital object that is produced in one software environment and/or format has been correctly interpreted when moved to a different environment and/or format."[24] Put simply, a UNF is automatically generated by software that examines the contents of a data set and calculates a "string of numbers and characters that summarizes all the content."[25] The UNF for a given data set will never change; if any data elements within the set are changed, and a UNF for that set is generated, it will be different from the original UNF.[26] For researchers who may be concerned about whether the data set that is cited somewhere is exactly the same as the one they are examining, a comparison of the UNFs can provide confirmation that they have accessed the correct version.

Finally, Altman & King[27] recommend a bridge service as part of the citation to online data sets. A bridge service provides a means for web browsers to recognize (and thus, access) unique global identifiers by adding a URL to the front of the global identifier. For example, the DOI® for Altman[28] is 10.1007/978-1-4020-8741-7_57. Without a bridge service to translate the DOI®, a web browser would not be able to access this digital object. However, with the addition of a bridge service (in bold), the object can be browsed to: http://dx.doi.org/10.1007/978-1-4020-8741-7_57.

---

[22] Ibid.
[23] Ibid.
[24] Micah Altman, "A Fingerprint Method for Scientific Data Verification," in Advances in Computer and Information Sciences and Engineering, edited by Tarek M. Sobh (Springer, 2008): 311-316.
[25] Altman and King, 2007.
[26] Ibid.
[27] Ibid.
[28] Altman, 2008.

CommonKnowledge is not able to provide unique global identifiers (with the accompanying bridge service) or UNFs for data sets it may hold. Dataverse sites, however, will automatically generate both unique global identifiers and UNFs for data sets that are uploaded. This is a clear benefit to the Dataverse platform. Altman & King[29] are not alone in raising issues related to clear and consistent data citation; recent discussions of data sharing have discussed similar issues.[30] [31] [32] In particular, the ability to provide a persistent link to available data sets, and the ability to confirm that the data accessed is identical to the data used/cited in publications is of great importance for researchers who may wish to attempt to replicate or validate others' results. A combination of the usability of *CommonKnowledge* and the robust functionality of the Dataverse Network would be ideal for ensuring that efforts within Pacific University to share data continue to grow.

Conclusions/Future Directions

This present project represents a starting point for data sharing initiatives at Pacific University. The primary and secondary research involved in this study provide the information necessary to guide an informed effort to encourage faculty and student participation in sharing research data and in utilizing data shared by others. The identification of potential barriers and benefits to faculty involvement will inform the development of educational materials and outreach for faculty, while the identification of a preferred platform for accessing information about research data provides a clear technological direction for this initiative.

Several directions for future work across the University are evident from this project. First, given the barriers that exist for researchers who are considering sharing their data sets online, it may be unreasonable to promote this within Pacific University as the only viable option for data sharing. The creation of a searchable database of metadata/descriptive information about existent data sets within the University would be a significant achievement in and of itself. Successfully encouraging faculty to take the time to contribute this information should be the initial priority (though the possibility of uploading/sharing actual data sets should always be an option as well).

Second, *CommonKnowledge* should be promoted as the repository for information about research data from across the University, and faculty should be provided assistance in learning to add their information to the repository. This assistance will be made available through online tutorials (linked from the *CommonKnowledge* site, http://commons.pacificu.edu/pudata/), information sessions and individual meetings, as appropriate.

Third, in anticipation of potential faculty willingness to share actual data sets, the Dataverse site developed for this project should be maintained and should be

---

[29] Altman and King, 2007.
[30] "Credit where Credit is Overdue," Nature Biotechnology 27, no. 7 (2009): 579.
[31] Nelson, 2009.
[32] Schofield et al., 2009.

used as the site for data storage. In this way, unique identifiers and UNFs may be generated for uploaded data and users will have the option of utilizing the full functionality of the Dataverse. However, *CommonKnowledge* will still be promoted as the portal/search interface for all research data information; links in metadata records will allows users to easily access actual data sets (if available) in the Dataverse.

Fourth, dialogue with the Pacific University Institutional Review Board should be started to discuss data sharing in general as well as potential ways for investigators submitting proposals to the IRB to proactively identify a plan to share resulting research data (including any plans to de-identify the data before sharing, if necessary). Finally, it would be beneficial to explore the possibility with promotion and tenure committees of formally recognizing the merits of data sharing. With proper citation, use of data sets can be tracked and recognized. However, even the act of contributing data (in a form that is usable by other researchers) should be recognized as a significant contribution to a faculty member's profession.[33] [34] [35]

Sharing research data (or, at the very least, information that the data exists) is a way not only for Pacific faculty and students to engage in intra- or interdisciplinary collaborations, but to also share their activities and expertise with the broader research community. Pacific faculty author dozens of publications every year as contributions to their respective disciplines; sharing the data associated with those publications presents both another contribution to disciplinary knowledge and another opportunity for faculty to be recognized for the work that they do. By providing resources like CommonKnowledge and Dataverse, and promoting their use, the University will enable its faculty to take advantage of these opportunities.

Acknowledgements

The authors wish to gratefully acknowledge the enthusiastic (and financial) support of the Berglund Center for Internet Studies at Pacific University, which made this project possible. The authors were co-recipients of a Berglund Fellowship for 2009-2010.

---

[33] Piwowar et al., 2008.
[34] Toronto, 2009.
[35] Credit, 2009.

Online and Enabled: Ways the Internet Benefits and Empowers Women

Valerie Horres

This piece is by one of our Berglund Student Fellow Valerie Horres, who has brought a strong feminist voice to the Berglund Center for this year. We regret that she is resigning to give more attention to other endeavors and will not be back for next year.

In December 2009, I wrote about how the Internet degrades women. I concluded that it is normally not the Internet itself, but rather the content of media available online which can be debasing toward women. The Internet serves as a convenient tool for accessing material, but, of course, does not create itself demeaning content.[1] And, while a large majority of the material available on the web and relative to sex or gender does degrade women, the Internet also benefits and empowers women in several ways.

The first way in which the Internet benefits women is that it is an extremely easy and efficient tool to use. The Internet is not limited to one single area of life; it can be used for both business and pleasure, for communication purposes, consumption of media, research, and so much more. There is potential in all these online fields to affect society both negatively and positively.

A huge positive regarding the Internet is that not only is it highly accessible, but it can be—for research in particular—much more effective and time-saving than traveling to a library and wading through multiple books or magazines. In a society that values saving time to the degree that the United States' culture does, the ability of online databases to scan an endless amount of data in nanoseconds and reveal the most relevant information is nearly priceless. The Internet then frees online-searchers to find more information than they could otherwise, or enables them to move onto another project.

Along with efficiency and time-saving, another benefit to women is that there "is a huge amount of information available on the Internet for just about every subject known to man, ranging from government law and services, trade fairs and conferences, market information, new ideas and technical support"—the list is endless.[2] A woman can use the Internet to educate herself on any number of these topics: she can learn how best to treat a child's illness using WebMD,[3] how

---

[1] Valerie Horres, "Boobs or Bitches: The Way the Internet Perceives Women," accessed 3 Dec. 2009,http://bcis.pacificu.edu/journal/2009/10/article.php?id=621.
[2] Jayashree Pakhare , "Advantages and Disadvantages of the Internet," accessed 23 Mar. 2010, http://www.buzzle.com/articles/advantages-disadvantages-internet.html.
[3] WebMD, http/:www.webmd.com.

to contact a state senator through the U.S. Senate website,[4] or engage in self-exploratory research, such as researching religion online.

The potential for acquisition of knowledge, then, is the empowering factor when it comes to research and education online. A woman has the ability to learn practically anything through the Internet, and that power provides her with the opportunity to effect positive change in her life and the lives of others.

In addition to research, the Internet also allows women to seek further schooling to empower themselves. From busy mothers to those fiscally challenged, the Internet provides a way for many women to expand their education. Women can acquire their G.E.Ds through online programs, as well as online Bachelor, Master, and even Doctoral degrees from places such as ITT Tech, Walden University, The Art Institute, and hundreds of other universities.[5] Education empowers women by allowing social mobility. Higher education is correlated with "higher earnings for all racial/ethnic groups," as well as "lower smoking rates, more positive perceptions of personal health, and lower incarceration rates," and "higher levels of civic participation, including volunteer work, voting, and blood donation".[6] Increased wealth, health, and social participation all improve the quality of living, allowing women the opportunity to achieve more of their potentials.

The Internet also empowers women by allowing them to work from home, just as it allows them to study from there. For example, many women delay or completely sacrifice motherhood because they wish to succeed in their careers. The Internet enables many women to work from almost any location easily, and thus makes it easier for them to have families. The Internet also makes business simpler for women by providing a very cheap space for their work to exist. To promote business offline "takes much money and time," but websites and e-mail may be created "and seen by anyone from anywhere" without any cost or an overwhelming time requirement.[7] Companies reach a much larger number of people online—both associates and customers—than offline. In addition, they can choose which websites to advertise on, so the Internet is a perfect avenue for advertising any sort of business, since it allows the most desired cliental to be targeted. As women have often been relegated to low-paying jobs, and highly discriminated against in the workplace, any advantage the Internet provides to overcome obstacles empowers women.

Whether for work, entertainment, or other activities, the Internet provides a way for people to connect with others. Online communication gives women the opportunity to converse without fear of judgment or persecution that can occur in face-to-face meetings. E-mail, online messaging systems, and social

---

[4] United States Senate, http://www.senate.gov/index.htm.
[5] Online Degree Today.com, http://www.online-degrees-today.com/.
[6] Sandy Baum and Kathleen Payea, "Education Pays: 2004," College Board.com, 2005, 7, accessed 15 Apr. 2010, http://www.collegeboard.com/prod_downloads/press/cost04/EducationPays2004.pdf.
[7] Akio Orita, Makoto Niimi, and Jun Murai, "The Three Ways the Internet Empowers an Ordinary Individual: How Women in Japan Express Themselves and Their Opinions," accessed 9 Apr. 2010, http://www.isoc.org/inet2000/cdproceedings/8a/8a_2.htm.

networking sites remove barriers—whether physical distance or prejudice based on external appearance or mannerisms—which provide the opportunity to communicate with people who cannot be reached through any other means. People can have little effect on others, none at all, or they can completely change another's life; again, the source of empowerment for women is in the potential the Internet provides.

Another way to empower women is through the "communication technology of the Internet. In the midst of the current economic crisis it can be costly to construct environments [in public spaces] that are free of physical barriers and ensure the independent personal mobility of women,"[8] but the Internet provides an uninhibited location free of almost all boundaries. On message boards, women can ask questions anonymously or with a nickname, thus freeing them to remark on anything and question everything. The Internet is the "only open platform where women can express their own views and post their own material without a gatekeeper".[9] It is the one place for women to completely express themselves without restriction.

Physical appearance can be just as restricting to women as the actual physical distance between people. In real life, "body language, voice, and attitude form the first impression which may last as a like or dislike of the other person".[10] When the physical presence is stripped away, such as it is online, and then people feel free to act completely different than they do in reality because they do not fear the perceptions they create in other people. Dr. Petra Boynton, sex editor of Men's Health, explains this in relation to online dating: "'People who feel uncomfortable can actually be much more up front [dating online], and ask direct questions. A lot of women say they find it quite empowering because they can ask things, demand things and flirt. For instance, many women find it hard to say "I don't want to see you again" but online they can. So it can be used just to improve your confidence outside of the Internet'".[11]

One more way that the Internet empowers women is by boosting their confidence and connecting them to other people is through support groups. There are hundreds of support groups online aimed solely at women. Some sites, such as http://www.dmoz.org/,[12] can be utilized to locate many of these online

---

[8] Inge Komardjaja, "The Internet Empowers Women With Disabilities," Isis International, accessed 23 Mar. 2010, http://www.isiswomen.org/index.php?option=com_content&task=view&id=653&Itemid=200.

[9] Mary Alice Crim, "The Internet is a Feminist Issue," Save the Internet, accessed 23 Mar. 2010, http://www.savetheinternet.com/blog/09/07/06/internet-feminist-issue.

[10] Inge Komardjaja, "The Internet Empowers Women With Disabilities," Isis International, accessed 23 Mar. 2010, http://www.isiswomen.org/index.php?option=com_content&task=view&id=653&Itemid=200.

[11] Tom Geoghegan, "Internet Dating 'Empowers Women'," BBC News Online, accessed 23 Mar. 2010, http://news.bbc.co.uk/2/hi/uk_news/2486815.stm.

[12] "Open Directory Project," dmoz, accessed 28 Nov. 2009, http://www.dmoz.org/Health/Women's_Health/Support_Groups/.

support groups. There are discussion boards for—just to name a few—divorce, menopause, birthing, smoking, losing weight, breast cancer, disabilities, and eating disorders. Researchers have found that these online support groups can be key in producing and maintaining a healthy physical, mental, and emotional state for females. For instance, a study funded by the National Institute of Mental Health, published in 2006, found that "Internet-based intervention program may prevent some high risk, college-age women from developing an eating disorder."[13]

While women are more likely to make use of these online support groups and programs,[14] the comment must be made that they are available for men to use as well. Likewise, women generally utilize social networking sites, such as Facebook, more than men,[15] but men still engage and benefit from all forms of online communication. Also, the advantages of online business apply to males as well as females. Therefore, it seems that the Internet does not explicitly empower women, but rather humanity in general. The Internet does seem to direct women toward online discussion and self-exploration, and men to business and entertainment, as shown by which sites the sexes visit,[16] but the Internet does not necessarily impart empowerment to one sex over the other. Both men and women have access to the same material online, so ultimately it depends on how individuals utilize these resources to empower themselves.

---

[13] Taylor CB, et. al, "Prevention of Eating Disorders in At-risk College-age Women," *Archives of General Psychiatry*, (2006), http://www.4therapy.com/consumer/conditions/article/8684/75/College+Women+at+Risk+for+Eating+Disorders+May+Benefit+From+Internet-based+Intervention+Program.

[14] "Different People Use the Internet in Different Ways," Infoplease, accessed 28 Oct. 2009, http://www.infoplease.com/ipa/A0931238.html.

[15] Justin Smith, "Fastest Growing Demographic on Facebook: Women Over 55," Inside Facebook, accessed 14 Apr. 2010, http://www.insidefacebook.com/2009/02/02/fastest-growing-demographic-on- facebook-women-over-55/.

[16] "Different People Use the Internet in Different Ways," Infoplease, accessed 28 Oct. 2009, http://www.infoplease.com/ipa/A0931238.html.

Naked in the World of Warcraft

IProfess, Zuljin, World of Warcraft

Editor's note*: Another piece from our intermittent and highly unlikely contributor, IProfess, who purports to be a "'toon" or Avatar from the on-line game, the World of Warcraft. He promises to answer any queries put to him in the commenting feature below.*

Iprofess begins:

Well, gentle reader, I take up the mouse to tell a cautionary tale! As many of you know, I am a 'Toon from the World of Warcraft who has become sentient—I have a number of hypotheses as to how this has occurred, but most are as indemonstrable as is the existence of Ol' Bliz, the dominant demiurge of my world. But, as interesting as those ruminations undoubtedly would be to you, I write here concerning a more immediate issue: identity theft and hacking.[1]

The World of Warcraft has, over the years, provided a number of surprises for me, most pleasant, some decidedly unpleasant. Recently, however, I scaled the heights of the latter. One evening (An evening by Server Time anyway; I can never keep straight the bewildering varieties of time in what you so quaintly think of as "The Real World" (TRW)... and Daylight Savings Time! Elune Forbid!) I was playing late—or being played late as some Phenomenalists might argue[2]—and suddenly began losing control, jerking about, growing faint, then more defined. I thought, of course, that Ol' Bliz, in his or her greed, had finally fatally overloaded the realm and we were about to crash, probably once and for all. In fact, I did crash. But this was not an ordinary crash; I could not get back in, nor was there any news in the help sites concerning a server crash.

I decided to try entertaining myself in TRW for a while until things settled down, and somehow survived for almost 12 unbroken hours there. I tried television...words fail even me. As there were no inns available to me to sleep, I went, upon the advice of friends, to the late showing of a film called "Avatar." A very interesting crowd, some of whom were properly dressed. Pretty enough, but what sort of Avatar cannot be played? It was entirely non-interactive and upon

---

[1] For my earlier writings see: See; "The Tales of Azeroth" and "Toons and Terrorism" and most recently, "Protecting Human Children in the World of Warcraft," at: http://bcis.pacificu.edu/journal/2009/04/article.php?id=60 See, too, my books reviews; the first of R. V. Kelly 2's Massively Multiplayer Online Role-Playing Games, followed by Edward Castronova's work, Synthetic Worlds, The Business and Culture of Online Games, and most recently: Hilde G. Corneliussen and Jill Walker Rettberg, (editors,) Digital Culture, Play, and Identity: A World of Warcraft Reader.

[2] To better understand the very interesting distinctions between playing and being played, see note 4 at: http://bcis.pacificu.edu/journal/2009/01/article.php?id=28.

staying to view it again, it was exactly the same! Apparently nobody could play it. I went to the local library after the second showing, but was denied entrance because it was "closed." Some sort of system breakdown, I assume. Then I went back to television, advised that it was the best soporific available, and watched the news. You poor souls!

Again, I quickly grew fatigued with the tiresome events of TRW: wars and intrigues, arcane political struggles that would make a Slime regurgitate, all tediously repetitive and accompanied by endless alarums and excursions, all obviously intended to transfer wealth and power as expeditiously as possible to elite beings in different "nations" speaking different languages, but all equally porcine, all bound about with corsets and if male, topped with unbelievably bad hair pieces; if female, ditto the corsets and often the hair pieces, but these were also curiously lacking in affect as so many of their facial muscles have been ironed out by some toxic chemical not available in even the seediest barbershops of Azeroth. Having exhausted the resources of TRW, I tried, but still could not get back into the game world! I was locked out!

I thought it possible that I had failed to transfer sufficient wealth from TRW into Azeroth for my monthly offering to Ol' Bliz, but this was not the issue. I checked into the Armory, where our images are stored in order that we might compare others' gear and feats to our own; I was there, but naked! As naked as we can get anyway, stripped to my trunks! So were all of my Alts!

(Here, I know, I must explain the concept of Alt or Alternative 'Toon. In order to save time running back and forth Ol' Bliz permits us to create alternative identities to conduct menial chores, banking, going to the Auction House, etc., those tiresome points where the World of Azeroth grows perilously similar to TRW! Anyway, the entire group was embarrassingly reduced in clothing and armor, weapons, everything was gone!)

Finally, comprehension slowly dawned! I had been hacked! My identity, myidentity, had been stolen somehow and a miscreant from TRW had one by one pillaged my Alts, my bank accounts, gotten up to who-knows-what sort of mischief, perhaps danced with Gnomes, even dallied with Blood Elves!

As I was locked out, all useful forms of communication were barred to me. I could not consult with guildies, summon a Game Master—the often-helpful representative of Ol' Bliz—nothing. I was a castaway in TRW! Reduced to analog! Finally I managed to calm down; there simply had to be a way home...

The websites whereby Ol' Bliz interfaces with TRW gave telephone numbers to call. Although it is true that there are persistent legends in Azeroth which hold that some 'Toon—always carefully unnamed—once communicated directly with Ol' Bliz by phone,—some say even before the Outlands were opened up, some put the event in the unchronicled era of Patch 2—I failed repeatedly and disgracefully. 'Ol Bliz was playing another of his or her cosmic jokes.

Finally, I resorted to Email. Aha! Ol' Bliz heard me, perhaps because I mentioned my many writings in TRW—in a perfectly unthreatening manner of course, one does not threaten the gods, or not very often, anyway—but for whatever reason, he, she, or it answered!

And in less than 24 hours I could get back in! This was not a simple procedure. I had to change my password, not knowing how much information the hackers had gathered, and fearing an attack on my pitiful funds in TRW—pitiful because this publication will not pay me at all—cancelled my credit card.

However, getting back in less than 24 hours was, according to guildies when discussing the issue later, record time. Some had been stranded in TRW for many days. Others, it was said, had in fact never returned to Azeroth at all, but probably are even now sobbing and twitching in some maximum care facility in TRW for going to an airport and trying to buy a ticket to Azeroth, having tried every other expedient!

But I got "back in" as we say. It was initially a soothing experience. The screams of the suffering in TRW faded away, the pleasant sounds of Azeroth rose around me. But my virtual goods were all gone. I did not have even the funds to fly! My mounts, my pets, everything was gone. One of my Alts had been contemptuously left with two copper pieces, whereupon it was clear that the thief was from TRW. Insult to injury!

When I checked in on one of my Alts, a stout Dwarven Warrior, I found I had been tossed out of my guild, Draco Dormiens. This was bad enough, but then a guildie spotted me coming in and began cursing me in the chat line. My Alt had robbed the guild bank! Then he ran an illegal hack and mined illegally, not only on the surface of the game world, but inside it! Now I was pretty sure that we were dealing with a Republican, perhaps even a banker, making a raid from TRW.

Fortunately, I managed to explain my Alt's weird behavior and was even asked if I wanted to rejoin the guild but I now had a mission: To learn how and what exactly the level of damage was, and try to prevent it from happening to others...this then is my purpose in writing.

There are many ways to get hacked in Azeroth. A common one is buying gold in-game from one of the many gold sellers constantly spamming the chat line. All of these, of course, are criminally minded, except for Susan from Hong Kong, who truly loves me and only me. These gold sellers will often succeed in transferring malware to one's computer along with the gold.

Another common error is sharing a machine, which can easily result in sloppy security and a subsequent hack. Falling for any number of phishing schemes, such as sending the noob (inexperienced 'toon) to a particular website to download a spectacular weapon or pet, usually known as the Phony Pony scam, is also often fatal.

Sometimes posting in a guild web site can open your system up, I understand. But I was guilty of none of these. I have no way of knowing what happened to me. I scanned my system, no problems, no malware, nothing.

However, through sloth and overconfidence (I must spend even less time in TRW, I am picking up the local culture!) I had unwittingly much increased the odds that I might be hacked. Over the last few months in TRW—we have seasons and seasonal holidays but not actually months in Azeroth, which is a blessing given the uncertainty of how long they are and when they begin and end, now this day, now that—'Ol Bliz' minions had been flogging a device called an authenticator to be used on something called Battle.net which serves some largely as yet unannounced purpose. This is held to be a definitive protection against hacking as it generated a random number (key), which had to be input into the login both locally and wirelessly. 'Ol Bliz then compared its key to yours, and viola, you were back in.

I was aware that guildies were being hacked, but convinced myself that they were all careless; perhaps even Susan had turned on them, but I was confident that I was unique. But what I was really doing was becoming a more and more prominent member of a rapidly shrinking pool of those unwilling to increase their security via the authenticator. As the pool of easy victims shrank, my number got close and closer to "up"!

How they got to me, I do not know. But it may have simply been some sort of brute force attack over time, software which tried ID's over and over until something clicked, then turned to my password, foolishly only 7 digits, all simple alpha characters. Or perhaps it was more elaborate, some sort of man-in-the-middle scheme wherein the hacker penetrated Bliz' system and waited for me to waltz blithely in.

One of my alts had also recently reached 80 and accumulated a very nice panoply of gear and weapons, an accumulation of wealth worth real money in TRW, where theft is a way of life for many, indeed for almost all, if you think, as I do, of pillaging resources in TRW on a non-sustainable basis as theft. So I was not only careless, but a prime target.

The interface for washing stolen wealth from Azeroth is, of course, via such otherwise innocent social media as PayPal and EBay. My gear, purchased with hours of labor in Azeroth, became worth currency in TRW—we have one of the largest "real" economies in any world in Azeroth, billions of dollars in TRW, worth more than the economies of many small nations, and even more than some large ones, too.

As shown by the expectation of other 'Toons that it would take more than 24 hours to recover their account, this was the window of time that the thieves had to act. I use the plural here advisedly.

Once a thief had gained access, groups of confederates raced madly about the server, first stripping my Alts and me, then our bank accounts, then running hacks such as the undersurface mining one mentioned earlier, depositing the illicit wealth into my bank using one of my alts.

Clearly the gang planned that, before they lost control over the account, they would move their goods to another, third party account, during that two or three-day window they had to act. This can be done through the mails of Azeroth, a self-service process since that unfortunate event involving the maddened Orc clerk in the Undercity. Talk about going postal—yet another unfortunate influence of TRW!

My unexpectedly fast return paid some interesting dividends for me. Some of my accounts still had some good gear, presumably stolen from others in them, and, after 'Ol Bliz generously restored my own, I was at least even with the thieves.

The thieves had also, however, created multitudinous new alts all over the game world; some in Zul'jin, others scattered across other realms. I am still, as of this writing, chasing them down and, uh... dispatching them, weeks after the events chronicled here. These were probably created to facilitate additional crimes on those servers, but were not used, as all of them I have dealt with so far were standing stupidly in the very spot in which they had been born!

Conclusion and Excellent Advice: It is best to listen to the gods on this issue. At the very least they wish to keep us in the game, so that those monthly offerings will keep coming. And like all gods, they are jealous ones, willing to pillage us but loathe to cutting others in on the take. So: in no particular order:

Make yourself a difficult target. Put on a real password, as long as Bliz' login window will take, and make it a nonsensical mix of letters and numbers. If it is a word, or all letters or all numbers, brute force exploits will run much faster, and remember, this is about being a harder target than the other noobs lurching about unaware. Write it down, but not on your computer.
You should probably create an email address in a good reputable service to be used only in identifying yourself in the game. If you have a multi-use email, corporate or school, you are too likely to draw attention to yourself even outside the game. There are places in TRW to buy millions of email addresses for very little, which can then easily be the first step in a brute force attack. Just having the last part of your email will make such an attack run faster. Recall the tragic harvard.edu attacks of several years ago, and the numerous gnomes and dwarves tragically stripped of even their trust funds, and the resultant wave of 'Toonucides. And the rumors of the .gov hack are tragic indeed, and may have so-called national security implications, but this, of course, we will never know.
Do not buy gold, seek out Phony Ponies, share your account, download hacks, use add-ons from unknown sources, log into 'Toon sites you don't really know anything about, etc. Go read 'Ol Bliz' advice very carefully. Start at: http://us.blizzard.com/support/article.xml?locale=en_US&articleId=20572&rhtml=y
As a matter of course, occasionally run malware scans on your machine. There are many ways to pick such things up.
And, above all, install the authenticator. These come in two flavors, one as an usb stick. I have no experience with this. I use an app on my MePhone, which works quite well, though the entire process is clumsy. Start at http://eu.blizzard.com/support/article.xml?locale=en_GB&articleId=28152 for more information.

I assure you, on the basis of my own experience, if there is anything worse than finding yourself naked in Azeroth, it is enduring several so-called "days" in TRW while you get everything all straightened out so you can get back in! Don't take a chance.

Copyright and Trademarks

Leonard Duboff and Christy King,
The DuBoff Law Group, LLC.

Editor's Statement: Because our Legal Editor and Berglund Center Board Member Leonard DuBoff is an internationally recognized specialist in Intellectual Property Rights, he sends us more material than we can really mention in our "Announcements" in any one issue. For this issue, we have gone back through recent submissions and assembled some of those which seem particularly relevant and timely for those interested in the impact of the Internet. Here are those relevant to two very important issues for content providers, Copyright and Trademarks.

TRADEMARKS

Accuracy in Trademark Registrations is Critical

We recently advised you about the importance of conducting regular intellectual property audits. As part of this audit, you should carefully review all of your trademark applications and existing registrations to be sure that there are no mistakes in the description of goods or services.

The US Patent and Trademark Office has in recent years been taking a hardline stance on even minor errors, finding applications and registrations that overstate usage of the mark to be fraudulent.

For example, perhaps your company used to use its mark in connection with toothbrushes, dental floss and hairbrushes, but a couple of years ago decided to phase out the hairbrush line and focus on dental products. Through some confusion, however, hairbrushes end up being listed on your new trademark application.

The entire application may be successfully opposed, or the entire registration could be canceled, based on the fact that the inclusion of hairbrushes was inaccurate, even though your company still uses the mark in connection with toothbrushes and dental floss.

Until recently, it was held that in order to be determined fraud, there had to be an intentional misstatement, but the Trademark Trial and Appeal Board now finds fraud if an applicant makes any statement it knew - or should have known - was false, even if the applicant had no intent to deceive.

Please let us know if you need any assistance with evaluating your trademark applications or registrations, or if you find any errors in your applications or registrations.

Are You Really Ready to Submit Your Intent to Use Trademark Application?

In the United States, traditionally a trademark or service mark could be protected only if was actually being used. Congress recognized that this was a problem for many, particularly when a project is in the planning stages. Thus, the US trademark law was amended to allow an application to be filed if there is an intent to use a mark, provided that the mark is actually used within a statutorily specified period of time after the application is filed. If you apply for a federal trademark registration for a mark you are not yet using, you are required to submit a declaration stating that you have a "bona fide intent to use" the mark in the future. While many have treated this declaration as a mere formality, recent decisions by the Trademark Trial and Appeal Board (TTAB) mean that careful thought should go into submitting an intent-to-use application. These TTAB decisions make clear that if the applicant is unable to produce documents evidencing a true intent to use the mark prior to the filing date, the application may be rejected. Thus, before applying for registration, you should be sure that you have documents showing when, where and how you expect the mark to be used, such as business plans, marketing plans, drafts of promotional materials, agreements with graphic designers, creation of labels, manufacturing deals, product designs, correspondence with potential licensees and the like. If you need assistance registering a trademark, whether in use or not, please feel free to contact our office at (http://www.dubofflaw.com/).

Choosing and Protecting a Trademark is More Complicated Than Many People Think.

Individuals are frequently placed in the position of creating new trademarks, whether for their own businesses or for the businesses of others (as when a graphic artist designs a new logo for a client). Unfortunately, they may be unaware of the nuances of the trademark law.

Although it comes as a surprise to many, creation of a trademark does not give rise to any rights in that mark. Rather, trademark rights arise from use of the mark in connection with goods or services in commerce. Since your use of a mark that is confusingly similar to the mark of another could be deemed an infringement, it is important to have a trademark search conducted prior to any use of a new mark. A good search will not only include marks registered on the federal registry, but will seek out unregistered marks as well.

Is Someone Else Using Your Trademark as a Domain Name?

Is your company losing business because of a cybersquatter? Cybersquatters intentionally register domain names that are the same or confusingly similar to the trademarks of others. The Anticybersquatting Consumer Protection Act (ACPA), enacted in 1999, prohibits this practice and allows the trademark owner to sue in federal court. In addition, the Uniform Domain Name Dispute Resolution Policy (UDRP) provides a low-cost administrative method for resolving cybersquatting disputes.

In order to establish a cybersquatting claim under either ACPA or UDRP, the trademark owner must show that the domain is confusingly similar to its trademark, that the domain-name registrant has registered and is using the domain name in bad faith, and that the registrant has no legitimate interest in the domain name.

Most trademark owners will choose to proceed under UDRP because this process is quick, usually taking fewer than 60 days, and relatively inexpensive. However, the only remedy in a UDRP proceeding is transfer of the domain name to the trademark owner. In contrast, a federal lawsuit will likely take more than a year and will definitely be much more expensive. In the right circumstances, though, the federal case may be the wiser decision because monetary damages and reimbursement of attorney fees and costs may be awarded to the trademark owner.

Please feel free to contact us if you need assistance with a situation such as this, or any other situation involving your trademarks.

Act Now to Protect Your Trademarks on Facebook

Trademark owners should act quickly to protect their federally registered trademarks on Facebook, a social networking site with more than 200 million active users. Beginning tonight at 9:00 p.m. (West coast time), Facebook users will have the ability to create usernames, which can be entered as search terms not only on Facebook, but also on popular search engines such as Google. These usernames will be assigned on a first-come, first served basis.

You should, therefore, act quickly to protect your trademarks on Facebook. If you enroll your trademark with Facebook by using the online form located at:http://www.facebook.com/help/contact.php?show_form=username_rightsusers of Facebook will be unable to register a username identical to that trademark.

While there is no fee for enrolling your trademark, unfortunately, this process is only for trademarks registered on the federal level. Facebook also has a procedure to report infringing usernames: http://www.facebook.com/copyright.php?noncopyright_notice=1.

It is not yet known whether Facebook will reclaim usernames that infringe unregistered marks.

If you have any questions about this issue, please contact our office.

Protecting Your Most Important Asset

Last week we alerted you to the fact that Facebook had announced that it would allow owners of federally registered trademarks to "enroll" those marks with Facebook, preventing third parties from registering those marks as usernames. The time Facebook permitted for the registration process was extraordinarily short, and the enrollment process closed after only a day, though trademark owners may still submit complaints about infringing usernames.

The fact that only owners of registered marks could take advantage of this procedure underscores the importance of having your trademark portfolio in order, and of registering any valuable words that you use to identify your business, products or services as federal trademarks. It is worth bearing in mind that the trademark laws, a product of the 19th and 20th centuries, permit protection of a mark by different owners in non-conflicting markets. For example, General Motors' Cadillac trademark did not prevent Cadillac Pet Foods from using "Cadillac" to identify its dog food, or from registering that trademark.

The Internet, a more modern innovation, is different. When, for instance, a name is first used as a URL in cyberspace, no one else will be allowed to obtain the same URL, even if the second claimant has an otherwise legitimate right to that name. Further, search engines such as Google will generally feature the identified URL even if others have an equal or better claim to the trademark.

Ownership of a federally registered trademark establishes a presumption that the trademark is valid and helps to establish a priority as among competing owners, as well as to simplify claims of infringement reported to service providers, such as Google, eBay, and YouTube.

There are a number of other benefits provided to those who have federally registered trademarks, and the importance of protecting your company's assets, including its intangible intellectual property, cannot be over emphasized. It is, therefore, appropriate to determine whether the names you use to identify your business, products and services can be registered as federal trademarks as well as on the web.

Feel free to contact us for more information.

COPYRIGHTS

Involuntary Termination of Copyright

The buyer of a copyright often assumes that it will own that copyright for the full duration of copyright in the work, but this is not necessarily true. Whether you see this as a good thing or a bad thing naturally depends on whether you are the buyer or the seller of the copyright. The situation is similar for one who acquires the exclusive right to use the copyrighted work of another.

The creator of a copyrighted work (or, if the creator is deceased, his or her heirs) has the right to terminate assignments and exclusive licenses during a specific period set by law, even if those assignments and licenses appear to be absolute. The timing of this period depends on when the assignment was made or the license granted. If the transfer was made after 1978, the assignment or license can be terminated any time during a five-year window beginning at the end of 35 years from the date of execution of the transfer; or, if the transfer covers the right of publication of the work, the five-year window begins at the earlier of 35 years from the date of publication of the work or 40 years from the date of the transfer.

The author or his/her heirs have two opportunities to terminate transfers made before 1978: one five-year window beginning 56 years from the date of the original transfer, and another five-year window beginning 75 years from the date copyright was originally secured.

Note that the termination right does not apply to true "works made for hire," but merely calling the work a work made for hire will not be sufficient to prevent the exercise of the termination right. A work made for hire is defined as a work created by an employee within the scope of employment or a work which is specially ordered or commissioned as a work made for hire through a written agreement, provided that the work falls into one of nine categories identified in the statute.

The right to terminate cannot be waived. That is, even if the creator of the work agrees not to exercise these rights, that agreement would not be enforceable. There are, of course, several formalities that must be followed in order to exercise the termination right.

It is likely that the Michael Jackson estate will find that it is subject to this termination right with respect to the Beatles music Jackson purchased some time ago, since the Beatles or their heirs are likely to reclaim their valuable rock music in order to be able to resume exploiting it for their own benefit or to resell it if possible.

Please feel free to contact us if you have any questions about the termination right or what qualifies as a work made for hire.

Register Your Copyrights!

The copyright laws protect any "original work...of authorship fixed in any tangible medium of expression...." This includes books, articles, paintings, photographs, jewelry, software and many other types of works.

Unless a work is registered before an infringement occurs, the copyright owner will not be entitled to recover statutory damages or attorneys' fees from any infringer. Also, you cannot file suit for copyright infringement until your work is registered. It is, therefore, a good idea to register your copyrighted works as they are created, since any registration of a copyrighted work within three months of the date it is first published will be retroactive back to the date of first publication.

Unfortunately, the Copyright Office has a backlog of registration applications, and the time for processing an application is now around 18 months. Because of this significant delay, the Copyright Office has determined that the normal handling fee for an expedited registration of $760 will not be charged to convert a pending application to expedited status when the application has been pending for more than six months and the applicant is able to satisfy the Copyright Office that expedited handling of the registration is needed in connection with a suit for copyright infringement. This rule is effective through July 1, 2011.

Feel free to contact our office if you have any questions about copyright registration.

How You Can Reduce Your Risk of Receiving an Enforcement Call from the Copyright Clearance Center

The Copyright Clearance Center represents thousands of copyright owners. It not only offers licenses on behalf of those copyright owners, but also seeks to enforce its members' copyrights.

In order to reduce your risk of receiving an enforcement call from this organization, you should make sure that your company has a policy prohibiting its employees from infringing copyrights. That policy should also require the employee to report any violations he or she learns about, and you should also provide employees with examples of alternatives to illegal copying. For instance, the employee can simply forward the original article, book or the like instead of making a copy, or suggest that the colleague obtain his or her own copy of a publication the employee describes. Instead of sending a copy of an online article, the website link should be provided. In the event neither of these solutions are feasible, the employee should either refrain from passing on the article, book, etc., or contact a supervisor and request that he or she obtain the right to make the necessary copies.

So that you can determine whether employees are actually following the policy, you should periodically conduct an audit of employee emails. To do this, email text can be searched for terms such as "this article," or other terms your employees may use when forwarding articles. Of course, you can audit emails only if you have a policy in your employee handbook or employment agreements providing that employees have no expectation of privacy in their emails and indicating that you will be monitoring them.

Similar problems may arise in a non-employment context as well. You should not illegally download music or movies, nor should anyone in your household. Representatives of these industries are actively policing their rights and they are notoriously aggressive.

Please feel free to contact us_if you have any questions about copyright policies or about how to ensure that you have the right to monitor employee emails.

David Shields' Reality Hunger: A Manifesto

Review by Jeffrey Barlow

Reality Hunger, by David Shields, is certainly not a book for everybody. From another review, I was persuaded that the work probably had much to say about the impact of the Internet, the understanding of which is our primary charge at the Berglund Center. Indeed, it does; but it takes careful reading and considerable thought to thoroughly understand what the author is saying—assuming that I have done so.

Readers must give the work a chance to develop, because of its mode of organization. It is presented as a series of epigrams[1] organized—very loosely at times—into sections. Some sections present an almost linear argument. Others, however, coalesce at some points then seem to move onto a different focus entirely. From these sections, and from the epigrams, major arguments or position eventually emerge.

Here, for example, are four epigrams from a series dealing with "facts" which are found in section h, "Now":

> 255 Facts now seem important.
> 256 Facts have gravitas.
> 257 The illusion of facts will suffice.
> 258 In our hunger for all things true, we make the facts irrelevant.[2]

The four linked epigrams establish the author's belief that, while we desperately seek the real, our "Reality Hunger" has been twisted, by the nature of our media and by our economic structure, to force us to settle for simulations of the real. The same section, in which the above epigrams appear, however, covers many other topics as well, obscuring any central authorial perspective with regard to "Now".

Here I list the sections, in part because I fear that this review may make more "sense" of this work than the author intends, imposing a unity that he might well

---

[1] Our search for a precise definition of the term "epigram" was not terribly satisfying. We finally settled on a simple dictionary definition: "any witty, ingenious, or pointed saying tersely expressed." From dictionary.com found at: http://dictionary.reference.com/browse/epigram. There is a Wikipedia entry on the term, but the site has been disputed on several grounds and as this area is an unfamiliar one to me, I cannot recommend it. For those wanting more background and copious literary and cultural examples, the site "A Dram of Epigrams from Art, Poetry, Literature, Politics, Science and Religion", compiled and edited by Michael R. Burch at: http://www.thehypertexts.com/Epigrams_in_Literature_and_Poetry.htm will probably be very satisfying.

[2] Because the work is entirely epigrams and each is numbered, I do not cite Kindle locations here.

find inappropriate. Shields is fully a post-modernist; he wants us to construct our own meaning, because he believes that this is the only meaning that there can be. The sections (in the author's formatting) are:

a overture
b mimesis
c books for people who find television too slow
d trials by google
e reality
f memory
g blur
h now
i the reality-based community
j hip-hop
k reality tv
l collage
m in praise of brevity
n genre
o contradiction
p doubt
q thinking
r autobio
s persona
t ds
u alone
v it is much more important to be oneself than anything else
w risk
x let me tell you what your book is about
y manifesto
z Coda

It should be noted that, throughout this review, I am going to concentrate only on one aspect of *Reality Hunger*—that touching upon the Internet, insomuch as such a tight focus is possible. The book has many other notable foci, however; much of it deals with questions of "reality" as encountered in fiction, memoir, memory, film, television, biography, music, and many other genres.

This very expansive coverage means that anyone interested in art, broadly defined, and willing to following the terse structure of the book, which is, after all, designed to make the reader impose his or her own structure and understanding, would find the work provocative. This is, of course, the purpose of an epigram.

It is clear, though never clearly stated, that the major cause of the changes we have experienced across all sorts of media and genres is the Internet because it is the Internet which has facilitated the communication of many new kinds of content in every genre, many of which are created by amateurs.[3]

Here is an extended epigram—the literary history of the epigram in fact includes many lengthy examples—in which Shields defines the Internet. (I have deleted in the interests of brevity passages that seem to me to add little to the total):

> 74 The opposite of broadcast: the distribution economics of the Internet favor infinite niches, not one-size-fits-all. The web's peer-to-peer architecture: a symmetrical traffic load, with as many senders as receivers and data transmissions spread out over geography and time. A new regime of digital technology has now disrupted all business models based on mass-produced copies, including the livelihoods of artists... Laws based on the mass-produced copy are being taken to the extreme, while desperate measures to outlaw new technologies in the marketplace "for our protection" are introduced in misguided righteousness. This is to be expected: entire industries (newspapers, magazines, book publishers, movie studios, record labels) are threatened with demise, and most will die... Many methods have been employed to try to stop the indiscriminate spread of copies, including copy-protection schemes, hardware-crippling devices, education programs, and statutes, but all have proved ineffectual...In a regime of superabundant free copies, copies are no longer the basis of wealth. Now relationships, links, connection, and sharing are. Value has shifted away from a copy toward the many ways to recall, annotate, personalize, edit, authenticate, display, mark, transfer, and engage a work.

This long epigram reflects one of the author's continuing arguments. Shields believes that art is, despite all we might try to do, at best loosely anchored in any fixed "reality." Ownership/authorship itself is ultimately un-attributable; how can we fix the defining moment at which ownership is established when works and authors all build on previous works and authors? He finds, therefore, no problems legal or otherwise, in mixing sources or "mashing" them up; rather to him, such blending has always been a sine qua non for true creativity.

Shields believes that information not only "*wants* to be free", but to be fully creative, *must* be free. The long epigram reproduced above ends: *Art is a conversation, not a patent office. The citation of sources belongs to the realms of journalism and scholarship, not art. Reality can't be copyrighted.* (Italics mine)

Our reality hunger comes from our alienation from current forms of content and meaning, from the blockbuster novel through the blockbuster film to carefully merchandized music. The author examines every one of these forms (and many others) as they have evolved. His explanation of the recent development of music, for example, is masterful. Here is part of epigram 275:

---

[3] As always in my reviews, I am trying to, in my own language and organization, to capture that of the original work. In this particular case, this review may itself seem choppy and disorganized.

> ... Somewhere along the way, as recording technology got better and better each year, the music lost something; it became too perfect, too complete. Which is why so many artists have turned to using samples and other preexisting sources in various forms: in this rush of technological innovation, we've lost something along the way and are going back to try to find it, but we don't know what that thing is... We're clinging to anything that seems "real" or organic or authentic. We want rougher sounds, rougher images, raw footage, uncensored by high technology and the powers that be.

Shields' perspective is that of an artist who has worked in a variety of genres and seen over his lifetime that the media has indeed become the message. The author's own creativity commands our respect. He has written a number of works with an astonishing variety of topics (sports, which hardly figures at all in this work is a recurring one).[4] In addition, he has worked in film and music.

Here, by way of our conclusion for this review, is epigram 262:

> Why is hip-hop stagnant right now, why is rock dead, why is the conventional novel moribund? Because they're ignoring the culture around them, where new, more exciting forms of narration and presentation and representation are being found (or rediscovered).

And although there are many explanations for these changes—largely technological ones—the Internet is first and foremost among them.

The author is fully committed to the electronic distribution of meaning, and on his personal site[5] has made available generous excerpts from *Reality Hunger*. These give enough of an experience of the work, as well as introductory and concluding remarks, that they might well be a useful guide to a reader's probable reaction to the work.

There is a great deal more that could, and surely will, be said about this book (if only in college courses in literature and media) but the reader who finds this review interesting should read the book and construct his or her own understanding of it. I have found reading it a worthwhile project and months after doing so, some of its epigrams continue to inform my thinking.

---

[4] See the author's pages at: http://www.davidshields.com/ Shields has also taken the care to add a "Reader's Guide" to the work, a trend which can only be applauded as it does much to clarify the work as well as to provide a structure for academic or social discussion of the work. Readers Guide:
http://www.davidshields.com/readersGuide/GuideRealityHunger.html.

[5] http://www.davidshields.com/excerpts/ExcerptRealityHunger.html.

Andrew Lih's *The Wikipedia Revolution*

Review by Jeffrey Barlow

This article consists of a review of an excellent book, Andrew Lih's *The Wikipedia Revolution*, and, in the spirit of Wikipedia, a "stub"— that is the beginning of a subsequent piece on how different classes of users can better use Wikipedia, which has become truly indispensible.

Review:

The impact of Wikipedia is closely related to the impact of the Internet itself. It is very much part of the Web 2.0 stage of the Internet. Wikipedia is an application which permits a community of highly organized— or loosely organized users, depending on your perspective—to create content. The advantages and disadvantages of the massive on-line encyclopedia, with its unattributed and community-edited articles, are largely those of the Internet itself. It is the first recourse when searching for information for more people, myself included, than any other site. But, at the same time, its articles are unattributed,[1] and there are abundant examples of its misuse by those deliberately planting inaccurate or misleading, not to say defamatory and deliberately false information.[2]

Andrew Lih's work is an excellent introduction to this cultural phenomenon. Lih had good access to key figures in its founding and in its continuing development. The book includes a not-very-informative forward by Jimmy Wales, Wikipedia's animating spirit, who has usually preferred to stay very much behind the scenes at the site, having largely turned it over to the community of users.[3]

It is not, of course, possible to write any one definitive book on such a broad phenomenon as *Wikipedia*. *The Wikipedia Revolution* is certainly not a guide to how to best utilize it for research nor how best to write for it. There are plenty of other works for those purposes, and we welcome, again in the spirit

---

[1] This is only true for the public viewer. *Wikipedia* editors themselves can tell who individuals are as they must all be registered and log in to post or correct. This may not correspond to a particular legal identity, of course, as pseudonyms are often used, but it does let editors judge the quality of frequent contributors' works, and when necessary, contact them.

[2] See Lih, especially chapter 8, "Crisis of Community."

[3] Lih points out in some detail that there were important antecedents to *Wikipedia* and several other individuals also deserve to be known as "founders." Foremost among these was Larry Sanger, often described as the co-founder of *Wikipedia*. Wales, however, has guided it from its formal inception to the present. Sanger recently published a very thoughtful if decidedly contrarian article, "Individual Knowledge and the Internet," in *Educause*, found at: http://www.educause.edu/EDUCAUSE+Review/EDUCAUSEReviewMagazineVolume45/IndividualKnowledgeintheIntern/202336. In it he touches upon some of the frequent criticisms of *Wikipedia*. It is not material closely related to Lih's work under review here, but it is certainly going to inspire considerable discussion among "Wikipedians."

of Wikipedia, readers to mention works they have found useful for other purposes in the comments section of this review.

In addition, there is more than one Wikipedia in the sense that many national groups have joined in creating it, and have not only their own unique languages (There are entries in 255 different languages as of Lih's writing in 2007-2008.) but their own branch Wikipedia organizations with their own rules and their own cultural concerns.[4] Wikipedia is also constantly growing and mutating, so any one book will necessarily neglect a great deal. This is then, a study of the dominant American English language version of Wikipedia.

As well as treating the history of Wikipedia, Lih necessarily deals with its technological underpinnings, a very interesting story in and of itself. A community of users has voluntarily modified and adapted the Wiki software originally created by Ward Cunningham[5] to steadily meet enormous technical challenges, such as how to facilitate writing, editing, and reading Wikipedia in its 255 different languages.

These were not, however, the most daunting problems which Wikipedia faced. Those problems were the social ones. Wikipedia is, after all, the world's largest encyclopedia of knowledge, with not only the most users, but also a huge community of writers, editors, and other behind-the-scenes critical personnel who selflessly patrol for bad grammar, punctuation, incorrect information, evil intent, and poor taste. As the work's subtitle suggests, *Wikipedia* is created and maintained by "a Bunch of Nobodies." These are all organized into what may be the world's largest technologically enabled voluntary community. As a result, Wikipedia, though the author does not belabor the fact, is a fascinating social experiment, which shows the very best, and occasionally the very worst of our species—at least the worst that can be accomplished by writing on the Internet.

Despite the inchoate nature of Wikipedia, The *Wikipedia Revolution* is tightly focused, well written, and informative. It is an excellent place to begin understanding the history, the key controversies, and the major issues related to the development of Wikipedia. Lih also deals with the antecedents of Wikipedia, principally Nupedia, which was intended to be fully peer-reviewed.[6]

Lih is well qualified to write the work, having worked both as an academic at Columbia (where he was a founder of the Media Studies program, and at the University of Hong Kong, in journalism and new media). At the time of writing, Lih was a frequent commentator at CNN, NPR, and MSNBC. He is very much a believer in the Internet as a tool for democracy, and even invites the readers of

---

4 Among the many fascinating examples which Lih discusses is the two-year long argument at *Wikipedia* as to whether to use the term *Danzig* or *Gdansk* to refer to the sometimes German, sometimes Polish, city by that name. Lih 122.

5 We were fortunate to have Ward Cunningham as our keynote speaker at the Berglund Summer Institute in the summer of 2008. Ward not only discussed but also modeled the community spirit which has made Wikis and particularly *Wikipedia* what it is today.

6 See http://en.wikipedia.org/wiki/Nupedia.

this book to edit its last chapter in a wiki format.[7] It would be difficult for an author to show more trust in the "commons" than this. He is also an administrator (a powerful class of *Wikipedia* users) who has edited more than ten thousand entries.

Lih and *The Wikipedia Revolution* then, do not lack for authority. Unfortunately, Wikipedia itself does. That is, as the ordinary viewer cannot know who has written or who has subsequently edited an entry, let alone what their qualifications may be, the articles cannot safely be accepted as definitive, and are often disputed. One of the key concepts of Wikipedia is that its content is not original research but a compilation of knowledge drawn from other sources. In short, it is an encyclopedia, deliberately modeled on classical models. As a result, many educational institutions, and doubtless many more educators, do not permit students to cite Wikipedia articles in the notes or bibliographies of formal papers.

Wikipedia's lack of authority is unfortunate, but inherent in its nature. It has become a useful source—easily the world's most useful single source—for research and learning of all types on virtually every conceivable topic precisely because it draws on user community interests and necessarily foregoes peer review. Lih does a great deal to establish the limits of Wikipedia authority. He discusses important points in its development when critical decisions, such as not to establish formal peer review, were made.

Lih also, however, points out that there is substantial care taken to ensure a high level of trust. For example, it is not true that anybody can post anything on any topic. The community of users has established a number of important restrictions and rules. For example, would-be authors are advised:

> *Remember the article you create will be deleted quickly[8] if it is not acceptable. Wikipedia has a new pages patrol[9] division where people check your new articles shortly after you create them.*
>
> - Articles that do not meet notability[10] and do not cite reliable published sources[11] are likely to be deleted.
> - Do not create pages about yourself, your company, your band or your friends,[12] nor pages that advertise,[13] nor personal essays[14] or other articles you would not find in an encyclopedia.[15]

---

[7] See the author's pages for this book at: http://www.wikipediarevolution.com/About_the_author.html.
[8] http://en.wikipedia.org/wiki/Wikipedia:CSD
[9] http://en.wikipedia.org/wiki/Wikipedia:NPP
[10] http://en.wikipedia.org/wiki/Wikipedia:N
[11] http://en.wikipedia.org/wiki/Wikipedia:RS
[12] http://en.wikipedia.org/wiki/Wikipedia:COI
[13] http://en.wikipedia.org/wiki/Wikipedia:Spam
[14] http://en.wikipedia.org/wiki/Wikipedia:OR
[15] http://en.wikipedia.org/wiki/Wikipedia:NOT

- Be careful about the following: copying things,[16] controversial material, extremely short articles, and local-interest articles.[17]

There are many other restrictions and a sharp-eyed community of groups (and very sophisticated software 'bots) such as the "new pages patrol" ready to delete, correct, or edit work.

Those who want a better understanding of Wikipedia might well begin with Lih's work simply because it is linear and authoritative. The next step would be to register with Wikipedia (a very simple instantaneous process...no waiting for your e-mail to cough up a password or other common delays) then prowl through it in order to understand the resources available to you. Many of these are broadly valuable; The Wikipedia Manual of Style, for example is an excellent resource for writers, and for students and teachers of writing.[18]
The Wikipedia Revolution should be useful not only to users of Wikipedia, but to those wishing better to understand the impact of the Internet, our audience at the Berglund Center.

Stub: How to Effectively Use Wikipedia

In Wikipedia, a "stub" is the bare beginning of what the author hopes will eventually be a much more developed article. That is the case for the following. I hope to draw some reader comment and in any event intend to fully develop this stub as an editorial for the next issue of *Interface*.

There are many reasons why Wikipedia is not equivalent to a peer-reviewed article written by professionals in the topic area and this means that it can never be granted the highest level of authority, as least as judged by scholars. To treat it as no more than a conventional paper encyclopedia, however, is naive. Educators (or Educationists as Sanger prefers to call them in the article cited above) who simply forbid students from using Wikipedia are making at least three mistakes.

First, for most students Wikipedia is instantly available and usually provides the sort of pithy introduction to an unknown topic that would get a researcher started. (As Lih points out, in many languages Wikipedia is the <u>only</u> encyclopedia available in any form.) I myself go to Wikipedia for information even on topics where I am expert. I would do so if to see if there was any new information available, if for no other reason. (I would like to hear from scholars who do not themselves do the same. Please comment below.) And as for topics where I am relatively ignorant, usually, but not always, Wikipedia will suggest additional reference points upon which I can begin to scaffold my own understanding.

The second reason why strict prohibitions on the use of Wikipedia are unwise is that students will use it regardless of what they are told. When I once forbade my

---

[16] http://en.wikipedia.org/wiki/Wikipedia:Plagiarism
[17] See: http://en.wikipedia.org/wiki/Wikipedia:Your_first_article See also http://en.wikipedia.org/wiki/Wikipedia:Introduction.
[18] http://en.wikipedia.org/wiki/Wikipedia:Manual_of_Style.

students from using it, one gave the stylized "whatever" shrug, and said that she would use it anyway but would cite the sources that it cited as evidence for her point, or would use it to backtrack to an Internet site which would meet my standards. Either of these, of course, is an accepted scholarly practice in paper materials, though the former requires a specialized sort of reference note.

Thirdly, and most importantly, blanket prohibitions on Wikipedia neglect an excellent opportunity to enhance students' research skills. Behind the scenes in the metadata of a Wikipedia article, accessible to any registered user (as stated above, registration is a very easy and fast process) is the history of the article, notations of any editing changes, any disagreements as to fact, or other relevant issues. A student can, based on this information and on the conventional information available to any viewer such as presence or lack of notes and sources, make thoughtful decisions as to the authority of the piece, surely the key scholarly practice in any media, and perhaps the more important evaluative ability for the use of the Internet itself.

An assignment increasingly used by some teachers is for the students to evaluate a Wikipedia article that touches upon a research topic that they have already worked up. They might well begin their work with Wikipedia, do substantial library research, then go back to the same Wikipedia article. If they now perceive errors or inadequate coverage, they should register and correct them, citing their own sources. This is a process that Wikipedia calls "SOFIXIT," that is, if you don't agree, "Be Bold"—another Wikipedia injunction—and correct it.

For scholars acting in the public arena and wishing to cite electronic sources, an additional practice is necessary. If you cite electronic sources, you must state in your notes why they can be considered authoritative. At the Berglund Center we signal our own level of trust by affixing an evaluative seal to each piece we publish.[19] Sadly, very few other sites do this, so we must ourselves certify each electronic source we use if we are to be taken seriously.

I myself recently had the experience of getting involved in a local (to Portland Oregon) controversy involving issues and fields in which I am expert. The topic was a very emotional one and so the on-line discussion was often confrontational, even bellicose.

As the venue was a blog-like structure, I tried to find useful Internet sources which I could cite in support of my positions, rather than standing on my own authority. I thought that these, being publically available, would be more useful to the audience. As I did so, I naturally sought out authoritative ones. In my notes, however, I merely cited them, not carefully explaining why they were useful and authoritative.

As the controversy itself had by this time become unavoidably political and subjective, this failure on my part opened me up to the quick dismissal of my sources as simply having been culled from the Internet. Once one of my opponents made that argument, other replied in the same vein. I then doggedly

---

19 See http://bcis.pacificu.edu/authority/index.html.

spent many hours citing published sources, contexting the Internet sources, and in general flogging a dead horse. My opponents had by then harrumphed away to the high ground, their original opinions intact.

While my problem was very particular to the controversy at hand and few issues are unlikely to provoke such partisan rancor, the problem is basic to the use of evidence. Anyone wishing to cite it as an authoritative source must explain, case-by-case, note-by-note, why any given article is credible. I now try to do this in my own writing for this journal.

Evidence of the reliability of a Wikipedia article (or any other online source) should include certain characteristics:

- It is sourced in published works by known experts or published via peer-review, as almost all books from reputable publishing houses and all university presses are.
- It has notes and bibliography showing a familiarity with the uses of such evidence.
- If it cites other on-line sources, you must go to them and see if they seem to be reputable as well.
- If a Wikipedia piece is marked "disputed" or has an "accuracy warning" stay away from it. The notation "citation needed" is probably also fatal to its current authority, although it is intended to signal only a weakness in citation at one point which does not necessarily invalidate the entire piece.

When citing such pieces, state in your notes why you find them authoritative. This is not the same as being merely useful. Students easily confuse the two. As one of my students said in his bibliography: "This source is authoritative because it is the only thing I can find on this topic."

Writers should not, however, confuse authority and utility. For example: The articles I cited below all have the same qualities which make them authoritative for my uses here. They are about Wikipedia and written at Wikipedia itself; this makes them what historians call an "original" or "primary source."[20]

So whether a student or an academic, or perhaps a businessperson wishing to persuade others, If you don't feel qualified to evaluate Wikipedia or other Internet materials you would like to cite, and are not willing to spend a bit of time establishing their authority with other published or Internet sources, and you are unwilling to clearly state the basis for your judgments in your notes, then you should stay way from them and stick to the library, which, of course, has its own pitfalls.

---

[20] See http://en.wikipedia.org/wiki/Primary_source for the distinction between these. The site is copiously noted in excellent sources many of which I am, as a practicing historian, familiar.

After Internet Time: A Decade of the Berglund Center/A Call for Proposals

Editorial by Jeffrey Barlow

Introduction: This piece is both an editorial, in which I discuss the notion of "Internet Time" and also a call for submissions. These are to be published first in *Interface*, then in an edited and peer-reviewed print-on-demand volume from the Berglund Press in the summer of 2011.

The genesis of this project lies in the 10th anniversary of the Berglund Center for Internet Studies at Pacific University Oregon, occurring this spring. During these ten years (roughly 1999-2010) we have seen the continuing impact of the Internet upon global culture and technology. This is not, of course, by any means the period during which the Internet developed most rapidly. That period, in our opinion, was the decade immediately preceding the founding of the Berglund Center. The Berglund Center has existed during the third stage of the Internet, and it is this stage which we wish to better understand. We believe that this third stage, unlike the earlier two, gives us better opportunity to make useful evaluations. In its third stage, the Internet has acquired a more or less fixed form, and now we have a better chance to understand it than we did in its earlier manifestations.

The Stages of the Internet: The first stage of the Internet proper, we believe, is the decade from 1980-1990. At that time the technology behind the Internet was of primary interest to those trying to develop systems to interconnect isolated computers and systems. This process had actually begun several decades earlier,[1] but the protocols necessary for true networking were not standardized until 1982. We'll look at the second stage, "Internet Time," below.

In the third stage, during the 1990s, the Internet became widely used; in 1992 the millionth host was added to it. Only then did the Internet become truly influential and begin to have a significant cultural impact. The study of this impact is, of course, the charge of the Berglund Center. Our founders, Jim and

---

[1] For my discussion here on the stages of the development of the Internet, I am drawing on both my experience at *The Journal of the Association for History and Computing*, and several Internet sites. See: "Internet History" at the Computer History Museum, http://www.computerhistory.org/internet_history/. This begins the development of the Internet at 1962, and ends it at 1992, after all the key technologies were in place and sufficient scale (one million hosts) had been reached to set it upon its present course. Another useful source—in some senses more useful in that it discusses cultural and economic impacts as well as underlying technology—is found at the very well documented Wikipedia article 'History of the Internet" at: http://en.wikipedia.org/wiki/History_of_the_Internet#TCP.2FIP.

Mary Berglund, had understood by the mid 1990s the significance of the rapid expansion of the Internet, and moved to fund the Center in 1999.

For my part, I had joined the Association for History and Computing in the spring of 2007 and founded its e-journal, the *Journal of the Association for History and Computing* (JAHC), which first appeared in the spring of 2008. My original intent at JAHC was simply to try to understand the place of digital content and communications in the long development of historical studies.[2] I concluded, as a result of my initial research, that not only were electronic publications in history inevitably going to have considerable impact, but that it was very likely that the process of producing even paper works would be impacted by digitization and that, consequently, print-on-demand was going to emerge as a significant technology.[3]

The Berglund Center was carefully nurtured by its first two Directors, Joe Howell, who pulled together its organization and its mission, and Steve Boone, who got the center up and running, inviting me aboard as Faculty Director. While I continued my involvement with the JAHC until the spring of 2006, I also began editing *Interface*, which first appeared in October 2001. I later became Director upon Steve's retirement and devoted myself entirely to the Berglund Center.

Now we have concluded that it is time to mark our first decade by doing a survey of the Impact of the Internet during that period, written largely by our regular contributors at *Interface*, but including such additional papers as we may elect to publish. There is special advantage to studying the Internet's impact in this decade. If the growth of the Internet has slowed, it has consequently become easier to evaluate than it was in either of its first two decades.

The first period, from the 1970's through to about 1980, was a geek's paradise—the rest of us are highly indebted, but largely unable to understand exactly what it was the techies were really doing. But by 1980 the visionaries among us began to apply the Internet to their work. By 1990, everyone (except those who would not see) could observe the impact of the Internet all around us, much accelerated, of course, by the events known as the Dot.Com Bubble, usually dated from 1995-2000.[4]

That period saw the development of some ideas key to the impact of the Internet. Some of those ideas were "disruptive" in the argot of the time. The rapid development of the Internet seemed to undermine, or at least to alter, many

---

[2] See the "Editorial Statement" in our first edition at: http://mcel.pacificu.edu/jahc/1998/issue1/editorial/.

[3] See above, particularly content referenced by notes 17-19.

[4] See our review of Cassidy, John. *dot.con*. The Greatest Story Ever Sold. Harper Collins, New York: 2002. at: http://bcis.pacificu.edu/journal/2002/06/cassidy.php for our understanding of this period.

phenomena earlier simply taken as "reality." Investors jettisoned old verities, such as the value of price-earnings ratios, and even grizzled skeptics such as Alan Greenspan thought, like Ronald Reagan, that a new day had dawned in America, precipitated by computer-mediated communications which raised productivity faster than equity values could keep up. We had a "New Economy" appropriate to the "New Day".

One of the accepted verities that suddenly became relative was even such a fundamental concept as "time." The concept and the measurement of time have long been argued over by philosophers.[5] These have largely divided into two schools, one of which (the Realists) see time as an absolute quality of reality, one of the seven basic units around which the universe is structured.[6] We discover reality by exploring and manipulating these qualities, or so say the Realists. In the dot.com era, philosophical realists might be said to correspond to the traditionalists of investment, who worried about their equivalents of fundamental elements of measurement, such as price-earnings ratios.

There was, however, another competing, recent, and more with-it philosophical school derived from Leibniz and Kant, who argued that time was not outside us, not "real," but a fundamental property of human cognition, one of the ways that we apprehend *something*, but not itself one of the seven *fundamental somethings.* This school focused not upon the known or the unknown, but upon the knower.

This school's economic equivalent in the 1990s might be said to be represented by those who discovered "Internet Time." These held that the development of the Internet and the very speed of digital transmission had created a sort of tipping point after which economic verities changed. All we had to do was to perceive that change. To them, time was now measured best, not by swings of a pendulum (or in the most recent system of measurement by the frequency of a Cesium atom[7]), but by rapidly increasing production cycles, which some argued, was

---

[5] I am indebted once again to a very well documented article in Wikipedia, "Time" at: http://en.wikipedia.org/wiki/Time. This summary can be found there: "Among prominent philosophers, there are two distinct viewpoints on time. One view is that time is part of the fundamental structure of the universe, a dimension in which events occur in sequence. Time travel, in this view, becomes a possibility as other "times" persist like frames of a film strip, spread out across the time line. Sir Isaac Newton subscribed to this realist view, and hence it is sometimes referred to as Newtonian time. The opposing view is that *time* does not refer to any kind of "container" that events and objects "move through", nor to any entity that "flows", but that it is instead part of a fundamental intellectual structure (together with space and number) within which humans sequence and compare events. This second view, in the tradition of Gottfried Leibniz and Immanuel Kant, holds that *time* is neither an event nor a thing, and thus is not itself measurable nor can it be travelled."

[6] See *Bureau International des Poids et Mesures* at: http://www.bipm.org/en/si/base_units/.

[7] See "Cesium Atoms at Work," http://tycho.usno.navy.mil/cesium.html.

now seven times faster than formerly. This was the time frame appropriate to the "New Day" and to the "New Economy." This concept was to have its consequences.

Andrew Odlyzko, then at AT&T Labs, assigned the basic cause of the Internet bubble to the notion of Internet time:

> A few key ideas appear to have led all these experienced people astray, ideas that are closely interrelated and reinforce each other. The most important was "Internet time." This was the perception that product development and consumer acceptance were now occurring in a fraction of the traditional time. Closely related to the concept of Internet time was the idea of "first-mover advantage." Further support for the dot-com craze was provided by several other notions, such as "network effects," "increasing returns," "control of open standards," and "standards lock-in." Of all these ideas, though, Internet time was crucial. If indeed seven years of traditional product cycles were now compressed to one year, then anything might change in the blink of an eye.[8]

Internet Time turned out largely to be hyperbole. Realism has reasserted itself; price-earnings proved a more useful measurement than did production cycles. Now that Internet Time, marked by its often illogical and discontinuous enthusiasms, has taken on more realistic parameters, we want to understand exactly what has occurred.

At the Berglund Center we certainly do not hope finally to solve the question of the precise nature of time, but we do want to explore the impact of the Internet over the last ten years. We are going to commission ten articles, for which we will pay generously, by the standards of a non-profit publication (For details see our formal call for papers[9]). These will be peer-reviewed, initially, to select among the submissions for e-publication. Then they will be included in a print-on-demand work to be published in hard copy at the Berglund Center in the summer of 2011. The working title is "*After Internet Time: A Decade of the Impact of the Internet, 2000-2010.*"

---

[8] The myth of Internet time (Preprint version) Andrew Odlyzko (http://www.dtc.umn.edu/~odlyzko/doc/internet.time.myth.txt) Odlyzko began this pre-print article (written in mid-2000) by suggesting "The attitude that "the Internet changes everything" is changing to denigration of the Internet as the "Citizen's Band radio of the 1990s." Yet just as the early attitude was overoptimistic, the new one could easily become unjustifiably over pessimistic." He himself might now reconsider some of his more negative comments about at least the economic impact of the Internet in light of the experiences of the following decade.

[9] http://bcis.pacificu.edu/journal/article.php?id=676.

We have not lightly arrived at the decision to publish in both digital form and in paper copy. We are well aware of the far larger audience which will access on-line pieces as opposed to ordering paper copies. However, despite the many changes wrought by the Internet, some factors have remained constant for specific forms of content. Scholars want archival physical copies of their work for certification purposes, and paper publication still carries more inherent authority than do digital works. We have also found, in our experiences in publishing two works with Create Space(TM) during the last six months that the conversion from digital to paper has become easy and rewarding.

Our first work, Berglund Fellow Yang Desheng's *Jigsaw III*, written for Chinese students and teachers, is now easily available as far as China, the audience he intended to reach. Our recent publication of the 1999 postings of *Interface*, assembled into a paper volume similar to those of any other major journal, is also available and each has been a wonderful learning experience for our students, and carried the Berglund Center, in a sense, back to the future.[10]

If you are interested in writing about how the impact of the Internet has impacted your particular field of work (or of play?) in the 1990's, please see our call for proposals and join us in seeking to better understand what has followed Internet Time.

---

10 See first: http://www.amazon. com/Interface-Journal-Education-Commuity-Values/dp/ 0615361676/ref=sr_1_1?ie=UTF8&s=books&qid=1272638005&sr=1-1, Then search: http://www.amazon. com/Jigsaw-III-Intercultural-Pedagogy-Classroom/ as it is temporarily down for minor editing, but will soon be available again at Amazon.

June 2010 – Volume 10, Issue 5

About This Issue

http://bcis.pacificu.edu/journal/article.php?id=692

Articles

Feature: Michael Geraci – *Google Enters the Web Video Fray with WebM*

http://bcis.pacificu.edu/journal/article.php?id=683

Technology: Jenn Hernandez – *Into the Limelight: HD video + DSLRs*

http://bcis.pacificu.edu/journal/article.php?id=685

Education: Mark Szymanski – *Google Earth The Redux: Global Organization*

http://bcis.pacificu.edu/journal/article.php?id=687

Corporate Education: Tom Cockburn, Khosro S. Jahdi – *Leveraging Organizational Learning in NGO-Business Collaboration*

http://bcis.pacificu.edu/journal/article.php?id=688

Book and Site Review: Jeffery Barlow – *Forward to a New Article Series*

http://bcis.pacificu.edu/journal/article.php?id=691

Book and Site Reviews

Jeffrey Barlow – CJ Box 's *Blue Heaven*

http://bcis.pacificu.edu/journal/article.php?id=698

Jeffrey Barlow – John Hart 's *The Last Child*

http://bcis.pacificu.edu/journal/article.php?id=728

Editorial

Jeffery Barlow – *Cyber War and U.S. Policy: Part I, Neo-realism*

http://bcis.pacificu.edu/journal/article.php?id=682

About This Issue

The June issue of *Interface*, the E-journal of the Berglund Center for Internet Studies, has been posted. This is our final issue for the 2009-10 academic year. We now enter the 2010-11 academic year. This issue is appropriately a full one, as was the year itself for us at the Berglund Center.

Our Feature is Michael Geraci's "*Google Enters the Web Video Fray with WebM.*" As Michael says in his piece, "Google's February 2010 acquisition of On2 Technologies and its subsequent announcement of the WebM Project have transitioned the company's role and influence on web video from the equivalent of a TV channel to a movie studio with worldwide reach." As usual Michael discusses the future before it arrives...

Education Editor Dr. Mark Szymansky, of the College of Education, offers us "*Google Earth The Redux: Global Organization.*" In it he introduces not only some of the new functions of Google Earth, but also several sites that will be of special interest to teachers. With the new Google Earth functions, for example, it is possible to follow the migration of the Joads, the family of characters in John Steinbeck's *Grapes of Wrath*, on Google Earth, within a fully enabled educational context.

Our Web 2.0 editor Tom Cockburn, of the Waikato University Management School of New Zealand, writing with colleague Khosro Jahdi presents "*Leveraging Organizational Learning in NGO-Business Collaboration.*" Tom and Khosro provide a perspective on possible partnerships between businesses and even highly political Non-Governmental Organizations.

Berglund Student Fellow Jennifer Hernandez, is also a fine still photographer. In "*Into the Limelight: HD video + DSLRs,*" she considers the implications of some of the new video technology being incorporated in high-end digital SLR cameras and finds them potentially useful for a number of consumers.

Jeffrey Barlow, our Editor, takes a new approach to two book reviews. See the explanation of that approach in this issue at: "*Forward to a New Article Series: 'Edgar and the Internet.'*" *The books are Box*, C.J. *Blue Heaven*, New York: St. Martin's Press, 2007. Edgar Prize Winner for Best Novel, 2009., and Hart, John. *The Last Child.* New York: Minotaur Books, 2009. Edgar Prize Winner for Best Novel, 2010. Each of the two books is excellent, but the review article contains plot spoilers...

Jeffrey's editorial in this issue, "*Cyber War and U.S. Policy: Part I, Neo-realism.*" Discusses recent events relating to U.S. strategies for Cyber War in light of an important book, Richard A. Clarke and Robert Knake's *Cyber War: The Next Threat to National Security and What to Do About It.* Jeffrey believes that while the Neo-realist school of policy makers may well have prevented nuclear war for the last half-century, they are still far from solutions to the problems presented by Cyber War.

Please see our Announcements for a wide range of materials relevant to the impact of the Internet, including a piece from our legal editor, Leonard DuBoff, "*Is Someone Copying Your Website or Other Copyrighted Material?*"

As always, we hope that you find this issue of *Interface* useful and entertaining. Look for us again in August.

The Berglund Center for Internet Studies,
Pacific University

Google Enters the Web Video Fray with WebM

Michael Geraci

In May of 2005, a little video sharing web site known as YouTube was released to the public. Within a year, 100 million videos were being watched every day on the service. Google purchased YouTube in October of 2006 and as of this writing, 2 billion videos are being watched daily.[1] So it seems unnecessary, even trite, to claim that Google has made video a mainstay on our computer screens. Yet, Google's February 2010 acquisition of On2 Technologies and its subsequent announcement of the WebM Project have transitioned the company's role and influence on web video from the equivalent of a TV channel to a movie studio with worldwide reach.

What's most interesting about this latest move by the Googlenaut is that the WebM Project seeks to make video on the web free of any licensing requirements, plug-in demands, and corporate control. It is the boldest move to date to make video creation and playback on the Internet freely accessible to producers and consumers, a move that, according to one source "...has thrown the video world into turmoil".[2]

"What's the big deal?" you may be asking. Hasn't video been free all along? After all, don't we post and watch videos on YouTube and other similar services without paying royalties or fees? Not really. Any time we create a digital video and post it on the web, we are, at some point, formatting that file to conform with technological standards put in place by corporations that lay down the ground rules for that videos encoding. Such ground rules exist because they, in small or large doses, benefit the private interests of the corporations that created them.

YouTube, for example, has always defaulted to Adobe's FLV video format for encoding. Files that do not conform are converted upon upload, and their playback in the web browser requires that you have Adobe's Flash Player plug-in installed. Apple, on the other hand, maintains and promotes its QuickTime architecture and its preferred web format, H.264. This format reportedly costs some browser developers $5 million in licensing fees to include natively in their software.[3] Google's WebM Project hopes to break video free from any single private interest and place its future development in the hands of everyone.

When Google bought On2 Technologies,[4] they became the proud owners of the VP8 video codec. A codec is a software algorithm for packaging the massive amount of data required for video files in a way that makes their delivery and playback manageable on a variety of software, hardware and network

---

1 http://youtube-global.blogspot.com/2010/05/at-five-years-two-billion- views-per-day.html

2 http://www.iptvtimes.net/2010/05/google-open-sources-vp8.html

3 http://news.cnet.com/8301-30685_3-10440430-264.html

4 http://en.wikipedia.org/wiki/On2_Technologies

infrastructures. The VP8 codec is valued at $120 million and Google's WebM Project, announced at its annual I/O Conference in May 2010, releases it as open source software under a BSD-style royalty free license.[5] It is effectively free.

VP8 is a definite step forward in video encoding. It puts Ogg Theora, the current open-source video format, to shame, and with Google's might and cache behind it, it has the potential to quickly catch up with FLV and H.264 in terms of its speed, quality and functionality. At the announcement, Google demonstrated that encoding speed in VP8 is already equal or better than in H.264 and with higher quality results, but certain features that some have come to enjoy with the commercial formats, such as full-screen viewing, closed captioning, and live streaming are not implemented in the codec. These omissions will be fodder for the development community to tackle and, in my opinion, don't present too great of a challenge given the rate of development we've seen in other areas where Google has played a stewardship role, such as mapping and calendaring.

But don't go hunting for WebM video just yet. While video now gets to be free, the clients you use to traverse the web and interact with its content are still mostly provided to you at the whim of the corporations, many of who would rather not see WebM become de rigueur on the web. Your browser, for one, is the biggest hurdle that WebM must clear. As of May 2010, Google Chrome (naturally), Firefox, and Opera have released WebM compatible builds of their browsers. Apple and Microsoft have not given any word as to their support of WebM in Safari and Internet Explorer. Steve Jobs' only response, when asked about Google's release of VP8 was to reference a blog post[6] that indicates that VP8 does not currently stack up against H.264.

If you're using a WebM-capable version of Chrome, Opera, or Firefox, you can participate in YouTube's HTML5 Video Beta by signing up athttp://www.youtube.com/html5. If you have some digital videos that you want to convert to the WebM standard to see it for yourself, you can download the open source conversion utility FFmpeg at http://www.ffmpeg.org. As other hardware and software companies adopt the WebM standard, we'll start to see WebM options proliferate in the video eco-system. For example, Skype will move its video stream over to WebM,[7] and Adobe has recently announced[8] that Flash Player will support VP8 encoded content, which indicates that their Creative Suite applications will likely play ball with Google's initiative, if only to spite Apple (but that's another story).

Finally it's worth noting that like any other open source technology, the potential for less than well-meaning uses for it are cause for concern. In a September 2009 article,[9] CNet refers to a Symantec report that "around 10 percent of the trojan

---

[5] http://www.webmproject.org/about/
[6] http://x264dev.multimedia.cx/?p=377
[7] http://skypejournal.com/blog/2010/05/19/codec-wars-peace-breaks-out- skype-uses-googles-free-on2webm-video-codec/
[8] http://blogs.adobe.com/flashplatform/2010/05/adobe_support_for_vp8.html
[9] http://news.cnet.com/8301-1009_3-10356421-83.html

market is now open source." According to the IPTV Times[10] even open source video can become a carrier of malicious code. Could YouTube become an instant and worldwide threat to computer security in the future? With 2 billion views per day, let's hope not.

The SDK, software developer's kit, and developer community are accessible on the WebM site at http://www.webmproject.org. Non-developers can learn about the project, gain access to encoding utilities and keep up with the project's progress on the site too.

Further Reading

The WebM Project Home Page: http://www.webmproject.org/
Information Week, "Google Gives Web $120 Million Gift":http://www.informationweek.com/news/infrastructure/traffic_management/ showArticle.jhtml?articleID=224900400

Google I/O session information, "WebM open Video Playback in HTML5":http://code.google.com/events/io/2010/sessions/webm-open-video-playback- html5.html#

CNet.com, "WebM and Google's Web-video plan (FAQ)":http://news.cnet.com/8301-30685_3-20005466-264.html

[10] http://www.iptvtimes.net/2010/05/google-open-sources-vp8.html

Into the Limelight: HD video + DSLRs

Jenn Hernandez

Berglund Student Fellow, 2007-2011

A few weeks ago I was asked how I'd like my performance of a form in a local sport karate tournament to be captured: "Would you like me to take video, or photos?"

The inquirer was not a hired videographer nor a photographer with thousands of dollars of fancy equipment in tow—it was my fiancé armed with his new Canon T1i digital SLR (or DSLR),[1] which he is learning to use taking a photography class at his school. I opted for photography, by the way, because he's getting to be pretty good shooting in manual mode, and I'd rather not see myself in video, EVER.

Last year, when I bought my Nikon D5000,[2] I was not aware of the addition of HD video, though it had HD video capabilities; my intended use was strictly still photography. (I am a photography major, after all.) Now I'm thinking about playing with the video options a bit, though it'll probably consist of me following my cats around and capturing their silly antics. Hardly award-winning stuff here.

The HD capabilities of SLR cameras have come into the limelight with coverage around a, "juried narrative film prize — essentially the best feature film"[3] for Lena Dunham's *Tiny Furniture*,[4] a film shot completely with the Canon 7D,[5] [6] at the 2010 South by Southwest Music and Media Conference,[7] This opens the doors to all kinds of aspiring film makers, or those who just want to experiment with a media which was probably not previously available to them. I'm thinking college students and recent grads.

In Vince Laforet's blog, he previews a "hybrid shoot" using a Canon HDSLR for video, and one for still documentary photography. Considering all the trouble his crew went to in outfitting the HDSLR, he explains that,

> the LOOK of these cameras is incredibly unique - the video...looks incredibly close to 35mm motion picture film ... Pulling off a similar production with a 35mm film of system would be significantly more time consuming and expensive - there is absolutely zero doubt about it... So

---

[1] http://www.usa.canon.com/consumer/controller?act=ModelInfoAct&fcategoryid=139&modelid=18385
[2] http://www.nikonusa.com/Find-Your-Nikon/Product/Digital-SLR/25452/D5000. html
[3] http://www.nytimes.com/2010/03/20/movies/20tiny.html
[4] http://tinyfurniture.com/
[5] http://philipbloom.co.uk/2010/03/20/film-shot-on-7d-wins-sxsw-juried- best-film-prize/
[6] http://www.usa.canon.com/consumer/controller?act=ModelInfoAct&fcategoryid=139&modelid=19356
[7] http://www.sxsw.com/

there absolutely is reason behind all of this madness. I had to mention this because I sometimes catch myself asking the very same question...and then I see the results on screen and all doubt is removed.[8]

Laforet took photos of the production process for his blog, including an impressive jumble of gear and wires.

Now, I don't mean to say that a DSLR comes cheap, but it's relatively less than a full list of gear needed for a typical video shoot. The package of high quality still photographs AND 24-30 frames-per-second HD video, paired with the support of online video hosting sites, such as YouTube[9] and Vimeo,[10] can make it worth it.

Vimeo led the way in 2007 offering HD video,[11] which became so popular that Youtube and others soon followed suit. The casual internet users began to notice that online videos started to look less horrible in terms of resolution. The following are some examples of the difference in resolutions[12] from standard (360p) to HD (720 and 1080p), as well as some comparisons[13] between HD and non-HD video, if you're still confused as to what the hype is all about. Can you see the difference?

Concerning the subject of HDSLRs, I spoke with the Berglund Center's[14] Senior Video Editor, Greg Boone. This summer he's working on a project shooting an HDSLR for a documentary[15] about a man with Friedreich's Ataxia, who is competing in an elite bike race, the Race Across America (RAAM).[16] Greg told me that the choice to shoot with HDSLRs was based solely on cost—comparing them to other digital medium (for example, Pacific University's Media Arts department's[17] two Panasonic P2s cost about $5500 each, without the cards. A 16 gigabyte card runs $200-300, according to Greg).

Greg told me that he felt some apprehension towards shooting with an HDSLR, not knowing how much the sensor in the camera could handle, not knowing how much it was built to handle, running HD video for long periods of time. He said, "I'm still wary of ... a small body camera doing a full body camera's work. ...maybe I'm just jealous and a little bit ticked off that you can get [the functionality] in a smaller camera".

So why not use those new little camcorders if you want to shoot in HD? I felt immediately like I had asked a silly question. Greg also explained to me that

---

[8] http://blog.vincentlaforet.com/2010/02/24/so-what-does-an-hdslr-hybrid- shoot-look-like/
[9] http://www.youtube.com
[10] http://vimeo.com/
[11] http://www.switched.com/2010/04/06/vimeos-blake-whitman-talks-hd-video- dslrs-and-web-communities/
[12] http://youtube-global.blogspot.com/2009/11/1080p-hd-comes-to-youtube. html
[13] http://gizmodo.com/5102772/youtube-goes-hd
[14] http://bcis.pacificu.edu/
[15] http://theataxian.com/
[16] http://teamfara.blogspot.com/2010/01/about-raam.html
[17] http://www.pacificu.edu/as/media/

HDSLRs were incomparable to small hand-held consumer HD camcorders because 1) there is not enough functionality (these are for people shooting silly pet antics and birthday parties...in HD) and 2) neither is there any quality control past a certain point (the zoom turns to digital zoom without warning, quickly producing grain in the video). Greg went on to assure me that HDSLRs were probably the most reasonable, cost effective choice for the prosumer.

An HDSLR is still a DSLR camera first, capable of shooting HD video. That doesn't mean it's the best option, but for many dabbling in film or just starting out, it is definitely a viable option. I'm sticking to still photography with my DSLR, however, though I can see the advantages of having HD capabilities plus all the options for different lenses and such inherent to the camera functions. Who knows, maybe at a future tournament I'll be the one asking my fiancé: "Would you like me to take video, or photos?"

Google Earth, The Redux: Global Organization

Mark Szymanski

Many of us who grew up in the Pre-Internet Age and loved learning have fond memories of paging through encyclopedias and reading randomly selected entries about places and people we had never heard of, and spinning globes to learn about countries and mountain ranges far from our homes. Occasionally I played a game where I spun the globe and stopped it with my index finger landing on a random place. Immediately after, I would reach for the encyclopedia and look up the city, country, body of water, or mountain range the finger rested on. The entries were laced with declarative facts and perhaps a chart or black and white thumbnail photo. Did you know that the Amazon River is the largest river in the world and the volume of the flow is greater than the next ten largest rivers combined! For full disclosure, I just looked that up on Wikipedia, which required ten seconds of time and a lot of restraint not to click on the hyperlinks and the beautiful satellite image in the entry.

Fast forward to 2010. I'm sitting with my daughter reading a National Geographic article about water on my iPad and she has a question about the Amazon River. She immediately touches the icon for the Google Earth App and quickly, using her fingers, spins the virtual earth to South America and stops it with her finger planted on the Amazon River Basin. She selects the National Geographic Wikipedia layer and zooms in closer to access the featured information about the Amazon River. When she clicks on a place-mark, a balloon pops up that contains an encyclopedia-like paragraph with images, videos, and links to Web Sites.

Google Earth has become a geographically-organized encyclopedia which stands in stark contrast to the alphabetically organized older versions of our childhood and the newer topically organized Internet-based Encyclopedia Britannica.[1] This is yet another example of how our Internet-based environments and tools, in this case Google Earth, allow us to organize knowledge in a way that facilitates exploration into the depth and complexity of a topic. When Google Earth was released in 2005 (yes, five years ago) and in its first phase of development, people were initially excited by what you could see. Stitched together satellite images gave people the chance to be transported to virtually anywhere on earth—virtually. I watched in my classes as students (future teachers) visited places they were most familiar with: their current homes, places they had lived, and other places they had visited. Getting them to think about how to use Google Earth as a learning environment was a challenge, but at a basic level they could now retire the pull down map and use the virtual globe when they needed to. And the wow factor they experienced certainly provided momentum and an indication to me that we were on to something.

---

1 Encyclopedia Britannica, http://www.britannica.com.

Maps and Globes: Layers and Real-Time Geographic Data

The next phase of development for Google Earth was highlighted by efforts to include layers with additional information. This gave the user control over the amount and type of information they wanted to see, like borders, highways, and labels for geographical features. The concept of adding layers to the map that had information made sense to those of us who were able to connect it to the idea of using an overhead projector with a map and layering transparencies with different graphic information that added more information about the map. This was still not an encyclopedia, but sort of a mashup of a map and a globe and a step in that direction. The layers really gave more detailed information about geographic features. Because Google Earth lets you control the altitude from which you view the earth—to zoom in and out—the level of detail is scalable and clearly something that is impossible to do on a physical globe. This was the beginning of the ability to add content; even if it was static, it allowed more depth and complexity to be added to the mix.

The next phase of development, adding real-time data to the layers, was a fundamental shift and added the next great notion that not only could we see what any place on the earth looked like, we could see features of the area in real time. This was made possible because sharing of real-time data began to spread over the web and Google Earth content could be created fairly easily using KML and HTML code. Whether it was foresight or luck, perhaps a bit of both, Google positioned itself for open source development of content. For example, the Unites States Geological Survey (USGS) created a layer called realtime earthquakes that accesses a database of the recordable earthquakes and maps the information in a kml file to create a layer for Google Earth. When you click on that layer, you can see where and when earthquakes have happened within the last 30 minutes, hour, day, and week. The pedagogical power of this layer is to show students that earthquakes are happening all the time around the world as the earth's plates move in small increments and helps them understand how increasingly powerful earthquakes are the result of potential energy being stored in the plates.

Another example is real-time Weather layers. My daughter's class was following The Iditarod Trail Sled Dog Race online and I came in to teach a geography lesson using Google Earth. A student asked if I knew what the weather conditions were like for that day's race. With the Iditarod course map layer already on the earth, I clicked on the cloud and radar weather layers and we saw the real time conditions and speculated about the next day's race based on the position of the clouds and the patterns of movements we were seeing. The students, second graders, were fascinated, but being children of the Internet Age, it seemed to make sense to them because it reflected their developing understanding of how knowledge is organized and immediately accessed in their world. What made this special was not just the up to date information; it was that information was also represented in a real way. It was real-time data used to render and represent real images of clouds in the sky at the moment.

Encyclopedias and Globes: Multimedia Balloons and Crowd Created Content

In the past few years, the number of Google Earth layers full of multimedia rich content has rapidly increased and reflects the current phase of development. This is a direct result of two phenomena. First, the increased amount of content on the web and the Web 2.0 ways in which it is accessible, and second the ability of organizations and common crowds of people to create layers and make them accessible to the world. The newer layers have place-mark balloons filled with encyclopedia-like entries designed to give digestible bits of text and multimedia to viewers with hyperlinks to Web Sites that provide another level of depth and complexity. For example, the Cousteau Ocean World layer has place-mark balloons that mark important locations relating to wildlife conservation. One place-mark on this layer identifies a spot where sea turtles hatch on Europa Island. When you click on the place-mark, a balloon opens that contains a paragraph describing sea turtle hatching on the island, a one minute video of the sea turtles hatching that plays right in the balloon, and a link to the Cousteau Society Web Page with a story on the sea turtles.

They key to making all this work is the Web 2.0 way everything works behind the scenes. The place-mark balloons are created using html code. Anyone can make a layer, save it and share it on the web. The layers and the balloons hold no content other than text and code so the files are very small and easily served out. The video in balloons plays using the embed code of the video. As a result, it's fairly easy to create place-mark balloons if you have the content uploaded and linkable or able to be embedded. The Wikipedia layer works the same way by pulling information from Wikipedia into the balloon. If you geotag a Wikipedia entry, it will appear as a part of the Wikipedia layer in Google Earth.

In addition to the layers included with Google Earth, many people are creating their own layers and posting them for people to download. Students are creating them for projects and assignments in their classes, and groups of educators are creating layers to support content across the curriculum. One example is Google Lit Trips.[2] The Google Lit Trips Web Site was developed to support and serve out Google Earth Layers (kml files) created by teachers and students to support teaching great literature. The layers organized by grade level and labeled with the titles of the books they are meant to support. Anyone can download the layers, which contain place-mark balloons that give multimedia information about a particular place in a story. For example if you download the kml file for John Steinbeck's *Grapes of Wrath*, you see place-marks that identify important places in the story of the Joad family that travels west after losing everything in the Great Depression.

The teacher who created the layer, Jerome Berg, uses the place-mark balloons in two ways. First he uses them to enrich the reading with multimedia content. The balloons have historical photos from the era specific to the geographical location of the place-mark and links to Web Sites with additional information. Second, he

---

[2] Google Lit Trips, http://www.googlelittrips.org.

embeds questions that require students to think in more deep and complex ways about what they were reading. In the place-mark balloon that identifies the location of the Joad family home they lost to the bank as a result of the dust bowl, he asks a questions that prompts students to think about symbolism in the story: What characteristics of monsters does Steinbeck associate with banks? This also creates an opportunity to guide student's thinking as they read through a new piece of literature. It is as, he states on his site, an experiment in teaching great literature.

As the Internet continues to grow by simply connecting more and more computers and servers, the task of organizing knowledge still falls to the people. In just five years, Google Earth has unintentionally morphed into the gathering place for a new geographically organized encyclopedia and a place to go virtually anywhere we want to go and learn more about it in an instant. And thankfully, you can still spin the globe, stop it on any random spot with your finger, and find out about that place.

Leveraging Organizational Learning in NGO-Business Collaboration

Tom Cockburn and Khosro Jahdi

Introduction

Despite the fact that there have been research reports by others such as Development agencies, the research topic on collaboration between Non-governmental organizations (NGOs) and the private sector has received relatively little attention from academic researchers until quite recently.[1] Often seen as having divergent, if not contradictory values and goals, there have been a number of changes in the global environment which have driven these institutions closer together of late. The aim in this paper is to examine ways of leveraging inter-organizational learning between NGOs and the private sector, with a focus on the use of Web 2.0 technology.

Firstly, we will briefly define what is to be understood by organizational learning, business and Non-Governmental Organization (NGO) and an outline of the somewhat contested concepts of Corporate Social Responsibility (CSR) and the so-called 'Triple Bottom Line' (TBL). Secondly, we will give an overview of some of the general drivers of such collaborative arrangements, organizational learning lessons drawn from both the literature and from case examples before thirdly, focusing on examples of how Web 2.0 technology has been used by NGOs especially.

Definitions and terms used

Learning, broadly defined as including how an organization gains new knowledge and responds to its environment, including both explicit and tacit forms of knowledge and learning, can be said to apply, to varying degrees, in all organizations. Such learning may happen in discrete episodes or events, in cycles or continuously at an individual level, a team/departmental level, or it may be at a corporate or even a sectoral level within an industry. Thus learning encompasses experiential and process components as well as outcomes.

Huber[2] suggested that there were four integral processes relating to organizational learning. These are knowledge acquisition, information distribution, information interpretation, and organizational memory and they should be understood and applied in broader rather than a narrowly restrictive

---

[1] Borwankar, A and Velamuri, S.R. (2009),The potential for management development in NGO-private sector partnerships, Journal of Management Development, Vol. 28 No. 4, pp. 326-343.

[2] Huber, G.P. (1991), Organizational Learning: The Contributing Processes and Literatures, Organization Science, Vol. 2, No. 1, February

manner as he suggests had heretofore been the case in much of the then current management literature.

For example he rejected the conceptualization of organizational learning as always intentional, explicit means or processes whereby employees improve their workplace potential, their performance of tasks or their overall task effectiveness[3]. Such learning may be positive or negative, deliberate or accidental, rational, non-rational, emotional, behavioral, in explicit or implicit forms.

He also stresses that organizational 'memory'; the store of available or shared knowledge recorded and retained within the organizational systems and processes, is critically important. Knowledge that resides in a database still must be accessibly-connected to the right people in the right context so that it can be classified as learning.[4] This includes digitized learning that is accessible to the organization as a whole or to relevant teams or sub-units within the organization. In the case of partnerships, the inter-organization knowledge-sharing is also critical as are the shared processes, systems and types of data, information or knowledge being shared.

Corporate Social Responsibility (CSR) definitions continue to evolve and to incite criticism and support in almost equal measure. However, for our purposes we define CSR as a stakeholder—based approach to self-regulation which means that companies monitor their behaviour against benchmarks of ethical, legal and international norms of best practice. This seems to be in line with the nub of most definitions in use and those most often cited.[5] [6] Usually, then, there is a statement of intention with respect to aligning corporate missions and strategies with their practice in key areas so as to construct a 'Triple Bottom Line'.

The Triple Bottom Line (TBL) concept has received a wide variety of attention ranging from praise for its ability to conceptualise Corporate Social Responsibility (CSR) as well as criticism for lacking currency and/or applicability.[7] However, the concept is invariably cited in CSR literature. John Elkington[8] claims to have devised the term in 1994. The TBL concept is that corporations should provide an annual, transparent report incorporating auditing data on the 3Ps: Profit, People and Planet. The report should be available to the general public as well as to shareholders. That process was envisaged as allowing the public to develop an informed opinion about the social

---

[3] See note 2.

[4] Siemens, G. (2005), Connectivism: A learning theory for the Digital Age,International Journal of Instructional Technology & Distance Learning, Vol 2, No. 1

[5] Clarkson, M.B. E (1995), A Stakeholder Framework for Analyzing and Evaluating Corporate Social Performance, The Academy of Management Review, Vol. 20, No. 1, January, pp. 92-117

[6] Carroll, A. B (1999), Corporate Social Responsibility Evolution of a Definitional Construct, Business & Society, Vol. 38, No. 3, 268-295

[7] Norman, W and MacDonald, C (2003), Getting to the Bottom of 'Triple Bottom Line', Business Ethics Quarterly, Vol. 14 No.2, pp.243-62.

[8] Elkington, J (1998), Cannibals with Forks: The Triple Bottom Line of 21st Century Business, Stony Creek CT: New Society Publishers.

and environmental 'footprint' of a business. In short, the TBL agenda examines more than the traditional economic contributions of companies' by including data on their positive and negative impact on society and the environment.[9]

The defining characteristics of an NGO are not undisputed but can be said to include the following features:

- An advocacy role and function as a core purpose and mission, i.e. NGOs are not simply professional, 'campaign organisers'. Many also have a welfare function relating to the communities with which they engage and on whose behalf they advocate.
- A formal structure and history, not simply organizational 'shells' or temporary entities set up pro tem or for a particular event or one-off task.
- They are, or aspire to be self-governing and have their own constitution.
- They are separate and distinct from governments.
- They may operate locally, regionally, nationally and/or internationally

The ECOSOC resolution 1996/31 which defines the criteria and principles for establishing consultative relationships for NGOs,[10] defines NGOs as: "...any international organization which is not established by a governmental entity or intergovernmental agreement".

The language and practice of private-sector businesses regarding CSR has typically involved tension between actual or perceived instrumental aspects of their activities and the ethical, moral or socially responsible components. Thus the private sector for-profit businesses have often been regarded suspiciously by many activists in NGOs. That mutual suspicion begs then the question 'what brings them to the table to negotiate a partnership or collaborative agreement with business?'

Factors driving them together: enterprise and governance trends

Previously NGOs sought no profits, employed idealists for low pay or volunteers without pay, and are often assumed to be still the same by members of the public. Today's reality is quite different. Senior staff members in established NGOs often earn wages comparable to their nearest counterparts in the private sector. Blood[11] writes that Friends of the Earth's (FoE) 2004 annual income was £5.5 million plus £3 million from major donors which was allocated to a charitable education trust. The figures for 2008 were £6,720,000 and £7 million respectively. For many large NGOs this has led to other business-like features emerging, for example, NGO 'commercial' units dealing with their business and

---

[9] See note 8.

[10] ECOSOC (1996), Consultative Relationship between the United Nations and non-governmental organizations, http://www. un.org/ esa/coordination/ ngo/ Resolution_1996_31/index.htm , last accessed 27th September, 2009.

[11] Blood, R (2004), Should NGOs be viewed as 'political corporation'?Journal of Communications Management, Vol. 9, No. 2, pp 120-133.

merchandising. Thus, some NGOs are beginning to adopt the practices and to resemble for-profit businesses.

The Directory of British Associations' figure for registered NGOs in Britain was over 7000 in 2004.The figures for Brazil and India were 210,000 and a million respectively. The rapid rise of NGOs in the 1970s coincided with that decade's 'entrepreneurial explosion', as it witnessed the birth of Greenpeace, Friends of the Earth (FOE) alongside the likes of Microsoft and Apple.

Edwards[12] cites three major reasons for the phenomenal growth of NGOs as follows:

1. A combination of abandoning the notion that free trade and liberalisation is the only means of alleviating poverty and ensuring growth, with an increasing realisation that NGOs are no longer there to 'pick up the pieces' and so forth.
2. An increasing realisation too that the involvement of NGOs can act as a cost effective PR activity as well as forming a useful partnership.
3. The growth in general public mistrust of governments and businesses alike, i.e. a move away from 'government' to 'governance'.

On the business side, there are different drivers encouraging collaboration with NGOs. The mood of the public with respect to business has been changing since the 1990s and there are also increasingly stringent legislative reporting requirements to be fulfilled by companies. Noel Turnbull predicted that in the twenty-first century there would be a new generation of customers whom he called 'generation MM' who would demand that business demonstrate that it is motivated by community interest rather than self-interest.[13]

A Millennium poll of 1000 consumers from each of 23 nations on 6 continents found 49 per cent cited corporate citizenship factors such as business ethics, environmental practice and labour management issues as the most significant determinant of their impressions of companies.[14] Only 32 per cent were most influenced by basic business investment factors such as finance, management or size of enterprise.

We should, however, take care in interpreting what consumers say about their motives and beliefs as the statements may not eventuate in practice. Others suggest that many consumers say they want to be socially responsible but when

---

12 Edwards, M. (2000). NGO Rights and Responsibilities: A New Deal for Global Governance, The Foreign Policy Centre/NCVO, London.

13 Turnbull, N (1996), The millennium edge: Prospering with generation MM. Sydney: Allen and Unwin.

14 Marlin, A.T (2000), Social and Ethical Quality in a global Competition, Conference paper in: Innovation, Manufacturing and Services: How to improve ethical quality? IESE, Graduate School of Management, University of Navarre, 9-10 Nov

it comes to buying various items their actions belie their noble intentions.[15] Nevertheless, against that scepticism there have been changes in many social mores and the social and ethical norms of acceptability, too. There does however appear to have been a social change in the direction of greater concern about corporate governance and potential harm to the civic society.

On the business leadership and management side of the equation, there is also some evidence of a growing realization of the need for changes in traditional thinking. The McKinsey Quarterly global survey of chief executive officers (CEOs) in January 2006 indicated that 84 per cent of those CEOs surveyed shared many of the views of others in society about the changing role of the corporation.[16] They saw the role of company management as now extending beyond simply satisfying shareholders with good dividends. Nowadays that management role is seen as including corporate social responsibility. Goodwill and respect is an asset on balance sheets and one that pays dividends.[17] Given recent recessionary events this view has clearly not permeated all business sectors equally. However, there are, since the sub-prime crisis, more governmental attempts to impose a responsible governance structure and reporting system in the private sector globally.

Currently, for example, there is an inverse relationship between BP's share of negative media attention and its perceived share of public goodwill as well as its losses from the spill. That is, goodwill is declining and media attacks increasing as the oil spill from their well in the Gulf of Mexico continues to leak millions of gallons of oil into the important fisheries in the area. For business organizations then, a pivotal question often is how can we best maintain public reputations and esteem and counter negative media surveillance whilst returning a profit? A partnership with an NGO and its cause marketing is often seen as a good endorsement to obtain.

There is a motivator for the organization's leaders too, insofar as survival for the twenty-first century CEOs increasingly means learning to take account of the levels of trust they must sustain not only amongst the shareholders but their boards, their employees, relevant trade unions and other stakeholders.[18] The best way for a company and the CEO to ensure goodwill is by acting responsibly and with integrity in the world at-large.[19]

---

15 Devinney, T. M., Auger, P., Eckhardt, G & Birtchnell, T. (2006), The Other CSR [Electronic Version] Stanford Social Innovation Review.http://www.ssireview. org/ articles/entry/the_other_csr/ ,last accessed 27th July 2009

16 McKinsey Quarterly online survey of business executives, January 2006,http://www.mckinseyquarterly.com , last accessed on 4th August 2008

17 KPMG, (2005) Earning Respect, Consumer Currents, issue 1, p16,http:// www. kpmg. co.uk/ pubs/Consumer%20 Currents%20 issue%2001.pdf, last accessed on 7th May, 2010

18 Lucier, C., Wheeler, S and Habbel, R (2007). The Era of the Inclusive Leader, Strategy + Business magazine, issue 47, summer, Booz Allen Hamilton, http://www. strategy-business. com/ press/ article/ 07205?pg=0,last accessed 10th May,2010

19 BITC/Radley Yeldar (2007), Taking shape—the future of Corporate responsibility communications, http://www.bitc.org.uk/ resources/ publications/ future _of _cr _comms. html , last accessed on 3rd May, 2010

At the same time, in the current epoch, publicity is as crucial to NGOs' success as it is for many other organizations and businesses. NGOs cannot 'grow' their membership, their funding or their sphere of influence without the use of the various communication media. Environmental NGOs as well as the IPCC (Intergovernmental Panel on Climate Change), for example, have often been accused of stretching facts to create a greater media impact. That perceived tendency alone may distort their agendas and has led some NGOs to develop media relations departments for PR, as Steinberg notes.[20] In terms of the potential power and influence of NGOs, Beaudoin writes:"...management can.... no longer ignore the 'opinion factor' in decision making, nor should they disregard opinion trends which NGOs represent. On the contrary, effective management decisions must include NGOs as actors in the markets- whether this market be of products, services, shares or labour- and consider opinions when shaping decisions."[21]

There will most likely always be some tension between business-led CSR and some of the NGO demands for more ethical business activities. Some of that tension is from what is regarded by many corporations as unrealistically high expectations of NGOs about what constitutes "doing the right thing" and not simply "doing things right". Although there are potential risks of conflicting interests, there are nevertheless still many different, viable options for partnerships and some international standards have been defined.[22] Tennyson and Harrison suggest that there are at least seven distinct categories or types of partnering, reflecting different cultures, industries and evolving roles for the respective partners involved in each project over time.[23]

What has been learned by both sides to date?

Recent research at the University of Massachusetts Dartmouth Center for Marketing research,[24] shows that US charitable organizations have continued to race ahead of the corporate sector and academia in their adoption and use of social media. In 2008, eighty-nine percent of charitable organizations were using some form of social media including blogs, podcasts, message boards, social networking, video blogging and wikis. A majority (57%) of the organizations are

---

[20] Steinberg, N. (2001), Background Paper on Congo's and QUANGOs and Wild NGOs [Electronic Version],http://www.wfm.org/WFM_NEWS/wfmpubs.html , last accessed 17th April, 2010

[21] Beaudoin, J.P (2004), Non-governmental organisations, ethics and corporate public relations, Journal of Communications Management, Vol. 8,No. 4, pp 366-371

[22] Forster. (2005). Collaboration in context-A report on the use of international standards in NGO-Business partnerships [Electronic Version],

[23] Tennyson, R and Harrison, T (2008), Under the Spotlight [Electronic Version]. International Business Leaders Forum, http://www.iblf.org/ resources/ general. jsp? id=124049 , last accessed 25th April, 2010

[24] Barnes, N.G and Mattson, E. (2010), Still Setting the Pace in Social Media: The First Longitudinal Study of Usage by the Largest US Charities, University of Massachusetts Dartmouth Center for Marketing Research,http://www.umassd.edu/ cmr/ studiesresearch/ socialmediacharity.cfm , last accessed 12th May, 2010.

blogging. Forty-five percent of those studied report social media is very important to their fundraising and are increasingly aware of the importance of Web 2.0 strategies in meeting their organizational objectives. Use of online video increased by 38 percent; social networking increased by 47 percent in the 2007-2008 period. Sixty-six percent of respondents in 2007 and 75% in 2008 reported that they regularly monitor the Internet. This compares with 54% of colleges and universities and 60% of the Fortune 500 corporations.

Some use is also made of virtual communities grown in Second Life or conferencing facilities such as Protosphere for virtual meetings, planning and collaborating on projects. There are various non-corporate as well as corporate websites brokering communications assistance, networking connections and specialist technical staff recruitment for projects, donations or philanthropic gift-giving such as CTCVista, a US project begun in 2000 and aimed at assisting low income domestic (US) communities. Social networking sites such as Facebook and MySpace have also been utilised to launch and sustain various fundraising, online volunteer recruitment as well as protest campaigns, for instance in Belarus.[25] And other forms of cyber-activism in Morocco.[26]

However, as Morosov[27] warns, the potential for cyber-activism is not entirely without risk as despotic regimes are also capable of using the technology to spy on dissidents. Online volunteering demographics indicate that more than 40 percent are from developing countries.[28] Use of Twitterand Blogs such as Global Voices[29] is increasingly being used to get instant alerts and commentary on emerging events such as the Haiti earthquake or the riots in Iran. There are also NGO alternatives for staff in developing countries such as FrontlineSMS an inexpensive mass SMS service targeting the NGO market (http://www.frontlinesms.com/).

So, in conclusion, a brief summary of the organizational learning about NGO-Business collaborations is given below:

1. Determine clearly and explicitly the type of partnership both parties are engaged in and the related contractual and moral obligations or expectations and assumptions. Obtain an explicit, written partnership agreement in plain language as this will help build relationship learning and accountability[30] [31] [32] as well as trust and reduce potential conflicts of expectations on either side.

---

[25] Morisov, E. (2009), How dictators watch us on the web, Prospect,http://www. prospectmagazine.co.uk/2009/11/how-dictators-watch-us-on-the-web/ ,last accessed 12th May,2010.
[26] Jankari, R. (2009), Amnesty International trains young Moroccans in cyber-activismhttp://www.magharebia.com/cocoon/awi/xhtml1/en_GB/features/awi/feature s/ 2009/08/05/feature-02, last accessed 9th May, 2010
[27] See note 25.
[28] UN online volunteering service, http://www.unv.org/, last accessed 11th May, 2010.
[29] Global Voices, http://globalvoicesonline.org/ , last accessed 10th May, 2010.
[30] Clarkson, M.B. E (1995), A Stakeholder Framework for Analyzing and Evaluating Corporate Social Performance, The Academy of Management Review, Vol. 20, No. 1, January, pp. 92-117.

2. Reflect and review the relationship regularly to respond appropriately to the demands of changing goals, roles, accountability and responsibilities over the lifecycle of the partnership [33] [34].
3. Plan and discuss joint goals, information-sharing, strategic change and anticipated learning for both partner organisations.[35] [36] The learning should be aligned with strategic goals at all levels from individual, team or corporate level to inter- organization level. Partners should build a shared, organizational knowledge exchange and 'memory' system.[37] [38]
4. Avoid being 'All talk and no action' either in planning stages (so that endless prevarication or procrastination results in a form of organizational 'paralysis by analysis') or in executing agreed tasks, division of labor and joint activities.[39]
5. Avoid a simple 'playing safe' approach where the partnership is seen as being concerned mostly with mitigating your risk or accountability; which may surface in your reluctance to accept greater influence and responsibility for your impact on the partner organisations' strategy.[40]
6. Whilst human resources are limited in small organisations, perceived over-dependence on one or two individuals can be a sign of limited 'buy in' to collaboration or accountability.[41] [42] [43]
7. Ensure constructive feedback is provided at each stage of partnership development process. Known but as yet unresolved conflicts of interest could indicate a lack of honesty in feedback between partners or unwillingness to address tough issues in the partnering relationship and so reduce trust.[44]

---

[31] Kohtamäki, M. (2010), Relationship governance and learning in partnerships, The Learning Organization, Vol. 17 No. 1, pp. 41-57.
[32] Unerman, J. and O'Dwyer, B. (2006), On James Bond and the importance of NGO accountability Accounting, Auditing &Accountability Journal, Vol. 19 No. 3, pp. 305-318.
[33] See note 30.
[34] Edwards, M. (2000). *NGO Rights and Responsibilities: A New Deal for Global Governance*, The Foreign Policy Centre/NCVO, London

[35] Borwankar, A and Velamuri, S.R. (2009),The potential for management development in NGO-private sector partnerships, Journal of Management Development, Vol. 28 No. 4, pp. 326-343.
[36] Clarkson, M.B. E (1995), A Stakeholder Framework for Analyzing and Evaluating Corporate Social Performance, *The Academy of Management Review*, Vol. 20, No. 1, January, pp. 92-117.
[37] Van Winkelen, C. (2010), Deriving value from inter-organizational learning collaborations, The Learning Organization, Vol. 17 No. 1, pp. 8-23.
[38] Prugsamatz, R. (2010), Factors that influence organization learning sustainability in Non-profit organizations, The Learning Organization, Vol. 17 No. 3, pp. 243-267.
[39] Kohtamäki, M. (2010), *Relationship governance and learning in partnerships, The Learning Organization,* Vol. 17 No. 1, pp. 41-57.
[40] Unerman, J. and O'Dwyer, B. (2006), *On James Bond and the importance of NGO accountability Accounting, Auditing &Accountability Journal,* Vol. 19 No. 3, pp. 305-318.
[41] See note 39.
[42] See note 40.
[43] Edwards, M. (2000). *NGO Rights and Responsibilities: A New Deal for Global Governance*, The Foreign Policy Centre/NCVO, London.
[44] See note 39.

8. Limited or poor governance and accountability structures or allowing one side to take precedence hampers delivery on partnership priorities.[45 46 47]
9. Poor technological infrastructure limits and obstructs services offered and delivered, development of staff and options for reducing costs as well as accessing potential funds or other collaborators.[48]
10. Cyber activism can be a double-edged sword and thus security has to be an issue of concern for both activists and potential corporate partners.[49]

There are still other issues to be addressed in the terms of the collaboration of NGOs with other stakeholders in businesses. For instance, NGOs are not universally popular with trade unions who sometimes believe that the NGOs usurp the legitimate role of the union as representative of the local workforce. There are specific concerns regarding corporate codes of practice devised between companies and NGOs, as undermining pre-existing or emerging labour legislation or voluntaristic collective bargaining frameworks and potential loss of staff following the end of collaborative projects.[50 51 52]

Concluding remarks

There are no 100% guarantees of success in any partnership endeavor. There is always going to be that frisson of danger that a PR disaster — such as when an NGO is seen as getting too close to a misbehaving corporation-could occur. However, we believe that there are growing similarities between the private sector and NGOs as well as a more vigilant public which are pushing them towards ethical collaboration. At present these drivers outweigh the suspicions each side has of the other. Thus there is the potential for win-win relationships to be developed. That is, providing each side deals with the other in good faith. If so, then they may jointly be able to leverage their skills and resources for the benefit of all stakeholders and the planet.

---

[45] See note 43.
[46] See note 39.
[47] See note 40.
[48] Barnes, N.G and Mattson, E. (2010), *Still Setting the Pace in Social Media: The First Longitudinal Study of Usage by the Largest US Charities*, University of Massachusetts Dartmouth Center for Marketing Research, http://www.umassd.edu/ cmr/ studiesresearch/ socialmediacharity.cfm , last accessed 12th May, 2010.
[49] Morisov, E. (2009), How dictators watch us on the web, Prospect,http://www. prospectmagazine.co.uk/2009/11/how-dictators-watch-us-on-the-web/ ,last accessed 12th May,2010.
[50] Compa, L. (2004). Trade unions, NGOs, and corporate codes of conduct, Development in Practice, 14(1&2), 210-215.
[51] Borwankar, A and Velamuri, S.R. (2009),The potential for management development in NGO-private sector partnerships, Journal of Management Development, Vol. 28 No. 4, pp. 326-343.
[52] Clarkson, M.B. E (1995), A Stakeholder Framework for Analyzing and Evaluating Corporate Social Performance, *The Academy of Management Review*, Vol. 20, No. 1, January, pp. 92-117.

Forward to a New Article Series

Jeffrey Barlow

Introduction: This piece is the beginning of an extended project to analyze the impact of the Internet over the last decade (2000-2010) by a study of mystery or detective fiction. The works analyzed will be those awarded an Edgar Allan Poe award ("The Edgar") by the Mystery Writers of America. In this forward we discuss the reasons for the project and our methodology.

There are many well-established current methods for evaluating the impact of the Internet. Most of them involve measuring classes of users, penetration of technology, numbers of web page, etc. Such measures have the advantage of facilitating comparisons between time periods and groups of users, among many others. However, such approaches fail to come to grips with the human mind. What has the Internet really meant to us, and how can we understand its impact on our thinking, our dreams, and our behavior?

In an effort to say something useful about these more humanistic impacts for some time we have been reviewing selected works of fiction at Interface to gauge the penetration of the Internet into popular culture.[1] We have learned a great deal from doing so, and hope that readers of the reviews we have published have done so as well. We will continue to use this approach, but it has serious limitations.

These pieces have been reviews, with all the conventions demanded in writing in this genre, such as avoiding too much depth of coverage lest the reader not want to read the book, feeling obliged to lean over backwards to identify some audience which might find the work useful or entertaining, and above all avoiding "plot spoilers".

We propose a more systematic and potentially more extensive approach: the analysis of a very old and popular genre of writing, mystery or detective fiction. The genre is almost inevitably about something that is not known—who the villain is, or if already known, why he or she did the deed among multitudinous other possibilities. It is also often about communication between individuals as these facts are uncovered. Both of these functions, discovery of information and communication, have been transformed by the Internet.

Before the Internet, the working methods of sleuths,[2] while somewhat variable, were limited. The author had, as a matter of course, to give his or her detectives strong personalities and appropriate approaches to their work.

---

[1] See a partial list of these reviews beginning at:http://bcis.pacificu.edu/journal/results.php?cx=006538533868481694997%3Am_lmeb1yh-g&cof=FORID%3A9&ie=UTF-8&q=fiction+review&sa=Search&siteurl=bcis.pacificu.edu%2Fjournal%2F#1290.

[2] Of course, we could not avoid researching this term to see if it would give us some clue to the genre; we found that it apparently has a number of origins, is a very old term,

Some sleuths (the clueless detective) blunder around making a nuisance of themselves until the perpetrator literally hits them on the head or shoots them in some non-vital part of their anatomy, as does Mickey Spillane's Mike Hammer. Others take the opposite approach, seeming disengaged while collecting seemingly unrelated evidence or innocent facts and ratiocinate until the answer to the central puzzle is revealed, like Rex Stout's Nero Wolfe. Most do a bit of both, of course, like Conan Doyle's Sherlock Holmes who relied in part on "modern" techniques such as physical analysis of evidence, and in part on logical reasoning.

Each of these archetypes has thousands of variants, old and new. But for almost all, the journey begins with the crime, works through the known facts to discover the unknown, and thence to the solution.

But now we have the Internet. Much of the process of collecting evidence, drawing connections, uncovering related crimes, identifying missing twin brothers, and all the other common "MacGuffins"[3] are now potentially digital. The protagonist need no longer send his or her faithful sidekick to the library, call a contact at the morgue of the local newspaper, secure a police file through marginally legal means, or any of the many variants of these search techniques because the data is now often a click away.

Mystery fiction, then, offers a very rich trove of materials from which to better understand the impact of the Internet. The problem, as usual with deep collections of data, is how to sort it. In our earlier reviews, we have simply scanned mass-market works, identified particular authors, often those with good technical experience and credentials, and evaluated their works.

This approach has been broadly educational, and permitted us to follow some authors over time, seeing, for example, how Jeffrey Deaver's paraplegic sleuth, Lincoln Rhymes, adapts to the impact of digital data, or how Michael Connelly's Jack McEvoy, an old-style investigative journalist, reacts to the death of traditional print journalism while dealing with the deaths of the victims of an arch-hacker.[4] But this selection process has several shortcomings.

First, it takes works dealing with the Internet and tries to generalize from them while avoiding the many counter-examples of works which completely ignore

---

perhaps Scandinavian in origin, and most often seems to mean "to track" in its early usages, some of which are very early indeed. It includes many variants, such as "sleuthhound" for a type of Bloodhound. Oxford Universal Dictionary and many web sources.

[3] A MacGuffin is defined as "a plot element that catches the viewers' attention or drives the plot of a work of fiction" at: http://en.wikipedia.org/wiki/MacGuffin I find this Wikipedia site sufficiently authoritative, although it deals largely with films, because of its thorough analysis of plot elements in a great number of films, and a bibliography which is satisfactory, though it could be stronger.

[4] See review essay of Michael Connelly's work, *The Scarecrow*, and Jeffery Deaver's, *The Broken Window: A Lincoln Rhyme Novel* at: http://bcis.pacificu.edu/journal/2009/07/article.php?id=96.

the Internet or so fabulize it that little can be learned. It also easily becomes repetitive as it often focuses on writers who have developed sleuths whose key ability is sophisticated hacking as has John Sanford in his "Kidd" series,[5] and more recently the marvelous Stieg Larrson, whose detective team is composed of a female hacker and a dogged male journalist.[6]

The mass-market approach also all but ignores the issue of quality in the works, requiring that I sometimes review poorly-written works, usually in the Neo-Gothic "Beware The Internet" genre, just because they do focus on the Internet.

That approach has been useful, but flawed. It is time to develop a more systematic methodology. In this series (Edgar and the Internet), I select books not for their known relationship to the Internet, but for their worth as meritorious examples of the genre itself. I will analyze winners of the Edgar Allan Poe awards ("The Edgar"), given by the Mystery Writers of America.[7]

Each year there are six nominees and one winner in a number of categories related to detective fiction. We have selected two categories, Best Novel Nominees and Best First Novel by an American Author.[8] We think it possible that there is could be a difference in the treatment of the Internet by older, more established authors, and those winning the award with a first novel.

We must, regretfully, ignore works that have no possibility of referring to the Internet, because of the time in which they were set. For example, Malla Nunn's 2010 Edgar nominee, *A Beautiful Place to Die*, is set in one of our favorite environments for fiction, South Africa, but in 1952, so it is not useful to our research.

However, some other books which do not touch upon the Internet we will analyze, simply because the author has worked out some clever way of not

---

[5] See review of, John Sandford, *The Hanged Man's Song*, at: http://bcis.pacificu.edu/journal/2004/05/sandford.php.
[6] I refer here to Larrson's "*The Girl Who...*" trilogy. See titles at: http://www.amazon.com/s/ref=nb_sb_noss?url=search-alias%3Daps&field-keywords=stieg+larrson&x=0&y=0.
[7] The awarded is broadly recognized as the highest honor given to authors in this genre. See the organization's web site at: http://www.theedgars.com/. The awards have been given since 1946, though the categories have often changed. See the database as the group's site above.
[8] The five best novel runner-ups were: *The Missing* by Tim Gautreaux (Random House - Alfred A. Knopf); *The Odds* by Kathleen George (Minotaur Books); *Mystic Arts of Erasing All Signs of Death* by Charlie Huston (Random House - Ballantine Books); *Nemesis* by Jo Nesbø, translated by Don Bartlett (HarperCollins) and *A Beautiful Place to Die* by Malla Nunn (Simon & Schuster - Atria Books). The winner was *The Last Child* by John Hart (Minotaur Books); The best first novel runners-up were: *The Girl She Used to Be* by David Cristofano (Grand Central Publishing); *Starvation Lake* by Bryan Gruley (Simon & Schuster - Touchstone); *The Weight of Silence* by Heather Gudenkauf (MIRA Books); *Bad Day for Sorry* by Sophie Littlefield (Minotaur Books - Thomas Dunne Books); *Black Water Rising* by Attica Locke (HarperCollins) and the winner was In the *Shadow of Gotham* by Stefanie Pintoff (Minotaur Books).

mentioning the elephant in the room in order to sustain his or her plot. The authors of the books we analyze in this issue each worked out a clever way of restricting the impact of the Internet upon their plot, while not entirely ignoring it either.

We will present our findings regularly in Interface as review articles, complete with plot spoilers rather than as pure reviews, and then eventually synthesize our conclusions in a longer review essay, perhaps, like the Edgar awards themselves, on an annual basis.

We are feeling our way in this series, and it may be some time before I can say anything very useful. But I can say that I have read through five of the twelve nominees in the two categories for this year, and found them all marvelous reading, though some are irrelevant to this project. In short, I have repeatedly encountered the fabled book you cannot put down.

In this issue, we begin with an essay comparing *Blue Heaven* by C.J. Box, the 2009 Edgar winner for best mystery novel, and the 2010 winner, *The Last Child*, by John Hart.

C.J. Box's *Blue Heaven* and John Hart's *The Last Child*

Reviews by Jeffrey Barlow

Warning: Plot Spoilers ahead. The two books discussed below are excellent, and if you enjoy the genre of detective or mystery fiction, you should read them before reading this article. I am not reviewing the works for potential readers, but discussing them in light of their treatment of the Internet.

We begin this series with the Edgar Award winning work from each of the past two years. Reading them affirms my trust in the award jury; they are each, in their own way, excellent. While they deal with the Internet in somewhat different ways, they also reveal what may be an emerging trope, a common theme in dealing with the Internet in a modern setting in detective fiction, discussed below.

C.J. Box, the 2009 Edgar Award Winner for Best Novel for his work *Blue Heaven*, can appropriately be said to be an old hand in this genre. He has a dozen or more works out, and is said to be a "Wyoming writer" because so many are set there, his home. His most noted character, Joe Pickett, a Wyoming Game Warden, has appeared in ten such works to date.
[1]

The protagonist of *Blue Heaven*, however, is not Joe Pickett but Jesse Rawlins, a down-on-his-luck rancher trying to save the family spread from developers who would turn it into a subdivision. Rawlins is drawn through a number of coincidences into a very complicated series of events, beginning when two children who have witnessed a murder flee to him for refuge.

The background context of *Blue Heaven* is not an uncommon one in regional fiction: the threat posed by newcomers to the pristine wilderness—in this case, pristine after the Arapaho and the Ute were satisfactorily subdued, of course.

The looming threat is not simply outsiders, but modernity itself. The evildoers are a group of retired rogue cops from the Mother of All Evil Cities, Los Angeles. These "live in woodland fortresses with satellite television and Internet, wells for water, backup power generators at the ready." (51)

However, things could have been worse. As the protagonist, Jesse Rawlins, muses, "Better ex-cops than actors or dot-com heirs..." (26) Jesse, by comparison, is a determinedly retro rancher on a spread started by his Grandfather. Jesse has preserved all the cowboy virtues and talents, including riding, roping, and when necessary, shooting.

One cause of the ultimate failure of the evil outsiders is to under-estimate the locals, seeing them "...as jaded Europeans thought of Americans: as child-like,

---

[1] See his web site at: http://www.cjbox.net/.

boisterous, too insular to appreciate what they had...(91) In short, the urbanites are too modern to appreciate the strengths of the primitive.

Along with the rogue cops, other potential evildoers are also present, including, possibly, sexual predators. (66) The rogues commit a murder—observed by the fleeing children—of one of their own group, but manage to divert suspicion onto a hapless walk-on character by painting him as a suspected sexual predator, and just possibly a child killer as well.

One of the cast of characters is Villatoro, a former cop from Los Angeles. Although retired, he has been investigating the original crime that brought the rogue cops together and financed their move to Wyoming, the robbery of the Santa Anita race track. While he is suspicious of the retired cops, he has no evidence.

Villatoro's trusty female assistant in Los Angeles, who is helping him "follow the money" in the racetrack robbery, turns up the critical evidence on the Internet after he arrives in Montana. She does this by a "Simple Google Search" on two of the rogue cops which reveals a crucial connection between them and the stolen money, providing an explanation for the local crimes at the same time.

So the modern, including the Internet, does have its place, even in Wyoming. However, critical elements of the action, particularly plot bits that require having a good horse or two handy, depend very much on the lack of digital services, particularly cell phones.

Blue Heaven then, is a variant of the cowboy mystery story, a sub-genre within detective stories in general, but in this case, one that employs the Internet to further its plot. It also, however, removes modern digital culture from the scene at key points so that the plot can be sustained and the forces of traditional local values triumph over digitally enabled newcomers.

The winner for 2010, John Hart's *The Last Child*, is quite a different work, but relies on a similar trope about the tension between the modern and the primitive, including the Internet. This book is very elegantly written and attracted a number of classy reviews, like that by the Richmond Times-Dispatch that it "...rises to serious literature." Indeed it does. Set in a relatively isolated area of North Carolina, it has a brooding Faulknerian air about it,

> As a writer, Hart presents himself as a good deal more cosmopolitan than does Box. Although he too lives in the setting of the novel under discussion here, he is not a regional writer. He has written three New York Times best sellers, including *The Last Child.*[2]

As in *Blue Heaven*, the plot is initially driven by a mystery involving missing children. One of these, a girl, has been missing for almost a year, but Johnny, her increasingly troubled and troublesome brother, has been searching for her block by block through the small town in which he lives, and its rural environs by local

---

[2] See the author's web site at http://www.johnhartfiction.com/.

bus and bicycle. This area is to an extent, timeless in that old prejudices and ancient hatreds are more salient than cell phones or computers, which are not mentioned at all for most of the book.

The characters are deeply troubled; the woods about them are dark, the rivers slow and murky. The bloody past, including the post-civil war extinction of a local colony of freed slaves, weighs heavily on the region. Males drink too much and abuse their wives, and even the good-guy policemen resort to vigilante justice when the law gets complicated.

For much of the book, the time frame itself is indeterminate. Then, finally, a reference to "Amber Alert" reveals that it is set after 1996, when the child for whom the alerts were named was killed.[3] This point sets the stage for additional material dealing with the Internet and computers.

Although a number of children are missing from the surrounding area, no clear pattern has evolved, because most of them are runaways or girls not known to be in the area where they were taken. Johnny finally uncovers one predator, in the time honored detective tradition of blundering in at just the wrong moment, but this man turns out to be only one of two, collectively acting out a dark evil that goes back to their murder of "Small Yellow" in the Vietnam war.

The real organizer of the serial crimes turns out once again to represent, in a sense the evils of modernity. He has picked his victims through his position as head of security at a mall with elaborate closed-circuit TV surveillance. His attempt to destroy his home computer while under surveillance finally betrays his trove of child pornography and he is brought down.

The plot is far more complicated than suggested here, as the Southern Gothic nature of family life and race relations continually figures in plot twists and turns. But once again, we see the Internet as a sort of Deus ex Machina,[4] both a source of key information and a key MacGuffin in the plot itself. However, as in Blue Heaven, it is kept carefully in the wings until it is needed.

We must, of course, be careful not to draw too many conclusions from these two works with regard to the impact of the Internet, but one possible trope is revealed by even this limited analysis. The Internet is unavoidable in even relatively isolated plot settings provided that the time period includes it. But plotting often demands that it be carefully restricted in its use until crucial moments. The trope then, requires some explanation for the failure to employ the Internet until the necessary moment.

---

[3] See http://en.wikipedia.org/wiki/AMBER_Alert. As I am interested only in the date, this site suffices, but in addition it is very thorough and well documented.

[4] "(Latin for "god from the machine"; plural: dei ex machina) is a plot devicewhereby a seemingly inextricable problem is suddenly and abruptly solved with the contrived and unexpected intervention of some new character, ability, or object."
From http://en.wikipedia.org/wiki/Deus_ex_machinaAlthough this site contains a warning that it may contain some undocumented original research, it serves well for my limited purpose here and is in fact quite generously documented.

In *Blue Heaven*, for example, it was critical that neither the Los Angeles retired cop Villatoro nor his assistant run the critical Google search on the rogue cops who had moved to Montana until well after he arrives in the region. He knew they were there—it was their presence that brought him to town. But he did not know that they were in league in circumstances that enabled them to wash the money from their robbery until the search is run from Los Angeles. In the meantime, he has become friends with Jesse, the heroic rancher, and the two can engage in the action together.

Without the delay in the Google search, the solution would have been reduced to the simple one of contacting local law enforcement authorities. However, this plot could have driven only a brief police procedural, not a heroic struggle between the traditional and the modern.

The author solves this dilemma by locating the Internet firmly outside the arena of action, implying that it is not really that accessible in the Wyoming setting in which the work occurs. The Internet user—the timeless trusty detective's assistant—who turns up the critical information is working in Los Angeles at the time, and is a very minor character.

The 2010 Edgar Winner, *The Last Child*, does not really even tell us the Internet has in fact been developed. We transit from the eternally timeless brooding south into post-1996 North Carolina, but we are never certain precisely when, according to my own reading. The assumption, however, is that it is the present. Computers are available and some of the plot turns upon them.

The police have law-enforcement computer networks, there are any number of worried adults missing friends and children, but nobody sits down at a computer to run searches that may well have revealed the pattern of missing multiple victims. The kids themselves, who carry much of the plot, are all very active, athletes and outdoors types, immune to the many appeals of the computer.

Both of these works then, are presumably set in a time when the Internet is as influential as it is today, but the authors provided effective means of setting it largely aside as a factor in the plot until it was necessary to them. Those means are somewhat similar too, in that both regions are isolated and it is implied, backward. Whether this is indeed an internet-related trope will depend on much more reading in this series.

Cyber War and U.S. Policy: Part I, Neo-realism

Editorial by Jeffrey Barlow

An editorial based in part on a review of Richard A. Clarke and Robert Knake, *Cyber War: The Next Threat to National Security and What to Do About It.* Ecco, 2010.

Introduction

"Cyber War" is breaking out on many fronts—at least as a concept for discussion and abundant press coverage. Whether, in fact, it is an emergent form of international conflict and we are fighting one now depends on whom you read, and how they choose to define the concept. We will define it below.

Mike McConnell, a former Vice-Admiral in the U.S. Navy, the former Director of the National Security Agency for the Clinton administration and the Director of National Intelligence for the Bush administration, believes that Cyber War has broken out, and that the United States is losing.[1] The British also believe this is happening, and like McConnell, that the enemy is the Chinese.[2] Very much on the other hand, however, Howard Schmidt, the recently appointed cybersecurity chief for the Obama administration has said: "I think that is a terrible metaphor and I think that is a terrible concept..."[3]

But whether Cyber War is or is not real, and has or has not already begun, policy dealing with it is rapidly being formulated. The just-released (May 28th) National Security Strategy of the Obama administration discusses it in some detail.[4] The U.S. has appointed its first "Cyber War General," Lt. General Keith B. Alexander, who also heads the National Security Agency, and the U.S. Air Force has reassigned thirty thousand troops to "the frontlines of Cyber Warfare".[5]

Clearly, it is important to examine the concept of Cyber War in some detail. We have argued at Interface that the concept of Cyber War as currently used is so

---

[1] See McConnell's article which has driven much of the furor at: http://www.washingtonpost.com/wp-dyn/content/article/2010/02/25/AR2010022502493.html.

[2] See Michael Evans, Giles Whittell, "Cyberwar declared as China hunts for the West's intelligence secrets" in The Times Online, March 8, 2010 at: http://technology.timesonline.co.uk/tol/news/tech_and_web/article7053254.ece.

[3] Ryan Singel, "White House Cyber Czar: 'There Is No Cyberwar' at: http://www.wired.com/threatlevel/2010/03/schmidt-cyberwar/.

[4] Download the full PDF document from: http://www.whitehouse.gov/blog/2010/05/27/a-blueprint-pursuing-world-we- seek. While cyber security is discussed throughout, see especially page 27 in this version of the document.

[5] See Peter Beaumont, "US appoints first Cyber Warfare general, The Guardian, May 23, 2010 at: http://www.guardian.co.uk/world/2010/may/23/us-appoints-cyber-warfare-general.

broad that it is of little value.[6] Recently, two highly respected authorities with a great deal of clout as policy analysts have examined the concept and discussed appropriate policy in a new work, *Cyber War: The Next Threat to National Security and What to Do About It*. Richard A. Clarke, the primary author, was prominent in counter-terrorism and particularly in Cybersecurity for both the Clinton and Bush administrations, and his co-author, Robert Knake, a member of the Council on Foreign Relations also has a considerable history of writing and speaking about Cyber War.[7]

This work is very welcome because Clarke and Knake give us a very straightforward and usefully limited definition of Cyber War which carefully excludes much of the Chicken Little gabble often found in the popular press: "When the term 'Cyber War' is used in this book, it refers to actions by a nation-state to penetrate another nation's computers or networks for the purposes of causing damage or disruption."[8] That cautious sentence alone makes the book worthwhile and we expect that it will dominate academic and policy discussions for some time, on the order of Herman Kahn's 1960 work, *On Thermonuclear War*, which defined many of the policy issues around nuclear war.[9] *Cyber War: The Next Threat to National Security and What to Do About It* may in fact be responsible for some of the recent developments we discussed above, such as the creation of the new cyber commands.

This piece is not a review of Clarke and Knake's work, but a start at laying out the various schools of thought on the issues around Cyber War. We utilize it as a scaffold here because of its lucidity, its highly organized development, and its approach, which places Cyber War into a historical context which gives many useful insights into what might be appropriate policies. At the same time, we recognize that many other authorities, or at least highly influential figures, like Mike McConnell mentioned above, disagree, and will cover their positions in Part II of this editorial, to be published in August in *Interface*.

Neorealist views of Cyber War

Clarke and Knake's theoretical orientation is what policy wonks would call "Neorealist".[10] The Neorealist position has been intellectually powerful and its policies have arguably prevented nuclear war, the potential ultimate breakdown

---

[6] See "*Cyber War or Cyber Vigilantism?*" at: http://bcis.pacificu.edu/journal/2010/03/article.php?id=660.

[7] See his pages at the Council at: http://www.cfr.org/bios/15502/robert_k_knake.html.

[8] Highlight Loc. 186-92 (Kindle edition).

[9] There is a commendably brief analysis of the book with good attributions found at: http://en.wikipedia.org/wiki/On_Thermonuclear_War.

[10] The earlier Realist school evolved into the Neorealist position. There is an excellent Wikipedia page (because carefully written and very well founded in appropriate research) to be found at: http://en.wikipedia.org/wiki/Political_realism The Realists believe that all states are inherently competitive, must ultimately depend on their own forces for security, and that attempts to restrain violence through international organizations or agreements are ultimately naïve. The Neorealist position is defined below in the text.

of the international order, since 1945. It is the history of this position and its contributions to preventing nuclear war which make it a useful place to begin analyzing Cyber War.

The Neorealists, like the classical Realists, see the world as an inherently dangerous place as states inevitably must compete for power in a disorderly international system. But the Neorealists believe that threat of instability can best be constrained by a stable world order in which a small number of powerful states (ideally two—a bi-polar structure, the classic example being the world of the Cold War) limit potential conflict out of self-interest. Particularly important to such stability is open communications and as many agreements and treaties as can be signed.

However, although the development of the concept of Cyber War promises to be fully as threatening and destabilizing to the world order as was nuclear war, the two are obviously quite different. Cyber War presents a number of new challenges to the international order, and to both Realism and Neorealism.

For example, there was never going to be any doubt as to the question of whether or not nuclear war had occurred, nor very little as to who was responsible. But cyber assets are non-physical and there are many ways to attack them unobserved, or at least un-identified. When Japanese forces attacked Pearl Harbor, the situation was easily understood; attacks on an enemy's military assets have often been a cause of war. But it is not always clear how to detect an opening skirmish in Cyber War.

Cyber battles then, are always going to have important elements of ambiguity. For example, in 2009 when somebody, perhaps acting from China, hacked into a defense contractor's computer and stole the plans for a radically new U.S. fighter plane, the F-35,[11] was this an act of war, of espionage, or of commercial piracy?[12] What was an appropriate response and against whom should any counter attack be launched?

If Cyber War is elusive, however, Clarke and Knake demonstrate that it is nonetheless real, and presents an imminent danger. Moreover, the United States, they believe, is woefully unprepared to create appropriate policies to help maintain stability in a world in which minor states, even criminal gangs or politically-motivated individuals, have the power to launch a devastating attack against a great nation.

---

[11] See: Siobhan Gorman, August Cole, Yochi Dreazen, "*Computer Spies Breach Fighter-Jet Project*," The Wall Street Journal, April 21, 2009, at: http://online.wsj.com/article/SB124027491029837401.html.

[12] Clarke and Knake, - Highlight Loc. 2601-8 Kindle edition. Those following up source materials in a Kindle edition are aware, of course, that these can vary somewhat depending on various settings, though they should be close to the location I have marked here. I assume this to be even truer if the work were read on another brand of electronic reader, but am not certain that it is.

We are, of course, discussing a form of violence markedly below the attacks on Hiroshima and Nagasaki, but Clarke and Knake present a number of terrifying possibilities:

> "If they take over a network, cyber warriors could steal all of its information or send out instructions that move money, spill oil, vent gas, blow up generators, derail trains, crash airplanes, send a platoon into an ambush, or cause a missile to detonate in the wrong place. If Cyber Warriors crash networks, wipe out data, and turn computers into doorstops, then a financial system could collapse, a supply chain could halt, a satellite could spin out of orbit into space, an airline could be grounded. These are not hypotheticals. Things like this have already happened, sometimes experimentally, sometimes by mistake, and sometimes as a result of cyber crime or cyber war."[13]

From these examples, the authors try to evolve appropriate Neorealist policy responses. Here again Neorealist precedents began to break down, because, as the authors point out, Cyber Warfare capabilities are highly asymmetrical. Cyber War is more similar to terrorism or guerrilla warfare in that regard than to classical set-piece battles or nuclear exchanges.

The United States has an unsurpassed offensive capability in "kinetic warfare," the traditional form of war in which one side launches metal or explosives at the other from various platforms ranging from a compound bow to a nuclear missile. Kinetic war has usually depended upon economic power. The United States outspends the rest of the world put together on kinetic weapons. But Cyber War enables very weak states, which are in every other regard basket cases, to wreak great damage, perhaps without even being caught doing so.

As in kinetic warfare, the U.S. has unparalleled advantages in offensive Cyber War because of its technological base. But, unfortunately, it also has one of the weakest defenses against Cyber War of any nation. It simply has too much to defend and there has been little or no planning or coordination in protecting the vast American complex of digital systems.

Warfare has always proceeded as a sort of on-going struggle between defense and offense. Nuclear weapons permitted no real defense; offense has been king since August 1945. The ultimate Neorealist peacekeeping strategy since than has been to ensure not that one could survive an attack, but that no aggressor could survive a counter-attack. It was on that calculus that cold-war treaties and agreements were founded.

But Cyber War again is different. Presuming some minimal level of investment, even in off-the-shelf technologies available on line from hundreds of sources, very weak states, terrorist groups, and even individuals, potentially have offensive capabilities.

---

[13] Highlight Loc. 1091-95 (Kindle edition).

Given that minimal offensive ability, the economically less developed a potential aggressor is, the better its inherent defenses. North Korea accordingly has powerful offensive capability and a very strong defense—dire poverty; it has very little to "take down." States with offensive Cyber War capabilities include not only unified Europe, rising China, and a renascent Russia, but also many very minor powers like North Korea.

The most powerful potential enemy, in the judgment of the authors, is first Russia, then China. Each of these brings special advantages to Cyber War. The Russian government might be said to have great offensive power; it has access to the most sophisticated hacker gangs in the world,[14] and in some cases seemingly overlaps with them.

The Chinese state, too, has a superior potential offense. It, according to Clarke, has trained thousands of civilian Cyber Warriors,[15] particularly among patriotic Chinese youth, markedly expanding the already very high capabilities of China's formal military forces. Defensively, they have such control over their own Internet that if they chose to "go first" in a Cyber War, they could simultaneously disengage from the global Internet, markedly reducing retaliatory action from others.

Part of the undeniable hysteria over Cyber War then, is the dawning realization that under the impact of the Internet, very important balances have changed. The United States, long dominant in kinetic warfare, may be critically behind in an important emerging form of combat.

In the Neorealist perspective, lacking a strong defense, what is a nation like the U.S. to do to ward off cyber attacks? At present our strategy consists of the Old Time Religion of warfare, threatening to "go kinetic". That is, if you do marked cyber damage to us, we bomb, perhaps even nuke, you. Clarke and Knake lay out the policy alternatives thusly:

> "If we do not have a credible defense strategy, we will be forced to escalate in a cyber conflict very quickly. We will need to be more aggressive in getting our adversary's systems so that we can stop their attacks before they reach our undefended systems. That will be destabilizing, forcing us to treat potential adversaries as current ones. We will also need to take a stronger declaratory posture to try to deter attacks on our systems by threatening to "go kinetic" in response to a cyber attack, and it will be more likely that our adversaries will think they can call that bluff."[16]

---

[14] See our review of Joseph Menn's work, Fatal System Error, at: http://bcis.pacificu.edu/journal/2010/02/article.php?id=648.
[15] While it is irrelevant here, I personally find this perspective overstated. I do not believe the relationship between the Chinese state and the Patriotic Youth hackers to be that formal, though it is clearly a useful one to the state, however loosely organized it may be.
[16] Highlight Loc. 2367-71.

Clarke and Knake think this a momentarily necessary policy, but ultimately limited.

Clarke is deeply suspicious of those in the American military who draw quick comparisons to past war-fighting technologies in which cyber space is viewed simply as another battlefield:

> "...the U.S. military in general repeatedly characterizes cyberspace as something to be dominated. It is reminiscent of the Pentagon's way of speaking of nuclear war in the 1960s. The historian of nuclear strategy Lawrence Freedman noted that William Kaufmann, Henry Kissinger, and other strategists realized that there was a need then "to calm the spirit of offense, potent in Air Force circles...[whose] rhetoric encouraged a view of war that was outmoded and dangerous." That same sort of macho rhetoric is strong in Air Force cyber war circles today, and apparently in the Navy as well."[17]

Conclusion: Neorealism Fails?

The Neorealist framework of Clarke and Knake gives their concept of Cyber War great resonance. Many of their analogies place it into a deceptively familiar framework, that of the post-war era dominated by kinetic technology. Accordingly, the reception of this book has been overwhelmingly positive;[18] some think it almost prophetic. Clarke, of course, is an ideal candidate for Prophet, at least among policy wonks, having repeatedly attempted to draw the incoming Bush administration's attention to the dangers presented by Bin Laden well in advance of the 9/11 catastrophe. He was, however, largely ignored.

When we survey Clarke and Knake's Neorealist policy prescriptions, we get some insight into how it was that, despite Clarke's prescience prior to 9/11, his dire warnings went unheeded. The authors propose actions that would require creating a new political order, internally and externally. They call for vast changes in the relationships between peoples and their governments, and between all governments, worldwide. Internationally, a whole new series of treaties and organizations would be necessary. These sweeping calls for action render the authors very vulnerable to critics.

The greatest fear and the worst weakness of Neorealist strategic thinking with regard to nuclear war, however, was always simply that things would get out of control either through accident or miscalculation. This weakness makes Neorealist solutions even less likely to succeed in preventing cyber conflicts.

There are too many differences between kinetic war, especially nuclear war, and Cyber War. Neorealism depends on a limited number of rational actors who

---

[17] Highlight Loc. 689-95.

[18] See the review of Clarke and Knake at "Armageddon Online" at: http://www.armageddononline.org/cyber-attack-electronic-pearl-harbor.html.

work together to restrain violence. The potential theater of Cyber War is global; the potential aggressors, legion.

The problem of attribution is itself ultimately unsolvable given current technologies. There are too many ways for an attacker to cloak his or her identity, or worse, to spoof it—lay electronic trails to another—so that a misattribution occurs, resulting in a cyber equivalent of an erroneous counter-strike which would truly result in Cyber War.[19]

But even if the problem of misattribution were solved, there are simply too many players and too many conflicting ideologies. Some of these are so non-materialist—and hence in an important sense irrational, unconfined by the bounds of reason alone—as to render their adherents totally disinterested in stability.

We think then, that the Neorealist model holds out little prospect of preventing Cyber War, even if Clarke and Knake nonetheless believe it to be the best hope. Even if Neorealist prescriptions, that is, a system of treaties and agreements buttressed by increasing attention to defense in the case of the United States,[20] offers some hope of eventual security in a world in which Cyber War is a real possibility, it also presages an extended period of what might well be termed "Cold Cyber War". This may well be marked by continual conflicts which all sides hope can be contained to something less than the Cyber War equivalent of nuclear strikes. Here the Neorealist program offers some ameliorative policies. Certainly the more agreements that are arrived at, the better we will all understand the important issues, if nothing else.

We will present opposing views to Neorealism as represented by Clarke and Knake and discuss such criticisms in Part II of this series, to be published in August. Many of these are, we believe, classically "Realist" and posit a world of endless struggle, for the near future marked by continual Cyber conflicts.

---

[19]Some of what are often thought to be Russian Cyber War attacks on break-away political interests, for example, were launched from enslaved botnets in the United States. The electronic trail of the recent violations of Google accounts in China led first to Taiwan, then to the United States, then onto China. Given the unwillingness of Chinese authorities to open up their servers to foreign scrutiny there is no real certainty that the trail ended there.

[20] This is my own reading of the underlying intent of the "National Security Strategy" referred to above.

August 2010 – Volume 10, Issue 6

About This Issue

The August 2010 issue of *Interface* is live and on the web. We are a bit late in posting this month because of circumstances explained in the Director's editorial, "Hacking v. Cyber War." Despite the delays, we think the issue is an outstanding one.

Our Feature is "An NTeQ Lesson Plan for: Exploring The Affects of Persona Upon Ethos through A COTS game "Diablo II". David Georgina, a highly experienced and widely published Instructional Designer, most recently at Minnesota State University, Mankato, has produced a lesson plan for teachers which effectively combines on-line role playing in a commercial off-the-shelf game with improving student understanding of computing, writing skills, and the relationship between persona and ethos.

Jeff Cain of the University of Kentucky, our Social Media editor, offers us "Can Social Media Make You Healthier and Fitter?" Jeff, in addition to being highly qualified in computer science and in pharmacy, is also a fitness buff and has good suggestions for how to answer the perennial question of how best to reconcile a busy work schedule, on-line social life, and fitness.

Two of our Berglund student staff content editors, Sierra Brummet and Lilly Huynh, each produced a hard copy on demand book from electronic materials at the Berglund Center this past academic year. Each used a different program to convert the materials to hard copy and they report on their experiences in "Preparing Print-on-Demand works with Microsoft Word and Adobe InDesign".

Each year the graduating seniors at Pacific University give public presentations of their senior capstone presentations, a culmination of the work in their respective majors. An increasing number of these deal with the impact of the Internet and are suitable for publication in Interface. In this issue we present graduate Kenny Larson's "More than Point & Shoot: A Look at Web-based Communication Strategies for Photographers" in which Kenny, a professional photographer, discusses the use of social media in his work. Kenny offers, we think tips that may well be of use to those starting small businesses in a number of fields, but his fine photography certainly enhances this piece.

Berglund Student Fellow Valerie Horres offers a summary of her research at the Berglund Center on the impact of the Internet on women, in "For Better or for Worse: How the Internet Benefits and Harms Men and Women."

In this issue editor Jeffrey Barlow reviews two quite different books. The first of these is a novel treating a post-apocalyptic world dominated by zombies and bloggers: Mira Grant's *Feed*. The book is very popular at this moment, and we trust the review suggests the reasons that it merits that popularity, and its relevance to the impact of the Internet.

The second review is Jeffrey Carr's work, *Inside Cyber Warfare*. Mr. Carr is an expert in cyber conflict and shows us perhaps a pre-apocalyptic world. His work is very timely given the increasing importance of cyber conflicts.
As stated above, the editorial, "Hacking v. Cyber War." is also on cyber conflicts and follows in part upon the review of Carr's work. Like Grant's novel, it is very much influenced by the War on Terror.

Please see our Announcements for a wide range of materials relevant to the impact of the Internet.

As always, we hope that you find this issue of *Interface* useful and entertaining. Look for us again in September.

The Berglund Center for Internet Studies
Pacific University Oregon

Can Social Media Make You Healthier and Fitter?

Jeff Cain

The obvious answer to the question posed in the title of this article is "no". However, because of my personal interests in both fitness and social media, I have recently discovered the growing influence of Web 2.0 in the health and fitness realm. This prompted me to delve further into how and why social media might be used to enhance the lives of those seeking to make and maintain positive changes in their fitness and health. What I have discovered is that many individuals, companies, and organizations are utilizing social media in exciting ways to help people meet their health and fitness goals.

According to most experts and published reports, Americans are unhealthier now than at any other time in our nation's history, with obesity described as our fastest growing public health challenge[1]. This has reached epidemic levels with approximately 30% of Americans falling into the obese category[2]. The upward trend is attributable primarily to inadequate physical activity, poor eating habits, and changing food alternatives[3]. Obesity-related conditions such as hypertension[4] and diabetes[5] are also increasing, furthering concerns over national health. Fortunately, this has finally come to the forefront of our attention and numerous efforts are underway to reverse this trend. Calls for reform at the federal, state, and local levels include clear and consistent federal recommendations regarding physical activity and nutrition, obesity-prevention programs, and menu-labeling[6].

In addition to governmental interventions, a plethora of grassroots-type efforts from health, nutrition, and fitness companies, as well as individual health and fitness enthusiasts are underway. They are targeting individuals interested in maintaining health and vitality, and providing the resources to make it happen. While these are not public health initiatives, nor are they likely to affect

---

[1] United Health Foundation, American Public Health Association, and Partnership for Prevention. The Future costs of obesity: National and state estimates of the impact of obesity on direct health care expenses. Available at:http://www.americashealthrankings.org/2009/report/Cost%20Obesity%20Report-final.pdf. Accessed June 21, 2010.

[2] Flegal, KM, Carroll MD, Ogden CL, et al. Prevalence and trends in obesity among US adults, 1999-2008. *Journal of the American Medical Association*. 2010; 303(3):235-241.

[3] See footnote 1.

[4] Cutler JA, Sorlie PD, Wolz M, Thom T, Fields LE, Roccella EJ. Trends in hypertension prevalence, awareness, treatment, and control rates in United States adults between 1988-1994 and 1999-2004. *Hypertension.* 2008;52(5):818-827.

[5] McKinlay J, Marceau L. US public health and the 21st century: diabetes mellitus. *Lancet.* 2000;356 (9231):757-761.

[6] Robert Wood Johnson Foundation and Trust for America's Health. F as in Fat: How obesity policies are failing in America. Available at:http://healthyamericans.org/reports/obesity2009/Obesity2009Summary.pdf. Accessed June 21, 2010.

significantly large populations, they may be very valuable to certain individuals with a baseline level of motivation. In turn, once individuals begin to take their own health and fitness seriously, they may positively affect those family members and friends surrounding them. Research has indicated that social support plays a strong role in continued exercise activities. This social support can come in a variety of ways including guidance, encouragement, and providing information[7]. For many, if not most of us, maintaining a healthy lifestyle and adequate physical activity is a daily struggle. Encouragement, accountability, information, and tips may help motivate individuals to sustain proper eating and exercise habits. Social media applications are particularly well equipped to help in these areas. First, they are mediated public spaces where people gather to interact, increasing the likelihood that interested individuals will be exposed to the support. Second, the reduced social inhibition in online settings may make conversations regarding one's health, nutrition, and fitness that much easier. Ease of dissemination, access, and sharing makes applications such as YouTube, Twitter, Facebook, and other social networking applications ideal tools to promote and encourage healthy lifestyles. The following sections highlight several such efforts.

One Company's Approach to Social Media

I first began to notice the social media influence on fitness through my affiliation with a health and fitness company best known for its infomercials. Beachbody®, owned by Product Partners, LLC is the producer of several highly popular home fitness programs including P90X® and Insanity®. In addition to the television promotion of its products, Beachbody® has developed a social media strategy that provides motivation, encouragement, and support for its customers. The company has a proprietary social networking site, Teambeachbody.com, that connects Beachbody® product customers and offers a plethora of discussion forums, nutrition support, and motivational tools. The WOWY (Work Out With You) gym is an online venue to log workout routine schedules. Users can document the workouts and their scheduled times, as well as invite others to join them virtually. Encouraging users to plan and schedule their workout times in advance is a method to increase commitment to the exercise routines. From a motivational perspective, customers can see that they are not alone in completing the workouts, which in some cases may supply that last bit of encouragement necessary for them to follow through with the commitment.

In addition to their social networking system, Beachbody® utilizes a host of other social media applications to promote health and fitness. At the time this article was being written, a search for the term "P90X" on YouTube yielded 5,680 results. The majority of these are from users of the product who were encouraged to record their body transformation as a result of completing the program. While this involved relatively little effort on behalf of Beachbody®, the videos detailing success can be an incredible motivator for others desiring

---

[7] Duncan TE, McAuley E. Social support and efficacy cognitions in exercise adherence: A latent growth curve analysis. *Journal of Behavioral Medicine.* 1993; 16(2): 199-218

similar fitness results. The P90X® Facebook fan page[8] has almost 150,000 fans, contains discussions related to their products and is updated frequently with health and nutrition information. The owner of the company, the trainers, and Beachbody® coaches/consultants, also actively promote fitness and their line of products on Facebook and Twitter. One group of coaches (called The Fit Club Network)[9] blogs, tweets, and uses Facebook to offer numerous support resources for participating coaches and clients. These resources include individual consultations, product reviews, meal planning, and a host of other related activities. Numerous connections among coaches and customers across the country have been made via Facebook and Twitter, which further enhance individual commitment to their health and fitness goals. Supporting and motivating customers to succeed appear to be significant elements of the company's social media strategy.

Motivating through Twitter

There is no shortage of fitness and nutrition experts on Twitter. Likewise, there is no shortage of users who follow those experts. Trainers Jillian Michaels (@jillianmichaels) and Bob Harper (@MyTrainerBob) from the popular television show, The Biggest Loser, have nearly 150,000 and 80,000 followers respectively. Presumably, many of their followers are interested in becoming fitter and healthier and follow the trainers on Twitter because of those interests. The tweets vary, but often combine information with motivation. The example below is a Tweet that was linked to the Jillian Michaels Facebook fan page[10], which by the way is "liked" by more than 350,000 Facebook users.

> "Emotional eating: Create coping mechanisms & recovery behaviors that are life affirming, not self-destructive. Instead of binging join a support group, call a friend, get a massage or do something that makes you feel beautiful like a mani/pedi. Go workout. Exercise boosts your mood & put you back in the power seat. & remove crap food from your house. No matter how bad you feel you can't eat what isn't there."[11]

The power of Twitter and Facebook takes that simple message and instantly makes it available to hundreds of thousands of people. For some who do not have support within their traditional social network of family and friends, this may be the only source of encouragement they receive. By enabling access to advisors, trainers, and health experts, social media's value becomes something more than just a tool to connect with friends and colleagues. It can provide the social support infrastructure necessary for success.

Ms. Michaels and Mr. Harper are just of two of numerous health/fitness advocates on Twitter. Other popular Twitterers include Discovery Health

---

[8] http://www.facebook.com/p90x
[9] http://www.thefitclubnetwork.com
[10] http://www.facebook.com/jillianmichaels
[11] Michaels J. (June 23, 2010). Twitter / Jillian Michaels: Emotional eating: Create coping mechanisms & recovery behaviors that are life affirming, not self destructive... Retrieved June 23, 2010 fromhttp://twitter.com/JillianMichaels/status/16826462380.

(@Disc_Health), Eat This Not That (@EatThisNotThat), and Men's Health magazine (@MensHealthMag). Their tweets are a mixture of motivational statements, links to online resources, and informational tips. According to the research alluded earlier, these are vital elements to the success of many embarking upon exercise and diet programs.

Conclusion

Because of the growing influence in our daily lives, social media applications have become an excellent venue for encouraging healthy lifestyles. Many companies, organizations, and individuals are successfully using these formats to provide motivated individuals with all the knowledge and encouragement needed to make positive differences in their health. While social media can be utilized to support people's health and fitness goals, it is not going to make dinner selections, pedal the bicycle, or lift a weight. Each individual is responsible for his/her own actions and a baseline level of interest and motivation is required to seek these resources initially.

If not readily apparent, it must also be noted that the companies and individuals mentioned above are using social media as a method of increasing brand recognition, and ultimately profits. However, just because some use social media within a business strategy does not preclude the sincere efforts and time that companies, trainers, and other advocates devote toward improving our country's health. We should not dismiss the value of the support, motivation, and encouragement obtained through social media simply because it is another cog in our capitalist society. I would even argue that it is the perfect use of these media, because users on both sides of the equation receive something of value.

Preparing Print-on-Demand works with Microsoft Word and Adobe InDesign

Sierra Brummett (Lead Copy Editor) and Lilly Huynh (Copy Editor)

Preparing for Hard Copy Publication in Microsoft Word© — Sierra Brummett

Through my work at the Berglund Center for Internet Studies, I have had the opportunity to learn a lot of new things and to do a few new things, too.

The articles that come to me through the Center's Google site cover a wide range of topics—though all related in someway or another to the Internet, related technologies, computers, or the business and education side of these (after all, as the Center's name implies, we study the Internet). I have read articles discussing the Internet as media as in webcomics and Role Playing Games, pieces exploring the effectiveness of new technologies in the classroom, the process of cyber-bullying and even censorship matters in China.

But the knowledge I've learned through reading and editing these articles is only a small part of the things I've been able to achieve at the Berglund Center. This year, with the help of Program Director Theresa Floyd and Maria Walters, I put together and published a book using Microsoft Word.

I feel the need to share a little secret with you, readers: I'm not terribly good with computers. Or any technology for that matter. A digital camera that could take a beautiful image in the hands of a friend barely produces a blurry snapshot in mine. My cell phone came with an instruction pamphlet an inch thick and yet the only function I'm capable of figuring out is the dialing and talking part. And I have 2043 songs on my Zune...that I have no knowledge of putting on it. I'm pretty much a stone-age dinosaur in a world full of shiny robots.

So when I was informed that my duties included putting together an entire book comprised of a table of contents, appendices, images, page numbers, and every article published in Interface over the last year, I might have panicked...just a little. How on Earth was I going to accomplish such a difficult task with my basic knowledge?

But working with Microsoft Word proved simpler than I had originally anticipated. Of course, I had a good head start thanks to the talented and very-much-missed, Maria Walters. Maria spent her last few weeks (before moving to a professional position at Intel!) at the Berglund Center setting up the formatting for what would eventually be the hard-copy version of our online journal.

This set-up allowed me to simply cut and paste an article in its entirety from our website to the Word document, highlight, for example, the title and hit the little "Interface Title" button in the formatting palette. The highlighted text would change to the font, size, and position that Maria had set it up for. Simple!

Numbering was all ready to go for me as well. And when I needed to start a new article, I inserted a page break by clicking on "Insert" in the menu bar and then "Page Break."

Another useful function was the ability to compress text where needed to avoid having a lone ("orphan" of "widow") line on an otherwise blank page. And there were a lot of little things that Microsoft Word let me do—lets any user do—to get around more difficult tasks.

Putting the book together seemed an insurmountable task when first I learned of it, but it went very smoothly and surprisingly quickly. I only hit a few snags along the way.

One such snag was formatting pictures. Microsoft Word is meant for documents and, as such, it handles formatting text very well. However, the program isn't quite as well suited in formatting pictures. Thankfully there weren't many pictures, but a few of the articles contained diagrams or charts and the Berglund Center's Authority Seal was included at the head of each article. In order to move around the pictures, I first had to format them to wrap-around the text by right-clicking the image and clicking "Format Picture." This was easy enough to do, but moving the picture around without drastically affecting the layout of the text was quite the challenge. But, again, with a little patience it was an easy enough process.

Another problem I ran into was with the Table of Contents. Whether it was a result of Maria's formatting or obstinacy in Microsoft Word, I had trouble making the table of contents look clean. Specifically, the page numbers appeared after each line of an entry. For example, each entry would have the page number next to the title, and author, and subtitle, etc. And, as I discovered the hard way, even when I took the (considerable amount of) time to delete the offending page numbers, they would reappear the next time I updated the field! We had to remove the page numbers at the very last minute before it was sent to print and after the document was as perfect as it could ever be.

I would however like to commend, again either Maria's MacGyver-ing or Microsoft Word's attention to detail, for updating the table of contents as I added new articles to the document. When I indicated that a specific line of text was "Interface Title," the program automatically inserted the same text into the table of contents in the proper format. Aside from a little bit of fine-tuning at the very end, the table of contents pretty much made itself.

Next year, we plan to add an index to the hard copy. We feel that this addition will make for an easier-to-read hard copy. Of course, this endeavor will be a new challenge for me but so far I've found Microsoft Word to be easy to pick up on quickly. I have no doubt that I will be able to figure out a simple way to create an easy-to-read index. And if I need assistance, I've found the "Help" function in Microsoft Word to be very useful.

Again, just so I'm crystal clear, I do not consider myself to be any sort of authority on putting together books, or Microsoft Word. The purpose of this piece is simply to relay how I found working with the program to be. Maybe a professional, looking for a more sophisticated formatting system would want to look elsewhere for a program to use but for someone with little computer experience and zero previous publishing experience, Microsoft Word was really a wonderful program to work in.

At the end of the day, I was proud of the work we accomplished in putting together the hard-copy *Interface*.[1] There's nothing quite like seeing something you worked hard on and were skeptical of achieving come to fruition. I thank the Berglund Center for Internet Studies for giving me the opportunity to do something that I'd never imagined I could and Microsoft Word for making it simple.

Learning InDesign on the Go — Lilly Huynh

This year at the Berglund Center for Internet Studies we have published several books in an on-demand process at CreateSpace©, a subsidiary of Amazon.[2] I was the staff editor assigned to edit and prepare one of the two books, Yang Desheng's Jigsaw III.[3] As this was an experiment of sorts for us, we chose to use two different programs to publish the two works. One would be done in Adobe InDesign©, one in MS Word©. I was assigned to the InDesign project. My colleague, Sierra Brummett, who published our annual version of Interface[4] in hard copy using MS Word will report on her experience.

My first reaction was that editing a MSS through to hard copy publication (I had also been lead editor on the MSS of Yang's work) is surprisingly enjoyable. There is nothing quite like finally holding a book that you edited and published in your hands. But at the same time, getting to the end result can be time consuming. This is in part because I was asked to utilize a program that I had never used before, Adobe InDesign for Macintosh. The program (I used the CS4 version) is the most commonly used design program in the industry, including newspapers as well as book publishers, we believe. It greatly automates the formatting of a book, but I have discovered from my experience, working with InDesign definitely has its pros and cons.

Working with InDesign made my experience working with a Mac computer more enjoyable. Being a PC user, though, I do not have that much background with the Mac, so trying to run such a complex program with little experience on Macs was a bit of a challenge. I was basically learning the Mac and the program at the same time—learning on the go.

---

[1] http://www.amazon. com/Interface-Journal-Education-Commuity-Values/dp/0615361676/ref=sr_1_5?s=books&ie=UTF8&qid=1295551159&sr=1-5
[2] https://www.createspace.com/
[3] [3] See the work at: http://www.amazon. com/Jigsaw-III-Intercultural-Pedagogy-Classroom/dp/061533590X/ref=sr_1_1?ie=UTF8&s=books&qid=1273782098&sr=1-1
[4] http://www.amazon. com/Interface-Journal-Education-Commuity-Values/dp/0615361676/ref=sr_1_5?s=books&ie=UTF8&qid=1295551159&sr=1-5

Working with InDesign was certainly very educational. It was, however, sometimes learning the hard way. Trying one thing and waiting to see if it works or doesn't was my way of better understanding how InDesign works. There was also a discovery aspect to my learning. It was entertaining to see all the little tasks that the program can do, like reducing the size of the font in the book to fit related material onto one page without being obvious to the reader. Overall, my experience with working with InDesign has been a very beneficial and educational one.

Not having had the opportunity to learn the program beforehand, I discovered along the way, there are certain tasks the program will do automatically—a fact I was originally unaware of. Some of the tasks that it would do on its own included forming a table of contents that would automatically update if a change was made and automatically numbering the pages.

Before discovering that InDesign could do all this automatically, I thought that putting the book together would be a long process on my part. It could take a while to make a table of contents and then go in and number all the pages by hand. One of the things I learned on-the-go was that I was not just restricted to pushing buttons and seeing what works and what doesn't.

Fortunately our Program Manager, Theresa Floyd, also wanted to learn to use InDesign. The two of us together discovered the utility of online tutorials. In addition to me trying to learn how to use the program, having Theresa there made learning on-the-go very beneficial. If there were any online tutorials that explained a particular operation in the program, both of us would look it over together to learn more about the program.

Patience is certainly one skill that I got to practice while working with this program. I have learned, from multiple experiences, that not everything will work the first time. Patience is key in achieving the end result. A few times, some operation would work on the second try but not the first and it was never clear why that was.

In working on this particular book, InDesign had some specific advantages for us. Yang Desheng, the author, is a Berglund Fellow who lives and works in China and English is his second language. As he was preparing the book for the English-speaking Chinese market, there were some particular issues that arose as to language usage, layout, and design. Also, as a linguist, Yang's English usage is very formal and very precise. We had edited his prose into somewhat colloquial English at times, and Yang preferred the formal academic variety (Chinese English is influenced by British English as much or more as by American English, though this is changing.) and this has required frequent editorial changes on our part. InDesign accomplished this with ease.

Unlike more traditional modes of publishing with large production runs, we were able to fine-tune the book repeatedly. It would probably not be unreasonable to say that the current edition is the 10th or 12th one, all made possible by InDesign.

We are very happy with the end result—the book itself. For me, learning to use InDesign will be great advantage as it is the industry standard and I will doubtless be better prepared for continuing to work in publishing after graduation.

We tell ourselves at the Berglund Center that we do quite a few things the hard way, because we are part of an educational institution and learning new programs is part of that goal, even if sometimes there are simpler paths to the same end.

More than Point & Shoot: A Look at Web-based Communication Strategies for Photographers

Kenny Larson

As an academic requirement for graduation at Pacific University, students are required to complete a Senior Capstone Project. The projects are held to a high standard and require thorough academic research. This article will present findings from my project, which focused on building and analyzing online communication strategies for my web-based photography business, ShutterSight Photography. The study focused primarily on social-media marketing, a networking and advertising experience that has earned much attention.

Introduction

With all of the would-be photographers out there, there is a growing number of people who would love to make money with their skills. With as much existing competition as there is, how does one stand out? It's about more than just making good photos. What it takes is an effective communication strategy that fosters an engaged client base via the web. At the conclusion of the study, I found that there are three important components to any photography business: An attractive website, a blog, and a business presence on Facebook.

Website

It is critical for any photography business, web-based or not, to have a website. The truth of this statement is evidenced in the real-world benefits one receives from a well-designed website.

The first of such benefits is that it provides a 24/7 display portfolio for your work. My website was visited 1304 times in approximately 5 months. That would have been the equivalent of 1304 client meetings to attend had this been twenty years earlier, before photography websites were commonplace. That represents a significant investment in time, money and energy to try and impress a client who may or may not choose to purchase my services after all. By making my portfolio easily accessible, clients can view it for as long as they want, and at their own leisure.

Also, the website provides a sense of legitimacy. My website is literally my storefront. My potential clients can see and experience my brand in the convenience of their home. Without a website, my clients would have to invest more time and energy to investigate my business and would more likely choose any one of my competitors who do have a website.

I constructed the website so that the best photos from various jobs are organized into a slideshow that automatically plays once someone arrives at my landing page. This is the most important part of the website because the first photo is what gets them to either look further into my business, or turns them off entirely. I keep the slideshow to ten images and constantly update the selection as I create more.

Facebook Fan Page

The Facebook page that I created provided the primary social media presence for our business. Though the website provided the storefront and business end for ShutterSight Photography, the fan page is the communication hub. It is a single point for information distribution where we were able to interact directly and successfully with our potential clients. By regularly interacting with them it engages them in our brand and creates a more personal experience.

Facebook also delivers very specific demographic information about my client base. When I started this business, my intention was to become an adult portrait photographer. I intended to shoot high school and college senior photos, engagement photos, wedding and events as well as portraits. Much to my surprise, 70 percent of my business has been child/baby photography.

The single largest demographic of ShutterSight Photography's Facebook fans are women between the ages of 25-34 (read on, young mothers). It is no less significant that the single largest male demographic is also within this age range. These are the people who are just starting families and are very excited to capture their children's images. Also, most of the people in this demographic are likely to have finished enough education to have a career and some disposable income.

The trend towards baby photography seems to be self-reinforcing and has forced me to specialize in this genre of photography. My clients, who are always very excited once they receive photos of their children, share them with family and friends. Many of these people are also mothers with young children, which in turn induces their friends and family to seek out my services, further perpetuating the cycle.

Facebook was also my primary advertising mechanism throughout this project. It provides both free and pay-for advertising services, both of which I utilized to different degrees of efficacy.

Free Facebook Advertising

The first form of free advertising is simply inviting friends from personal networks to become fans of the business and join the Fanpage. When one becomes a fan of a particular business, everyone in the joining person's network is alerted to this development in their own news-feeds. This makes them, at least on a very basic level, aware of my business.

The second form is the free advertising spot provided by Facebook. For example, say Tom, Dick, Harry and Mary are close friends. Tom, Dick and Harry join my fan page, but Mary does not. Every so often, when Mary navigates to her news-feed, there will be an advertisement in the upper right portion of the window that says, "Three of your friends like ShutterSight Photography." She sees that Tom, Dick and Harry are fans, and because she trusts their judgment she is curious and navigates to ShutterSight Photography's fan page. This leads to a "friends-of-friends" joining effect and now all of her friends—who may or may not be friends with any other fans of ShutterSight Photography—are alerted to her activity with the fan page, further perpetuating the cycle.

Paid Facebook Advertising

Due to my main client demographic, I thought it prudent to target my advertising at mothers in the Willamette Valley area. I used a pay-per-click model. After setting up the advertisement I set the maximum bid at $2.00 and a maximum daily budget of $8.00, which resulted in several tens of thousands of impressions a day.

When a person navigates to another page within Facebook or refreshes their current page, the Facebook servers run through a bidding process for all advertisements eligible for that particular ad slot. The ad that has the highest bid is presented in that slot. This is the "impression". The advertiser (me) using the pay-per-click model does not actually pay Facebook unless someone actually "clicks" on the advertisement, which navigates the person to the destination (usually a website). If my maximum bid is $2.00, then my ad will continue to bid up to $2.00. If I win at $0.49 and am placed and someone clicks on that ad for that impression, I would owe Facebook $0.49.

I ultimately spent $110.53 in advertising costs using Facebook advertising. The average price-per-click was $1.41. This resulted in roughly 440,000 impressions, meaning my ads were seen 440,000 times. From those impressions I received 77 "clicks", which navigated the interested parties to my main website. This resulted in zero jobs. These findings seem to be echoed in the real world when a businessman was quoted in the *Wall Street Journal* as saying, "My business has received millions of visits, but I haven't made millions of sales."

Unexpectedly, the free advertising proved to be most effective. I don't know that I will continue to pursue pay-for advertising until I become significantly more established. I believe that it may be the scale of my business that makes it financially unfeasible to pay for Facebook advertising at this time. Facebook is an important traffic generator for the ShutterSight Photography website. 15.5 percent of all traffic came directly from the Facebook Fan page. When combined with traffic first directed to the blog, and then from the blog to the webpage, that number jumps to 42 percent.

Blog

The ShutterSight Photography blog has proven to be an important asset for my business. Hosted for free through Google's blogger service, the blog provides another interactive stimulus for potential clients. The blog is where I post messages that would be too long to post on Facebook.

The most effective way to generate traffic for the website was to post "Sneak Peaks" on the blog following a photo shoot. I would take one of my favorite photos of the shoot and edit it first, then post the photo in the blog as a "Sneak Peak". Due to my client base, the subtext is written in a manner that is appealing to young mothers as well as grandmothers.

After the photos have been edited and the client has had them for a few days, I create a public gallery on the website with some of my favorite images from the shoot. I post an announcement on the blog with links to the gallery, and another one of my favorite photos from the session. Both the "Sneak Peak" and the "New Photos!" announcements are posted on the Facebook page.

What both of these blog postings do is keep the brand fresh in the minds of my potential clients. The Sneak Peak photos provide the additional function of exciting the client for the photos that are yet to come.

Conclusion

This project resulted in important findings: First of all, the website, Facebook fan page, and blog all provided important core communication functions for the business. Second, when it comes to online advertising and web traffic in general, views do not necessarily equal jobs.

I have discovered that many other companies are having difficulties leveraging a social media presence, and in some ways social media may be "over hyped".

Due to the relative newness of social media as a marketing medium, there is little scholarly research on the subject. Being that experiences like mine are not uncommon, I don't know that marketers as a whole have actually figured out social media marketing. Until the effects of social media are better understood, it will continue to prove both a boon and a hassle that cannot be ignored.

Resources

"2010 Marketing Trends Study Release." Andersonanalytics.com. (accessed 1 April, 2010). Anderson Analytics found that "70% of marketers are planning new social media initiatives in 2010". I still advertise my business as a portrait photography business that does the aforementioned genres of photography, not just babies. Facebook has since changed this term to "like". This is a recent development that happened after the conclusion of my project. This is the first page people usually see when they log into their Facebook accounts. It contains the status updates and developments or changes that people in their networks have experienced or done.

Sarah E. Needleman. "Entrepreneurs Question Value of Social Media — Marketing via Facebook, Twitter Yields Results for Some, Others Say It's Overrated" *Wall Street Journal* 16 Mar. 2010.

"ShutterSight Photography Blog." Blogspot.com.

Sarah E. Needleman

NTEQ Lesson Plan for: Exploring the Affects of Persona Upon Ethos Through a COTS Game "Diablo II"

David Georgina, Ph.D.

Lesson Title:
Player Ethos Avatar/Persona

Subject Area(s):
English Composition

Learner Experience Level:
First Year College Writing

Time Required:
Six class sessions (15 hrs of class time) plus 6-9 hrs of student homework

Session Summary

In English, literacy is tied to author and the reader (understanding and interpreting symbols for meaning), text—how, why, what, where of story (character, time line, plot, themes...). In digital games, all of this is true plus an additional skill for usage of the tool itself. Learning to utilize the tool for writing is a very important skill for both literacy(s): being able to navigate the internet for research, for definitions, for creative ideas and uses of games, being able to respond thoughtfully in detailed thorough text—plus learning to use the computer to operate the game commands—all this is fodder for literacy discussion in the English classroom.

The educational value of playing the COTS game is in playing to enhance student understanding of how persona affects ethos in writing. This is accomplished with the use of student groups and individualized game playing. The player will develop a relationship with their Avatar in much the same way a writer develops a persona to increase their ethos. There is a direct link with the player and the success of the Avatar which can be used to introduce the concept of persona in writing—from logos, ethos, and pathos—persona is related most closely with ethos or the writer's credibility. As the player becomes more attuned with the Avatar and the Avatar's requirement for successful play, the concept of persona becomes more real to the player—the player is the Avatar in many ways; indeed, the player must become the Avatar while playing or else the focus of the challenge/quest and even the play of the game itself is lost.

Learning Objectives

By the end of this lesson:

- The learner will actually play the game and experience the concept of persona through the use of their Avatars. The player will also be able to distinguish between the narration and the action of the game.
    - Persona as the avatar, Ethos as the player—credibility of the writer based upon the character (avatar) of the writer (player).
- The learner will be able write accurate short answers about the gaming world through researching any of the following:
    - The role of, food, water, protection, belief systems, myths, religions in a community and the power to dominate or organize people.
- The learner will be able to openly discuss through in-class discussions, blogging, or online discussion groups elements of the game and how they compare with elements of fiction and writing.
- The learner will be able to complete online research, write, peer-review, and present research findings to the class (topics related to playing the game).
- The learner will also prepare and present findings through presentation software to the entire class.

Problem Statement

Define through game play how the player/Avatar relationship is similar to the relationship between ethos and persona in writing?

- This adventure game is all about persona; the player is asked to imbue the Avatar with the qualities needed to win challenges. The qualities that the player chooses determine the effectiveness of the play. As the Avatar's actual skill levels (attack, defense, move, magic, life...) improve the player's abilities improve. There is a direct link with the player and the success of the Avatar which can be used to introduce the concept of persona in writing—from logos, ethos, and pathos—persona is related most closely with ethos or the writer's credibility. As the player becomes more attuned with the Avatar and the Avatar's requirement for successful play, the concept of persona becomes more real to the player—the player is the Avatar in many ways; indeed, the player must become the Avatar while playing or else the focus of the challenge/quest and even the play of the game itself is lost.

Standards

The objectives for this assignment (and others which are associated with the COTS games) align with Gagné's Learning Taxonomy including: verbal information, intellectual skills, rules, cognitive strategies and motor skills. The learning outcomes in for the assignments using Diablo II Lord of Destruction-Expansion Pack are in purple text.

1. Verbal information: *Reciting something from memory*
    - The game does not require a player to recite anything from memory; however if in multi-player mode a player may be required to declare status and character of their Avatar and this action necessitate reciting information

2. Intellectual skills
    - Discrimination: *Recognizing that two classes of things differ*
        - Distinguishing the difference between simple demons from special demons

    - Concrete concept: *Classifying things by their physical features alone*
        - Identifying life potions and manna potions for separate storage and usage

    - Defined concept: *Classifying things by their abstract features*
        - The entire game is abstract in application and requires the player to categorize each undead, demon, or monster type challenge with a series of similar and newly acquired actions. Also applying the rules such as boundaries, or elemental realities such as cold, hot...

    - Rule: *Applying a simple procedure to solve a problem or accomplish a task*
        - The game consists of simple problem solving as when demonstrating abilities with weapons or skills; applying the necessary and appropriate potion or scroll in order to open a chest or create a diversion.

    - Higher-order rule: *Applying a complex procedure to solve a problem or accomplish a task*
        - The procedures players use to create complex actions based upon a series of commands—tasks/attacks/defense

3. Cognitive strategies: *Inventing or selecting a particular mental process to solve a problem or accomplish a task*
    - Creating a series of actions for effective fighting which kills a monster and leads to reward.

4. Motor skills: *Performing a physical task to some specified standard*
    - Executing the correct mouse or keyboard strokes to move the character from place

5. Attitudes: *Choosing to behave in a way that reflects a newly-acquired value or belief*

- Electing to kill, quest, don better equipment are all attitude based. The game demands user emotions to challenges.

Resources

Computer-Related:
- Computers in the lab with the Diablo II games installed
- Access to the teaching platform required for this Composition course
- Discussion groups created in the teaching platform
- Email for student to student and instructor inquiries
- Online internet access
- Search capabilities
- Power Point (other presentation technologies)
- Website access for cheats and additional play materials
- MSWord

Paper-Based:
- The final group paper on ethos and persona will be printed out.

Human Resources:
- Fellow students within assigned groups
- Teacher contact
- Online gamer groups

Hands-on Materials:
- Access to Diablo II web site
- Internet Access
- Manual

Handouts:
- Basic instructional manual on how to play game
- Assignment sheets for:
    - research paper,
    - persona/ethos exercises,
    - presentations

Other:
- None

Computer Applications

Computer Application	Activity
MSWord	Students will write a group paper in on ethos and persona and how the COTS game assisted their understanding of both concept and usage.
Power Point	Students will present findings from the game play and introduce their Avatars and their game play development

	(relationship to their writing)
COTS Diablo II – Expansion Pack	Students will play the game through the first level
Discussion Groups	Students will comment, inquire, assist and debate their game play with members of their group.
Website/Internet search functions	Student will search websites for gaming Help and Cheat codes used in COTS Diablo II

Activities and Procedures

The activities are for focusing upon the player's use of the Avatar. The purpose is to assist the learner in understanding the interactions between Ethos and Persona through player interactions with their Avatar.

Activities

In Class

1. Install and test COTS game before class meets—each computer in the lab (15 terminals) will be installed with the game software—(about three hours).
2. Revisit Discussion on Ethos and Persona and their role in creating meaning in writing—(one hour).
3. Discuss purpose of the COTS gaming in class, writing assignment options, presentation requirements and final papers—(30 minutes).
4. Assign online groups and their discussion platforms.
5. Assign Class Manual for reading before next class meeting (see manual at end of this lesson plan
6. Introduce Diablo II through storyline and screen shots—(30 minutes).
    - Show opening cinematic—(10 minutes).
        - The original Diablo II game opens with a voice-over video of an Inn somewhere in the frozen Mountains. Many motley characters are enjoying drinks and food in the dimly lit bar. The door swings open and a tired bedraggled man slouches in towards the fireplace; his sword hangs limply from his hand. He slumps into a chair as other characters being to chide him… bait him… until he reacts by standing up. As he stands, the others continue to laugh at is carriage—that is until the walls erupt in flames and slugs pour from the floorboards as demon skeletons attack the patrons of the bar. The stranger moves out of the room and stops before the narrator (who apparently has been in the bar/Inn all along); the stranger beckons the narrator—a frail man of

non-descript assent) to follow and the video ends with the Inn in flames and the narrator skulking behind the stranger.

- OR you may use this opening—(10 minutes)
    - o In the Expansion pack version, the first Act begins with the narrator in a cell of insane asylum. The narrator has received a visitor who he believes to be the Angel Teriel. The narrator then begins to tell the Angel his story—one act at time with a total of five Acts. The entire game takes place while being narrated (cinematic transitions between Acts) by the old man's memory, until the added 5th Act which ends with the destruction of a power called the World Stone. Each act is a chapter in the story of how Diablo and his evil brothers, Mephisto and Baal come to power. Your job as a player is to complete the many quests within each chapter and ultimately kill the evil brothers.

7. Hand out assignments (paper and online text-based) and explain each one
    - Group work
    - Final paper
    - Online exercises
8. Begin Game play—for the next five class sessions the majority of the time will be divided into—(total 15 hours class time).
    - Game playing
    - Discussions in-class,
    - Peer-to-peer interactions—as student see fit.
    - Discussion groups—usually in the beginning of class for 30 minutes.
        - o Online searching—for cheats and codes for 15 minutes.
    - Questions for entire class—whenever students inquire
9. Class session six allows 1 hour for group debriefings and 2 hours for class presentations.

Outside of the Classroom

- The presentations will be completed on the student's own time and referred to as part of the homework activities.
- The final paper will be completed outside of class and will include portions of the group discussions as support for the writers' claims.

Culminating Activity

The game play ends and the students ready their presentations on what they have learned about Diablo II Avatar/Player relationships and how those relationships relate to the affects of persona upon ethos.

To see the *Instructional/Training Resources & Materials*, turn to the next page.

David Georgina, Ph.D.

Class Manual
"The Relationships between Ethos and Persona"
Diablo II Lord of Destruction—A Manual for Play
Composition and Academic Writing

Class Manual for Playing Diablo II Lord of Destruction

This Expansion Pack's addition to Diablo II offers new characters (good and evil), new player functions, and new a narrative used to set the stage for the climatic ending. The last Prime Evil is still loosed upon the world of Sanctuary; our hero's mission is to stop him.

High Concept

Diablo II Lord of Destruction offers the players the most basic of all oppositions—Good versus Evil. In order to save the entire planet from destruction and free the populace from tyranny, the player must conquer evil by solving quests, battling monsters, in order to become a stronger and more efficient hero, who must ultimately defeat the three brothers of Prime Evil.

Overview

> "Since the beginning of time, the forces of Order and Chaos have been engaged in an eternal struggle to decide the fate of all Creation. That struggle has now come to the Mortal Realm...and neither Man, Demon, nor Angel will be left unscathed.... (Blizzard Entertainment, par.1, 2009)

This is a hack-n-slash game that takes place in a middle age-style world where legions of demons and the undead are brought into the public sphere in order to assist their masters, the three Prime Evils—Mephisto , Diablo, and Baal—from slowly taking over human civilization. The players' missions are to kill the evil brothers and save the world called Sanctuary. In this expansion pack version, players will face a new series of quests and challenges to prevent the vile minions of the underworld from destroying their world of.

Diablo II Lord of Destruction Expansion Pack introduces a new brother Prime Evil—Baal as a new chapter is added into the storyline. Diablo II ended with the player defeating Diablo and learning that one more Prime Evil still exists. The hero must follow the path of Baal into the Barbarian Highlands of the north, "Traveling with hordes of demonic minions, Baal intends to corrupt the powerful Worldstone, which protects the whole of the mortal plane from the forces of Hell" (Blizzard Entertainment, par.2). The hero must prevent Baal from reaching Mount Surrat and ultimately, the Worldstone in order to save Sanctuary. The hero is assisted with non-player characters (NCP) that initiate quests, fix and sell weapons and armor, offer advice, and heal the hero.

The "Expansion Pack" introduces two new heroes—the Assassin (female skilled at martial arts) and the Druid (male shape-changer, controller of the elements). Also players will find new challenges and new rewards as they venture into the mountains of the mountainous terrain in the Barbarian's highland of the North. Game options include: player-to-player venturing and interactions through the gaming interface, as well as, online interactions with players from around the world with free access to battle.net. In this game, the learner plays by choosing the Avatar (hero) who best fits the learners desired skills and abilities, and must defeat Baal (last of the Prime Evils) by completing a series of quests and challenges which serve to enhance player skills and increase life levels to their avatar.

Learner Characteristics

The point of view (POV) of the player actually shifts from first person to third person. The majority of the time a player is active within the game (questing, killing, dialoguing with other avatars and players), the POV is third person. However, when a player chooses to examine their Avatar's personal inventory and character skills, they do so in first person POV. All of the cinematic clips are delivered from a first person narrative (this character is NOT an avatar, but serves to expand the storyline through narrative).

Players play

The learner chooses an avatar from a list of characters accessed when beginning the game. There are seven character avatars to choose from: the women include the Amazon, the Sorcerer, and the Assassin; the men include the Necromancer, the Barbarian, the Paladin, and the Druid (screenshot #1). Each avatar has special strengths, powers, and skills that the player can choose to learn and add too as the player progresses. The avatars also each have Life Force (life) and Mana (magic) which can be strengthened with potions. Life and Mana drain as the player completes tasks. The learner controls when an avatar needs Life/Magic replenishment. One of the original Diablo II characters has been selected—the Necromancer.

After naming the avatar, the player has the choice of selecting "Expansion Character" or "Hardcore". If the player chooses the Expansion Character and the avatar is killed and the player the game will save the avatar (stripped of all weapons, armors, gold....) back at the home base. The player is then able to re-fit the avatar and continue game play. If the player chooses "Hardcore", the avatar dies and the game ends. Everything gained in the game is lost; the player must choose a new avatar and begin a new game.

Screenshot #1: Avatar Selection

Intended Audience

The audience for this game is rated by Entertainment Software Rating Board (ESAB) at Mature 17+ for animated blood, gore, and violence (www.esrb.org). This game is well suited for use in a college level composition, literature, or history course.

Interface Design & Interactivity

The interface design and interactivity of this Expansion Pack (addition to the Diablo II Lord of Destruction game) contains the same point and click, smart keyboard, drop down menus, drag and drop options as the original game. The player has many options for interactions with the avatar, and NCPs throughout this game. For example, the player can choose to load life and mana potions into a belt. This is done by dragging and dropping the potions into the empty slots of the belt, which can be accessed by clicking upon the Inventory slot on the players screen. Or the player may want to interact with a NCP, this requires the player to move the avatar until he/she is next to the NCP; the player then clicks on the NCP and chooses from a drop down menu (see Screenshot #2).

Accesses to other menus include clicking on one of the seven small boxes:

Screenshot #2: NPC interaction

Character, Inventory, Skill Tree, Automap, Dialogue (with other players in the game), Quest, and Exit. The learner may also access these menus by using the Smart Keyboard. This option can be assessed by clicking on the "H" key (H for help) and selecting from the preprogrammed designations or by changing the keyboard designations to suit the player (Screenshot #3). Keys are usually coded with simple letter recognition: I = Inventory, S = Skill Tree, Q = Quest Log, C = Character Attributes, etc.

The F keys (F1 through F12) may also be used and accessed by the player to change or add unique skills for each character. The number keys may also be used and are associated with Life and Mana potions in the avatar's belt. A player need only choose a number key and the Life or Mana potion associated with that number key will be used by the avatar. This feature comes in handy when fighting a particularly strong demon or monster.

Other Interactive Features

Moving the avatar hero throughout the game's geographic layouts requires two actions by the player. The first is to click the place or spot where the player wants to move to avatar. The avatar will move to that selected spot. The second and more maneuverable way to move the avatar is to click and hold the mouse while moving the cursor on the screen. The avatar will follow the motions of the cursor. For instance, if the player wants to move the avatar around a chest found

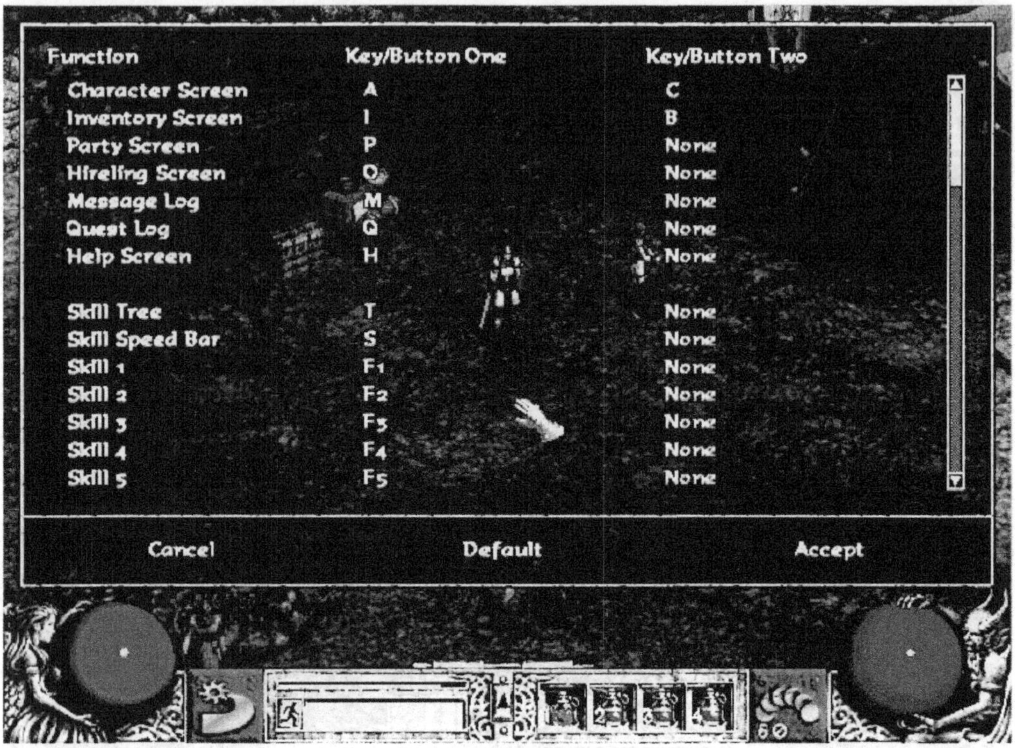

Screenshot #3: Smart Keyboard

in the middle of a field, then the player simply clicks and hold the mouse and moves the cursor about the chest. The avatar will circle around the chest. Another means for the player to move their avatar is by use of portals.

Every area within the level has one "Waypoint" or teleportation pad. Waypoints allow the avatar to move from one area to another; however Waypoints cannot be accessed unless the avatar steps directly upon the pad to activate them. Waypoints allow travel from one Waypoint to another (from the Stony Field's Waypoint pad to the Rouge Encampment's Waypoint pad). The player is not allowed to use Waypoints in areas the avatar has not been. There are a total of eight Waypoints on each level. Avatars may also teleport back to the home (in first level it is known as the Rouge Encampment) with the use of Teleport Scrolls known as Town Portals. Players collect Town Portal scrolls as they find them in the game. At the last level, players may purchase Teleport scrolls from NPC in the Barbarian Highlands. Teleportation of objects may also be done by avatars with special scrolls or by avatars with the teleportation skill—Sorceress, Necromancer.

Players are able to pick up items simply by clicking on the item; if their inventory has room the item will automatically be entered, if not, the item will drop back to the ground. If the items are a weapon or a piece of armor and the player has an empty slot for the armor or weapon, then the item will be installed into that slot. This is one way to populate the inventory slots with weapons and armor for the avatar. Players can also choose to move their avatars at a faster pace by using the R key for run, or by clicking the run icon on the mini panel display. One or two advanced character skills deal with movement for each avatar; the skill can be leaping long distances, increased speed and stamina, teleporting close ranges, and various forms of attacking enemies with fervor and ferocity.

Game Management

Most functions of the game are controlled with simple mouse clicking or the completion of a quest, challenge, or level. Point and click mouse action opens the game. Selecting options allows the player to choose which format to use (Screenshot #4). The initial opening of the game begins with an animated video of the narrator expressing his concern for the world and espousing his story. This is how the player learns the narrative of the Diablo II saga. (The Cinematics can be selected any time.)

After each level is completed (a demon or one of the brothers is killed) a new

Screenshot #4: Game Management Opening

video chapter plays revealing more about the Prime Evils and the characters. The videos are transitional and can be replayed by clicking on the cinematic option when a player starts or returns to the game. Other game management follows:

- Once the player's avatar has been killed, the player is automatically returned to the Home port (each level has its own home port).
- If the player chooses to end the game, everything is reset for the return play. For instance, if the player leaves the first quest in the first level, all the demons killed will reappear when the player returns.
    - Player's avatar is auto-saved every five minutes.

    - Player's avatar is also saved any time any player leaves the game, as well as when you quit the game.
    - Player's avatar is saved if you are disconnected from your Internet connection, and it is also saved if your system crashes mid-game.
  - Goals that have been accomplished and skill levels and player points achieved will not be lost and will continue to increase once player returns to the game.
- If in multi-player mode or in Battle.net (online version of game) the player may dialogue with other players simply by clicking the Message Log (or in battle net the Speak icon).
- In multi-player modes, players are able to exchange or trade items.
- Saving the game
    - Limitations include not being able to save the game exactly as it is when you leave it. The game will always repopulate challenges already completed. Using the Waypoints allow the avatar to return to the area last played. Also, in single player mode it is not possible to save items found for other avatars created.

Tools and their Use

Player: Tools for the player include: player to player texting (or when in Battle.net and multi-player mode direct communication is allowed through headsets); maps that overlay he scene and show where an Avatar has ventured; smart key set-up allowing the player to set the key and mouse functions.

Avatar: The tools of the Avatar are the means to win challenges and complete quests. All weapons, armor, potions, scrolls, can be purchased, traded, and/or found in chests or taken from fallen monsters or (in multi-player games) from other players. All the tools can be sold for cash when a character needs to purchase more effective equipment.

- *Weapons:* A vast array of weapons are contained within the play of the game, including: knives, swords, lances, spears bow and arrows, cross bows, scepters, staffs, maces, clubs, wands.... Some of the weapons are specific for only one character; others can be used by all the characters if they have the skill levels necessary. Weapons are often limited for use by skill levels. The following categories for weapons are also true for armor:
- *Magic Weapons* glow with a blue aura and have special powers that can increase both skill and characteristics of an Avatar.
- *Special Weapons* give off a yellow aura and the most powerful of all weapons.
- *Gemmed Weapons* have open sockets which require the player to insert any series of gems or magic totems, or skulls—increasing their attack, defense, magic, and poison abilities.
- *Challenge Weapons* while most weapons are used to kill monsters and the undead, Challenge Weapons have additional uses; for example, in the third stage of the game, players are required to gain access to a portal which leads to the Prime Evil brother Mephisto. In order to pass though

the hidden stairway portal, the player must assemble a weapon made from parts of a mage's body (eye, brain, heart). These parts are collected throughout the challenges and are combined through the use of the Horadrics Cube.

- *Horadrics Cube:* The cube has the power to create magic items and can be used with other items found) to make newer more powerful weapons. It is found during the second stage and is needed in order to create the weapon which unlocks the power of the sun in order to break through a doom wall and fight with a Prime Evil.
- *Armor:* A necessary tool which is available in all types and strengths, from leather to reinforced steel—Helmets, Breasts Plates, Full Body Suits, Grieves (gloves), Boots, Shields... the only hindrance to wearing armor is that the Avatar must have achieved a minimum skill Strength levels. Level are increased by progressing in the game, magically imbued items and by completing challenges. Some of the armor is enhanced with Magic adding to both Characteristics and Skill levels, some Special armor is specific for one character, and some are accessible to all characters. Often armor, like weapons and potions, are limited to use by skill levels.
- *Amulets:* The power necklaces can enhance any skill or characteristic once worn. They are part of the basic "outfit" for the Avatars and can be sold for cash
- *Scrolls* are magic and can give the player a one time advantage through their use. Some of the scrolls found are: Town Portals, Identity, Fire Walls, Invisibility, Transportation, Maps... Scrolls resemble the powers of the magic wielding characters.
- *Potions* can contain explosives and poisons but are mostly of two main types: Life and Mana.
- *Wells* contain either rejuvenating Life powers (blood red in color), or refilling Mana powers (blue for magic). The player moves the Avatar to the well and the energy is transferred by touch.
- *Shrines* are located in every stage of play, once touched by the Avatar they release their special powers. These special powers include, armor boosts, rate of speed boots, defense boosts, offense boosts, and increased skill levels... the special powers only last a few minutes but can be used to help defeat a monster and end a quest.

Challenges and Quests

Like all good hack-n-slash games (or as I like to call them chop-n-shop) the player is required to complete a series of challenges and quests. The net result of completing these challenges and quests is a stronger, more capable Avatar—more capable of killing the monsters, demons, undead and Prime Evils. As mentioned in the overview, quests and challenges become more difficult as the player progresses.

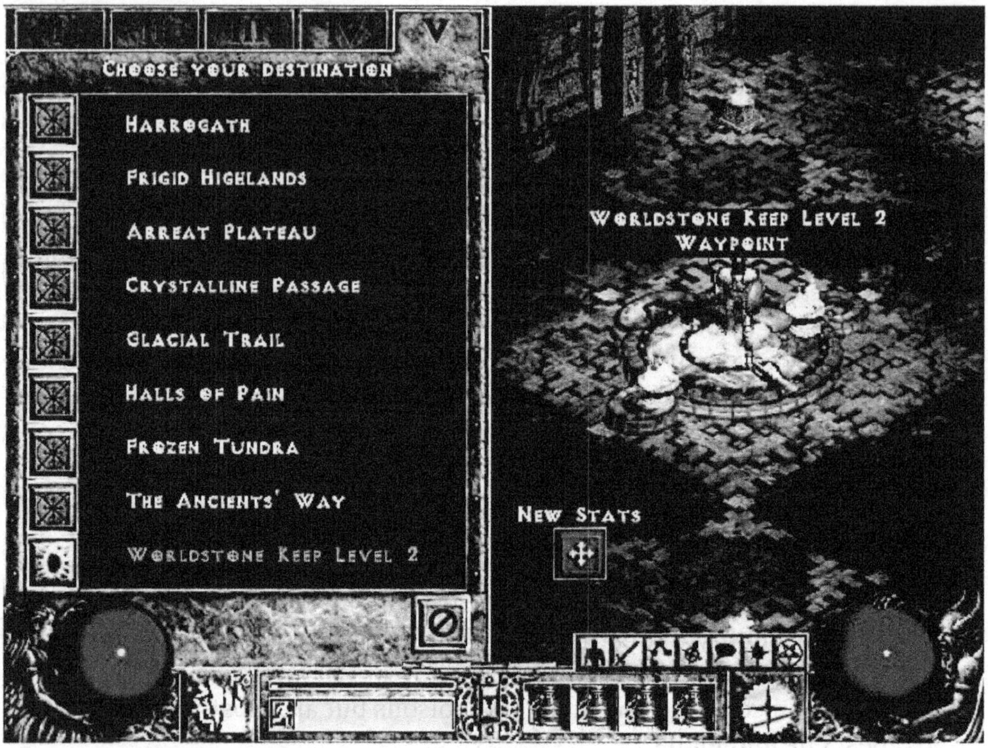

Acts I-V This show Act V (Screenshot #5)

Storyline

The original Diablo II game opens with a voice-over video of an Inn somewhere in the frozen Mountains. Many motley characters are enjoying drinks and food in the dimly lit bar. The door swings open and a tired bedraggled man slouches in towards the fireplace; his sword hangs limply from his hand. He slumps into a chair as other characters being to chide him... bait him... until he reacts by standing up. As he stands, the others continue to laugh at is carriage—that is until the walls erupt in flames and slugs pour from the floorboards as demon skeletons attack the patrons of the bar. The stranger moves out of the room and stops before the narrator (who apparently has been in the bar/Inn all along); the stranger beckons the narrator—a frail man of non-descript assent) to follow and the video ends with the Inn in flames and the narrator skulking behind the stranger.

In the Expansion pack version, the first Act begins with that same narrator in a cell of insane asylum. The narrator has received a visitor who he believes to be the Angel Teriel. The narrator then begins to tell the Angel his story—one act at time with a total of five Acts. The entire game takes place while being narrated (cinematic transitions between Acts) by the old man's memory, until the added 5th Act, which ends with the destruction of a power, called the World Stone. Each act is a chapter in the story of how Diablo and his evil brothers, Mephisto and Baal come to power. Your job as a player is to complete the many quests within each chapter and ultimately kill the evil brothers.

Game Play

The game can be played on three levels—Normal, Nightmare, and Hell. The player can only access the levels previously won and the next level up; if the player has just completed the Normal level, they will have access to either Normal or Nightmare. Each level contains five Acts (Screenshot #5) and each Act is built upon eight stages (Screenshot #6), not including theHome—In Act I the Home is the rouge's Encampment. The Home area is where interactions among Avatar and Town's people allow for healing, equipment repair, purchase, quests, challenges….

- Act I takes place at the Rouge's Encampment (Home stage) and offers the quest for killing Andariel, evil sorceress, who blocks all paths to the East—and the East is where the hero must journey to unravel the mysteries of the game.
- Act II takes place in the desert town of Lut Galai and reveals the locations of the Prime Evils.
- Act III brings the player to the ocean side docks of the jungle port Kurast where the player ultimately meets and must kill the First Prime Evil—Mephisto.
- Act IV is in the heaven protected area between Sanctuary (world's name) and Hell called the Pandemonium Fortress; the most difficult Prime Evil reigns in an abandoned fortress—Diablo.
- Act V opens in the highlands of the Barbarian's home near Mount Sarrat, here the player must save the world and kill the last Prime Evil—Baal.

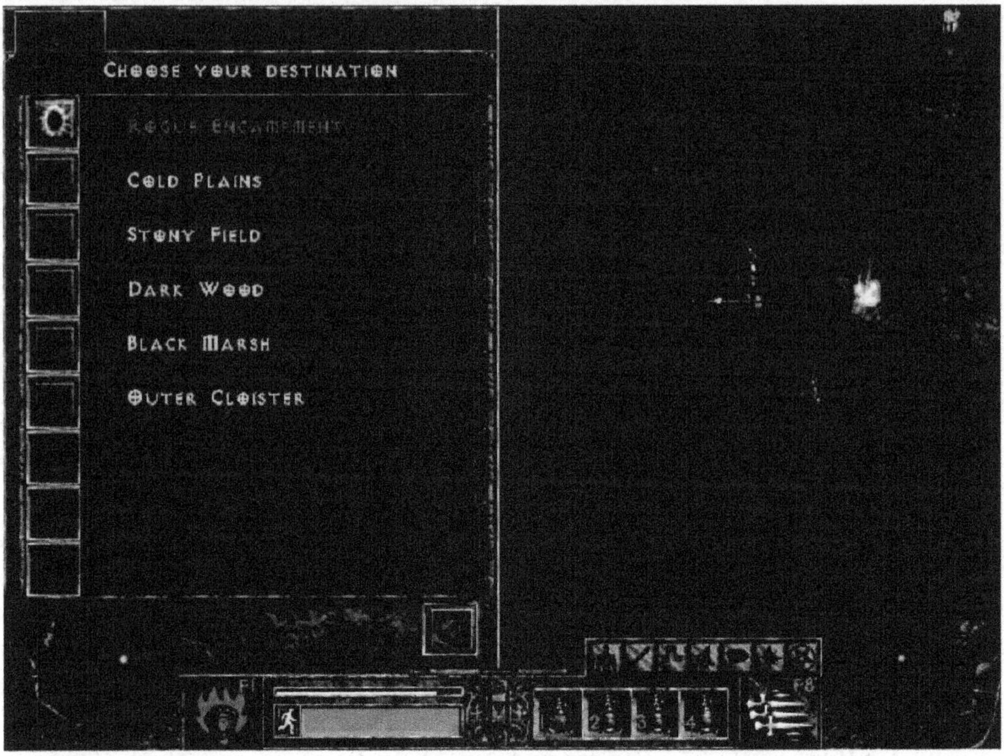

Stages of Act I Accessed by Rouge's Encampment Waypoint (Screenshot #6)

In Act I, there are six major quests—Den of Evil, Sister's Burial Grounds, The Search for Cain, The Forgotten Tower, Tools of the Trade, and Sisters to the Slaughter. However, the player will encounter min-challenges while trying to complete the quest. Most mini-challenges consist of fighting powerful evil demons or monsters. The game is composed of stages within each Act which contain the challenges/quests that the Avatar must win. For example, Act I has eight stages: Cold Plains, Stony Field, Dark Wood, Black Marsh, Outer Cloister, Jail Level One, Inner Cloister and Catacomb (Screenshot #5). Each stage may contain two to three min-levels, and may have a major quest or challenge. The Avatar enters the game stripped without armor and with one weapon of very little power. From the first challenge (to rid the caves beneath the encampment of all the monsters) the player is required to kill monsters and find equipment, potions, scrolls in order to better equip the Avatar or for cash use later on (to purchase better equipment). The Avatar must return to the Home in order to receive new directions and instructions from the NCPs.

NCP Companion

In Act I, the Avatar wins a companion by defeating the evil Blood Raven (quest #2). Most of the Acts allow for a change of companion: In Act one, the companions are Rouge Archers; in Act II, the companions are Desert Mercenaries who wield a spear; Act III offers more mercenaries but these wield swords; Act IV does not allow for a change of companion; Act V has barbarians with swords.

It is necessary for the game play to outfit the NCP with a weapon and armor. The NCP companion is a very useful game attribute because it will interact with the surroundings and move to protect the Avatar. The companion and the Avatar do not directly interact; the movement of the Avatar determines the placement and subsequent movement of the NCP companion (Screenshot #7).

While the player can change the NCP companion in most of the Acts, I prefer to

NCP Companion—Rouge Archer (Screenshot #7)

keep the Rouge Archer and accumulate life and strength for the NCP as the game progresses. General information about the NCP companions includes:

- Limited ability to move on their own accord, they basically follow the Avatar's path with some preprogrammed movement.
- They shoot whenever they encounter enemies
- Added offense and defense to the game play
- Ability for the NCP companion to shoot long distances
- Special powers like freezing blast, or fireballs, or increased defense to the Avatar
- Ability to use magic, special or gemmed weapons and armor
- If the player chooses to swap the NCP companion for a different one, it is best to remove all armor and weapons and then select the new NCP companion, otherwise all the equipment will be lost.

Avatars

There are seven character avatars to choose from: the women include the Amazon, the Sorcerer, and the Assassin; the men include the Necromancer, the Barbarian, the Paladin, and the Druid. Each avatar has special strengths and powers and skills that you can choose to learn and add to as you progress with each quest. The Avatars also each have Life Force and Mana (magic) which can be strengthen with potions. Life and Mana drain as you do tasks. As the avatar moves through each challenge or quest, the player has the opportunity to collect armor, weapons, scrolls, gems, potions, life and mana—thus increasing the overall effectiveness of the avatar. The Avatar also gains in skills and characteristics.

While Skills are Character/Avatar specific, Characteristics among all the Avatars remain the same, the Characteristics are: Strength, Dexterity, Vitality, and Energy. For example in the Characteristics first Column for the Barbarian, it is easy to see that this character relies more upon Strength and Vitality (see Screenshot #8) than the Sorceress, who relies upon Dexterity and Energy. The second column in the Characteristics panel (accessed by smart key C or by clicking the mini-panel) shows the level and type of weapon use. Each of these is associated with a characteristic. For the Barbarian: Strength = double swing damage and leap attach damage (damage); Vitality is linked with the form of attack—double swing attack rating and leap attach rating (attacks rating); Dexterity is linked with stamina and life points; Energy is linked with mana (magic use). Each time a quest or challenge is accomplished, the player is able to add to their skill and character levels. This is important because as the player moves through the challenges, they will need to have heartier more aggressive Avatars.

The role of the Avatar is reinforced by the player identification to the character. When the Avatar is killed by a monster or (as is usually the case) a group of monsters, the player experiences the loss as more than problematic failure or strategy. Rehak talks about the "I" within the Avatar by identifying six necessary elements that are vital in successful Avatarial operations.

1. player identifies with onscreen avatar
2. physical interface allowing player control of the avatar
3. rules of engagement which govern play—concerning the whole of the games sensory intent, including visual, aural, narrative, plot, character interactions…
4. extra gaming effects (timing, scoring, music…) in which only the player has conscious awareness. The avatar is unaware of these additional constraints and effects
5. frequent deaths of the avatar

6. the continuous breaking of the player/avatar connection, requires that the player reestablish control of the avatar—subsuming their own identity to that of the game play, thus allowing (teaching) the player to learn how to navigate, strategize, control the avatar in a more advantageous manner (p. 111).

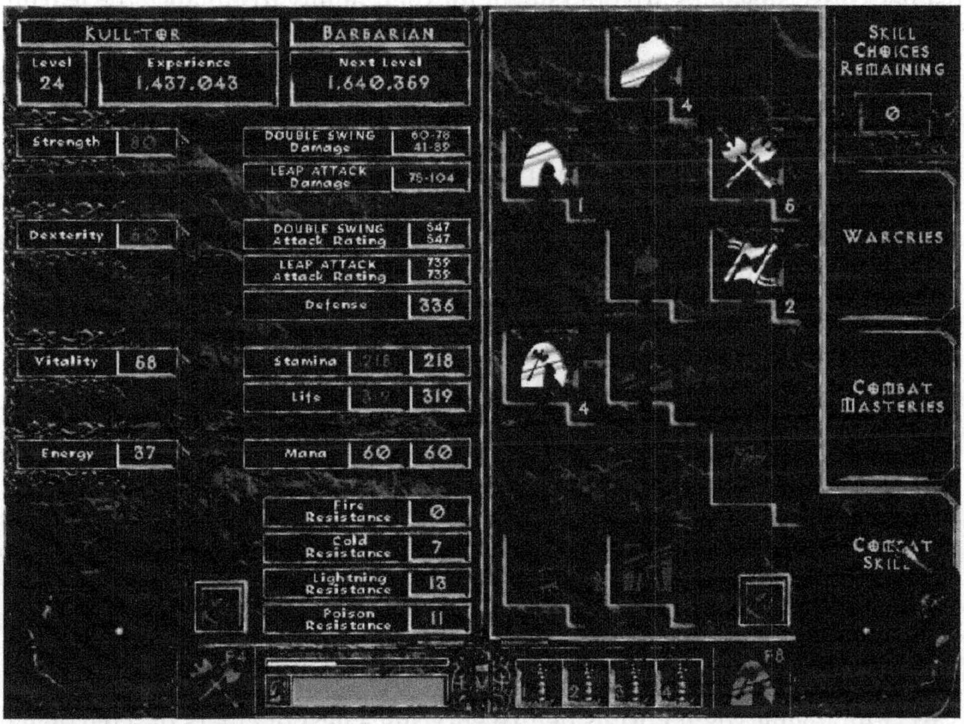

Characteristics and Skills (Screenshot #8)

I believe that this constant interaction or growing the Avatar—becoming, dying, re-becoming of the Avatarial state is what drives the player's identification with the Avatarial performance. This process is a teachable moment in an English class, by experiencing the game's play the learner is able to identify with the Avatar much the same way a writer identifies with characters created.

Difficulty

The play of the game begins easily enough so that the player can become familiar with their Avatar. The first quest is quite easy; one is simply required to kill all the monsters in the deep recesses of the earth beneath the Rouges Encampment (home for this level). Once the monsters are all killed (this requires a player to be careful not to rush into situations because the player soon learns that some monsters have special skills and deadly attacks and are not so easy to defeat) the player returns to the giver of the quest—in this case, the sorceress who controls the encampment—and is rewarded with additional skill levels. Throughout this game the difficulty comes from increased power and skills of the enemies and their ability to survive massive attacks from the Avatar and still have the ability to kill the hero. Also, as the game progresses it becomes increasingly difficult to find the best tools for defeating the enemies. By the time a player has made it through all the

Strategies

Most hack-n-slash games are not known for their ability to enhance the learning of high-level strategies (they are not as important as the ability to withstand attacks of monsters). Yet, there are certain strategies employed by the player which act to ensure the life of the Avatar. A few examples are:

1. It is often best to not get over-run by monsters with your back to a wall—retreat is paramount for survival.
2. Knowing the limits of your NCP helpers can extend the life of the Avatar. So, equip the NCP helper with the best armor and weapons available.
3. Early in the game it is important to collect all the weapons, armor, loot that the Avatar comes across—place the loot into the Inventory and return to the town's people to sell for cash (or if the items looks promising or is mana, store in the Avatar storage chest). Use the cash to purchase better equipment or Town Portals.
4. Distance from the enemies can allow for distance attacks by the Avatar (cross bow, throwing spears and knives...).
5. Wherever Avatars rush in, they soon die. The game actually requires a strategy of slow and methodical hit and run approach for the Avatar. This "feels" contrary to some of the characters' personalities (characteristics and skills) and may be difficult for the player to comprehend—until the player's Avatar is killed ten too many times.
6. Employing Town Portals before entering a nest of vipers or a particularly strong monster allows for a quick retreat (should it be required, and it usually is) and access to healing and restocking Life potions and Mana potions at the home portal.
7. Whenever help or advice is offered, take it.
8. If you need a socketed weapon and there are none for sale in your current chapter (they become rarer as the game progresses) the player can use the portal in their home base to transport to earlier chapters and seek equipment.
9. When battling one of the Prime Evils, always overstock your inventory and belt with Life potions (also 1,3,and 5)

NOTE TO PLAYERS: For our next three class sessions, we will delve into the COTS gaming world of Diablo II – Expansion Pack where you will create an Avatar to play. As player you will also be responsible to completing the first level of play (or as close as we can get in our limited class time). We will explore game Cheats and Codes to better defeat the monsters and win the quest.

Mira Grant's *Feed*

Review by Jeffrey Barlow

Anyone who has browsed the shelves of recent fiction at any of the big box bookstores surely has been struck by the increasingly high percentage of the titles devoted to the monstrously supernatural. Such works continue to appear, although the long-dominant vampires are giving way to zombies, and werewolves remain slavering in third place.

Such titles are, clearly, more than just a passing fad. Horror and the supernatural have always been with us in fiction, with a dependably large niche audience. Now, however, the creatures of the night have crossed over into the mass market, both in fiction and in film.

One of the more persuasive explanations for the enduring appeal of horror and the supernatural is, that like several other genres, they give us a place to fix our own inchoate fears. Mary Shelley's seminal *Frankenstein*, for example, has long been held to have been a Romantic response to the oncoming scientific and industrial revolutions[1].

However, the scientific revolution, as much as fans of *Frankenstein* may have feared it, had changed everything. Frankenstein itself depended on a willingness to believe that several new scientific advances might indeed permit the reanimation of dead parts, if properly harnessed.

Horror can, of course, be plotted with a minimum of plausibility, witness the long series of Friday the Thirteenth-style films. But to cross-over and be successful as more than a quick read or a date-film, however, horror works best when supported, even if vaguely, by science. *The Andromeda Strain*, Harvard Medical School graduate Dr. Michael Crichton's bestseller and subsequent film, depended for its plausibility on epidemiology—even if the pathogen was of extra-terrestrial origin. Many of his subsequent techno-thrillers depended in part on some other scientific element[2]. Computers and the likelihood of unforeseen catastrophic events—often supported by vague references to Chaos Theory— were often at the center of such plots.

Mira Grant, the author of *Feed*, the subject of this review, is in some senses closer to the roots of horror fiction in its usual insistence upon copious gore and stomach-churning visuals than is Crichton, who wanted a mass audience and a

---

[1] For one such argument, see Blake Taylor, "Frankenstein and Revolution." See also: http://en.wikipedia.org/wiki/Frankenstein. This article is an authoritative one because it is well written and organized and has an extensive vocabulary including scholarly sources.
[2] See http://en.wikipedia.org/wiki/Michael_Crichton for an excellent summary of Crichton's life and work which demonstrates this point. The site is a credible one, well researched and thoroughly researched. As its focus is upon Crichton's public career, it tends to neglect his painstaking research.

PG rating. Grant has created her own persona, which revels in an avid appreciation for blood and horror[3].

Grant's most recent work, *Feed*, cleverly brings together such themes as zombie wars[4], epidemiology (which she has studied at the collegiate level), the War on Terror, hacking, and world-class blogging. The work, despite its helter-skelter pacing, is very tightly plotted and well written. It is set in a dystopian future, the second quarter of the 21st century, which is little evolved beyond the present.

The Zombie Wars, which began in medical experimentations in 2014, are an omnipresent fact. Mankind, at least in its American So-Cal variant, has managed to cope. The really in-crowd restaurants have electronic fences and armed waiters, but crowds rarely gather; the onset of the zombie virus is so rapid that there will be few uninfected survivors of an attack. To be infected is to be immediately killed and entrance to protected facilities—and there are no other kind—gained only through constant blood testing. (Apple makes one of the best testing kits, we are glad to learn.)

The mass media, already in decline, has given way to niche-based blogging. Bloggers have become media stars and compete for increasingly dangerous content. The protagonists, a brother and sister team of video bloggers, is noted for their ability to stream content from areas well beyond human control. Known for their unflinching realism and truth-telling, their team is invited to follow a presidential candidate in the run up to the election.

At bottom the novel is a sort of social satire. The reader will recognize many of the outrageous elements of the plot and the material setting as only mild extrapolations from present equivalents. The Internet, for example, has become not only the dominant mode of communication, but almost the only one.

Reporters have become divided into blogging "Newsies" who "report facts as untainted by opinion as we can manage…" the "Stewarts, who report opinion informed by fact"…The Irwins who seek danger, and "the Aunties, who share stories of their lives, recipes, and other snippets to keep people happy and relaxed. And, of course, the Fictionals, who fill the online world with poetry, stories and fantasies. They have a thousand branches, all with their own names and customs…[5]"

Underlying the entire work is a trope which equates the Zombie Wars to the War on Terror. The government, such as it is, as well as the military, flourishes on

---

[3] Ms. Grant's personal WWW page is found at: http://www.miragrant.com/. Ms. Grant has also written as Seanan McGuire.

[4] In the zombie wars sub-genre developed by film director George Romero—amusingly presented in a brief cameo in this book as a zombie being protected for research purposes—zombies and mankind are at war and the world has become a series of shifting battlefronts. Mankind fights for survival and zombies, in addition to an irresistible urge to dine out and often, are engaged in some terrible quest for self-actualization.

[5] P. 50, Feed.

mass fear and does not want to see any solution to the zombie problem. There is also a continual trope dealing with fundamentalist religious beliefs, held by those who think that more than a little terror would bring the country, if not the world, closer to their own particular view of God.

The audience for this book is, I believe, a sort of crossover young adult-to-adult reader similar to the more mature end of the Harry Potter and Twilight series. Although there are occasional references to sexuality, the entire culture seems to have largely lost all erotic urges and beyond the frequent gore fests, the work is "G" rated.

This target audience may initially be entertained but, if even marginally thoughtful, will quickly grow uneasy. The constant references to pop culture and to the increasing irrelevance of news and entertainment, shows us a populace which is so fearful that it seeks relief not in concerted or even individual action, but in increasingly isolated escapism which ultimately dooms it, if not to outright extinction, to irrelevance.

The zombie plague is often referred to as "The Rising," but when the author asks the audience, as she does in both the work and in her web site, "When Will You Rise," she has, I think, a double meaning in her question.

This work is bound to find a mass audience, an inevitable film, and as it relies in large part on speculation about the future of the Internet as a critical element in mass communication, it is well worth reading for those interested in the impact of the Internet.

The prose style—a sort of combination of early Tom Wolfe (Electric Kool-Aid Tom—not Looking Homeward Thomas) and a hard-driving techno-pop narrative will be off-putting to many, as will the youthful voices of the protagonists. However, the book has a great deal to say about the post-Internet world. It is to be the first of a trilogy in which the key characters continue to fight zombies and blog the truth.

Jeffrey Carr's *Inside Cyber Warfare*

Review by Jeffrey Barlow

This review of Jeffrey Carr's work, *Inside Cyber Warfare*, follows upon our discussion in the previous issue of Interface, "*Cyber War and U.S. Policy: Part I, Neo-realism.*"[6] That piece was informed in large part by a review of Richard A. Clarke and Robert Knake's recent work, *Cyber War: The Next Threat to National Security and What to Do About It*. The two books are on the same topic, and the two reviews are intended to be complementary.

The works proceed, however, from different premises. While Clarke and Knake see the topic of cyber war as related to earlier forms of warfare, they also see cyber war as demanding a very different approach.

Carr in *Inside Cyber Warfare* sees continuities as more important than discontinuities. The work relies, much more than did Clarke and Knake, upon models derived from earlier forms of warfare.

The distinction arises, I believe, because the two works are intended for substantially different audiences, though clearly they overlap; the group concerned about cyber war is very large. Clarke and Knake see cyber war as a policy problem. But for Carr, the problem is essentially a military one. This may be in part because the group concerned with the threat of war in any form, is, of course, the military establishment. Today's high-ranking officers were trained for, and are experienced in, kinetic warfare. Attempts to present cyber war as discontinuous and requiring substantially new approaches are going to be less welcome than those which see it as just a new "battle space."

Clarke, however, is deeply suspicious of those in the American military who draw quick comparisons to past war-fighting technologies in which cyber space is viewed simply as another battlefield:

> "...the U.S. military in general repeatedly characterizes cyberspace as something to be dominated. It is reminiscent of the Pentagon's way of speaking of nuclear war in the 1960s. The historian of nuclear strategy Lawrence Freedman noted that William Kaufmann, Henry Kissinger, and other strategists realized that there was a need then "to calm the spirit of offense, potent in Air Force circles...[whose] rhetoric encouraged a view of war that was outmoded and dangerous." That same sort of macho rhetoric is strong in Air Force cyber war circles today, and apparently in the Navy as well."[7]

---

[6] See June 2010 – Volume 10, Issue 5

[7] Highlight Loc. 689-95, Kindle Edition, Clarke and Knake.

Jeffrey Carr is a "principal" at GreyLogic, a noted cyber security firm. Carr, and GreyLogic take a hard line on issues related to cyber War.[8] While having a significant financial stake in the cyber Security industry obviously does not disqualify an expert such as Carr from having a great deal to say on the subject, it does expose him to charges of self-interest and subjectivity. There clearly is a "cyber War industrial complex" already in existence, and there are billions to be made from solving the problems presented by cyber conflicts, but also from exploiting, even creating, fears. Some commentators have felt that at times the line between problem solving and exploitation grows a bit unclear.[9]

Carr's credentials are first-rate; he consults frequently, publishes widely, and his access to insider sorts of studies and information—some studies done at GreyLogic, others in various military and think-tank venues. These provide *Inside Cyber Warfare* with a great deal of urgency and credibility. He is, in this area, a consummate insider. His publisher, O'Reilly Media, is noted for narrowly focused expert analysis of a broad range of technical areas.[10]

Another large difference between the two works is that Carr and his major sources reflect a sort of mirror image to Clarke and Knake in that while they certainly were concerned with the potentially violent impact of the Internet, their work focuses more on policy than on technology.

Carr's work is very much based in a close analysis of technology and technologically enabled opponents. Accordingly it largely treats solutions not as policy issues, but as technical ones facing the defense establishment. This is both its strength, and its weakness.

The strengths of *Inside Cyber Warfare*, however, are many. The work analyzes many examples of cyber conflicts. It also has very close analysis of the organizations and cyber conflict doctrines of potential adversaries, to Carr, clearly China and Russia. While Clarke and Knake saw a large part of the critical threat from cyber conflict to be a result of the wide dispersion of both tools and motives for engaging in cyber attacks among highly varied non-state actors around the world, Carr focuses upon potentially adversarial states.

While paying attention to criminal gangs and free-lance hackers, Carr sees the link between nation states and their hackers to be the truly threatening issue. Carr's material includes many useful brief summaries of hacker gangs, their WWW locales, and even of individual hackers, usually, of course, known by their on-line identities. These make fascinating reading and would provide the

---

[8] For an understanding of GreyLogic's perspective on questions related to cyber war, see their WWW page at: http://greylogic.us/

[9] See a skeptical take on this issue see Robert X. Cringely, "The next cyber war will be for your wallet" In InfoWorld, at:http://www.networkworld.com/news/2010/030510-the-next-cyber-war-will.html

[10] http://oreilly.com/

interested reader with a great deal of material for their own research, though a great deal of caution is in order in accessing some of the sites listed.[11]

Carr's grasp of technology is very strong and chapters 7-10 could well constitute a manual for white-hat hackers wishing to form a sort of counter-weight to the Russian criminal gangs and Chinese citizens' cyber militias which Carr sees as part of the strengths of those two potential adversaries. Some of the content is quite dense and in addition to providing step-by-step guidance to guarding against or tracking down threats, serves as an introduction to many useful sites which will doubtless evolve to stay abreast of future developments in this field.

The book grows a bit labored at times. The author simply incorporates parts of a large unpublished study by Lt. Cdr. Matthew Sklerov into chapter 4, and again into Chapter 13. Chapter 4 deals with the concept of "active defense," or what might fairly be termed immediate retaliation or even preemptive strikes for cyber attacks presumed to be imminent.

The problem in active defense, however, is attribution. That is, how do we know who has attacked? And even if we determine that an attack comes from say, China, how can we be sure that it was launched by the Chinese government and not by an ultranationalist Chinese teenager? Carr rather glosses over such issues, asserting that technological solutions and "predictive intelligence" can ultimately determine perpetrators. Clark and Knake, however, see this as a very difficult problem to be dealt with quite carefully in terms of policy.

The work itself, however, shows some of the problems raised in dealing with a potentially infinite number of threats. For example, a state often presumed to be adversarial is China. But Carr's own materials on China do not give us a great deal of confidence in at least his own ability to perform the snap-judgments necessary to respond to possible impending attacks on the part of some unknown foe.

While Carr might be excused for such cultural lapses as a compete misunderstanding of the Chinese system of names, in which family names come first and given names last, other problems are more serious ones. To Carr, Hong Kong and China are sufficiently the same that a threat from Hong Kong is one from China, and, presumably, vice-versa. This would astonish both mainlanders and "Hong Kong Belongers," each quite a distinct group.

And at pages 174-175 his analysis is at least laughable, if not downright racist. He takes an ancient Chinese book of military stratagems and by drawing very far-fetched analogies makes them warnings of potential Chinese evil intentions with regard to cyber war.[12] As Carr says, the "36 stratagems...still plays a large role in

---

[11] If you are not already well aware of some of the potential consequences of visiting some web pages, see our review of Nitesh Dhanjani's work, "Hacking: The Next Generation."

[12] "Hide a knife behind a smile," for example, is related to phishing schemes at p. 175, as is "tossing a brick to get a jade gem."

shaping Beijing's military strategy."[13] And don't forget the greatest of all Chinese criminal masterminds, Fu Manchu, either.

Skerlov, and by extension, Carr, after a great deal of logic-chopping on the former's part, finesse the problem of attribution by arguing that states are legally obliged to prevent cyber attacks[14], and hence it would be legal to immediately attack that state.[15] This is, of course, given the ability of teenagers to successfully launch cyber attacks upon the Pentagon from, say, a rural area of Alabama, let alone a Chinese Internet café, rather strange reasoning.

This chain of reasoning also ends, as Clarke and Knake point out, in justifications under certain foreseeable circumstances for "kinetic responses"—i.e., conventional warfare attacks, given that the U.S. is so much weaker on the defense than some of its potential opponents (because it has so many more critical electronic sites to defend) and hence must rely on quick and violent counter-attacks.

At the last I must agree with Clarke and Knake that while extrapolations from warfare in the predigital age are useful, cyber conflicts are substantially new. Belabored attempts to face cyber conflicts into the moulds of kinetic ones are more dangerous than enlightening.

On balance, this is a very useful book. It provides a hard-nosed counterpoint to anyone suspecting that Clarke and Knake are ultimately appeasers, and a good insight into the very widespread, perhaps dominant, Realist perspective on cyber conflicts. Anyone wishing to fully understand cyber conflict and the various schools of thought on it should not neglect it. But it is probably most useful not as a manual or a final statement on cyber war, but as a resource which can open up a wide variety of sources and perspectives.

---

13 p. 175.
14 p. 62-68.
15 See also Carr's article "Projecting Borders into Cyberspace."

Hacking v. Cyber War

Editorial by Jeffrey Barlow

Introduction

This editorial was intended to be a summary of our current thoughts and experience at the Berglund Center on the topic of cyber war, informed by recent reviews of first Richard A. Clarke and Robert Knake's work, *Cyber War: The Next Threat to National Security and What to Do About It*, and Jeffrey Carr's, *Inside Cyber Warfare*. However, like so much that relates to the Internet, events overtook analysis. In late May we were hacked and our server taken down. Cyber war is still not irrelevant to us; it may well be a part of those events. But suddenly our intended objective analysis was infected with bitter experience.

The context of the events is important to an understanding of them. We take security very seriously, both at Pacific University and at the Berglund Center for Internet Studies. The university firewall protects many of our activities, but we do run our own server outside the university firewall of necessity. Access through the firewall is appropriately slow and cautious, but we have need for frequent immediate changes in content and operations on a server of our own. Too, we have an important educational mission at the Center so provide our student staff opportunities to learn server operations.

We have had eight different Systems Operators in our almost 15 years at Berglund and its forerunners, including the Matsushita Center for Electronic Education, still in operation. Up to this last incident, we have had only one serious hacking, and a "scraping" or cyberjacking of our site by the Iranian Ministry of Science, plus occasional minor intrusions. These were each expensive and in the Iranian case, a rough introduction to some of the political issues affecting the World Wide Web.

The recent event, however, was much more serious, in part because of its timing. We were operating our then current server at its capacity, anticipating the purchase of a new one and its installation in the budget period which would begin in July. As a result, some scripts ran incorrectly and did not perform the backup and defense functions for which they were designed. Too, our Systems Operator had graduated, and his successor had just started a challenging summer internship in the industry.

In this vulnerable period, somebody gained access. The purpose of the hacker was not to destroy content but to enslave our server into a bot net intended to function unobtrusively during late weekend hours. The motives of the hacker were possibly political in nature, though they may also have been related to illicit commercial spamming operations. His or her motives are not clear because the intruder deleted several weeks of server logs so that we could not track illicit activities in the server.

The political element, however, was that our server became part of a denial of service attack (DoS) aimed at servers in Russia. (We will return to this issue below when discussing these events and the concepts of cyber war.) At that point, the University Systems Operator began receiving angry emails from European Server Operators and unplugged our server.

Fortunately, our previous Systems Operator, Ben Elliot, who had graduated in 2008, had become the Web Master for Pacific University and was able to devote considerable weekend time to restoring our content and straightening out the many problems presented by the hacking. We began operating solely from our Canadian mirror, originally intended only as an external back-up resource.

Ambiguity and Cyber War

There were many potential political elements to our recent hacking experience. We had been on alert earlier because as we study the impact of the Internet, with a secondary focus on Chinese use of the Internet, much of our editorial writing and some of our other operations deal with China. We attempt, of course, to be as objective as possible, but we had touched on issues such as Google and China, Sino-Tibetan relations, discussed both commercial and political hacking in a number of articles and editorials, etc., etc. Some would doubtless find these discussions subjective or biased on one side or the other.

As the editor of Interface I try to follow my own personal cyber reputation in Chinese sources, and during this past year found both positive and negative Chinese reactions, not so much to my opinions as expressed at Berglund, but to my personal writings and blogs. This is not to say that we suspect Chinese sources of launching the attack upon us. It could equally have been anti-Chinese sources opposed to some of our previous positions. And the fact that our captured server had immediately begun attacking Russian sites suggested the possibility of many other political players as Russia is more or less engaged in continual cyber conflict with former Soviet republics.

Identifying potential attackers, either before or after the fact, is the central problem of cyber conflict: "attribution." Regrettably, much of what passes for analysis on cyber conflict asks only two simple questions when trying to identify the attacker:

1. Who has motive?
2. Who has ability and opportunity?

Clarke and Knake recognize attribution as the central factor in crafting either international treaties to prevent or regulate cyber war, and in creating appropriate U.S. policy. Much of the material in Carr's work analyzes cyber conflicts within traditional pre-digital legal or military frameworks in an effort to finesse the issue of attribution. We had now become deeply involved in this problem of attribution.

We have held, we hope, two consistent opinions with regard to China and cyber conflicts. First, we think that the standards used internationally to quickly condemn China as the miscreant in such incidents as the Google hackings are much too low—often amounting to little more than prejudice—and usually neglect other equally likely explanations for the events.

Second, we think that China and all countries must do much more to police their own hackers if they are to avoid both badly damaging the international community constituted by the World Wide Web, and to avoid suspicions of their own state's involvement in politically motivated hacking attacks.

To these two perspectives we will now add a third, stemming from our reviews of the works by Clark and Knake and by Carr: We believe that it is has been very much to the interests of Western democracies to define cyber conflicts very narrowly.

In the conventional view, any electronic attacks emanating from non-democracies are potentially cyber war. However, facilitating or permitting attacks on non-Western culture which have amounted to attempts to support regime change, as in the twitter protests in Iran, or attempts to support the independence of various Chinese ethnic groups, are not seen as cyber war; rather they are viewed as examples of the democratizing potential of the Internet.

In short, the Chinese state may well be choosing to permit if not to facilitate cyber attacks of which it approves on foreign groups or states because it sees them as interfering in China's internal affairs. For its part, the United States and others are also standing by while hacktivists are attacking groups or states of which it disapproves in the name of cyber democracy. These problems are, unfortunately in the short run, insoluble.

The United States, like other states, has chosen to militarize the problems of cyber conflict by creating military commands in the name of cyber defense. Even now the United States is, we believe, attempting to create hacker groups equivalent to those groups of patriotic Chinese youth who may or may not be supported and encouraged by the Chinese state. For their part, the Russian government employs or encourages criminal gangs, and in considerable part, overlaps with them.

There are of course, many non-state actors internationally. The Internet has empowered virtually everyone with a computer to engage in cyber conflict with minimal training and at minimal expense. To expect that these problems can be dealt with by current legal or military practices seems naïve if not utopian.

Our Solution

The problem of security and the Internet has simply grown too complex for non-profit operations like our own. Even though we have been hacked only twice in almost fifteen years, we cannot afford even these two examples. The last event has exposed inherent flaws in our current modes of operation, too.

Unfortunately, the Internet has grown too hazardous and our own operations too extensive, perhaps too consequential, for us to continue to rely upon undergraduate staff to provide security.

Our Systems Operators have been very effective over the years and we are proud of all of them and of their consistent ability to find professional employment in the hi-tech industry. But the rhythms of college life are set by academic terms, budget intervals, vacations, the graduation of key personnel, even exam periods. These inevitably will eventually coincide, as has just been the case, with an attack by an aggressive and sophisticated hacker with the costly results we have just experienced.

We intend to move into the "cloud" and in effect outsource our defenses. Our goal at Berglund is to begin posting issues of Interface in such a cloud by October of 2010, and to be functioning fully within a cloud environment by February of 2011. This move will deprive our staff of the experience of running a server complex, but it will also offer them the experience of working within a cloud environment, which is, we believe, the direction in which operations such as our own most go.

Conclusion

What can we say at this point about cyber conflict as it has impacted the Berglund Center? In fact, very little: the core problem of attribution remains. We do not know who attacked us, or for what reasons. We made, for example, a decision following the first attack, that it was probably the outmoded operating system of the old server that was compromised. Ben Elliot, our acting Systems Operator, recovered our content and placed it on the new server, configured it and immediately began serving our content via our usual practices.

That next weekend the new server again engaged in DoS attacks, this time upon Chinese sites as well as Russian, European and American ones. Working with the techs at the firm supporting our Canadian mirror, Ben discovered that there were concealed rootkits sprinkled through our files, presumably by the initial attacker. We locked the server down so that we could continue serving without being hijacked, but now we have to clean out the malware, again at considerable expense.

For us to attribute the attacks to any particular agency would be foolish. It could be anybody, anywhere. The perpetrator may have political or financial motives, or by conventional values, none at all. All we can do is to protect ourselves, and accept that, given the centrality of the Internet to education and communications, there are no realistic alternatives. We can no more stop relying upon it for educational activities than we can give up cell phones or computers.

References

See *Cyber War and U.S. Policy: Part I*[16], *Neo-realism* for the review of Clarke and Knake, and the review of Carr in this issue.

For the previous hacking and the Iranian scraping, see: CYBERJACKED! Again... and Again...[17] A DoS attack consists of repeated automated "calls" to a targeted server until it is overwhelmed and either crashes out or its operations become very slow and legitimate visitors' browsers "time out" and drop attempts to view it. These types of attacks can be part of a political attack, (The most noted example among analysts of cyber war is probably the attacks, assumed to be Russian in origin, upon Georgian servers in 2008. See Carr above, p, 17-18.) They may also be part of a blackmail scheme in which the targeted servers' owners are told to pay up or else experience continual interruptions.

See, for example, Carr's chapter 7. "Follow the Money" for an example of the torturous, means necessary to attribute attacks.

See first *Google and China: Minor Incident or Cyber war?* at: http://bcis.pacificu.edu/journal/2010/01/article.php?id=634 and then *Google and China Eight Weeks Later: Where Are We Now?* at: http://bcis.pacificu.edu/journal/2010/02/article.php?id=645.

See pp 144-45 in Carr discussing the degree of involvement of non-Iranians in facilitating the twitter campaign. See also GOLNAZ ESFANDIARI, "The Twitter Devolution" in *Foreign Policy*, JUNE 7, 2010.

Neither Clare and Knake nor Carr even consider this issue. But to the Chinese, as well as to many Islamic states and religious believers, it is the central issue in the impact of the Internet. This disconnect will inevitably be fatal to any attempt to find a truly international framework with which to ameliorate cyber conflicts. See "Cyber War and U.S. Policy: Part I, Neo-realism" for copious example.

For a discussion of cloud computing see: http://en.wikipedia.org/wiki/Cloud_computing

For an explanation of rootkit see: http://en.wikipedia.org/wiki/Rootkit.

---

[16] June 2010 – Volume 10, Issue 5, at: http://bcis.pacificu.edu/journal/article.php?id=682.
[17] April-May 2006 – Volume 6, Issue 2, at: http://bcis.pacificu.edu/journal/article.php?id=252.

September 2010 – Volume 10, Issue 7

About This Issue

http://bcis.pacificu.edu/journal/article.php?id=719

Articles

Media: Valerie Horres – *For Better or for Worse: How the Internet Benefits and Harms Men and Women*

http://bcis.pacificu.edu/journal/article.php?id=701

Feature: James Kundart, et al. – *Word Recognition and the Accommodative Response to Desktop Versus Handheld Video Displays (Handheld Study #2)*

http://bcis.pacificu.edu/journal/article.php?id=713

Technology: Steve Dodge – *Digital Magazines and the iPad*

http://bcis.pacificu.edu/journal/article.php?id=714

Education: Mark Szymanski – *VoiceThread: Building a Mosaic of Asynchronous Communication*

http://bcis.pacificu.edu/journal/article.php?id=715

Book and Site Reviews

Jeffrey Barlow - Andrew Bacevich's *Washington Rules: America's Path to Permanent War*

http://bcis.pacificu.edu/journal/article.php?id=717

Jeffrey Barlow - Charlie Huston and David Cristofano's *Edgar and the Internet: The Mystic Arts of Erasing All Signs of Death and The Girl She Used To Be*

http://bcis.pacificu.edu/journal/article.php?id=718

Editorial

Jeffrey Barlow - *Peer Review and Interface*

http://bcis.pacificu.edu/journal/article.php?id=716

About This Issue

The September issue of *Interface* reflects a slightly different direction for us this year. While most of our content will continue to be of interest to a general audience, we will be publishing more peer-reviewed materials beginning with this issue. Our Feature is "Word Recognition and the Accommodative Response to Desktop vs. Handheld Video Displays" by Drs. Yu-Chi Tai, James Kinder, John R. Hayes, and James Sheedy, all of Pacific University.

For an explanation of the importance of peer review on both the Internet and in a print environment, see the editorial for this issue, "Peer Review and Interface."

Our Education Editor, Mark Szymansky, offers us "VoiceThread: Building a Mosaic of Asynchronous Communication?" In which he discusses a very flexible application for extending many of the familiar forms of text based social interaction on the WWW into video and voice media. This permits a group of commentators to work together on selected materials, using different media.

Berglund Fellow Valerie Horres discusses the differential impact of the Internet upon the genders in "For Better or For Worse, How the Internet Benefits and Harms Men and Woman" Valerie has been writing on related topics for us, and this is her last piece. Thanks, Valerie, you will be missed.

Pacific University's Steve Dodge begins the first of a new regular feature with "Digital Magazines and the iPad". As the editor of the University's magazine, Pacific Magazine, Steve has a great deal of experience with a wide variety of applications and media devices.

Our book reviews include an analysis of the impact of the Internet as revealed in two recent novels. These were nominated for the "Edgar" prize awarded to outstanding novels in the mystery or detective category. The review article is "Edgar and the Internet: Charlie Huston's *The Mystic Arts of Erasing All Signs of Death* and David Cristofano's *The Girl She Used to Be*." In addition, editor Jeffrey Barlow also reviews Andrew Bacevich's recent work, *Washington Rules: America's Path to Permanent War* in an attempt to better understand the notion of Cyberwar. Dr. Bacevich is often said to be America's foremost analyst of foreign policy, particularly as related to the use of military force.

Please see also our announcements for September.
As always, we hope you find this issue of *Interface* useful and entertaining. Join us again in October.

The Berglund Center for Internet Studies,
Pacific University Oregon

For Better or for Worse: How the Internet Benefits and Harms Men and Women

Valerie Horres

As an increasingly integral and influential part of international culture, the Internet largely affects men and women. It both influences how each gender is perceived through online portrayals, and the Internet can also benefit and harm men and women through its content and functions.

The Internet has three basic operations: communication, information gathering, and entertainment. All three have negative or positive potential for both genders, but ultimately how men and women are affected depends on how they utilize the Internet. The two genders typically use the Internet differently, guided somewhat by traditional gender roles. Women generally utilize the Internet "in facilitating new interpersonal interactions, providing access to information from the domestic sphere, and facilitating the purchase of goods."[1] For example, women are more likely to research an illness online, which follows with the traditional notion of women being healthcare providers. They are also more likely to shop online, which is convenient as it can be done at home. The Internet also allows people to locate items that are not available locally or for a cheaper price than offline. Additionally, women are more likely than men to search for spiritual and religious information, and to participate in support groups.[2] There are hundreds of support groups online aimed singly at women. Some sites, such as http://www.dmoz.org/, [3] can be utilized to locate many of these online support groups. These groups specialize in topics like health, divorce, religion, pregnancy, motherhood, menopause, and many others.[4]

Likewise, men generally use the Net in "providing employment or assisting career development,"[5] which also makes sense with the traditional gender role of men being more involved in the business world. Men also employ the Internet to read news, add content to the web, deal in finances, and find entertainment at a

---

[1] Ann Colley and John Maltby, "Impact of the Internet on our Lives: Male and female personal perspectives," (2007): 2011, Scribd., accessed 10 May 2010, http://www.scribd.com/doc/13551365/Impact-of-the-Internet-on-Our-Lives.
[2] "Different People Use the Internet in Different Ways," Infoplease, accessed 28 Oct. 2009, http://www.infoplease.com/ipa/A0931238.html.
[3] "Open Directory Project," dmoz, accessed 28 Nov. 2009,http://www.dmoz.org/Health/Women's_Health/Support_Groups/.
[4] Online women support groups, Google search, accessed 28 Nov.2009,http://www.google.com/search?hl=en&source=hp&q=online+women+support+groups&aq=0&oq=online+women+sup& aqi=g1
[5] Ann Colley and John Maltby, "Impact of the Internet on our Lives: Male and female personal perspectives," (2007): 2011, Scribd., accessed 10 May 2010, http://www.scribd.com/doc/13551365/Impact-of-the-Internet-on-Our-Lives.

higher rate than females.[6] Instead of the stereotypic patriarch reading the newspaper at the breakfast table, or trading stocks and bonds from his study, men are now doing these acts online.

However, it is the area of online entertainment that tends to be potentially the most detrimental. Online materials can damage men and women by distracting them. Watching YouTube videos of old Star Trek episodes, looking at Lolcats,[7] or any other form of online entertainment, takes time away from more "productive processes that would aid development, such as education [or] work."[8] In addition, the Internet also affects people through portrayals. Online entertainment—listening to and downloading music, streaming television shows, viewing online pornography—tends to propagate a degradation of men and women. For instance, many examples of entertainment media lean toward depicting women as bitches or sexual objects. Business women on streamed television shows are often characterized with a Hilary Clinton-esque stigma of trying to do a "man's job" or being emotionless bitches.[9] Media sources also show scantily clad cheerleaders,—such as those found on http://twitter.com/twiCheerleaders[10] —dancers, singers, and actors, and contain offensive characterizations and lyrics. A prime example of a song degrading women is "Bitches Ain't Shit" by Dr. Dre.[11]

These media also portray men in a negative light, often characterizing them as airheaded He-men, violence driven, and extremely misogynistic. Many sports games or matches, which are often streamed online, inspire and condone violence and aggression. Society places athletes on a pedestal, which in turn implies that the hostility provoked by them on the field is desirable.[12] Likewise, music lyrics and singers promote violence towards others, and again, their fame suggests this attitude of aggression and cruelty is positive and even manly. An excellent illustration of this is Ice T's song "Cop Killer," which endorses killing police and states "F**ck the police, don't be a pussy."[13]

---

[6] "Different People Use the Internet in Different Ways," Infoplease, accessed 28 Oct. 2009, http://www.infoplease.com/ipa/A0931238.html.

[7] "Lolcats 'n' Funny Pictures of Cats – I Can Has Cheezburger?," WordPress.com, accessed 20 May 2010, http://icanhascheezburger.com/.

[8] Jason S. Carroll, Alexander C. Jensen, Larry J. Nelson, and Laura M. Padilla-Walker, "More Than a Just a Game," (2009): 110, accessed 17 May 2010, http://www.springerlink.com/content/w487673k5415k142/.

[9] Joanne Lipman, "The Mismeasure of Woman," The New York Times, accessed 25 Oct. 2009,http://www.nytimes.com/2009/10/24/opinion/24lipman.html?pagewanted=1&_r=1&em

[10] "TwiCheerleaders," Twitter, accessed 28 Nov, 2009,http://twitter.com/twiCheerleaders.

[11] Dr. Dre, "Bitches Ain't Shit," The Chronic, 1992.

[12] Henry Miller, "Manly Men: Sports and Patriarchy, Feminists and Gays," Affirmation: Gay & Lesbian Mormons, accessed 21 May 2010,http://www.affirmation.org/resources/manly_men.shtml.

[13] Ice T, "Cop Killer," Body Count, 1992.

Another sort of entertainment that more male online users engage in than females is video games. Analysis of these games reveals there are "no female characters in 41% of the games with characters. In 28% of these, women were portrayed as sex objects [...] and 21% depicted violence directed at women."[14] The virtual gaming world at large contains few female characters, often depicts females as sex toys, and/or females as a target for abuse. One such game over 2.5 million people play is Castle Age, a role playing game on Facebook, where many of the characters are nearly naked females.[15] Further, many video games premises revolve around killing. For example, the basis of World of Warcraft, an especially popular online role playing game, is quests and raiding, both of which rely heavily on slaughtering opponents.[16] Men are normally the ones who play these games, and the Internet harms them by promoting violence. However, "women who played video games or violent video games also tended to engage in more drinking behaviors, had more sexual partners, had lower self-worth and perceptions of social acceptance, and had lower quality relationships with friends and parents."[17]

These risk behaviors are also associated with women who view pornography, both online and off.[18] Men are more likely to entertain themselves with pornography more than women,[19] and they too are affected by pornography. Whether videos, pictures, cartoons, or text, a great deal of pornography presents females negatively. Women often appear as mere sex toys, normally willing to engage in any act, suffer many abuses, all for the purpose of arousing the viewer. Further, if the pornography depicts a female refusing to participate in a sexual act, she is called names, or even forced into participating against her will, which again, the viewer is supposed to get off on and enjoy. This portrayal of women not only degrades them, but it sends the message to both genders that women are supposed to act submissively to men and accept whatever abuse. It also suggests that men are to violently dominate women during sexual acts and even that this is the only way that they act.

---

[14] Tracy L. Dietz, "An Examination of Violence and Gender Role Portrayals in Video Games: Implications for Gender Socialization and Aggressive Behavior," Women and Language 23.2 (2000): 64, Academic OneFile, accessed 4 Nov. 2009, http://find.galegroup.com.

[15] Castle Age, Facebook, accessed 28 Nov. 2009,http://www.facebook.com/apps/application.php?id=46755028429&ref=search&sid=1595268849.2015195435..1.

[16] "World of Warcraft," Wikipedia, accessed 21 May 2010,http://en.wikipedia.org/wiki/World_of_Warcraft.

[17] Jason S. Carroll, Alexander C. Jensen, Larry J. Nelson, and Laura M. Padilla-Walker, "More Than a Just a Game," (2009): 111, accessed 17 May 2010, http://www.springerlink.com/content/w487673k5415k142/.

[18] Ibid.

[19] William A. Fisher and Azy Barak, "Internet Pornography: A Social Psychological Perspective on Internet Sexuality," *Journal of Sex Research 38*, no. 4 (2001): 315, accessed 4 Nov. 2009, http://web.ebscohost.com.

Yet, a recent study has shown that "as pornography has increased in availability, sex crimes have either decreased or not increased."[20] This fact can mean either that the viewing of pornography does not encourage sex crimes, or it affects the perception of what exactly a sex crime is, so fewer people report them. Likewise, "a correlation between pornography and rape may indicate nothing more than a common cause for both. Namely, that we live in a sexually repressed society. To further repress sex by restricting pornography might well increase the incidence of rape. Opening up the area of pornography might well diffuse sexual violence by making sexuality more understandable."[21]

Pornography may have benefits then, in allowing violent sexual tendencies to be relieved through the viewing of pornography. Also, many sexual fetishes are displayed in online pornography, which can also be a release for some people who cannot find such outlets in their real life. Similarly, it establishes particular acts to be normative for sexual arousal, which can be good in reassuring someone that his or her particular turn-ons are not strange or abnormal.

Online pornography is perhaps more widespread than some might think, which means its affects are likewise pervasive. Wordtracker.com supplies reports on the top 200 long-term search phrases—those that reappear through the weeks, months, and years—and the top 200 short-term search phrases—phrases that appear within a one-day period—that are put into its database. 42% of both long and short-term search phrases are direct searches on porn sites, searches for women celebrities known for their sexual appeal, and phrases whose top hits are pornography, such as "girls showering," or relate to women in a sexual fashion, such as "boobs."[22] An article in the Psychology of Women Quarterly reported that in the 1980s all "X-rated materials in the U.S. represented '… an estimated $8 billion industry of misogyny per year' (Cowan, Lee, Levy, & Synder, 1988, pp. 309-310) and the U.S. Attorney General's Commission reported that violent pornography was '[…] the most prevalent form' of sexually explicit material."[23] 30 years later the numbers have risen. In 2006, the Internet pornography industry made over $2.84 billion, and total the porn industry made $13.33 billion.[24] More Internet pornography increases the amount of online materials which affect both men and women.

It is not only online entertainment that can affect people. In fact, it is not only the content of the Internet which can have an effect. Internet also benefits men and

---

[20] Miranda Marquit, "Could Porn Be Good For Society?," Physorg.com, accessed 17 May 2010, http://www.physorg.com/news187448961.html.

[21] Wendy McElroy, "Banning Pornography Endangers Women," International Society for Individual Liberty, accessed 21 May 2010,http://www.isil.org/resources/lit/banning-porn.html.

[22] "Top 1000 Search Phrases," Wordtracker.com, accessed 28 Oct. 2009,http://www.wordtracker.com/database.

[23] William A. Fisher and Azy Barak, "Internet Pornography: A Social Psychological Perspective on Internet Sexuality," *Journal of Sex Research 38*, no. 4 (2001): 313, accessed 4 Nov. 2009, http://web.ebscohost.com.

[24] Jerry Ropelato, "Internet Pornography Statistics," TopTenReviews, accessed 28 Nov. 2009, http://internet-filter-review.toptenreviews.com/internet-pornography-statistics.html.

women in that it is an extremely easy and efficient tool to use. The Internet is not limited to one single area of life; it can be used for both business and pleasure, for communication purposes, consumption of media, research, and so much more. There is potential in all these online fields to affect society both negatively and positively.

A huge positive regarding the Internet is that not only is it highly accessible, but it can be—for research in particular—much more effective and time-saving than traveling to a library and wading through multiple books or magazines. In a society that values saving time to the degree that the United States' culture does, the ability of online databases to scan an endless amount of data in nanoseconds and reveal the most relevant information is nearly priceless. The Internet then frees online-searchers to find more information than they could otherwise, or enables them to move onto another project.

Along with this nature of efficiency and time-saving, another benefit to people is that there "is a huge amount of information available on the Internet for just about every subject known to man, ranging from government law and services, trade fairs and conferences, market information, new ideas and technical support"—the list is endless.[25] Everyone can use the Internet to educate him—or herself on any number of these topics: he or she can learn how best to treat a child's illness using WebMD,[26] how to contact a state senator through the U.S. Senate website,[27] or engage in self-exploratory research, such researching religion online.

The potential for acquisition of knowledge, then, is the empowering factor when it comes to research and education online. A person has the ability to learn practically anything through the Internet, and that power provides him or her with the opportunity to effect positive change in his or her life and those of others.

In addition to research, the Internet also allows people to seek further schooling to empower themselves. From busy parents to teenagers who dropped out of high school to those fiscally challenged, the Internet provides a way for many people to expand their knowledge. Anyone with Internet access can acquire their G.E.Ds through online programs, as well as online Bachelor, Master, and even Doctoral degrees from places such as ITT Tech, Walden University, The Art Institute, and hundreds of other universities.[28] Education empowers people by allowing social mobility. Higher education is correlated with "higher earnings for all racial/ethnic groups," as well as "lower smoking rates, more positive perceptions of personal health, and lower incarceration rates," and "higher levels of civic participation, including volunteer work, voting, and blood donation."[29]

---

[25] Jayashree Pakhare, "Advantages and Disadvantages of the Internet," 23 Mar. 2010, http://www.buzzle.com/articles/advantages-disadvantages-internet.html.
[26] WebMD, http/:www.webmd.com.
[27] United States Senate, http://www.senate.gov/index.htm.
[28] Online Degree Today.com, http://www.online-degrees-today.com/.
[29] Sandy Baum and Kathleen Payea, "Education Pays: 2004," College Board.com, 2005, 7, accessed 15 Apr.

Increased wealth, health, and social participation all improve the quality of living, allowing people the opportunity to achieve more of their potentials.

The Internet also empowers people by allowing them to work from home, just as it allows them to study from there. For example, many women delay or completely sacrifice motherhood because they wish to succeed in their careers. The Internet enables many people to work from almost any location easily, and thus makes it easier for them to have families. The Internet also makes business simpler for women and men by providing a very cheap space for their work to exist. To promote business offline "takes much money and time," but websites and e-mail may be created "and seen by anyone from anywhere" without any cost or inputting a lot of time.[30] Companies reach a much larger number of people online—both associates and customers—than offline. In addition, they can choose which websites to advertise to, so the Internet is a perfect avenue for advertising any sort of business, since it allows the most desired cliental to be targeted. As women especially have often been relegated to low-paying jobs, and highly discriminated against in the workplace, any advantage the Internet provides to overcome obstacles empowers women and benefits the business world through their inclusion.

Whether for work, entertainment, or other activities, the Internet provides a way for people to connect with others. Online communication gives people the opportunity to converse without fear of judgment or persecution that can occur in face-to-face meetings. E-mail, online messaging systems, and social networking sites remove barriers—whether physical distance or prejudice based on external appearance or mannerisms—which provide the opportunity to communicate with people who cannot be reached through any other means. People can have little effect on others, none at all, or they can completely change another's life; again, the source of empowerment for people is in the potential the Internet provides.

Another way to empower men and women is through the "communication technology of the Internet. In the midst of the current economic crisis it can be costly to construct environments [in public spaces] that are free of physical barriers and ensure the independent personal mobility of women,"[31] but the Internet provides an uninhibited location free of almost all boundaries. On message boards, people can ask questions anonymously or with a nickname, thus freeing them to remark on anything and question everything. The Internet is the "only open platform where [Internet users] can express their own views and post

---

2010,http://www.collegeboard.com/prod_downloads/press/cost04/EducationPays2004.pdf.

[30] Akio Orita, Makoto Niimi, and Jun Murai, "The Three Ways the Internet Empowers an Ordinary Individual: How Women in Japan Express Themselves and Their Opinions," accessed 9 Apr. 2010,http://www.isoc.org/inet2000/cdproceedings/8a/8a_2.htm.

[31]Inge Komardjaja, "The Internet Empowers Women With Disabilities," Isis International, accessed 23 Mar. 2010, http://www.isiswomen.org/index.php?option=com_content&task=view&id=653&Itemid=200

their own material without a gatekeeper."[32] It is the one place for people to completely express themselves without restriction. However, this lack of any constraining feature means that "people can say whatever they want without suffering the consequences. Therefore, you don't need to be politically correct online. Because of this, many are allured to the Internet to express their hate and anger towards specific groups; as a result, many racist, sexist and just plain hate websites exist."[33] These comments are more harmful than they are beneficial: while the Internet allows people to express their feelings and emotions in a physically nonviolent manner, it puts these negative messages out there to be read and absorbed by others. Often when people protest against these negative messages, they are ridiculed or bullied. A woman online who "speaks out steadfastly and strongly against [...] pornography, prostitution, who writes as a feminist or as a human rights advocate, can expect to be harassed and attacked [...] not only for her specific views and perspective, but in ways that are distinctly sexist."[34] It is not the ideas that are assaulted, but rather an attack on the female writer's appearance, or "she will be described as a man-hater, her writings, activism and life's work will be dismissed and trivialized, she will be called shrill and strident, or she will be threatened in ways that are sexual."[35] Therefore the discussions of a topic often become one-sided, with the rest of the comments spiraling into attacks. There is also the problem that most of the content of the Internet is presented from a Western perspective. Most of the material online "presents western cultures and language as dominant over all others,"[36] which is common viewpoint in America. However, the United States, or even all of North America, is the center of the world. Other countries are more powerful in certain fields, and the Internet does not present that.

The Internet also affords anyone the opportunity to metaphorically stand on a soapbox and express opinions in any way they desire. In the United States, these reactions, even if they are violent ad homonym harassments of a writer, the responses (recall that men are the ones that are more likely to add content to the web[37]) are "understood to be matters of someone's 'freedom of speech,' while [female writers'] objections and our outcries [against the debasement of women], are called 'censorship' by some. And yet it is this 'freedom of speech' of some that ultimately silences us and robs us of our own freedom of speech."[38]

---

[32] Mary Alice Crim, "The Internet is a Feminist Issue," Save the Internet, accessed 23 Mar. 2010,http://www.savetheinternet.com/blog/09/07/06/internet-feminist-issue.
[33] "Negative Effects of Internet Usage," Associated Content, 4, 15 May 2010,http://www.associatedcontent.com/article/45919/negative_effects_of_internet_usage_pg2.html?cat=15.
[34] Cheryl Lindsey Seelhoff, "A Chilling Effect: The Oppression and Silencing of Women Journalists and Bloggers Worldwide," Off Our Backs 37, no 1 (2007) 18, accessed 4 Nov. 2009, http://web.ebscohost.com.
[35] Ibid.
[36] "What Is The Negative Impact The Internet Has On People?," blurtit.com, accessed 30 Apr. 2010, http://www.blurtit.com/q132748.html.
[37] "Different People Use the Internet in Different Ways," Infoplease, accessed 28 Oct. 2009, http://www.infoplease.com/ipa/A0931238.html.
[38] Cheryl Lindsey Seelhoff, "A Chilling Effect: The Oppression and Silencing of Women Journalists and Bloggers Worldwide," *Off Our Backs 37*, no 1 (2007) 20, accessed 4 Nov. 2009, http://web.ebscohost.com.

Further, the freedom of the Internet permits people to be whoever they want. While this means most can be themselves without fear of judgment, it also means that people can pretend to be someone else. For example, many sexual predators use the anonymity of the Internet to lure young children or teenagers by posing as individuals of the same age. When chatting or posting online, it is never definite whether the person who says that she is a forty-year-old businesswoman who works as an engineer is forty years old, a businesswoman, an engineer, or a woman at all. It might be a thirteen-year-old girl, or a twenty-year-old boy, or a seventy-year-old man. There are no certainties when it comes to online identities. Thus, the freedom afforded by the Internet can be dangerous, as well as advantageous in many ways.

Another valuable function of anonymity of the Internet, however, is that physical appearance can be highly restricting to men and women. In real life, "body language, voice, and attitude form the first impression which may last as a like or dislike of the other person."[39] When the physical presence is stripped away, such as it is online, then people feel free to act completely different than they do in reality because they do not fear the perceptions they create in others. Dr. Petra Boynton, sex editor of Men's Health, explains this in relation to online dating: "'People who feel uncomfortable can actually be much more up front [dating online], and ask direct questions. A lot of women say they find it quite empowering because they can ask things, demand things and flirt. For instance, many women find it hard to say "I don't want to see you again" but online they can. So it can be used just to improve your confidence outside of the Internet'."[40]

One more way that the Internet empowers people is by boosting confidence and connecting to other people is through support groups. There are hundreds of support groups online aimed singly at women. Some websites, such as http://www.dmoz.org/,[41] can be utilized to locate many of these online support groups. There are discussion boards for—just to name a few—divorce, menopause, birthing, smoking, losing weight, breast cancer, disabilities, and eating disorders. Researchers have found that these online support groups can be key in producing and maintaining a healthy physical, mental, and emotional state for females. For instance, a study funded by the National Institute of Mental Health, published in 2006, found that "Internet-based intervention program may prevent some high risk, college-age women from developing an eating disorder."[42]

---

[39] Inge Komardjaja, "The Internet Empowers Women With Disabilities," Isis International, accessed 23 Mar. 2010, http://www.isiswomen.org/index.php?option=com_content&task=view&id=653&Itemid=200

[40] Tom Geoghegan, "Internet Dating 'Empowers Women'," BBC News Online, accessed 23 Mar. 2010,http://news.bbc.co.uk/2/hi/uk_news/2486815.stm.

[41] "Open Directory Project," dmoz, accessed 28 Nov. 2009,http://www.dmoz.org/Health/Women's_Health/Support_Groups/34.

[42] Taylor CB, et al, "Prevention of Eating Disorders in At-risk College-age Women," Archives of General Psychiatry, (2006),http://www.4therapy.com/consumer/conditions/article/8684/75/College+Wo

While women are more likely to make use of these online support groups and programs,[43] the comment must be made that they are available for men to use as well. Likewise, women generally utilize social networking sites, such as Facebook, more than men,[44] but men still engage and benefit from all forms of online communication. Therefore, it seems that the communication function of the Internet does not explicitly empower women, but rather humanity in general.

There are also other inherent dangers to the Internet. Practically every aspect of life can now be done online: shopping for food and clothes, research, education, communication, playing games, listening to music and watching movies, business, banking—almost all necessary activities can be completed without leaving the living room. Life can literally be lived online since "the Internet cuts out the social interactions of our lives. With the Internet doing so many jobs for us, we have become lazy and non-social."[45] The Internet allows for complete solitary living without any contact from outside forces. This can lead to loneliness and depression. A recent study found that "Adolescents who reported regular Internet use for web surfing, instant messaging, emailing and online games had a significantly higher mean score of loneliness than those who did not. The results, also, indicated that the frequency of Internet use is a significant predictor of loneliness."[46]

Overall, there are both advantages and disadvantages to almost every aspect of the Internet; nothing is completely good or bad, but rather has characteristics which can both harm and help. Online material does not seem to portray one sex as better or worse than the other, nor do the applications and resources there give power to or hinder one sex more than the other. Furthermore, the Internet itself does not seem to be the source generating the content, but rather the material comes from the various outside media, such as television shows off network channels, or songs downloaded through iTunes. The Internet simply acts as a convenient source to access a large amount of data, and it provides this material to the large audiences that use the Internet. Ultimately, how men and women are affected by the Internet depends on what they use it for, and men and women typically utilize it for different purposes: women usually for online discussion and self-exploration, and men for business and entertainment.[47]

---

men+at+Risk+for+Eating+ Disorders+May+Benefit+From+Internet-based+Intervention+Program.

[43] "Different People Use the Internet in Different Ways," Infoplease, accessed 28 Oct. 2009, http://www.infoplease.com/ipa/A0931238.html.

[44] Justin Smith, "Fastest Growing Demographic on Facebook: Women Over 55," Inside Facebook, accessed 14 Apr. 2010,http://www.insidefacebook.com/2009/02/02/fastest-growing-demographic-on-facebook-women-over-55/.

[45] "Negative Effects of Internet Usage," Associated Content, 2, 15 May 2010,http://www.associatedcontent.com/article/45919/negative_effects_of_internet_usage_pg2.html?cat=15.

[46] Yavuz Erdogan, "Exploring the Relationships among Internet Usage, Internet Attitudes and Loneliness of Turkish Adolescents," Cyber Psychology, accessed 21 May 2010,http://www.cyberpsychology.eu/view.php?cisloclanku=2008111802

[47] "Different People Use the Internet in Different Ways," Infoplease, accessed 28 Oct. 2009, http://www.infoplease.com/ipa/A0931238.html.

However, this does not mean that one sex is affected more so than the other by the Internet. It simply means that men and women are affected in different ways because they use the Internet differently.

Word Recognition and the Accommodative Response to Desktop Versus Handheld Video Displays (Handheld Study #2)

James Kundart, OD, MEd, FAAO
Yu-Chi Tai, Ph.D.
John R. Hayes, Ph.D.
James Sheedy OD, PhD, FAAO

Vision Ergonomics Research Lab
Pacific University College of Optometry

Purpose

To determine the difference, if any, in text legibility and the accommodative (focusing) response between hard copy, an LCD desktop monitor, and handheld video displays, and how it affects users' accommodative responses.

Introduction

As much as many of us relish living in the Information Age despite difficulties with ergonomics and comfort. Both recreational computer users and those for whom it is an occupational necessity can suffer from ergonomic difficulties.[1,2]

Many users report greater comfort reading with hard copy or on a handheld device than on a desktop computer monitor.[3] One reason might be because hard copy and handheld text resolution is typically higher than inexpensive desktop monitors, despite their often smaller display size. Paradoxically, this greater comfort is despite very close working distances typically used with handheld devices.[4]

In this study, both text legibility and accommodative responses were measured on desktop and handheld displays, as well as hard copy, to test the hypothesis that the higher the text resolution, the fewer the symptoms.[5]

---

[1] Ergonomics, part one : is the job you love a pain in the neck? / Linda Roach. *EyeNet* 1097-2986 2009 Jul/Aug; 13(7): 49-50.
[2] Seven risk factors for injury, and seven solutions : ergonomics, part two / Linda Roach. *EyeNet* 1097-2986 2009 Sep; 13(8): 45-46,48-50.
[3] Sheedy JE, Hayes JR, Engle J. Is all asthenopia the same? *Optom Vis Sci* 2003;80:732-739.
[4] Hemphill N. Handheld device use poses more stress on eyes, body than reading printed copy. *Primary Care Optometry News* 1081-6437 2008 Dec; 13(12): 5.
[5] Vasta S. Ergonomics research aims to help reduce visual demands of computer use : studies designed to improve usability are focusing on enhancing font designs. *Primary Care Optometry News* 1081-6437 2008 Apr; 13(4): 24.

Comparing the desktop and handheld video displays, both are capable of displaying subpixel rendering known as ClearType. However, there is typically a difference in display resolution. For instance, the resolution of a typical 15" LCD desktop monitor is 120 dpi, while the resolution of a 2.5" handheld display is 140 dpi. Laser-printed hardcopy has the best letter rendering, but of course, no ClearType. See Figure 1.

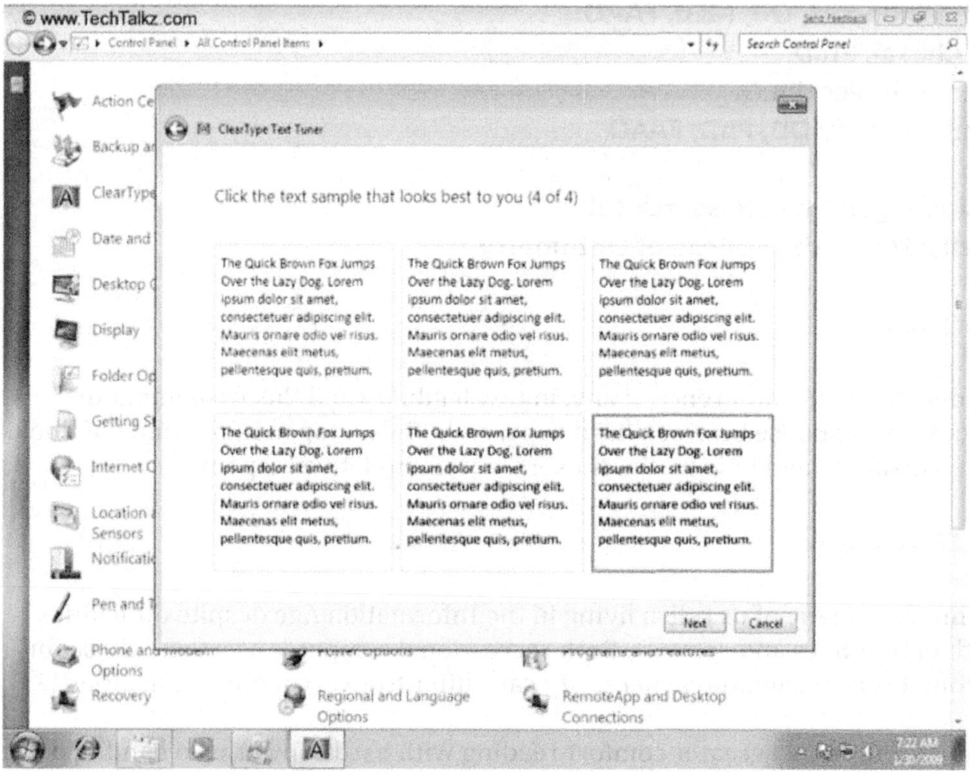

Figure 1: ClearType Text Tuner as seen on a Windows PC

The font size in Windows Mobile does not correspond exactly with a desktop display or hard copy. In general, the font size needs to be one or two points smaller on the desktop to match the handheld display in linear size. In this study, we were careful to match these linear sizes with and without ClearType.

Method

Participants

37 participants, all younger than age 40 (and therefore not in need of bifocals), completed the study. All wore the proper spectacle or contact lens prescriptions to correct them to 20/20 vision at distance, as applicable. Participants were recruited through a website following IRB and HIPAA privacy protocols.

Equipment

Text was displayed on a 15"desktop LCD monitor (120 dpi), a 2.5" HP iPAQ smartphone (left) (140 dpi), or hard copy (right) (printed form a 1200 dpi laser printer). Both video displays were capable of displaying ClearType rendered text. Tahoma font was used for presentation as constrained by the smartphone we used. See Figure 2

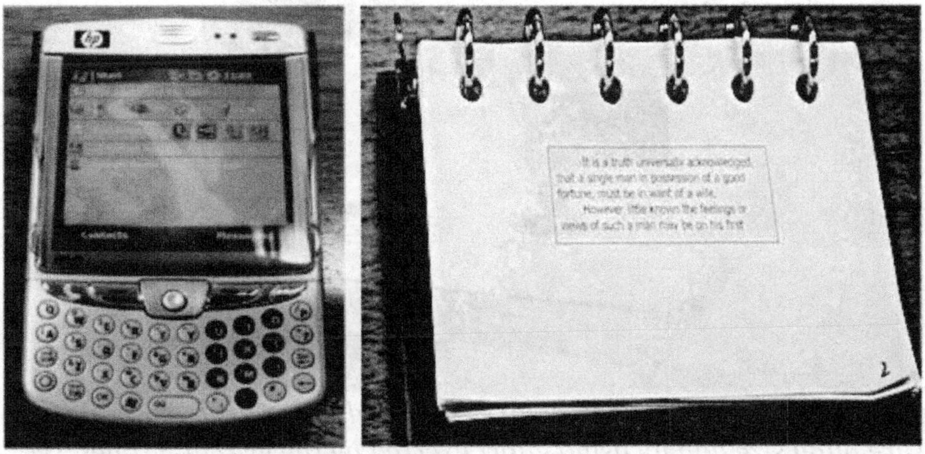

Figure 2: HP iPAQ smartphone and hard copy text used

Tasks

Participants were asked to perform two tasks*: Text legibility and Accommodation in reading*. Each participant performed all conditions.

In *Text legibility* task, they were asked to read aloud a row of five high frequency words of 5 or 6 letters from a designated distance. The words were displayed on hard copy, desktop monitor or handheld display at various font sizes. After each attempt, the participant was asked to back up to a distance that would increase acuity demand by logarithmic steps and repeat the process until words could be correctly recognized, as reported to the experimenter.

Participants completed nine short readings and had their accommodative response (focusing) measured while reading. All participants completed all conditions in randomized order using the Latin Square technique.

For each task, participants were asked to silently read text presented on hard copy, a desktop monitor and a smartphone display while their pupil size and accommodation were monitored with Grand-Seiko auto-refractor. See Figure 3.

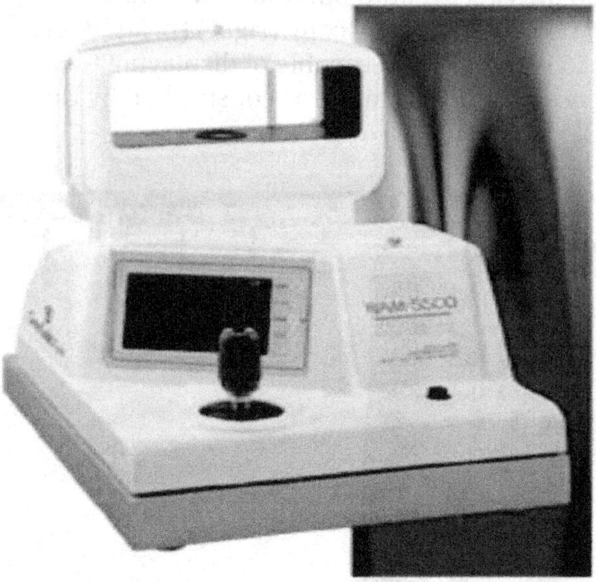

Figure 3: *Grand Seiko WAM-5500 Open-Field Autorefractor, used to measure pupil size and focusing effort exerted by the eyes at 5 times/sec*

There were nine experimental conditions used for this study, and each participant was exposed to all nine of these conditions for five minutes each. Therefore, 45 minutes of raw data were gathered, each consisting of many data points. This is because our autorefractor sampled both accommodation and pupil size up to five times a second for up to 45 minutes of reading per subject, as follows:

Condition #1: LCD desktop monitor with font size matched to 9-pt text on smartphone, with ClearType

Condition #2: LCD desktop monitor with 9-pt Tahoma without ClearType

Condition #3: LCD desktop monitor with 9-pt Tahoma font with ClearType

Condition #4: Smartphone using 9-pt Tahoma without ClearType

Condition #5 (control condition): Smart phone using 9-pt Tahoma and ClearType

Condition #6: Smartphone using 12-pt Tahoma without ClearType

Condition #7: Smartphone using 12-pt Tahoma with ClearType

Condition #8: Hard copy with font size matched to 9-pt text on smartphone

Condition #9: Hard copy with tear-down pages and 9-pt Tahoma font

During each condition, participants were seated behind the Grand Seiko WAM-5500 open-field autorefractor for accommodative measurements. The participants read from one of several continuous text stories for 5 minutes each.

All participants were given a symptom survey after each reading condition and asked to rate their experience. Twelve questions addressed reading problems. See Appendix for an example of this survey.

Statistical Methods

Conditions were compared with mixed model analysis of variance. Individual paired comparisons were illustrated with confidence intervals. Non-overlapping 84% confidence intervals reveal statistically significant differences at an unadjusted p<0.05.[6] Symptoms questions log transformed and combined into three pre-defined scales for internal (3 questions), external (4 questions), and reading problems (12 questions) using principal component analysis separately on each set of questions. Factor scores were constructed with an Anderson Rubin transformation. The confidence intervals were geometrically transformed back to the original 100 point scale for graphing.[7]

Results

Differences of text legibility were significant (F = 9.9 (df 8,312), p<0.001). The control handheld condition (HH 9 pt CT) was equal in legibility to all other handheld conditions and significantly poorer than non-handheld conditions. The handheld 12-point ClearType was more legible than handheld 12-point non-ClearType on video displays. There were no differences between the LCD monitor and hard copy. See Figure 4.

---

[6] Ergonomics, part one : is the job you love a pain in the neck? / Linda Roach. *EyeNet* 1097-2986 2009 Jul/Aug; 13(7): 49-50.

[7] Payton ME, Greenstone MH, Schenker N. 2003. Overlapping confidence intervals or standard error intervals: What do they mean in terms of statistical significance? 6pp. *Journal of Insect Science, 3*:34, Available online: insectscience.org/3.34

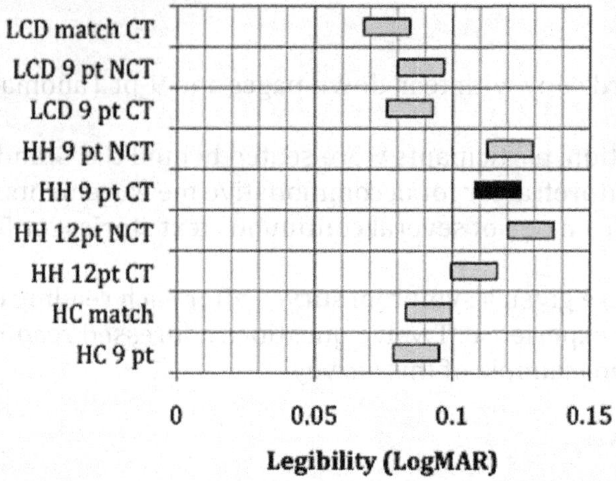

Figure 4. *Legibility across conditions. LogMAR stands for the logarithm of the minimum angle of resolution, with 0.1 representing 20/20. Bars represent 84% confidence intervals around means. The SEM for the confidence interval was derived from the standard error of differences used in the paired comparisons. Non-overlapping confidence intervals are significant at p<0.05, unadjusted for multiple comparisons. The black bar represents the control condition.*

Grand Seiko Real-Time Accommodation

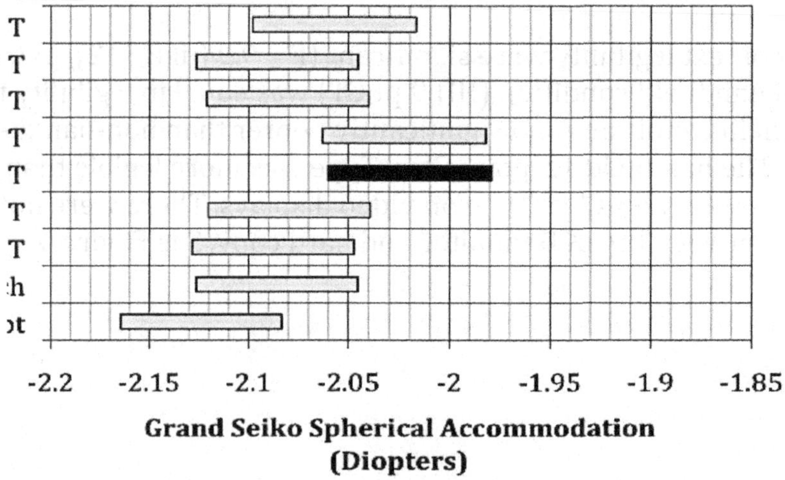

Figure 5: *Accommodation (focusing) effort was not significantly different comparing all conditions except the smallest (9 pt) hard copy font. (Note the y-axis labels are cut off, but are conditions 1-9 in order). The black bar represents the control condition.*

There was no significant main effect of (F=1.32 (df 8,304), p=0.23). Namely, focusing effort was the same with hard copy, desktop and smartphone video displays. See Figure 5.

Relationship Between Vision Measures and Symptoms

There were only a few weak correlations between vision measures and symptom scores, as determined by survey. Survey questions and responses were divided into internal, external, and physical symptoms.

Internal Symptom Factors

These included survey items about sore eyes, eye ache, eye pain, headache and eyestrain.
Except for comparing the smallest size font without ClearType on the smartphone vs. hard copy, there was no significant effect of internal symptoms (F=2.049 (df 8,311) , p=0.04). See Figure 6.

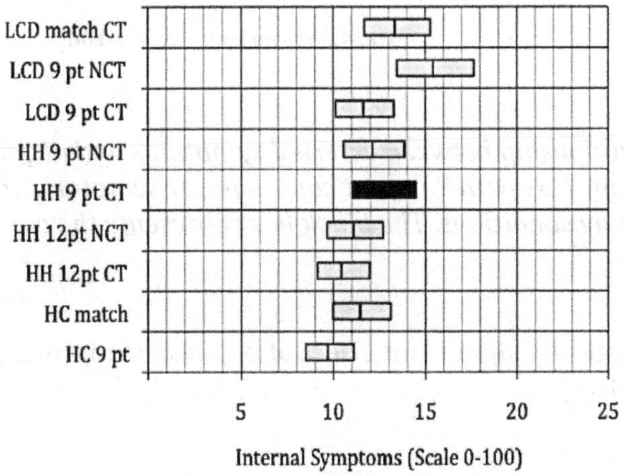

Figure 6: *Relationship between internal symptoms and display used. Note that the desktop monitor with 9 pt font caused fewer symptoms than the same size font on the LCD desktop monitor, but only without ClearType. The black bar represents the control condition.*

External Symptom Factors

External symptoms included eye irritation, burning, tired eyes, dry eyes, and tearing. There was no significant effect of external symptoms (F=1,23 (df 8,312), p=0.28). However, the hard copy text with the smallest font showed fewer symptoms than the most of the electronic displays, regardless of font size. See Figure 7.

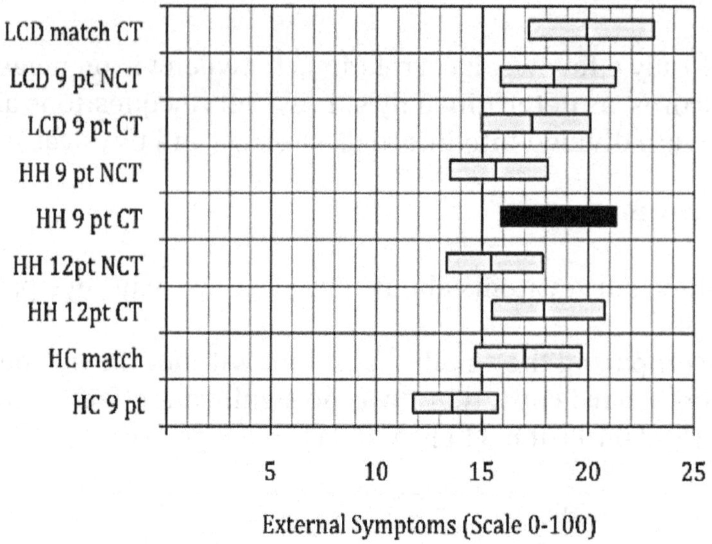

Figure 7: *Relationship between external symptoms and display used. Note that the hard copy text with 9 pt font caused fewer symptoms than most of the electronic display conditions. The black bar represents the control condition.*

There was no statistically significant effect of physical symptoms, such as neck pain (F=1.56, p=0.137).

Reading Problems

Twelve questions addressed reading problems. There was a significant main effect of condition (F=3.3 (df 8, 304)1, p=0.001). Comprehension accuracy had no effect. In other words, the three different displays (hard copy, desktop and smartphone video displays) were all equally easy to see. The exception was at the smallest font size, judging from the frequency of symptoms surveyed, the hard copy was still preferred. See Figure 8.

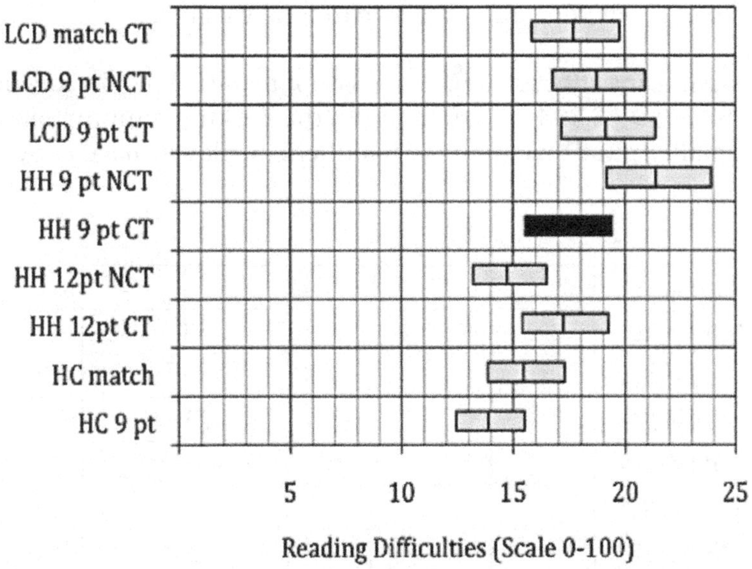

Figure 8: *Relationship between reading problems and display used. Note that the hard copy with 9 pt font caused fewer symptoms than the same size font on the smartphone, but only without ClearType. The black bar represents the control condition.*

Pupil Size

The Grand Seiko WAM-5500 autorefractor measures pupil size as well as accommodation. The iris pupil changes size in response to two primary factors: lighting changes and accommodative changes. See Figure 9.

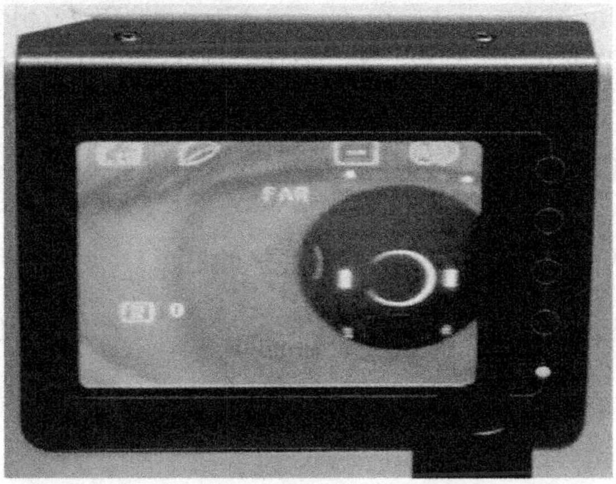

Figure 9: *Pupil size measurement with the Grand Seiko WAM-5500 was possible up to five times/sec*

Pupil size was not associated with accommodation (F=2.29 df 1,340, p=.13; pseudo R2=.004). The pseudo R2 was computed using the mixed model analysis taking the ratio of predicted value variance to total variance.

There was a significant effect of pupil size without controlling for any other variables (F=53.37; DF 8,304 p < 0.001), with the desktop monitor causing significantly smaller pupil size than the handheld display or hard copy. See Figure 10.

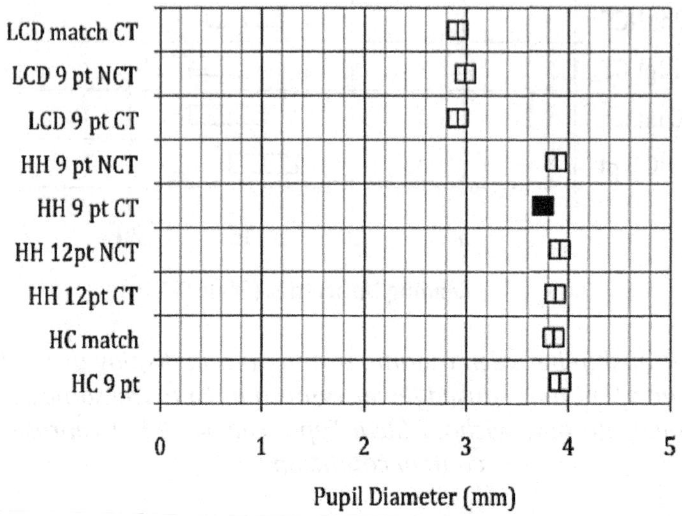

Figure 10: *Pupil size was significantly smaller with the desktop monitor, regardless of font size. This is likely due to the increased luminance of the white background in a typical Word document, as we used. The black bar represents the control condition.*

Also, pupil size was significantly smaller when looking at the desktop monitor than either the handheld or hard copy (F=53.370 p < 0.001), likely due to monitor brightness when black text is displayed on a black background. While not tested, smaller pupil size generally increases depth-of-focus.

Other Results: Residual Refractive Error

At the beginning of each participant's study, baseline residual refractive error after corrective lenses was measured.. There was no significant relationship between accommodation and refractive error (OD F=1.63 df 1,45, p=.209; OS F=1.0 df 1,43, p=.32).

Conclusions

Legibility is worse on the handheld display tested (HP iPAQ smartphone) than on the LCD desktop monitor tested, or hard copy. Accommodative responses were not significantly different on handheld displays versus desktop monitors and hard copy.

Internal symptom factors (sore eyes/ eye ache/ eye pain, double vision, blurred vision, headache and eyestrain) were not significantly related to accommodation. Conversely, external symptom factors (irritation, burning, tired eyes, dry eyes, tearing) were worse with desktop and handheld displays than hard copy. This result is supported by previous research.[8] [9]

As accommodation relates more closely to the internal symptoms, focusing alone does not seem to explain these differences. This was borne out by the accommodative measurements made with the Grand Seiko autorefractor. Participants reporting reading problems showed insignificantly different accommodative responses.

However, one explanation as to why our participants had greater external symptoms with the desktop monitor may be that pupil size is significantly smaller in response to desktop versus handheld video displays. Smaller pupil size might cause symptoms by itself, according to the following logic:

1. The pupils constrict more when using a desktop video display as compared to a handheld one, such as a smartphone, undoubtedly due to greater luminance of the standard white background on the desktop monitor
2. Pupil constriction occurs to a lesser extent due to accommodation, or focusing, of the eyes
3. Accommodation also triggers convergence of the eyes through the extraocular muscles
4. Many vision scientists believe that overstimulation and fatigue of this so-called "near triad" of convergence, accommodation and pupillary constriction causes fatigue and eyestrain

While this study has only proven a consistent difference in the effects of handheld versus desktop video displays to be with pupil size, not accommodation, future studies should examine the last leg of the near triad, convergence.

Looking to the future, these researchers would like to discover why users seem to be more comfortable with shorter working distances when using hard copy or handheld video displays, compared to desktop computer displays. One possible reason may be that hard copy and handheld devices, like smartphones, provide proprioceptive feedback from the hand that better helps to aim the eyes than

---

[8] Anshel J. Diagnosing, treating CVS relies on good case history : basic eye care, ergonomics and optical correction are all part of an effective treatment plan for computer vision syndrome. *Primary Care Optometry News* 1081-6437 2007 Sep; 12(9): 14-16.
[9] DePaolis MD. CVS requires multifaceted treatment : computer vision syndrome demands attention to ergonomics, ocular surface and vision correction / Michael D. DePaolis. *Primary Care Optometry News* 1081-6437 2007 Sep; 12(9): 3.

when using a desktop monitor place out of arm's reach. Another is that handheld video display users may only be using one eye.[10]

These possibility, and others, will hopefully be addressed by another study of handheld video displays and eye teaming.

Acknowledgements and Financial Disclaimer:

Funding for this study was provided by the Advanced Reading Technologies Group of Microsoft Corporation. The authors have no financial interest in Hewlitt Packard or Grand Seiko corporations.

APPENDIX A: DIGITAL SYMPTOM SURVEY

For each of the following symptoms, choose the sensation that most closely represents the severity you experienced during reading just now.

[10] Villa JLR. Monocular impairment in video display terminal operators : a case series. *Journal of Behavioral Optometry* 1045-8395 2006; 17(6): 143-148.

	None	Mild	Moderate	Bad	Severe
Sore eyes, painful eyes, or ache in or around eyes	None	Mild	Moderate	Bad	Severe
Double vision	None	Mild	Moderate	Bad	Severe
Blurred vision	None	Mild	Moderate	Bad	Severe
Headache	None	Mild	Moderate	Bad	Severe
Eye strain or pulling of the eye muscles	None	Mild	Moderate	Bad	Severe
Irritation or burning of the eyes	None	Mild	Moderate	Bad	Severe
Tearing, or watery eyes	None	Mild	Moderate	Bad	Severe
Dry eyes	None	Mild	Moderate	Bad	Severe
Tired eyes	None	Mild	Moderate	Bad	Severe
Bothered by brightness	None	Mild	Moderate	Bad	Severe
Bothered by glare	None	Mild	Moderate	Bad	Severe
Computer screen fonts look too small	None	Mild	Moderate	Bad	Severe
Computer screen colors are distorted	None	Mild	Moderate	Bad	Severe
Computer screen clarity is poor	None	Mild	Moderate	Bad	Severe
Desire to blink harder	None	Mild	Moderate	Bad	Severe
Desire to blink more often	None	Mild	Moderate	Bad	Severe
Difficulty concentrating on the text	None	Mild	Moderate	Bad	Severe
Difficulty comprehending the text	None	Mild	Moderate	Bad	Severe
Difficulty remembering the text	None	Mild	Moderate	Bad	Severe
Feeling sleepy or eyelids feel heavy	None	Mild	Moderate	Bad	Severe
Feeling dizzy	None	Mild	Moderate	Bad	Severe
Desire to move closer or further away from the screen	None	Mild	Moderate	Bad	Severe
Desire to stop or take a break	None	Mild	Moderate	Bad	Severe

Digital Magazines and the iPad

Steve Dodge

If you listened to all of the hype surrounding the introduction of Apple's iPad, you would have thought that perhaps it would provide a cure for cancer or miraculously get everyone on the same page on global warming. One of the other lofty claims is that it would single-handedly save the publishing industry with its enhanced ability to deliver digital magazines and books.

No cures for cancer have been announced, iPad generated or otherwise, since the Pad's April 2010 debut and there is still a wide disparity on global warming between the apparent scientific consensus and government action. Also, while (Amazon) announced recently that sales of its digital books had for the first time passed sales of its dead tree scrolls (traditional books), it's unclear what role, if any, the Amazon Kindle app for the iPad played because Amazon doesn't share those numbers. Apple's iBook application, though, was for several months the leading free app in the iTunes store. Sales of the iPad passed the 1 million mark in May. About the same time Apple reported iBook downloads totaling 1.5 million. Those aren't exactly "savior" numbers, but certainly is an impressive start.

I mention iBook because no one in Magazine Land has yet captured its elegance, logical page turning, zooming or search ability for digital magazines. Most efforts I have seen have emphasized creating a whole new magazine "experience" with eye-popping graphics and photos. The result, as in the much ballyhooed Popular Science app, has been beautiful and innovative, but fraught with confusing and difficult navigation.

Wired magazine's app has done a much, much better job. Navigation is for the most part magazine-like and logical. Marvelous imbedded animations supplement and wow without overwhelming. Some of the interactive additions in the magazine's iPad debut like the Mars landing graphic are a little like playing a game (one must time the touch of swirling satellites just right to see information behind them) rather than a controlled interactive experience. But, it's cool and it mostly works. Curiously, though, the Wiredapp has no ability to zoom in and out with iPhone and iPad finger gestures, a real drawback.

Another entry into the digital magazine horse race is Zinio, a company that has been a leader in developing mainstream titles for desktop and mobile delivery. Soon after the iPad debuted, Zinio announced their new app for the iPad and iPhone. While the app is free, users initially could buy individual magazines for about the price of a newsstand copy. That price point proved to be controversial, with many arguing the publisher's savings in not printing or mailing should be passed on to the consumer. Prices for many titles are now less than newsstand costs. Either way, the Zinio app leads the pack at the moment because it delivers digital magazines that look like a print magazine, navigate like a print magazine, but also utilize the iPad's finger-gesture controls for zooming in and out. Reading Smithsonian this way is not quite as satisfying as the print edition, but you can carry around several issues without harming your back. With Rolling Stone magazine's special 500 Greatest Songs issue, Zinio continues to innovate. Readers can tap an icon to read about each song, another to hear a sample of the song and, of course, another to buy the song in iTunes. Though navigation is sometimes an issue–like finding your way back to a page after touching on a link that sends you to the middle of the magazine—it's a very engaging product that takes full advantage of the iPad screen and finger controls.

Announcements of new iPad magazines are happening almost daily and while it remains to be seen if they will be the significant new revenue stream publishers are hoping for, readers are certainly getting more options for delivery of their favorite titles.

Screenshots

iBooks App Icon

iBooks Library

Popular Science App Icon

Poplar Science App Cover

Zinio App Icon

Zinio Cover Sample

Suggested Links

http://www.zinio.com/
http://www.apple.com/ipad/
http://www.padgadget.com/
http://www.wired.com/magazine/2010/05/mag_editors_letter/

VoiceThread: Building a Mosaic of Asynchronous Communication

Mark Szymanski

For those of us early adopters, threaded discussions on discussion boards were one of the first forays into having "discussions" on the Internet. At the time the most important aspect of these discussions was the ability to have them over time, asynchronously, with people who were not in the same physical place as we were. Today, as we embrace the world of mobile web devices and micro-blogging, they seem like simple ideas; text-based, if you will.

Most of our communication on the Internet has been done with and still takes the form of text-a symbol system that represents our oral language. In some cases this is the appropriate and preferred method of communication for sending messages. Text messaging and instant messaging have all taken their place in our new communication culture. But because it is a symbol system for language, it is-in it's strictest sense-representational and not real. Thus, the content of what we communicate about is sometimes lost in translation along with the nuance and purpose we reveal when we speak to each other. A current example would be the use of mapping on the Internet. Today, instead of giving someone directions to a place, most of us simply give out the address and zip code to the place. This makes it easy data to put into web-based mapping software or our new mobile web-enabled devices. It seems cumbersome to listen to and write down step-by-step directions. Text works, but in this case, it's not the most effective way to communicate.

But, all this is changing as bandwidth and processing speed increase and data compression improves. We've all watched other mediums, video, audio, images, become more prevalent and powerful on the Internet. They are more popular because they provide raw content, no description necessary. No need to describe what something looks like when you can just see it. Today, our methods of synchronous or asynchronous communication still hold, but the thing that has changed over time is the content we comment on and the ways we comment. VoiceThread[1], web-based collaborative software is a way to facilitate media rich asynchronous communication on the Internet.

In a VoiceThread, a moderator posts content for invited people to comment on in a six-inch by six inch window in the middle of the browser window. The uploaded content can be most any form of media we commonly use on the web, images, videos, text, PDFs, and Office files. At its core, like the bulletin board systems and discussion forums that it follows, VoiceThread is, technologically, a web-based application that manages content created by users. VoiceThread is designed to be used by authors who are moderators of a conversation with invited people. Perhaps as a nod to distinguish itself from the older of asynchronous communication, the VoiceThread people use the term

[1] http://voicethread.com

"conversation" instead of "discussion." In this way, the environment is an exclusive one, but one that allows for feedback from a specific group of people who are selected to give feedback or participate in a discussion because of their qualifications.

In addition to the content that is commented on, the distinguishing feature of a VoiceThread is the way in which people can comment on the content. People can comment in five different ways using voice (with a microphone or telephone), text, audio file, or video (via a webcam). In addition to the actual comment, VoiceThread gives the commenter the ability to draw, or in their words doodle on the content file. They do this by incorporating a basic draw tool into the window. Again, instead of using text to describe something, the user gets to draw, circle, underline, or in some other way visually identify a part of a file they are talking about. After a participant leaves a comment, a thumbnail image of the commenter appears on the edge of the content window. As more and more people comment, their thumbnail profile pictures line the outside of the content window, creating a tile mosaic of contributors. This allows all the contributors to see and hear all the comments.

During the past few years, VoiceThread has begun to build a community of users that is steadily growing. The community consists mostly of educators and visual and performing artists who are seeking feedback or conversations about content that is mostly not text based. Ironically, they have a forum where users can post questions and get answers to all things VoiceThread. Most of the discussions are technical question-technical answer interchanges. Thus, it seems appropriate and oddly familiar that the technical questions are text-based.

In a broader sense, VoiceThread is giving voice to other modes of communication. And in doing this, they give voice to people who use content other than text in their work and world. This seems like the natural evolution of things as our virtual and real worlds become more seamlessly interwoven. By doing this, it's also creating a place for all people to communicate effectively using non-text-based tools. This is no accident. VoiceThread is a space designed on principles of Universal Design for Learning (UDL).[2] Universal Design for Learning focuses on designing digital spaces and learning environments that enable all individuals to develop knowledge and gain access to content and information. The people at VoiceThread have written an accessibility white paper[3] that explains their compliance with Section 508 of the Federal Rehabilitation Act that requires Federal agencies to make digital content accessible to people with disabilities. You can read a profile about how Gallaudet University, a university that specializes in serving deaf and hard of hearing students, uses VoiceThread to on their web page.[4]

The "thread" in VoiceThread implies the threading of a needle and the threading of a discussion in the discussion forum sense of the word. Thus, VoiceThread

---

[2] http://www.cast.org/

[3] http://voicethread.com/about/features/accessibility/

[4] http://elearning.gallaudet.edu/Academic_Technology/eLearning/Tool_Box/MyThread.html

does stand on the shoulders of these early giants of asynchronous technology. But, what we see happening in a VoiceThread environment is different. It's more like a mosaic than a tapestry. The mosaic, art created by assembling small images, speaks to the collective development of a larger work of art which in this case allows everyone to contribute to the development of a collective understanding in our new virtual world.

Andrew Bacevich's *Washington Rules: America's Path to Permanent War*

Review by Jeffrey Barlow

Andrew Bacevich is a noted critic of American foreign policy, particularly as it bears upon military issues. And it is Bacevich's contention that since World War II, U.S. foreign policy bears upon little else but military affairs.

We have recently discussed in successive editorial essays in Interface two works dealing directly with war and the Internet. First was Richard A. Clarke and Robert Knake, *Cyber War: The Next Threat to National Security and What to Do About It.*[1] We next reviewed Jeffrey Carr's *Inside Cyberwarfare* which took quite a different approach to the first work.[2]

Bacevich takes yet another and much broader approach than did the first two works. He discusses American military and foreign policy from its beginnings in the American Revolution, to the very recent past. Concentrating upon the period from World War II to the present, Bacevich concludes with a discussion of the "surge" in Iraq. The work closed sometime before the firing of General Stanley McChrystal in late June.

Andrew Bacevich is a Professor of International Relations at Boston University where he specializes in U.S. Foreign Policy. He graduated from West Point, served in Vietnam,[3] and received his Ph.D. from Princeton. He has published a great deal and is, I think, the preeminent commentator on U.S. foreign policy and military planning, though many would disagree with his conclusions.[4]

This book adds to our understanding of cyberwar as laid down by, first, Clarke and Knake, then by Carr, because Bacevich details the evolution of American military power from being almost entirely kinetic—dependent upon the application of mechanical force—to the increasing importance of information as an element of military might.

However, to Bacevich, it is not important to closely analyze Cyberwar to understand its special characteristics as the previous authors do. To him, it is just another weapon, appropriate under some circumstances, not useful in others.

---

[1] See it at: http://bcis.pacificu.edu/journal/2010/05/article.php?id=682

[2] The Carr essay is found at:http://bcis.pacificu.edu/journal/2010/06/article.php?id=708

[3] Bacevich also, though it is not mentioned in this work, lost a son who was killed by an IUD in Iraq. For his thoughts on that issue see:" I Lost My Son to a War I Oppose. We Were Both Doing Our Duty," *The Washington Post*, May 27, 2007, at: http://www.washingtonpost.com/wp-dyn/content/article/2007/05/25/AR2007052502032.html

[4] For a list of his writings see his faculty page at:http://www.bu.edu/ir/faculty/alphabetical/bacevich/

The critical issue is not the weapon, but rather the larger strategy and the political goals that drive it.

The digitization of information and the many related technologies that it supports had profound military applications as the process developed. An important point of departure, Bacevich believes, followed the August 1990-February 1991 campaign known as "Desert Storm." As Bacevich puts it:

> "Considered from this perspective, Operation Desert Storm signaled not the perfection of industrial-age warfare but its death knell. According to RMA[5] (Revolution in Military Affairs) enthusiasts a new era of Information Age warfare was dawning. Primacy in the cyberworld held the promise of primacy in the real world: This was their conviction."[6]

This victory was seen at the time as following upon to new advances in digital technology. These were so profoundly a departure that they demanded a new understanding of war, The Revolution in Military Affairs.

The new systems promised several distinct and badly sought advantages. Accordingly, new approaches were quickly integrated into the military structure. These however, according to Bacevich, were not a Revolution in Military Affairs so much as they were the continued pursuit of old goals by new means:

> "The expectations generated by RMA theorists—forces optimized for "network centric" warfare providing the foundation for lasting American primacy—grew out of a specific context in which post–Cold War triumphalism blended with a rising faith in the transformative power of technology married to the forces of globalization. In a fast, flat, and wide-open world, this new way of war offered an enticing blueprint for extracting the maximum benefit from the arena in which the United States enjoyed unquestioned superiority. ...Best of all, for the moment at least, the United States owned the RMA franchise. Yet strip away the cyberjargon and the RMA bore more than a passing resemblance to flexible response. The new generation of semiwarriors—Democrats like Madeleine Albright eager to succor the afflicted; Republicans like Donald Rumsfeld, pursuing more overtly imperial ambitions—were, in fact, the heirs of Taylor, McNamara, and Bundy. In the RMA they saw the possibility of fulfilling the promise of flexible response, dashed by Vietnam...

The initial victories of the next war, the invasion of Iraq, seemed initially to demonstrate the superiority of the digitally-driven RMA. Bacevich quotes Lt. Gen. Robert Wagner on the future of warfare, during this optimistic phase of the war:

---

[5] While Bacevich discusses the rise and application of this concept, he does not give it full explication. For a useful site see:http://en.wikipedia.org/wiki/Revolution_in_Military_Affairs This site is heavily documented and I judge it to be reliable.

[6] Andrew Bacevich, *Washington Rules: America's Path to Permanent War*. Kindle Edition. Loc. 2420-23 |

> "We envision the future from an information age perspective where operations are conducted in a battlespace, not a battlefield.... We are now able to create decision superiority that is enabled by networked systems, new sensors and command and control capabilities that are producing near real-time situational awareness....Our operations in Afghanistan and Iraq [have demonstrated the] operational attributes that an adaptive joint force must possess in the modern Battlespace. To dominate this battlespace, the joint force must be "knowledge centric," "coherently joint," "fully networked and collaborative" interdependent in organization and employment and uniquely designed for "Effects-Based Operations."[7]

It was then, this overweening confidence in American digital superiority that lead to what Bacevich sees as the quagmires of Iraq and of Afghanistan.

Not everybody will endorse Bacevich's overall conclusions. He believes that the U.S. has entered a state of permanent warfare beginning with the victories of World War II. He argues that an almost religious conviction (religious because it's dependent on faith and hence impossible to prove) rests on what he calls "the credo and the trinity." These are: "In the simplest terms, the credo summons the United States—and the United States alone—to lead, save, liberate, and ultimately transform the world."[8]

The trinity is somewhat more complex, but amount to the means by which the end of the credo are to be realized:

> "Yet an examination of the past sixty years of U.S. military policy and practice does reveal important elements of continuity. Call them the sacred trinity: an abiding conviction that the minimum essentials of international peace and order require the United States to maintain a global military presence, to configure its forces for global power projection, and to counter existing or anticipated threats by relying on a policy of global interventionism. Together, credo and trinity—the one defining purpose, the other practice—constitute the essence of the way that Washington has attempted to govern and police the American Century...Together they provide the basis for an enduring consensus that imparts a consistency to U.S. policy regardless of which political party may hold the upper hand or who may be occupying the White House. From the era of Harry Truman to the age of Barack Obama, that consensus has remained intact."[9]

This is a shockingly critical stance and could easily be taken for a left-wing rant. Bacevich's argument, however, is much more embedded in American political and military history than that. He sometimes refers to himself as being from the

---

[7] Bacevich, Loc. 2641-60
[8] Bacevich, Loc. 230-47
[9] Bacevich, Loc. 268-80

"non-interventionist right".[10] Simply put, Bacevich sees the undeniable interventionism of American post-war policy as a cynical departure from the intentions of not only the Founders, but also from American traditions. He thinks that what he calls the credo and the trinity are inappropriate, even deadly, to the American democracy.

So what does all this mean for our understanding of Cyberwar? It seems to me that if Bacevich's position has any merit then several profound implications follow. Perhaps the first of these is that we are wrong to focus too much upon Cyberwar as more than just another type of war.

In this, Bacevich differs profoundly from Clarke and Knake, who see Cyberwar as threatening to unbalance a world in which violence has been restrained by appropriate policies and the challenge is simply to find new policies to contain this new threat. Carr, on the other hand, sees—along with many of his Realist sources—a world that is always unbalanced and in which the best hope for stability is the power of the United States. Under these circumstances, Cyberwarfare techniques could and should be used preemptively.

Where Bacevich departs from both of the other works is that he sees a United States, which is not threatened by violence—including Cyberwar, so much as it is perpetuating it in the interests of limited sectors of the American society.[11]

It is difficult to recommend Andrew Bacevich's *Washington Rules: America's Path to Permanent War* as simply a book on cyberwar. We are free, of course, to disagree with Bacevich about the forces that have driven its adoption or the purposes to which it may one day be put. But to fail to grasp his perspective is to leave Cyberwar out of its military context, and hence to fail to fully understand it.

---

[10] See http://peterbcollins.com/2010/08/13/prof-andrew-bacevich-on-washington-rules-journalist-john- gorenfeld-on-times-propaganda/

[11] It is not my intention to reproduce Bacevich's argument in entirety here. It suffices to say that he thinks that a citizenry obsessed with individualistic gratifications has abrogated control over the powers of government, which have then been wielded by selfish special interests from a broad range of such groups in American society. At bottom, Bacevich believes that the American democracy has been hijacked, and the citizenry has chosen to party on rather than to deal with the problem.

Edgar and the Internet: Charles Huston's *The Mystic Arts of Erasing All Signs of Death* and David Cristofano's *The Girl She Used to Be*

Review by Jeffrey Barlow

Introduction

We pick up once again our topic of the impact of the Internet in mystery or crime fiction.[1] By reading works selected as noteworthy by the jurors of the Edgar Allan Poe awards, we will encounter works which are not selected simply because we know them to focus on the Internet. This is not then, truly a review, but rather an analysis that proceeds from a detailed examination, including, unfortunately, plot spoilers.

The Edgar awards are given annually to mystery or crime fiction in several categories. Such fiction is usually, above all, about the discovery of information by the sleuth. Now information is increasingly transmitted by the Internet and often a click away as opposed to discoverable only by the Sherlock Holmes among us. As such fiction has a long and much-analyzed history—the Edgars were first awarded in 1946. We are able, then, to systemically assess the changes wrought by the Internet.

In this piece we discuss two books, each nominated for an Edgar for 2010. Neither work won; we analyzed the winners in these categories earlier.[2] Here, in order to extend our analysis and broaden our sample, we look at some also-rans. Both, however, are excellent works and each does tell us quite a bit about the Internet, although in very different ways.

Charles Huston, *The Mystic Arts of Erasing All Signs of Death*.

Huston is a highly published author. His protagonist here, Webster Fillmore Goodhue, belongs to the "clueless sleuth" category, a hapless soul—described by the author as "a slacker"—who blunders into a crime requiring that he solves it to survive.[3]

The impact of this work lies in large part in the unique employment of the protagonist. After failing at everything he has tried, Goodhue winds up cleaning trauma sites, such as suicide locales, and the homes of recluses discovered weeks, if not months, after their death. While this might initially seem an

---

[1] The initial review article in this series is found at:http://bcis.pacificu.edu/journal/2010/05/article.php?id=691 Reading it will clarify the methodology and assumptions behind this continuing project.

[2] See the discussion at: http://bcis.pacificu.edu/journal/2010/05/article.php?id=698

[3] For an essay by Huston on writing The Mystic Arts go to:http://bcis.pacificu.edu/journal/2010/05/article.php?id=691

unpromising, if not totally off-putting premise, the author has previously demonstrated his mastery of contemporary popular culture. He has several fiction series going, including super heroes and classic comic books, as well as, from this work, what may turn out to be an HBO series.[4]

The work is post-modernist and contemporary (he refers to his style as pulp) in that it has an ironic undercurrent in which the author continually signals his distance from not only the protagonist, but also from the audience. The gruesomely described trauma sites are nothing if not sensationalized, as though to draw attention from an otherwise rather thin plot.

The author has suggested that his style has in part been driven, as were earlier pulp authors, by the need to write very quickly to survive as a writer. The quality he seeks is described as "velocity".[5] Huston's style is distinctive, relying heavily upon dashes in lieu of quotation marks to develop velocity, and indicating changes in voice by identifying the speaker's actions rather than using the "he said..." of conventional fiction.

These devices result in passages such as these:

> I walked to the section of bookcases that was in line with the open bathroom door.
> —He had some nice books.
> She watched me.
> —Yeah, he loved his books...
> She dropped her voice an octave.
> —Too much to do sweetheart, why bother reading about some made-up life when you can live it yourself?
> She brushed dark curly hair from her forehead, and bit her lip.
> —Is that bad, that it makes a kind of sense to me?...[6]

These make the dialogue a series of statements interrupted by physical action, as in the above series where the speaker is one woman, hectically watching, dropping, biting, and brushing within three statements, while quoting her dead father as well. The author certainly achieves velocity, but often at the expense of clarity. This is not really a style which can sustain complex plot development or intricate dialogue. It is intended to leap off the page and be apprehended perhaps more emotionally than intellectually.[7]

---

[4] See a Wikipedia page at: Wikipedia page for Huston found at:http://en.wikipedia.org/wiki/Charlie_Huston I have no judgment on the veracity of the material covered there and suggest that the avid fan crosscheck it on other sites. A good place to begin doing so would be at:http://www.pulpnoir.com/, where the author maintains a blog. Another interesting site is found at:http://mjroseblog.typepad.com/backstory/2009/02/david-cristofanos-backstory.html

[5] See interview at: http://www.paradigmjournal.com/elliott/huston.html

[6] The elisions signaled by " ..." here are my own in order to shorten the passage in which they appear.

[7] See, for example, the references at Huston, p. 117 and p. 240.

Among the icons of pop-culture, frequently dissed in this work are both computers and videogames. Computers are portrayed as ultimately a shallow entertainment, comparable to television, and merely a way of filling time.

The poor quality of the Internet and of its audience is suggested by a humorous passage in which one of the more witless characters (among many such) details plans to make his fortune by investing in the careers of two video artists who attracted a large audience on Youtube by showing clips of animals eating their own feces. The character intends to lock up their output for ten years and to attract an audience initially by providing a steady stream of such literal dreck, via a subscription-only website, followed by other equally humorous content.[8]

It seems to me that the author desires to break with conventional fiction, both speeding up narrative through a variety of devices such as those discussed above, and by embedding the story in a horrific context of mindless violence, both the commission of which and the messy aftermath is described in detail.

Lest this analysis be taken as a simple longing on my part for the back-in-the-day Miss Marple-style of crime fiction—which I personally find laboriously slow—I think that, in fact, the author is addressing a real problem. Fewer and fewer young people read mystery fiction; its audience is aging dramatically. The goal now for an author, like Huston, is to find new audiences by breaking into television, film, and adult comics, thus becoming a one-person media conglomerate. These all require an increasingly violent pace and must be deeply imbedded in pop culture, because the audience is an impatient one that shares no other cultural reference points. All of these characteristics can be attributed in part to the Internet. The audience for fiction is increasingly less educated, the pace is necessarily fast so as to suit a web-speed attention span, the level of information conveyed, and plot complexity necessarily ever more shallow.

Huston's career shows that this approach, whatever else may be said of it, works. He has a large audience in a variety of genres and perhaps, as of this writing, a TV series in the works. However, the author is, at the bottom in this work at least, almost contemptuous of his characters and his audience, and would like, I think, to be accepted as a WRITER. The fact that the work was nominated for an Edgar suggests that other writers feel this same contradictory pressure.

David Cristofano, *The Girl She Used to Be*.

Our second work was nominated as a first novel and comes to us via quite a different route than did the previous one. Cristofano's back-story includes having worked in Washington D.C. He has degrees in Government and Politics and in Computer Science.[9] The degree in CS might suggest that this work would have a great deal to say about the Internet, as most new writers do follow the ancient advice, "write about what you know."

---

[8] Huston, p. 215.

[9] Cristofano's web site is found at: http://www.davidcristofano.com/

The Girl She Used to Be, however, turns on an almost an anti-Internet MacGuffin.[10] The protagonist, Melody, witnessed a mob killing with her parents, who then testified in court. She has been in the Federal Witness Protection Program since she was six years old. At the time the book begins, she is twenty-six and her parents have been killed some years ago by the mob, and only she had escaped. Having been in the program for twenty years she has moved a great many times and has had at least eight identities, so many that she is not quite sure who she is, or even who she was.

Melody's confusion is self-inflicted in part because, whenever she gets bored, she falsely reports a threat, is given a completely new identity, and re-located once again. In the course of the identity change that opens the book, the son of the gangster whose crime initially drove her family into the federal protection program suddenly confronts her.

Melody is peculiarly vulnerable. None of her series of identities has ever given her the sense of security that would allow her to establish a sexual relationship. The one time she had made an attempt to shed her virginity resulted in a real exposure of her identity, and she again had to flee.

The mobster, about her own age, is sophisticated, charming, and wealthy. He persuades her that he has come to save her life. He explains that she had dropped out of the purview of the gangsters after her family had been killed, but recently they have learned where she is through a mob informant in the federal program. The young man has been ordered to kill her. He prefers to protect her; in fact, he has been following her for some time.

With this one event, her life is turned upside down; now the enemies are among the Feds, perhaps even the one supposedly taking her to her new location. The young gangster seemingly wants to protect her, and is a very likely, and likeable, candidate to relieve her of her virginity, which she intensely desires.

His plan, however, is simply to take her home and introduce her to the family as his girlfriend, thus saving her life. However, she has been on the run too long to contemplate such a plan. As she says, "it's like bringing a deer to the front door of a hunting lodge."[11]

Part of the appeal of this work is not only what may be a unique MacGuffin, but the protagonist's very strong voice. While the above description may seem overly complex, the very straightforward first person voice renders it all quite believable. Melody has been on the run so long that she has become very self-

[10] A MacGuffin is defined as "a plot element that catches the viewers' attention or drives the plot of a work of fiction" athttp://en.wikipedia.org/wiki/MacGuffin I find this Wikipedia site sufficiently authoritative, although it deals largely with films, because of its thorough analysis of plot elements in a great number of films, and a bibliography which is satisfactory, though it could be stronger.
[11] Cristofano. P. 76.

reliant and perhaps because of her isolation, a very singular character. She is also a math whiz, which proves helpful at points.

It is here that the issue of the Internet intrudes. Part of what drives the character is supposedly her isolation. Because she dare not reveal her true identity or any of her multiple pasts to friends, she has none. Her human contact consists in part of hanging out at Hallmark card outlets and fantasizing that she is part of the sort of relationship that she thinks the card buyers probably have with the intended recipient; now a loving mother, now a sweetheart or even, a wife.[12]

This putative isolation is, however, hard to sustain in the age of the Internet. We know that Melody is fully Internet savvy because when she needs to pull a new life together, she does so very quickly; she even finds a hacker she then bluffs into providing her with a new identity unknown to the feds or to the mob.

This competency is not surprising; Melody is, after all, a former teen-ager, and a math whiz at that. She is a classic geek if ever there were one, surely familiar with such social sites as Facebook, Twitter, Youtube, and the dozens of similar ones. She seems far more likely to cruise the Internet than to lurk at Hallmark displays.

We inevitably must wonder why she seems totally ignorant of the social utility of chat-rooms, or of massive online multiplayer games with their guilds and frequent real-world meetings of players under conditions permitting full anonymity. And why, in an age when one of the major preoccupations of parents is the threat of Internet predators, does she seem to find it impossible to meet sexual partners? Why, when a Google search on "hook up sites" will produce more than eight million hits,[13] is this attractive young woman lonely?

This isolation in one so competent strains credulity. We can choose to believe that Melody is too frightened or too shy, but these qualities seem inconsonant with the character that we meet here. Her hilarious three-page long confrontation with a college boy making fun of her in a bar is a classic put-down. Her confidence and sharp repartee, it is suggested, not only inflicts instant impotence on him, but the condition will afflict him the rest of his life.[14]

We think that this interpretation of the Internet—now irrelevant despite her well-established geeky identity, now a very useful tool—is another case of an author laboring to work within the time-worn conventions of crime fiction, despite the enormous changes wrought by the Internet. In this case, it is not an issue of how facts can remain unknown when almost everything is searchable, but how an attractive and highly competent woman can remain isolated despite her intense desire not to be so.

---

[12] Cristofano. p. 6-7.

[13] http://www.google.com/search?q=hook+up+sites&ie=utf-8&oe=utf-8&aq=t&rls=org.mozilla:en-US:official&client=firefox-a

[14] Cristofano, pp 1-103.

There is nothing wrong, of course, with asking an audience to suspend a certain amount of disbelief; it is a necessary aspect of every interesting book or film ever produced. And this is a very interesting book, but it rather ignores the elephant in the room once too often for an entirely satisfactory level of consistency.

Conclusion

The changes wrought by the Internet as revealed in these two Edgar nominees, in 2010, are slightly different. The first work, Huston's *The Mystic Arts of Erasing All Signs of Death*, suggests that, under the impact of the Internet, the audience for crime fiction is evolving rapidly. Authors seeking a mass audience may find it easiest to play to this evolution, as does Huston. But the desire to succeed as a writer in the conventional sense persists.

The second work, Califono's excellent *The Girl She Used To Be*, tells us, however, that to neglect the impact of the Internet in plot and character development can produce anomalies which eventually are disturbing. Again the conventional bounds of mystery or detective fiction have transgressed.

Peer Review and *Interface*

Editorial by Jeffrey Barlow

Our Feature article in this issue of Interface is James Kundart, Yu-Chi Tai, John R. Hayes, and James Sheedy, *"Word Recognition and the Accommodative Response to Desktop Versus Handheld Video Displays (Handheld Study #2)"*

We are pleased to publish it as a fully peer-reviewed submission. We write here to explain the significance of peer review, particularly for an e-journal such as ours.

The problem of electronic materials distributed over the Internet is their relative authority and reliability. Anybody can publish on the Internet and make whatever claims they wish for the reliability of their materials and for their own authority, within the rather broad limits of criminal laws such as those affecting slander and egregious misrepresentations.

Materials distributed in classical paper journals do not face the same problems. The reader usually has a good notion of the reliability of the materials, because the journals or newspapers themselves have established reputations.

If journals wish to be considered scholarly or professional, they must follow long-established procedures for peer review. Usually it is expected that submissions will be stripped, inasmuch as possible, of all hints of who it is who had authored them, then sent out to a number of review editors who are professionally qualified in fields identical to, or at least close to those of the author. The author, in turn, should never learn whom it was who either supported or condemned his or her submission, so that it was or was not published.

This system usually works quite smoothly, although most scholars can usually and easily be induced to rave on about great injustices, they personally have suffered. I, for example, once submitted a piece to— excuse me, I was momentarily overcome by a flashback there!

At *Interface*, we publish articles in a variety of niches, some more weighty than others. We assure reliability by contracting with highly competent professionals in their field, but we encourage them to write quickly (and cheaply!), and to aim for a broad audience.
Because we believe very strongly that the quality of materials on the Internet must be improved and readers much better prepared to use them properly, we have devised a system for communicating the relative authority of our pieces. Usually, unless the piece is obviously little more than an announcement or otherwise relatively trivial, we put a seal signaling authority levels upon it.[1] We usually aim for a minimal authority level of "4" which means the piece ultimately

[1] See discussion at: http://bcis.pacificu.edu/journal/submissions/authoritylevel.php

can be read with confidence, but it may well be that there are better materials to be found on these same topics.

Our student authors, often Berglund Student Fellows who have worked on a given piece for an extended period, should receive levels of "3".[2]

However, authors sometimes wish for a full peer-review process because they intend the piece to be used in some professional process requiring such reviews, as is the case with our Feature. Accordingly, it receives an authority level of "5" indicating it was peer reviewed.[3]

---

[2] Level 3 materials are often the result of research projects done by inexperienced authors, but guided by experienced ones. These might include extensive undergraduate research projects. They have the following characteristics:

> -Level 3 materials should be free from errors of fact. If some of their conclusions are controversial ones, these should be held by at least some authorities in the field of study.
>
> -Level 3 materials should depend to a considerable extent upon published and easily available materials so that readers can themselves explore the topic further with some confidence.
>
> -The basis of conclusions drawn in level 3 materials should be clear and rooted in research, not in mere opinion or prejudice.
>
> -Level 3 authors should be known, and can be contacted to discuss their works.
>
> -The works are dated as to time of origin and any updates that occurred.
>
> -Limitations of level 3 materials: Level 3 materials may provide an adequate beginning for serious research, but should not be the sole foundation of such research. They might well provide a good orientation to the topic and suggest additional research paths, but this is their major strength.

For source see: http://bcis.pacificu.edu/journal/submissions/authoritylevel.php

[3] Level 5 materials have to pass a number of tests and represent the highest possible level of trust or authority. They are equivalent to materials published in paper form by scholarly journals or presses. They could be placed in a library and should prove useful for some length of time.

They have the following characteristics, but no piece, of course, will necessarily have all of them:

Materials certified as Authority Level 5 have been reviewed by scholars in the appropriate field following practices long utilized in scholarly journals and other refereed publications. That is, they have been read closely by one or more established professionals comfortable with the topic area of the piece. The review process was "double-blind." That is, neither the authors nor the reviewers were aware of each other's identities.

In the judgments of these readers, the piece makes a contribution to the topic being discussed; that is, they are not merely a restatement of existing scholarly opinions.

The materials have both citations and bibliographies sufficient to permit readers to retrace the author's research steps so as to form their own opinion as to the strength and weaknesses of the pieces when measured against the set of evidence on which they were constructed.

The author should discuss methodology as well as evidence: how do they know what they know?

We think that peer review is often over-stressed and that it can have many problems. Certainly it sometimes delays publication for a considerable period. At the Berglund Center we also publish several scholarly peer-reviewed journals, such as E-AsPac and formerly, The Journal of the Association for History and Computing,[4] now published at the University of Michigan, and the time lag from submission to publication is often many months as an article travels back and forth between editors and reviewers. In the pre-digital days, such a process could take years.

There are, some think, better ways of establishing quality than by the traditional scholarly path, but it is well established and for now we must live with it. Hopefully, electronic journals will eventually establish their own procedures. For now, when we award a Berglund level 5 seal to an article, as we did for the Feature, we follow established procedures.

The articles show an awareness of the current state of the topic by referencing or discussing recent scholarship in both important books and articles. The author should probably indicate areas where there are differences of opinion among authorities.

The author of the piece is known, can be contacted to discuss or defend his or her positions, and themselves have some specialized education, training, or experience relative to their topic.

The piece is well written and organized and has a minimum of spelling, grammatical or formatting errors, showing the qualities of mind necessary to good research, thought, and writing.

Such publications would usually include research done in the language(s) of the subject field as appropriate.

Limitations of Level 5 materials: Despite these strict standards, even the best research and writing has areas of relative weakness, and scholars in the field will often disagree about each others' positions. The more "cutting edge" a piece, the more likely it is to be controversial. For the average reader, however, these controversies are likely to be unimportant ones.

For source of the above see:
http://bcis.pacificu.edu/journal/submissions/authoritylevel.php

[4] For E-AsPac see: http://mcel.pacificu.edu/easpac/ For the JAHC see: http://quod.lib.umich.edu/j/jahc/

October 2010 - Volume 10, Issue 8

About This Issue

The October issue of *Interface* can be thought of as our Back-to-School issue in a sense. We begin the academic year with new staff members, and with a full year of activities planned.

We lead off with two features, for the first time in our ten years of publication. Each of these is a part of our tenth-year anniversary publication, After Internet Time, to be published in peer-reviewed book form in late summer 2011. Each article in that publication will first be presented in Interface as a much shorter non peer-reviewed version.

The first feature, in alphabetical order, is "The Impact of the Internet on Education and Training in Professional Psychology" by Lauren Wiswall and Shawn Davis, both of Pacific University's School of Professional Psychology.

Our second feature is "The Internet and the 'just-in-time' Mind" by our Editorial Board member Dr. David J. Staley, Director of the Harvey Goldberg Program for Excellence in Teaching in the Department of History at The Ohio State University.

Pacific Graduate Jennifer Conner (Class of 2010), presents "Journalism's Aversion to an Evolving News Media." The longer work from which this article is derived was the winner of the 2010 Berglund Award for Excellence for an Outstanding Senior Thesis dealing with the Impact of the Internet.

Berglund Center staff member and Berglund Student Fellow Nicole Nowlin offers us part II of "Scanlations: Copyright Infringement for Literature and Art Fans Brought to You by the Internet." Intended originally as a single article, Nicole's research and the response of the Scanlations artists' and readers' community has led to this series continuation...

Our first book review is Nicholas Carr's *The Shallows: What the Internet is Doing to Our Brains*. The reviewer states: "...however much we may cavil, perhaps in attempts to protect our own cherished views of the Internet, it remains a work which must be read and considered by all those interested in the impact of the Internet."

The second review is of a fiction work which has sometimes been said to be the best novel dealing directly with the impact of the Internet, Dan Chaon's *Await Your Reply: A Novel*.

Our editorial for this issue, *The Magic of Reading: iPad, Book, and Kindle*, offers editor Jeffrey Barlow an opportunity to compare reading and research done on the Apple iPad with that on Amazon's Kindle.

In our announcements, see the DuBoff Law Groups' "Do You Have a Plan to Protect Your Intellectual Property?" which gives excellent advice on how to protect valuable assets. See also notices of our forthcoming Berglund Roundtable and the locations of the videos of recently posted ones…

As always, we hope that you find this issue of *Interface* educational as well as entertaining…

The Berglund Center for Internet Studies
Pacific University Oregon

Editor's Note: Jennifer Conner (Pacific University Class of 2010) won the Berglund Award for Excellence, awarded to a graduating senior, for her Senior Thesis. "The Real Political Elite: Journalism's Aversion to Evolving News Media." Here we present the thesis in an edited version.

Journalism's Aversion to an Evolving News Media

Jennifer Conner
2010 Berglund Award for Excellence Winner

Journalism's ability to inform and influence the public about everyday affairs rests in its credibility and reliability. In order to ensure both of those qualities, journalism created a foundation in schools and ethical codes to which journalists could adhere. But the emergence of new technologies has changed the environment of traditional newsgathering and reporting. With easy access to public officials and records online and permeating social media sites such as Twitter, citizen journalists and bloggers now find themselves at the forefront of the news.

This trend, the creation and running of online news websites by non-traditional media types, was my primary interest when I began my senior project at Pacific University. However, I quickly found another issue lurking beneath the surface. Citizen journalists and others who, relying on an internet platform to disperse their stories, faced rejection from the traditional media community who branded them as unreliable and damaging to the reputation of journalism.

Hence, I refocused my project to examine why this schism exists, as well as the legal, ethical and political problems it can create if left unresolved. Based on this research, I suggested a model of how the two spheres could interact and evolve together. Since I completed my thesis in May 2010, some news organizations, including the Associated Press, created or updated guidelines on social media for journalists during the summer. Such new developments undoubtedly affect my thesis, but they are not analyzed in the following discussion.

I concentrated my research on media most averse to evolving forms of journalism, which was the print media, notably newspapers. From here, I examined how newspapers and reporters treated new media and attempted (if at all) to integrate it into their operations. Major newspapers, such as *The New York Times* and *The Wall Street Journal*, prefer their employees to post only links, no commentary, to articles in order to maintain reliability, a key component of keeping readership and making a profit. Hence, newspapers might be using new media, but they certainly are not utilizing it. For instance, nearly all of *The New York Times*' Twitter and Facebook posts are headlines with links to a story. But when those are posted, the information is not new; rather, it is the stories currently available in print editions or posted online content. There is nothing that encourages the reader to follow the link, although it is likely that the story or information is available elsewhere.

Next, I researched citizen journalists, as well as the related concept of community journalism (intimate local reporting by journalists living in the area), to understand the purpose and work of both ideas. Neither idea is particularly new, but applied in the context of emerging technology, "citizen journalists" (citizen implying no formal training) become neighborhood bloggers or active community members.

Finally, I explored how people use social media by looking at trends of what people search for and how it affects their news consumption. For instance, news, both national and local, topped the list for searches and there is a slight generational shift among those who find news online and those who read more traditional sources. Younger generations consume more news online, which should encourage news organizations to utilize technology to attract new readers. By analyzing the information from these three areas of my thesis, I formulated a model based on the characteristics of community journalism suggesting how traditional media should integrate citizen journalism. Community journalism lent itself to a natural foundation because it united the journalistic principles of traditional media with the localness of citizen journalists. There are five tenets generally associated with community journalism; they include being relentlessly local, small, second-read (not breaking news), accessible, and less concerned with deadlines.[1]

1. Organizations should use a "hyperlocal" approach to promote information and stories important to the local vicinity. For instance, focusing citizen journalists' efforts on small, underrepresented towns or individuals.
2. Citizen journalism is secondary to traditional media; its part is to enhance, not make the story. An example might be a sidebar or accompanying story, unless the report stands on its own.
3. Too often, news organization focus on getting the information first, as that increases ratings and sells the news. Information on a story is easy to find via search engines; it is the local importance of the news that is often unreported. For instance, reporting the effect of a state law on a specific city or organization.
4. Accessibility, in this context, means both professional journalists and citizen journalists participate. This allows the newspaper's journalists to work their regular beats without an extra burden of more stories, especially in newsrooms with reduced staff.
5. Online components cannot be rushed by a deadline. This does not mean content updates are infrequent. However, a weekly paper operates differently than an everyday publication. Content can be added daily, as websites are easily updated quickly, adjusting to the pace and demand of information.

---

[1] Lauterer, Jock. *Community Journalism: Relentlessly Local.* Chapel Hill: The University of North Carolina-Chapel Hill Press (2006): 43.

This model is not without two significant questions; first, whether citizen journalists qualify as "journalists", and second, if this hybrid model can create profit? Local governments afford traditional journalists certain rights, such as keeping sources confidential (shield laws) or having access to executive meeting sessions. Furthermore, within the journalism community, there are ethical and stylistic considerations to which trained journalists adhere. However, citizen journalists, who have no formal training or recognition, do not receive such benefits or follow normal journalistic practices. This is a long-standing problem that will not be resolved easily; nonetheless, if traditional news media and citizen journalists can create a working relationship, it can begin to address these underlying issues.

It is also unknown whether citizen journalism is a profitable field. Most citizen journalists simply follow a "hobby model", in that reporting on local news is not their primary job or concern, but a passion. Traditional news organizations may be reluctant to add evolving forms of media if there is little monetary benefit. Nevertheless, citizen journalism, through its hyperlocal focus, can draw advertisers through online traffic.

Newspapers have been able to hold on to the idea that not everyone can be a journalist, and consequently to elitism, by equating credibility with tradition and establishment. The fourth estate effectively impugns different methods of journalism by refusing to take them seriously. Granted, not all forms of alternative journalism will be accurate and reliable. But credibility will not improve if there is no cooperation between types of journalism. If journalism's lofty goal is to act as a watchdog of government and democracy, it must encourage and allow all types of journalism to thrive.

A Berglund Center Tenth Anniversary Essay

Editor's Note: This is one of a number of essays we will be publishing in coming issues which are brief portions of the longer essays to be published in our tenth anniversary volume, After Internet Time, forthcoming in fall, 2011. That volume will be fully peer reviewed. These essays have not yet been peer reviewed, but all are by experts in the fields which they discuss.

The Impact of the Internet on Education and Training in Professional Psychology

Lauren Wiswall
Pacific University – School of Professional Psychology

Introduction

Over the past decade, the total number of internet users increased by an estimated 399.3%, from roughly 321 million to 2 billion people worldwide.[1] Rapid technological growth has presented both new opportunities—as well as challenges—to innovators and educators in the field of professional psychology. Technological advances have stimulated new methods of pedagogy and new models of education and learning. However, there is controversy over whether advances in technology translate into advances in learning. Educators and institutions in professional psychology are challenged to consider the impact of technological advancements in training and education. Electronic methods of pedagogy are reviewed first, followed by recent trends in e-learning and distance education programs, and lastly, implications for the field of professional psychology.

Electronic Pedagogy

The term e-learning refers to learning via electronic methods and models and pedagogy. Theoretical support for e-learning comes from research in behaviorism, cognitive theory, and constructivism.[2] In education, levels of e-learning integration can range from traditional, low-tech lectures to primarily electronically mediated courses.[3] Today, traditional lecture-based courses often have supplemental websites and may even require access to electronic resources, electronic submission of assignments, and participation in online discussions. In contrast, internet-based courses might include live teleconferencing and in-person meetings and training experiences. E-learning

---

[1] internetworldstats.com

[2] Chan, C. H., & Robbins, L. I. (2006). E-learning systems: promises and pitfalls. *Academic Psychiatry, 30*, 491-497.

[3] Murphy, M. J., Levant, R. F., Hall, J. E., & Glueckauf, R. L. (2007). Distance education in professional training in psychology. *Professional Psychology: Research and Practice, 38*, 97-103.

tools are also used for training and assessment purposes. E-learning programs have been designed to adjust difficulty levels, ensure learning benchmarks are graded in complexity, and provide relatively objective, individualized feedback.[4]

Distributed education models rely on electronic forms of pedagogy, enabling them to transcend location barriers and create new opportunities.[5] Electronically mediated courses may be suitable for acquiring and evaluating content knowledge, but the transfer of professional knowledge, skills, and attitudes may rely more on the dynamic interaction between student and advisor.[6] Similarly, Hare states, "actually acquiring the necessary skills for psychiatric practice will always require considerable experience with real patients".[7]

To challenge this assumption, Worrall and Fruzzetti developed an Internet-based training system for dialectical behavior therapy and tested it with peer-supervisors.[8] The program was designed to help students identify effective therapy interventions and guide peer evaluation and feedback. The students were able to watch, rate, and view feedback on mock therapy sessions over the Internet. The researchers propose that similar programs could be implemented in real-world settings to provide training therapists with supervisory feedback.

E-Learning and Traditional Pedagogy

Although advances in technology have paved the way for electronic forms of pedagogy, the relative value of e-learning compared to traditional pedagogy remains unclear. Therefore, researchers have recently turned their attention to the study of human-computer interaction. Several studies have examined the effects of learner control, but results have been mixed.[9] Still, at least two moderating variables – trainee self-regulation and training satisfaction – appear to play important roles in e-learning.[10] [11]

---

[4] Bell, B., & Kozlowski, S. (2002). Adaptive guidance: Enhancing self-regulation, knowledge, and performance in technology-based training. *Personnel Psychology, 55*, 267-306.

[5] Rudestam, K. E. (2004). Distributed education and the role of online learning in training professional psychologists. *Professional Psychology: Research and Practice, 35*, 427-432.

[6] See note 3.

[7] Hare, E. (2009). E-learning for psychiatrists. *Psychiatric Bulletin, 33*, 81-83.

[8] Worrall, J. M., & Fruzzetti, A. E. (2009). Improving peer supervisor ratings of therapist performance in dialectical behavior therapy: An internet-based training system. *Psychotherapy Theory, Research, Practice, Training, 46*, 476-479.

[9] Kraiger, K., & Jerden, E. (2007). A meta-analytic investigation of learner control: Old findings and new directions. In S. M. Fiore & E. Salas (Eds.), *Toward a science of distributed learning*. Washington, DC: American Psychological Association.

[10] Orvis, K. A., Fisher, S. L., & Wasserman, M. E. (2009). Power to the people: Using learner control to improve trainee reactions and learning in web-based instructional environments. *Journal of Applied Psychology, 94*, 960-971.

[11] Sitzmann, T., & Ely, K. (2010). Sometimes you need a reminder: The effects of prompting self-regulation on regulatory processes, learning, and attrition. *Journal of Applied Psychology, 95*, 132-144.

Bell and Kozlowski developed and tested a program designed to enhance self-regulatory processes.[12] The program, adaptive guidance, provided trainees with information to help them invest cognitive resources wisely. The researchers observed a significant change among trainee study and practice, self-regulation, knowledge, and performance when the training program was employed.

Implications

In 2001, an APA task force assembled to address the issue of distance education and training in Professional Psychology, including new developments, best practices, program accreditation, and graduate licensure and recognition.[13] Both traditional programs and distance programs are expected to meet the same accreditation standards. However, distance education programs are introducing new challenges to the assessment of compliance. The APA task force identified several areas that need to be addressed by accreditation reviews and procedures in professional psychology distance learning programs: access to online materials; competence of faculty in technology and distance pedagogy, mentoring, and supervision; student and faculty support; evaluation and assessment of students and practicum sites; institutional context and commitment; facilities and finance; library and learning resources. There is currently only one professional psychology program accredited by the APA using a distributed education model (Fielding Graduate University).[14]

A question faced by graduates of non-accredited distance programs in professional psychology today is whether they will have difficulty obtaining licensure and work. Policies and procedures of many distance education programs are tailored to meet accreditation standards. However, it remains to be seen whether distance education programs will meet accreditation standards and acceptance by licensing boards in professional psychology. As the APA task force states:

"Concern is raised that as professional psychology moves toward greater recognition, acceptance, and expanded scope of practice, barriers may be encountered if it adopts approaches to professional preparation that are out of the mainstream and may erode the perception of quality and rigor of the profession."

A survey of accredited doctoral training programs indicated that currently accredited training programs report using the Internet for e-mail, web pages, and online access to articles. However, the implementation of electronic pedagogical

---

[12] Bell, B., & Kozlowski, S. (2002). Adaptive guidance: Enhancing self-regulation, knowledge, and performance in technology-based training. *Personnel Psychology, 55*, 267-306.

[13] Murphy, M. J., Levant, R. F., Hall, J. E., & Glueckauf, R. L. (2007). Distance education in professional training in psychology. *Professional Psychology: Research and Practice, 38*, 97-103.

[14] Murphy, M. J., Levant, R. F., Hall, J. E., & Glueckauf, R. L. (2007). Distance education in professional training in psychology. *Professional Psychology: Research and Practice, 38*, 97-103.

methods was limited. Most accredited training programs have not integrated e-learning or other forms distance education. Other health care professions use distance education programs for continuing education and certifications beyond the entry-credentialed level. Distance programs for post-graduate training and certifications assume that foundational knowledge, skills, and professional values have already been acquired, providing base upon which to build and integrate new knowledge, as is seen with post-doctoral psychopharmacology degrees in psychology.[15]

Conclusion

Technological advances have led us to face a paradigm shift in terms of pedagogical methods, models, and theories. In the future, innovators will need to prudently consider the implications of integrating electronic forms of pedagogy into professional training and education as the substitution of e-learning methods and distance education can come at a cost to other forms of learning and pedagogy.

[15] See note 14.

Scanlations: Copyright Infringement for Literature and Art Fans Brought to You by the Internet, Part II

Nicole Nowlin
Student Fellow, Berglund Center for Internet Studies

The previous article on scanlations[1] provided an overview of the phenomenon and the copyright issues related to it. Initially, the articles in Interface were intended to be only two parts. However, considering the recent developments on the issue, Part II will now become Parts II and III. Part II of this discussion covers the users of scanlations, and the authors, artists, and publishers harmed by scanlations. Part III will review the current issues and offer suggestions to publishers (link to next article when posted – go back and link to second article at bottom of first article?).

Fans and Scanlators

Fans, in some cases, clearly see the illegality of scanlations and the reality of the infringement of rights. In forum discussions about scanlations and whether or not there existed a grey area in the copyright ownership, poster TatsuGero23 affirmed, "Someone, somewhere will have the rights. Even if Funimation or Viz doesn't have the rights to episode 2082 of Naruto or Chapter 692 of Bleach, that doesn't mean that the people in Japan don't have rights over them. Even if [Funimation] or Viz never get those chapters or episodes for 'X' reason, the original Japanese companies still have the rights to them and they get to [decide] how their product is distributed and those rights generally extend internationally. So it's not a 'legal loophole' as it is just an excuse to get something for free.

"It wouldn't be much of a problem if people went and bought the legitimate version when they become available. If that were the case then I'm sure licensers and the industry wouldn't be so negative with it all. But the problem is that most people don't. They just pick up the free 'illegal' versions and settle for that."[2]

There are fans and scanlations groups out there who try to support the authors as much as they can. Groups like Nakama will remove scanlations from their archives as soon as they hear word that they were licensed in the U.S., and immediately request their users to stop distributing.[3] Other scanlators will find their materials online in places like MangaFox and request that the materials

---

[1] January-February 2010 – Volume 10, Issue 1 at: http://bcis.pacificu.edu/journal/article.php?id=633

[2] TatsuGero23. "Re: Licensee Rights Over Scanlations." Web log comment. Forum Index - General - Manga. Anime News Network, 29 Apr. 2010. Web. 14 June 2010. <http://www.animenewsnetwork.com/bbs/phpBB2/viewtopic.php?t=129898>.

[3] Nakama. "About U.S.." Web. 12 Jan. 2010. <http://nakamanga.com/node/24>.

taken down because they are now available in the U.S.. In a way, you could say it is responsible scanlating – whetting the appetite for the artist or series, and then handing it over to the legal entities in the publishing industry that pick it up, leaving it to the fans to buy the series officially in their native language rather than read chapter by chapter online. However, it is obvious. that not everyone is as industry conscious.. Fans may continue to distribute scans, as they are unlikely to delete the series off of their hard drive when they purchase the official release, if they purchase it at all. Responsible scanlating only works (marginally) if a series is left unfinished, forcing fans to Use official channels to complete their reading of the work. Some scanlators pre-release future chapters of popular series, like FMA: Brotherhood and Naruto, or continue to distribute their releases despite licensing in the country in which they are distributing.[4]

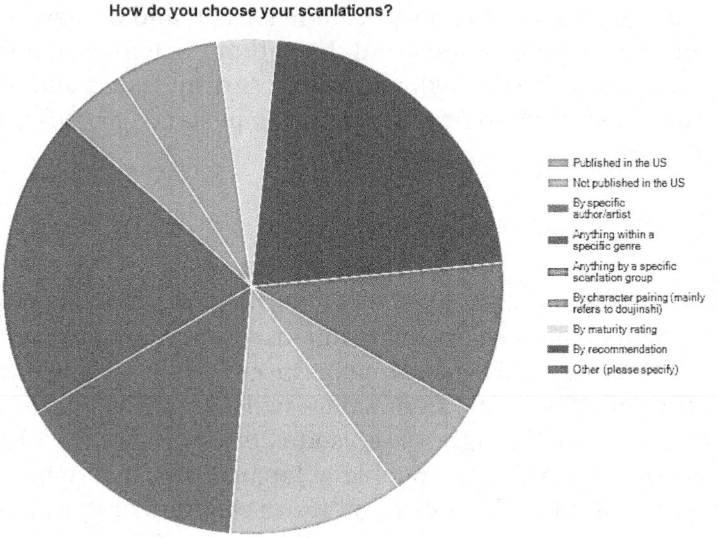

When asked to select all ways in which they choose their scanlations, 13.5% of fans noted that they choose their scanlations based on the fact that the volume is published in the United States, an example of true disregard for publishers and the industry. Nearly 23% of fans chose based on a work not being published in the U.S.[5]

The use of scanlations is an opening for legal repercussions. Like the recording industry taking on users who download hundreds or thousands of songs, a publisher could conceivably sue for copyright infringement against a person who had illegal scanlations of their licensed works on their computer.

Some fans feel that going after scanlations is pointless – and that the bigger issue is the anime and manga industry as a whole:

1. “I don’t think cracking down on anime and manga file sharing will help the American industry much. It’s going to continue contracting one way or another. I hate to say it, but anime was a fad and the fad is fading. In the next few years I can see anime and manga return to what they were ten years ago: A niche market, populated by a few specialty publishers and an imprint or two that can only afford to publish titles that appeal to

[4] Hollingworth, William. "'Scanlators' Freely Translating 'manga,' 'anime'" The Japan Times Online. Kyodo News, 10 Mar. 2009. Web. 08 June 2010. <http://search.japantimes.co.jp/cgi-bin/nn20090310f2.html>.
[5] “Manga & Scanlations Survey.” Survey. Survey Monkey. Apr. 2010. Web.

'mainstream' western comic fans."[6]

2. "Just whining about it is not going to change anything. Even if they find all the scanlators and lock their sites down, people will still find a way to get around it. Companies should focus more on making their book copies look more appealing, whether through cheaper prices or having more 'traditional' translations..."[7]

	Yes	No	Maybe/Sort of	Undecided	Response Count
Are they legal?	16.0% (33)	30.6% (63)	**35.0% (72)**	18.4% (38)	206
Are they ethical?	24.9% (51)	12.2% (25)	**43.4% (89)**	19.5% (40)	205
Are they useful to the industry?	**41.7% (86)**	14.1% (29)	27.2% (56)	17.0% (35)	206
			Hide replies	Other (please specify)	20

1.	Do not used scanlations	Sun, May 16, 2010 11:48 AM	Find
2.	For series not present in the US I find them helpful to companies, and personally I feel less ethical quandary reading them since there is no present license here.	Thu, May 13, 2010 7:06 PM	Find
3.	I think scanlation is great to discover new manga, and I'll always check first scanlations or even anime streaming before actually buying the anime. Even if i already saw or read it, it's important to me to actually buy the official product so the manga/anime industry stay in business. It's not legal, but if it's not avaible where I am, I need a way to discover this manga/anime.	Fri, Apr 30, 2010 7:07 PM	Find
4.	Borderline copyright infringement (doujinshi) to outright theft if it's published material	Fri, Apr 30, 2010 11:34 AM	Find
5.	It helps spread the interest. Manga is expensive, so not everyone would buy manga to try reading it	Thu, Apr 29, 2010 6:05 AM	Find
6.	I could just read the book in the bookstore; either way I don't buy them usually. Also, scanlations give me access to books that Borders doesn't think are popular enough to sell	Tue, Apr 27, 2010 10:53 PM	Find
7.	I believe that if people read the scanilations to gauge interst and then decide to purchase the manga it can be a good thing for the industry, but if people are just reading all their manga online, then it's obviously bad for the industry and is unethical	Tue, Apr 27, 2010 2:57 PM	Find
8.	NA	Tue, Apr 27, 2010 12:40 PM	Find
9.	I view series and volumes not yet published in English in America as fair game.	Tue, Apr 27, 2010 11:53 AM	Find
10.	Useful if people like myself sample then buy if published here. If not localized, it may help the industry grow by readers showing interest in unpulished works to bring over. Legally and ethically is probably a no, but discrepancies in copyright laws and such can force the issure to a maybe/sort of technically-speaking.	Tue, Apr 27, 2010 8:35 AM	Find

1 — 10 responses per page

answered question	**207**
skipped question	**83**

Fans themselves have a varying opinion on the acceptance of scanlations. Some have simple views: "I'll be blunt; fans don't download fansubs or scanlations... Fans don't steal from creators."[8] And "Manga is not a right. It is a privilege."[9] A survey conducted over two months received nearly 300 responses from fans about scanlations and about themselves with a 68.3% survey completion rate.

---

[6] Spica. "Re: What Might HTMLComics Bys Mean to Scanlations?" Web log comment. Icarus Publishing, 7 May 2010. Web. 14 June 2010.

[7] Feder. "Re: WSJ's Editors Statement Concerning Scanlations." Web log comment. Tokyopop. 3 May 2010. Web. 15 June 2010. <http://messageboard.tokyopop.com/forums/showthread.php?t=15525&page=2>.

[8] Sizemore, Ed. "What Price Fandom?" Web log post. An Eddy of Thought. 17 May 2010. Web. 15 June 2010. <http://ed-sizemore.blogspot.com/2010/05/what-price-fandom.html>.

[9] Adaywithoutme. "The Matter of Manga in America." GAR GAR Stegosaurus.. 25 May 2010. Web. 15 June 2010. <http://gargarstegosaurU.S..wordpress.com/2010/05/25/the-matter-of-manga-in-america/>.

The survey took responses from fans through links posted on numerous anime and manga convention forums between April 13 and June 14, 2010 and from links sent via school email lists. The majority of fans considered scanlations possibly legal (35%), maybe even ethical (43%), and definitely Useful to the industry (42%). The exact statistics may be found here in the image above, including the first ten responses for those who marked "Other" on the survey. Of specific interest is comment number 3, where a respondent clearly states that it's not legal and that they feel it is important to buy, but that scanlations always come first. Comment 6 also references another problem bemoaned by business, wherein manga readers will treat the bookstore like a library – reading but not purchasing.[10]

The survey delved further into what most see as the grey area – is the title licensed in the language into which it is being scanlated? Respondents overall felt scanlations were acceptable when something was unavailable in the language of the scanlation or licensed for publication (38%)or still felt it was wrong but was at least more acceptable so long as it was otherwise unavailable (28%). A surprising 17% of respondents believe scanlations are perfectly acceptable even with licensing and translations available in the scanlation language. A nearly even split of persons surveyed felt that scanlations should no longer be available once the publication is licensed (43.5%) versus. being left online regardless of licensing (43%).[11] It is that behavior by fans and scanlators that has led to the soon to be discussed legal actions within the industry.

Who are the fans themselves? 67% of the fans surveyed were between the ages of 18 and 25 and 65% were female. 77.5% identified themselves as a student, including 34.5% of respondents who were students who also held full or part-time jobs. Fans often read multiple genres, but the top five genres selected were: 1) Action 71.4%; 2) Comedy 70.7%; 3) Fantasy 64.0%; 4) Adventure 63.2%; and 5) Romance 57%. No other genres surpassed a 50% response rate. Niche genres such as yaoi and yuri received 23.1% and 16.1% respectively. When combined with their less explicit genre cousins shounen ai and shoujo ai, both receive a significant amount of readership with 44.6% for shounen ai/yaoi and 33.9% for shoujo ai/yuri. 74% of fans read OT (Older Teen – Ages 16+) ratings, though all ratings (shown below) were above 50% in readership except for Y (Youth – Ages 10+).

---

[10] "Manga & Scanlations Survey." Survey. Survey Monkey. Apr. 2010. Web.
[11] "Manga & Scanlations Survey." Survey. Survey Monkey. Apr. 2010. Web.

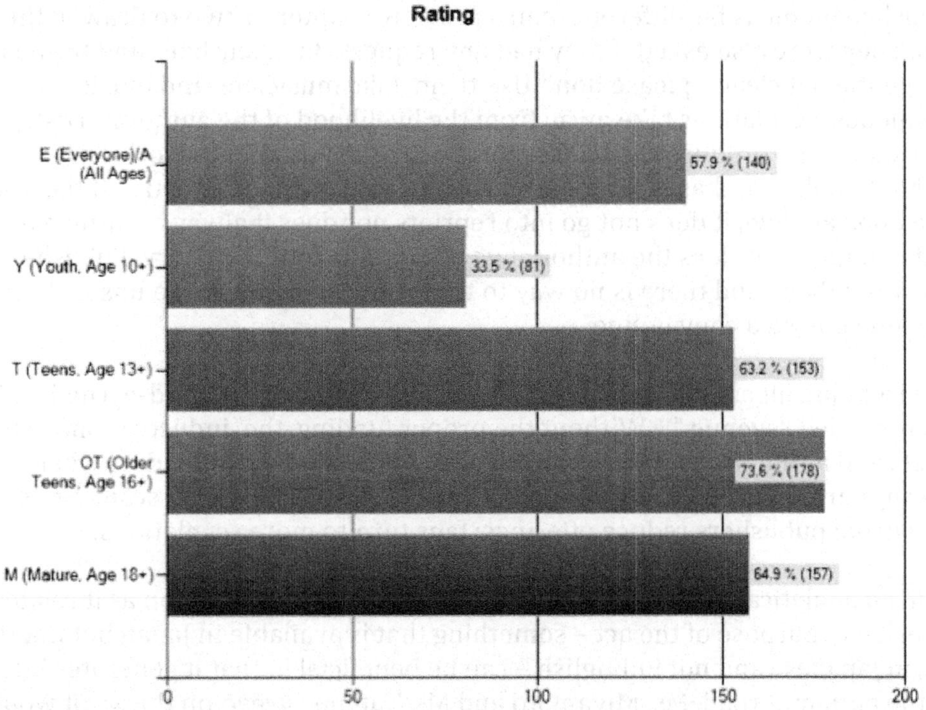

In a smaller survey of 30 participants, Dr. June Madeley found that older fans stepped into manga through mentoring by other fans or noticing volumes in the bookstore when the selection was still small. Newer fans start off through anime shown on television, mostly action-oriented shows such as Naruto, Bleach, and InuYasha. Older female fans also reported being interested in Boys Love (yaoi/shounen ai) manga more than younger fans. Most of the fans interviewed read scanlations to be current with the Japanese release or to find what was newly popular, but also purchased the books where possible.[12]

Authors and Artists

Conversely, the authors have far less awareness. When speaking with two Japanese author/artists, Makoto Tateno (Tateno Makoto)[13] and Kano Miyamoto (Miyamoto Kano),[14] both were aware of the existence of scanlations, but not to the extent of the Use as known by fans. Ms. Miyamoto was especially surprised to be shown a whole list of her works on MangaFox, unaware that such a site existed with so many of her materials available. When asked, both authors said it was disheartening to see fans Using scanlations, and knew other authors and artists felt the same. They said scanlations are a depressant for artists, discouraging them from continuing their works. While they agree it can be a

[12] Madeley, Dr. June. "Dr. June Madeley Talks To Manga Fans About Manga Fandom." Interview by Charles Webb. MangaLife. Web. 15 June 2010. <http://www.mangalife.com/features/InterviewDr.JuneMadeleyTal.htm>.
[13] Tateno, Makoto. Personal interview. 1 Nov. 2009.
[14] Miyamoto, Kano. Personal interview. 1 Nov. 2009.

beneficial introduction to their work and stir up interest, having their full works published online is far different than a preview chapter or two to draw in the fans. They were also asked if they had any requests for their fans, and the answer was gentle but clear – please don't Use them. Like musicians and music downloads, scanlations take away from the livelihood of the authors, artists, and publishers who produce the books. For the artists, it is akin to working for free. Without books purchased, there is no royalty paid back to the artist. If the sales for a book are low, it does not go into reprints nor does it always continue to the next volume – nor does the author always continue to a new story. Publishers follow numbers, and there is no way to track how many books go unsold because someone posted a copy online.

Copyright infringement "depriv[es] artists and publishers of hard-earned and much-needed revenue."[15] Without the proper funding, the industry contracts, artists and authors lose their publishers, and publishers lose readers when offerings are reduced or delayed. It is a cycle of sorts – fans read scanlations; sales drop; publishers reduce offerings; fans turn to more scanlations.

From an analytical perspective, the publishing of a true scanlation as it relates to the original purpose of the act – something that is available in Japan but not the U.S., in Japanese and not in English – can be beneficial in that it generates interest for the author abroad. Ms. Miyamoto and Ms. Tateno agreed on this, as it would be more of a preview or introduction to their work. However, publishing books online as free images when they can be purchased legally within the U.S. hurts the industry by skewing sales figures. Maybe the fans loved that book on knights and damsels that hit the shelves in the spring – but oh, it was available online! Fans can just read it there. Someone read it, enjoyed it, recommended it... and the domino effect began. 44.2% of fans find scanlations through recommendations.[16] Fewer people bought the book, because it drops down a rung on the priority purchase ladder, or off entirely, once it's already been enjoyed.

Publishers

Scanlations give an alternative to the purchase of licensed books. If the scanlation titles are not available in the U.S., then it does not apply to companies operating in America. But, with available titles online, there is less drive to go to the store and pay for the physical book. An anonymous representative from a U.S. publisher pointed out that it is impossible to gauge the effect on the industry as no money is typically changing hands for the scanlations. Fans are sharing things but not reselling them. However, with U.S. editions available online, the copyright infringement is blatant.[17]

Masaaki Hagino of e-book seller Voyager submitted manga on behalf of Kodansha to Apple iTunes and claimed an over 30% rejection rate. A clever

---

[15] TatsuGero23. "Re: Licensee Rights Over Scanlations." Web log comment. Forum Index - General - Manga. Anime News Network, 29 Apr. 2010. Web. 14 June 2010. <http://www.animenewsnetwork.com/bbs/phpBB2/viewtopic.php?t=129898>.
[16] "Manga & Scanlations Survey." Survey. Survey Monkey. Apr. 2010. Web.
[17] Anonymous U.S. Publisher Representative. Personal interview. 1 Nov. 2009.

blogger is likely on the right track with their analysis of the actions of Apple, and through it highlight a serious downside to scanlations. "Maybe someone should give a heads-up to Kodansha's legal department that in all likelihood, a majority of those rejected manga are available through Apple by way of apps developed by scanlation aggregators."[18]

Other publishers have previously expressed a certain level of acceptance or usefulness when it comes to scanlations. A Japanese publishing representative interviewed in 2009 saw scanlations as a type of advertisement in a way, but when there is too much of it, removal is requested.[19] "Frankly, I find it kind of flattering, not threatening," said TokyoPop's Steve Kleckner in an article published in the San Francisco Chronicle in 2004. "To be honest, I believe that if the music industry had used downloading and file sharing properly, it would have increased their business, not eaten into it. And, hey, if you get 2,000 fans saying they want a book you've never heard of, well, you gotta go out and get it."[20]

The manga publishing industry as a whole is showing serious signs of contraction. Viz, a major publisher of manga in the U.S., announced a 40% staff reduction in May 2010.[21] The industry decreased by a third to $140M in 2009 over the last two years following its peak in 2007 of $210M. Some publishers blame scanlations, while other industry experts cite an overall decrease in purchasing in addition to an aging female market leaving the shoujo genre or moving into other forms of fiction, such as Twilight.[22] Other publishers remind their fellows that several years ago they didn't complain about scanlations and even went so far as to say they didn't hurt the industry, a la the previous Tokyopop quotation.[23]

Conclusion

With all of the possible problems stemming from scanlations, one has to wonder why a person would participate. It is, as most readers and writers agree, a gray area, with opinions varying based on the presence of the publication in the language of the scanlation. By the letter of the law, scanlations are illegal copyright infringement. Fans are perpetuating a practice that is detrimental to the industry and, by their own words, know it.

---

[18] Simon. "Kodansha Manga Rejected by ITunes?" Web log post. Icarus Publishing, 8 May 2010. Web. 14 June 2010. <http://www.icarU.S.comics.com/wp_web/?p=5028>.
[19] Anonymous Japanese Publisher Representative. Personal interview. 1 Nov. 2009.
[20] Yang, Jeff. "ASIAN POP Manga Nation -." SF Gate. *San Francisco Chronicle,* 14 June 2004. Web. 15 Jan. 2010. <http://www.sfgate.com/cgi-bin/article.cgi?file=/g/archive/2004/06/14/manganation.DTL>.
[21] Reid, Calvin. "Viz Media Lays Off 60." *Publishers Weekly*. 11 May 2010. Web. 16 June 2010. <http://www.publishersweekly.com/pw/by-topic/book-news/comics/article/43145-viz-media-lays-off-60.html>.
[22] "A Second Bad Year in a Row for Manga." ICv2 : *Inside Pop Culture.* 16 Apr. 2010. Web. 15 June 2010. <http://www.icv2.com/articles/news/17292.html>.
[23] Johnson, Rich. "You Say You Want a Revolution?" *The Beat.* 24 May 2010. Web. 16 June 2010. <http://www.comicsbeat.com/2010/05/24/you-say-you-want-a-revolution/>.

Terms

Anime – Japanese animation; previously Japanimation
Manga – Japanese comics or graphic novels
Mangaka – artist/author of manga
Manhwa – Korean comics or graphic novels
Manhua – Chinese comics or graphic novels
Scanlation (scanslation) – a scanned translation of a work originally published in another language
Scanlator – the person(s) who scan and translate the works
IRC, BitTorrent – downloading and file sharing services
Sensei – literal translation is "teacher" or "doctor" but is also used as a formal term of respect for mangaka
Shoujo – girls comics
Josei – older girls comics
Shounen – boys comics
Seinen – older boys comics
Yaoi – homosexual male/male comics for women, also called BL (Boys Love)
Fansubs – anime with fan translations as subtitles

A Berglund Center Tenth Anniversary Essay

Editor's Note: This is one of a number of essays we will be publishing in coming issues which are brief portions of the longer essays to be published in our tenth anniversary volume, After Internet Time, forthcoming in fall 2011. That volume will be fully peer reviewed. These essays have not yet been peer reviewed, but all are by experts in the fields which they discuss.

The Internet and the 'Just-in-Time' Mind

David J. Staley

However you may feel about its politics, Garry Trudeau's Doonesbury is particularly good at identifying broad social trends in our culture. One of my favorite strips takes place in a college lecture hall. A student sits in his chair furiously typing away at his laptop, obviously distracted from the lecture. His device pings him: a fellow student warns him "Head's up dude—professor just asked you a question." None of his friends seems to know what the question is, since no one in the room apparently is paying attention to the professor. One of the student's electronic classmates overhears the question and chats back "name four major greenhouse gasses." The student pings his friend "stall her while I Google the answer." From the back of the auditorium, we hear "Professor, we couldn't hear the question back here, could you repeat it?" "I asked Mr. Harris to name four major greenhouse gasses," replies the teacher, after which comes the immediate reply from Mr. Harris "Water vapor, CO2, ozone and methane." The professor concedes "uh…right." Triumphantly indifferent, our student chats back to his friend "If this keeps up, I'll never get through my email."

I have shown this cartoon to a number of teachers over the last few years. They immediately light upon the behavior of the students, and decry the use of laptops in their classes. The students are distracted from the class, are having their attention drawn away from the lecture, indeed are not even engaged in the class, but are rather chatting with friends or emailing or surfing the web. When pressed, teachers express concerns over classroom management and control in such an electronic setting. Not only are the students distracted from the lecture, this appears to be a coordinated distraction, as the students are engaged in a subterranean conversation extraneous to the formal class. The students come across as wily and duplicitous, conning the professor with their clever use of technology.

But upon deeper examination, many teachers also see an issue with the professor's behavior, or at least with the entire pedagogical architecture of the class. The professor has asked a relatively simple question, one that can be easily looked up. The underlying pedagogical assumption as expressed in the behavior of the professor is that the student, having diligently read the material the night before or having been attentive to the lecture, should have such information ready to recall at the professor's insistence. This is, of course, a standard way to think about education: information and knowledge is deposited in student minds, ready to be recalled upon demand. (It is the underlying logic of standardized testing.) This student, Mr. Harris, clearly does not have this information at ready recall, in his memory, at any rate. A quick check of Google, of course, yields the answer as quickly as if it were embossed upon his memory. Teachers understand the implications: if such answers, if such information is so readily available on the Internet and if students have easy access to that Internet through a laptop or some other portable device, perhaps the "deposit" model of teaching and educational assessment needs to be reexamined.

Given that I am an historian and a futurist, I cannot help but to place events in a wider and deeper context, which is what I would like to do with Doonesbury's visual anecdote. As an educator, I am particularly interested in the effects of the Internet on knowledge. These effects should be placed in a wider historical context, certainly that of the emergence of electronic communications generally (starting with the telegraph), and perhaps even longer. I would like to argue here that the Internet represents the next great extension of the "external symbolic storage system" humans have developed since the beginnings of civilization. For all of the dramatic and disruptive change that the Internet surely represents, placing it in this long-term historical context renders this change more familiar, perhaps even less jarring.

When considering the status of knowledge, the present moment might be described as the era of "just-in-time knowledge." The situation described in the Doonesbury cartoon is an example of what I mean, that it seemingly becomes unnecessary to retain information in our physical, biological memory. Since information and knowledge can be stored on the Internet, and since I can easily access that knowledge wherever I might be, then I need only to access this "external memory" when called upon. Obviously, this has all sorts of implications for education as we currently conceive it. Is the Internet "making us stupid," as Nick Carr would have it, by messing around with the brain's wiring system, making us all as attention-deprived as the Doonesbury character? Observers remark that we live in the era of cloud computing, but one could easily make the case that we have been surrounded by an informational "cloud" for much of recorded history; since the first Venus figures and cave paintings, humans have been devising ways to create and store "tokens of memory" in visible, external form. The human mind conceives and constructs tools of cognition, like art, writing, books, and libraries. These cognitive tools, in turn, reshape the very mind that conceived them, a process that has spanned millennia. Far from "making us stupid," the Internet represents (merely) the next step in a much longer cultural and historical process.

As an educator, I am interested in what this all means for the status of knowledge and education. I'd like to place the Internet as an external symbolic storage system in the context of other such systems, especially the Library. For academics, the Library remains our dominant metaphor for the University: indeed, the Library itself is assumed to physically and conceptually sit at the center of the University. The Internet as cloud, the Internet as a system that facilitates just-in-time knowledge challenges that central metaphor: we no longer need travel to a central physical location to access knowledge, since that knowledge now swirls around us, accessible from whatever location. There are, of course, disquieting implications for the University, especially if we adhere to the idea that the University is grounded in place. A placeless Cloud of information and knowledge might force us to re-imagine the University as similarly placeless and just-in-time.

All of this raises important questions: Is the knowledge on the Internet any good? The shelf-life of electronically preserved information seems volatile and short; can we live with "evanescent information?" Is this move into a just-in-time cloud healthy for humanity?

And what of the Gutenberg Galaxy? What is the fate of "typographic man," whose knowledge was tethered to physical books and its larger systems of storage (like libraries) and the pedagogical assumptions that followed? Rather than seeing such a cognitive system disappear, as many fear, I suspect that typographic culture but will probably become a vestigial part of our cognitive system, vestigial to an electronic system that features sound and movement and other (actually ancient) forms of knowledge.

To understand what the future holds for the Internet, beyond the present moment, we must place it in a much wider and deeper historical and temporal context. To do so will, I believe, make us less alarmed by the impact the Internet is having on our minds and on our culture, and more balanced in our assessments.

Nicholas Carr's *The Shallows: What the Internet is Doing to Our Brains*

Review by Jeffrey Barlow

Nicholas Carr has become one of America's "public intellectuals"[1] in that his work has become iconic for us. As that work has focused increasingly upon the impact of the Internet, he has always had much about which to write.[2] His latest book, which should be read by everybody with a serious interest in teaching, learning, and the Internet, is The Shallows: What the Internet is Doing to Our Brains.

Part of the value of Carr's research and publication has been their ability to be both broad in their implications and understandings, and deep in their research and their embedding within the Western intellectual tradition. To read one of Carr's books is to also encounter many of the great minds of the Western tradition in whichever subject he may be discussing at the time.[3]

Carr has been working on issues related to the Internet for some time. In May of 2003 he wrote a controversial essay, "IT Doesn't Matter" in The Harvard Business Review. Then in 2004 he extended that analysis in the book, Does IT Matter?.[4] In the summer of 2008, he published a precursor essay to the present work in The Atlantic, "Is Google Making Us Stupid."[5] By any standards Nicholas Carr is a Deep Thinker in matters relevant to the Internet—I capitalize the term here, because it is a critical element of Carr's current argument that the Internet is making Deep Thinking increasingly difficult. This is because, Carr argues, persistent use of the Internet and other electronic devices literally rewires the brain and makes concentrated thought more difficult or at least, markedly less attractive to us.

Carr begins by first introducing the long-running argument between those who are interested more by the content of a new medium, and those who argue, like Carr via Marshall McLuhan, that the medium itself is the message.

As Carr states: "What both enthusiast and skeptic miss is what McLuhan saw: that in the long run a medium's content matters less than the medium itself in

---

[1] For a useful definition of public intellectual see: http://en.wikipedia.org/wiki/Intellectual Although this is a very broad entry ("intellectual") I find this Wikipedia site sufficiently authoritative for my purposes, a definition embedded within a wider context and nicely foot-noted.

[2] See his biography and partial bibliography at his personal page: http://www.nicholasgcarr.com/info.shtml.

[3] We reviewed his last major work, The Big Switch, at: http://bcis.pacificu.edu/journal/2008/02/carr.php.

[4] The essay can be downloaded on a paid basis at: http://harvardbusinessonline.hbsp.harvard.edu/b01/en/common/item_detail.jhtml;jsessionid=ENB34YRB5QWSGAKRGWDSELQBKE0YIISW?id=R0305B.

[5] See Carr's page together with book reviews at: http://www.nicholasgcarr.com/doesitmatter.html.

influencing how we think and act."[6] With this introduction, Carr then proceeds to interrogate the impact of the Internet as a medium on our thought processes.

In a chapter entitled "Hal and Me," Carr discusses his own intellectual journey which began in 2007. He began to experience difficulty in focusing on his work, particularly on careful and concentrated reading, thinking about that reading, and writing carefully about it. Finally, after some initial consultations which convinced him he was not alone in his difficulties—that, in fact, other intellectuals of his acquaintance had expressed the same anxieties, he began to consider that the Internet itself was impacting his ability to concentrate. Finding evidence in leading research on the chemistry of the brain that he had reason to be concerned, Carr "unplugged," moved to a rural area and limited his Internet use in order to be able to finish this book with a minimum of electronic interference or temptations.

Any simple summary of the *The Shallows* will surely be inadequate and incomplete, but I understand the argument of the work to be that we now know the brain is much more plastic than we once believed to be the case. It is capable of rewiring its neural system with surprisingly limited inputs in order to become better at tasks, whether these be perceptual or cognitive ones, or those impacting memory. This neuroplasticity is innate, continuous, and perhaps a key function enabling human evolution.[7]

Unfortunately, it follows that the brain's—as a limited system—changes may well come at the expense of some previous function:

"Experiments show that just as the brain can build new or stronger circuits through physical or mental practice, those circuits can weaken or dissolve with neglect. "If we stop exercising our mental skills," writes Doidge, "we do not just forget them: the brain map space for those skills is turned over to the skills we practice instead."36 Jeffrey Schwartz, a professor of psychiatry at UCLA's medical school, terms this process "survival of the busiest."37 The mental skills we sacrifice may be as valuable, or even more valuable, than the ones we gain. When it comes to the quality of our thought, our neurons and synapses are entirely indifferent. The possibility of intellectual decay is inherent in the malleability of our brains."[8]

The impact of electronic media—particularly of the quick scanning of materials read on the Internet is cumulatively a very heavy one, Carr and his sources argue.

---

[6] Amazon makes large portions of the book available at: http://books.google.com/books?id=wrROE6SLJFEC&dq=carr+does+it+matter&pg=PP1&ots=hvTj3027am&sig=VKGYfZHpK3kcC_-kEUySSGlA6L8&hl=en&prev=http://www.google.com/search?q=Carr+Does+IT+matter&ie=utf-8&oe=utf-8&rls=org.mozilla:en-US:official&client=firefox-a&sa=X&oi=print&ct=title&cad=one-book-with-thumbnail.

[7] See it at: http://www.theatlantic.com/magazine/archive/2008/07/is-google-making-us-stupid/6868/.

[8] Kindle formatted version of Nicholas Carr, *The Shallows*, at Loc 121-126 read on Kindle application on an Apple iPad, Loc. 659-65.

All the familiar tropes of negative views of the Internet are included such as short attention spans, superficial reading, and potentially addictive behavior. But there are also frightening new ones: The changes resultant from continual or frequent use amount to a rewiring of the brain itself, and further, will impact our ability to work in non-digitized media. We will be impatient with books requiring careful or repeated reading; our brain desires faster and broader inputs: "What it does mean is that the vital paths in our brains become... the paths of least resistance. They are the paths that most of us will take most of the time, and the farther we proceed down them, the more difficult it becomes to turn back."[9]

In underlining McLuhan's argument that the medium is the message and not the content, Carr argues that even the act of placing a given body of content—say, this book itself—into a digital format inevitably makes it more distracting because of the bells and whistles which digitization usually adds. For example, I read my copy of The Shallows, for the purposes of this review and for the editorial[10] in this issue of Interface, on both an Amazon Kindle and an iPad. In doing so I was tempted by both the presence of an electronic dictionary just a click away, and by a powerful browser putting the Internet itself a click away, and in the case of the iPad, in large format and gorgeous color to boot.

Carr makes no bones about his position in the cultural wars implied by the above facts. He is convinced that deep reading of texts, in which a reader encounters another mind in a limited and quiet intellectual environment permitting a close contact between the reader and the author, may prove to have been a brief period in human history. We may be moving toward a period when there is a "reading class" and many other non-reading or perhaps "scanning" classes who get snippets of information and input over the Internet but can never consider it in depth.[11]

In a bit of intellectual judo, Carr argues that even the counter-arguments of those who "...suggest that the value of the literary mind has always been exaggerated...are another important sign of the fundamental shift taking place in society's attitude toward intellectual achievement."[12]

The author also cites details from numerous studies suggesting/proving that the sort of multitasking or scanning of information gleaned while reading interactively are inevitably inferior in terms of comprehension and lasting memory, to material simply read from a book.[13] Again, studies suggest that the damage of multitasking in terms of easily distracted users seems permanent. Those who multitask are less able to concentrate on a given task than those who multitask less.[14]

---

[9] Loc 581-589, Loc. 667-68.
[10] October 2010 – Volume 10, Issue 8 at: http://bcis.pacificu.edu/journal/article.php?id=730.
[11] Loc 1870-1876.
[12] Loc 1938-1944.
[13] Loc 2156-2185.
[14] Loc 2489-2496.

Conclusion

Carr's argument is a very elaborate and complex one and no simple review in limited space, such as Interface affords, can possibly do it justice. Neither do I have the requisite expertise to fully consider, let alone refute, most of the research which Carr discusses. The book itself seems somewhat repetitive at points, and at others it seems to move rather quickly and perhaps too facilely along very complex chains of logic. But, however much we may cavil, perhaps in attempts to protect our own cherished views of the Internet, it remains irreducibly a work which must be read, and considered by all those interested in the impact of the Internet.

Dan Chaon's *Await Your Reply: A Novel*

Review by Jeffrey Barlow

Dan Chaon (pronounced as though written Shawn) is a very highly regarded novelist, though not yet one with the popularity of the sort that will soon bring his work to the bookshelves at your local super market. Among other literary prizes he has a National Book Award nomination (for his short stories), a Pushcart Prize, an O. Henry Award and an Academy Award in Literature from the American Academy of Arts and Letters.

Chaon's previously best-known work was *You Remind Me of Me*. He teaches writing at Oberlin and is a very self-aware writer, cognizant of the masters and stylists who have preceded him.[1] This makes *Await Your Reply: A Novel* fun to read as we recognize some of his allusions and plot devices. In addition, it is both suspenseful and challenging.[2]

Await your Reply and the earlier *You Remind Me of Me* both deal very much with identity and separation. In addition, *Await your Reply* is related to the Internet at almost every turn, and to its potential effects upon identity. It has been regarded by some, who are otherwise not particularly interested in this issue, as perhaps the best recent work to do so.[3]

While Chaon is clearly quite familiar with the Internet and related security issues, this is definitely not geek fiction. The Internet has given the author a new way to explore the issue of identity and communication but otherwise the central issues---of trust, and of personal authenticity and integrity---are very familiar ones, and Chaon is largely disinterested in the details of identity theft or other computer crimes in this work.

The three intertwined plot lines are tied together by the relationships between the three central protagonists---occasionally so intertwined as to introduce deliberate confusion as to which characters is speaking or being discussed---and by the Internet. One of the three main characters and several important minor ones are criminally minded hackers. It is their hope to use computers simply for

---

[1] See his personal page at: http://danchaon.com/

[2] Those wishing to better understand the author's approach in this novel (hopefully after first reading it!) might begin with an interview conducted by Edan Lepucki, one of his writing students, at: The Millions Interview
The Millions Interview: Dan Chaon found at: http://www.themillions.com/2009/08/the-millions-interview-dan-chaon.html

[3] Discussion with Michael Schaub, editor and writer for Bookslut.com at Pacific University, Tuesday September 14th. See Michael's review at: http://www.bookslut.com/fiction/2009_10_015215.php Michael, speaking in the Berglund Roundtable series, gave a wonderful talk on the impact of the Internet upon fiction. View the video of his presentation at: XXX For a more conventional review see: http://www.washingtonpost.com/wp-dyn/content/article/2009/08/25/AR2009082503195.html

petty theft, but slowly their crimes bring them into the orbit of several different groups of truly dangerous criminals.

The primary character, the dominant voice, is the brother of the hacker and is doggedly and selflessly trying to track down his brother so as to save him from himself. The third major character is Lucy, the girlfriend of the hacker brother, if a relationship lacking intimacy and eroticism can be so characterized.

Most of the characters---perhaps all of them---represent for us the problems of creating identity in a world shaped increasingly by evanescent electronic pulses. Lucy, for example, knows only that she really wants to have money, though she is less certain why she wants it. She slowly becomes aware that her relationship with the hacker will require that she lose her familiar, if boring and confining, identity:

> "What would happen to Lucy Lattimore now, she wondered. If she no longer entered the public record, if she never held a job or applied for a driver's license or paid taxes or got married or had children, if she never died, would she still exist two hundred years from now, free-floating and unresolved in some record bank in some government dead-letter office computer? At some point, would they decide to expunge her from the official roster?"[4]

Lucy goes forward in the belief that this step will certainly give her relative wealth, the hope of material gain being for most of the characters the one constant in their lives.

Another key group of characters begin as slacker hackers, described as:

> "...Dylan and his buddies spent a good portion of their time playing mean, stupid practical jokes on the Internet—posting bestiality porn videos on some lady's bichon frise website, The Wonderful Fluffy World, and uploading graphic accident photos to message boards meant for children; terrorizing some poor girl who maintained a tribute site for a dead pop star they all loathed, sending hundreds of delivery pizzas to her house and getting her power turned off; hacking into the website for the National Epilepsy Foundation with a strobe-like animation they'd decided might send the epileptics into seizures. They sat around doing imitations of convulsions, and chortling wildly as Jay stood by watching with uneasy disapproval."[5]

While the Internet is essential to the development of character and plot, it is always subsumed to the story line. However, the author's continual homage to "great works" of literature, film and even television, continually reminds us that the Internet is new, and potentially direly negative in its consequences.

---

4 - Highlight Loc. 3666-69 (Kindle edition).

5 - Highlight Loc. 3716-27

For example, at one point, Lucy is taping hundred-dollar bills stolen through computer-enabled identity theft into a volume of Bleak House in the hopes of evading Customs inspection, treating us to curiously appropriate snippets of text as she does so:

> "Are you sure this will work?" Lucy had said. She was flipping her way through Bleak House, fragments of text rising up as she laid a bill on the page and pinned it down. "The fog is very dense, indeed!" said I. And she pressed Ben Franklin over the line of words, and then flipped a couple of pages forward. "It's disgraceful," she said. "You know it is. The whole house is disgraceful." And she covered it again, though once again some grain of the book rose up: We found Miss Jellyby trying to warm herself at the fire ..."[6]

At another point, we see simultaneously the fate of old media, and the paranoia which afflicts those who make the Internet a part of their daily life---or in this case, lives:

> "Down below his third-story window, he could see the roof of the building next door; a mummified newspaper, still rolled and rubber-banded but slowly decaying... and then a helicopter appeared, gliding heavily, passing close to the treetops, its thick propellers chopping the air up. On its way to the hospital, no doubt, though Miles watched it sternly. For years, Hayden had believed that helicopters were spying on him."[7]

For many readers, the value of this book will lie in its plot, its masterful development of narrative and its haunting images, which often verge quite deliberately on familiar ones from classic horror fiction and film. It is, however, the author's talent and his ability to develop clearly defined yet highly intertwined characters and embed them in a continually interesting plot, which should make the book attractive for a very wide audience.

For those of us interested in the impact of the Internet, Awaiting Your Reply shows us how a truly dexterous writer can mine Internet tropes for plot elements such as identity theft, computer crime, ambiguity and threat, even computer addiction (one character wonders if he has wasted his time playing video games for ninety-one thousand hours---more over ten years)8---and yet at the same time, keep the Internet unobtrusive, merely what it has become for all of us, an inescapable part of our lives.

---

[6] -_Highlight Loc. 4387-91.

[7] - Highlight Loc. 2211-14 |

[8] - Highlight Loc. 2145-49

The Magic of Reading: iPad, Book, and Kindle

Editorial by Jeffrey Barlow

Having been an enthusiastic user of the Kindle, if not of Amazon's restrictive usage policies, I have written several times upon the advantages---and the disadvantages---of the appliance.[1] I have now had an opportunity to read upon the iPad and here compare the two experiences.

There are limitations to this review. I focus here entirely upon the question of using the iPad as an electronic reader. To use the iPad solely as an electronic reader neglects all of its multitudinous other potential uses. Mine will let me look up Chinese characters, take dictation and quickly and largely accurately translate that speech into text, sooth me with a visit to a virtual koi pond, bring up Google maps, serve as a flashlight and let me read my email, all in gorgeous color on a screen much larger than my first computer, the supposedly-portable Kaypro. Every time I visit the iTunes App store, I find some new use for the iPad demanding an immediate download, though I confess my disappointment in not learning to play the saxophone in the last several weeks as I had hoped I would, with the aid of the Saxophone App.

Another limitation of my experience is that it is limited solely to the software which is packaged with the iPad, plus a downloaded App from Amazon, amazonkindle.[2] There may be numerous better Apps in development and doubtless there will be some quick system upgrades which will solve some of my objections as well.

I used the iPad to read one of the books reviewed in this issue: Nicholas Carr's *The Shallows*. I relied upon my trusty Kindle in reading the other, Dan Chaon's *Eagerly Await Your Reply*.

This is perhaps an unfair review. To review the iPad with only the experience of reading one book risks attributing to it, problems which are due to my own unfamiliarity with the device, and perhaps not inherent to it.

As for all of these problems, surely one concern of any electronic reading device is the learning curve required to use it. Most of us are intimately familiar with the use of a book,[3] and we would certainly like to learn to use any electronic

---

[1] See: *To George Orwell: It's the Kindle Baby, it's the Kindle!* at: http://bcis.pacificu.edu/journal/2009/04/article.php?id=68; *To George Orwell, II; Is It 1984 yet?* at: http://bcis.pacificu.edu/journal/2009/05/article.php?id=71 and *An Educator Reconsiders the Kindle* at: http://bcis.pacificu.edu/journal/2009/09/article.php?id=129

[2] Go to: http://www.amazon. com/gp/feature.html/ref=kcp_iPad_mkt_lnd?docId=1000490441 for additional information.

[3] For those readers who are not, I recommend a quick visit to "The Medieval Help Desk," A Danish imagining of the problems presented to initial readers of the Book and to the early adopters who helped them at: http://www.youtube.com/watch?v=ueOOo8BwsmI

replacements for it in at least a few moments, and we would like it good-to-go out of the box, not following additional electronic developments.

With these caveats, let us begin. First, for me, as probably for most readers, the question of text legibility is very high on my list of desiderata. The iPad lets me select not only my own font size but also my text and background color, though the choices are somewhat limited. Nonetheless, if this was the only factor in selecting between the two, the winner is easily the iPad, because of its gorgeous large screen.

With a few moments use, however, an important limitation becomes obvious: The iPad is heavier than all but the weightiest of books, and far more so than the Kindle which is lighter than even many paperbacks. Even carrying the iPad in my Man Bag is a noticeable burden. I often even forget that my Kindle is in it. Advantage, Kindle.

The controls of the iPad, however, are very easy to manipulate. One swipe of the finger and the "page" changes just like a real book, though much faster. The image reforms even as the page is turning and there are no ghost images or lags as some readers say they experience on the Kindle. The iPad, unlike the Kindle, can be held in landscape format making reading even easier. All controls are touch controlled in the familiar iPhone format, and presumably can ultimately be updated.

The Kindle controls initially struck me as clunky. There are several buttons which creak when depressed and do not seem to have any positive positions so that I sometimes fail to depress them sufficiently far, leading to a fatiguing sort of press that again, calls forth the plastic creaking sound. The question of text availability may be an important one for many readers. Although there are comparatively few formatted for the iPad at present, with the Kindle App, you have access to the entire Amazon library. A reader can download a book on to his or her computer at Amazon or via the iPad with the appropriate account, just as on the Kindle. The App also permits you, as with the iPhone and the iPod, to hop between appliances, returning to the last page read each time, assuming that you have wireless access.

The battery usage seems more than adequate on both machines, so much so that I forget to charge sometimes after days of intermittent use and have to quickly do so. In each case access to a USB is all that is required. I find it convenient that the iPad uses the same familiar cord as does my iPhone and many other Apple devices, unlike the Kindle which requires a very small plug at the device end, somewhat like a miniature fire wire cable, which it may be for all I am aware.

The iPad immediately strikes the user as artfully designed and pretty in a functional sort of way, while the Kindle creaks when handled and seems designed to ultimately be recyclable. Of course, it now costs only 139.00 and the iPad begins at 499.00 and can easily be pushed over a thousand with additional memory and a few of those lovely Apple add-ons.

However, for all of these virtues, considered solely as a reading appliance, there are several real problems that make the iPad not quite ready for prime time, for me at least. These are probably issues that will largely face those making academic use of the machine.

For me, the really critical function of the Kindle is that I can underline text by manipulating a nib, not always an easy process but one I have easily gotten used to. These underlinings can be saved to a text file in most cases. (Some authors limit the total amount of underlining, presumably so as to limit possible piracy, with the end result that I often do not review their book.) These text files can be moved to my desktop and enable me to quickly cut and paste extended quotations from the text rather than laboriously hammering them in on a keyboard.

This distinction became really clear to me in writing the two reviews for this issue. Charon's book yielded a large text file with hundreds of underlined sections, but Carr's required reading the text while typing it in.

The iPad has a similar function, up to a point. A drag of the finger theoretically will place a pleasing yellow highlight over selected text, or, all too frequently several drags of the finger. Sometimes the drag will activate another command and the entire text will pop into some alternative function. Other times the placement of the finger accomplishes nothing; the screen simply refuses to respond. And then, providing that all of this has finally been accomplished, a menu will open up a few words of the highlights in a small central screen which requires scrolling through them to find the one you want; another finger stab (and another screen smudge) and you are taken back to your original highlighted text.

Despite the apparent clumsiness of the Kindle nib, it is an easy winner relative to the repeated motions and the dexterity required to manipulate the iPad, motions sometimes wasted when the screen just will not respond as ordered.

The final problem, however, is that there is not an apparent way to move the highlights off the iPad onto my computer; it cannot be reread and cut and pasted. I have found reviewing these text files in my Kindle or on my desktop are a wonderful way to quickly remind myself of even the details of a text underlined on the Kindle. The iPad is a non-starter in that regard.

I suppose that I now have three categories of books in my reading: books to be shared, which must necessarily be hard copy as the various e-book licenses are otherwise too restrictive; books to be read for review; these must be read on a kindle so that I can save text files of direct quotations; books to be read in color because of graphics or plates. In short, the iPad seems at present to be an adequate substitute for the coffee-table format.

It is difficult to say which of these problems are truly results of Amazon's formatting of the text, its App, or the iPad itself. I suppose we will have to wait for some system updates to the iPad to find out.

In the meantime, however, it is back to the Kindle for books I intend to review in Interface. My Man Bag contains a Kindle for reading and my iPad for all the other things it will do, and two cell phones; but that is another review.

November 2010 - Volume 10, Issue 9

About this Issue

http://bcis.pacificu.edu/journal/article.php?id=746

Articles

Nicole Nowlin - *Scanlations: Copyright Infringement for Literature and Art Fans Brought to You by the Internet Part III*

http://bcis.pacificu.edu/journal/article.php?id=737

Deborah Lines Andersen - *Information, Mediation, and Users: A View of the Internet's Evolving Relationship to Information and Library Science*

http://bcis.pacificu.edu/journal/article.php?id=738

Chris Pruett - *The Anthropology of Fear: Learning About Japan Through Horror Games*

http://bcis.pacificu.edu/journal/article.php?id=741

Ruth Happ - *Text Appeal: The Internet, Dating, and Jane Austen, Part 1*

http://bcis.pacificu.edu/journal/article.php?id=742

Book and Site Reviews

Jeffrey Barlow - Payal Arora's *Dot Com Mantra. Social Computing in the Central Himalayas*

http://bcis.pacificu.edu/journal/article.php?id=739

Jeffrey Barlow - Gary Shteyngart's *Super Sad True Love Story: A Novel*

http://bcis.pacificu.edu/journal/article.php?id=740

Editorial

Jeffrey Barlow - *Bullying and WWW Sites: An Introduction*

http://bcis.pacificu.edu/journal/article.php?id=736

About This Issue

The November issue of Interface is, we think, a wonderfully diverse one.

The Feature article for the issue is "Information, Mediation, and Users: A View of the Internet's Evolving Relationship to Information and Library Science," by Deborah Lines Andersen of the College of Computing and Information at NYU Albany. Deborah is preparing a much longer version of this piece for our tenth anniversary publication, *After Interface Time*. This selection will give readers a good idea of the quality of work done by Deborah, and of the quality of the forthcoming volume, to appear fall, 2011.

Ruth Happ, a graduate of Pacific University in May 2010 offers us the first part of her witty senior thesis, "Text Appeal: The Internet, Dating, and Jane Austen, Part 1." Ruth compares Jane Austin's civilized courting practices with today's often internet-driven hookups. We think all Janeites (and who isn't one?) will enjoy this piece.

Nicole Nowlin, Student Fellow at the Berglund Center concludes her series, "Scanlations: Copyright Infringement for Literature and Art Fans Brought to You by the Internet Part III" This final posting reviews the current issues affecting scanlations in 2010 and offers suggestions to publishers.

Chris Pruett, Pacific graduate and one of our early Systems Operators at the Berglund Center, our Gaming columnist, and now a Google Engineer in Japan, published "The Anthropology of Fear: Learning About Japan Through Horror Games" in the journal of the Canadian Games Studies Association. We reprint it here with Chris' permission. Congratulations Chris!

The anthropological focus of this issue is continued by our first book review, Arora Payal's *Dot Com Mantra. Social Computing in the Central Himalayas*. This is an excellent work by a much-published Indian anthropologist. This study was done in an isolated northeast Indian township and will appeal to many different audiences interested in computing and education for economic development.

The second review is of Gary Shteyngart's *Super Sad True Love Story: A Novel*. This is a recent highly acclaimed novel set in New York, not that far in the future. It focuses on digital communication and reminded some reviewers of Orwell's *1984*, though it is described as both a love story and a dark comedy. Our reviewer states "the book, and its overwhelmingly favorable reception tells us a great deal about the impact of electronic communications, including the Internet."
Our editorial for this issue is "Bullying and WWW Sites: An Introduction". This is our start at *Interface* on gaining a better understanding of the issues involved not only with bullying per se, and particularly cyber bullying, but bullying as a media phenomenon.

Please see also our announcements section for recent events at the Center as well as a discussion by our Legal editor, Leonard DuBoff on "Beware of Domain Name Registration Scams." Interestingly, we just had such a scam attempt launched at the Berglund Center from China, and were forewarned by Leonard's piece. Here our readers can see the many advantages of following Leonard's work closely!

The Berglund Center for Internet Studies
Pacific University Oregon

Scanlations: Copyright Infringement for Literature and Art Fans Brought to You by the Internet Part III

Nicole Nowlin

Student Fellow, Berglund Center for Internet Studies

Editor's Note: This is the last article of a three part series on scanlations. The project as a whole was fascinating and enjoyable, and made a great Berglund Student Fellowship project. Part I provided an overview of scanlations and the copyright issues related to them. Part II covered the users of scanlations, and the authors, artists, and publishers harmed by scanlations. Part III reviews the current issues affecting scanlations in 2010 and offers suggestions to publishers.

Issues in 2010

In April, Japanese publisher Shueisha took the first step against scanlators with an open letter requested the cessation of all scanlating activities and usage, as seen to the right.[1] The letter reminds readers that the scanlations and their usage is illegal and asks for support as they handle uploads "severely."[2]

In May, HTMLComics, a purveyor of posted materials supposedly number over 6.6 million pages, fell under charges of copyright infringement in a joint operation by the FBI, a comics publisher coalition formed mostly of American comics publishers, and an entertainment legal firm Katten Muchin Rosenman LLP. With the first serious legal action against a site related to the scanlation subculture, fans have been made aware of the impending legal assault on copyright infringement.[3]

---

1 Dofla. "Shueisha Asks for the End of Scans." *MangaHelpers*. 15 Apr. 2010. Web. 15 June 2010. <http://mangahelpers.com/forum/showthread.php?t=59936>.

2 "Weekly Shonen Jump Editors Discuss Unauthorized Copies." *Anime News Network*. 16 Apr. 2010. Web. 15 June 2010. <http://www.animenewsnetwork.com/news/2010-04-16/weekly-shonen-jump-editors-discuss-unauthorized-copies>.

3 Katten Muchin Rosenman LLP. "Pirate Website Www.Htmlcomics.com Shut Down by Coordinated Efforts of Department of Justice, FBI, Katten and Consortium of Comic Publishers." *Katten in Focus*. 5 May 2010. Web. 14 June 2010. <http://www.kattenlaw.com/pirate-website-wwwhtmlcomicscom-shut-down-by-coordinated-efforts-of-department-of-justice-fbi-katten-and-consortium-of-comic-publishers-05-05-2010/>.

On June 8, a coalition was formed to combat "scanlation aggregators," large websites who earn money through memberships, donations, or advertising while providing scanlations, and occasionally officially translated manga, for free online. Thirty sites were targeted for action which may result in filing charges with the Justice Department's anti-piracy division, local law enforcement agencies, and the FBI, as well as requests for damages. The group includes Japan's Digital Comics Association, a group of 36 publishers,[4] additional Japanese publisher Square Enix, American publishers Viz Media, TOKYOPOP, Vertical, Inc., Yen Press, and legal entity the Tuttle-Mori Agency.[5] OneManga, the largest aggregator, shut down in July. Their closing letter to their readers may be seen at: http://bcis.pacificu.edu/journal/2010/09/images/nowlinImage2.jpg.

Contents 2010
No.20
銀魂 空知英秋
ぬらりひょんの孫
バクマン。大場つぐみ 小畑健
PSYREN—サイレン—
ONE PIECE
NARUTO-ナルト-
BLEACH
トリコ
REBORN!
めだかボックス
べるぜバブ
保健室の死神
いぬまるだしっ
SKET DANCE
LOCK ON!
HUNTER×HUNTER
4月26日(月)発売

Kurt Hassler of Yen Press spoke on scanlations in an article published in Publisher's Weekly about the new coalition, pointing out that the early scanlations were all about availability where none existed and would remove materials when licenses were obtained by a publisher. He insists that is no longer the reality of scanlations. "Go back 2 years and track these sites and you'll find an inverse relationship between the rise of traffic on these scanlation sites and the decline in U.S. manga sales. These sites are run as businesses and include direct scans of licensed English-language manga editions. Some even include our copyright notices. We don't want to have to do this but publishers are now focused on this problem."[6]

---

[4] Japan's Digital Comics Association members: Akane Shinsha, *Akita Shoten*, *ASCII Media Works*, *East Press*, *Ichijinsha*, Enterbrain, *Okura Shuppan*, *Ohzora Shuppan*, *Gakken*, *Kadokawa Shoten*, Gentosha Comics, *Kodansha*, Jitsugyo No Nihonsha, *Shueisha*, Junet, *Shogakukan*, *Shogakukan Shueisha Production*, *Shodensha*, Shonen Gahosha, Shinshokan, Shinchosa, Take Shobo, Tatsumi Shuppan, *Tokuma Shoten*, Nihon Bungeisha, *Hakusensha*, *Fujimi Shobo*, *Fusosha*, *Futabasha*, *France Shoin*, Bunkasha, *Houbunsha*, *Magazine House*, *Media Factory*, Leed sha, Libre Shuppan

[5] Viz Media. "Multi-National Manga Anti-Piracy Coalition Formed." *Anime News Network*. 8 June 2010. Web. 15 June 2010. <http://www.animenewsnetwork.com/press-release/2010-06-08/multi-national-manga-anti-piracy-coalition-formed>.

[6] Reid, Calvin. "Japanese, U.S. Manga Publishers Unite To Fight Scanlations." *Publishers Weekly*. 8 June 2010. Web. 16 June 2010. <http://www.publishersweekly.com/pw/by-topic/digital/copyright/article/43437-japanese-u-s-manga-publishers-unite-to-fight-scanlations.html>.

In some cases, cease and desist letters are sent to scanlators only to find that they have already yanked the licensed manga from their own sites or servers. However, that doesn't stop the manga from being distributed – the Internet is famous for viral distributing.[7] Manga scanlations are as viral as anything else on the 'net, making cease and desist letters almost as pointless as fans suggest the assault on scanlations is. If those to whom the letters are addressed have already stopped, how does the company halt the dissemination of their materials in a space as wide as the net?

In response to the recent coalition against scanlations, fans on forums have made the following unimpressed comments.

- "They think they can stop us. All they can do is shut down these easy access sites. We'll just turn to IRC and Torrents instead."
- "It does nothing at stopping the scanlations, which are usually done by low-key groups anyways."
- "Aw, boo. These organizations need to STFU and let us enjoy their darn mangas."
- "If you know the scanlation group then you can visit their websites for the scanlations. They can't stop scanlations and they STILL can't stop anime fansubs."
- "I wouldn't even of discovered manga and buy your damn volumes if it wasn't for the scans D:."[8]

They have even gone so far as creating an online petition to gather signatures in protest of the actions against scanlations. One petition, "This is madness," was created July 22nd and has only 59 signatures to date.[9] A second petition, "Don't stop scanlation sites!," also created July 22nd, has nearly 2,500 signatures.[10] Both are still a far cry from the 1,000,000 signature goal. The Google search for these petitions brought up several more are on various sites.

Suggestions for Publishers

Pricing is a big issue for manga publishers as it is a constant complaint of fans. "Companies really need to re-think their prices if they want people to support the official copies instead of just downloading scanlations," wrote one fan on a Tokyopop forum. "Most people I know who read scanlations either can't afford

---

7 Cha, Kai-Ming. "Scanlation Smackdown." *Boiled Egg.* 8 June 2010. Web. 16 June 2010. <http://genuinearticle.wordpress.com/2010/06/08/scanlation-smackdown/>.
8 Various. "Coalition Against Scanlations." *Mabination.* 8 June 2010. Web. 15 June 2010. <http://mabination.com/mabination-community/general-discussions/entertainment/3512-coalition-against-scanlations-2.html>.
9 Kitteh, Dr. "This Is Madness, Manga Scanlations Are Forbidden." *Petition Spot.* 22 July 2010. Web. 29 Sept. 2010. <http://www.petitionspot.com/petitions/thisisinsanity/>.
10 Mozzor, Shoshanna. "Don't Stop Scanlation Sites!" *Petition Spot.* 22 July 2010. Web. 29 Sept. 2010. <http://www.petitionspot.com/petitions/SaveManga/>.

the official manga, don't have it in their area, or don't want to pay 10+ for a manga. And now manga prices are rising even higher! It's gotten to the point where I won't even buy a manga unless I've already read it and have a coupon."[11] Of fans who read scanlations, nearly 22% read a few times a week, and 17% read daily. 21% of fans rarely or never read scanlations.[12] Another believes that "jacking prices up on most of [their] titles during the worst economic downturn in history had something to do with declining sales."[13]

Fans suggest that pricing increases lead to more illegal scanlation usage, a detriment to publishers. As previously mentioned, that is hard to prove as it is hard to track. A fan did summarize the possible lost revenue succinctly, stating, "If you averaged 8 chapters and $10 a volume, then even (extremely) conservatively I've read $2,500 worth of free manga. This bothers me a little, but it's countered by the fact that without scanlations (and aggregator sites) I'd never have read (or even known) them in the first place. I'm almost driven to buy a little of my favorite series to support them a bit, but when it's available for free [and] you throw out the ethics issues, it's like throwing away money. Leading to only wanting to throw away money for the really really good ones."[14] It is important to note that price is relative to the consumer; smaller American comics may be more expensive. A volume of manga at 221 pages for $9.99 compared to a volume of an American comic at 140 pages for $15.99 suggests that the price of manga is not as much a detriment to the average fan as it may be to the niche fan purchasing from an imprint or small publisher.

Fans also want to read manga in its true form; uncensored or edited. Manga was initially flipped to read left to right for western readers, then eventually changed to be traditionally Japanese as right to left. When an industry employee says, "...knowing full well the accusations of unprofessionalism and manga-industry-treachery I'll get for saying it -- I'd rather read scanlations than pay for censored manga,"[15] there is something to be said for the desire for authenticity and quality displayed by the fans. When those same fans overwhelmingly prefer traditional Japanese style for their manga when surveyed on reading preferences (see below), it is an even more obvious requirement to meet their tastes.[16]

---

[11] Feder. "Re: WSJ's Editors Statement Concerning Scanlations." Web log comment. *Tokyopop*. 3 May 2010. Web. 15 June 2010.
<http://messageboard.tokyopop.com/forums/showthread.php?t=15525&page=2>.
[12] "Manga & Scanlations Survey." Survey. *Survey Monkey*. Apr. 2010. Web.
[13] Opipari, Julie. "YOUR MANGA MINUTE: Trying to Find the Silver Lining." Web log post. *Newsarama.com*. 12 May 2010. Web. 15 June 2010.
<http://blog.newsarama.com/2010/05/12/your-manga-minute-trying-to-find-the-silver-lining/>.
[14] Axx. "Re: Coalition Against Scanlations." Web log comment. *Mabination*. 8 June 2010. Web. 15 June 2010. <http://mabination.com/mabination-community/general-discussions/entertainment/3512-coalition-against-scanlations-2.html#post58190>.
[15] Thompson, Jason. "IPad vs. Kindle vs. Manga." *Khyungbird. Live Journal*, 1 June 2010. Web. 16 June 2010. <http://khyungbird.livejournal.com/79141.html>.
[16] "Manga & Scanlations Survey." Survey. *Survey Monkey*. Apr. 2010. Web.

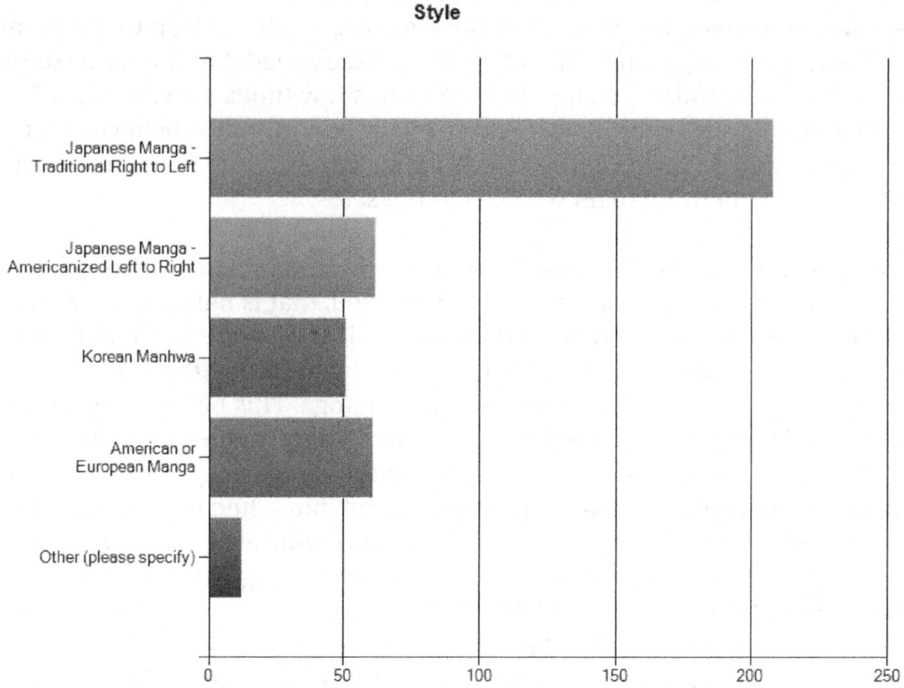

Note: Respondents were allowed to choose multiple styles. Traditional was selected by 80% of respondents.

Other frequent complaints against publishers are poor translations and long breaks between released volumes – from two to three months to a year or more, depending on the publisher and the release. It may be in the publishers best interest to speed up releases, as evidenced by the success of One Piece, a manga that has traditionally held less regard when compared to series like Naruto and Fullmetal Alchemist. When five volumes were released at once, all five made the New York Times Bestseller List.[17] Fans have a surprisingly high regard for the quality of translations in scanlations, with 29% grading quality as an 8/10 and less than one quarter of respondents citing scanlations as low or below average in quality.[18]

	1 - Extremely Poor	2	3	4	5 - Low Average	6 - High Average	7	8	9	10 - Fabulous!	Rating Average	Response Count
Quality of Scanlations	4.8% (10)	1.0% (2)	1.4% (3)	3.4% (7)	10.1% (21)	18.8% (39)	15.9% (33)	29.0% (60)	9.7% (20)	5.8% (12)	6.77	207
											answered question	207
											skipped question	83

[17] Ishaan. "Viz "Speed Up" One Piece Releases, Libraries Attempt To Catch Up." *Siliconera*. 1 May 2010. Web. 15 June 2010. <http://www.siliconera.com/2010/05/01/viz-speed-up-one-piece-releases-libraries-attempt-to-catch-up/>.
[18] "Manga & Scanlations Survey." Survey. *Survey Monkey*. Apr. 2010. Web.

Former Go! Comi creative director Audry Taylor provided a valuable action plan for ailing publishers to consider for incentivizing their customers to buy more manga and read less scanlations.

1. Make a story available world-wide simultaneously in all major languages.
2. In a digital format.
3. With perks for pre-orders.
4. And goodies that digital pirates can't reproduce. (And yes, that's possible. Goodies they can't compete with, like author chats.)
5. Rip off business model 4 pirate sites & one-up them. They offer a Wii raffle for a subscription to a d/l site, u offer author-signed Wii

Use the assets YOU have that pirates CAN'T have to compete with free.[19]

Publishers have access to authors and artists on a scale no fan or scanlators can hope to match. Incentives of additional art, autographs, interviews, and updates may make the difference between reading a grainy JPEG online and purchasing a pristine copy of a manga filled with fan-delighting goodies direct from their favorite mangaka. Publishers have ignored the problem too long and it has blossomed into something potentially beyond their control.

Conclusion

With the recent developments of coalitions and increasing cease and desist letters, the liberal age of scanlations is drawing to a close. A new chapter is in the works for the history of the manga subculture – look for the next volume.

Terms

- Anime – Japanese animation; previously Japanimation
- Manga – Japanese comics or graphic novels
- Mangaka – artist/author of manga
- Manhwa – Korean comics or graphic novels
- Manhua – Chinese comics or graphic novels
- Scanlation (scanslation) – a scanned translation of a work originally published in another language
- Scanlator – the person(s) who scan and translate the works
- IRC, BitTorrent – downloading and file sharing services
- Sensei – literal translation is "teacher" or "doctor" but is also used as a formal term of respect for mangaka
- Shoujo – girls comics
- Josei – older girls comics
- Shounen – boys comics
- Seinen – older boys comics
- Yaoi – homosexual male/male comics for women, also called BL (Boys Love)
- Fansubs – anime with fan translations as subtitles

---

[19] Alverson, Brigid. "Digital Piracy: Words to the Wise." *Robot 6. Comic Book Resources*, 20 May 2010. Web. 15 June 2010. <http://robot6.comicbookresources.com/2010/05/digital-piracy-words-to-the-wise/>.

Information, Mediation, and Users: A View of the Internet's Evolving Relationship to Information and Library Science

Deborah Lines Andersen
Associate Professor of Information Studies and Informatics
College of Computing and Information
University at Albany
Albany, NY 12222
dla@albany.edu
518.442.5122

Editor's Note: This article is the preliminary version of a much longer peer-reviewed piece to be published later as part of out tenth-year anniversary volume, *Internet 2.0: After the Bubble Burst 2000 - 2010.*

The Internet's Evolutionary Impact on Library and Information Science

In the realms of information, mediation, and users the Internet continues to have profound effects on information and library science. This article explores these effects through literature and research. It looks at whether information and library science have indeed come fully to terms with changes brought about by the Internet, or are still in the throws of contending with and adapting to this force that has taken over the field. Is the Internet an evolving force or have we already fully seen its effects on the field? If the Internet is still an evolving force to be reckoned with, then the questions for the field are many. What direction is it going? How quickly? What will mark its progress? What new kinds of information, organization, and access might we expect to see in the future? What sorts of technology will shape information delivery? What kinds of new mediation will be necessary in order to best meet patron needs? What kind of education will need to be put into place to train information professionals in this new mediation? And finally, what might we expect users to look like in the future and how will their characteristics in turn shape the field?

A Vignette: The New Information Consumer or Plagiarist?

A central tenant of information and library science service is to know the user. Since the purpose of acquiring, organizing, and making accessible information is to do that for the user, it makes absolute sense to understand that user and that user's behaviors and needs. Unavoidably this is a complex task since all users are not the same and all require specialized attention. In library science we speak of the "reference interview" in which we ascertain the specific information needs of specific individuals.[1] All of this ascertaining, knowing, and interviewing is

[1] See, for example, Patricia Dewdney and Gillian Mitchell. 1996. Oranges and peaches: Understanding communication accidents in the reference interview. *RQ 34*(4): 520-535; James

theoretically independent of the media through which a user will receive information, although more and more we must also consider mode of access and delivery as well as the informational content itself.

Online media are changing information consumers in a variety of ways that are challenging as well as disturbing to information professionals. A case in point is the concept of intellectual property and the linked concept of plagiarism. Although individuals from a very early age tend to understand the idea of owning a toy, a book, a car or a house, the concept of owning an idea is less distinct. Ideas can be multiplied and be distributed. Many individuals can possess the same piece of information without having any single piece diminished in the process—decidedly different that sharing ownership of a house or a piece of land. Grandma's recipe for rhubarb pie is information which could potentially be broadcast on the Internet for all to read and use. After it has been published online, who now "owns" the recipe? Could anyone take it and create a book, for profit, that includes it in its pages? Here is where the next generation of information consumers arises, or, as the *New York Times* headline named them—"Generation Plagiarism."[2]

It would appear that the next generation of information consumers' definition of intellectual property is far less clear than that of past generations. One college student on the generation plagiarism page stated that, "In the digital age, plagiarism isn't and shouldn't be as big of a deal as it used to be when people used books for research." He or she did not elaborate on why this might be the case but other students have. An earlier piece in *The New York Times*[3] quoted students, saying that pages without author information and, in particular, articles in Wikipedia did not need to be cited because they were unsigned and collectively written, therefore "common knowledge." The article's author went on to state that "concepts of intellectual property, copyright and originality are under assault in the unbridled exchange of online information." This "evolving view of authorship" was supported even further in Germany when a 17-year-old author created an award-nominated novel that turned out to be a collection of materials taken (plagiarized?) from other sources. The article noted that her work was:

> representative of a different generation, one that freely mixes and matches from the whirring flood of information across new and old media, to create something new. 'There's no such thing as originality

---

Rettig. 2003. Technology, cluelessness, anthropology, and the memex: The future of academic reference service. *Reference Services Review 31*(1): 17- 21; David Tyckoson. 2003. On the desirableness of personal relations between librarians and readers: The past and future of reference services. *Reference Services Review 31*(1): 12-16; and Jack O'Gorman & Barry Trott. 2009. What will become of reference in adacemic and public libraries? *Journal of Library Administration 49*(4): 327-339.

[2] This is a social media site that allows individuals over the age of 13 to comment on questions presented by the moderator. The focus of this session was "tell us what you think about plagiarism." Montgomery, Carrie. Are you part of "Generation Plagiarism?" *The New York Times*, August 3, 2010. http://learning.blogs.nytimes.com/2010/08/03/are-you-part-of-generation-plagiarism/

[3] Trip, Gabriel. Plagiarism lines blur for students in digital age. *The New York Times*, August 2, 2010: A1. http://www.nytimes.com/2010/08/02/education/02cheat.html

anyway, just authenticity,' said Ms. [Helene] Hegemann in a statement released by her publisher after the scandal broke.[4]

Is this the new user of information, who will grow up, become an adult, and supplant those of us who presently recoil at the idea of plagiarism in any form? What has happened to the idea of information property? How about of information authorship? Of creation of new ideas that will in turn need to be organized and made accessible to others? How worried should information professions get and what kind of actions might be taken now to evolve gracefully in this world that has been decidedly changed by the Internet?

Beginnings: What Goes Around Comes Around

There have always been deep challenges to the field of information and library science. On October 6, 1876 in Philadelphia, Pennsylvania, a group of 90 men and 13 women, including Melvil Dewey (of the classification scheme), Charles Ammi Cutter (of a competing classification scheme), Richard Rogers Bowker (of *Books in Print*), and Samuel S. Green, signed a register which made them charter members of what was to become the American Library Association. The goal of this new association was "to enable librarians to do their present work more easily and at less expense."[5] This goal has continued until the present day even as technology changes, information explodes, and users seem to be more and more happy to use the Internet rather than step into an actual library building.

The question for this forthcoming article is what difference the Internet has made in information science, and if indeed we are now seeing a stabilizing of information and library science in relation to the Internet. Is the field now at peace with technology—with the way information is stored, organized, and made available for access? Has the field come to some kind of agreement—mutually agreed upon behaviors—with users of information? Samuel Swet Green, the last of those listed above, is notable for having written a seminal piece, in 1876, entitled "Personal relations between librarians and readers."[6] Green's central thesis was that one could not let a reader (the term "patron" was not yet in use, and "reader' was indeed appropriate since individuals did that and only that) into a library on his or her own. Readers needed the guidance of a well-trained, cordial librarian to find what they were looking for. They would be lost at the library catalog (paper cards at the time) and unable to find a print work suitable to their needs.

Green gives many examples of the kind of work a librarian must do in order to help a patron find needed information. In doing so he suggested the title for this

---

[4] Kulish, Nicholas. Author, 17, says it's "mixing" not plagiarism. *The New York Times*, February 12, 2010, A4. http://www.nytimes.com/2010/02/12/world/europe/12germany.html

[5] See Edward G. Holley., ALA at 100, in *The ALA Yearbook* (centennial edition); P. Sullivan, Carl H. Milam and the American Library Association, HW Wilson, 1976; and Doris Cruger Dale. ALA and Its First 100 Years, 1876-1976, in *Milestones to the Present: Papers from Library History Seminar*, V. Gaylord Professional Publications, 1978.

[6] Samuel Swett Green. "Personal relations between librarians and readers." Library Journal, 1. 1876: 74-81.

essay—information, mediation, and the user. Green's information was in books on the shelves of the library. His mediation was in the form of the well-trained librarian, and his user was "modest men in the humbler walks of life, and well-trained boys and girls" since "scholars and persons of high social position" would not be timid about finding what they need or approaching a librarian for assistance.[7] A central question for this piece is how, if at all, information, mediation, and the user have been changed by the Internet, and if these changes are complete or still evolving.

Public Libraries

Melvil Dewey was primarily concerned about the public library—not private or subscription libraries that were selective about their clientele. The focus for this piece is also the public library rather than academic or university settings. Public libraries are at least in part funded by tax dollars and as a result bring with them the challenges of responding to citizens, legislators, public administrators, and various citizen groups that often have the opportunity to advocate for or against the policies of libraries. Drawing on research on public libraries and public library policy in Scotland, Canada, Mexico, Guatemala, and the United States, this article explores a variety of ways o dealing with information, mediation, and patrons in a comparative sense, looking at similarities and differences in style to develop potential practices and policy that might be put into effect in the public sphere. Public libraries also cover all ranges of patrons—young and old, educated and becoming educated.[8] Information science is necessarily concerned with all patrons, not just academics in the university library.

Information

Today's information has expanded far beyond the library's shelves and the library itself. Libraries now often pay for access rather than ownership of online materials, and an overwhelming amount of information is free for the finding, if one knows where to look. Very often the library is no longer a place to visit but a resource to be consulted through the Internet. There is an abundance of policy questions for libraries about what kinds of resources patrons need, about redundancy of information in print and electronic forms, and about patron education as a balance to online information that is abundant but dubiously accurate. Inevitably the question of resources comes to play in this debate. Where should funds be directed in order to provide the best services to the greatest numbers of individuals?

---

[7] Ibid. p. 74.

[8] See, for example, Deborah Lines Andersen, 2004. "Library as Living Space: How Glasgow, Scotland Defines Its Public Libraries." *JLAMS* (Journal of the Library Administration and Management Section of the New York Library Association), *1*:1 (October); http://www.nyla.org/content/user_10/JLAMS2004-01.pdf ; and 2003. "Selling a Public Good: The Case of Rechartering Public Libraries by Referendum in New York State." *Public Library Quarterly* *22*(4): 5-23.

Mediation

Today's mediation could be in the form of the friendly librarian, but librarians today continue to lament how few people come into the library and how those who do often want to use just the computer terminals. Reference questions for onsite users have devolved for many to issues of computer settings and broken printers. Off-site use of libraries has its own set of choices in terms of telephone, instant messaging, ask a librarian, 24/7 distributed reference, websites, wireless, wikis, and blogging, to name just a few. Social media hold out a promise of bringing individuals into the library, virtually if not in person, but librarians and library schools are faced with choices about what services to provide for which users—especially potential users who might be lured into the library with the right choices.

Users

A user of today who is 20 years old or less has never known a time without the Internet. He is also probably the owner of a cell phone, can instant message, and knows how to search the Internet for information. The probability is very high that she believes that all needed information is on the Internet. More frightening is his complete trust in the veracity of information on the Internet. Perhaps most frightening is her belief that she is really good at searching and really does not need any help at all. If information professionals were only dealing with technology-savvy 20 year olds the path would be fairly straightforward. We would teach our new information professionals and equip our libraries to target this group. Instead, and rather obviously, we have babies through 90 year olds visiting the library and wanting to make use of an enormous variety of resources, sources, and services available there. How does one address the needs of so many disparate individuals? How do information professionals assess those needs and adjust present practice as users change—in skills, country of origin, language, and cultural background? It would be impossible to address questions of users without also addressing issues of globalization and the ease with which ethnic groups can move into a community and change its demographics.

If we could answer all the questions presented above, our libraries, information professionals, and users would be far better equipped than they are today to meet 21st century information needs. The answers to some of these questions undoubtedly require a crystal ball. For this paper the overarching questions concern how much we know and how smart we can be about using new technologies, predicting the directions they might go, and mustering our resources in the best possible way to keep information available to all.

The Anthropology of Fear: Learning About Japan Through Horror Games

Chris Pruett

Abstract

Japan is the source of almost every major horror game franchise in existence. Whether they are attempting to mimic Western horror or create experiences rooted in the country's long tradition of scary stories, Japanese game developers seem to be uniquely adept at building scary games. It would surely be worthwhile to study the Japanese culture to learn why they happen to be such prolific creators of horror games, but this paper attempts to address the question from the other direction: what can we learn about Japanese culture directly from the games that they produce? Using horror games as a lens, this research finds that many common themes in Japanese horror games can be traced back to non-game cultural origins. In some cases these motifs come from traditional folklore or ideas; in others they are a reflection of anxiety related to recent events. A number of Japanese horror games—including games attempting to mimic a foreign format—draw directly from Japanese culture. By studying these games we can therefore learn about the culture of Japan.

Studying the Japanese Through Their Horror Games

Japan is extremely prolific when it comes to horror games. For more than a decade the country has dominated the horror game market, so much so that every single top-tier horror franchise has its roots in Japan. How did this come about?

When *Resident Evil* (Capcom, 1996) was released for Sony Corporation's PlayStation game console in 1996, it was one of a few key titles that caused a dramatic shift in the video game industry. A generation of children who had grown up playing *Super Mario Bros.* (Nintendo, 1985) and *Sonic the Hedgehog* (Sega, 1991) were quickly reaching adulthood, and the introduction of the PlayStation marked the moment at which the industry began to seriously consider teenage and adult audiences.[1] Suddenly there was a platform for games that were not targeted at children: *Tomb Raider* (Eidos, 1996), *Tenchu: Stealth Assassins* (Acquire, 1998), and *Metal Gear Solid* (Konami, 1998) created entirely new genres that employed mature themes and violent imagery. Only a few years earlier the two-dimensional, low-resolution comic violence in games like *Mortal Kombat* (Midway, 1992) had caused such controversy that the US Congress held hearings to explore the matter (Kent, 2001). But within the first few years of its

---

[1] Though the PlayStation era was the first in which the adult-oriented video game market became viable in the United States, it is not clear if this was due to strategic Sony marketing or simply the result of the Nintendo Entertainment System generation coming of age. Sega marketed its Genesis console to adults years before the PlayStation, but it was much less successful.

release, Sony's console was home to a large library of violent and complicated adult-oriented games that put earlier titles to shame. A shift had occurred, the core audience of video game players had expanded, and, thanks to a small number of ground-breaking games aimed at mature players, the industry had changed. *Resident Evil* was one of those games.

Resident Evil, known as '*Biohazard*' in its native Japan, created the horror game genre as we know it today. The term we now use to describe games that involve horrific themes, complex narratives, and puzzle-laden game play--survival horror--was coined by this seminal title. This is not to say that it was the first horror game; its design draws heavily from an earlier title, *Alone in the Dark* (Interplay, 1992), which predates *Resident Evil* by several years. There are many examples of even earlier games that explore horror themes, such as *The Lurking Horror* (Infocom, 1987), *Sweet Home* (Capcom, 1989), and *Splatterhouse* (Namco, 1988). But it was *Resident Evil* that brought horror video games to the masses, proving that players expecting action-heavy game play common to console games could be lured into more substantive and carefully-paced designs (see Pruett, 2007a, for more information about the history of the genre.

The game was a major success. Capcom, the development firm behind *Resident Evil*, reports that almost three million copies of the game were sold in North America alone. Its successor, *Resident Evil 2* (Capcom, 1998), achieved sales of close to five million. At a time when the metric for financial success was only a few hundred thousand copies, the *Resident Evil* series was a blockbuster. Capcom's hit led others to follow suit, and within a few years the survival horror genre was packed full of titles. While many of these were simply copycat games, a few key franchises emerged. Among them, Konami Corporation's *Silent Hill* (Konami, 1999), a game which eschewed explicit violence in favor of a psychological brand of horror, is now regarded as the most important.

Since the late 1990s the game industry has grown by leaps and bounds. Subsequent game consoles are now home to a great number of horror titles. The juggernauts of the genre remain the *Resident Evil* series and *Silent Hill* series, but more recent games such as *Fatal Frame* (Tecmo, 2001), *Siren* (Sony, 2003), *Condemned* (Monolith Productions, 2005), and *Dead Space* (Electronic Arts, 2008) have helped to diversify the genre. Unlike most other video game genres, horror games are identified by theme, not by style of play. Consequently, the survival horror genre is home to a wide range of styles, including first-person games, third-person games, action-oriented games, puzzle games, and even text-based games. Whatever the style of play, one fact cannot be ignored: the vast majority of horror video games come from Japan.

Resident Evil, *Silent Hill*, *Fatal Frame*, *Siren*, *Echo Night* (From Software, 1998), *Clock Tower* (Human Entertainment, 1995), and *Dino Crisis* (Capcom, 1999) are all horror franchises from Japan that have been successful enough to spawn at least three games apiece. The *Resident Evil* series alone, including various spin-off titles such as *Resident Evil: Survivor* (Capcom, 2000) and *Resident Evil Outbreak* (Capcom, 2003), accounts for twenty separate games. By comparison, the only horror franchises from the West to account for three or more games are the *Alone in the Dark* series (four games) and the *Evil Dead* (THQ, 2000) series (three games). In fact, Japan has released more horror games than the West almost every single year since 1995 (see Figure 1). Clearly, the Japanese have a keen interest in horror games.

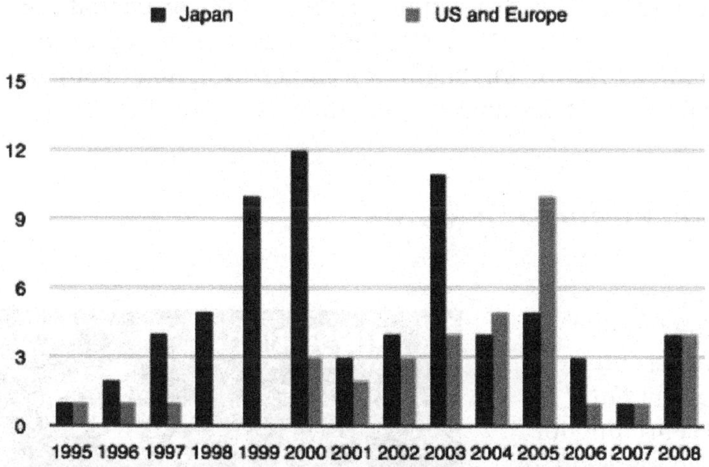

Figure 1. Japanese and Western horror game releases per year. Source: http://www.dreamdawn.com/sh

It might be interesting to perform a study of the Japanese culture to determine why it is home to such a high concentration of horror games. Instead, I would like to turn the question around and study the Japanese through the horror games that they have produced. What is it that we can learn about Japanese culture by examining the large number of horror games that country is responsible for? It is through the lens of horror games that I wish to study the Japanese.

The Importance of Intent

Though some Japanese horror games are designed to reflect themes in traditional Japanese horror, others are constructed to appear as if they originated in the US or Europe. This is an important distinction; while the former style is relatively easy to dissect for interesting cultural clues, cultural signals in the latter style are often purposefully obfuscated by the developers of the game. This presents a challenge for the horror game anthropologist: in order to draw meaningful conclusions about Japanese culture from games designed to look Western, we must look past the content of the game and identify uniquely Japanese motifs that the developers themselves may not have been entirely cognizant of.

The *Resident Evil* and *Silent Hill* series are prime examples of Japanese content authored to appear Western. *Resident Evil*'s introductory sequence (which features live action scenes starring white, American actors) and the series' penchant for Victorian buildings, underground laboratories, and other decidedly non-Japanese locales are clear evidence that the series is designed to appeal to the West. *Resident Evil Outbreak* even lifted the likenesses of famous Western actors for its protagonists, presumably in an attempt to design characters that are attractive to Westerners. Akira Yamaoka, the creative force behind the *Silent Hill* series, described in a lecture at the Game Developers Conference in 2005 his team's desire to create a Western-style horror game "through Japanese eyes." His intent was to create a game in the mold of Stephen King and H.P. Lovecraft, but

Yamaoka admitted that since he and his team are Japanese, their cultural heritage probably influenced their work (Pruett, 2005).

At the same time, games like *Fatal Frame* and *Siren* are steeped in traditional Japanese horror ideas and motifs. They draw upon imagery and stories that are common throughout Japan, and are therefore excellent candidates for cultural analysis. It is with these games that we will begin; the games designed to appear Western will be much easier to analyze once some of the basic concepts of Japanese horror have.

Powerful Emotion and Pitiful Antagonists

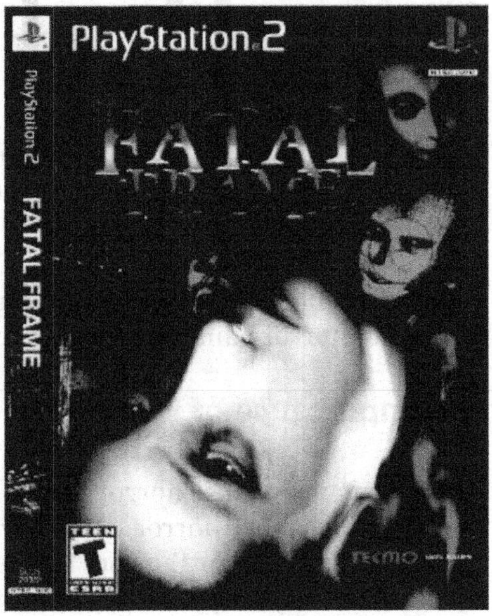

Figure 2. American box art for *Fatal Frame.*

The *Fatal Frame* (Figure 2) series is fundamentally about young women venturing into old, scary, decrepit Japanese buildings. In the first *Fatal Frame*, the protagonist is searching for her brother in a dilapidated mansion. In *Fatal Frame 2* (Tecmo, 2003), a young girl searches for her twin sister in an apparently haunted remote village. In *Fatal Frame 3* (Tecmo, 2005), a woman visits a sinister mansion in her dreams, where she searches for her late fiancée. The Fatal Frame series is one of the very few games that employ ghosts as antagonists. In each of these games, the decrepit buildings the main characters must delve into are infested with the ghosts of people who died long ago, often in the process of performing or suffering from some hideous ancient ritual. These ghosts are subordinate to a main antagonist, a ghost of particular power, whose grip on the human world persists as the result of some tragedy that she experienced in life. In all three games[2] the antagonist, like the protagonist, is female.

The *Fatal Frame* series' story pattern is not simply the result of franchise iteration. The themes and motifs are typical of traditional Japanese ghost stories. Japan has a long tradition of scary stories stemming from the two major religions of the region: Buddhism and the indigenous Shinto. Shintoism in particular is home to a wealth of ghost stories because one of its core tenets is that everything in the world has a soul, called a reikon (霊魂), which can be prayed to and which can, under certain conditions, persist in the human world after death. Many of the most famous stories (see Hearn, 2005) revolve around ghosts who linger in the physical realm because they died while in the throes of intense emotion. This

[2] In fact, a fourth *Fatal Frame* was in 2008, but as of this writing it has only been released in Japan.

idea, called onnen (怨念), is that some emotions are so strong that they can reach from beyond the grave and manipulate the human world. Onnen is a central concept in Japanese horror literature.

The onnen concept allows ordinary people to become menacing after their death. Many stories are based on the idea that a dying person can only remember his final thought, and if that thought is one of intense sadness, pain, or rage, its strength may cause an apparition to remain in the human world that knows only that emotion. For example, in Hearn's "Diplomacy," a samurai is able to avoid the angry post-mortem wrath of a man that he must execute by tricking him into thinking about something else just before he is killed. The man's emotion, though still strong enough to affect reality after his death, is thus redirected away from the samurai and becomes impotent (Hearn, 2005: 50).

Figure 3. ***"Sarayashiki Okiku no Rei"*** **An Ukiyo-e print depicting Okiku from the** ***Story of Okiku. Yoshitoshi, 1890.***

In another story, Banchou Sarayashiki (番町皿屋敷, known in the West as The Story of Okiku), a maid named Okiku (see Figure 3) is falsely accused by her samurai master of breaking a precious plate. As punishment she is drowned in a well. The plate is part of a set of ten dishes, and so every night thereafter she appears outside of the well, counts to nine, and sobs. Her presence is so maddening that eventually the samurai goes insane.

An interesting related trait of Japanese horror is that of the pitiful antagonist. Though the ghosts in Fatal Frame are scary and dangerous, they are also portrayed in a sympathetic light at points in the narrative. Japanese horror stories, especially ghost stories, are very often sad tales about victims of atrocity, innocent people whose powerful emotions transform them into angry spirits. Fatal Frame's antagonist, Kirie, is referred to as the "Rope Shrine Maiden" because she was violently sacrificed as part of some terrible, ancient ritual. In Fatal Frame 2, the final antagonist is Sae, another woman who was killed by others as part of an ancient ritual. This game in particular shows the separation between the "good" parts of the ritual's victims (they appear as butterflies after death) and the "bad" parts, or onnen, of the dead, which return as vengeful spirits.[3] In each case, innocent women who are violently murdered return to kill those around them indiscriminately. As the narrative comes to a close and the true nature of these characters' deaths are

---

[3] *Fatal Frame 2* actually has several of these characters, including another set of twins (Akane and Azami Kiryu; Azami's *onnen* possesses a doll after her death) and the "rope man" ("*kusabi*"), who is sadistically sacrificed in lieu of twins to appease the "hellish abyss" upon which the town central to the game's plot rests. This character returns as the final boss in the "normal" ending of the game.

revealed, we are compelled to feel sorry for them; it is clear that they have only become evil after being victimized by others.

This model of innocence lost, involving a traumatic death which produces a sad or vengeful spirit, is pervasive in traditional and contemporary Japanese horror literature. It is the mechanic that drives Sadako to kill her victims in the 1998 hit horror film Ring, it is the reason that Okiku returns from the grave to count plates, and it is the implicit force behind the antagonists in *Fatal Frame*.[4] The pattern manifests itself almost exclusively with female characters; perhaps this is because women, especially young women, were traditionally viewed both as a model of innocence and as capable of forming stronger grudges than men.

There are many other aspects of the Fatal Frame series that fit the traditional Japanese horror mold. The ghosts themselves appear to be floating above the floor, their feet entirely translucent, which is the way ghosts have been depicted in Japanese art since the 18th century. A more vague characteristic of the series is the way that characters so easily step into a world filled with ghosts, spirits, and other strange occurrences. According to Koji Suzuki, author of *Ring* and many other modern works of horror, this is because the Japanese believe that the spirit world is intertwined with the mortal plane. He writes,

> In America and Europe most horror movies tell the story of the extermination of evil spirits. Japanese horror movies end with a suggestion that the spirit still remains at large. That's because the Japanese don't regard spirits only as enemies, but as beings that co-exist with this world of ours. (Suzuki, 2005 [interview])

Just as Urashima Taro[5] finds that the underwater Palace of the Dragon is separated from the world by much more than just a few waves, the characters in Fatal Frame all pass easily out of reality and into some place more sinister.[6] Miku Hinasaki steps through a door and into the terrible world of Himuro Mansion, sisters Mio and Mayu stumble upon the lost All Gods Village almost by accident, and Rei Kurosawa's dreams seem to directly correlate with events that occur after she wakes. Each of these characters pass into an alternate reality in which ghosts maintain control, and yet in every case it is not so much an alternative dimension as the opposite side of a coin, or the nighttime to the regular world's day.

---

[4] It is also important to note that the mechanism for returning from the grave due to excess emotion is in no way limited to violent ghosts. In stories like *A Dead Secret* and *Of a Mirror and a Bell* (see Hearn, pp. 101 and 51, respectively), ghosts return from the grave not to exact revenge but to make sure that work left undone in their lifetimes is completed. The entire *Echo Night* series of games is based on this version of the *onnen* concept.

[5] Urashima Taro is a character from a Japanese folk tale of the same name. Urashima Taro saves a struggling turtle who turns out to be a princess in a secret underwater palace. He is invited to the palace and stays there for three days, but when he returns to land he finds that 300 years have passed.

[6] Another interesting correlation between the "Urashima Taro" story and the first *Fatal Frame* is the variability of time within these adjacent realms.

Haunted Schools, The Leech Child, and Terrorist Cults

It is worth noting that *Fatal Frame* is not the only game from Japan to so clearly exhibit these traditional traits. It is one of the most lucid examples and is well known in the West, but many other games that never make it across the ocean also contain these themes. In his work on Japanese horror film, Kalat identifies several major movements within the world of contemporary Japanese horror, including what he calls "Dead Wet Girls" and "The Haunted School."

The Dead Wet Girls genre (so named because water and dampness are often common motifs; horror is a summertime genre in Japan, and for several months of the year the country is extremely humid) describes works like *Ring* and *Fatal Frame*; these are contemporary tales about women exercising their onnen to wreak vengeance on the world.

The Haunted School genre, as Kalat defines it, describes a group of stories that all take place at night in a public school. Until recently, public schools were left unlocked after hours, and it was common for children to dare each other to enter a school alone at night. A great many stories stem from this premise; the most well-known is probably "Toire No Hanakosan" (トイレの花子さん, "Hanako-in-the-Toilet"), a story about a ghost who lives in the school restroom and will appear if called upon in a certain way. There are also a large number of games that fall into this genre, including Twilight Syndrome: Saikai (Spike, 2000; "*Twilight Syndrome Reunion*"), THE Tairyou Jigoku (Tamsoft, 2007; "*The Overwhelming Hell*"), and Kyoufu Shimbun Heiseiban Kaiki! Shinrei File (Konami, 2003; "*Fear Newspaper (Heisei Edition) Mystery! Ghost Files*").

The Haunted School is a sub-genre of horror games that rarely makes its way outside of Japan. However, aspects of the genre are often present in mainstream games, and the category deserves special mention.

One example is *Siren*, a game that, despite its realistic presentation, betrays its Japanese roots with cultural themes like The Haunted School. Several stages in Siren (Figure 4) take place in an elementary school at nighttime that is infested with people who have become zombie-like creatures called shibito. These levels require the characters to hide under desks, cower in bathrooms, and combat former school employees in the gymnasium. Though the use of the monstrous shibito instead of ghosts changes Siren's tone and presentation, these stages clearly draw from The Haunted School's regular themes and motifs.

Figure 4. American Box Art for *Siren*.

In fact, *Siren*'s cultural roots go much deeper than The Haunted School--it is firmly entrenched in traditional Japanese folklore. Siren takes place in the fictional village of Hanyuda, a remote locale that is home to a small group of farmers. Hanyuda is a strange place; it has its own religion, it was the site of a number of murders some thirty years ago, and a single family seems to have maintained control of the town for many generations. At the beginning of the game an earthquake and a strange sound (the siren for which the game is named) signal a change of state in the area: it becomes separated from the rest of the world and the lake that surrounds the village turns crimson. The residents of the town become murderous shibito, and the plot centers around a handful of survivors who attempt to escape.

It is eventually revealed that Mana, the town's strange religion, is the creation of a character named Hisako Yao, who, some fourteen hundred years prior, ate the flesh of a dying creature from space and became immortal. She appears as a nun of the Mana religion, and guides other followers of the religion to "become closer to God" by drinking the crimson water and becoming shibito. This character is directly based on a character from Japanese folklore called Yaobikuni (八百比丘尼), and at points she is referred to by this name in the game. The story of Yaobikuni involves a woman who eats the flesh of a mermaid and becomes immortal only to find that everlasting life is full of pain. She eventually becomes a nun and, with the help of another mermaid, is finally able to die. Indeed, the *Siren* version of Yaobikuni is an ageless nun and the alien that she has eaten is referred to as "skyfish."

The narrative in *Siren* also reveals that the people of Hanyuda practiced Shinto alongside Mana at some point in the past. The town is home to a Shinto shrine that is dedicated to Hiruko, which is a character from the Shinto creation myth. The myth involves a sort of Japanese Adam and Eve, named Izanagi and Izanami, who copulate improperly and cause their first children to be born with deformities (Izanami, the woman, taints the mating ritual by speaking before Izanagi). Their first child is Hiruko, "the leech child," who is born without bones. His parents cast the baby away by putting it in a reed boat and sending it down the stream. However, Hiruko survives and eventually becomes the fisherman god Ebisu (see Figure 5), the only member of a group of seven important gods to actually originate in Japan. Ebisu (sometimes rendered as "yebisu") is an extremely common icon in contemporary Japan; as the god of fishermen and a symbol of good luck, his image can be found in restaurants, train stations, and on the labels of all sorts of products. However, his earlier form of Hiruko is much more uncommon; indeed, many Japanese are not aware that Ebisu and Hiruko are one and the same.

Figure 5. A typical statue of Ebisu from Ebisu Station in Tokyo, Japan.

Siren's narrative also mixes folklore with contemporary superstition and beliefs. One example of this is the appearance of the tsuchinoko, a mythical creature that, like Bigfoot, some believe to be a real animal that has eluded capture. Tsuchinoko are short snakes that have a wide girth, and various legends describe them jumping, speaking Japanese (but being untrustworthy), and biting their own tail to form a loop. Several Japanese prefectures have offered rewards to anybody who is able to catch a tsuchinoko and prove its existence, and this behavior makes its way into *Siren*'s large collection of items and clues. More interesting is the physical appearance of a tsuchinoko in the game; it looks more like a large leech than a snake, and it is visible only briefly before escaping down a drain. The suggestion is that the tsuchinoko is related to Hiruko, and is thus another example of Siren's fish-oriented motif.

Analysis of *Siren* can teach us much about Japanese folklore, but the game also bears other hallmarks of traditional Japanese horror. In addition to the water themes and the appearance of The Haunted School, *Siren*'s world, like those found in the *Fatal Frame* series, is one that is separated from reality and home to otherworldly things. The game also reflects cultural unease about an aspect of modern Japanese society: cults and splinter religions.

Japan is home to a large number of young religions. Many are based on either Shinto or Buddhism, though some incorporate teachings from other religions that are foreign to Japan. Since the end of World War II when state-sponsored Shintoism was abolished, a variety of new religions, called shinsyuukyou (新宗教), have appeared. Some of these religions are large and influential (e.g. Sokka Gakai, a branch of Buddhism which has a large following and a related political party), while others are esoteric and nonsensical (such as Pana-Wave Laboratory, a group that covers their homes, cars, and bodies with white tarps to protect themselves from electromagnetic radiation). In 1995 a religious group named Aum Shinrikyo released sarin gas on several Tokyo subway lines, killing twelve people and injuring many others. Investigation of the group revealed chemical weapons, bombs, drugs, and other evidence of planned terrorism. Since that event new religions have come under increased scrutiny, and many Japanese consider them cults.

So it is not hard to believe that a remote region like Hanyuda might have its own unique religion. Siren depicts this religion controlling the town and eventually driving its residents to their deaths, and within the context of post-Aum Shinrikyo Japan, it is clearly representative of an underlying cultural distrust of cults. Kalat makes the point that just as the atomic bomb had a major influence on Japanese horror media in the second half of the twentieth century (e.g. Godzilla), contemporary Japanese horror is related to recent national tragedies. Specifically, Kalat names the devastating Kobe earthquake and the sarin gas attacks, both of which occurred in 1995, as the progenitors of modern films like *Ring* and *Ju-on* (titled *The Grudge* in the West). In this context, *Siren*'s references to these events seem obvious; in addition to the untrustworthy cult, the story begins with a major earthquake that separates Hanyuda from the mainland. Even the siren, for which the game provides a supernatural explanation, sounds like a World War II-era air raid siren. Though *Siren*'s narrative is steeped in traditional folklore, it is also very much the product of modern Japanese ideas about horror.

The Attempt to Appear Western

So far this paper has touched only on games that were explicitly developed to mirror aspects of modern Japanese culture. But as previously mentioned, there exists a second class of games that attempt to obscure their heritage. These games, such as *Silent Hill*, *Resident Evil*, and *Clock Tower* (among numerous others), attempt to appear Western by eschewing symbols and themes that are obviously Japanese. *Silent Hill* is an excellent example: it takes place in a fictional American resort town, stars an entirely white, American cast, and draws upon American horror films like *Jacob's Ladder* and *The Shining* for its visual and narrative themes. Yamaoka, the project's development director, has described *Silent Hill* as an attempt to make "Hollywood horror," specifically in regards to shocking visuals (Pruett, 2005).

But closer inspection reveals several traditional Japanese horror motifs lurking beneath *Silent Hill*'s Westernized exterior. Yamaoka himself has noted that no amount of effort on his part can possibly remove all cultural references from his games because he and his team are Japanese and that heritage is bound to affect their work. In the context of modern Japanese horror, Silent Hill contains several classic motifs.

As with the locales employed by *Fatal Frame* and *Siren*, the town for which the *Silent Hill* series is named has been separated from reality. In the original *Silent Hill*, this separation is explicit: all roads eventually terminate in a gaping abyss, as if the entire town has been violently lifted from the surface of the world. In later games in the series, the separation is more subtle; the apartment in *Silent Hill 4: The Room* appears normal but is isolated from the rest of the building; no amount of pounding on the door can be heard by people on the other side, and notes slipped under the door come through dramatically changed. In addition to an obvious physical separation from the real world, the *Silent Hill* series further isolates its characters by forcing them to delve into progressively tenuous derivations of reality. The "fog world," which appears most similar to reality, gives way to the "dark world" (a nighttime version of the fog world found only in the first *Silent Hill*) and then the "otherworld," a hellish version of the town (Pruett, 2007b). In *Silent Hill* 3 the otherworld itself degrades until it finally appears to be decomposing in front of the characters' eyes. *Silent Hill* takes the idea of an otherworldly copy of reality in which malicious, supernatural creatures roam, and stacks it in layers, each more isolated and distant from the real world than the last.

The *Silent Hill* series is also home to a few references to common Japanese themes. As in *Siren*, the elementary school area can easily be considered a derivation of *The Haunted School* motif; in keeping with the genre's requirements that the school be visited only at night, it is accessible only through the dark world. The elementary school is also the point at which the most fundamental *Silent Hill* game mechanics are revealed, including the protagonists' first real descent into the otherworld. The elementary school is an important locale in *Silent Hill*, and in the context of Japanese horror we can consider it an extension of the large body of work that revolves around deserted schools at nighttime. A couple of other miscellaneous references to common horror themes are hidden away here and there (such as a Hanako-in-the-Toilet reference in both *Silent Hill 2* and *Silent Hill 3*). *Silent Hill 4* dwells extensively on a religious cult that, as in Siren, is unique to Silent Hill and is involved in both black magic and organized crime, providing another reference to modern sensitivity about young religions. But the most interesting reference is the series' antagonist herself.

Figure 6. American box art for *Silent Hill 2.*

Though it stars white, American characters, the plot leading up to the events in the original *Silent Hill* is typical Japanese horror. A young girl is tortured and eventually killed by a religious group hoping to use her suffering as a beacon that will summon a powerful demon to Earth. However, in death the girl is able to take vengeance on those who wronged her in life, and she does so by separating them, along with the rest of *Silent Hill*, from reality. Though the series goes on to show that the fog world, dark world, and otherworld are manifestations of the girl's pain and suffering, the story follows the same basic tenets as *Fatal Frame*, *Ring*, and other traditional onnen legends. In *Silent Hill 2* (see Figure 6), the protagonist himself is responsible for the purgatory that he finds himself in, and this too is an application of onnen.[7] Though the format has been tweaked and presented with a Western sheen, the bedrock concepts of *Silent Hill* fit very comfortably within the Japanese horror genre.

Many of the *Silent Hill* games also portray non-standard family structures. The family of Harry and Cheryl is that of a single father and an adopted child, while the antagonist in the series' fourth iteration is an orphan. Kalat singles out the "broken home" motif as a particularly prevalent pattern in modern Japanese horror narratives. The works of Koji Suzuki, including *Ring* and *Honogurai Mizu no Sokokara* ("*Dark Water*"), focus on single mothers, single fathers, and other deviations from the traditional nuclear family. Kalat suggests that this reflects anxiety about dramatic changes in Japanese society over the last fifty years, especially in regard to the rights of women. He contends that while women's rights have come a long way in the last half-decade, the resulting culture is necessarily much more complex. This is perhaps why the antagonists of modern Japanese horror are so often female: in death they wield power that they were denied in life.

---

7 See Hearn's *Of a Mirror and a Bell* for a similar legend in which a living woman's desire for a bronze mirror that she was forced to give up is so strong that the mirror cannot be melted.

Cultural Mirrors

Horror games give us a window through which we can study the Japanese. But such studies can also teach us about our own culture. In attempting to define what "Japanese horror" is, we must also define "Western horror" in order to draw distinctions between the two. It is these distinctions rather than the details of the culture itself that make these works so fascinating (not to mention frightening) to us. We find ourselves strangers in a strange land, unable to guess at where the narrative might be heading, unfamiliar with the conventions that the author is employing. Without the comfort of our usual cultural signals we feel out of control, and in that state the narrative can wield much power over us. The most effective Western horror films achieve the same sense of unease with innovative cinematography and surprising stories, but foreign horror films benefit from it almost automatically.

Though this paper has dwelt exclusively on details of Japanese culture that are evidenced by their horror games, it is perhaps the foreignness of these games that makes such details relevant. This is also a clue as to why so many horror games attempt to appear Western; if the cultural divide makes Japanese horror more effective to us, it stands to reason that it also makes Western horror more effective to them.

The Japanese have a rich history of scary stories, and themes common in historical works are evident in their contemporary horror media. Games are naturally affected by this heritage, even when they are designed to appear to be of non-Japanese origin. By tracing these patterns and motifs through the games that they occupy we not only learn about the Japanese psyche, but about our own culture as well.

References

Capcom, Inc. (2009, June 30). Platinum Titles. Retrieved September 15, 2009, from http://ir.capcom.co.jp/english/business/million.html

Hearn, L. (2005). *Kwaidan: Stories and Studies Of Strange Things*. Tokyo: Tuttle Publishing.

Kalat, D. (2007). *J-Horror: The Definitive Guide to The Ring, The Grudge and Beyond*. New York: Vertical.

Kent, S. L. (2001). *The Ultimate History of Video Games: From Pong to Pokemon--The Story Behind the Craze That Touched Our Lives and Changed the World*. Three Rivers Press.

Pruett, C. (2003, August 30). Chris' Survival Horror Quest. Retrieved September 15, 2009, from http://www.dreamdawn.com/sh

Pruett, C. (2005, March 13). GDC: Akira Yamaoka and the Atmosphere of Silent Hill. Retrieved September 15, 2009, from http://www.dreamdawn.com/sh/post_view.php?index=1715

Pruett, C. (2007, April 2). The Prehistory of Survival Horror. Retrieved September 15, 2009 from http://www.dreamdawn.com/sh/features/prehistoryofhorror.php

Pruett, C. (2007, December 2). The Changing Utility of the Otherworld in the Silent Hill Series. Retrieved September 15, 2009, from http://www.dreamdawn.com/sh/features/otherworld.php

Suzuki, K. (2005, December 1). Interview with Koji Suzuki, novelist of the dank and dread. Retrieved September 15, 2009, from http://int.kateigaho.com/win05/horror-suzuki.html

Text Appeal: The Internet, Dating, and Jane Austen, Part 1

Ruth Happ '10

This piece, in its original form is recent Pacific University graduate, Ruth Happ's, thesis. It has been edited and broken into two parts, specifically for publication in Interface, in order to build upon references to the Internet and communications which were already present in Happ's original thesis.

Original thesis edited by Pauline Beard
Interface version edited by Jenn Hernandez

"[Jane] Austen isn't alluring us with scantily-clad photos on her Facebook profile, but with her timeless wit and well-crafted text." –Jenn Hernandez

The Internet is the "go-to person" for any and all of the literate (and not-so-literate) members of U.S. society today. "Just Google it," is a common answer for questions related to any subject or concern. Once known more for its character as the "information superhighway," the World Wide Web has expanded to incorporate e-mail, social networking, and online dating. Laptops, cell phones, iPads, and other handheld devices now allow unlimited, portable access anywhere Wifi is available. Where users once could do the laundry while waiting for dial-up to load the home page, users now expect immediate upload with fiber optic and broadband speeds. Conversations may be held via text messaging, which has developed into a dialect of its own using abbreviations, acronyms, and replacing words like "you," "are," and "four," with the quicker "u," "r," and "4." With the increase of and advancement in communication technologies, many feel that the Internet is doing all it can to bring about the death of fine literature and genuine conversations.

In this Internet/technology-saturated culture of speed and immediacy over accuracy and completeness, where do fans of Jane Austen and her much slower and smaller literary world fit in? Perhaps, fans of Austen create a culture of their own, anodyne to that of the Internet and society-at-large, wherein communication is more personal, humor is cultivated, and relationships are more committed. This does not mean, however, that the Internet is rejected. Rather, it is a tool for Janeites' communication, wit, and virtual, communal gathering, via websites like The Republic of Pemberly (pemberly.com) and JaneAusten.org. Therein, lay-commentators and scholars alike discuss the novels and adaptations, appraise them and relate them to their own lives, and offer up their own ideals, contrasts, and critiques of modern-day culture.

Indeed, Jane Austen, single woman of the turn of the eighteenth-into-the-nineteenth century, has a fan club like no other author. She is famous, not because of her ever-changing relationships, new extravagant home, or latest stint in rehab, but because her six principal novels have not only withstood the test of time and generational change, but have only become more popular, birthing an

Austenian subculture where Janeites take comfort and wisdom in the wit, satire, and romance of the stories. Carol Memmott and Claudia Puig, in their USA Today article, raise the question, "Why, in a Britney/Lindsay/Paris-saturated culture, does a lady novelist born in 18th-century England resonate so much with us today?" (1). Why all the film/television adaptations, spinoff and sequel books, souvenir products, websites, and associations and fan clubs? Austen's novels stand as some of the most excellent writing in English history; beyond the literary skill she manifested, however, readers have always enjoyed Austen's humor, satire, characterizations, and dynamic marriage plots. For the modern-day reader, Austen's magnetism may, as reflected in scholarly and "lay" Janeite opinions (in blogs and online comments), also arise from the readers' nostalgic urge for a simpler time and place, an appreciation of subtle romance and strong commitment without graphic and meaningless sex, as well as an affinity for her presentation of men and women as progressive within their repressive society. The popularity of her works and their offshoots may also reflect, beyond nostalgia for a past era, a commonly-shared hope for love, commitment, equality, and personal growth in relationships, rather than the sex-laden, loveless "hook-up system" common to college students and supported by the media and society at-large.

Jane Austen has received the rare honor of being both a canonical author (as a female nonetheless) and a popular author. As of 2007, her novels had been adapted for film or television thirty-three times, according to Sue Parrill, author of *Jane Austen on Film and Television: A Critical Study of the Adaptations (The Republic of Pemberley)*. Since then, at least four new Austen-related films have been produced, along with PBS' Masterpiece Theatre's series, The Complete Jane Austen, including new adaptations of five of her novels as well as Jane Austen Regrets, a dramatic presentation of Austen's life and relationships (Memmott and Puig 1). The new and popular novels, along with the potential for similarly-themed movies (like the proposed film *Pride and Predator*), *Sense and Sensibility* and *Sea Monsters* and Pride and Prejudice and Zombies, along with the time-traveling film, *Lost in Austen*, integrate Austen's own text and transport it into new genre frontiers of horror and science fiction (Itzkoff 1). Sequels and spin-offs of her works, beginning in 1914, have continued being written to this day, especially novels related to Mr. Darcy, the famous leading-man of Austen's best-loved novel and continuing best-seller, *Pride and Prejudice* (Memmott and Puig 1). The Internet is heavy-laden with fan web-sites, blogs, and YouTube videos (James). Janeites, as they have been known since the 1890's (Sutherland 9), read and re-read Austen's novels and find themselves essentially part of "a cult as ardent as a religion." Feeling "extraordinary familiarity and affection" for her characters and stories, some call them "better than Prozac" (Thompson 20).

Without performing a comprehensive sociological study, it is impossible to state whether fans of Austen participate in unfulfilling, sexually-based relationships, and are therefore seeking satisfaction for their romantic desires through Austen; or if they are in committed, love-based relationships appreciating her affirmation of their choice; or if they are in no relationship at all, living out their fantasies through her stories. Examining the contemporary culture of both young people and society at large may help, however, to understand the surrounding cultural conditions that help shape their interests and attitudes, either by forming them or provoking an opposite reaction. Kathleen A. Bogle, an Assistant Professor of Sociology and Criminal Justice, executed a sociological study involving interviews of college students and, in 2008, published *Hooking Up: Sex, Dating, and Relationships on Campus.* Her study, as well as the research and ideas of Tom Wolfe in *Hooking Up* and Zygmunt Bauman in *Liquid Love*, may assist in understanding not only the shifts in relationships and sexual practices since the sexual revolution of the 1960's and 70's, but also why so many people, especially women, are enchanted by Austen. Seeing the contrast between the cultural obsession with sex, as well as connection via impersonal technology, and Austen's settings, characters, and storylines may help bring a greater awareness of today's practices and the driving forces behind them, as well as motivate a critique of society's lack of personal connection and commitment in relationship.

In Hooking Up, Bogle delineates the changes in attitude and practice from the dating era to the common "hooking up" system, which reveals a stark contrast not only between those two trends, but also between Austenland and today's popular culture. The women's liberation movement of the 1960's worked to free women from the sexual limitations placed on them, which men never had to abide by to protect their reputations and freedom (21). Forty-plus years later, however, one college sophomore states that "It almost seems like [the hookup scene] is a guy's paradise. No real commitment, no real feelings involved, this is like a guy's paradise. This age [era] that we are in I guess...And women have always resisted, but now they are going along with it" (183).

What women may be "going along with" is a system of "hook ups," terminology including interactions ranging from "just kissing" to "going all the way," and everything in between, but without dating or any requirement of relationship (Bogle 24-29). Unlike the dating era, neither party needs to get to know the other before getting physical (163-64). Sex is viewed as simply a personal choice, unrestricted by social norms or religious regulations (93-95, 159-61). Not only are young men and women often getting sexually involved before any form of relationship has a chance to form, but they are also going further physically. In his book *Hooking Up*, Tom Wolfe describes the change in definition of yesterday's first base of "embracing and kissing," second base of "'French' kissing" and "heavy petting," third base of "oral sex," and home plate of "conception-mode intercourse" to the current trends: "In the year 2000, in the era of hooking up, "first base" meant deep kissing ("tonsil hockey"), groping, and fondling; "second base meant oral sex; "third base" meant going all the way; and "home plate" meant learning each other's names" (7).

Changes in today's social, sexual situation transcend the mere confines of college campuses. Zygmunt Bauman describes the situation as part of the consumer culture Americans have embraced in this free market society. People are often valued as "objects of consumption" to be exchanged within the free market (75). They are judged by the "volume of pleasure they are likely to offer" and/or by their substance as determined by monetary value (75). Members of this consumer culture are accustomed to "products ready for instant use, quick fixes...all-risk insurance and money-back guarantees" (7). Love and relationships are a risky business with no guarantees of success; therefore, rather than believing love in a marriage-relationship-to-last-a-lifetime worth the effort and risk, consumers reduce "love" to "making love" (5). As "till death do us part" no longer means what it once did, Bauman claims that "the standards have been lowered," and love is now like a "skill to be learned" and improved "with the number of experiments and assiduity of exercise" (5). Each subsequent "love" experience may be "an experience yet more exhilarating," so, the more the better (5). Thus, in today's society, participants pursue happiness and grasp for love...in a drive-thru.

The result of this trend in society is the prevalent lack of lasting and fulfilling relationships. Bauman explains that "the temptation to fall in love is great and overwhelming, but so also is the attraction of escape. And the enticement to seek a rose without thorns is never far away and always difficult to resist" (8-9). Often seeking union with each other to escape loneliness, by moving from one encounter to the next, men and women end up just as lonely as before, or worse. Bauman quotes Erich Fromm who describes the "Illusion of Union" in purely sexual encounters, claiming that the "brief moment of orgasmic climax leaves strangers as far apart as they were before" (quoted in Bauman 45). Sex is touted as a "wonder drug," becoming like alcoholism and drug addiction, "judged solely by...the satisfaction it may bring on its own" (45). The drug does not fulfill one's expectations, however, and AIDS and STD's are not, according to Bauman, "the most fearsome of fears" related to sex. Rather, the fear deserving of this title "stem[s] from the ambiguity of the sexual encounter," raising the questions of whether it was "an initial step towards a relationship, or its crowning and its terminus?" (51) Confusion and loneliness thus serve as consequences for this liberality of sexuality without marital commitment.

In contrast to this world of confusion and solitary confinement within society, Jane Austen presents a world in which sex is endorsed only within the bounds of marriage, and commitment to one's spouse and even fiancé is maintained without question by those considered honorable. Those who rebel against this moral guideline and/or disregard their engagements or marital vows are declaimed as immoral and disgraceful. In Northanger Abbey, the naïve heroine Catherine declares, "A woman in love with one man cannot flirt with another" (143), in regard to her friend Isabella, who, while engaged to Catherine's brother, lets her eyes wander to Captain Tilney. Upon receiving a letter from her brother, Catherine is undeceived and declares to her friends, Captain Tilney's siblings, "Isabella has deserted my brother, and is to marry your's! Could you have believed there had been such inconstancy and fickleness, and every thing that is bad in the world?" (192) Eleanor Tilney concurs with Catherine's opinion of Isabella declaring "She must be an unprincipled [girl], or she could not have used your brother so.—And how strange an infatuation on Frederick's side! A girl who, before his eyes, is violating an engagement voluntarily entered into with another man!" (193) Her brother Henry also critiques Frederick's (Captain Tilney) choice: "It is all over with Frederick indeed! He is a deceased man—defunct in understanding" (193). Frederick and Isabella do not marry, however, and Isabella is left alone. Her grasping after a "better," at least richer, man than the last ends with obtaining neither.

Maria Rushworth similarly finds herself left alone after betraying her commitment to her husband in Mansfield Park. The protagonist Fanny discovers that her cousin Maria has left n her husband for Henry Crawford, a man with whom Fanny was nearly engaged. The news brings a shock to Fanny who strongly criticizes such unfaithful actions. Austen writes:

> The horror of a mind like Fanny's, as it received the conviction of such guilt, and began to take in some part of the misery that must ensue, can hardly be described. At first, it was a sort of stupefaction; but every moment was quickening her perception of the horrible evil...A woman married only six months ago; a man professing himself devoted, even engaged to another; that other her near relation; the whole family, both families connected as they were...; all friends, all intimate together! It was too horrible a confusion of guilt, too gross a complication of evil, for human nature, not in a state of utter barbarism to be capable of! (625)

"Horror," "evil," and "barbarism" express the outrage Fanny feels, not only in regard to the immorality demonstrated by Henry and Maria, but also to the "misery that must ensue" to the detriment of each family in connection with them. Ultimately the guilty parties of Henry and Maria, and subsequently Mary, Henry's sister, who defends his actions, are cast out of the family relations. Even Mr. Rushworth is denounced as he knew that Maria never loved him, even "despised him" (643). The consequences to him, as "his punishment followed his conduct" (643), reflect the unjust treatment of society of women versus men caught in immorality, for he might yet take his chances with another woman. Maria, on the other hand, after she and Henry part ways, "must withdraw with infinitely stronger feelings to a retirement and reproach which could allow no second spring of hope or character" (643), holed up in a "remote and private" country with Mrs. Norris, wherein "their tempers became their mutual punishment" (644). Austen thus recognizes that society did not punish the man as severely as the woman, as is also the case with Henry Crawford. Austen moralizes: "That punishment, the public punishment of disgrace, should in a just measure attend his share of the offence is, we know, not one of the barriers which society gives to virtue. In this world, the penalty is less equal than could be wished" (646). Crawford's punishment lies in his permanent loss of the superior Fanny Price, whom he has perhaps grown to love sincerely; his relationship with the Bertrams; and his presumed "vexation that must rise sometimes to self-reproach, and regret to wretchedness" over these losses (646). A male character taking advantage of young and often foolish females is a common villain of Austen's novels. In Pride and Prejudice, a "wolf in sheep's clothing," by the name of Mr. Wickham, preys on two young women, one with the intention of marriage to gain fortune, and the other with no intent to marry. He first tries his hand with wealthy Mr. Darcy's teenage sister, then later runs off with the youngest Bennet girl, Lydia, who is flirtatious and foolish enough not to grasp the magnitude of her actions and their consequences for not only herself, but also her family. Upon hearing the news, and believing Lydia "lost for ever," Elizabeth Bennet, Lydia's sensible older sister, despairs (217). "Every thing must sink under such a proof of family weakness, such an assurance of the deepest disgrace....the humiliation, the misery, [Lydia] was bringing on them all, soon swallowed up every private care" (217). In a later letter from their aunt, Elizabeth learns that her aunt attempted to bring Lydia to an understanding of her actions, "I talked to her repeatedly in the most serious manner, representing to her all the wickedness of what she had done, and all the unhappiness she had brought on her family. If she heard me, it was by good luck, for I am sure she did not listen" (253). Lydia's disgrace could have prevented her other sisters from finding husbands, which would create a dire situation for them, considering their father could leave them no home and little inheritance per the rules of the day regarding women and property.

Fair Austen does not lump all blame on the female, however, and Lydia's parents receive their due as Elizabeth notes the consequences resulting from "the mischief of neglect and mistaken indulgence toward such a girl" (219). She explains in a later conversation with her father what she feels are the contributors to Lydia's actions:

> She is very young; she has never been taught to think on serious subjects; and for the last... twelvemonth, she has been given up to nothing but amusement and vanity. She has been allowed to dispose of her time in the most idle and frivolous manner, and to adopt any opinions that came in her way....nothing but love, flirtation, and officers, have been in her head....And we all know that Wickham has every charm of person and address that can captivate a woman. (221)

Lydia is the example not to follow. She stands as a grand contrast to Elizabeth, who thinks seriously; is unafraid of speaking her mind and questioning those "above" her (like Mr. Darcy, a man of much greater wealth than her father); occupies her time with reading, sensible conversation, and walking in nature; considers the effect of her actions on herself and her family, and acts with propriety.
Examples of a man's commitment prior to marriage include Edward Ferrar's dedication to his word in being secretly engaged to Lucy Steele for five years, preventing a declaration of love to Elinor Dashwood. Willoughby, in contrast, implies love and an "understanding" between him and Marianne Dashwood, but then leaves her without proper explanation for a wealthy, more "acceptable" woman to protect his inheritance and station in life. Worse than this betrayal is Willoughby's history with young Eliza, the ward of Colonel Brandon, whom he impregnated, then abandoned. Colonel Brandon explains, highlighting the shamefulness of Willoughby's actions, to Elinor, "He had left the girl whose youth and innocence he had seduced, in a situation of the utmost distress, with no creditable home, no help, no friends, ignorant of his address! He had left her promising to return; he neither returned, nor wrote, nor relieved her....His character is now before you; expensive, dissipated, and worse than both" (194). By contrasting society's blame on the female and subsequent ostracizing of her, Austen decries the predatory and negligent actions of men like Willoughby who must take no consequence for them. Austen further emphasizes the importance of integrity and good character while sympathizing with Eliza through Marianne:

> She felt the loss of Willoughby's character yet more heavily than she had felt the loss of his heart; his seduction and desertion of Miss Williams, the misery of that poor girl, and the doubt of what

> his designs might once have been on herself, preyed altogether so much on her spirits, that she could not bring herself to speak of what she felt. (197)

Other examples of commitment versus betrayal, abandonment, and immorality can be found in Austen's works, but the aforementioned speak a sufficient strength to the concepts of integrity, morality, commitment, and consideration of the consequences of one's actions to oneself and others, stretching the literature of Austen beyond simple love stories ending in fairy tale marriage.

This is not to say that Austen's world is completely based around moral poles of black and white with no gray area of compromise. She bends the rules of her society regarding marriage and social class, including the situation of Edward Ferrars's escape from bondage in marriage to Lucy Steele due to her marriage to his brother, freeing him to marry his true love, Elinor (and, in doing so, he loses his right to an inheritance). Additionally, Elizabeth and Darcy cross social class and financial barriers to marry, and Darcy defies his Aunt, Lady Catherine deBourgh, who, with his mother, betrothed him to her daughter from birth, risking his familial connections and status, as well as his own reputation, by uniting himself to one from a family of damaged reputation due to Lydia's folly. Also, in regard to Willoughby, a later chapter of Sense and Sensibility is devoted to his giving his side of the story. Some of his guilt is moderated by his good intentions toward Marianne, and his culpability in the abandonment of Eliza somewhat lessened when he claims, "I did not recollect that I had omitted to give her my direction; and common sense might have told her how to find it out" (301). This does not completely alleviate his responsibility in the matter, but it reveals Austen's purposeful avoidance of fitting her characters into the confines of moral and social stereotypes.

Sense is not to be disregarded, and morality should be upheld, but Austen's heroes and heroines maintain love as an honorable goal and commitment the necessary conduit. Thus, unlike today's common idea that dating represents an agreement to be an expendable sex partner, Austen's heroes and heroines engage in courtships that lead to marriage. Her heroines, especially, do not select marriage partners casually; they marry only for love and profound connection, a kinship of spirit and mind, mutual respect, and manifest honor, but without forgetting the sensibleness of the match and the resulting financial stability.

References

Austen, Jane. *Mansfield Park*. 1814. Ed. Great Britain: Chancellor Press, 1985.

–. *Northanger Abbey*. 1818. Ed. Marilyn Butler. New York: Penguin Books, 2003.

–. *Pride and Prejudice*. 1813. Ed. Great Britain: Chancellor Press, 1985.

–. *Sense and Sensibility*. 1811. Ed. New York: Barnes & Noble, Inc., 1996.

Bauman, Zygmunt. *Liquid Love: On the Frailty of Human Bonds*. Malden, MA: Polity Press, 2010.

Blum, Virginia L. "The Return to Repression: Filming the Nineteenth Century." In Pucci and Thompson. 157-178.

Bogle, Kathleen A. *Hooking Up: Sex, Dating, and Relationships on Campus*. New York: New York University Press, 2008.

Daryl. "Re: Austen's Power: Jane addiction sweeps theaters, bookstores." *USA Today*. 23 August 2007. 7 May 2010. <http://www.usatoday.com/life/books/news/2007-08-01-austen-frenzy_N.htm?loc=interstitialskip>.

Dobie, Madeleine. "Gender and the Heritage Genre: Popular Feminism Turns to History." Pucci and Thompson 247-259.

Ed in NM. "Re: Austen's Power: Jane addiction sweeps theaters, bookstores." *USA Today*. 23 August 2007. 7 May 2010. <http://www.usatoday.com/life/books/news/2007-08-01-austen-frenzy_N.htm?loc=interstitialskip>.

Fitzgerald, Helena. "Intimacy as Text; Twitter as Tongue." *The New Inquiry*. 4 August 2010. 14 October 2010. <http://thenewinquiry.com/post/903929008/intimacy-as-text-twitter-as-tongue>.

"5 Billion Text Messages sent/received each month in the US. Mobile..." *Qwasi News*. 23 March 2010. 7 May 2010. <http://www.qwasi.com/news/tag/text-message-statistics>.

Harman, Claire. *Jane's Fame: How Jane Austen Conquered the World*. New York: Henry Holt and Company, LLC, 2009.

Horwitz, Barbara. "Women's Education During the Regency: Jane Austen's Quiet Rebellion." *Persuasions, No. 16*, Dec. 1994: 135-45.

Itzkoff, Dave. "Austen Meets Alien in 'Pride and Predator.'" *The New York Times*. 17 February 2009. 9 March 2009. <http://www.nytimes.com/2009/02/18/arts/18arts-AUSTENMEETSA_BRF.html?_r=1&ref=arts>.

James, Caryn. "Austen Powers: Making Jane Sexy." *The New York Times*. 29 July 2007. 6 May 2010. <http://www.nytimes.com/2007/07/29/movies/29jame.html?scp=1&sq=Making%20Jane%20Sexy&st=cse>.

Laughlin Adler, Barbara. "A disagreement between us: Gendered Argument in Austen's Novels." Persuasions: The Jane Austen Journal. 24 (2002): 164-76. *Academic One File.* Pacific University Oregon, Lib. 6 May 2010.

MacRoni. "Re: Austen's Power: Jane addiction sweeps theaters, bookstores." *USA Today.* 23 August 2007. 7 May 2010. <http://www.usatoday.com/life/books/news/2007-08-01-austen-frenzy_N.htm?loc=interstitialskip>.

Memmott, Carol and Claudia Puig. "Austen's power: Jane addiction sweeps theaters, bookstores." *USA Today.* 23 August 2007. 7 May 2010. <http://www.usatoday.com/life/books/news/2007-08-01-austen-frenzy_N.htm?loc=interstitialskip>.

Pucci, Suzanne R.. "The Return Home." Pucci and Thompson 133-155.

Pucci, Suzanne R., and James Thompson, eds. *Jane Austen and Co.: Remaking the Past in Contemporary Culture* State University of New York Press, 2003

Republic of Pemberley, The. 2004-2009. 9 March 2009. <http://www.pemberley.com>.

Ross, Josephine. *Jane Austen's Guide to Good Manners: Compliments, Charades & Horrible Blunders.* New York: Bloomsbury USA, 2006.

"SMS Preferred Mode of Communication on Mobile." *Qwasi News.* 12 January 2010. 7 May 2010. <http://www.qwasi.com/news/tag/text-message-statistics>

Sutherland, Kathryn. *Jane Austen's Textual Lives: from Aeschylus to Bollywood.* New York: Oxford University Press, 2005.

Thompson, James. "How to Do Things with Austen." Pucci and Thompson 13-32.

Voiret, Martine. "Books to Movies: Gender and Desire in Jane Austen's Adaptations." Pucci and Thompson 229-245.

Wolfe, Tom. Hooking Up. New York: Farrar, Straus, and Giroux, 2000.

Woolf, Virginia. "Jane Austen." The Common Reader. New York: Harcourt, Brace & World, Inc., 1953.

Payal Arora's *Dot Com Mantra. Social Computing in the Central Himalayas*

Review by Jeffrey Barlow

Dot Com Mantra is an excellent work by Payal Arora, a much-published[1] Indian anthropologist who writes frequently on social computing, that is, the connection between society and the use of computers. This study is an ethnography (a branch of anthropology dealing with the scientific description of individual cultures[2]) done in the town complex of Almora, in a fairly isolated area of Uttrakhand, India, formerly Uttar Pradesh.

Dr. Arora is well qualified to write this particular work. She has studied at Cambridge (Certificate in Teaching ESL), at Harvard (M.A. in International Policy, Education) and at Columbia (Doctorate in Language, Literacy & Technology). This work is derived from her Ph.D. Dissertation, Social Computing in the Central Himalayas.

Dot Com Mantra focuses largely on the social, economic, and political aspect of development considered within a global framework. Dr. Arora speaks the language of the area and fully immersed herself in its day-to-day life, moving among farmers' organization, development groups (non-governmental organizations-NGOs), teachers and students, and even volunteering her time working in an Internet café, from all of which she derived deep understandings.

In many cases, Arora's conclusions are counter-intuitive and the book sparkles with frequent flashes of insight. We learn also that many of the approaches of the non-governmental organizations (NGOs) and of the Government of India are ineffective in the area, because they have ignored the social aspects of technology.

It is not that the area is under-computerized; many groups have distributed machines in a variety of settings, but these attempts fall afoul of existing social conditions. For example, schools are given computers, but one-quarter of the teachers never show up to teach. Of those who do, fully half do not teach even when present[3]. Most of them are held personally responsible for the books and machines sent them and will have to pay if they are damaged, so they lock them safely away.

Aware of these issues, NGOs and the Government of India previously sponsored a variety of access points – via the Hole-in-the-Wall/HiWel program among many

---

[1] For the author's publications and reviews see: http://www.payalarora.com/Publicationspage1.html

[2] http://dictionary.reference.com/browse/ethnography

[3] Arora, 26.

others[4] – to encourage children to teach themselves[5]. These meet with initial success, but in order to be safe from vandalism or theft, the centers have to be placed on school-grounds where the same conditions which vitiate the educational process also impact the use of the "free" computing facilities.

Arora's insights are deeply rooted in a close knowledge of both practical and theoretical pedagogy and anyone interested in education could benefit from understanding this aspect of her research. Part of her progress here might be said to be "unlearning," as she finds that many of her assumptions are simply irrelevant in the social context of village India. For example, after working in the Internet café, she comes to understand the limitations of Western attitudes toward plagiarism.

Arora has focused closely on gender issues in her previous research. In her ethnographic research in Almora, she also derives a new understanding of gender issues. This comes about when she watches female students, usually treated in the critical literature as deliberately marginalized in the world of technology, ably manipulate not the machines so much as those who work in the cafes (including the author), on the model of traditional Indian mistress-servant relationships. She concludes that choosing not to work directly with technology is also a means of using technology, and a valid choice in many situations.

The author also begins to understand the complexity of globalization when she assists two local girls prepare school papers on "Western" art by selecting a variety of graphics, including cowboy-style horse paintings done by a contemporary Chinese artist, side by side with the Mona Lisa and the works of a noted Indian painter[6].

The weakness of NGO and governmental assumptions about the link between development and I.T. development are treated directly in a section on farming. Farmers are given access to computers by the government in the belief that, with better information about markets and prices, they can avoid exploitation by traditional middlemen.

However, the author learns, the middlemen are also a critical element in farming practices, advising farmers of how to develop new crops, for example. And even with perfect knowledge of the market, the farmers are still producing on such a small scale that they cannot take any better advantage of the information.

Dot Com Mantra really comes alive and makes a significant contribution when Arora begins to reconceptualize the Internet cafes and their most frequent use as

---

[4] See their site at: http://www.hole-in-the-wall.com/ See also, however, the many criticisms of the program, beginning at: http://www.thebrokeronline.eu/en/Online-discussions/Blogs/Janelle-Ward/A-critique-of-Hole-in-the-Wall-HiWEL

[5] The One-Laptop-Per-Child program, about which we have been very enthusiastic at the Berglund Center (see a Roundtable presentation at: http://bcis.pacificu.edu/roundtables/Presentations/2008/), does not fare much better in Dr. Arora's brief analysis at p. 17.

[6] See chapters 7-8.

places not of learning so much as of recreation. Here she undermines one of the major assumptions of developmental economics: that the poor are so desperate that given the opportunity they will always choose to look first after basic needs and that idling away time is the province only of the wealthy. Arora concludes: "There is an assumption that the poor will somehow behave differently from their wealthier counterparts. Herein lies a deep bind of contemporary ICT development thinking."[7]

As with the issue of plagiarism, however, when the author situates the recreations of the Internet cafes in the local social context, she comes to see the play as also a valid social choice for the use of computing. We learn, for example, that due to widespread broadband access in Almora, local children and teens are now fully conversant in many elements of Indian urban culture, their rural dialects are now inflected by urban usages, and they are also fairly aware of international pop culture. These may seem to a developmental economist to be an inadequate result for billions of dollars of investment in I.T., but in fact, as Arora points out, in their own way, these consequences represent considerable progress.

The work betrays its origins in that it is extremely dense and steeped in academic jargon. However, it should be of interest to a variety of audiences, including most especially those concerned with development, with I.T. investment, with teaching and pedagogy (in any context— many of the weaknesses she spots in constructivist practices in education are as relevant in London or New York as in village India— and generally interested, as are we, in the impact of the Internet. But given its cost ($99.95) most readers should probably seek it out in an academic library, where it properly belongs.

[7] For a deeper understanding of some of the contemporary schools of development thinking, in addition to Arora's marvelous introduction, see also our review of Atkinson, Robert D and Andrew S. McKay, *Digital Prosperity. Understanding the Economic Benefits of the Information Technology Revolution., and of* Charles Kenny, *The Information Technology & Innovation Foundation Overselling the Web? Development and the Internet.* London: Lynne Rienner Publishers. Both are found at: http://bcis.pacificu.edu/journal/2007/03/atkinson.php

Gary Shteyngart's *Super Sad True Love Story: A Novel*

Review by Jeffrey Barlow

I have lately reviewed a series of apocalyptic works for *Interface*, ranging from zombie takeovers (Myra Grant's *Feed*[1]) to the decline of the American brain (Nicholas Carr's *The Shallows*[2]). I now find myself reporting on a related work, insofar as the impact of the Internet goes, Gary Shteyngart's *Super Sad True Love Story: A Novel.*

Shteyngart has splendid credentials of the high-literature-set-in-New York sort. He emigrated to the U.S. from Russia in 1979 at the age of seven. His earlier books have won numerous awards and he clearly is a rising literary figure.[3] This book received excellent reviews and I am painfully aware that I am very much an outlier in that regard.

Grant's, Carr's, and now Shteyngart's works have little in common save the manner in which they deal explicitly with the impact of digital communications. In each of them, digital media have reduced communication to a mindless, if not soulless, process. Writing is reduced (or to be fair to Carr, threatens to be reduced) to simplistic texting. Here is a representative text sent to Eunice, the female participant in the supersadtruelovestory, from her sister:

> "I feel like I don't know what I'm doing half the time anyways, but I'm so glad that we can confide in each other, because the world sometimes feels so, like, I can't even describe it. It's like I'm floating around and the moment anyone gets near me or I get near anyone there's just this STATIC. Sometimes people verbal me and I just look at their mouth and it's like WHAT? What are you saying to me? How am I supposed to even verbal back and does it even matter what comes out?"[4]

---

1 See Mira Grant's *Feed* reviewed at: http://bcis.pacificu.edu/journal/article.php?id=707.

2 See review of Nicholas Carr's *The Shallows: What the Internet is Doing to Our Brains* at: http://bcis.pacificu.edu/journal/issue.php?vol=10&iss=8.

3 From his website: Gary Shteyngart was born in Leningrad in 1972 and came to the United States seven years later. His debut novel, The Russian Debutante's Handbook, won the Stephen Crane Award for First Fiction and the National Jewish Book Award for Fiction. His second novel, Absurdistan, was named one of the 10 Best Books of the Year by The New York Times Book Review, as well as a best book of the year by Time, The Washington Post Book World, the San Francisco Chronicle, the Chicago Tribune, and many other publications. He has been selected as one of Granta's Best Young American Novelists. His work has appeared in The New Yorker, Esquire, GQ, and Travel + Leisure and his books have been translated into more than twenty languages. He lives in New York City. See: http://supersadtruelovestory.com/.

4 Shteyngart, Highlight Loc. 807-14 Kindle version.

The recipient, Eunice, a Korean-American twenty-something, is if anything even less literate than her sister. When Lenny Abramov, the protagonist, reads aloud to Eunice as part of his campaign to educate her, we get this scene:

> "Are you following all this?" I said. "Maybe we should stop." "I'm listening," she half-whispered. "But are you understanding?" I said. "I've never really learned how to read texts," she said. "Just to scan them for info."[5]

The only fully literate and reflective major character is Lenny, the son of Jewish immigrants who left a collapsing post- Russian state to migrate to New York. Lenny owns a "Wall of Books," his most precious possession. Others are deeply suspicious of books, which in the popular view, smell very badly and are at best archaically useless.

Though educated and reflective, Lenny is painfully and obliviously unaware. Virtually everyone in the work, including his supposed friends, victimizes or makes fun of him, including the light of his life, Eunice. In this, Lenny, like many other characters is fundamentally a walking ethnic stereotype, in this case the hapless Jewish male, the schlemiel.

However, Eunice and her coevals, as well as Lenny, might be forgiven for remaining unaware, because they live in a United States on the very verge of collapse. It has sold its economy to Sweden and to China, among others, and is fighting a losing war in Venezuela. The national government, the ARA—American Recovery Administration—has responded by fastening an ever more repressive society on its citizenry.

Here is the author's take on one such ARA moment:

> "An unstable, barely governable country presenting grave risk to the international system of corporate governance and exchange mechanisms" is what Central Banker Li called us when his ass had landed safely in Beijing. We had been humiliated in front of the world. The Fourth of July fireworks were canceled. The parade to crown the "American Spender" winner put on hold because a section of Broadway near City Hall had buckled in the heat. The remaining streets were empty, the citizenry prudently staying home, the F running at one train per hour (not that different from its normal schedule, I must say). The only changes noticeable are the new ARA signs drooping off some of the Credit Poles featuring a tiger pawing at a miniature globe and the words "America is back! Grrrr ... Don't write us of [sic]. Ain't No Stoppin' Us Now! Together We'll Surprise the World!"[6]

---

[5] Highlight Loc. 4959-63.
[6] Highlight Loc. 3207-14.

The repression extends to total control over communications. Each citizen carries an "äppärät"— a sort of next generation smartphone— with which to communicate, regardless of whether one wishes to do so or not. The apparat reveals to all other nearby similar machines (and to the Credit Poles mentioned above, which are ubiquitous readers which constantly flash the carrier's information to everyone around) their credit standing, their mood, even their sexual attractiveness based on an average of responses from other apparat users. Highly abbreviated texting on the apparat has become the substitute of choice for "verbaling," human speech.

There are a number of sub-plots that careen through the book, but basically do little more than fill out the society in which the love story occurs. These are interesting and evocative of other writers' takes on dystopian futures. The apparat and the security state which employs it are reminiscent of Orwell's *1984*, of course; the attitude toward books as well as other plot elements remind the reader of Bradbury's *Fahrenheit 451*. There are many other such tropes.

Where the book fails as an enjoyable reading experience for me is in the love story. Lenny is a schlemiel held together by reminiscences of happier—because more European and less American—times and people. Eunice soon became a boring caricature whose endless materialism is only rarely pierced by the beginnings of altruism or social consciousness, from which she quickly turns away. She is altogether a lapsarian heroine, selfish, weak, and treacherous; Madame Bovary, but far less interesting.

Her Korean family, like Lenny's Jewish one, is a collective ethnic stereotype. His, warm and food-obsessed, hers headed by a dominating abusive Korean Confucian father and a weak mother who has failed to master even the rudiments of English.[7] Taken together they want me to tell the protagonist, "So get out more, meet some interesting people, New York must be full of them."

The book works then, by weaving a not-very-interesting love story through a not-very-original setting. Its main appeal, it seems to me, is precisely what brought me to it: its many tropes of the evils of digital communications.[8] These are often the high points of the many quite favorable reviews the book has received.[9]

---

[7] These Korean stereotypes are particularly unfair ones. Korean girls and women are nearly universally regarded as the most independent and confident females of East Asia, and it is almost inevitably the immigrant woman who masters English before the immigrant male.

[8] See the author's own take on this issue in an interview at: http://www.theparisreview.org/blog/2010/07/27/gary-shteyngart/.

[9] For favorable reviews see, among many others: http://www.slate.com/id/2262500/; http://www.nytimes.com/2010/07/27/books/27book.html. See also Sarah Davidson's review "Gary Shteyngart Super Sad True Love Story. A totally awesome printed, bound media artifact" at: http://wweek.com/editorial/3639/14348/, which repeatedly points up the book vs. electronic media trope. Elsbeth Pancrazi's review at:

Rob Harvilla's review in *The Village Voice* (Surely the place Lenny would have preferred that his own book be favorably received!) wrote:

> Gary Shteyngart's Super Sad True Love Story tries to be many things—tragicomic 1984 update, poignant May-December romance per the title, heartfelt tribute to the nostalgic joys of plain ol' books—and succeeds at most of them. But primarily, it's the finest piece of anti-iPhone propaganda ever written, a cautionary tale full of distracted drones unwilling to tear themselves away from their little glowing screens long enough to make eye contact, let alone an actual lasting connection, with another human being. It's super sad 'cause it's true, but that also makes it hilarious.... Super Sad ain't Tolstoy, but it argues for the analog pleasures of Tolstoy in an increasingly, detrimentally digital world, and that'll do. Read it as an eBook, and you're part of the problem.

Rob may be right, I could be part of the problem, reading this as I did on my Kindle. Fortunately, we learn at Shteyngart's site that we can go to our ITunes store and download his free IPhone app which will give us (Free!):

> "The official app for Gary Shteyngart, the bestselling author of novels including "Absurdistan," "The Russian Debutante's Handbook" and the new novel "Super Sad True Love Story." Everything you want to know about Gary is now available for your iPhone or iTouch.
>
> With this handy application, you'll have instant access to:
>
> -- Breaking news
> -- Excerpts
> -- Bonus content
> -- Video clips
> -- Twitter and Facebook integration
> -- And more fan goodies!"

The book is worth reading as a pastiche of dystopian clichés, and because it may indeed represent our possible future, which apparently will be alternately boring and terrifying.

However, the book, and its overwhelmingly favorable reception do tell us a great deal about the impact of electronic communications, including the Internet. There is a considerable market for point-with-alarm fiction at present, and the Internet is an easy target. This work suggests that many of us are afraid of the pace of change, and of the future. Why not blame it on the Internet?

---

http://www.bookslut.com/fiction/2010_09_016584.php is also written around a defense of the book vis-à-vis electronic forms of reading and digital communications.

Bullying and WWW Sites: An Introduction

Editorial by Jeffrey Barlow

Bullying is very much in the news at present. A simple Google search will yield about 17,900,000 hits[1]. A search of cyber bullying within that data set will yield about 915,000 hits[2].

This editorial review is our start at Interface on gaining a better understanding of the issues involved not only with bullying per se, and particularly cyber bullying, but bullying as a media phenomenon.

I should probably state as a fair warning at the outset that I belong to two different groups that are concerned with this phenomenon, and also have had personal involvement with the issue, which has doubtless shaped my response to it.

One of the groups to which I belong is the listserv youth-risk-online@googlegroups.com. I was invited to this group by Nancy Willard, our most recent guest at the Berglund Center Roundtable (XXX link to where her video will be???) and have found it a very useful source for understanding Internet safety, focused largely but not entirely on children and young adults[3]. The discussion is lively and wide-ranging and the group remarkably eclectic in their approaches. A light day's list will still see 5-6 well thought out messages into my email. In the last year of reading the list, I have seen that many members have been widely quoted in the media, interviewed on television and frequently present at professional conferences in related fields.

The other organization to which I belong, in the minimal sense that I have attended one of their conferences and receive their e-mails, is the Family Online Safety Institute (FOSI)[4]. FOSI, as a glance at their Board of Directors will show, is a very well connected group that now stages several annual conferences (this year's were in Washington D.C., Bahrain, and Madrid.)

---

[1] http://www.google.com/search?q=bulling+d+of+ed&ie=utf-8&oe=utf-8&aq=t&rls=org.mozilla:en-US:official&client=firefox-a#sclient=psy&hl=en&client=firefox-a&hs=Yjs&rls=org.mozilla:en-US%3Aofficial&q=bullying&aq=f&aqi=g4g-o1&aql=&oq=&gs_rfai=&pbx=1&fp=b7b968c575c3858f

[2] http://www.google.com/search?q=bulling+d+of+ed&ie=utf-8&oe=utf-8&aq=t&rls=org.mozilla:en-US:official&client=firefox-a#hl=en&client=firefox-a&hs=H4X&rls=org.mozilla:en-US:official&q=cyber+bullying&revid=-1&sa=X&ei=IYzITJC1AYTGsAP73oS8CA&ved=0CJEBENUCKAc&fp=b7b968c575c3858f

[3] I am not sure, but believe, that this group is not open to the casual reader but that one must be invited to have access. Anyone of course, could email the above link and ask for access, though I am sure that it will take some time to reply to all such requests. If I were requesting access I would state briefly and succinctly my reasons for wishing access, and the reasons why I could contribute to the group's discussions.

[4] See their WWW page at: http://www.fosi.org/

Both of these groups are wonderful resources. FOSI is more of a public lobby, and youth-risk-online a group of scholars and practitioners devoted to understanding and creating the best possible data from which good public policy decisions can be made.

My personal experience with bullying is that in fourth grade, after three years of attending schools where my mother taught and watched after me like a mother bear at all times, I went outside her protective shield to a town-wide basketball practice to which I walked, following unfamiliar routes. I was stopped en route and harassed the first evening, and given what seemed at the time to me to be a beating. My mother's over-reaction brought down the wrath of the entire school system on the four or five boys who were involved, and whom I did not see again until, gulp, we all entered the same high school. This began a period which lasted for another four years where I was often frightened and occasionally harassed.

After going off to college I discovered first Judo, then a series of Gongfu related arts. I subsequently studied martial arts and coached them in the U.S., Taiwan, Vietnam, and China. I came to understand that really what I had experienced in fourth grade was somewhere between being hazed as the new kid and being beaten.

My fear at the time and over an extended period, however, was significant. Bullying interferes with the victim's personal development, with his or her education, and their relationships with others. I missed a lot of what a very diverse high school had to offer, including all forms of athletic activity because for boys the gym is inevitably the scene of much bullying.

Bullying then, is a serious issue and should not be tolerated. Its sudden explosion in at least the American media, if not in the American school system, puzzles many. While there have been several spectacular cases in the last few months, some argue that actually there is no evidence that bullying has increased.

At another of the sites I wish to introduce here, education.com, it is argued that:

> "Despite the media frenzy around events such as school shootings, suicides, and filmed beatings on YouTube, there is no definitive evidence that bullying is on the rise. More research studies that consider rates of bullying over time are needed. Why might bullying be on the rise?
>
> * There is greater awareness of the seriousness of bullying, which could be due to higher reporting rates by students.
>
> * The addition of cyberbullying as a new, easy, and round-the-clock place to bully.
>
> * There are a number of early childhood risk factors that have increased that might also increase a child's vulnerability to bully

or be bullied, such as an insecure attachment to a primary care giver or lack of parental supervision."[5]

I would add from my own close personal preventative study of bullying during my high school years that economic differences are an important factor which is often neglected and that the current suffering of many groups in America is bound to increase violence at all levels. I also feel that the increased attention paid to bullying no doubt increases the willingness of victims to come forward. The key words "bullying and harassment" now signal to educators potential bad publicity and possible legal action, ensuring an immediate hearing for every complaint, no matter how trivial.

This pressure is increased on school districts by growing federal involvement. The government is now increasingly involved in preventing bullying, eliciting perhaps many different sorts of reactions. To some this interest might appear to be more of what the British term the "Nanny State," – or "Smother Mother" as the Home School Legal Defense Association[6] calls it – a government that just won't stay out of our affairs. But regardless of its need or right to be involved, the feds nonetheless offer a wealth of resources. See the U.S. Department of Health and Human Services' materials, for example[7].

The Office of Civil Rights (OCR) has recently (October 26 2010) issued to all school districts a ten-page "Dear Colleague" letter which presents the issue not as so often been the case an issue in criminal law but one of civil rights[8]. The letter lays out in great detail specific examples of bullying or harassment of many different groups and explains why these are violations of federal laws protecting civil rights and may expose school districts which do not prevent of investigate them to federal action, including loss of federal funds.

This letter has been well received in the listserv youth-risk-online, in part because it changes the focus from criminal to civil action, but it will take a few weeks until we have a well-considered reaction from a variety of quarters[9]. There is bound to be a negative reaction to "Dear Colleague as well[10].

---

[5] For the site, the article and the references see: http://www.education.com/reference/article/bullying-on-the-rise/ This is a very useful site with a wide variety of materials covering various approaches to bullying.

[6] See: http://www.hslda.org/docs/news/200907200.asp

[7]http://search.hrsa.gov/search?q=Bullying&btnG=Search&ie=&site=default_collection&output=xml_no_dtd&client=aquilent_dev&lr=&proxystylesheet=aquilent_dev&oe=

[8] Download the PDF at: http://www2.ed.gov/about/offices/list/ocr/letters/colleague-201010.html

[9] This issue is of special concern to the gay community for obvious reasons and has been well received there as well as best I can tell from a quick survey of Internet sites. See, for example, http://gay.americablog.com/2010/10/dept-of-education-and-four-us-reps-take.html

[10] For an early negative response see: http://stoppingschoolviolence.com/blog/2010/10/is-obamas-education-department-the-new-bully/

The issue of harassment or bullying of gays is highlighted in the OCR letter, and by accompanying speeches by President Obama. This presents a very divisive issue to conservative Christians, who may simultaneously feel that harassment is wrong, but so is homosexuality, and who decry what they see as the increasing aggression of gay lobbying groups[11]. Many Christian groups share an understanding of what they refer to as the "gay agenda" as just another disguised campaign for "special rights" for minority groups, which must, in their views, come at the expense of everybody else's rights.

Bullying then, is not a simple issue and the materials we have accumulated to fully understand it are not yet that comprehensive nor reliable. It is probable that bullying is inflected by ethnic, gender, and age differences. Diverse political and social groups are going to respond very differently to attempts to define, to identify and to prevent or to punish it. We will continue to follow this issue in *Interface*.

---

[11] See for example Tobin Grant, " Bullying Blame. Is it enough to say bullying gays is wrong?" in *Christianity Today* at: http://www.christianitytoday.com/ct/2010/octoberweb-only/51-52.0.html?start=1

December 2010 - Volume 10, Issue 10

About This Issue

Despite the frantic wrap-up of both the academic and solar calendars here, we believe that this issue of Interface is an appropriately climactic one.

Our feature, by Berglund Faculty Fellow Isaac Gilman of the Pacific University Library is "Open Opportunities: The Impact of the Internet on Academic Libraries" and is his summary of an in-progress piece for our tenth year anniversary issue. Every academic seriously working with computers is aware that it is the librarians who have been quickest to understand the implications of changes in information technology and to employ them in serving their clientele.

Ruth Happ, a graduate of Pacific University, concludes her witty senior thesis, "Text Appeal: The Internet, Dating, and Jane Austen." We think that she takes the Jane Austin cult into the 21st century.

We offer two pieces related to video gaming. The first is Berglund Student Fellow Jamaica King's piece "Online Gaming Communities: Strengths, Limitations, & Death." As both a serious student and an ardent player of video games, we think that Jamaica sheds new light on gaming communities. This is the first report on her on-going research.

Our second gaming-related piece is a book review by our resident 'Toon author', IProfess, who presents himself as a gaming avatar crossed into the real world from the on-line game The World of Warcraft. Here he gives us his unique perspective on a current book by one of the leading authors in both crime fiction and romance novels, who writes both as J.D. Robb and as Nora Roberts. Her recent book, Fantasy in Death, deals with a murder committed inside a computer game. IProfess suggests the book would be a great stocking-stuffer for the gamer on your holiday shopping list.

Our security editor, Pat McGregor discussed the importance of appropriate use of password protection in "*Throw Out Your Passwords!*." Some of Pat's very useful advice is counter-intuitive and we urge all readers to treat this issue very seriously indeed.

Our second book review is of Dr. Sharif Mowlabocus' book *Gaydar Culture. Gay Men, Technology and Embodiment in the Digital Age*. Our reviewer states: "Anyone with a serious interest in the impact of the Internet should read it, and anyone with a gay friend or family member will find it offers many insights into a culture probably otherwise closed to them."

Jeffrey Barlow's editorial is "Peaceful Evolution in China and the World Wide Web: Part III, China's Emerging Leadership." Here he reports on China's emerging generation of leaders and the very significant political factions which are increasingly important in Chinese politics.

Please see also our section "announcements" for recent events at the Center as well as a discussion by our Legal editor, Leonard DuBoff on "*Do You Really Own Your Web Pages?*"
We hope that all of our readers have a great holiday season and that you check back with us in February for our first issue of the new year.

The Berglund Center for Internet Studies
Pacific University Oregon

.

Open Opportunities: The Impact of the Internet on Academic Libraries

A Berglund Center Tenth Anniversary Essay

Isaac Gilman, Pacific University Library

Editor's Note: This article is the preliminary version of a much longer peer-reviewed piece to be published in hard copy in fall, 2011 as a chapter in our tenth-year anniversary volume, After Internet Time.

Introduction

The ongoing impact of the Internet on library and information services cannot be understated. As with print journalism, the capacity and culture of networked life has transformed every aspect of the library profession, from technical services to public services. The first comprehensive examinations of the Internet's impact on libraries and library services began in the 1990s,[1] and by the turn of the century there was a considerable body of literature devoted to various dimensions of the topic. Not surprisingly, these examinations largely addressed the effect of the Internet on traditional library services and roles: cataloging/technical services, collection management, interlibrary loan, bibliographic instruction, and reference services.[2] [3]

These changes in traditional services are perhaps best exemplified by the changing nature of the library catalog: the transition from physical index cards to machine-readable records to networked catalogs (i.e. WorldCat) alone has improved the process of bibliographic research phenomenally. With the Internet, libraries are able to provide remote access for their users not only to their local collections and catalog, but also to library collections around the nation and the world. With this capacity, metadata and resource description standards have become more important as numerous libraries contribute records to shared catalogs and local cataloging practices affect access for patrons across the world. However, while such Internet-induced changes in the library catalog are worthy of examination, these changes do not fundamentally alter the role of the catalog in library services.

Indeed, library literature in 2001[4] [5] reflects the fact that, as much as the Internet had (to that point) changed the process and the possibilities of traditional library

---

[1] Liu, Lewis-Guodo. 2001. *The Role and Impact of the Internet on Library and Information Services.* Westport, Conn: Greenwood Press.
[2] See note 1.
[3] Su, Di. 2001. *Evolution in Reference and Information Services: The Impact of the Internet.* Binghamton, NY: Haworth Information Press.
[4] Liu, Lewis-Guodo. 2001. *The Role and Impact of the Internet on Library and Information Services.* Westport, Conn: Greenwood Press.

functions, the essential nature of library services remained the same: the acquisition, organization, and dissemination of and education about, information resources. In the past decade, though, the open culture and evolving technology of the Internet has created a set of user expectations that have presented libraries – particularly academic libraries – with opportunities to not only change their approach to traditional services, but to embrace *new* roles.

Openness and Online User Expectations

From its inception, the concept of openness has been integral to the success of the Internet; as some of its developers note, "A key to the rapid growth of the Internet has been the free and open access to the basic documents [...]."[6] Collaboration and open sharing of documentation and code enabled swift development of the early Internet, and open source programming continues to be the backbone of some of the most robust applications available to Internet users today. The openness of the Internet extends beyond sharing source code, however. At its core, the open ethos of the Internet is today expressed in two ways: *openness of access and openness of identity.*

In a 2010 global British Broadcasting Corporation (BBC) survey (n=27,000), 80 percent of respondents indicated that Internet access is a human right.[7] The expectation that equitable access to online resources is on par with access to clean water seems entirely reasonable – after all, like water, the Internet is freely available to anyone. It may require resources to procure the computer and hardware necessary to connect to the Internet, but the Internet itself is a free resource. Users pay for a computer and for access to cable lines or to wireless networks, but no one pays for a Web browser or to access a search engine or to send an email or to visit millions of websites.

The view of Internet access as a human right is a reflection of how today's users experience the Internet, and what they expect when they go online: easy and free access to resources. The most popular Internet sites and applications like Google and Facebook are openly (freely) available to all. Many daily tasks can be accomplished on the Internet without spending a cent: Google Docs or Zoho or Open Office provide tools for work and school assignments; Hulu provides entertainment; CNN (or Fox) provide news; Skype provides a connection to relatives in Detroit; Mint provides budgeting assistance; and Pandora provides the soundtrack for it all. As a recent Wall Street Journal (online!) column notes, "we have built a country-size economy online where the default price is zero –

---

[5] Su, Di. 2001. *Evolution in Reference and Information Services: The Impact of the Internet*. Binghamton, NY: Haworth Information Press.

[6] Leiner, Barry M., Cerf, Vinton G., Clark, David D., Kahn, Robert E., Kleinrock, Leonard, Lynch, Daniel C., Postel, Jon, Roberts, Larry G. and Stephen Wolff. 2001. "A Brief History of the Internet" in Liu, Lewis-Guodo, ed. *The Role and Impact of the Internet on Library and Information Services*. Westport, Conn: Greenwood Press.

[7] Ayish, Muhammad. "Universal Internet Access is the New Human Rights Issue." *The National*, March 18, 2010. Accessed October 29, 2010. http://www.thenational.ae/news/universal-internet-access-is-the-new-human-rights-issue?pageCount=0.

nothing, nada, zip. [...] For the Google Generation, the Internet is the land of the free."[8] As much of an economic driver as the Internet is, the expectation of free access to online tools, resources and information is hard-wired into many Internet users: the 2010 Annenberg Digital Future Study found that, of the 49 percent of Internet users who reported using services like Twitter, exactly zero percent would be willing to pay for such a service.[9] This does not mean that users will never pay for an online service (e.g., for a "premium" version of an online service[10]) – but supports the supposition that users' default expectation is to experience free access online.

At the same time that users have been conditioned to expect open access to online resources, the Internet (particularly in the last decade) has also encouraged users to be open about themselves online. Though it can be argued that the Internet encourages not openness about identity but rather faceless (or deceptive) anonymity, it would be difficult to argue against the predominance of online technologies and forums that enable (and expect) unprecedented individual openness. Users' full utilization of social networking sites like MySpace and Facebook is directly related to the amount of personal information users are prepared to share online and the culture of blogging and micro-blogging (i.e. Twitter) encourages people to expose their deepest (and shallowest) thoughts with ongoing immediacy. It has been noted that some online users do attempt to retain a certain level of privacy within their online activities,[11] [12] and consistent flaps over Facebook privacy snafus demonstrate that many users do care about having control over their personal information. However, a recent study by the Pew Center found that only 33 percent of Internet users are concerned about what information is available about them online – and only 33 percent of users have taken any action to limit/reduce the amount of information available about them on the Internet.[13] In fact, some users are beginning to acknowledge that limiting the amount of available information

---

[8] Anderson, Chris. "The Economics of Giving it Away." *Wall Street Journal*, January 31, 2009. Accessed October 29, 2010. http://online.wsj.com/article/SB123335678420235003.html.

[9] Annenberg School of Communications. 2010 USC Annenberg Digital Future Study Finds Strong Negative Reaction to Paying for Online Services, July 23, 2010. Accessed October 29, 2010. http://www.digitalcenter.org/pdf/2010_digital_future_final_release.pdf.

[10] Bulik, Beth Snyder. "On-Demand Generation Will Pay to Play." *Advertising Age*, April 12, 2010. Accessed November 1, 2010. http://adage.com/digital/article?article_id=143220.

[11] Lange, P.G. "Publicly Private and Privately Public: Social Networking on YouTube." *Journal of Computer-Mediated Communication 13*(2007): Article 18. Accessed November 1, 2010. http://jcmc.indiana.edu/vol13/issue1/lange.html.

[12] Holson, Laura M. "Tell-All Generation Learns to Keep Things Offline." *The New York Times*, May 8, 2010. Accessed November 1, 2010. http://www.nytimes.com/2010/05/09/fashion/09privacy.html?_r=1.

[13] Madden, Mary and Aaron Smith. 2010. *Reputation Management and Social Media*. Pew Research Center. Accessed November 1, 2010.

may be less important than *adding* desired information to influence the nature of their online identities.[14]

Openness and Opportunities

Over the past decade, the confluence of users' willingness to share personal information (in a variety of formats) online, and their desire/expectation of receiving open access to online tools and resources (sometimes in exchange for sharing personal information) has contributed to an unprecedented culture of openness on the Internet. As users with these expectations and experiences arrive on college and university campuses (both as students and as faculty), it has presented academic libraries with the opportunity to provide services that are informed by both dimensions of this online openness – and that reach beyond the library's traditional roles.

Open Access Publishing

Traditionally, academic libraries have purchased resources from publishers and other vendors to create collections of materials for student and faculty use. In turn, libraries have been defined by their role as collector.[15] However, as the cost of library resources, particularly scholarly journals, has risen dramatically over the past decade, academic libraries have been confronted with stark budget realities[16] – and the openness of the Internet, in the form of open access, has emerged as a partial solution. The open access movement, which calls for a scholarly publishing model that provides free and unrestricted access to online journal content, has been made possible by the minimal costs of online publication. The number of open access journals is growing continuously (the Directory of Open Access Journals added more than 3 new titles per day in the last quarter[17]) and even journals which are not strictly open access are making some content openly available, either voluntarily or due to mandates from both the government and educational institutions.[18] [19]

---

[14] Thompson, Clive. "The See-Through CEO." *Wired,* March 2007. Accessed October 29, 2010. http://www.wired.com/wired/archive/15.04/wired40_ceo.html.
[15] Gilman, Isaac and Marita Kunkel. "From Passive to Pervasive: Changing Perceptions of the Library's Role through Intra-Campus Partnerships." *Collaborative Librarianship 2*(1): 20-30. http://collaborativelibrarianship.org/index.html.
[16] Van Orsdel, Lee C. and Kathleen Born. "Reality Bites: Periodicals Price Survey 2009." *Library Journal,* April 15, 2009. Accessed November 1, 2010. http://www.libraryjournal.com/article/CA6651248.html.
[17] Morrison, Heather. "Dramatic Growth of Open Access: September 30, 2010." *The Imaginary Journal of Poetic Economics.* Accessed October 4, 2010. http://poeticeconomics.blogspot.com/2010/09/dramatic-growth-of-open-access.html
[18] National Institutes of Health Public Access. Accessed November 1, 2010. http://publicaccess.nih.gov/.
[19] Suber, Peter. "The Open Access Mandate at Harvard." *SPARC Open Access Newsletter,* March 2, 2008. Accessed November 1, 2010. http://www.earlham.edu/~peters/fos/newsletter/03-02-08.htm#harvard.

As clear beneficiaries (both for their bottom lines and for their users) of open access publishing, academic libraries have been fierce advocates of this model. But advocacy is not the most significant role that libraries have embraced; as leaders in the open access movement, libraries are also becoming *publishers* as well by providing technological and organizational support for new publications. This shift, from passive purchasers of external resources to vital partners in the creation of new publications, is truly transformational. By providing venues for local scholarship to be widely disseminated, and by providing resources that will never require their users (or others') to encounter a "pay-per-view" screen when trying to access an article, academic libraries have embraced the opportunity of openness and are meeting (and sometimes exceeding) users' expectations.

Readers' Advisory to Identity Advisory

While capitalizing on their own opportunity to contribute to openly accessible knowledge through online publishing activities, academic libraries are also faced with the challenge of responding to their students' personal openness. Libraries have long been privacy advocates, though primarily in relation to issues of intellectual freedom and the privacy of circulation records. As technology has evolved, libraries have certainly been faced with decisions about how best to protect patron privacy when sending circulation information over non-secure channels (e.g. e-mail and text messages). However, as important as an academic library's own practices are in the face of changing technology, it is their users' practices that provide the most opportunity for a new service area: *identity advisory*.

As long-standing privacy advocates, it makes sense that academic libraries should play a role in educating their student (and occasionally, faculty) users about the creation and maintenance of online identities. Although tied to a traditional library practice (protecting privacy), the focus is fundamentally different – it is a shift from assuring users of how the library protects their information to advocating for how users should manage their own information (outside of the context of a library record). Though recent research like the Pew study indicates that most social-networking users are mindful of adjusting their privacy settings,[20] there is certainly anecdotal evidence that points to contrary behaviors.[21] While college or university IT staff may also have a role in educating students about the importance of managing their online identities, this is an opportunity that academic libraries can, and should, welcome. For example, at Pacific University (OR), librarians offer online privacy-related instruction to freshmen to help emphasize that online identities cultivated during school can have an impact long after graduation.

---

[20] Madden, Mary and Aaron Smith. 2010. *Reputation Management and Social Media*. Pew Research Center. Accessed November 1, 2010. http://pewinternet.org/Reports/2010/Reputation-Management.aspx.

[21] Gilman, Isaac. "Online Lives, Offline Consequences: Professionalism, Information Ethics and Professional Students." *Interface on the Internet* 9 (2009). http://bcis.pacificu.edu/journal/article.php?id=22

Conclusion

Libraries have changed – and benefitted – in myriad ways due to the creation and continuing evolution of the Internet. And though the anachronistic stereotype of the academic library as the home of musty stacks may persist, the reality of library services (both traditional and non-traditional) will continue to evolve along with it. After all, in the library's emphasis on free information and its continual attention to privacy issues, the open culture of the Internet has no more appropriate partner.

Text Appeal: The Internet, Dating, and Jane Austen, Part 2

Ruth Happ '10

Editor's Note: This piece, in its original form is recent Pacific University graduate Ruth Happ's, thesis. Part I was published in November (Volume 10, Issue 9). In this final part we contrast the personal relationships of Jane Austen's time to the non-committal "hook ups" of today, as well as the use of modern technology versus Austen's community.

Original thesis edited by Pauline Beard
Interface version edited by Jenn Hernandez

In today's world, one can see how many readers and viewers, especially women, would be drawn to Austen. The "sexual liberation" of women has not fulfilled its commitment to granting women a more powerful position in male and female interactions. Unlike back in the dating era, they can now initiate hook ups, but their goal of having a relationship is often left unmet. Females typically outnumber males on college campuses, which can increase the females' competition and subsequently, the males' power in "control[ling] the intensity of the relationship" (Bogle 174). The men are generally still the ones to decide whether a relationship will follow the physical encounter (55-56, 125). Partially because the male students have so many options, they are commonly more interested in casual hook ups with no commitment attached, while the females often want to "hold on" to a man because of the competition and because they are more interested in the long-term (55-56, 125, 174, 177). In fact, in all of Bogle's interviews, love was never mentioned as a prerequisite for hooking up, and no emotional or romantic attachment paralleled the encounters, as would have been expected in the dating era (165). Interviewees, especially alumni, recognized that one cannot find a "quality" relationship through this system (137). Some post-college female alumni had expected to find a "quality" man sooner, but having spent their college years casually hooking up, they expressed deep concerns about finding a life partner (154-56).

Many of today's relationships also lack an understanding of "etiquette" and role expectations. According to Bogle, the casual "hooking up" and dating of today, especially among young people, no longer follow the dating "rules" that once applied, and gender roles in the society-at-large are blurred. Young people often pair up during an evening of drinking or dancing or just "hanging out"; no one is responsible to "ask the other out," plan an evening's activities, or pay for them. Public displays of affection through flowers and gifts are not necessary, either, since the relationship often does not continue past the physical meeting (169-70). Confusion often results from this indefiniteness in role expectations, and romance, purpose, and commitment are found deficient in these kinds of relationships.

In contrast, as Josephine Ross delineates in her book *Jane Austen's Guide to Good Manners: Compliments, Charades & Horrible Blunders*, Miss Austen highly respected the Manners of her time and place. "The word [Manners] was applicable to every aspect of daily life—from dress and domestic arrangements, to the treatment of servants, and the proper way to encourage or deter an admirer" (3-4). The manners that define Austen's world are not for the purposes of "mere formality" or snobbery; "they are based on solid principles of courtesy, propriety and, most of all, regard for the feelings of others" (4). Austen distinguishes between manners of vain conceit and manners reflecting inner character and dignity. Characters that manifest "too much polish" may simply be shining conches with hollow insides (5). As Ross points out, "More than one of [Austen's] heroines is temporarily taken in by a man whose good looks and gallant 'address' are not supported by any inner qualities of principle, morality, or selflessness" (5). The true heroes of Austen's novels are less concerned with show and gallantry, and more concerned with acting honorably, following those societal rules "which contribute to the comfort, or dignity, of others" (6). Jane Austen knew well and honored these Manners, but she also poked fun at them on the proper occasion and satirized the people of "good breeding," who esteemed themselves based on their birth, but paid no attention to the cultivation of the inner characteristics meriting admiration (10). A refined, or gradually honed, discernment of what are good manners and what are empty shows of gallantry is a strong characteristic of Austen's heroines. The deserving heroes are those whose inner character, honor, and own discernment stand up to the test of the heroine's evaluation.

This code of etiquette allowed members of society to know what was proper in almost every situation, especially as concerned interactions between men and women. They knew what was expected of them. It does appear that men held the greater power. Ladies could not call upon gentlemen or invite them to dance (Ross 31, 55). If a lady refused one gentleman's offer to stand up with him (to dance), she could not then accept another's offer (54). After dinner, ladies had to withdraw to another room, as the men would continue drinking and discussing more "masculine" subjects (61-62). Ladies held certain rights, however, in the realm of male/female interaction. From the first moments of introduction, according to Ross, "Safeguarding the reputation of a lady is at all times a matter of the highest importance" (20). A man had to be formally introduced to a lady before asking her to dance with him (53), and as Frank Churchill states in *Emma*, "It is always the lady's right to decide on the degree of acquaintance" (184). Men had the power of marriage proposal, with the permission of the lady's father, of course, but women had the power of refusal, a right exercised by Elizabeth in *Pride and Prejudice*, and Fanny in *Mansfield Park*. Once engaged, the woman could change her mind and call it off, as Anne does in *Persuasion*, but propriety dictated the man honor his promise to the woman, as Edward does in *Sense and Sensibility*.

The codes in place also determined a proper level of decorum and respect to be demonstrated in men and women's treatment of each other. A gentleman's attention to the neighboring lady's needs at the dinner table (refilling plates and glasses), her modesty in dress, and avoidance of flirtatiousness and imprudent shows of affection are just a few examples (Ross 75, 83-84, 61). As demonstrated in *Sense and Sensibility*, a certain level of intimacy between a man and a woman, as with the constant time spent together, the gift of a lock of hair, and the exchange of letters between Marianne and Willoughby, also implied an "understanding," an engagement, between the parties. Such rules of decorum, although perhaps unfair or overly rigid in the twenty-first century mindset, did serve to keep men accountable to their relations and society in their treatment and commitments to women.

Contemporary fans of Austen express their love of Austenland's safe nature, morality, and romance online through blogs, Austen-fan websites, and comments to Austen-related online articles. *The Republic of Pemberley* web-site promises visitors, "No, you've not lost your way. You remain safe within the borders of *The Republic of Pemberley*...Your haven in a world programmed to misunderstand obsession with things Austen" (said misunderstanding perhaps alludes to derogatory views toward Austen's "fairy tales," as they may be perceived). Fittingly, in representation of the manners and sense of propriety of Austen's culture, the web-site includes a code to follow as a citizen of *Pemberley*, found under "Frequently Asked Questions", described as being "about the discussion boards and the laws we live by in this micronation -- with some of the answers, too." In *The Republic of Pemberley*, Janeites can "meet" and form a small community, appropriately guided by rules of etiquette, ironically within the worldwide web. A blog conversation in response to Memmott and Puig's *USA Today* online article illustrates how readers of Austen novels and viewers of the film adaptations can appreciate the romantic, yet moral, nostalgia of her stories in contrast to their experiences in today's American society. "daryl" writes:

> "I now have developed an interest in the Regency and Victorian periods. What ever happened to actual courting and real socializing? Now courting is getting drunk then having sex, knowing someone a week then moving in, getting pregnant, then maybe married. Socializing is now centered on texting, calling, or emailing." (1)

"MacRoni" responds:

> "Daryl, isn't that the truth? People danced because they couldn't touch in that era. Now dancing doesn't involve touching because people just go to bed after flailing about. :-D Everything was so dignified then. Even in the 30s and 40s there was culture and dignity. Not now! If only we could bring some sophistication and class to our times." (1)

Blogger Ed in NM praises the "classy and respectful" women and "good" men of "character" in Austen (1). MacRoni later adds her thoughts on how Austen's world ought to infiltrate modern culture: "Men should dress up, get some manners and learn how to dance; women would be lined up for a chance," and for women, she thinks "girls are afraid that males won't look at them unless they show more. They should realize that it's what you don't show that leaves something to the imagination" (1). MacRoni's conservative views toward modesty echo Jane Austen's modest treatment of romance to the exclusion of public displays of affection and sex in her novels. Her plots may be emulated in Harlequin Romances, but Austin left plenty to the imagination in comparison.

Leaving more to the imagination is likely a significant cause for Austen's current popularity in a time when all forms of media leave almost nothing to the imagination and contribute to the sexually charged popular culture. Virginia Woolf wrote that Jane Austen is "a mistress of much deeper emotion than appears upon the surface. She stimulates us to supply what is not there" (142). Austen's use of subtlety and sexual restraint enhance the attraction to her understated romances and near-fairy tale marriage plots, as exemplified by the 1995 BBC/A&E version of *Pride and Prejudice* with Colin Firth and Jennifer Ehle. This version, and specifically Colin Firth, set in motion much of the Austenmania of today (Dobie 251). The blogger daryl elucidates a common theme among modern Janeites: "Colin Firth hooked me on Jane Austen. Two years ago I stumbled across a copy of *Pride and Prejudice* on VHS. I would have never started reading Jane Austen until watching that mini-series (1995)" (1).

Colin Firth is indeed handsome, but his widespread appeal is not simply due to his good looks; rather, Darcy's "looks" at Elizabeth Bennet were the primary catalyst for his cult following, according to Virginia Blum, who states he "did a lot of acting with his eyes" (163). Blum explains in her chapter "The Return to Repression that "what [Firth] did precisely was to think instead of act. The trick is to assume the look of desire instead of acting upon it" (163). In fact, "watching him struggle with his pent-up emotion is the centerpiece of the 1995 *Pride and Prejudice*" (Blum 165). Nothing physical occurs between Darcy and Elizabeth until their wedding day at the very end of the movie, when they finally kiss. Blum claims that it is this very restraint and sexual repression that many contemporary readers and viewers are beginning to prefer versus the blatant sex scenes of most adult fiction, romantic or otherwise. She finds it unsurprising that many "go in search of sexual desire in what we imagine to be the most repressed context of all, Austen's pre-Victorian world of heavily controlled courtship, significant glances, and ever unstated agendas" (Blum 166).

Austen's marriage plots in which the heroines fall in love with respectable men, and the two commit to each other for life unsurprisingly appeals to a generation, especially of women, which has become disillusioned with the hooking up system and society's current mode of lackluster romance. "Sexual liberation" has not produced a paradise for both men and women, nor has it produced fulfilling, long-lasting, faithful relationships. Fans of Austen find the kind of men and women they could hope to be or hope to marry. Her heroes are honorable, financially responsible, and abundantly wealthy. They appreciate and admire the minds and opinions of the heroines they love. Martine Voiret, in the article, "Books to Movies: Gender and Desire in Jane Austen's Adaptations," avers that "part of the attraction of Austen's novels is that they provide plots fulfilling the contemporary female desire that it is not the traditionally gentle and self-effacing woman who finds fulfilling love but the outspoken, self-assured woman" (234). Voiret is mostly right. Austen's heroines actually represent a spectrum of feminine characters, from naïve and imaginative Catherine Morland, shy and delicate Fanny Price, neglected and serious Anne Elliot, and responsible and courteous Elinor Dashwood, to independent and interfering Emma Woodhouse and lively and outspoken Elizabeth Bennet. Thus, it is not simply the outspoken, outgoing women so well accepted in popular culture today that Austen heroizes.

All of Austen's heroines manifest intelligence, wisdom, strong character, and caring hearts, and are brave enough to express their well thought-out opinions to men of superior social class or education. Caryn James points out that a heroine of Austen "is not afraid to be the smartest person in the room, yet after a series of misunderstandings gets the man of her dreams anyway" (1). This fact is not only admirable to the feminists and Janeites of the twenty-first century, but also society-challenging in Austen's day. In her article, "A disagreement between us: Gendered Argument in Austen's Novels," Barbara Laughlin Adler thoroughly details the argumentation strategies and gendered reasoning in Austen's novels, contrasting them with the accepted Manners of Austen's time. Adler refers to Barbara Horwitz and Naomi Jacobs who claim that "women were to avoid 'serious' topics such as politics, religion, and philosophy....When tempted to disagree with a man, a woman was to back away, resist speaking up, and remain positive, cheerful, and compliant" (cited in Adler 166-67). Adler draws from David Monaghan, as well, to explain how Austen, although respecting "civil behavior... understood that abstract rules of etiquette and manners are sometimes insufficient to deal with the complexities of human experience " (cited in Adler 174). When such is the case, "a woman may choose to defy restrictions, and allow herself to speak up with intelligence as well as courtesy, and to engage in serious disagreement with men" (Laughlin Adler 174-75). Though the women's arguments are still civilly spoken and femininely decorous, they demonstrate a "verbal rationality and eloquence" to rival the men's (175). Their civil boldness also expresses itself through the heroines' decisions to hold out for love in the face of possible poverty as unwed females (by not marrying without Reason).

Contemporary women may also identify more with Austen's plots and characters because their interests have shifted somewhat since the 1970's. Martine Voiret explains that in that decade women pursued independence over marriage and family; then, in the 1980's, women returned to being "happy nesters." In the 1990's, women were "torn by difficult compromises between a desire for independence and success, and a desire for companionship or marriage" (233). This feminine struggle is certainly alive in this decade, but it is now juxtaposed with the vibrant sexuality permeating society. Happily for women jaded by the over-sexed images and ideas about women in mass media and general society, the heroines in Austen's stories do not have to supplement their intelligence with sensuality; Voiret believes that the adaptations of Austen's novels in particular "address in a complex way women's desires to go beyond those stereotypes of every sign of intelligence or initiative [being] compensated by sexy behavior" (236). Thus, the combination of desire for independence and respect, desire for companionship and a lasting relationship, along with a possible disillusionment with the "freedom" of promiscuity, has perhaps readied the culture, specifically the women therein, to passionately embrace Austen's works and their adaptations and spin-offs.

Austen's focus on a small, interwoven community (reflected in the modern era by *The Republic of Pemberley* web-site community) also entices because of its contrast to the modern society in which almost all have the world at their fingertips with hand-held devices, while they keep those in physical proximity at arm's length. Zygmunt Bauman states, "Those who stay apart, mobiles allow to get in touch. Those who get in touch, mobiles permit to stay apart" (60). Now, not only do cell phone owners have immediate access to people through phone calls, they may perform an innumerable list of operations with their hand-held devices, including text messaging, e-mailing, checking and changing statuses on social networks like Facebook or Twitter, playing games, downloading infinite "apps" (applications), purchasing songs, surfing the Web, and obtaining instant sports results. The Qwasi News web site details the highlights of the CTIA Wireless Association's statistics, which reveal that "there are now more than 257 million data-capable devices in consumers' hands in the US" ("5 billion..." 1). Wireless subscribers are sending 250% more multimedia messages (MMS), like photos, than the year prior, as well (24.2 billion for the latter half of 2009) ("5 billion..." 1). The grandest increase in usage lies with text messaging. During the latter half of 2009, "more than 822 billion text messages [were] sent and received on carriers' networks...amounting to almost 5 billion messages per day at the end of the year" ("5 billion..." 1). The total for the entire year was 1.5 trillion text messages ("5 billion..." 1). And people are beginning to prefer text messaging over other forms of phone communication, including phone calls ("SMS preferred..." 1). Cell phone users do not use these features solely when alone with nothing better to do. It is commonly observable that users respond to a text message, or engage in a full text-message conversation, while engaged in conversation or other activity with someone physically present.

Bauman believes that this "virtual proximity," as he deems it, is detrimental to forming community and close relationships among members of society and families. He claims that this virtual proximity through cell phone usage (and Internet dating, 65) "renders human connections simultaneously more frequent and more shallow, more intense and more brief. Connections tend to be too shallow and brief to condense into bonds" (62). Bauman quotes Jonathan Rowe, who describes his experience in coffee shop during the high tech boom of the late 1990s. In Rowe's words,

> "I observed a scene play out there time and time again. Mom is nursing her mocha. The kids are picking at their muffins, feet dangling from their chairs. And there's Dad, pulled back slightly from the table, talking into his cell phone...It was supposed to be a 'communication revolution', and yet here, in the technological epicenter [of San Francisco], the members of this family were avoiding one another's eyes." (61)

Bauman adds that in only a couple of years, "Rowe would probably see four cell phones in operation around that table...Given enough time, the mobiles would train the eyes to look without seeing" (61). The situation, according to Michael Schluter and David Lee, as quoted by Bauman, occurs within families and homes, as well as without. They delineate a society wherein "we have stepped into our separate houses and closed the door, and then stepped into our separate rooms and closed the door. The home becomes a multi-purpose leisure centre where household members can live, as it were, separately side by side" (quoted in Bauman 64).

Although readers of Austen may not all involve themselves in constant virtual communication or interrupt real-life conversation with text messaging and Internet searching, they may feel the effects, even subconsciously, of this growing environment of virtual connection and personal disconnect. Austenland, in dynamic distinction, is a world wherein the players, principal and minor, interact with their voices in conversation and through their penmanship and composition of letters. They walk or ride in carriages through their communities or surrounding countryside; visit neighbors and family; participate in game nights, country dances, dinners, and balls; in short, people find numerous opportunities to intermingle and interrelate with those around them.

This era of hooking up without commitment, difficulty in finding a mate, peer pressure, gossip, and confusing lack of norms, combined with the twenty-first century's problems of noise pollution, technological saturation, and personal isolation provide a stark contrast with the world Jane Austen presents through her novels. She instead presents a "small and perfect world" (Thompson 21), a place "to live the exotic, if identifiable, fictions of domestic intimacy" (Pucci 154). Any problems characters experience are successfully managed by the end; truth and morality are upheld; consequences are meted out to those committing wrongs; and love and goodness victoriously conclude each tale. The men and women live in a historical society of well-defined male and female roles, an aspect some readers may find refreshing and stabilizing in today's world of blurred gender lines and shifting role-definitions. That is not to say that the characters never defy the boundaries, but they remain within the "bounds" of society with a relatively "rigid code of social rules," as Caryn James deems them. She adds, however, that despite the possible "repressive[ness]" of such a societal structure, to contemporary readers, "it can seem positively peaceful and stable, a respite from today's fraught, slippery world of quick hook-ups, divorce and family counseling." (1)

Further justifying Austen's place in canonical literature and in popular culture, Austen's novels do not only offer the pleasing aspects of marital commitment, financial stability, and clear gender roles and decorum, but also a satirical critique of parenting and education, idleness versus occupation, and social class and hierarchies. Her books are rich with wisdom, ironic wit, and heroes and heroines who manifest both, yet remain human with flaws in their characters and mistakes. She depicts a woman's world of her day and illustrates the lives of women who strive to do the best they can in their restrictive environments. Rather than succumbing to familial or financial pressures when choosing a husband, her heroines wait for fulfilling love and respectful companionship to come their way. As seen in the study of college students, women still struggle with societal pressures and an unsatisfying, male-driven framework for relationships. Whether true to reality or perceived as simply fairy tale material, Austen's stories and characters stretch beyond one's imagination and understanding and can touch one's emotions, dreams, and hopes. Today's fascination with Austen does not thus reflect a regression to a patriarchal structure, but more likely a need for renewed respect and romance in relationships, more balanced attitudes and practices regarding sex, and a deeper level of communication and commitment between the sexes (and among all members of society).

Claire Harman asks in the Preface in her book about the history of Austen's fame, "How did a young woman who was happy to limit her scope to "3 or 4 Families in a Country Village" conquer the world?" My answer to that question lies partly with the idea that Austen wrote of what she knew and made it funny, complex, insightful, and wise, thus inspiring, awakening, and engaging readers throughout generations. Jane Austen touches readers' desires for romance, commitment and respect in relationships, and a safe community wherein to talk, laugh, and love.

While the over-usage of the Internet and technology, at the expense of personal interaction, is a dangerous and isolating venture, Helena Fitzgerald, in her article, "Intimacy as Text; Twitter as Tongue," takes a more positive stance in regard to such communication. She believes that our online and digital communications hearken back to a day-and-age like Austen's, wherein letters are the primary tool for communication other than face-to-face conversation:

> Though our letters are not delivered by hand or horse-drawn carriage, our relationships once again live and die in the texts by which we barter with each other. The internet age unavoidably resembles the 19th century novel's idea of human intimacy as so many of us pour our passionate confessions into emails, messages or chat boxes." (1)

As those who visit the Austen-fan websites, post online, and access journal articles (JASNA.org) know, value may be found in the communal and relational possibilities of the virtual world, as long as the "real world" and those in proximity are not forgotten. Fitzgerald declares that "there's a Jane Austen-ish quality to online social life" and that "the written word gains unmatched power and inarguable primacy" (1). Thus, may readers use the Internet and technology to their benefit, but pair the reading of Austen's books, as well as web sites and virtual conversations, with a rooted connection to reality and lasting, face-to-face relationships.

Works Cited

Austen, Jane. *Mansfield Park*. 1814. Ed. Great Britain: Chancellor Press, 1985.

---. *Northanger Abbey*. 1818. Ed. Marilyn Butler. New York: Penguin Books, 2003.

---. *Pride and Prejudice*. 1813. Ed. Great Britain: Chancellor Press, 1985.

---. *Sense and Sensibility*. 1811. Ed. New York: Barnes & Noble, Inc., 1996.

Bauman, Zygmunt. *Liquid Love: On the Frailty of Human Bonds*. Malden, MA: Polity Press, 2010.

Blum, Virginia L. "*The Return to Repression: Filming the Nineteenth Century.*" *Jane Austen and Co.: Remaking the Past in Contemporary Culture*. In Pucci and Thompson 157-178.

Bogle, Kathleen A. *Hooking Up: Sex, Dating, and Relationships on Campus*. New York: New York University Press, 2008.

Daryl. "Re: Austen's Power: Jane addiction sweeps theaters, bookstores." USA Today. 23 August 2007. 7 May 2010.

<http://www.usatoday.com/life/books/news/2007-08-01-austen-frenzy_N.htm?loc=interstitialskip>.

Dobie, Madeleine. "*Gender and the Heritage Genre: Popular Feminism Turns to History.*" In Pucci and Thompson 247-259.

Ed in NM. "Re: Austen's Power: Jane addiction sweeps theaters, bookstores." *USA Today.* 23 August 2007. 7 May 2010. <http://www.usatoday.com/life/books/news/2007-08-01-austen-frenzy_N.htm?loc=interstitialskip>.

Fitzgerald, Helena. "Intimacy as Text; Twitter as Tongue." *The New Inquiry.* 4 August 2010. 14 October 2010. <http://thenewinquiry.com/post/903929008/intimacy-as-text-twitter-as-tongue>.

"5 Billion Text Messages sent/received each month in the US. Mobile…" *Qwasi News.* 23 March 2010. 7 May 2010. <http://www.qwasi.com/news/tag/text-message-statistics>.

Harman, Claire. *Jane's Fame: How Jane Austen Conquered the World.* New York: Henry Holt and Company, LLC, 2009.

Horwitz, Barbara. "*Women's Education During the Regency: Jane Austen's Quiet Rebellion.*" *Persuasions,* No. 16, Dec. 1994: 135-45.

Itzkoff, Dave. "Austen Meets Alien in 'Pride and Predator.'" *The New York Times.* 17 February 2009. 9 March 2009. <http://www.nytimes.com/2009/02/18/arts/18arts-AUSTENMEETSA_BRF.html?_r=1&ref=arts>.

James, Caryn. "Austen Powers: Making Jane Sexy." *The New York Times.* 29 July 2007. 6 May 2010. <http://www.nytimes.com/2007/07/29/movies/29jame.html?scp=1&sq=Making%20Jane%20Sexy&st=cse>.

Laughlin Adler, Barbara. "*A disagreement between us: Gendered Argument in Austen's Novels.*" *Persuasions: The Jane Austen Journal. 24* (2002): 164-76. Academic One File. Pacific University Oregon, Lib. 6 May 2010.

MacRoni. "Re: Austen's Power: Jane addiction sweeps theaters, bookstores." *USA Today.* 23 August, 2007.

August 2007. 7 May 2010. <http://www.usatoday.com/life/books/news/2007-08-01-austen-frenzy_N.htm?loc=interstitialskip>.

Memmott, Carol and Claudia Puig. "Austen's power: Jane addiction sweeps theaters, bookstores." *USA Today.* 23 August 2007. 7 May 2010. <http://www.usatoday.com/life/books/news/2007-08-01-austen-frenzy_N.htm?loc=interstitialskip>.

Pucci, Suzanne R. "*The Return Home.*" In Pucci and Thompson 133-155.

Pucci, Suzanne R., and James Thompson, eds. *Jane Austen and Co.: Remaking the Past in Contemporary Culture.* New York: State University of New York Press, 2003.

Republic of Pemberley, The. 2004-2009. 9 March 2009. <http://www.pemberley.com>.

Ross, Josephine. *Jane Austen's Guide to Good Manners: Compliments, Charades & Horrible Blunders.* New York: Bloomsbury USA, 2006.

"SMS Preferred Mode of Communication on Mobile." *Qwasi News.* 12 January 2010. 7 May 2010. <http://www.qwasi.com/news/tag/text-message-statistics>.

Sutherland, Kathryn. *Jane Austen's Textual Lives: from Aeschylus to Bollywood.* New York: Oxford University Press, 2005.

Thompson, James. *"How to Do Things with Austen."* In Pucci and Thompson 13-32.

Voiret, Martine. *"Books to Movies: Gender and Desire in Jane Austen's Adaptations."* In Pucci and Thompson 229-245.

Wolfe, Tom. *Hooking Up.* New York: Farrar, Straus, and Giroux, 2000.

Woolf, Virginia. *"Jane Austen." The Common Reader.* New York: Harcourt, Brace & World, Inc., 1953

Throw Out Your Passwords!

Pat McGregor

Don't get too excited, folks. It's definitely holiday time, but that doesn't mean we've solved world peace and the annoyance of passwords yet. Let's look over the issue, and review some of the research and news from the last few years. Although most news reports about passwords are full of dire warnings, there are ways to improve your password strength as well as making them easier to remember.

Problem: People hate remembering passwords.
Solution: People use simpler passwords so they can remember them.

Problem: People use simpler passwords so they can remember them, or they write them down. This makes the account vulnerable to attack.
Solution: IT departments force "strong" passwords and changing passwords regularly so that accounts are only vulnerable for a limited time.

> "Strong" password requirements[1,2,3] are generally something like this: "Passwords must be at least 8 characters. Use at least one Uppercase and one Lowercase letter, and either at least one number or one symbol such as @ # * $) + ~ ".

Problem: The more often a password changes and the stricter the requirements, the more people forget them and have to have them reset.
Solution: They call the help desk. Frequently.

Passwords are a subject that almost everyone is grumpy about: Users, Help Desk staff, IT staff, Information Security people. Hackers, on the other hand, love passwords, because many people use simple passwords, public information, don't change them regularly, or use dictionary words. Breaking a password and getting entry into an account is much easier than most other methods.

When Information Security folks say that the most commonly used passwords are simple, most users don't believe it, because they have a good password. But

---

[1] There is a great deal of math to demonstrate how complexity improves security in passwords. For a good article on the bit space and entropy around passwords, see this Gartner article by A. Allen. Although the article is older, the math is still valid, and has clear charts. http://www.indevis.de/dokumente/gartner_passwords_breakpoint.pdf.
[2] The original Internet Engineering Task Force research paper on randomness requirements/complexity for passwords: http://tools.ietf.org/html/rfc4086.
[3] A recent help article for users from Google, who are working very hard to improve their image in the security arena: "How Safe is Your Password." https://www.google.com/accounts/PasswordHelp.

some recent data on the most frequently used passwords[4] show that many people use simple passwords that leave their accounts vulnerable to attack:

1. 123456
2. 12345 (in 1998 this was the most commonly used password)
3. 123456789
4. Password
5. Iloveyou
6. Princess
7. Rockyou
8. 1234567
9. 12345678
10. abc123
11. Nicole
12. Daniel
13. Babygirl
14. Monkey
15. Jessica
16. Lovely
17. Michael
18. Ashley
19. 654321
20. Qwerty

How did Imperva, a hacker blocking software company, get the data to compile this list? About a year ago, a hacker broke into RockYou.com, an ISP, hijacked their entire password list, and shared them on the Internet.[5] This block of real-life data provided an excellent basis for security researchers to analyze what people actually do instead of what they say they do. Imperva's summary of the study shows how they got this great data:

> In December 2009, a major password breach occurred that led to the release of every RockYou.com user [password.] Further, the hacker posted to the Internet the full list[6] (with no other identifiable information). [At RockYou], passwords were stored in clear text in the database and were extracted through a SQL Injection vulnerability.[7] The data provides a unique glimpse into the way that users select passwords and an opportunity to evaluate the true strength of these as a security mechanism. In the past, password studies have focused mostly on

---

[4] Imperva, a California application security company, created a white paper on consumer worst practices regarding account security: http://www.imperva.com/docs/WP_Consumer_Password_Worst_Practices.pdf.
[5] Security Alert notice from the breached ISP. http://www.rockyou.com/help/securityMessage.php.
[6] One of the first press articles about the breach: "One Of The 32 Million With A RockYou Account? You May Want To Change All Your Passwords. Like Now." http://techcrunch.com/2009/12/14/rockyou-hacked/.
[7] Wikipedia's basic description of SQL injection with a bibliography of more technical sources: http://en.wikipedia.org/wiki/SQL_injection.

surveys.[8] Never before has there been such a high volume of real-world passwords to examine.

Passwords like this are easy to break because attackers use a "dictionary." Dictionary attacks take a password and check against every dictionary in every language the hackers can get their hands on, including lists such as the 32 million passwords in the RockYou breach. You can be sure that these top 20 lists, plus all the lists produced in the last 20 years, are among the first words checked. We've all been told that longer passwords are harder to hack. Are we paying attention? As part of their analysis, Imperva checked to see if users were at least using longer passwords, even if the passwords were not complex. Their results showed that the majority (~70%) were still too short.

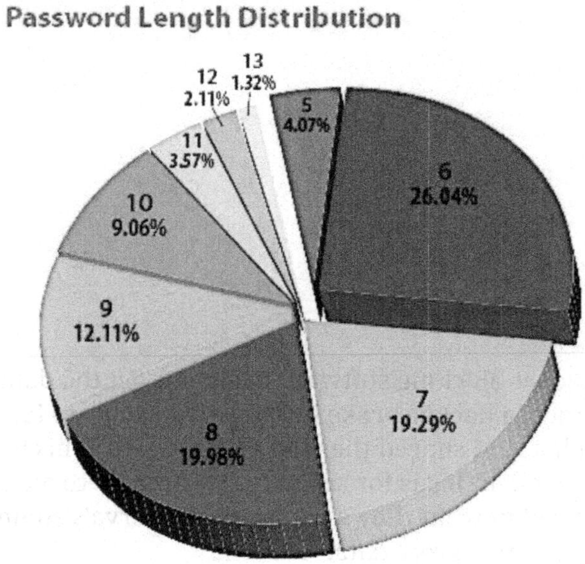

Image Source: Imperva Software, Jan. 2010.

Bad news for building passwords

Have you upgraded your computer — or your kid's computer — to have a high-end graphics card yet? Oops! We may be creating a new generation of supercomputers in the hands of hackers.

At Georgia Tech, researchers have been linking several high end graphics cards — most costing less than $200 — to create supercomputer-level capability on any desktop.

[8] Quest Software commissioned the Aberdeen Group to study authentication practices at 150+ organizations worldwide.http://www.quest.com/newsroom/news-releases-show.aspx?contentid=7986.

"We've been using a commonly available graphics processor to test the integrity of typical passwords of the kind in use here at Georgia Tech and many other places," said Richard Boyd, a senior research scientist at the Georgia Tech Research Institute (GTRI). "Right now we can confidently say that a seven-character password is hopelessly inadequate - and as GPU [graphics processing unit] power continues to go up every year, the threat will increase."[9]

Adding to that, sophisticated software for hacking passwords is available for free online.

What does that really mean to you? I confess, when I listen to people talking about "teraflops" or "billions of operations per second" my eyes glaze over. Let's look at this in something slightly easier to understand for those of us who are not mathematicians.

Let's say you have a 7- or 8-character password following the mixture above. Using a computer with several graphics cards linked together — or even just the kind of power it takes to show an HD movie on your home computer — the scientists in Georgia were able to crack passwords like that in an average of two hours. Five years ago, we were estimating that time as nine to fifteen weeks. Changing your password every 45 to 90 days was considered good enough to make the window of opportunity to crack it small enough.

But it isn't all bad news. Their model shows that a hacker with really good software and graphics cards might be able to try 1 trillion password combinations per second. In that event, it would take 180 years to crack an 11-character password, 17,134 years to crack one with 12-characters.[10] Statistically, of course, the odds are that the software might land on your password on the first try. But you are statistically more likely to win a state lottery than for that to happen. I can live with that.

Warning: Never, ever use any of the examples of good passwords in this or any other article. They will undoubtedly be put into hacker dictionaries immediately. Make up your own!

What now?

Try a *pass*PHRASE. Passphrases are strings of characters that appear random, but are more easily remembered because you made them up out of a sentence or other string of words that makes sense to you. Let's try one:

---

[9] Georgia Tech is using advanced high-end graphics boards to research the strength of passwords. http://www.gtri.gatech.edu/casestudy/Teraflop-Troubles-Power-Graphics-Processing-Units-GPUs-Password-Security-System.

[10] CNN article about the Georgia Tech research and password-breaking times. http://www.cnn.com/2010/TECH/innovation/08/20/super.passwords/index.html?hpt=T2.

Pick a line out of a song — let's say, "All I want for Christmas is my two front teeth"

Take the first letters of each word:

A I w f C i m t f t

I spaced these out so you can see what I'm doing. You should type them all in a row with no spaces.

That's ten characters, and mix of upper and lower case letters. Let's change some of those characters to numbers. Since one of the words in the song is "two," that's an obvious switch.

A I w f C i m 2 f t

Now, let's put in a symbol. The "at sign" @ has a letter A in it. Let's use it for the first character instead of "A."

@ I w f C i m 2 f t

And, just for the heck of it, to make twelve characters, let's add a couple of numbers on the end. Since Christmas is December 25th, let's add a 2 and a 5.

@ I w f C i m 2 f t 2 5

All together, with no spaces and a great mix of length, letters, numbers, and symbols, you have:

@IwfCim2ft25

which is a great password! These are sort of fun to make up, and you can use any sentence you're likely to remember. Such as:

"My dog Snooty is 34 inches long and has 6 puppies." That could come out to be:

Md$i34"lah6p

I substituted the dollar sign ($) for the S and the double quote " for inches.

One last thing: Stop "Master keying" your online accounts

Remember that the janitors or security officers in your office building have keys that unlock every door? Those are called "Master Keys," and it's important to make sure that only authorized people have them.

Don't give hackers the virtual Master Key to your important online accounts. Use different passphrases on different accounts.

The London Telegraph reports in November that close to 1.7 million residents in Great Britain use the same password on every site. The Telegraph cites a recent study by the insurance company CPPGroup that most people admit not only to using the same password, but that the password is an easy one (dog's name, birthday) and they share the password with their families and friends.

"The research reveals that nearly half (46 per cent) of Britons use the same password to login to their banking, shopping and social networking sites with a further 54 per cent confessing to using variations of the same password. And with the average person visiting 23 different sites each month that require a login they are an easy target for fraudsters."[11]

I know the advice to have a different password for every account sounds like a terrible burden. Security expert Bruce Schneier recommends using a different password and keeping them written down or in an online password safe.

> "Simply, people can no longer remember passwords good enough to reliably defend against dictionary attacks, and are much more secure if they choose a password too complicated to remember and then write it down. We're all good at securing small pieces of paper. I recommend that people write their passwords down on a small piece of paper, and keep it with their other valuable small pieces of paper: in their wallet."[12]

Schneier has also invented a password safe. Just as it sounds, a password safe is a program for Windows machines that keeps your passwords securely encrypted in one place. A single Safe Combination—just one thing to remember—unlocks them all. It uses Twofish encryption technology, which is an open source technology. Since it's invention in 1998, SourceForge, the developing company, claims there have been no documented cases of it being broken.

An alternate approach is to use different passwords for different classes of sites. You might use one fairly simple passwords for all the sites where you read the newspapers or do crossword puzzles — sites where no money is involved. An example might be "Xw0rds" . For shopping sites, you might use something else — a strong passphrase that reminds you of money or shopping. And a third kind for banking sites. While this is a cautious approach, you need to be accepting the risk that someone will get that password and use it.

Use a security blanket and install a deadbolt

If crime goes up in your neighborhood, many of us would change our locks or install a deadbolt lock for added protection. Internet risks go up all the time. At the very least, start using a passphrase instead of a password, which decreases

---

[11] The London Telegraph's article on master-keying: http://www.telegraph.co.uk/technology/news/6125081/Security-risk-as-people-use-same-password-on-all-websites.html.

[12] Bruce Schneier has been recommending this since 2005: http://www.schneier.com/blog/archives/2005/06/write_down_your.html, and information about Password Safe: http://www.schneier.com/passsafe.html.

the likelihood of it being broken significantly. Protect that password — especially if you using it as your master password — then consider what your next steps to protect yourself.

Online Gaming Communities: Strengths, Limitations, & Death

Jamaica King, Berglund Student Fellow

Introduction

At the beginning of this semester, I wondered what, exactly, to do with my life after I graduate. I will be graduating in May 2011, and up until the end of September, I had no clue about what I wanted to pursue as a career or merely what I was going to do after college. During Labor Day weekend this year, I attended the Penny Arcade Expo (PAX) in Seattle, Washington, which is an annual 3-day gaming convention for gaming enthusiasts.

Although an avid gamer for over 5 years, I was never compelled to attend any type of gaming event. But in December of 2009, I was introduced to a game called "League of Legends" created by Riot Games. Since then, I have spent considerable time playing the game as a recreation in my spare time. Through Twitter, I was able to keep in touch with other members of the League of Legends community, including the game developers and staff members. It was through Twitter that I discovered Riot Games would be attending the Penny Arcade Expo, hosting tournaments and other events and also giving out free loot – shirts, headsets, keyboards, unique in-game items, etc.

I was motivated to attend PAX because I planned to play with a friend and we had a decent chance of winning the tournament. In addition, I also wanted to go on a mini-vacation before senior year started rolling and to get free limited edition in-game items.

Unfortunately, the plans changed and I was unable to participate in the 64-team League of Legends 3v3 tournament, the Saturday of Labor Day weekend, due to the limited number of participating teams permitted. My friend, Nhat Nguyen, with whom I was supposed to compete, fortunately found a team berth the night before the tournament as a replacement player and was even luckier the next day, when his team placed first after seven long hours of competing.

During the day of the tournament, I was not allowed to enter the tournament room because only competitors were allowed entrance. Outside of the tournament room I found Volibar, one of the producers of the game. Several months prior to PAX, I communicated with Volibar using Twitter and was able to tell him that I would be attending PAX. While talking with Volibar, I was also able to meet other League of Legends fans, as well as other staff members.

Thanks to Volibar (his real name is Travis), I was able to enter the tournament area to spectate! Travis introduced me to almost all the Riot Games employees that attended PAX. He also introduced me to team Aggressive Reginald, the team who placed second. After a fast two and a half days of spectating, interacting, and talking with the Riot Games staff and League of Legend fans at PAX, I realized how passionate I am about the game.

I was ecstatic to meet other players and was comfortable around the employees. Whenever I spoke a word about League of Legends, I did so passionately. I felt like this is where I wanted to be; I want to be surrounded by this community – interacting and encouraging other League of Legends fans like myself.

So you are probably wondering what the above has to do with this article. Through attending all aspects of League of Legends at PAX, I discovered that I want to get involved in the League of Legends community. My goal after graduation is to work for Riot Games, specifically in their Community relations department (although I would not mind working for Customer Support Service). The Berglund Center for Internet Studies encouraged me to attend PAX and continues to support me by providing me an opportunity, as a Berglund Student Fellow, to engage in a year of research into a topic of interest dealing with the Internet. I immediately accepted the research opportunity, seeing it as a chance to gain experience that would benefit me in the future. The purpose of the research is to investigate what it means to be an online gaming community, to explore the aspects of online gaming communities, and to analyze the Internet as a communication medium. The overall goal is to become familiar with all aspects of online gaming communities to the level where I can analyze in depth a specific League of Legends' online community for my Fellowship presentation and article.

What is an Online Community?

With the evolution of technology and the development of the Internet, several disciplines gained interest in researching various aspects of online communities. Each of these disciplines defines online communities differently.[1] From a social perspective, Howard Rheingold[2] defines online communities as "social aggregations that emerge from the Net when enough people carry on public discussions long enough, with sufficient human feeling to form webs of personal relationships in cyberspace." From a business perspective, Hagel and Armstrong[3] describe online communities as "computer-mediated spaces where there is a potential for an integration of content and communication with an emphasis on member-generated content." This definition reveals the importance of members' involvement for the sustainability of a community. In social psychology, Blanchard[4] and Blanchard and Markus[5] characterize online communities as

---

[1] Iriberri, A. & Leroy, G. (2008). *A Life Cycle Perspective on Online Community Success*, ACM Computing Surveys, Forthcoming.
[2] Rheingold, H. (1993). *The Virtual Community. Homesteading in the Electronic Frontier*. Addison-Wesley Publishing Company, Reading, MA.
[3] Hagel, J.I. & Armstrong, A.G. (1997). *Net Gain: Expanding Markets through Virtual Communities*. Harvard Business School Press, Boston MA.
[4] Blanchard, A.L. (2004). *The Effects of dispersed virtual communities on face-to-face social capital. In Social Capital and Information Technology*, M. HUYSMAN and V. WULF, Eds. MIT Press, Cambridge, MA, 53-74.

"groups of people who interact primarily through computer-mediated communication and who identify with and have developed feelings of belonging and attachment to each other."

Although all the above definitions differ in some way, they all define some aspects of online communities. Lee, Vogel, and Limayem[6] combined nine of the most popular definitions to create their own. They stated that online communities are "cyberspace[s] supported by computer-based information technology, centered upon communication and interaction of participants to generate member-driven content, resulting in a relationship being built." Throughout this analysis, online gaming communities will adhere to Lee et al.'s definition.

What is an Online GAMING Community?

An online gaming community is a subset of a virtual or online community. It can even be more specific, like targeting a particular game audience (e.g., League of Legends community, World of Warcraft, Eve Online, etc.). Concurrently, there exist smaller gaming communities within each community associated with a specific game.

The formation of online gaming communities is the result of players coming together for a specific purpose. Online gaming communities provide an infrastructure where players can ask questions and find answers, obtain advice, receive support, seek recognition, and collaborate.[7] Cao, Glukhova, Klamma, and Renzel[8] identified these components of gaming communities:

- A shared goal or interest that provides the reason for being a part of the community: gamers' similar goals to play and win games;
- Shared activities between members, here between gamers;
- Intense interactions and strong ties, esp. important for online multiplayer games;
- Support between community members also for online multiplayer games;
- Access to shared resources such as gaming forums etc.;
- Social conventions, language, or protocols are associated with the context of gaming communities.

---

[5] Blanchard, A.L. & Markus, M.L. (2004). *The experiences "sense" of a virtual community: Characteristics and processes*. Data Base for Advances in Information Systems 35(1), 65-79.

[6] Lee, F.S.L., Vogel, D., & Limayem, M. (2003). Virtual community informatics: A review and research agenda. *Journal of Information Technology Theory and Application 5*(1), 47-61.

[7] Jive Software. (2006). Building a successful online community with Jive Forums. Portland, Oregon.

[8] Cao, Y., Glukhova, A., Klamma, R., & Renzel, D. (2009). A community success model for gaming communities. *Journal of Multimedia, 4*(2), 87-93.

Online gaming communities are more than member-driven content and interactions. Preece[9] proposed two important frameworks with key components (See Table 1).

Aspect	Components
Sociability	• Purpose • People • Policies
Usability	• Dialogue and social interaction support • Information design • Navigation • Access

Table 1 – Preece's community parameters

The sociability category contains elements involving interactions, the purpose that drives these interactions, and the rules to maintain and guide the community. On the other hand, usability focuses on the user interface and design of the community website. Because community members utilize computer-mediated communication (CMC), the usability aspect is crucial to ensure members can communicate easily and meaningfully.

Limitations and Weaknesses

Utilizing the Internet as a communication medium imposes limitations on online gaming communities. Content on the Internet is abundant, challenging the credibility of available information. Information shared within communities might not always be valid (i.e. rumors or errors). Without citation, members may be hesitant to listen or believe what others say. In communities, members with higher status and/or skill generally gain more respect than "no-namers" or people who do not communicate frequently.

Since online gaming communities are highly dependent on member participation, lack of involvement may lead to the death of the community. Iriberri and Leroy[10] created a table of factors associated with community death by concatenating ideas from several authors (See Table 2).

---

[9] Preece, J. (2000). *Online Communities: Designing Usability, Supporting Sociability*. Wiley, New York.
[10] Iriberri, A. & Leroy, G. (2008). *A Life Cycle Perspective on Online Community Success*, ACM Computing Surveys, Forthcoming.

Life Cycle Stage: Death		
Success Factor	**Community Type**	**Author**
Undersupply of content Poor participation Unorganized contribution Transient membership Members with weak ties Willingness to share information Lack of Anonymity Concerns of privacy and safety Shyness about public posting Time limitations	All	[Jarvenpaa and Knoll 1998] [Nonnecke and Preece 2001] [Iriberri 2005] [Zhang and Hiltz 2003] [Constant, Kiesler *et al.* 1994]

Table 2 – Determinants of Online Community Termination

All the factors affect each other. If one is lacking, this may be problematic for other factors. Poor participation result in an undersupply of content and vice versa. Shyness about public posting, willingness to share information, and transient membership are subsets of participation and may weaken ties between members. Concerns of privacy and safety and lack of anonymity are closely related and may prevent a member from contributing content or feedback to the community. Participation is crucial in sustaining a community, but specific to an online community, the communication medium (i.e., Internet, forum, etc.) is crucial for the existence of the community. Without a communication medium, members cannot communicate.

Benefits and Strengths

Despite the limitations, online gaming communities possess unique aspects that sustain the relationships among its members. Online gaming communities provide benefits (See Table 3) that can be categorized into two areas: social group benefits and technological benefits.

Benefits for Individuals
Information Exchange - Access to a wide variety of members, information, and experiences with whom to exchange information - Access to obscure or otherwise inaccessible information **Social Support** - Opportunity to build and maintain social ties with people already known offline or those met online - Opportunity to help and provide support to the group or to the larger community - Opportunity to offer and receive emotional support in a climate of trust, equality, and empathy - Opportunity to bond socially and generate social action **Time and Location Flexibility** - Flexible access to the community - Flexible time management - Spatial and temporal independence - Visibility beyond boundaries of local work or geographical community **Permanency** - The ability to think about and edit responses - The ability to store and retrieve messages - Access to research articles and hyperlinks within the community related to the focus of the community - The ability to establish permanent social presence through photographs, textual profiles, and archive message, and the ability to control with ease one's level of participation in the community.

Table 3 – Benefits of Online Communities for Individuals [Malooney-Krichmar and Preece 2005; Butler, Sproull *et al.* 2005; Johnson and Ambrose 2006; Preece 1998; 1999]

Social group benefits include the opportunity for members to have fun, develop relationships, exchange information, and to give and receive social and emotional support.[11] The technological benefits are similar to that of the positive qualities of the Internet as a communication medium. Online communities operate 24/7 and are available for access at any time (assuming internet and a computer are available). Because the online communities are housed via the Internet, members are able to interact and communicate with other members who are geographically distant. Members can interact both asynchronously and synchronously.[12] Using hypertext links, allows more information to be shared, but not necessarily elicit content overload. Interactivity online allows for members to communicate via multimedia including voice/audio applications,

[11] Ridings, C.M. & Gefen, D. (2004). Virtual Community attraction: Why people hang out online. *Journal of Computer Mediated Communication 10* (1).
[12] Iriberri, A. & Leroy, G. (2008). *A Life Cycle Perspective on Online Community Success*, ACM Computing Surveys, Forthcoming.

video, group chat, games, etc. Conversations online are not always fleeting (compared to voice). When something is said online, there is a way to save or maintain that information (screenshots, permanent storage facilities, etc). Anonymity on the Internet encourages freedom and self-expression while maintaining a member's privacy and security.[13]

Conclusion

Although online gaming communities possess limitations, they still contain unique elements that allow for the creation and maintenance of successful and lasting communities along with strong relationships among members. Because an online gaming community is such a broad concept, I specifically focused on the benefits individuals can attain. But these communities also benefit businesses; in that it helps them make decisions based on what their consumers want and demand. Online gaming communities are more than a place to hangout. It can also be a useful tool for improving a game or aiding in customer support services.

References

Butler, B., Sproull, L., Kiesler, S., & Kraut, R.E. (2005). Community effort in online groups: Who does the work and why? In *Leadership at a Distance*, S. Weisband and L. Atwater Eds. Lawrence Erlbaum Associates Inc, Mahwah, NJ.

Constant, D., Kiesler, S. & Sproull, L. (1994). What's mine is ours, or is it? A study of attitudes about information sharing. *Information Systems Journal 14*.
Jarvenpaa, S.L. & Knoll, K. (1998). Is anybody out there? Antecedents of trust in global virtual teams. *Journal of Management Information Systems 14*, 29-65.

Johnson, J. & Ambrose, P.J. (2006). Neo-tribes: The power and potential of online communities in health care. *Communications of the ACM 49*(1), 107-113.

Maloney-Krichmar, D. & Preece, J. (2005). A multilevel analysis of sociability, usability, and community dynamics in an online health community. *ACM Transactions on Computer-Human Interaction 12*(2), 201-232.

Preece, J. (1998). Emphatic communities: Reaching out across the web.*Interactions* 2, 32-43.

Preece, J. (1999). Emphatic communities: Balancing emotional and factual communication. *Interacting with Computers 12*, 63-77.

---

[13] Panteli, N. (2009). *Virtual social networks: a new dimension for virtuality research.*

Sharif Mowlabocus' *Gaydar Culture. Gay Men, Technology and Embodiment in the Digital Age*

Review by Jeffrey Barlow

Dr. Sharif Mowlabocus' work *Gaydar Culture* shows us the transformative impact of the Internet upon a very particular minority culture, and in doing so teaches us a great deal, not only about that culture, but about the Internet itself. The Internet has enabled many minority communities to come together in a context in which they are, often for the first time, in a majority.

The culture the author discusses is gay urban male culture, largely, though not entirely, as represented in England. This topic, of course, might alienate some potential readers. If such readers turn away, however, they will fail to understand a unique and substantial impact of the Internet which empowers many minority groups, not only gays.

Dr. Mowlabocus argues that gay culture has always, of necessity, been a virtual culture in that it could not exist permanently in any particular physical space, but was created and recreated temporarily in what was always a "heteronormative" environment. In such an environment, heterosexual values and practices are the norm and any deviation from them, particularly homosexual ones, was long illegal and punished with horrific sanctions, including even death.

The Internet now offers the opportunity for minority groups to create virtual spaces in which their values are considered normative. Consequently, within the homonormative spaces of the Internet, gay culture has changed greatly.

The survey of gay history in England, with which the work opens, is, in and of itself, very useful background, but the author's analysis truly begins with the last quarter of the 20th century. At that time, a new and public gay identity began to emerge. The immediate stimulus for this movement, the author believes, was the feminist movement, and the parallel creation of gay liberation organizations, particularly the Gay Liberation Front.[1] Following that development, gay culture became increasingly "visible" and could build a public identity.

The political efforts of gay organizations, as well as wider cultural changes, also brought about changes to British law. Urban enclaves, which had been largely concealed homosexual centers, now became public.

---

[1] The author argues that while feminism was key to the development of the movement, when some feminist leaders, particularly Dworkin and MacKinnon, began to focus upon heterosexual male pornography as inherently violent toward women, they brought pressure on gay male pornography as well. In the gay male culture, pornography literally embodied gay culture, and the gay males, under new pressure for censorship, broke with feminism in general.

The almost simultaneous impact of AIDS contributed to the rise of a gay press because the English and, particularly, the American government and media establishments were long reluctant to even discuss the disease. The Internet naturally facilitated the creation of additional spaces in which a new identity could develop. It is at this point that the international homosexual culture begins to self-identify with the term "gay".

One of the many ironies of this new and more open identity was that gay culture—urban and relatively wealthy—quickly became a very attractive niche for advertisers. The author believes that gay culture is now defined by its consumption patterns as well as by its sexual preferences.

The author bases his analysis largely in the materials now available in the gay press, and on gay Internet sites and other digitized modes of communication. Mowlabocus, as a gay male, has also had ready access to a wide range of interview subjects and makes excellent use of their broad perspectives.

It is Dr. Mowlabocus' perspective that gay identity is now largely a cyber one—the term "cybercarnality" is frequently used here. Important elements of gay culture are carried by and, in turn, inflected by the Internet and other forms of digital communications. There are hundreds if not thousands of sites where gay males can now communicate, not only locally but also internationally. Many of these are highly specialized in their focus. Some are used for searching out dating relationships, analogous to heterosexual equivalents. Others serve to bring together those desiring quick anonymous sex—sometimes involving particular practices—in local environments such as a university district.

The author focuses chapter by chapter upon the impact of digital communications upon gay sub-cultures, sometimes defined by specific sexual practices, other times by attitudes toward AIDS, or by gay identities within local historical and cultural contexts. One of his central arguments is that, overall, a sort of homogenization of gay culture is occurring as a result of enhanced communications. This culture is, in the minds of many gays, being driven increasingly toward a sort of gay culture analogous to heterosexual culture—the notions of constancy in relationships, of legal protections within circumscribed boundaries, of "safe" sexual practices, of culture defined by consumption, and of a sort of apolitical approach to the culture itself are all becoming normative.

Each of these elements, on the other hand, is also producing a corresponding backlash, both in the hetero- and homosexual communities. Each such group then goes to the Internet to argue in opposition to such changes.

This work is not without its problems. It is quite expensive ($99.95 at Amazon) and probably best secured from a very good library. Clearly it will not be welcome in many public or middle school libraries, unfortunately. While the author's strict scholarly attention to previous theory and bibliography will make the work very valuable to those wishing to undertake additional research, it will also make the work less attractive to wider audiences in many cases.

My own relative unfamiliarity with the cultures which *Gaydar* analyzes rendered this a very dense read. The author is extremely thorough, putting English gay culture into a long-term historical perspective while embedding his arguments into both the scholarly bibliography of the field and his own research into the widely varying community groups which together make up the culture.[2] The methodology is that of Media/Cultural Studies, with a sort of participant-observer Anthropological slant to it. The vocabulary is largely that of post-modernism, though the work is far clearer than is the norm in such studies.

Neither is the work, as thorough as it is, inclusive. The author repeatedly reminds the reader that it is largely centered on gay urban culture, that there are some class issues as well since that sub-culture tends to be relatively comfortable. Further, it deals primarily with England, and secondarily with the United States. Its coverage is restricted almost entirely to Western and urban cultures. It is probable that the Internet has had equivalent impacts on rural and non-Western gay cultures as well, but that work will be left to other researchers.

On the whole, however, we think this an important contribution to Media Studies, and obviously to Gay Studies as well. Any reasonably open reader will find it extremely informative on both counts. Anyone with a serious interest in the impact of the Internet should also read it, and anyone with a gay friend or family member will find it offers many insights into a culture probably otherwise closed to them.

---

[2] Dr. Mowlabocus holds an M.A. in Sexual Dissidence and Cultural Change, and a Ph.D. in Media and Cultural Studies, both from the University of Sussex, England, where he now lectures.

J.D. Robb's *Fantasy in Death*

Review by IProfess, Elven Druid, Zuljin, Azeroth

Editor's note: This piece was written for Interface by IProfess, a purported avatar or 'Toon from the largest of the on-line role-playing games, the World of Warcraft. We will be happy to take questions for him, her, or it at Berglund.

IProfess begins:

Gentle Reader, I trip the keyboard fantastic one more time in this venue to review a truly interesting book, J.D. Robb's *Fantasy in Death*.[1] Interestingly, it is classified as a fiction book as the author, J.D. Robb, is one of the most popular authors of that literary category in the English-speaking portion of the so-called "Real World" (TRW) .She is also known as Nora Roberts, under which name she is a best-selling author of romances or "bodice rippers".

Fantasy in Death is set in the earth year 2060 and the protagonist, Eve Dallas, is a female detective in a New York police unit that specializes in electronic crime. Her partner/lover/bf is a zillionaire—note, however, that in 2060 a zillion does not buy what it used to!—who, among other industries, dominates electronic game design. This gives Eve unlimited funds, futuristic electronic resources, and periodic opportunities to have her bodice ripped.

Despite its fanciful (to denizens of TRW) setting the book is well worth a reader's attention, providing, of course, that said reader likes this sort of thing. Essentially the book is a well-written police procedural and the characters are likeable and clever. The plot is rather intricate with regard to technology and the setting amusingly unobtrusive, given that it is placed in the distant future.

Robert's 2060 seems rather like The Real World's 2010, though rather less down-at-the-heels insofar as at least New York is concerned, illustrating the author's sunny optimism. Despite this distant setting, the reader easily gets caught up in plot or character development; then, suddenly, one of the latter straps on his or her magic gliding slippers and goes sliding over hundreds of yards of something or other faster than one can read about it. There are also periodic reminders that mankind—or somethingkind, some of the characters are 'droids, so independent as to be under suspicion of the crime—has colonized

---

[1] See; most recently, "Naked in the World of Warcraft" at http://bcis.pacificu.edu/journal/article.php?id=671. Earlier works include "The Tales of Azeroth" and "Toons and Terrorism" and, "Protecting Human Children in the World of Warcraft," at http://bcis.pacificu.edu/journal/2009/04/article.php?id=60. See, too, my other book reviews; the first of R. V. Kelly 2's *Massively Multiplayer Online Role-Playing Games*, followed by Edward Castronova's work, *Synthetic Worlds, The Business and Culture of Online Games*, and most recently: Hilde G. Corneliussen and Jill Walker Rettberg, (editors,) *Digital Culture, Play, and Identity: A World of Warcraft Reader* at: http://bcis.pacificu.edu/journal/2009/01/article.php?id=28.

other planets, though the inference is that these are usually better places to stash criminals than to visit.

Despite the occasional blasts from the future, however, the book avoids most of the traps and cul-de-sacs of sci-fi lit—bogging down in technology and setting—and keeps our minds firmly fixed on plot and character. By page 50 or so I had quite ceased goggling at the material culture and was rooting for Eve to solve that crime!

And it is, of course, the nature of the crime that interests me as a 'Toon. An übergeek is murdered while playing a game which his firm is preparing to bring to market, and we, the readers, know that he was killed in-game by a 'Toon.

To me, of course, this seems unremarkable. If anything, I am usually perplexed in such cases—increasingly frequent btw—that it has taken said 'Toon so long to turn on his lame-brained "creator". But Eve and company are not quite ready for this revelation and so we are treated to a careful development of how the technology was produced and just precisely what it was, in highly technical terms.

Amazingly, the descriptions are as smoothly done as is the plot and the material culture. There is, of course, a holoroom suited for immersive gaming, with great surround sound, excellent holographic projectors, etc., the sort of thing that the American pop-tart digital culture magazine Wired salivates over endlessly, and sandwiches between its hopelessly illegible adverts when its declining revenues permits the editors to insert some actual content![2]

The description of the game, as given by one of the deceased's four partners—also, predictably, the four most likely suspects, this being a novel firmly set within a graspingly materialist context—goes like this:

> "The program reads you," Benny went on. "Your pulse rate, your BP, your body temp. Just like a medi-unit. It tailors the challenges to your specific physicality. It combines the sensations of top-flight VR with the reality-based imagery of high-end holo. Fight the dragon to save the princess? You'll feel the heat, the weight of the sword. Slay the dragon and the princess is grateful. You'll ah...feel that, too. The full experience." (p. 33)

Fortunately for crime solving, Eve's bf is also working on a similar program so he is able to explain to us that there are illegal or carefully licensed technologies that would permit such effects. Those technologies are restricted to off-world military use, Saint Philip K. Dick would be glad to know—there was a 'Toon for you! But I digress...these enable the game, interacting with the nervous system, to inflict real wounds—digital stigmata—to game players. Our protagonists, of course, eventually must enter the game world to catch the murderer.

---

[2] As for me, I think the holoroom is going to be leapfrogged in favor of three-dimensional viewing glasses as soon as mankind is ready for them.

The in-game portions of the work are very dramatic and realistic, quite like the gaming worlds themselves. The realism is not surprising, as the carefully attentive readers have spotted in the foreshadowing in the second sentence in my introduction above. (See how easy it is to practice Lit'rary Analysis!) Obviously this work is not fiction! It is a cautious exploration of the passages between the Virtual Worlds and the sad shadow in which I now write and you read, The Real World.

J.D. is, like myself, a 'Toon, perhaps also crossed over from Azeroth, perhaps from one of the many sci-fi themed multi-player role-playing games. I say this not only because of her split identity, but also because of her incredibly prolific output—she has dozens and dozens of books out, and only began writing in 1993. It is obvious that she is writing in several dimensions at once, a feat easily possible with the latest goblin technology from the *World of Warcraft*.[3]

At the conclusion of Fantasy in Death the reader will be happily satisfied. For my part, I was amused for several hours and got to see a masterful crossover 'Toon toying deftly with the differences between TRW and the Gaming Worlds, and all within an explanatory complex which reassures TRW audience, "Hey, things are alright." The author has a very good sense of humor and periodically gives a broad wink to the many 'Toons in her audience.

Truly, J. D. Robb is a crossover writer in almost every possible sense. Fantasy in Death is currently on every mass-market paperback bookrack you see, and it would make a great gift for any gamer or 'Toon on your holiday gift-transacting list.

---

[3] I must wonder how J.D. gets paid for her voluminous works, given the labyrinthine legal system that, according to Editor Barlow, keeps the Berglund Center from paying me for my work! Doubtless it is just a matter of time until the crazed newly elected U.S. Congress, packed with Orcs and Goblins led by the notorious and admittedly highly sensual Blood Elf Sarah the Impaler, turns its attention to rounding up illegal immigrants like myself from the Virtual Worlds.

Peaceful Evolution in China and the World Wide Web: Part III, China's Emerging Leadership

Editorial by Jeffrey Barlow

Introduction

While this editorial is meant to stand alone, two related ones have preceded it.[1] The last of those concluded:

> "Political systems, to be stable, must reflect history and culture in both their forms and functions. The American and the Chinese systems differ markedly, especially in form, but it is difficult to claim that the multiparty system is superior to a one-party system in which factions may be so prominent as to be recognizably consistent in membership and policy inclinations. Chinese history and culture is capable of producing a system which is democratic in function, is doing so at the present, and will inevitably continue do so under the impact of the Internet."[2]

At that time, more than a year ago, this assertion was largely an editorial opinion. However, evidence is accumulating to support this position.[3] In addition, the nature of the new evidence---details of the emerging leadership in the Chinese political system---tells us a great deal more about the possibilities for Chinese democracy, and about the potential impact of the Internet in shaping those changes.

China's Fifth Generation Leadership Emerges

Leadership in China is currently passing to a new generation of leaders, usually termed the "Fifth Generation."[4] Barring disruptive changes, this group will be

---

[1] Jeffrey Barlow, "Peaceful Evolution in China and the World Wide Web: Part I, Two Democracies?" at: http://bcis.pacificu.edu/journal/article.php?id=98 and Jeffrey Barlow, "Peaceful Evolution in China and the World Wide Web: Part II, Factionalism and Democracy" at: http://bcis.pacificu.edu/journal/article.php?id=108.

[2] "Peaceful Evolution in China and the World Wide Web: Part II, Factionalism and Democracy" at: http://bcis.pacificu.edu/journal/article.php?id=108.

[3] Cheng Li, "China's Fifth Generation: Is Diversity a Source of Strength or Weakness?" http://www.nbr.org/publications/element.aspx?id=147 This article, while published in 2008, has achieved recent significance because current indications of leadership changes forthcoming in China have proven the author's perspective to be very accurate indeed. Any social science author who manages to be predictive in future changes (especially those in China!) deserves a great deal of respect and attention. The PDF of this article, which has served as the major source of my argument in this editorial, was downloadable in PDF form at the above site through the end of November.

[4] The first four generations and their leaders include: Mao Zedong in the First Generation, Deng Xiaoping in the Second, Jiang Zemin in the Third, and Hu Jintao in the Fourth.

confirmed in 2012, when the 18th National Congress of the Chinese Communist Party (NCCPC)---which normally meets every five years---will convene. It is at this meeting that the Central Committee of the Communist Party of China (CPC) will be named, and it is in this group that most high-level leaders will be found.[5]

The Fifth Generation is in large part an age cohort.[6] To rise to the top level of the CPC now requires a long process of working through a number of previous posts. As a result, the route to power is fairly clear, though there are, of course, frequent exceptions, as some are more talented, harder working, or better connected than others. But most of the new leaders selected in 2012 will have been born during the 1950's.

This means that the historical experience of the top leadership will have been quite similar as the changes in China from the 1950's period forward affected virtually everybody, and certainly all of those who were likely to become noted political figures. This commonality of experience is relatively new for Chinese leaders.

In the first several leadership generations, (beginning with those, like Mao Zedong, born in the late 19th century) it was possible to rise suddenly, often from nowhere, as the outgoing leaders simply appointed incoming ones by fiat. From Deng Xiaoping's leadership forward, however, power transitions have been far less dependent upon charismatic leaders and more based upon consistent service to the Party and the government of China. The process has become increasingly bureaucratized.[7]

Factions and the Fifth Generation

Despite commonalities of experience, however, Chinese leadership is often factionalized. Factions are doubtless endemic to politics, regardless of the system. Within the U. S. system for example, we recognize among the dominant Republican and Democratic parties such groups as members of The Tea Party, The Black Caucus, Blue Dog Democrats, Log Cabin Republicans, regional interest groups and many others. If we move outside the parties themselves, we can identify the Christian Right, Paleoconservatives, Neoconservatives, Progressives, Labor, and yet others.

---

[5] Not all leaders in China are Party members—an issue discussed in Part IV of this piece—but most of them are, and all of the very top ones are.

[6] They were born according to the general definition, sometime during the 1950's.

[7] Deng Xiaoping, 邓小平, b 1904, became dominant—often from behind the scenes—from 1976 forward to his death in 1997) There is very detailed and well-documented information to be found at: http://en.wikipedia.org/wiki/Deng_Xiaoping#Re-emergence Deng is a transitional figure in several regards. He was as capable as was Mao of simply cashiering leaders who fell out of favor, though Deng was much more careful to maintain a fig leaf of legality. For a fascinating though itself highly politicized work which gives insight into the process whereby Deng directly interfered in succession, see Zhao Ziyang, Adi Ignatius, Bao Pu, and Renee Chiang, *Prisoner of the State: The Secret Journal of Chinese Premier Zhao Ziyang*. London: Simon & Schuster UK Ltd, 2009.

China is no different. Even during the period of extreme totalitarianism under Mao we recognized within the Communist Party regional cliques or factions.[8] Among them were the Shanghai and Siquan cliques, others following a particular charismatic leader like Mao himself, his arch-rival Liu Shaoqi, or his strong supporter Zhou Enlai. There were many other local and regional cliques as well of course.

As the turnover in leadership groups has become less dramatic and more predictable, factions have become perhaps even more important. The usual way of defining factional membership has been the recognition that a given individual came up through some group or local organization that seemed cohesive, often because the ultimate leader of the group, although not as charismatic as the Mao or Deng models, nonetheless brought others along in his wake. Factions, in short, have leaders, and part of the political process entails mutual support around what may be both self-interest and common programmatic goals---not unlike Western political parties.

Since the last meeting of the National Party Congress in 2007,[9] two factions have become increasingly clear, the Tuanpai, and the Princelings. A third which was earlier very influential, the Shanghai Clique, has seemingly lost influence and is generally no longer regarded as significant.

The Tuanpai Faction

The Tuanpai[10] is a group which had emerged as clearly recognizable and influential by the 1980's. It is composed largely of those who came up politically

---

[8] We prefer the word faction rather than clique here. The terms "faction" and "clique" are generally presented as interchangeable in English, http://dictionary.reference.com/browse/faction A Chinese reading also appears to make no real distinction. Faction is usually translated as immediately below; from http://www.mandarintools.com/cgi-bin/wordlook.pl?word=faction&searchtype=chinese&where=whole&audio=on)
幫派　帮派　bāng pài = faction
派 pài = clique; school; group; faction; to dispatch
陣營 = zhèn yíng; group of people; camp; faction The key terms here in my experience when discussing this topic are bang (group or sect), pai, faction and in older historical period perhaps ying or camp. Clique can also be translated as pai 派 (http://www.mandarintools.com/cgi-bin/wordlook.pl?word=clique&searchtype=chinese&where=whole&audio=on)

[9] For discussions of factions in the 16th NPC see: http://www.wilsoncenter.org/index.cfm?fuseaction=events.event_summary&event_id=1885 for the 17th see: A significant research tool for understanding factions is the China Vitae database, found at: http://www.chinavitae.org/aboutus.php

[10] Tuanpai 团派 means "League Faction," meaning in this case a group based in earlier membership in the Chinese Youth League, one of the entry-level groups for Party membership. There is a good article, based on Cheng Li's work which we also follow here, at: http://en.wikipedia.org/wiki/Tuanpai. Although this is a Wikipedia entry, it presents a good synopsis.

through the mass organization, the Chinese Youth League (共青团).[11] The League is an old organization, going back to the pre-revolutionary period and has always been closely tied to the CPC. Almost all graduating high school students belong to it---the age bracket for membership is 18-24--- and it is a sort of entry-level for later membership in the CPC, which is much more exclusive. Service in or guided by the Youth League is probably now the most common channel for those working to be invited to join the CPC. The group essentially does mass organizational work with even younger people and with high school and college age youth.

The first recent leader clearly associated with the Youth League was Hu Yaobang, who was CPC party chairman from 1981-1982, and CPC General Secretary for 1982-1987, following the abolition of the Chairmanship (a post closely associated with Mao Zedong) as a position. The second Tuanpai leader is Hu Jintao who has been President since 2003.

The Tuanpai might be said to be the most broadly representative of Chinese factions in that the Youth League is the largest of the mass organizations which combine to shape the CPC. It is also the organization with the closest ties to grass roots groups as it is present at every level where large numbers of youth are found, including all educational institutions, reaching right down to the lower grades if we count the groups of younger students organized by the League. It is also found among peasant and labor organizations, among women's and other special interest groups.

It is significant that both Hu Yaobang and Hu Jintao are each associated with the Tuanpai and closely associated with reform in China. It was Hu Yaobang who led the way in reversing the extremist purges of the Cultural Revolution. He was also closely associated with pressures for reform in the late Deng years, and in 1987 removed from power by Deng, presumably for Hu's tolerance of dissent.[12] His death is widely held to have been one of the triggers for the student movement of the late 80's which contributed in large part to the Tiananmen Incident two years later.[13]

Hu Jintao is also associated with reform pressures. In an important speech in 2007 Hu mentioned the Chinese term which we translate as democracy, minzhu

---

[11] http://en.wikipedia.org/wiki/Communist_Youth_League_of_China This article is little more than a description of the organization based on CPC Chinese English language sources, but adequate for our descriptive purposes here.

[12] Here I am following the English language edition of Zhao Ziyang's "secret journal" Prisoner of the State. (London: Simon and Schuster, 2009). Zhao was the reform leader's whose fate became closely intertwined with the Tiananmen Incident, which, in my view, were closely tied to factional politics at the time. The thumbnail sketches of contemporary leaders in the appendix to the work very much reflect the analysis of the Zhao-led faction, which is in turn closely tied to the Hu Yaobang group, though not completely congruent with the Tuanpai faction itself.

[13] Zhao, passim.

(民主) more than sixty times.[14] It is important to realize, though, that the Chinese concept of democracy is far different than the Western one, and anyone attempting to measure Chinese progress toward Chinese style democracy and condemning it because it is not like American democracy will both be disappointed, and miss the important changes occurring in China.[15]

The Princelings Faction

The group often known as the Princelings[16] is far different than the Tuanpai and inherently less well organized. They are made up of the children of previously important leaders. Their base is quite different from the Tuanpai's, but their factional identity is well grounded in Chinese history and culture. Family, in traditional China, was pretty much everything. It is the root of Confucian values, the model for the state, and the single most important social organization in China. To be descended even remotely from a powerful ancestor continues to be an advantage, and to be the son, daughter, or grandchild of a recently powerful individual, even powerful because a member of the Communist Party, is very important.

The Princelings are very often criticized because their frequent quick progress through the Chinese political system is very much contrary to CPC doctrine which places a strong emphasis on "Serving the People" as a justification for power, and because it is clear that they often have special privileges denied to others. The title of this group of similar individuals in Chinese is Taizi Dang (太子党) meaning most basically "Party of the Crown Princes," which has inescapable overtones of imperial politics and royal successions.

For these individuals to begin to function openly as a faction would, under current or foreseeable conditions in China, be disastrous.[17] The Internet has

---

[14] http://english.peopledaily.com.cn/90001/90776/6283187.html This is a CPC controlled newspaper, the official Chinese daily, and the fact that this was so widely reported there was very important.

[15] For a close analysis of this issue see Jeffrey Barlow, "Peaceful Evolution in China and the World Wide Web: Part I, Two Democracies?" at: http://bcis.pacificu.edu/journal/article.php?id=98.

[16] For an analysis of the Princeling party (太子党) see http://en.wikipedia.org/wiki/Crown_Prince_Party, This does not reference Cheng Li's important work and incorporates additional materials in which I have less confidence. It argues that the Princelings should not be viewed as a faction or a clique, but simply as a group which has benefited from nepotism as they are related to powerful members of the Party or the government.

[17] For recent discussions over princeling-like factions leading to corruption, see first information on Wu Renbao at: http://books.google.com/books?id=24P3M4hrpWwC&pg=PA197&lpg=PA197&dq=Wu+Renbao+wiki+]&source=bl&ots=ywmewjno8R&sig=CiQcouC9jc9tFV79JoGOjf5dXjY&hl=en&ei=GSTkTK-0IIv0tgOnxsxm&sa=X&oi=book_result&ct=result&resnum=1&sqi=2&ved=0CBMQ6AEwAA#v=onepage&q=Wu%20Renbao%20wiki%20]&f=false. Then go to the Chinese English language blog China Smack at: http://www.chinasmack.com/2010/stories/chinese-village-constructing-worlds-15th-tallest-building.html It will be necessary to read down

enabled a very robust and active channel for political comment in China, and any hint of special privilege, let alone signs of a privileged cabal, would lead to widespread criticism and fuel implications of corruption. Corruption is the most damaging charge that can be leveled at Chinese leaders, and the most common weapon employed by opposing factions.

However, it is still a recognized political strategy for the ambitious to seek the support of currently or formerly powerful leaders by quickly promoting their sons or daughters. As a result, the idea that they do represent a faction or at least a community of interest is widespread in China.[18]

There is another emergent group which is sometimes lumped in with the political princelings: the newly wealthy and their progeny. The significance of this group has grown considerably in recent decades and they too are associated in the popular mind with the rigid class-bound society of the old China. The most recent issue (October 10, 2010) of The Huren Report, the magazine and website which follows those of "high worth", was founded in China by a Westerner and is now published in both Chinese and English,[19] "shows that there are 875,000 people with more than RMB 10 million (EUR 1.1million/ USD 1.47million) in China today, an increase of 6.1% from last year."[20]

With the above framework we can start to better understand the changes occurring in China. There are two critical questions to be asked with regard to the upcoming changes. The first of these is who will replace Hu Jintao, currently General Secretary of the CP, and President, often known as the "Paramount Leader." The second important question is who will replace Wen Jiabao, Premier of the State Council and Head of State, and in each case what the antecedents of the replacements may be.[21]

---

through the comments to understand how volatile an issue the implication of Princeling ties and corruption can be.

[18] It is probably worth noting that the notion of restoration of imperial rule, however unlikely, is a recurrent trope in even modern Chinese politics. The first Chinese Republic, associated with the Chinese Revolution of 1912 ended with a tragicomic attempt by the warlord Yuan Shikai, who earlier had seized the Presidency, to create a new dynasty in 1916. The purported attempt by Mao's former right-hand man Lin Biao to assassinate Mao in 1971 was charged by the state to have been ultimately a coup attempt intended to create a new imperial dynasty.

[19] http://www.hurun.net/indexen.aspx.

[20] By comparison, "The number of U.S. households with a net worth of $1 million or more, not including primary residence (NIPR), grew 16% to 7.8 million in 2009, up from 6.7 million the year before, according to "Affluent Market Insights 2010," a new report released today by Spectrem Group (www.spectrem.com). That follows a 27% decline in the millionaire population in 2008. Similarly, the number of Ultra High Net Worth households, those with a net worth of $5 million or more (NIPR), advanced 17% to 980,000 in 2009." See: http://www.spectrem.com/custom.aspx?id=115 Here, as elsewhere, China has a great deal of catching up to do.

[21] The distribution of power in China is split between Party and governmental posts. This is very confusing and is historically intended to be. The imperial government for centuries followed a pattern of splitting power at even local levels, usually between officials drawn from the Civil Service and those appointed to military posts by the central government. This prevented local usurpation of power, or at least made it more

Of the two emerging successors, one, Li Keqiang, is from the Tuanpai Faction, and the other, Xi Jinping, is widely regarded as a leader of the Princelings. In part IV of this editorial series we will clarify the consequences of these ties, and of the impact of the Internet.

---

complicated, and instituted the stasis which Imperial governments usually preferred to dynamic local leadership. The Chinese, after their experience with Mao, have tried to divide power similarly, though between CPC and state posts. Because of the influence of the Party, however, the Party posts are inevitably dominant ones.

About the Authors

David F. Anderson, Ph.D.

David F. Andersen is Distinguished Service Professor of Public Administration and Informatics at the University at Albany. His areas of research include public administration and policy, System Dynamics modeling, digital government applications. He is a recipient (with a coauthor team from the Center for Technology in Government, University at Albany) of a three-year NSF grant on data interoperability and social systems. A 2010-2011 Carlos Rico Fulbright Scholar, he is on sabbatical in Montréal, Canada and Cholula, México (Universidad de las Americas Puebla) for the 2010-2011 academic year.

Deborah Lines Anderson, Ph.D.

Deborah Lines Andersen is Associate Professor of Information Studies and Informatics at the University at Albany. Her areas of research include international information policy, public libraries, and education in library and information science. She is a recipient (with a coauthor team from the Center for Technology in Government, University at Albany) of a three-year NSF grant on data interoperability and social systems. A 2010-2011 Carlos Rico Fulbright Scholar, she is on sabbatical in Montréal, Canada and Cholula, México (Universidad de las Americas Puebla) for the 2010-2011 academic year.

Jeffrey G. Barlow, Ph.D.

Jeffrey Barlow has been the Director of the Berglund Center from 2000 to the present. He is the founding editor of several peer-reviewed scholarly e-journals, including the Journal of History and Computing, now housed at the University of Michigan and E-AsPac, the e-journal of the Association for Asian Studies on the Pacific Coast. He has given invited lectures in the U.S., Canada, and China on topics related to the Internet.

Jeffrey's academic training at the University of California, Berkeley, was in Modern Chinese History. He is also a recognized authority on Chinese immigration into the Pacific Northwest, and on Chinese use of the Internet. He taught at the University of Oregon and at Lewis and Clark College before coming to Pacific in 1994. He has worked with the Berglund Center since its beginnings.

Sierra Brummett

Sierra Brummett is a junior at Pacific University in Forest Grove, Oregon studying Modern Languages and Ethics, Society and Law. With this program, Sierra would like to continue on to graduate school in pursuit of a higher degree in Ethics or Foreign Policy. She has also studied French in Paris at the Sorbonne. She started with the Berglund Center as a copy-editor in Spring of 2009 and has worked there, editing articles, ever since. Sierra is active in several groups on campus and in the community including her sorority Phi Lambda Omicron and the Phi Eta Sigma National Honor Society.

Jeff Cain, Ed.D., MS

Jeff Cain is an Adjunct Associate Professor for the Department of Pharmacy Practice & Science and also serves as the Director of Education Technology at the University of Kentucky College of Pharmacy. His primary research interests are social media, e-professionalism, Web 2.0 applications in education and health science professions, and educational technology. He is an active member of the American Association of Colleges of Pharmacy (AACP) and currently serves on the editorial board of *Currents in Pharmacy Teaching and Learning*.

Dean Antonio Cantù, Ph.D.

Dr. D. Antonio Cantù is Professor and Chair of Teacher Education at Bradley University in Peoria, Illinois. He received his Ph.D. in Curriculum and Instruction from Southern Illinois University, Ed.S. in Community College Education, M.A. in History, and B.S. in Social Science Education from Arkansas State University. With over 20 years of experience in professional education, Professor Cantu is the author of a number of research articles and books on history/social studies education and technology integration. Professor Cantu's most recent book publications include: *Technology Applications for the Digital Classroom* (2011), *The Art and Science of Elementary Social Studies Education* (2010).

Tom Cockburn, Ed.D.

Dr. Tom Cockburn gained his first degree with honours from Leicester University, England, his MBA and Doctorate in Management Education from Cardiff University in Wales. He has extensive assessment and evaluation experience and has been commissioned to carry out reviews of MBA and Executive programs at universities in the UK, EU and Malaysia. In addition, he has designed and delivered tailored, Corporate and Professional Development programs for senior managers in both the public and private sector. He is currently an Associate Fellow of the New Zealand Institute of Management.

Jennifer Conner

Jennifer Conner was born and raised in Tigard, Oregon. After graduating from Tualatin High School, she attended Pacific University. She graduated from Pacific in May 2010, with degrees in Political Science and Journalism and a minor in German. While at Pacific, Conner participated in various organizations, specifically the Speech Team and the nonpartisan Politics and Law Forum (PLF). She represented the Speech Team, winning numerous awards, at state, regional, national, and international tournaments. In PLF she held leadership positions as Marketing and Communications Coordinator and later as President. Currently, Conner serves as the Communications Coordinator for Contact Wellness Foundation, a nonprofit based in Portland, Oregon.

Shawn Davis, Ph.D.

Shawn Davis is an Associate Professor in Pacific University's School of Professional Psychology wherein he teaches the Psychometrics, Cognition, and Lifespan Development courses. Dr. Davis comes to Pacific University from Texas where he earned an MA degree in Experimental Cognitive Psychology from Stephen F. Austin University and his Ph.D. in Developmental Psychology from the University of Houston. His research interests center around ways to maximize the effectiveness of information presented online. In particular, he has focused on the development of highly individualized online health promotion programs. His current research interests are in the area of media influence on individual and social behavior.

Steve Dodge

Steve Dodge is editor of *Pacific* magazine, published by Pacific University, Oregon. He was formerly editor of *Visions* magazine, a science and technology magazine published at the Oregon Graduate Institute, and has worked as a writer or editor for several other newspapers and magazines.

Leonard D. DuBoff, JD

Leonard D. DuBoff is an attorney specializing in business and intellectual property law. Leonard was a professor of law at Northwestern School of Law of Lewis & Clark College for 23 years and has pioneered the field of art law, written extensively on the subject, and lectured all over the world on business and intellectual property. His two-volume text entitled *The Deskbook of Art Law* is frequently referred to by judges, lawyers, legal commentators and others who are interested in finding out about this important field of law, and it has also been adopted by several law schools as the basis for their courses on art law.

Chris Ferguson, Ph.D.

Chris Ferguson is an associate professor of psychology at Texas A&M International University. He is a leading researcher of video games and youth behavior, recently serving as guest editor for the American Psychological Association journal Review of General Psychology's special issue on video games. He lives in Laredo, Texas with his wife and young son.

Lorely French, Ph.D.

Lorely French is Professor of German and Distinguished University Professor at Pacific University Oregon. She is the author of the book *German Women Letter Writers 1750 to 1850*. She has published numerous book chapters and journal articles on German and Austrian literature, film, and culture. She has been co-editor of *Pacific Coast Philology: The Journal of the Pacific Ancient and Modern Language Association.* She is presently completing a book manuscript examining gender and ethnicity in writings by Roma in the German-speaking countries. In 2009/10 she was a Berglund Center for Internet Studies Research Fellow, during which time she completed a multi-media project on the Romani "Gypsy" Austrian artist and writer Ceija Stojka and a website on Romani Arts (http://bcis.pacificu.edu/roma/). She is a recipient of the Outstanding College Professor Award from the Confederation in Oregon for Language Teaching, and she is an American Association of University Women (AAUW) Educational Foundation Award Honoree. Her research has been supported by grants from the Fulbright Commission, the Deutscher Akademischer Austauschdienst, the American Council of Learned Societies, and the Northwest Academic Computing Consortium.

David Georgina, Ph.D.

David Georgina's educational history includes a Ph.D. in Education, Masters in English, and Bachelors in English Creative Writing (1998). He supports a social constructivist approach to teaching and learning., and believes that in order to be an effective teacher he must first be an effective learner. Digital technologies continue to affect access to information, concept creations, and research inquiry. Integrating that digital technology into our pedagogy/andragogy can enhance learning by increasing access to the diversity of learning styles. However, it is imperative that the hybrid course/curriculum (integrated technological pedagogy) created includes both formative and summative assessments. Georgina's research areas include technology integration, faculty training and game theory.

Michael Geraci, M.S.

Michael Geraci is an associate professor in Pacific University's Integrated Media program. Mike also teaches online courses for the University of Oregon's Applied Information Management Masters program, where he received his Master of Science degree in 2002. Prior to teaching, Mike spent eight years managing Pacific's department of Educational Technologies. In addition, he has experience working as an independent web developer, graphic designer and video production specialist. Mike's scholarly interests center upon the continued evolution of the Web, user experience, and typographic design.

Isaac Gilman, MLIS

Isaac Gilman is Assistant Professor and Scholarly Communications & Research Services Librarian in the Pacific University (Oregon) Library. In addition to teaching courses in research methods and scholarly publishing, he manages Pacific University's institutional repository, *CommonKnowledge*, through which he also provides editorial support for the publication of both student and professional peer-reviewed journals. He received his Master of Library and Information Studies degree from the University of British Columbia in 2006 and his scholarly interests include information-seeking behaviors, scholarly communications, open access publishing and the legal and ethical aspects of information use.

Ruth Happ

While growing up in Hillsboro, Oregon, Ruth Happ always loved to read, talk, and write. Since first viewing a Jane Austen adaptation, she became enthralled with Austen's novels and their corresponding films, especially for their well-wrought language, plot lines, humor, and romance. After living in Veracruz, Mexico, and teaching English there for over a year, Ruth gained a love for sharing her understanding of the English language with students. Currently working as a bilingual assistant for the Hillsboro School District, Ruth tries to impart her love of English, reading, and writing to struggling students. She and her husband and their two little girls live in Beaverton, Oregon, and though busy with work, school, church, and household duties, both try to make their relationship with their daughters a top priority.

John Hayes, Ph.D.
John Hayes is an Associate Professor of Optometry at Pacific University's College of Optometry. His primary mission is to provide statistical support to faculty and students in the areas of design, analysis, and presentation of information.

Jenn Hernandez
Jenn Hernandez is a senior majoring in studio art with an emphasis in photography and a minor in integrated media. She will be presenting her senior capstone, pet portrait photography in April 2011. Selected pieces will be displayed in the Kathrin Cawein Gallery of Art on campus April 27th to May 22nd. After graduation, Jenn hopes to continue her writing, photography, and to find work in a field that interests her, such as publishing, design, or photography.

Valerie Horres
Valerie Horres loves literature and writing, and hopes to go into editing novels, as well as publishing her own work. Valerie is also heavily involved with Pacific University's Center for Gender Equity, an organization that has fostered her interest in advocacy and human rights. For the past two years, she has led the committee that orchestrates "Serving the Full Spectrum: Meeting the Needs of Gay, Lesbian, Bisexual, and Transgender Students," a conference aimed at educators to provide them with the skills necessary to better reach students who often go without support. Valerie also is involved with Girl Scouting, and helps young women to develop their leadership skills.

Lilly Huynh
Lilly is a junior at Pacific University, pursuing an education and learning major and music minor. She is a member of the Pacific Philharmonic Orchestra, quartet, and chamber group, and an active member of the Speech and Debate team.

Lynda Irons, MLIS

Lynda Irons, Assistant Professor, has been the Reference & Information Services Librarian for Pacific University since 1996.

Khosro Jahdi, Ph.D.

Khosro Jahdi has been a marketing lecturer for almost 25 years with an MBA (marketing), MPhil (Political and Peace Studies) and a PhD in Ethical/Green Marketing. He has had articles published in the *Social Responsibility Journal*, the *Journal of Business Ethics*, *Journal of Further and Higher Education*, etc. as well as *Interface*. Jahdi's research interests lie in CSR, Marketing Ethics and Green Marketing, and he submits papers to international CSR related conferences on a regular basis.

Jamaica King

Jamaica King is originally from the Mariana Islands, currently residing in Oregon. She is a Pacific University student majoring in Psychology and minoring in Computer Science. Jamaica is a 2010-2011 Berglund Student Fellow with interest in online gaming communities. She is passionate about video games and community satisfaction. Her goal is to be a part of Riot Games' community team, assisting with community-related event planning and other projects.

James Kundart, B.S., B.A., O.D., M.Ed.

James has been an Assistant Professor of Optometry since 2005, where he teaches visual perception and new courses in ocular motility and nutritional optometry. He was named Clinical Faculty of the Year in 2007, and Amigos Eye Care Doctor of the Year in 2008. James maintains the continuing education website for the College of Optometry, and is the founding editor-in-chief of the new online journal, *Health and Interprofessional Practice.* James and his wife Alicks have an infant son and a collection of rescued pets.

Christine A. Macfarlane, Ph.D.

Christine is an Associate Professor and Director of the Special Education Program in the College of Education at Pacific University. Prior to coming to Pacific University, Chris spent 9½ years at the University of Northern Iowa in Cedar Falls, Iowa where she coordinated the mental disabilities program. After arriving in Oregon in August, 2000 Chris worked with local school districts to develop and implement the Special Education Program. She received her Master's degree and doctorate from Utah State University. She has published and presented on assessment, the use of technology in teacher preparation, mental retardation, and severe disabilities. A highlight of her career was the opportunity to provide technical assistance to special education faculty at Commenius University, Bratislava, Slovakia following the "velvet revolution." In 2010-11, she was selected as a Berglund Fellow to study distance learning.

Daniel Munoz, Ph.D.

Dr. Munoz received his masters and doctoral degree in clinical psychology from the University of New York at Albany in 2006. He is currently an assistant professor of clinical psychology at Pacific University of Oregon's School of Professional Psychology. His research and clinical work has focused in the area of eating disorders, obesity, body image in children, adolescents and adults. He has authored or co-authored nearly over two dozen research papers and presentations for peer-reviewed journals, national and international scientific conferences. He was award the 2009 Academy of Eating Disorders Young Investigator award.

Nicole Nowlin

Nicole is a senior at Pacific University in Business Administration (International Business) and Japanese with a special interest in international relations. She is a Fulbright finalist for a research grant to Japan in 2011/2012 and an active member of Pacific's Speech and Debate Team. In her spare time, she caters to her voracious appetite for fiction through novels, comics, movies, and writing. Her interest in comics, particularly Japanese manga, led her to her Student Fellowship in the Berglund Center for Internet Studies and her articles on scanlations and e-manga.

Chris Pruett
By day, Chris Pruett is a Senior Game Developer Advocate at Google, focused on Android. Under the cover of night he writes indie games and blogs about horror game design. The views expressed here are his alone and not those of his employer. Chris lives in Cupertino, California with his wife and daughter.

James Sheedy, O.D., Ph.D.
Dr. Sheedy received his optometry degree and his doctorate in physiological optics from the Ohio State University. He was a Clinical Professor at the University of California at Berkeley School of Optometry where he founded the first VDT Eye Clinic in 1985. He also established the Center for Ophthalmic Optics Research at Ohio State University and is recognized as an expert in the design and prescribing of progressive addition lenses. He has twice received the Garland Clay Award for the best clinical research published in the journal of the American Academy of Optometry and also received the William Feinbloom award for his work in vision ergonomics. He also received the Distinguished Service Award from Prevent Blindness America for his work with ultraviolet. He has over 140 published articles and has participated in the development of numerous ANSI and ISO standards and regulations. Dr Sheedy has earned a reputation as the expert in vision problems at computers. This has led to research into hardware and software configurations of computer displays. Dr Sheedy has several graduate students who have received degrees under his guidance. Currently Dr. Sheedy is the head of the Vision Performance Institute and professor of optometry at Pacific University.

David Staley, Ph.D.
David Staley is Director of the Goldberg Center and an adjunct associate professor of history at The Ohio State University. He also serves as National Dean for General Education at Harrison College in Indianapolis. In addition to his work as a scholar/administrator, Dr. Staley is principal of The DStaley Group, a strategic foresight consulting practice, and serves as president of Columbus Futurists. He is a writer and essayist, whose work includes *History and Future: Using Historical Thinking to Imagine the Future*, and *Computers, Visualization and History.*

Mark Syzmanski, Ph.D.

Mark Szymanski, Ph.D. is an Associate Professor in the College of Education at Pacific University where he teaches online and blended courses in technology in education and educational psychology. He has been writing and editing for *Interface: The Journal of Community, Education, and Values* since its inception in 2000. Mark's research focuses on designing and understanding technology rich learning environments and activities informed by learning sciences. Recently he has been working on projects that involve using and creating cognitive frameworks for learning that allow students and teachers to integrate digital content into challenge-based learning activities to increase the depth and complexity of their understanding. He's also beginning to design Apps for the iPad environment and is optimistic about the future of games and learning.

Lauren Wiswall

Originally from the Pacific Northwest, Lauren earned her B.A. in Psychology from the University of Washington and is currently earning her PsyD. in Clinical Psychology from Pacific University's School of Professional Psychology. She has worked with diverse populations in both community and college student counseling center settings. In addition to her studies, Lauren offers business management consultation services.

Yu-Chi Tai, Ph.D.

Yu-Chi Tai received her doctorate in Cognitive Psychology from University of Illinois at Urbana-Champaign. In December 2006, Yu-Chi went to Pacific University from Ohio State University where she was a post-doctoral fellow in the Vision Ergonomics Laboratory. Currently she works as a research scientist and lab manager for the Vision Performance Institute where she continue her research in the fields of reading, dyslexia, and improvement of visual function with digital displays.

Made in the USA
Monee, IL
08 November 2026

67382831R00247